Institutions and Economic Theory

*Economics, Cognition, and Society*

This series provides a forum for theoretical and empirical investigations of social phenomena. It promotes works that focus on the interactions among cognitive processes, individual behavior, and social outcomes. It is especially open to interdisciplinary books that are genuinely integrative.

Titles in the Series

Ulrich Witt, Editor. *Explaining Process and Change: Approaches to Evolutionary Economics*

Young Back Choi. *Paradigms and Conventions: Uncertainty, Decision Making, and Entrepreneurship*

Geoffrey M. Hodgson. *Economics and Evolution: Bringing Life Back into Economics*

Richard W. England, Editor. *Evolutionary Concepts in Contemporary Economics*

W. Brian Arthur. *Increasing Returns and Path Dependence in the Economy*

Janet Tai Landa. *Trust, Ethnicity, and Identity: Beyond the New Institutional Economics of Ethnic Trading Networks, Contract Law, and Gift-Exchange*

Mark Irving Lichbach. *The Rebel's Dilemma*

Karl-Dieter Opp, Peter Voss, and Christiane Gern. *Origins of a Spontaneous Revolution: East Germany, 1989*

Mark Irving Lichbach. *The Cooperator's Dilemma*

Richard A. Easterlin. *Growth Triumphant: The Twenty-first Century in Historical Perspective*

Daniel B. Klein, Editor. *Reputation: Studies in the Voluntary Elicitation of Good Conduct*

Eirik G. Furubotn and Rudolf Richter. *Institutions and Economic Theory: The Contribution of the New Institutional Economics*

Lee J. Alston, Gary D. Libecap, and Bernardo Mueller. *Titles, Conflict, and Land Use: The Development of Property Rights and Land Reform on the Brazilian Amazon Frontier*

Rosemary L. Hopcroft. *Regions, Institutions, and Agrarian Change in European History*

# Institutions and Economic Theory

## The Contribution of the New Institutional Economics

Eirik G. Furubotn and Rudolf Richter

*Ann Arbor*

THE UNIVERSITY OF MICHIGAN PRESS

330
F992ia

First paperback edition 2000
Copyright © Eirik G. Furubotn and Rudolf Richter 1998
All rights reserved
Published in the United States of America by
The University of Michigan Press
Manufactured in the United States of America
⊗ Printed on acid-free paper

2003   2002   2001   2000      6   5   4   3

*A CIP catalog record for this book is available
from the British Library.*

Library of Congress Cataloging-in-Publication Data

Furubotn, Eirik Grundtvig, 1923–
    [Neue Institutionenökonomik. English]
    Institutions and economic theory : the contribution of the new
institutional economics / by Eirik G. Furubotn and Rudolf Richter.
        p.   cm. — (Economics, cognition, and society)
    Includes bibliographical references (p.     ) and index.
    ISBN 0-472-10817-4 (cloth : acid-free paper)
    1. Institutional economics.   I. Richter, Rudolf, 1926–   .
II. Title.   III. Series.
HB99.5.F8713   1997
330—dc21                                                97-30103
                                                            CIP

ISBN 0-472-08680-4 (pbk. : alk. paper)

Originally published in German as *Neue Institutionenökonomik* by Rudolf Richter and
Eirik Furubotn. Tübingen: Mohr Siebeck Verlag, 1996.

*To Elisabeth and Florence,*
*whose help was essential*
*to the writing of this book*

# Contents

Acknowledgments    xi

Preface    xiii

Chapter 1. Introductory Observations    1
    1.1. Some Basic Assumptions and Terms    2
    1.2. The Strange World
        of Costless Transactions    8
    1.3. The Ideal Type of the Classical
        Liberal State    11
    1.4. The Ideal Type of Market Socialism    12
    1.5. Constructed or Spontaneous Orders?    14
    1.6. The Work of the Invisible Hand Can
        Be Accelerated    15
    1.7. Rational Incompleteness    17
    1.8. Enforcement    19
    1.9. The Political Process    21
    1.10. Agency    22
    1.11. Institutional Stability    23
    1.12. Once More with Feeling    25
    1.13. The New Institutional Economics and
         Modern Institutionalism    29
    1.14. Some Notes on the History of the Old
         Institutional Economics    33
    1.15. Suggested Readings for Chapter 1    37

Chapter 2. Transaction Costs    39
    2.1. The Concept of Transaction    41
    2.2. Transaction Costs: Illustrations and Attempts
        at Definition    42
    2.3. Guesstimating the Size
        of Transaction Costs    49
    2.4. Modeling Transaction Costs:
        The Activity "Transaction"    54

2.5. Some Notes on the Development of the
Transaction-Cost Literature   62

2.6. Suggested Readings for Chapter 2   67

Chapter 3. Absolute Property Rights: Ownership of
Physical Objects   69

3.1. The Property-Rights Approach: Some
Basic Concepts   71

3.2. Property Rights: Illustrations and Attempts
at Definition   76

3.3. Property in Physical Objects: The Private
Property Issue   85

3.4. Common Pool Resources   98

3.5. The Emergence of Property Rights   104

3.6. The Economic Analysis of Property Rights:
Some Notes on the Literature   114

3.7. Suggested Readings for Chapter 3   119

Chapter 4. Relative Property Rights:
Contractual Obligations   121

4.1. Basic Principles of
Contractual Obligations   123

4.2. Diverse Types of
Contractual Obligations   127

4.3. Some Elements of Contract Theory from the
Economist's Viewpoint   140

4.4. Three Types of Contract Theory   147

4.5. Resume   169

4.6. The Economics of Contract Law and
Contractual Behavior: Some Notes
on the Literature   172

4.7. Suggested Readings for Chapter 4   176

Chapter 5. Contract Theory   179

5.1. Overview of the Types of Contract Theory to
Be Discussed   181

5.2. Managerial Theory of the Firm: The
Expense-Preference Model   183

5.3. The Principal-Agent Model:
Moral Hazard   186

5.4. The Principal-Agent Model:
Adverse Selection   202

5.5. Implicit Contracts   227

5.6. The Incomplete Contract Model    232
5.7. Self-Enforcing Agreements    239
5.8. Looking Back    246
5.9. Bibliographic Notes on Formal
Contract Theory    250
5.10. Suggested Readings for Chapter 5    262

Chapter 6. The New Institutional Economics Applied to
Markets, Firms, and the State: General
Remarks    265
6.1. The Elementary Rules of a Private
Ownership Economy    266
6.2. General Remarks on Organizations: The
Firm, the Market, and the State    269
6.3. A Brief Guide to the Literature on Order
and Organization    278
6.4. Suggested Readings for Chapter 6    281

Chapter 7. The New Institutional Economics
of the Market    283
7.1. The Market as Organization    284
7.2. On Price Rigidity    285
7.3. Market Organization as a Result
of Market Cooperation    287
7.4. Some Views of Neoinstitutionalists on
Market Organization    291
7.5. Markets: Conclusion and Outlook    312
7.6. A Brief Guide to the Literature
on Market Organization    314
7.7. Suggested Readings for Chapter 7    319

Chapter 8. The New Institutional Economics
of the Firm    321
8.1. The Orthodox Neoclassical Firm    321
8.2. The Incentive to Integrate    328
8.3. The Limits of Integration    336
8.4. Ownership and Control    342
8.5. Institutional Models in the Tradition of the
Neoclassical Theory of the Firm    354
8.6. The Traditional Soviet Firm    366
8.7. The Socialist Labor-Managed Firm    375
8.8. Codetermination    389

8.9. The New Institutional Economics of the
      Firm: Forerunners and First Steps    404
8.10. The New Institutional Economics of the
      Firm: Summary and Main Literature
      beyond Coase    405
8.11. Suggested Readings for Chapter 8    410

Chapter 9. The New Institutional Economics
      of the State    413
9.1. A Simple Neoclassical Theory
      of the State    414
9.2. The Role of Political Institutions    417
9.3. Political Markets    420
9.4. International Relations    423
9.5. A Brief Guide to the Literature on the
      Economics of the State and
      International Relations    430
9.6. Suggested Readings for Chapter 9    434

Chapter 10. Future Development of the New
      Institutional Economics    435
10.1. Institutionalism as Extended
      Neoclassical Theory    439
10.2. The Initial Approach Reconsidered    441
10.3. The Basis of a New Paradigm    464
10.4. Modern Institutionalism: The Opportunities
      for Progress    477

Glossary    483

References    497

Author Index    539

Subject Index    547

# Acknowledgments

Numerous individuals and institutions have assisted our work over the years, and we should like to offer our sincere thanks for their generous contributions of time and resources. First, the University of Saarland is to be mentioned. The university, despite a difficult budgetary situation, has given consistent support to the Center for the Study of the New Institutional Economics and has done its best to advance our programs. This assistance has been crucial because the Center, located at the university and directed by the authors, has proved a stable base for our diverse activities. Important support has also been received from the Minister of Education of the Saarland, the President of the Landeszentralbank im Saarland (later Rheinland, Pfalz, and Saarland), the Deutsche Forschungsgemeinschaft, the Volkswagen Foundation, the Thyssen Foundation, the Stifterverband für die Deutsche Wissenschaft, the James L. West Chair at the University of Texas at Arlington, and the Private Enterprise Research Center at Texas A&M University. These individuals and organizations helped to make possible the twelve international seminars, and the seven summer schools on the New Institutional Economics that the Center has arranged. Without these scholarly activities, and without the continuing assistance of Georg Siebeck, publisher of the *Journal of Institutional and Theoretical Economics* (JITE), the present book would never have come into existence.

Despite the existence of modern communications techniques, personal meetings of the authors and periods of local coauthoring were unavoidable. Fortunately, such needed association was made possible by the financial support of the Deutsche Forschungsgemeinschaft and the Thyssen Stiftung. Grants enabled Eirik Furubotn to confer with influential German economists at Konstanz, Jena, Trier, and elsewhere. Similarly, the Hoover Institution at Stanford University and the Department of Economics at the University of Michigan (Ann Arbor) provided several visiting appointments for Rudolf Richter, which, among other things, permitted him to visit scholars at various points in

---

*The Journal of Institutional and Theoretical Economics* was edited by Rudolf Richter from 1978 to 1994.

the United States and gain insights into some of the current research being done in the area of the New Institutional Economics.

Numerous friends and colleagues influenced our thinking about neo-institutionalist issues. Thus, we should like to thank especially Armen Alchian, Kenneth Binmore, Holger Bonus, Ronald Coase, Thrainn Eggertsson, Bruno Frey, Victor Goldberg, Herbert Hax, Christian Kirchner, Barbara Krug, Gary Libecap, Siegwart Lindenberg, Douglass North, Timothy Roth, Thomas Saving, Erich Schanze, Ekkehart Schlicht, Dieter Schmidtchen, Urs Schweizer, and Oliver Williamson. As for our own contribution, the book is a genuine joint product. To signal this, and to avoid getting involved in a case of alphabetical discrimination, we use in the English edition the name sequence Furubotn and Richter and in the German edition Richter and Furubotn.

Finally, we should like to recognize the contributions of Barbara Thimm-Maldener, who provided organizational assistance and did much of the manuscript typing at the Center in Saarbrücken. On the other side of the Atlantic, in Texas, Heidi Duckworth performed valuable secretarial and typing services for the book. Significant help with the manuscript was also provided by Susanne Lipinsky and Teri Bush of Texas A&M University.

Eirik G. Furubotn
Rudolf Richter

Center for the Study of the New Institutional Economics
Universität des Saarlandes
66041 Saarbrücken
Germany

# Preface

The last two decades have seen some very significant changes in the direction of development in economic theory. Although neoclassical analysis has continued its domination of mainstream thinking in the profession, there has been a growing insistence on the part of certain contemporary scholars that we reconsider the acceptability of rigid neoclassical assumptions and reassess the role that institutions play in shaping economic behavior. Indeed, special emphasis has been placed on the importance of viewing institutions as endogenous "variables" that have to be explained within the framework of the ruling economic model. It is reasonable to say, then, that a new analytical style is in the process of being developed, a style that is about to complement, if not replace, conventional neoclassical doctrine. Differently expressed, the point is that it no longer seems possible to justify the use of "frictionless" models of competition and imperfect competition that are based on assumptions of costless transactions, perfect individual rationality, and exogenously given institutional structure.

In general discussion, the generic term *modern institutional economics* is used to describe various new theoretical approaches that have some connection with institutional issues. The present book is concerned with this broad area but will confine its attention to one particular form of institutional analysis—the New Institutional Economics (NIE), which is, at times, also referred to as the New Theory of Organization. The fundamental idea animating this school of thought is quite simple; it is that transaction costs exist and necessarily influence the structure of institutions and the specific economic choices people make. With respect to institutions, it is abundantly clear that their use (as well as their formation) requires the input of real resources. Here, consideration of transaction costs cannot be avoided. Or, viewing things from a somewhat different standpoint, we can say that property-rights allocations condition the economic results produced by a society and that transaction costs are responsible, in part, for the way in which property rights are allocated and enforced. In short, the introduction of transaction costs into the orthodox model of production and exchange is highly significant and demands a fundamental reorientation in our thinking about economic processes.

It seems amazing that the recognition of transaction costs, an obvious phenomenon, took so long to come about. Yet, in fact, this home truth was disregarded not only by the representatives of classical and neoclassical economics but also by their various critics—for example, writers of the German Historical School, the Old American Institutionalism, and more recently the Keynesian School. Certainly, the role of "frictions" was mentioned at various points in the earlier literature. We see this in monetary economics in the work of John Stuart Mill (1857) and later in that of Hicks (1935). Nevertheless, the theme was not picked up and developed further in the general literature.

It was Ronald H. Coase (1937, 1960) who first appreciated the central importance of the concept of transaction costs for the economic analysis of institutions. Moreover, this general line of analysis led logically to improved understanding of the role that property-rights allocation plays in affecting incentives and economic outcomes. Although the significance of the Coasian insights was not recognized immediately, Coase ultimately did receive the Nobel Prize in Economics (1991) for his pioneering contributions. His "discovery" of transaction costs had impact on various specialized fields in economics and tended to change the prevailing views and the orientation of research in these fields. Among the areas influenced were economic history, under the leadership of Douglass North (1981, 1990), and industrial organization, under the leadership of Armen Alchian (1965a, 1965b), Oliver Williamson (1975, 1985), and others. Interestingly, North was honored with a Nobel Prize in 1993 (together with Robert W. Fogel). The fact that North, an exponent of the new institutionalism, was awarded the prize only two years after Coase suggests the increasing respect with which the new research approach is being held by the profession. The importance of the New Institutional Economics is also shown by the growing number of newly founded journals dealing with modern institutional issues and by the increasing time given to such issues at conferences such as the 1995 meeting of the American Economic Association in Washington, D.C.

The present book views the New Institutional Economics as an amalgam of transaction-cost economics, property-rights analysis, and contract theory, and it is on this interpretation of the field that the book will focus. Our objective is to introduce, and assess critically, the major theoretical contributions that have shaped thinking in the NIE since the field's early beginnings in the 1960s. Particular attention will be given to the theory of relational or incomplete contracts, which has wide applicability in the real world. The volume is directed toward professional economists who are interested in these new developments as well as toward graduate students who may be seeking a promising area of research in which to write dissertations. To achieve our purposes, we try, in the first five chapters, to bring some order to the multifarious and ever growing literature on the NIE and explain how the various theoretical strands discussed fit into the general fabric of modern institutionalism. After this background material is in place, the book attempts to illustrate the application of the existing concepts to the economic analysis of three basic types of institutions—markets, firms, and states. A final chapter deals with an adumbration of what we believe are the primary problems and questions that have to be resolved in the future development of the New Institutional Economics.

This book was inspired and nurtured by the discussions that took place during twelve international seminars on the New Institutional Economics organized by the authors between 1983 and 1994, in which the leading representatives of modern institutionalism participated. Among those who attended the seminars on a number of occasions were Armen Alchian, Ronald Coase, Douglas North, and Oliver Williamson. The papers and proceedings of these conferences were published in the March issues of the *Journal of Institutional and Theoretical Economics* over the period of 1984 to 1995. Some of the more formal analysis that appears in the book was influenced by the work undertaken during eight summer school sessions for European doctoral students that the authors organized during the years 1988–94. Contract theory was the main topic dealt with in these sessions, and it was taught by Benjamin Hermalin, Bengt Holmstrom, Paul Milgrom, Michael Riordan, and Jean Tirole.

The present volume is, essentially, the English-language version of the book *Neue Institutionenokonomik*, by R. Richter and E. G. Furubotn, published in Tübingen by J. C. B. Mohr (Paul Siebeck) in 1996. In preparing the English edition, however, the authors took advantage of the revision process to extend coverage of the growing literature and further clarify some of the arguments put forward by neoinstitutional writers. Thus, while no fundamental changes have been made, the new work does reflect more fully the present state of discussion on institutional questions.

# CHAPTER 1

## Introductory Observations

> If the project of turning economics into a hard science could succeed, it would be worth doing. . . . There are, however, some reasons for pessimism about the project. (Solow 1985, 331)

The central message of the New Institutional Economics is that institutions matter for economic performance. This is, of course, an old and inherently plausible intellectual position. Even writers in the strict neoclassical tradition such as Marshall (1920, 200) have recognized that institutional structure exerts an important influence on behavior. In more recent times, however, as the technical development of neoclassical theory has progressed and economic models have become increasingly abstract, institutional phenomena have received less and less attention. Thus, in what may be regarded as mainstream theory through the 1980s (exemplified by welfare economics and the general equilibrium models of Arrow-Debreu), institutions play virtually no role at all. Emphasis is on allocative efficiency, and different institutional arrangements are seen merely as "alternative means" for meeting the conditions required for Pareto optimality.

> The optimality conditions, being simply technical requirements, contain no ideological implications. They apply equally to capitalism, socialism, or any other "ism." Whatever the political ideology of a country, it could make all of its citizens better off by ensuring that production and allocation satisfied the optimality conditions. (Lancaster 1969, 276)

On this accounting, microeconomics is, in effect, institutionally neutral, a circumstance that represents both a strength and a weakness of neoclassical economics. The orthodox approach is useful because it permits the theorist to show the basics of economic efficiency under ideal-typical conditions of perfect information and foresight. Moreover, the role of relative prices in economic decision making can be made clear despite the absence of any institutional analysis. Contemporary theory, however, does have sharp limitations. Its weakness resides precisely in its institutional neutrality or its predisposition to neglect serious consideration of institutional constraints and transaction costs. Neoclassical economic theory, therefore, can only be applied in a highly abstract sense to questions of resource allocation.

The deficiencies of neoclassical theory were, of course, not unknown to earlier generations of economists. Indeed, dissenters to the classical and neoclassical theoretical line have always existed in the profession, and, at times, these critics have had substantial influence. Representatives of the German historical school such as Roscher, Hildebrand, and later Schmoller reacted strongly against English classical economics, as did American institutionalists such as Commons. But these writers were basically hostile to abstract theoretical work in the sense of marginalism, utility or profit maximization, and the weighing of alternatives.[1] By contrast, the exponents of modern institutional economics apply the analytical apparatus of neoclassical theory (and newer techniques) to explain the workings and evolution of institutional arrangements and thus to expand the scope and predictive power of microeconomics.

## 1.1.  Some Basic Assumptions and Terms

The body of thought that is now known as the New Institutional Economics began simply as an attempt to extend the range of applicability of neoclassical theory. During the postwar period, there was increasing dissatisfaction with, and criticism of, the traditional models of production and exchange. Nevertheless, neoinstitutionalism did not come into being as a result of any planned or coordinated effort to develop a new doctrine. In particular, marginalism was not rejected. What was desired primarily was change in certain key assumptions. Thus, modern institutionalism, while similar in many respects to standard neoclassical analysis, is distinct and is characterized by a significantly different perspective on microeconomic phenomena.

The following concepts and hypotheses are particularly relevant in modern institutional economics.

1. *Methodological individualism:* An entirely new interpretation is given to the role of individual decision makers. Methodological individualism emphasizes that people are different and have different and varied tastes, goals, purposes, and ideas. Hence, the implication is that "society," "the state," "the firm," "political parties," and so on are *not* to be understood as collective entities that behave as though they were individual agents. The organization or collectivity per se is no longer the main focus. Rather, it is thought that a theory of social phenomena must start with and base its explanations on the views and

---

1. On the German Younger Historical School, of which Schmoller was the leading figure, see for example, the critical remarks by Wagner (1907, 15): "political economy dissolves into a descriptive economic and cultural history."

behaviors of the individual members whose actions give rise to the phenomena being studied.

2. *The maximand:* Individuals are assumed to seek their own interests as they perceive them and to maximize utility subject to the constraints established by the existing institutional structure. Contrary to conventional practice in neoclassical theory, the dichotomy between the theory of consumer choice and the theory of the firm is ended by extending the utility maximization hypothesis to *all* individual choices. It follows, therefore, that a decision maker, whether he be the manager of a capitalist firm, a state bureaucrat, a politician, or whatever, is presumed to make his own choices and pursue his own goals within the limits allowed by the organizational structure in which he is operating.

3. *Individual rationality:* The neoinstitutionalist literature reveals that at least two distinct approaches are taken by economists in current attempts to interpret the concept of "individual rationality." The situation can be understood as follows. First, there are theorists who adhere closely to the traditional neoclassical view of *perfect individual rationality.* The assumption here is that all decision makers possess consistent and stable preferences—whether they are consumers, entrepreneurs, or bureaucrats. In other words, it is possible to conceive of an ideal case in which individuals display purposeful, rational behavior of a very high order. Thus:

> A completely rational individual has the ability to foresee everything that might happen and to evaluate and optimally choose among available courses of action, all in the blink of an eye and at no cost. (Kreps 1990b, 745)

Such complete or perfect individual rationality is assumed in the earlier work of representatives of the New Institutional Economics, and the view still dominates thinking in agency theory, the economic analysis of law, and public choice theory.

To approach the conditions of the real world more closely, contemporary writers have given increasing attention to the idea of *imperfect individual rationality.* From this perspective, the preferences of decision makers are recognized as incomplete and subject to change over time. Among the new institutional economists, this point is stressed particularly by North (1978, 972ff.).[2] What must be recognized, however, is that once positive transaction costs are

---

2. "The study of tastes—or writ large, ideology—can certainly be ignored by economists in dealing with many economic issues; it cannot be ignored by economists exploring the political and judicial process and certainly cannot be ignored by economic historians studying the changing constraints of an economic system over time" (North 1978, 973).

introduced into a microeconomic model, the universe being considered changes fundamentally, and decision makers cannot be assumed to be "completely" informed. The acquisition of unlimited knowledge simply becomes too expensive, or plainly impossible, insofar as future developments are concerned. Moreover, when transaction costs are posited, it is an easy step to the further understanding that individuals have restricted ability to handle data and formulate plans. Simon (1957) uses the term *bounded rationality* to signify the fact that decision makers are not omniscient and have real difficulties in processing information. Thus, while people can be seen as intendedly rational, they are not "hyperrational."

The assumption of imperfect individual rationality is dominant in transaction-cost analysis, in the more recent work on property rights, and in the new institutional approach to economic history. Williamson (1985) has consistently emphasized the importance of transaction costs in economic relations, and he has pointed out that, inter alia, limited rationality means that all economic exchange cannot be organized by market contracting. The situation under bounded rationality (and nonzero transaction costs) is such that it is impossible to deal with complex reality in all contractually relevant respects. As Kreps (1990b, 745) says:

> A boundedly rational individual attempts to maximize but finds it costly to do so and, unable to anticipate all contingencies, and aware of this inability, provides ex ante for the (almost inevitable) time ex post when an unforseen contingency will arise. Given this insight, the theory of incomplete contracts emerges as an inevitable development.

4. *Opportunistic behavior:* Qualities other than rationality per se have been attributed to decision makers. For example, Brunner and Meckling (1977, 71) describe the model of man developed in economics as the "resourceful, evaluating, maximizing man" (or REMM). This characterization implies that man is more than a brainy but heartless calculating machine. The literature also recognizes, however, that not all human qualities are attractive or praiseworthy. As Williamson has argued (1975), some individuals are likely to be dishonest in the sense that they may disguise preferences, distort data, or deliberately confuse issues. The existence of such behavior is important because, while bounded rationality prevents the writing of complete contracts, there could be general reliance on incomplete contracts if economic agents were *wholly trustworthy.* But realistically, since there is, in Williamson's phrase, "self-seeking with guile," and since it is normally very costly to distinguish opportunistic from nonopportunistic actors ex ante, comprehensive contracting must break down.

5. *Economic society:* From the most general standpoint, economic society can be said to involve individuals and a set of rules or norms that assign sanctioned property rights to each member of society. Property rights, in the economist's widest sense of the term, embrace the right to use and gain benefits from physical objects or intellectual works and the right to demand certain behavior from other individuals. The latter condition implies that contract rights exist—for example, in the requirement that the promised performance of a labor contract or loan agreement be fulfilled.[3] Society must, of course, be concerned with contract rights and the social arrangements that regulate the transfer of property rights.

Characteristically, neoclassical economics considers a special type of society in which the transfer of property rights by the use of physical force or other forms of compulsion is excluded. This convention means, inter alia, that the formation of pressure groups is ruled out. In other words, no attention is given to those coalitions whose purpose is to improve the welfare of their memberships at the expense of other individuals in the system through the use, for example, of government authority. In the neoclassical world, the only coalitions considered operate so as to produce Pareto improvements for their members by adhering to the principle of voluntary association and voluntary exchange.[4] Competition and free choice are assumed to dominate. Thus, transfer payments (including taxes) are to be understood as voluntary transfers within a cooperative coalition.

6. *Governance structure:* At any time, the property-rights configuration existing in an economy is determined and guaranteed by a governance structure[5] or order.[6] The latter can be understood as a system of rules plus the instruments that serve to enforce the rules. In general, an order may be enforced by "purely subjective" mechanisms (value-rational, religious, etc.) or by "the expectations of specific external effects" (Weber 1968, 33). Institutional economics usually deals with the second case—specifically, with a system that

---

3. Fisher (1912, 20) explains this as follows: "Lawyers distinguish between property rights and personal rights; but, to the economist, all rights are proprietary . . . logical convenience is served by adopting the broader definition of wealth, which includes human beings even when free, and by adopting also a coexistensively broad definition of property so as to include all rights known to jurisprudence. This being premised, it follows that every right is a property right. . . . Property rights, then, consist of rights to the uses or services of wealth." These are necessarily future services and they are therefore uncertain: "A strictly complete definition of property rights, therefore would read as follows: A property right is the right to the chance of obtaining some or all of the future services of one or more articles of wealth . . . Wealth and property . . . are correlative terms. Wealth is the concrete thing owned; property is the abstract right of ownership."

4. Essentially, that is the main concern of the theory of the core.

5. See Williamson (1979).

6. Weber uses the term *legitimate order* (1968, 31). Terms such as *structure, system,* and *social organization* have also been used (see Coleman 1991, 8).

restricts the possible behaviors of individuals through the use of sanctions. The sanctions are themselves established either by law or by custom (including the social enforcement of ethical and moral codes of conduct).

7. *Institutions:* It is tempting to try to secure some precision in formulating a definition for so basic a concept as the "institution," but, as Arrow has noted, "since research in this area is still in its early stages, undue exactness must be avoided" (1970, 224). In any event, for the purposes of this book, an institution will be defined as a set of formal and informal rules, including their enforcement arrangements (Schmoller 1900, 61). The purpose of an institution is, of course, to steer individual behavior in a particular direction. And, insofar as it is successful in realizing this objective, an institution provides structure to everyday activity and thus reduces uncertainty (North 1990, 239). In effect, institutions "define the incentive structure of societies and specifically economies" (North 1994, 4). This general conception of an institution can be elaborated, and it may be useful now to introduce Ostrom's fuller definition:

> "Institutions" can be defined as the sets of working rules that are used to determine who is eligible to make decisions in some arena, what actions are allowed or constrained, what aggregation rules will be used, what procedures must be followed, what information must or must not be provided, and what payoffs will be assigned to individuals dependent on their actions. . . . All rules contain prescriptions that forbid, permit, or require some action or outcome. Working rules are those actually used, monitored, and enforced when individuals make choices about the actions they will take . . . (1990, 51)

Schmoller (1900, 61) understands an institution to be

> a partial order for community life which serves specific purposes and which has the capacity to undergo further evolution independently. It offers a firm basis for shaping social actions over long periods of time; as for example property, slavery, serfhood, marriage, guardianship, market system, coinage system, freedom of trade.

How institutions come to be established is another question of interest, and the literature suggests at least two basic explanations. At one extreme, institutions are said to arise "spontaneously" (as a spontaneous order) on the basis of the self-interest of individuals. In such cases, they may organize themselves "without any agreement, without any legislative compulsion, even without any consideration of public interest" (Menger [1883] 1963, 154). Hayek (1973, 5) uses the term *evolutionary rationalism* to describe the situation. It is also recognized, however, that at the other extreme institutions may be the product of deliberate design. Some authority (parliament, a dictator, an entrepreneur, a team, etc.), acting with complete rationality, may be able to introduce a particular institutional structure that it deems appropriate. In the words of Hayek (1973), this is the case of a "made order" as opposed to a "spontaneous" or "grown order." Williamson (1991, 3) speaks of the respective situations as "intentional" and "spontaneous" governance. Coleman (1991, 8) uses the terms *constructed* and *spontaneous* social organization.

Institutions so defined are, so to speak, the grin without the cat, the rules of the game without the players. The functioning of an institution, though, depends in part on the individuals who use it. Thus, it follows that: "You cannot construct foolproof institutions" (Popper 1957, 66). Indeed, as Popper further notes: "Institutions are like fortresses. They must be well designed *and* properly manned" (66).

From the standpoint of institutional economics, there is interest not only in studying the characteristics of institutions but in making them integral elements of a general economic model. The endogenization of institutions is, therefore, crucial to the ongoing program of the New Institutional Economics.

8. *Organizations:* Institutions together with the people taking advantage of them are called organizations (North 1990) or in Schmoller's (1900, 61) terms "the personal side of the institution." Relative to the two explanations of institutional evolution mentioned above, the following associations hold. We speak, in the constructivist case, of formal organizations (a firm, a city council, etc.) and, in the spontaneous case, of informal organizations (such as a market community). De facto, there are neither pure formal nor pure informal organizations[7] to be found in the real world. Modern institutional economics deals with both institutions and organizations—that is, with institutions sine and cum people. Therefore, the New Institutional Economics includes, as a special case, the so-called new economics of organization (Moe 1984; Williamson 1991). A formal organization is defined by Arrow (1970, 224) as "a group of individuals seeking to achieve some common goals, or, in different language, to maximize an objective function." The problem of organizational control is, according to Arrow (225), answered by what we have termed an order.[8] Ideally, the order is constructed in such a way as to precisely maximize the organization's objective function. If this interpretation is accepted, it would seem that the economic theory of formal organizations (i.e., those that are deliberately "made") has some elements in common with neoclassical theory but still fits into the general body of institutional economics.

---

7. This terminology follows Weber (1968, 40, 48).

8. In the words of Arrow (1970, 225), this consists of a set of operating rules "instructing the members of the organization how to act" and a corresponding set of enforcement rules "to persuade or compel them to act in accordance with the operating rules."

It is apparent that real resources are required in order to create and operate any institution (or organization) and guarantee obedience to its rules. In other words, costs are involved, and these costs are referred to, broadly, as *transaction costs*. Once the assumption of a "frictionless" economic system is abandoned, analysis must change radically. Given frictions, property or contractual rights cannot be defined, monitored, and enforced instantly and without the use of resources. Rather, all of these essential activities imply transaction-cost outlays. Similarly, if property rights or contractual rights are to be transferred, transaction costs are inevitable. Specifically, there are costs attached to using the market (e.g., search and bargaining costs), and there are the costs of administrative coordination within a hierarchical organization (Chandler 1977, 490), including the setup costs of hierarchies. In short, transaction costs are both ubiquitous and significant in a modern economic system.

## 1.2. The Strange World of Costless Transactions

Although the fact has not always been recognized explicitly, the neoclassical model is based squarely on the assumption that transaction costs are zero. At first glance, such a simplification may appear to be both innocuous and highly useful to analysis. This assessment, however, is dubious. The concept of costless transactions has very far reaching consequences for microeconomic theory and leads to a model of the economic universe that is difficult to interpret consistently. In the rarefied world of zero transaction costs, decision makers can, supposedly, acquire and process any information they wish instantly and costlessly. They possess perfect foresight and, hence, are able to write complete contracts—contracts that can be monitored and enforced with absolute precision.[9] Force, in all its forms, is perfectly monopolized by the state. Consequently, there can exist no strikes, no boycotts, no sit-ins, no need for political correctness or other forms of social pressure. The power of coercion is exclusively in the hands of the state. Quite simply, then, it seems that, under neoclassical thinking, the setting in which economic activity is assumed to take place is remarkably specialized and remote from reality. While abstraction can be useful, there is good reason to believe that the neoclassical approach is overly abstract and incapable of dealing adequately with many current problems of interest to theorists and policymakers.

It is important to note that the assumption of costless transactions has great significance for the way institutions are viewed by neoclassical theory. The general impression conveyed is that institutional arrangements play an inconsequential role in the economic process. There is recognition that politi-

---

9. Note that "perfect foresight" does not necessarily imply that a decision maker knows precisely what the future will bring. Normally, the term is used to mean that the decision maker is aware of all future contingencies and knows the probabilities attaching to these contingencies.

cal, legal, monetary, and other institutions exist, but they are regarded as *neutral* in their effect on economic outcomes and largely ignored. In other words, institutions are taken as "allocationally neutral" in the sense that it does not matter, for example:

1. whether goods and services are exchanged by the use of money or otherwise (Samuelson 1968)
2. how production is organized—by the price mechanism across markets or within a hierarchically organized firm (Coase 1937)
3. whether the factors of production are owned or rented by their users (see Samuelson 1957, 894: "Remember that in a perfectly competitive market it really doesn't matter who hires whom: so have labor hire 'capital,' . . .").
4. who holds property rights in the productive factors, individuals or society (see, e.g., the arguments in favor of market socialism by Lange [1938] or of the labor-managed economy by Vanek [1970])
5. whether or not the ownership and control of a firm are separated (the market value rule is imposed by the forces of the market for corporate control, e.g., through the threat of hostile takeovers [Manne 1965])
6. whether the factors of production employed by a firm are financed by money loans or shares ("the market value of any firm is independent of its capital structure and is given by capitalizing its expected return at the rate . . . appropriate to its risk class" [Modigliani and Miller 1958, 268])
7. whether transactions are undertaken singly as transactions between "faceless strangers" or are repeated frequently between the same parties (Macneil 1974)
8. whether a good is supplied by a monopolist or by a large number of independent firms (in either case, unrestricted bargaining is said to lead to a Pareto-efficient equilibrium (Buchanan and Tullock 1962, 88; Demsetz 1968b, 61)[10]
9. whether legal rights are assigned to the party generating an externality or the party harmed by the externality (whatever the law, the allocation of resources will be identical [Coase 1960] because "people can always negotiate without cost to acquire, subdivide, and combine rights whenever this would increase the value of production" [Coase 1988b, 14])
10. whether an economy is based on the operations of decentralized individuals who rely on price signals and require no extensive infor-

---

10. From a game-theoretical viewpoint, this implies that every individual knows every other individual's payoff (utility, profit, or whatever function of the strategies played [Arrow 1979, 24]).

mation on the system's data or by a command structure based on a central agent who possesses complete knowledge of individual preferences, technological alternatives, resources, and so on.

Given the diversity and importance of the cases just summarized, it is clear that the idea of neutral institutions is strongly entrenched in neoclassical theory. It may be true that, in some instances, the downplaying of institutional arrangements does not seem to make much difference to the conclusions that can be reached by economic analysis. What has to be remembered, however, is that all of the explanations in points 1 through 10 are tied to the assumption of costless transactions, and this assumption implies that decision makers operate with perfect information and perfect foresight. But the presumption that hyperrational individuals exist necessarily affects outcomes. The precise and unambiguous solutions that can be reached in a frictionless world are simply not possible in the real world. As Stigler has said: "The world of zero transaction costs turns out to be as strange as the physical world would be without friction" (1972, 12). The central inference to be drawn is that, because of its treatment of institutions, neoclassical theory will not be able to discriminate between certain economic situations that are, in fact, quite different. For example, if the conventional neoclassical position is taken, a money-using economy cannot be distinguished from a barter economy or a private-ownership economy from a socialist economy. Yet we know that, in these cases, systems having the same initial data will show quite different results.

It should also be noted at this point that, in neoclassical theory, the price system is the *only* (explicitly modeled) device that is identified as a means for coordinating different activities. Administrative coordination is disregarded because it is generally not thought to be necessary in a market-driven system. Thus, coordination within institutions such as firms is viewed as taking place in a "black box." That is, whatever is presumed to happen beyond straightforward market transactions is not modeled.[11]

In general, the representatives of the NIE have not been content to merely criticize orthodox neoclassical theory. Rather, they have attempted to produce new theoretical constructs capable of explaining areas of economic life that have previously been ignored and of showing why certain neoclassical theorems cannot be validated in real life. A first step was to consider why the existence of positive transaction costs makes it necessary to view institutions as endogenous variables in the economic model. The answer, of course, is that in the real world institutional structure affects both transaction costs and individual incentives and hence economic behavior. Once this set of relations is

---

11. Arrow (1970, 232) says: "Some intra-organizational transactions will have the same economic content as price-mediated transactions . . . [but] there are limits to its application."

acknowledged, it follows that new, more refined economic models must appear. In the chapters that follow, this book will attempt to describe some of these innovations.

### 1.3.  The Ideal Type of the Classical Liberal State

General equilibrium theory can be understood as an approach that tries to establish the main features of the ideal type of liberal capitalist state in terms of a system of simultaneous equations. The state or society envisioned here is supposed to

> abstain from all attention to the personal wealth of its citizens and to go not a step further than necessary to secure its citizens against themselves and foreign enemies; for no other final purpose the State should restrict their freedom. (Humboldt [1792] 1967, 52)

Consequently, the elementary *constitutional rules* are based on the principle of the inviolability of individual property rights. This demands an elementary legal order, plus its enforcement mechanism, regulating: (1) the *property rights* of individuals according to the general principles of private property, (2) the *transfer* of these rights by consent according to the principle of freedom of contract,[12] and (3) individual *liability* for contractual obligations or in case of tortious acts.

Unfortunately, freedom of contract does not necessarily guarantee "voluntary exchange." To secure the latter, at least in general equilibrium theory, the principle of freedom of contract has to be *limited.* Individuals must not be permitted to contract in order to form coalitions whose purpose is predatory. That is, any coalition that is organized so as to improve the lot of its members at the expense of individuals outside the coalition must be ruled out. This restriction means, technically speaking, that there will be no resource allocations outside the core.[13] As a practical matter, there can be no pressure groups, no cartels, or, indeed, any coalition possessed of monopoly power. As noted, force is monopolized by the state, but the state's power of coercion is strictly limited by law—that is, by the state's constitution. Nevertheless, even if the state's powers are perfectly controlled, there remains the problem of the formation of pressure groups and the control of private coercive power.

The principle of freedom of contract can destroy itself through the evolution (via contract) of pressure groups, monopolies, and so on—Eucken (1952,

---

12. The individual has the right to regulate his contractual relations with a freely chosen partner in a mutually binding agreement.

13. Zero transaction costs do not imply the nonexistence of pressure groups. Actually, because of zero monitoring and enforcement costs, pressure groups are quite imaginable. See Furubotn (1991).

48), therefore, rightly demands that the constitutional state must protect its citizens not only from the coercive power of government but also from arbitrary acts by other citizens.[14] It follows that the formation of the institutional framework of the economy should not be left to itself.[15] Finally, the observance of this elementary legal order for the liberal state can be perfect provided that all activities can be monitored and proper behavior enforced at *zero cost.*

The basic legal structure implicit in the neoclassical model leaves room for the creation of "law" (*Recht*) by *private individuals,* and it is assumed that individuals take advantage of this opportunity. Given the existence of zero transaction costs (and the consequent full information status of decision makers), any private contracts made will be complete in the sense that they account for all contingencies. As a result of the private activity, the honeycomb of the legal order provided by the state is filled out by a network of complete (classical) contracts between individuals. Collectively, these contracts constitute a "voluntary legal order" built up spontaneously from below by utility-maximizing individuals (Hippel 1963, 27). In effect, freedom of contract is the institutional counterpart of the principle of economic decentralization—which is presupposed by competitive market models.[16]

According to the logic of the decentralized capitalist model, individual "atoms" negotiate with each other until they reach a state of the economy in which no one can improve his position without hurting someone else—that is, until Pareto efficiency is achieved. Since pressure groups are excluded by assumption and the number of bargaining parties is very large, the principle of free contracting described in this section is also the optimal means of achieving fair conciliation of interests. In other words, the presumption is that private contracting will be undertaken in such a way that the content of contracts will not be dictated by the more powerful agents in society.

## 1.4.  The Ideal Type of Market Socialism

From a technical standpoint, general equilibrium models are institutionally neutral, but, in much of the literature, such models are discussed against the background of a competitive capitalist system. Consequently, the first-best configuration of the economy, which is supposed to be attained when all of the

---

14. "If the constitutional State (Rechtsstaat) was able to protect its citizens from arbitrary acts of the State itself, it was unable to save them from the arbitrary acts by other citizens" (Eucken 1952, 52). Eucken warns that the constitutional state is only able to succeed completely if together with its public legal order an "adequate" economic order is realized (52).

15. Eucken has noted that: "The realization of the laissez-faire principle causes the tendency for its abolition" (1952, 55).

16. German legal literature speaks in this context of *Privatautonomie,* the principle that each individual is free to regulate the circumstances of his life himself.

Pareto conditions are met, is associated with idealized capitalism. This association, however, is not necessary or inevitable. As some socialist writers have attempted to show, the same general equilibrium model may also be used to characterize the role of prices (or shadow prices) in the democratic socialist state (whose operation mimics that of a laissez faire system). In the socialist case, of course, the elementary legal framework has to be changed accordingly. Perhaps the best-known model of the socialist market economy is the one Lange (1938) proposed in seeking to answer Mises's assertion that a socialist economy could not provide for consistent and efficient factor allocation. Under socialism, the material means of production belong to "society" or the state—which may be regarded as a coalition of all individuals who are members of the economic system under consideration. Unfortunately, this arrangement leads to the loss of normal (capitalistic) markets for production goods, natural resources, and so on, but, as Lange argues, artificial markets can be created. That is, the state planning authorities, with the aid of so-called industry managers, can set arbitrary prices and then, through a trial-and-error process, range in on meaningful scarcity prices.

Since the liberal socialist blueprint normally provides for free markets for consumer goods and labor, only certain sectors of the system require the use of the trial-and-error approach. In any event, if all activities go forward as Lange suggests, the economy will achieve a first-best equilibrium solution and show allocative efficiency equal to that promised in an ideal capitalist state. Moreover, certain added advantages are said to hold for socialism. Pressure groups such as unions do not exist and are not necessary. Since all enterprise profits revert to the state, the socialist economy is able to pay "social dividends" to the public at large and bring about a more egalitarian (and supposedly more "fair") distribution of income than that found in capitalist societies. Ownership and control of capital are perfectly separated in the socialist case. This separation, however, poses no problem in a zero-transaction-cost world. Of course, "ownership" under socialism has limited meaning; ownership rights are severely attenuated, and no private individual possesses either permanent or transferable rights in collective assets. Finally, what must be emphasized here is that the assumption of costless transactions is crucial to the results Lange and other theorists obtain. Given an environment in which perfect monitoring and enforcement are possible, even an authoritarian socialist state can be made to seem appealing.

The literature indicates that it is possible to construct other elementary legal orders and secure variant types of economic systems. Thus, for example, the institutional framework of socialist labor management has been studied, by Vanek (1970) among others. The system envisioned relies heavily on the existence of competition and is similar to capitalism in that profit maximization by firms is encouraged. Workers are accorded certain control rights in the firm and are expected to make key decisions for the firm.[17] Reward is based on the success of the firm's operations but is limited to usus fructus. In all cases, the productive capital required is leased to the labor-managed firms at a centrally or democratically determined leasing rate (Vanek 1990, 191), which, in the end, will become equal to the long-run equilibrium rate.

It is interesting to note that, in the zero-transaction-cost world of neo-classical economics, the two economic systems that have been viewed as the arch rivals of this century, capitalism and socialism, can be modeled by general equilibrium systems. Granted, the analysis of the respective cases proceeds only with regard to the role of the price system as a device meant to coordinate activities. No real attention is paid to the significance of changes in ownership (or property rights) for economic behavior. And this is true despite the fact that ownership, in another sense, constitutes a central issue for socialism. Indeed, the complete disregard of the economic role of ownership is astounding. To "prove" the workability of a socialist market economy by means of an institutionally neutral model (e.g., the Walrasian system) is as meaningless as if we were to use this model to "prove" that a barter economy is in reality as efficient as a monetary economy.

The essential point to be noted is this. In attempting to answer the question of whether a competitive market economy with or without private ownership rights in firms is the more efficient social arrangement, one needs a model in which property-rights structure plays a central role. Institutionally neutral general equilibrium theory is simply not appropriate for the purpose of comparing different institutional arrangements (Richter 1992a). In general, the concept of economic efficiency needs rethinking when something other than the frictionless neoclassical world is considered. And the problems of efficiency definition are compounded when the issue is one of proper institutional choice (Furubotn and Richter 1991, 11ff.).

## 1.5.  Constructed or Spontaneous Orders?

Earlier discussion indicated that there exist, in principle, two types of (formal) institutions—one created and protected "from above" by the central agent of an organization, the other created "from below" by independent individuals but also protected "from above." In the case of the classical liberal state, the two types of formal institutions are: (1) institutions in the sense of *law* (e.g., the German constitution or the German Civil Code), and (2) institutions in the sense of *rights* (e.g., concrete claims arising out of a voluntarily agreed upon labor contract).

---

17. The principle of freedom of contract excludes labor contracts for productive purposes and trade in land and capital goods.

In the neoclassical world of costless transactions and perfect foresight, such institutions, (constitutions, laws, individual contracts, and so on) are complete and perfect. Their provisions, which are perfectly enforceable by law, will be observed with absolute precision. Courts work without cost in resources and time. Moreover, in this special environment, it is known in advance how courts will decide in the event of litigation. Lawsuits could be carried out by computers because of perfect information and perfect laws and contracts. Strictly speaking, there will be no need for lawsuits because decision makers understand the conditions of the system and act with perfect rationality. This, then, is the neoclassical vision. It is the ideal world of the public administrator who dreams of perfect social engineering.

In real life, of course, neither the formal rules of society nor individual contracts are perfect, and individuals do not behave with complete rationality. Characteristically, the gaps in the formal constraints are covered, to some degree, by informal rules. The latter, however, cannot be fully enforced by law. From a historical standpoint, we know that informal conventions existed before the formal, legally enforceable rules came into being. In tribal societies, "a dense social network leads to the development of informal structures with substantial stability" (North 1990, 38). These arrangements make exchange possible, though only on a limited scale.[18] Since people have limited capacities to acquire and process information, uncertainty and asymmetric information must exist, and these conditions represent unavoidable obstacles to "perfect" institutional design.

As a result of the imperfections found in the real world, formal institutional arrangements such as constitutions, laws, contracts, and charters are inevitably *incomplete.* This inherent limitation should be recognized and dealt with as far as possible. Important instruments of the type noted should be written in such a way as to leave room for their rapid adaption to unforseen circumstances through the spontaneous development of informal rules. Following this flexible approach, the difficulties caused by uncertainty and asymmetric information can be reduced. Thus, during the last ten to fifteen years, the New Institutional Economics has placed increasing emphasis on the need to view institutional design from the perspective of unavoidable incompleteness.

### 1.6.  The Work of the Invisible Hand Can Be Accelerated

The invisible hand, if unaided by supporting institutions, tends to work slowly and at high cost. For example, we know that in primitive societies the absence of effective government contributes to limited exchange in property (Posner

---

18. For a good description, see Collson (1974).

1980). Fortunately, however, the work of the invisible hand can be accelerated substantially, and transaction costs lowered remarkably, by planned collective action undertaken through either public or private auspices. The "construction" of institutions is feasible because certain factors that are important to the successful fashioning of institutional arrangements are relatively well known to the public and largely independent of future events.

In the first place, a community normally has knowledge of the elementary "objects" in the system that require regulation or control through the functioning of institutional rules. Characteristic regulatory objects would include property, money, marriage, and contracts. Elementary property laws or rules, for example, have to regulate the use of an asset (usus), the appropriation of the returns from an asset (usus fructus), and the change of its form, substance, and location (abusus). The last element implies that the owner has the freedom to transfer some or all of his property rights in an asset to another individual at a mutually agreed upon price (as in selling or renting a house).

When money is introduced into a barter economy or when a new monetary system is created (such as the planned European Monetary Union), rules are again necessary. An elementary monetary order has to regulate four basic issues: the unit of account, its real anchor (i.e., the standard of coinage or the price target of monetary policy), the means of payment, and the organization of the money supply.[19]

Second, in addition to general knowledge of the regulatory objects of any particular institutional arrangement, society can have a rather clear understanding of how, on the average, individuals behave under certain circumstances. That is why comedies or tragedies can be written so convincingly that, sometimes at least, people in the audience laugh or cry at the right moment. That is also the reason why economics, as a science, is feasible at all. In trying to forecast tomorrow's interest rate, or the levels that will be reached by the prices of shares, economists have no great advantage over others. But economists can predict with some confidence what is likely to happen to a piece of property, say a forest, that operates as a common property resource. And economists know that the fate of the forest would be quite different if it were privately owned and subject to sale by its owner to any qualified purchaser. Similarly, reasonable predictions can be made of the circumstances under which a vendor will, on the average, adhere to his promises (or at least avoid gross infringements of the rules of good faith and fair dealing) and when not. Further, relative to the use of money, we can imagine quite well how, in general, the individual money user will protect his financial assets in the case of serious inflation. We can also tell broadly what kind of problems will arise if a manager does not own the business he runs.

---

19. See Richter (1989a, chap. 4).

In all of these illustrative cases, it is necessary to consider "human nature as we know it" (Knight 1922, 270) to make good forecasts. In particular, we have to identify "moral hazard" as an endemic condition with which economic organization must contend. The ideal of the perfectly honest, or perfectly controllable, homo oeconomicus of neoclassical theory cannot be sustained. This conclusion is basic to the approach taken by modern institutional economics.[20]

## 1.7.  Rational Incompleteness

Several thousand years of human history have made it clear that a lawmaker, however dedicated and ambitious, must accept incompleteness in any fabricated order. All of the contingencies of real life cannot be anticipated ex ante. Thus, a rational lawmaker does not try to regulate everything to the last detail. Rather, he recognizes the wisdom of leaving reasonable gaps in his design. The gaps in question can be closed over time, as circumstances dictate, by for example, "jurisprudence and legal practice."[21]

As noted, the fundamental problem in this area arises because of our relative ignorance. If everything were known in advance, "something could be done and specified in advance by rule. This would be a world fit for 'mechanical jurisprudence'" (Hart 1961, 125). But, as we know: "Plainly this is not our world; human legislators can have no such knowledge . . ." (125). One technique to deal legally with the difficulties created by "gaps" is to apply certain accepted principles—for example, the common judgment of what is "reasonable." Hart says: "The most famous example of this technique in Anglo-American law is the use of the standard of due care in cases of negligence" (129).

For obvious reasons, a judge is not free to decide cases according to his whims. He has to apply some principle[22] that, ideally, is understandable,

20. Although institutional economics is still in the process of development, economists are able to make predictions about how particular institutional arrangements affect behavior and economic outcomes. Indeed, in some areas, as in state ownership of the means of production, we know with considerable precision what the consequences of given institutional frameworks are likely to be.

21. A typical example of this general approach is found in German civil law. In Article 929 of the German Civil Code, which is concerned with the transfer of physical objects, the phrase "agreement and delivery" is used. Whether "agreement" in this context is to be understood only in the sense of "contract" (i.e., contractual transfer of ownership) or has a broader meaning is left to the dictates of "Wissenschaft und Praxis" (Motive 1888, 332).

22. Legal principles, not rules, are cited by courts as justification for adopting and applying a new rule. On the role of principles in reaching particular decisions of law, see, for example, Dwarkin (1977, 28ff). He discusses the positivists' tenet "that the law of a community is distinguished from other social standards by some test in the form of a master rule" (44). North

reconstructible, and predictable. Unavoidably, bargaining is pervasive. And this process seems to obey some implicitly or explicitly agreed upon principles. In any case, the rational lawmaker knows that additional rules will evolve over time. Changes will come about partly by the extension of judge-made law, or through the writing of individual contracts, and partly through the generation of informal rules. This informal area is the sphere in which the invisible hand still works, slowly but powerfully. Such action may help to stabilize a necessarily incomplete formal institutional structure (as in the development of property laws in the West), or it may destabilize a system (as in the property regulations in the East under socialism). In either case, the inevitable residual activity of the invisible hand, via the continuous bargaining between private or public agents, is an important source of institutional change.

Not only constitutions and formal bodies of law but also private contracts are necessarily incomplete. Indeed:

> The parties [to a contract] will quite rationally leave out many contingencies, taking the point of view that it is better to 'wait and see what happens' than to try to cover a large number of individually unlikely eventualities. Less rationally, the parties will leave out other contingencies that they simply do not anticipate. Instead of writing very long-term contracts the parties will write limited-term contracts, with the intention of renegotiating these when they come to an end. (Hart 1987, 753)

It is true, of course, that in considering contracting activities decision makers are forced to take due account of transaction costs.

The parties to a contract must agree, either explicitly or tacitly, "about the procedure [the 'constitution'] that will be employed to deal with problems that may arise in the future" (Macneil 1974, 753). Moreover, it is accepted that negotiations on matters of concern will be carried on more or less continuously. Many of the different types of contracts found in the business world have emerged on the basis of this set of procedures. In the academic literature, Williamson (1985) especially has stressed the ongoing nature of contractual relations and has criticized models that assume all contractual problems are solved, once and for all, during the initial period.

Room for the development of informal rules in a formal organization is generally of vital importance. Barnard (1938, 120) has argued that "formal organizations are vitalized and conditioned by informal organizations. . . .

---

(1978, 976) suggests that it is useful to analyze "legal principles" from the standpoint of "ideology." See section 1.10.

[T]here cannot be one without the other."[23] All this has obvious significance for the New Institutional Economics. The evolution of informal rules is seen, once again, as the force that in the end may lead to institutional change. Informal rules, as expressed by certain empirical uniformities, are called "custom" (*Sitte*) if the practice is based upon long-standing behavior (cf. Weber 1968, 29). Important for the viability of a custom is what Schlicht (1997) calls the "clarity of its informal rules."

Any custom refers to regularities that must be perceived, learned, memorized, and passed on. Unclear and complicated rules cannot be handled in this way and cannot, therefore, be coded by custom. This constrains possible customary patterns. Clarity eases encoding, while unclarity smothers it (Schlicht 1997).[24]

## 1.8. Enforcement

Bounded rationality makes institutional incompleteness inevitable, and the existence of incompleteness causes problems not only for the design of an institution's behavioral rules but also for its enforcement rules. The basic difficulty is that, in the case of an incomplete institution, legal enforcement is of limited use. The perfect constitutional state (*der "perfekte Rechtsstaat"*) simply does not exist in practice. Thus, legal enforcement rules must be supplemented by extralegal guarantee instruments such as hostages, collateral, tit-for-tat strategies, reputation, and so on. In other words, various "private" guarantees against "bad" behavior by an institution's members are needed during their unavoidably ongoing relationship. The rational designer of an incomplete institution has to take into account a priori the human tendency toward opportunistic behavior—that is, the predisposition toward self-seeking with guile (Williamson 1985, 47).

It is true, of course, that conflicts may also arise because of honest disagreement among parties (Alchian and Woodward 1988, 66). In general, then, the rational designer of an incomplete institution must plan for strategic or "noncooperative" behavior on the part of the participants during their ongo-

---

23. One of the indispensable functions of informal organizations operating within a formal organization is communication. "Another function is that of maintenance of cohesiveness in formal organizations through regulating the willingness to serve and the stability of objective authority. A third function is the maintenance of the feeling of personal integrity, of self-respect, of independent choice" (Barnard [1938] 1962, 122). Barnard also stresses the importance of personal knowledge on the part of management. The "clarity view" of custom is elaborated by Schlicht (1997). The clarity view stresses the motivational aspect of custom as well as its unifying force.

24. *Bargaining,* understood in the widest sense of the word, includes as a limiting case the possibility of delegating all decision making to one party, an "authority."

ing bargaining process.[25] The designer has to make sure that the members or parties of an institution agree ex ante to guarantees against ex-post opportunism (noncooperative behavior). As might be expected, transaction costs play an important role in this context. Because they require resources, activities undertaken to enforce an institution's operating rules should be treated as a standard economic problem (Wiggins 1991). And this cost issue looms large in comparative institutional analysis. Differences in institutional design may be attributed in large degree to the need to overcome enforcement problems. Full understanding of institutions must, in fact, rest on a more complete understanding of the enforcement process (Wiggins 1991, 33).

In a general sense, the enforcement problem turns on the matter of how to make incomplete agreements "binding" and thus credible. The credibility problem was "discovered," as an important issue, by economic theorists pursuing different specialties. For example, monetary economists were concerned with credibility in their analysis of monetary policy formation (Persson and Tabellini 1990). Similarly, industrial organization economists focused on this issue in their research on the purchase of experience goods (Klein and Leffler 1981).[26]

Characteristically, the establishment and enforcement of institutional norms requires some kind of *collective* action, private or public. This is precisely what the New Institutional Economics analyses, and it is this recognition of the need for collective action that sets the NIE apart from orthodox neoclassical theory. The latter accepts the metaphor of the invisible hand and supposes harmony of individual actions because enforcement is seen as automatic in a zero-transaction-cost world. Once frictions are posited, however, the operation of the invisible hand cannot be accepted without qualification. In what follows, then, economic behavior will be assumed to include the development of enforcement rules and the necessary collective action to support the rules.

Arrow mentions the role of ethical and moral codes in connection with the enforcement problem. "It is useful for individuals to have some trust in each other's word. In the absence of trust, it would become very costly to arrange for alternative sanctions and guarantees, and many opportunities deriving from mutually beneficial cooperation would have to be foregone. Banfield (1958) has argued that lack of trust is indeed one of the causes of economic underdevelopment" (Arrow 1969, 62).

The observations made by Arrow represent a recognition of the instru-

---

25. Commitment problems play a central role in shaping the structure of firms, contracts, and most long-term relationships (see Wiggins 1991).

26. See also Dewatripont (1986) on the problem of "renegotiation proofness" in the context of labor markets.

mental role of morality, the overlap of economics and practical ethics.[27] Social morality (or trust) cannot simply be bought. Within limits, it can be produced through "education"—a collective undertaking that requires a considerable amount of real resources and time to become effective. Such education may be costly, but it is crucially important for keeping society together.

## 1.9. The Political Process

The political process is intimately involved in bringing about institutional change, but many economists, at least in this century, have tended to abstract from political phenomena in conducting their analyses. Realistically, though, political and economic processes cannot be separated.

People are not merely consumers and producers; they are also citizens in a variety of polities that not only regulate markets but can expropriate directly the resources markets allocate. Correspondingly, it is impossible to predict market outcomes without also predicting the political response that alternative outcomes engender (Ordeshook 1990, 9). That is the hard lesson for people who favor free markets. The hard lesson for socialists is that "whatever institutional structure the state takes, the laws governing market forces cannot be abrogated—the forces of supply and demand operate regardless of culture, ethnic identity, socialization patterns, ideology, and political system" (9). It is therefore apparent that the NIE is related to the New Political Economy in the sense of Black 1958, Downs 1957, Buchanan and Tullock 1962, Olson 1965, and so on. But, strangely, these authors have not shown much interest in utilizing the methods of the NIE for analysis. On the other hand, among the representatives of the NIE, North (1990) probably comes closest to dealing with the subject matter of Public Choice Theory with his observations on what he calls the "institutional environment." Some political scientists, too, such as Keohane, Shepsle, Weingast, and Levi, have concerns with institutional questions and have produced works that show affinity with the neoinstitutionalist approach.

Political and economic decisions are necessarily interconnected in the real world where positive transaction costs exist and no party has a complete monopoly on violence. Decisions are constrained by formal economic and political rules. Both have to be consistent, and both are necessarily incomplete. That is, informal rules develop in both fields through the functioning of the "invisible hand." The problem with state and governmental activity is that "formal political rules, like formal economic rules, are designed to facilitate

---

27. For example, Adam Smith [1776] 1976) has spoken of the great importance of rules of conduct: "Those general rules of conduct, when they have been fixed in our mind by habitual reflection, are of great use in correcting misrepresentation of self-love concerning what is fit and proper to be done in our particular situation" (quoted in Sen 1990, 87).

exchange but democracy in the polity is not to be equated with competitive markets in the economy" (North 1990, 51). Dealings in the arena of "power" are, apparently, much more difficult to explain by means of the workings of some sort of invisible hand than are market phenomena in the case of economic exchange. Nevertheless, even in the political sphere, decentralization, and thus competition, is possible, too. As a political counterpart to the market economy, one may consider a federalist state such as Switzerland. Federalism may enhance political competition (Weingast 1995) and thus help to check the power of the state as the owner of some kind of "monopoly of violence." However, the transaction costs associated with political markets are high, and for this reason institutional inefficiency tends to persist (North 1990, 52).

Another important point to consider is that the coercive power of the state can be used to economize on transaction costs (Arrow 1969, 60). And, as Arrow points out: "Political policy is not made by voters. . . . It is in fact made by representatives in one form or another. Political representation is an outstanding example of the principle-agent relation" (61).

Disregard of the interrelationship between economic development and political processes by Western academic advisers is responsible for the malaise of development economics and the slow and hesitant economic transformation of postcommunist countries. As Riker and Weimer (1995, 85) point out, Western advisers have not been as alert to the political side of political economy as they have been to the economic. Consequently, they "initially proposed reforms for a well-operating market for free trade. But when these reforms were undertaken, without solicitation of popular political support for the new economic system, the voters often became hostile to the reforms, which seemed to offer immediate suffering for only the prospect of future benefits." The authors continue: "Only in the Czech Republic . . . did the government undertake economic reform balanced with a search for political support" (85).

### 1.10. Agency

The legal construct of agency plays a prominent role as an analytical concept in modern institutional economics. The basic idea conveyed is simple. The agent acts on behalf of the principal, but the principal faces difficulties in trying to monitor the actions of his agent. What the principal sees, essentially, are results. For example, if the principal is the owner of a firm and the agent serves as the firm's manager, the results are the profits at the end of the year. Provided there were no exogenous disturbances (e.g., variations in the weather), the principal could assess the firm's results and draw conclusions about the behavior (e.g., the effort level) of his agent. However, if outside disturbances that could influence results did occur, the agent may have valid excuses for bad results, and the principal cannot determine definitively what the reason is for the results observed.

In theory, a situation can be envisioned in which the principal is "blind" as a direct monitor of his agent but otherwise has full knowledge of his agent's personality (the agent's preference function) as well as precise knowledge of the distribution function of the external shocks (disturbances). Under these special circumstances, the principal can design a remuneration plan for the agent that could induce or "bribe" the agent to act advantageously for the principal. This is, broadly speaking, what the economic principal-agent theory is about.

Of course, informational difficulties (i.e., transaction costs) are ubiquitous in real life and not confined to one or a few activities. Indeed, once we reject the notion of the omniscient decision maker who is "completely rational" (Kreps 1990b, 745), the existence of positive transaction costs everywhere in the system is assured. The implication is that complete agency contracts (in the sense of the preceding paragraph) will be impossible. Incomplete contracts must rule in practice. Thus, one of the central interests of the New Institutional Economics is the search for optimal incomplete agency contracts.

The field of application of the principal-agent model is very wide. What can be included, besides the familiar problem of separation of ownership from control in the firm, is, for example, the issue of rules versus discretion in economic policy making. A basic point is this: insofar as positive transaction costs and incomplete foresight exist, it is not feasible to write a complete set of rules that monetary or fiscal policymakers must observe. Discretionary powers for agents are, within limits, unavoidable. The problem, then, is how principals in the form of money users or taxpayers can protect themselves against opportunistic behavior on the part of their agents (the policy authorities).

### 1.11. Institutional Stability

The problem of institutional stability becomes evident once consideration is given to the possibility that institutions may evolve and show changes in their structures over time. Change (or distortion) can come to any type of institution (constitution, contract, etc.) and, in each case, it is important to understand the causes and consequences of change. For formal institutions (so-called made orders) key questions are: what set of informal rules will grow into the gaps in the formal institutional framework and how long will the spontaneous growth process continue? Is it likely that some stable endpoint will be reached that represents a *complete* institutional arrangement? And, if such an endpoint does appear, can it be viewed as a true institutional equilibrium position?

Presumably, an institutional equilibrium would mean that an original set of formal rules remains in active use despite the fact that a supplementary set of informal rules and enforcement characteristics has grown up to complete the total structure. Then, an institutional equilibrium may be said to be essentially stable: (1) if it is achieved "automatically" in the sense that the informal rules reach some stable endpoint of the new (complete) institutional arrangement without destroying the original formal framework, or (2) if, after a disturbance of an initial institutional equilibrium, a new institutional equilibrium (not necessarily the original) will be reached. The central concern expressed here is with the adaptive capabilities of institutions such as markets (Hayek 1945) or hierarchies (Barnard 1938).[28]

It should be noted that a theory of institutions may not lead to the conclusion that unique institutional equilibria will always emerge (Schotter 1981, 12). Note further that political and economic processes cannot be separated in this context. The New Institutional Economics is therefore closely related to the new political economics (public choice and constitutional economics) and political science proper.

Even a tentative understanding of the nature of institutional stability permits us to recognize that it is impossible to impose any ad libitum constructed institutional framework on people and expect that it will function normally. In general, we know that institutional change can be the result of institutional instability in the sense of "bad design." Change may, however, come about as a consequence of economic growth or decline or because of technical, intellectual, or cultural shifts. History suggests that there is no easy way to forestall institutional instability; certainly, attempts to simply arrest change through the use of force have proved ineffective.[29]

An example of institutional instability drawn from experience can be instructive. Thus, consider the European Monetary System (EMS) of 1979. It

---

28. Barnard was particularly interested in the adaptability of internal organizations. He writes that "the survival of an organization depends upon the maintenance of an equilibrium of complex character. . . . [This] calls for readjustment of processes internal to the organization. . . . [Hence] the *center of our interest* is the processes by which [adaptation] is accomplished" ([1938] 1962, 6). Williamson asks in this connection: "If, however, the 'marvel of the market' [Hayek] is matched by the 'marvel of internal organization' [Barnard], then wherein does one outperform the other?" (1991, 163)

29. In considering the Platonic State, Popper makes the comment:

Arresting political change is not the remedy, it cannot bring happiness. We can never return to the alleged innocence and beauty of the closed society. Our dream of heaven cannot be realized on earth. Once we begin to rely on our reason, and to use our powers of criticism, once we feel the call of personal responsibilities, and with it, the responsibility of helping to advance knowledge, we cannot return to a state of implicit submission to tribal magic. For those who have eaten of the tree of knowledge, paradise is lost. The more we try to return to the heroic age of tribalism, the more surely we arrive at the Inquisition, at the Secret Police, and at a romanticized gangsterism. Beginning with the suppression of reason and truth, we must end with the most brutal and violent destruction of all that is human. (1945, 1:200) formally was organized in such a way that no "key currency" existed. The system, however, developed so that the D-mark "automatically" assumed the role of a key currency and the Bundesbank the role of a "stability leader" for the system. The general result was that the formal part of the European Monetary System was not stable in the sense described. The informal rules that grew into the formal institutional framework led to an institutional disequilibrium manifested by the desire of some members of the EMS to create the European Monetary Union (EMU). The motivation for this suggested change in structure was presumably the wish on the part of some member states to avoid German monetary hegemony. This, of course, represented a political rather than an economic reason. What can be expected now is that the formal institutional framework of the European Monetary Union will, again, be necessarily incomplete. The question that arises, then, is what kind of informal institutional extension will grow into the new formal hull of the EMU. Will the EMU, given the present individual interests of Europeans and in light of their individual endowments, organization, and technical knowledge, move to a stable endpoint, to an institutional equilibrium? To answer this question, both political and economic forces have to be taken into account. There are, however, good reasons to expect that the EMU will not be a stable system—provided it will in fact be realized.

### 1.12.  Once More with Feeling

In the discussion so far, it has been argued that the working of the "invisible hand" can be accelerated by the introduction of a set of rationally designed formal institutions into a system. It is true, however, that even the best attempts at such construction cannot be expected to yield perfect or "complete" institutions. Rationally designed formal institutions have to leave room for the development of informal arrangements. Moreover, if the so-called made institutional framework is to be *stable,* the structure must be established so as to take account of "human nature as we know it" and must, of course, remain open for the inevitable growth of informal process and enforcement rules.

Affectual social relationships "determined by the actor's specific affects and feeling states" have a role to play in shaping the general environment in which economic activity takes place, as do the traditional social relationships that are determined by "ingrained habituation" (Weber 1968, 25). Feelings or traditions cannot be created ad hoc by rational acts, and time often is involved. To illustrate this point, it will be useful to consider the phenomenon of trust among people. Without a large measure of general trust, "society itself would disintegrate" (Simmel 1978, 178). Obviously, trust cannot be created instantaneously—for example, by the use of force or money. Trust is the product of an evolutionary process that takes time. Among other things, it requires the development of common values (social consensus) and the adaptation of values to new conditions. Credible commitments by the agents of society are also crucial in this connection. We know that, to a great extent, the past rules the present, that history matters.

Take the institution of money; without trust, money transactions would collapse. Simmel argues that it is important to think of trust not only in the sense of, for example, confidence in next year's harvest, but also as

> a further element of social-psychological quasi-religious faith. The feeling of personal security that the possession of money gives is perhaps the most concentrated and pointed form and manifestation of confidence in the sociopolitical organization and order. (Simmel 1978, 179)

Dasgupta (1988, 51) speaks of "trust" as involving correct expectations about the *actions* of other people who influence one's own choice of action when that action must be chosen before it is possible to *monitor* the actions of these others. He emphasizes that the inability to monitor others' actions in his definition of trust is crucial. Logically, this is "trust" viewed in terms of the "moral hazard" version of the principal-agent problem previously described.

From the standpoint of motivation, it can be argued that feelings and emotions are the proximate causes of most behavior (Frank 1990). The psychological reward mechanism that guides individual choices can and does compete with feelings that spring from rational calculations about material payoffs. Frank's thesis is that understanding of this interaction has direct relevance for the commitment problem that underlies the matter of trust.

Commitment problems in close personal relationships are better solved by moral sentiments than by awkward formal contracts. The best insurance against a change in future material incentives is a strong bond of love. If ten years from now one partner falls victim to a lasting illness, the other's material incentive will be to find a new partner. But a deep bond of affection will render this change in incentive irrelevant, which opens the door for current investments in the relationship that might otherwise be too risky (Frank 1990, 76).

Presumably, the ideal outcome just described can be realized only if feelings are equally strong on both sides. There are, of course, clues to behavioral predispositions, but it is also true that emotional attitudes can be falsified and misleading signals given. In any event, Frank finds it useful to distinguish between the *commitment model* and the *self-interest* model. As suggested, the former relates to situations in which seemingly irrational behavior may be explained by emotional predispositions that help solve commitment problems, while the latter concerns situations in which people always act "efficiently" in the pursuit of narrow self-interest.

Feelings are important not only in the context of private relationships but also in the public domain. Thus, the connection between feelings and ideologies must be considered. Ideologies, or comprehensive systems of cognitive and moral beliefs, figure prominently in social life and require study (North 1978, 972ff.).[30]

Ideologies are shared frameworks of mental models possessed by groups of individuals that provide both an interpretation of the environment and a prescription as to how that environment should be ordered (North 1994, 363, n.6).[31]

They may be understood as implicit agreements about informal rules for social action that help to reduce uncertainty. They may or may not become social norms or "ethical systems." Whatever the outcome here, the quality of trust an individual has in the word of others is correlated with the quality of the system of informal rules established in society in the large or in the small. The formation of implicit agreements (social relationships) leads to a structure that has some persistence over time. These agreements need not only be seen as components of social structure but as resources for individuals. Indeed, the term *social capital* has been used to describe these resources (see, e.g., Schlicht 1984; and Coleman 1990, 300).[32]

Of course, change in ideology, or implicit agreements, can take place over time and a hysteresis effect may be observed. As Arrow has pointed out:

> [Social] agreements are typically harder to change than individual decisions. When you have committed not only yourself but many others to an enterprise, the difficulty of changing becomes considerable . . . (1974, 128)

---

30. North argues that: "The study of ideology has been bedeviled by its origins in the writings of Marx . . . and Mannheim . . . on the relativity of knowledge to one's social position. . . . But ideology can be studied as a positive science, and empirically testable propositions can be derived as Robert Merton (1949) pointed out . . . in examining the literature on the sociology of knowledge" (1978, 975). North goes on to suggest two propositions about ideology that bear exploration by economic historians. These are: (1) all societies invest substantial resources to convince their constituents that the existing system is legitimate, and (2) the political and judicial structure results in legislators and judges making many decisions about property rights (and therefore resource allocation) based on their set of moral and ethical views about the "public good." It follows, from the latter point especially, that: "Any study of the independent judiciary must make ideology central to analysis" (976).

31. Schmoller (1900, 70), like North, argues that: "The nature of Weltanschauung, the moral system, is to give a holistic view of the world. Such a system therefore always contains some hypothesis and belief . . ."

32. Other such terms are *moral capital* (Schlicht 1984) and *organizational capital* (Weizsäcker 1971).

He goes on to say that what may be hardest of all to change are unconscious agreements, agreements whose very purpose is lost to mind.

> A commitment to war or revolution or to religion is typically one that is very hard to reverse, even if conditions have changed from the time when the thing started. Even if experience has shown the unexpectedly undesirable consequences of a commitment, the past may continue to rule the present. (128)

Examples are provided by contemporary developments in Eastern Europe. For the reasons indicated, then, rational institutional change cannot help but be path dependent. The working of the invisible hand can be accelerated only within limits by "piecemeal social engineering," as Popper (1957, 64) calls it.[33]

Popper's arguments in favor of policies that seek only modest change in social arrangements seems to speak against a restructuring of the Eastern European economy by means of shock therapy. There is little doubt that attempts at swift and radical change pose dangers, and this fact must be kept in mind even though it seems essential to repair the consequences of misleading socialist ideology and to reestablish modern market economies in Eastern Europe. Some grounds for optimism may exist because these troubled societies had functioning market systems fifty to eighty years ago, and reversion to a historically known position is not quite the same thing as moving into a completely new and untried institutional framework. Nevertheless, a new social consensus, a consensus ideology, has to be developed, and a new system of informal rules has to grow into the gaps of the formal market framework, if a successful economic reconstruction of Eastern Europe is to be achieved. At best, this transformation will take time and resources and is, politically, a tricky exercise. Reconstruction requires, besides patience and sufficient popular confidence in the new policy, substantial specific investments in the political, educational, intellectual, and other sectors of these societies.

To summarize the main themes of this general line of discussion, we can say the following. The rules and enforcement characteristics of specific institutions involve elements that can, for the most part, be "rationally expected" by lawmakers, contracting parties, organizers, and so on. The basic objects of regulation are known in advance. Moreover, as for the rules to be applied for these objects, we know pretty well from experience and introspection how individuals behave on the average under certain circumstances. Inferring from this, we are able to formulate general principles according to which the rules

---

33. This is understood to be distinct from what he calls "holistic" or "utopian" engineering. "It aims at remodeling the 'whole of society' in accordance with a definite plan" (Popper 1957, 67).

and enforcement characteristics of a particular institution are to be written. Differently expressed, the presumption is that society is able to use incentive and disincentive effects rationally in setting up the basic structure of an institution. It is also understood that complete or perfect rationality is impossible in social planning because of transaction costs and an unavoidable lack of knowledge of what the future will bring. Institutional arrangements will, of necessity, be incomplete, and therefore they should be planned from the outset, as incomplete. That is, institutional arrangements should be sufficiently flexible and open ended so that they will be able to adapt swiftly and at low cost to new circumstances. Enforcement through credible commitments plays a vital role in this connection. Costs also have to be considered because considerable amounts of real resources are needed to establish, operate, and adapt institutions.

Brief mention can be made of other factors that affect institutional development. Agency relationships influence social processes and raise special problems because of informational asymmetries. Inevitably, there are important interconnections between economic and political activities. And, finally, we know that history matters for the success or failure of institutional change and that there are limits to institutional engineering. The path dependency of institutional change and the ideological and emotional predispositions of the public always have to be taken into account.

## 1.13. The New Institutional Economics and Modern Institutionalism

The various issues described in the preceding sections illustrate the types of problems addressed by modern institutional economists. Such writers, however, do not all follow the same analytic approach. Rather, they deal with problems selectively and often use quite different methods. Thus, it is important to emphasize that, in the present book, we shall concentrate attention on one particular mode of analysis—the New Institutional Economics. This line of investigation, also called the New Theory of Organization, is associated with the work of Armen Alchian, Ronald Coase, Douglass North, Oliver Williamson, and others.[34] Analysis here is based on the elementary insight that the creation of institutions and organizations, and their day-to-day use, requires the input of real resources. In short, the existence of transaction costs is recognized. And nonzero transaction costs mean, in turn, that resources have significance at several levels. Resources serve as transaction inputs in production and distribution activities and as necessary factors in maintaining the framework within which all economic operations take place. It follows, of course, that the

---

34. The term *New Institutional Economics* was coined by Williamson (1975, 1).

assignment and formation of individual property rights in resources have direct influence on the economic results achieved by a society.

*Transaction costs, property rights, and contractual relations* constitute basic elements in the literature of the New Institutional Economics. All these concepts have far-reaching consequences that require exploration. For example, it is possible to argue that, because of transaction costs, the neoclassical assumption of perfect rationality has to be abandoned and replaced by some notion of "bounded rationality." Thus, consistent with these understandings, the following chapters are organized around the three themes just noted. We begin with a chapter each on transaction costs and property rights and continue with two chapters on contract rights. The first of the contract chapters covers writings cast largely in literary terms, while the second takes up contributions made in the mathematical style by information or contract theorists such as Stiglitz and Holmstrom. Uniformity of approach does not obtain in these fields, and, indeed, disagreement exists about how the research should be pursued. On the new institutionalist side, there is skepticism concerning the usefulness of the formal approach. This is so primarily because formal contract theory stays relatively close to neoclassical preconceptions and assumes, inter alia, that decision makers possess a capacity for highly rational behavior. It is this rationality assumption that neoinstitutionalists see as unacceptable because it is inconsistent with their belief that transaction costs and bounded rationality make anything like mathematically precise economic calculation impossible for individuals.[35] Nevertheless, in order to present a full survey of the divergent methods applied in the New Institutional Economics and its immediate neighborhood, an investigation of formal contract models is unavoidable. (This presentation will be undertaken in simplified form so that readers possessing basic knowledge of standard microeconomic theory will be able to follow it readily.)

As planned, the first part of the book is devoted to a description and explanation of the analytical tools of the New Institutional Economics. In the second part, the objective is to illustrate the application of the new research style to certain significant problems. Specifically, understanding of three fundamental types of institutions will be sought—namely, the market, the firm, and the state. It is hoped that the examples provided here are sufficiently diverse to give the reader an idea of the flexibility of the new institutionalist research procedures and to show how they can be applied to a variety of real world problems. Given this background, the power of the NIE approach to yield valuable insights into economic phenomena should become evident.

---

35. Indeed, some leading figures in the new institutionalist group, such as Frey and Williamson, argue that formalization may actually be counterproductive and impede further advances in the understanding of basic institutional questions.

The analytical methods based on the fundamental building blocks of the New Institutional Economics were, of course, not developed at one stroke in the systematic manner outlined in this book. The new approach, which is still in the process of refinement, came about as the result of groundbreaking studies in various subfields of what is now known as modern institutional economics. These subfields included the following.

1. *Transaction-cost economics:* Transaction costs arise in connection with the exchange process, and their magnitude affects the ways in which economic activity is organized and carried out. Included within the general category of transaction costs are search and information costs, bargaining and decision costs, and policing and enforcement costs. Transaction-cost economics is concerned particularly with the effect such costs have on the formation of contracts. Contributors in this area include Coase, Williamson, Alchian, Klein, Demsetz, and Barzel.

2. *Property-rights analysis:* The system of property rights in an economic system defines the positions of individuals with respect to the utilization of scarce resources. Since the allocation of property rights influences incentives and human behavior in ways that are generally predictable, a basis exists for studying the impact of property-rights arrangements on economic outcomes. Contributors in this area include Coase, Alchian, Demsetz, DeAlessi, Furubotn, and Pejovich.

3. *Economic theory of contracts:* As a "relative" of both transaction-cost economics and property-rights analysis, contract theory deals with incentive and asymmetric information problems. The latter fall into two distinct categories. There can be asymmetric information between the parties to a contract and asymmetric information between the contractual parties on one side and a third party (e.g., the court) on the other. Accordingly, we may distinguish between two variant types of contract theories.

a. *Agency theory* deals with problems of asymmetric information between contractual parties. The asymmetric information in question can exist either before or after a transaction has taken place. The theoretical approach adopted in these cases may rely largely on verbal analysis or on the use of formal models. Contributors to verbal ("positive") agency theory include Jensen, Meckling, Fama, Alchian, and Demsetz. Contributors to the mathematical ("normative") agency literature include Stiglitz, Holmstrom, Spence, and Shavell.

b. *Relational and incomplete contract theory* focuses on informational asymmetries that can arise between the parties to a (usually longer-term) contract on one side and a third party on the other. An important objective of such contracts is to overcome the postcontractual opportunism that may result from the difficulties courts or other third parties face in verifying the execution of contractual obligations. Credible commitments and self-enforcing commitments are important topics in this field. Contributors to relational contract theory include Macauly, Macneil, Goldberg, Williamson, and Alchian. Writers such as Grossman and Hart have contributed to the literature of formal incomplete contract theory, while Telser, Klein, Leffler, and Kreps have produced less formal models of self-enforcing contracts.

4. *The new institutional approach to economic history:* The work of economic historians following this methodological line is concerned with the application and extension of concepts such as transaction costs, property rights, and contractual relationships to historical experience. One important objective is to establish a theory of the institutional structure of society as a whole. As would be expected, writers in this field are especially concerned with making institutions endogenous variables within a general economic model. Contributors in this area include North, Thomas, Wallis, Weingast, Hoffman, Eggertsson, Libecap, and Greif.

5. *The new institutional approach to political economics:* In recent years, the New Institutional Economics movement has given impetus to the development of the so-called New Economics of Organization (NEO). This approach, pioneered by Williamson and drawing on ideas developed independently by North, has been applied in various fields of political science. The areas affected include the theory of the state (Levi 1988), government organization (Shepsle and Weingast 1987), public administration (Weingast 1984; Moe 1990), international organization (Keohane 1984), and the emergence and change of (political) institutional arrangements (Knight and Sened 1995), among others. In general, it can be said that the close relationship between the political and economic sides of social systems, which has been the basic object of study for political economy, is now viewed from the perspective of transaction costs and their effects on property rights and contractual arrangements. These observations provide a link to constitutional economics.

6. *Constitutional economics:* Buchanan (1987, 585) describes this field as one that attempts "to explain the working properties of alternative sets of legal-institutional-constitutional rules that constrain the choices in activities of political and economic agents." Moreover, since these "rules" can be interpreted as formal or informal social devices that constrain behavior, procedures for making selections among alternative constraints must be examined along with the constraints themselves. In particular, interest attached to the study of how society chooses the rules for making the rules under which the system operates ("public choice"). This focus on institutional choice suggests that some of the recent work on constitutional economics may be regarded as an American version of German Ordnungspolitik. American representatives include Buchanan, Wagner, and Tollison. German representatives include Eucken, Böhm, Miksch, and Watrin. Significantly, the new view of pressure groups initiated by Olson (1965) has developed into an important topic of its own.

It is also interesting to observe that in recent years there has been an increased willingness among sociologists to apply rational-action-based theory to social problems. This movement has stimulated the development of areas of mutual interest among economists, including representatives of the NIE and sociologists. According to Swedberg (1990), economists with sociological interests include such scholars as Becker, Akerlof, and Williamson. On the other side, Coleman, White, Granovetter, Lindenberg, and Opp can be mentioned as sociologists with economic interests.

These various subfields, which underlie our presentation of the New Institutional Economics, overlap to greater and lesser degrees. Collectively, they comprise a considerable part of modern institutional economics. Nevertheless, subsequent discussions in this book will give only limited attention to some of these specialties. Complete coverage is not feasible (and is hardly desirable) in a book of limited size. Further, certain important subareas of institutionalist scholarship, such as the economic analysis of the law and the field of public choice, will not be covered at all. We believe that these areas of concern are somewhat remote from our central interest in the methodology and application of transaction-cost/property-rights analysis. It is also true, of course, that in both of the fields just mentioned there already exist good systematic surveys and introductory books. On the economic analysis of law, there are volumes by Posner (1972b) and Cooter and Ulen (1988); on public choice, a number of works are available.

Finally, we must point out that two other interesting areas of study, ones that lie close to modern institutional economics, have been largely disregarded in the present book. These fields are neo-Austrian economics (e.g., Kirzner 1973) and the evolutionary approach to economics (e.g., Nelson and Winter 1982). Although the writings in these areas project lines of thought that complement the research program of the New Institutional Economics, the two fields are sufficiently distinct in their essential content to warrant separate treatment. Langlois (1986) provides a useful introduction to some of the parallelism here.

### 1.14. Some Notes on the History of the Old Institutional Economics

An excellent review of this area has been provided by Hutchison (1984). The old institutionalists, he writes, "were a rather loose and mixed group of economists, and institutionalism, as a brand, or type of economics, is a rather fuzzy, opaque term" (20). It is true, of course, that institutions or organizations were never totally excluded from consideration by economists; institutions played a role in the work of "orthodox" theorists such as Adam Smith, J. S. Mill, and Alfred Marshall, though not a central one. The adjective *institutional* was applied, expressis verbis, to the American economists Veblen, Commons, and Mitchell. Of these three, John R. Commons was the most important from the standpoint of the NIE. This is so because his work, due to its direction, had particular significance for the development of modern institutionalism. He advanced the proposition that the *transaction* (the transfer of ownership) should be regarded as the ultimate unit of economic investigation. This view contrasts with classical economic theory, Commons (1934, 57) argues, whose units were "commodities and individuals with ownership omitted." To Commons, the "collective control of individual transactions" represented the basic conceptual contribution of institutional economics to political economy (6). Commons argued that classical and neoclassical doctrine was misleading because it failed to recognize that it is not harmony but "conflict of interests" among individuals that is predominant in transactions. Unlike Marx, however, he did not believe that conflict of interests represented the only relevant principle. Also important are mutual dependence of people and maintenance of order by collective action. Indeed, Commons defines an institution as "collective action in control of individual action" (69).[36]

According to Commons's analysis, cooperation emerges, in the end, not as a result of any presupposed harmony of interests, as in classical or neoclassical economics, but as a consequence of deliberate action designed to bring about a new harmony of interests among the hoped-for cooperators (1934, 6). A major objective of Commons was "to give to collective action, in all its varieties, its place throughout economic theory" (5).

Also helpful to the development of modern institutional economics was the work of Knight (1922). He acknowledged the importance of studying "human nature as we know it" (1922, 270) and identified "moral hazard as an endemic condition with which economic organization must contend" (quoted in Williamson 1985, 3).

The German Historical School might be classified as still another branch of "institutional" economics. Gustav Schmoller, the leader of the so-called Younger German Historical School, assumed the most prominent role in this intellectual movement. Significantly, Schumpeter (1926, 355) described him as the "father" of American institutionalism. Schmoller's critique of classical economics is strikingly similar to that made more recently by Ronald Coase—the "father" of the New Institutional Economics. Selected quotations from the writings of these two influential economists illustrate the parallelism in their thinking. Thus:

---

36. Collective action ranges all the way from unorganized custom to many organized going concerns such as the family, the corporation, the holding company, the trade association, the trade union, the federal reserve system, the "group of affiliated interests," and the "State" (Commons 1934, 69).

The old [classical] economics, submerged in the analysis of prices and the phenomena of circulation, represents the attempt to provide an economic physiology of the juices of the social body without anatomy. (Schmoller 1900, 64)

The objection [to what most economists have been doing] essentially is that the theory floats in the air. It is as if one studied the circulation of the blood without having a body. Firms have no substance. Markets exist without laws. . . . (Coase 1984, 230)[37]

Consistent with this thinking, Schmoller (1900, 64) insisted on the importance of comparative institutional analysis—something the exponents of the NIE insist on today. He also considered such topics as evolution, feelings, and norms, as some modern institutional economists do. Yet Schmoller's model of man is more that of homo sociologicus, whose behavior is driven by passions (26–41) and controlled by norms (41–59), than of homo oeconomicus, the self-seeking, purposive, rational individual of classical and neoclassical theory. Indeed, Schmoller abhorred the latter theories (92). In general, then, Schmoller's *Grundriss* (1900) offers a sociological analysis of institutions (linked to strong ethical goals) not an economic one.[38] Max Weber (1968), a representative of the "Younger" Historical School (Schumpeter 1955, 816), developed an institutional theory similar in spirit and scope to that developed recently by North (1990). Hamilton and Feenstra (1995, 59) point out that:

Weber assumed that participants in the market economies reach decisions based on rational means-end calculations of interests. These calculations occur in institutionalized contexts, where only a range of specific options and an array of specific economic organizations are present. In such contexts, economic calculations are conditioned by the fact that economic actions are "carried" by an existing set of "economic orgnizations" (i.e., corporations, cartels and business groups) and are channeled by an existing set of "economically regulative organizations," a category including everything from "medieval village assocations" to "the modern state."

What may be interpreted as a mixture of English classical economics and the teachings of the German Historical School forms the intellectual base for

---

37. See Richter 1996a for similar parallels between the writings of Douglas North, and Schmoller.

38. "The natural forces of the economy, as far as they concern human action, go back not only to natural feelings but to feelings transformed through spiritual and moral evolution to ethicized instincts, to an ordered combination of natural and higher feelings, that is, essentially moral feelings, to virtues and habits (which are due to the ethical community life)" (Schmoller 1900, 60). For further details, see Richter 1996a.

the Freiburg School. The leading economist of the Freiburg group was Walter Eucken (1952), about whom Lutz remarks that his "academic training followed, in the first instance, the lines of the Historical School. What was best in the Historical School he absorbed as part of his intellectual make-up: that is, the urgent concern with the real world" (quoted in Hutchison 1984, 22). It should be said, however, that in general Eucken was strongly opposed to Schmoller's research methods (Eucken 1940).

As is well known, Eucken was one of the originators of German "Ordnungspolitik." The fundamental idea behind this theoretical approach is to create and maintain an institutional framework that guarantees the proper functioning of a free market economy. As guidelines to this end, Eucken developed a set of principles to be observed by lawmakers and public administrators. These principles include the three classical concepts of private ownership, freedom of contract, and acceptance of obligation (Hume [1739–40] 1969, 542). In addition, stress is placed on the need for open markets, the stability of economic policy, and the primacy of monetary policy. It can be observed that, in general, the teachings of German Ordnungspolitik (cf. Schmidtchen 1984) are quite similar to those of American constitutional economics as represented in more recent years by Buchanan (1987).

Ordnungspolitik, rather than Keynesian macropolicy, was applied at the time of the West German currency reform of June 1948 and achieved great success. Similarly, it proved valuable during the following years of the Wirtschaftswunder (Richter 1979). Nevertheless, Ordnungspolitik is open to criticism because it tended to disregard the costs of establishing and running institutions—as did American institutionalism and the German Historical School. The failure to account adequately for costs is no small matter. The German public (and a large part of the economics profession) learned this through experience after German reunification! If there were any doubts previously, it is now abundantly clear that the reorganization of an institutional framework, the creation of viable markets, is an extremely costly and time-consuming affair.

On the classical or neoclassical side of old institutional economics, we have to mention the evolutionary approach in the tradition of the Austrian School: Carl Menger ([1883] 1963) and later Mises and Hayek. This approach involves the application of the concept of convention (a regularity in behavior) between rational individuals to explain the spontaneous evolution of such institutions as language, law, and money.

The idea can also be found in David Hume's ([1739–40] 1969) explanation of the origin of "justice and property." Hume writes that it is human conventions without promise that gradually establish institutions like the three just mentioned plus those of property rights and obligation. Famous became his example of two men pulling the oars of a boat in rhythm by convention, "though they have never given promises to each other" (542). In technical terms, we have here cooperation without ex ante binding promises. This is a rather special case that assumes a harmony of interests. In the more general case, cooperation between individuals may not be possible without ex ante binding agreements, that is, without enforcement characteristics. To consider this became a major issue of the New Institutional Economics.

## 1.15. Suggested Readings for Chapter 1

Chapter 1 deals with general issues, and the readings should be correspondingly general. We suggest the following.

One may begin with some introductory readings on formal organizations. An excellent beginning is provided by Arrow's presidential address delivered to the international meeting of the Institute of Management Science, Tokyo, in 1963 (Arrow 1970) in combination with his booklet on *The Limits of Organization* (1974). Somewhat special but also very readable is Arrow's statement prepared for the Joint Economic Committee of the Ninety-first Congress, first session, on "The Organization of Economic Activity" (Arrow 1969), which is one of the first contributions in which transaction costs and general equilibrium theory are confronted. With regard to institutions, in the sense of institutional frameworks (rules of the game), North (1990) provides a fine introduction to the problems involved. Also stimulating is the presidential address to the Royal Economic Society by R. C. O. Matthews (1986) on "The Economics of Institutions and the Source of Growth." A short introduction to the early history of the New Institutional Economics is provided by Williamson (1985, 1–14; 1996, 3–20).

As for the history of thought of the old institutional economics, we would suggest, as a first step, to read David Hume, *A Treatise of Human Nature,* part 2, section 2, of *The Origin of Justice and Property.* Hume explains justice and property as the result of human convention. One could continue with Carl Menger ([1883] 1963), who argues along the same lines and attacks the German Historical School. Schmoller's (1883) unfavorable review of this book and Menger's (1884) bitter reply began the original Methodenstreit. The differences in methods stemmed from fundamental differences in worldviews, with the individualist outlook of Menger standing in sharp contrast to the more collectivist outlook of the German Historical School. For readers who know German, it would be interesting to read Schmoller's exposition on custom, law, and morality and on the relationship between economic and ethical life in his *Grundriß der Allgemeinen Volkswirtschaftslehre* (1900, 48–72). A more balanced view of the two positions is given by Commons (1934), whose introductory chapter 1 is a suggested reading.

Institutional economics helps to improve understanding of economic history, and therefore plays an increasing role in modern economic history, as illustrated by North (1990). Still, the warning by Popper in his book *The Poverty of Historicism* (1957) should not be forgotten. No scientific theory of historical development can serve as a basis for historical prediction (which Popper calls historicism). Of particular interest here is the section on "Piecemeal versus Utopian Engineering" (64–70) together with the rest of the chapter.

CHAPTER 2

# Transaction Costs


A distinguishing feature of the New Institutional Economics is its insistence on the idea that transactions are costly. This change from the neoclassical position seems straightforward enough. But, from a theoretical standpoint, it is important to recognize that the move to positive transaction costs is also a move to a different, more realistic conception of decision makers. To say that individuals have to use time and resources to secure information, and that they have limited ability to process data and formulate plans, is merely to make reasonable assumptions concerning the nature of the decision makers in an economic system. While there may be questions about the precise meaning of the term *bounded rationality,* it is not unreasonable to say that human beings are, in a significant sense, boundedly rational in their behavior. But insofar as people are conceived as possessing limited and bounded rationality, it is clear that they must incur what we call "transaction costs" and that nonzero transaction costs will be incurred no matter what sector of an economy decision makers are conducting operations in and what type of activity they are performing. Because of their human limitations, their restricted knowledge, and their tendency to make errors, real-world decision makers will always function inefficiently relative to the hypothetical decision makers of neoclassical theory. In short, transaction costs attributable to this inefficiency must arise. Transaction costs are encountered *universally* because of the character of the individuals who make decisions. Quite simply, then, the relationship between imperfect human agents and the costs of running an economy should be kept in mind when considering the phenomenon of transaction costs.

Not only do positive transaction costs exist, but they are, in fact, quantitatively substantial. According to some estimates, transaction costs in modern market economies comprise as much as 50 to 60 percent of net national product. And these figures do not include the setup costs of new institutions and organizations. The situation has obvious implications for economic theory; the need to model transaction costs cannot be viewed as a minor exercise in extending neoclassical economics. Indeed, the "discovery" of transaction costs by Ronald Coase (1937), and his use of them as a heuristic device, started (after an incubation period of some twenty-five years) a revolution in microeconomic thinking. The ideas generated by Coase gave major impetus to the development of the field of the New Institutional Economics. Because of the importance of transaction costs, we begin our more detailed presentation of the NIE with some illustrations and further discussion of this key concept.

As noted in chapter 1, transaction costs include the costs of resources utilized for the creation, maintenance, use, change, and so on of institutions and organizations. In any event, a closer view of transaction costs requires us to focus on the various contexts in which such costs appear. When considered in relation to existing property and contract rights, transaction costs consist of the costs of defining and measuring resources or claims, plus the costs of utilizing and enforcing the rights specified. Applied to the transfer of existing property rights and the establishment or transfer of contract rights between individuals (or legal entities), transaction costs include the costs of information, negotiation, and enforcement.

A typical example of the costs of using existing rights is found in the case where outlays have to be made by an entrepreneur desirous of exercising his right to give orders within his firm (e.g., on the basis of existing labor contracts.) Next, a standard example of the costs associated with the transfer of rights is this. An individual interested in hiring labor would have to use the market, and such use entails costs. For example, there are definite costs of establishing a labor contract. Of course, it is also necessary to be aware of the large costs that must be met for the creation or change of more basic organizations. The setup costs incurred in establishing a structure of property and contract laws, together with the investments in social capital required to ensure the proper functioning of the system, must represent a large sum, but such transaction costs are unavoidable.

As the preceding examples illustrate, some transaction costs are "variable" in the sense that they depend on the volume or number of certain transactions (e.g., sales registered or hours worked), while others are "fixed" (e.g., the setup costs of a new basic organization). Current developments in the former communist states of Eastern Europe suggest how great the problems of setting up new basic organizations can be. Attempts to organize Western-style market economies already give evidence of being extremely costly in terms of both the amount of resources and the time required for programs to reach fruition. It is also clear that the *maintenance costs* of a basic organization like the state are substantial. Inter alia, there are expenses for external and internal security, the administration of justice, and the provision of a minimum level of education.

In a general sense, "transaction costs are the costs of running the economic system" (Arrow 1969, 48). Such continuing costs, together with the costs associated with the establishment or change of a system's basic political organization, represent the essential components of the transaction cost category. From the standpoint of neoclassical theory, these are the costs that have to be *added* to production and transport costs—the costs normally recognized in, for example, the orthodox theory of the firm. All this appears quite straight-forward. In fact, however, the introduction of positive transaction costs into the standard neoclassical model has far-reaching implications and changes the interpretation that must be given to the model. Moreover, in practice, transaction costs are not easily distinguished from production or transport costs or, indeed, any other type of cost. It has been suggested, though, that in a rough way at least we can get an idea of the order of magnitude of transaction costs by looking at such things as the spread between factory and retail prices (corrected for transport costs), the spread between the interest paid on bank loans and the amount paid on bank deposits, the overhead costs of firms, the expenditures of the state for its basic tasks, and so on.

## 2.1. The Concept of Transaction

One way to improve understanding of transaction costs is to proceed slowly and consider, first, the meaning of the basic term *transaction*. Williamson has offered the following definition:

> A transaction occurs when a good or service is transferred across a tech-nologically separable interface. One stage of activity terminates and an-other begins. (1985, 1)

According to this interpretation, the term is restricted to situations in which resources are actually transferred in the physical sense of "delivery." Such delivery may occur within firms or across markets. Thus, it is possible to speak of internal and external transactions or of intrafirm and market transactions. They can be seen as resulting largely from the division of labor.

The basic idea of the intrafirm transaction is nicely described by the pin example of Adam Smith ([1776] 1976). He notes that the work of the pin maker is divided into a number of operations: "One man draws out the wire, another straights it, a third cuts it, a fourth points it, a fifth grinds it at the top for receiving the head, . . ." (4). In this example, it is clear that a "transaction" takes place each time a pin changes hands within the factory.

In the case of market transactions, an important dictum is that the division of labor is limited by the extent of the market (Smith [1776] 1976, 17). Trans-actions occur accordingly. It is true, of course, that, broadly interpreted, the transfer of a good or service may be understood to include such activities as the transfer of pieces of information or batches of knowledge, for example, in connection with advisory or educational services, research and development, and so on.

Another description of the term *transaction* is given by Commons. For him, transactions "are the alienation and acquisition between individuals of the *rights* of future ownership of physical things" (1934, 58). Again, the definition deals with the transfer of resources but now in the legal sense—namely, the transfer of sanctioned property rights. Contract rights should be added, though, and in fact they are included by Commons in his later interpretation of his concept of transaction (1934, 64).

Both transactions in the legal sense and in the sense of delivery are interrelated. Nevertheless, when analyzing transaction costs, we may find it useful, practically, to view the respective cases as reflecting two separate types of resource transfers or economic transactions. Thus, in recent years, the number of transactions in the sense of *delivery* has attracted the attention of both cost accountants and academic scholars. From this perspective, delivery is understood as exchanges of material and/or information that move production along but do not result in physical products (Miller and Vollmann 1985).

The objects of concern in the economic analysis of institutions are not only economic transactions but also certain other "social actions" (Weber 1968, 22ff.). Of special importance are actions necessary to establish, maintain, or change social relationships. In this sense, economic transactions are a special kind of social transaction, that is, social actions that are necessary for the formation and maintenance of the institutional framework in which economic activity occurs. Formal or informal rules, plus their enforcement characteristics, are involved here. And political transactions would seem to be especially significant. That is, it is essential to account for the transactions between politicians, bureaucrats, and interest groups and consider the bargaining and planning of these groups about the exercise of public authority ("political exchange"). Also to be considered is the routine exercise of political authority by officials in the form of judicial decisions and administrative acts.

Following Williamson (1979, 239), both economic and political transactions can be characterized by the following three critical features: (1) uncertainty, (2) the frequency with which transactions occur, and (3) the degree to which transaction-specific investments are involved. Neoclassical theory has long recognized uncertainty as an important factor affecting exchange, but it has paid very little attention, if any, to the roles played by the frequency of transactions or by transaction-specific investments. Under the New Institutional Economics, of course, all three dimensions of transactions are understood to exert systematic influence on economic behavior.

## 2.2. Transaction Costs: Illustrations and Attempts at Definition

Transaction costs involve the use of real resources—specifically, the resources required to carry out the social transactions (including the economic transactions) just described. As noted, Arrow defines transaction costs as the costs of running the economic system (1969, 48). But transaction costs embrace, in addition to such routine costs, the costs of establishing, maintaining, or changing a system's basic institutional framework. Thus, relative to formal institutions, we can say that transaction costs are the costs that arise from the establishment, use, maintenance, and change of: (1) institutions in the sense of law (e.g., the German constitution or the German Civil Code) and (2) institutions in the sense of rights (e.g., a concrete claim based on a voluntarily agreed upon labor contract). Moreover, additional transaction costs appear here because of the informal activity connected with the operation of the basic, formal institutions.

Typical examples of transaction costs are the costs of using the market and the costs of exercising the right to give orders within a firm. In the first case, we shall speak of *market transaction costs,* in the second of *managerial transaction costs.* As far as institutions in the sense of law are concerned, what must be considered is the array of costs associated with the running and adjusting of the institutional framework of a polity. For want of a better term, we shall speak in this case of *political transaction costs.*

For each of these three types of transaction costs, it is possible to recognize two variants: (1) "fixed" transaction costs, that is, the specific investments made in setting up institutional arrangements; and (2) "variable" transaction costs, that is, costs that depend on the number or volume of transactions. Before going further in describing market, managerial, and political transaction costs, one more general remark should be made. We know that production costs are interpreted as the costs associated with the activity "production." Similarly, transaction costs can be considered to be the costs of the activity "transaction." Then, if productive activity is described by a production function, transaction activity can be described by a transaction function. This approach to transaction costs will be developed more fully in the ensuing material.

### 2.2.1.  Market Transaction Costs

To begin the discussion of this topic, we can do no better than to quote Professor Coase:

> In order to carry out a market transaction it is necessary to discover who it is that one wishes to deal with, to inform people that one wishes to deal with and to what terms, to conduct negotiations leading up to a bargain, to draw up the contract, to undertake the inspection needed to make sure that the terms of the contract are being observed, and so on. (1960, 15)

Market transaction costs consist primarily of information and bargaining costs. Information costs are clearly important, but the magnitude of bargaining costs should not be underestimated. Thus, Dahlman (1979, 148) probably goes too far when he says that one need speak of only one kind of transaction cost— "resource losses incurred due to imperfect information." On the other hand, it is true that the complete absence of transaction costs (as in neoclassical models) is connected with the assumption of complete information. However, this orthodox interpretation does not seem to be entirely correct either. Presumably, more than information is needed to enforce fully an existing assignment of private property rights. In reality, information is, of course, substantially incomplete. There exists *market* uncertainty.[1] No decision maker knows immediately and automatically who will buy or sell each commodity or under what conditions.

In general, anonymous exchange across perfectly competitive markets does not take place. Characteristically, potential traders must search each other out, and, once such interested parties have made contact, they must try to find out more about each other. Specifically, each has to determine who the other party is and whether he is willing and able to live up to any agreement that may be reached. Negotiations are needed to find an efficient exchange relationship and to establish the detailed conditions of the exchange. Quite possibly, there may be a need to provide legal safeguards. Since errors may occur, the fulfillment of the contract must be supervised. It may even be necessary, in some cases, to enforce the fulfillment of contractual obligations by legal means or other sanctions. The costs of using the market may be classified in more detail as follows: (1) the costs of preparing contracts (search and information costs narrowly defined), (2) the costs of concluding contracts (costs of bargaining and decision making), and (3) the costs of monitoring and enforcing the contractual obligations.

A brief discussion of these three types of transaction costs will be taken up next.

1. *Search and information costs:* An individual contemplating a particular market transaction must search for a suitable party with whom to deal, and the search process inevitably results in costs. These costs may arise because individuals make direct outlays (on advertising, visits to prospective customers, and so on), or costs can arise indirectly through the creation of organized markets (stock exchanges, fairs, weekly markets, and so on). Also included are the costs of communication among the prospective parties to the exchange (such as postage, telephone expenses, and outlays on sales representatives). Still other costs relate to the gathering of information about the prices demanded by different suppliers of the same good[2] and the costs in-

---

1. On this concept, see Hirshleifer and Riley (1979, 1376).
2. The problem is a typical one of search theory, which has been developed on the basis of an article by Stigler (1961). For a survey, see Lippman and McCall (1976).

curred in testing and quality control. In the case of services, quality control would involve some assessment of the credentials and suitability of the service supplier.[3] A major problem in the service area, of course, is the search for qualified employees, an activity that is increasingly costly and time consuming. From a theoretical standpoint, questions about search and information costs are dealt with, in one form or another, by the special field of the economics of information.[4] The issues addressed have clear importance because, inter alia, the use of resources to secure information helps decision makers avoid costly mistakes.

2. *Bargaining and decision costs:* Costs in this category relate to the outlays that must be made when a contract is being written and the concerned parties must bargain and negotiate over its provisions. Not only is time required for the process, but such things as expensive legal advice may be needed. In cases in which informational asymmetry exists (i.e., the bargaining parties possess private information), inefficient outcomes can result (Kreps 1990b, 760). Depending on the particular case, a contract may be legally more or less complicated and correspondingly more or less difficult to negotiate. Decision costs include the costs of making any information gathered usable, the compensation paid to advisers, the costs of reaching decisions within groups, and so on. Finally, it should be mentioned that, just as in other areas, the complexity and costliness of contracts will be conditioned by competition.

3. *Supervision and enforcement costs:* These costs arise because of the need to monitor the agreed upon delivery times, measure product quality and amounts, and so on. Information plays an important role here. There are costs involved in measuring the valuable attributes of what is being exchanged and costs involved in protecting rights and enforcing contractual provisions. Insofar as there are high supervisory and enforcement costs, violations of contracts are to a certain degree unavoidable. Of course, cheating or opportunistic behavior by the parties to a contract has bad consequences. Such deviant behavior not only has redistributive effects but also causes losses in the general level of output or welfare. Opportunistic behavior that is potentially avoidable through appropriate institutional arrangements constitutes a drag on the system. Williamson (1985) considers issues of this type in connection with his discussion of ex ante and ex post contractual activity.

---

3. The concept of "market signaling" is to be mentioned here: "higher quality workers signal by acquiring education (even if education does not contribute to productivity), on the hypothesis that employers know that higher quality workers can more easily and cheaply undergo the education ordeal" (Spence, quoted in Hirschleifer [1973, 37]; see also chap. 5.

4. For a survey, see Hirshleifer (1973, 37ff.), as well as Hirshleifer and Riley (1979) and Bössmann (1978). See also chapter 5.

### 2.2.2.  Managerial Transaction Costs

What is of concern here are the costs of implementing the labor contracts that exist between a firm and its employees. For convenience, assume that employment contracts have already been concluded and must now be acted upon. According to our basic scheme, the costs arising in this connection belong to the category of market transaction costs. Managerial transaction costs reduce to the following:

1.  The costs of setting up, maintaining or changing an organizational design. Such costs relate to a rather wide array of operations. Thus, there are costs of personnel management, investments in information technology, defense against takeovers, public relations, and lobbying. These are typically fixed transaction costs.
2.  The costs of running an organization, which fall largely into two subcategories.
    a.  Information costs—the costs of decision making, monitoring the execution of orders, and measuring the performance of workers, agency costs, costs of information management, and so on.
    b.  The costs associated with the physical transfer of goods and services across a separable interface (Williamson 1985, 1)—examples are the costs of idle time in the handling of semifinished products, the costs of intrafirm transport, and so on.

The costs in (2) are characteristically variable transaction costs. The various costs noted in this discussion of managerial transaction costs have begun, in recent years, to play a role in cost accounting known as "activity-based costing" (Prozesskostenrechnung). Accounts of the new thinking are to be found in Miller and Vollmann 1985; Cooper 1988a, 1988b; and O'Guin 1990. The purpose underlying activity-based costing is to discover ways to save on the ever increasing manufacturing overhead costs that seem to plague modern industry. It is argued that transactions are responsible for most overhead costs, and that, in consequence, the key to managing overhead is to control the transaction activity that drives overhead costs (Miller and Vollmann 1985, 146). Presumably, transactions can be "managed" by thinking carefully about which transactions are appropriate and which are not. In this way, overhead reduction is envisioned.

In this general context, the literature distinguishes between various types of transactions, for example:

> *Logistical transactions:* ordering, executing and confirming the movement of materials

*Balancing transactions:* ensuring that existing supplies of materials, labor, and capacity are equal to the demand

*Quality transactions:* quality control, indirect engineering, procurement, and the development of relevant data

*Change transactions:* updating basic manufacturing information systems to accommodate changes in such things as engineering design, schedules, and materials specification (Miller and Vollmann 1985, 145ff).

### 2.2.3. Political Transaction Costs

Market and managerial transactions are assumed to take place against a well-defined political background. That is, institutional arrangements consistent with a capitalist market order hold, and this means that a particular local, national, or international organization of the political community exists. Of course, the provision of such an organization and the public goods associated with it also involves costs. These are political transaction costs. They are, in a general sense, the costs of supplying public goods by collective action, and they can be understood as analogous to managerial transaction costs. Specifically, these are:

1. *The costs of setting up, maintaining and changing a system's formal and informal political organization:* Included here are the costs associated with the establishment of the legal framework, the administrative structure, the military, the educational system, the judiciary, and so on. But, in addition to these commitments, there are the costs associated with political parties and pressure groups in general. In effect, all these costs are the nontrivial outlays made in order to achieve the "domestication of coercive force" or the realization of a "monopoly of organized violence."[5]

2. *The costs of running a polity:* These are current expenditures for those things formerly specified as the "duties of the sovereign" (Smith [1776] 1976, 689, 709, 723, 814). Involved are current outlays for legislation, defense, the administration of justice, transport, and education. Just as in the private sector, these governmental undertakings have to bear search and information costs, the costs of decision making, the costs of giving (official) orders, and the costs of monitoring and enforcing the observance of official instructions. Levi (1988, 12) describes political transaction costs as "the costs of measuring, monitoring, creating, and enforcing compliance." Also to be added to the total here are the costs of running organizations that participate or try to participate in the political decision-making process (Olson 1965, 46). Organizations of this type include political parties, labor unions, employers' associations, and pressure

---

5. The first step in the process of state creation "is to build a monopoly of organized violence" (Levi 1988, 42).

groups in general. Finally, the costs of bargaining have to be taken into account.

It is important to note that the costs of the "domestication of force" or the "building of a monopoly of organized violence" are completely disregarded in the neoclassical zero-transaction-cost world. Force, any kind of force, is assumed to be perfectly under control in the neoclassical environment. Hence, transfers of property rights occur only under conditions of mutual agreement. Pressure groups are assumed either not to exist or to neutralize each other (Commons 1934).[6]

To a certain extent, both managerial and political transaction costs can be interpreted as agency costs, or the costs that arise in a principal-agent relationship. An agency relationship between two (or more) parties is understood as one in which one party, the agent, acts for, on behalf of, or as a representative of a second party, the principal. Of course, given the pervasiveness of opportunism, the agent will not always act fully in the interest of the principal. The latter, however, can attempt to limit divergences from his interest by establishing appropriate incentives for the agent. He can, for example, incur monitoring costs designed to reduce the aberrant activities of the agent or share the benefits that are created by the activity. Moreover, as Putterman has noted: "In addition it will pay the agent to expend resources (bonding costs) to guarantee that he will not take certain actions that will harm the principal . . . " (1986a, 212). Nevertheless, there will, in general, remain some divergence between the agent's decisions and those that would maximize the welfare of the principal. The dollar equivalent of this difference has been termed the "residual loss." Jensen and Meckling define agency costs as the sum of the monitoring expenditures of the principal, the bonding expenditures of the agent, and the residual loss (1979).

From what has been said so far, it appears that transaction costs are, essentially, the costs of specialization and the division of labor. It is also clear that the real resources needed for transaction purposes have to be financed and, insofar as they do, transaction costs bind financial capital. We may, therefore, speak of *transaction capital*. This category includes the capital investments (transactional investment capital) required for the setting up of markets, firms, and polities and the current capital (current transaction capital) required for the day to day running of the market and political systems. Since capital is directly involved, capital theory may be applied to the problems of this area. Austrian capital theory, in particular, would seem to be useful because time plays a

---

6. The view of Commons was, as Olson (1965, 115) points out, that the market mechanisms did not of themselves bring about fair results and that disparities in the bargaining power of market participants could not be removed by the government. "Thus pressure groups were to Commons virtually an indispensable means for the achievement of a just and rational economic order."

crucial role—especially in the case of institutional change. Special interest attaches to the concept of transaction capital when consideration is given to development economics and the economics of socialist transition to market capitalism.

Another interesting aspect of transaction costs is that their level depends, inter alia, on the behavior of individuals. Monitoring and enforcement costs, in particular, will tend to be low if mutual trust predominates in the society. Under favorable conditions, property rights will be respected, and comparatively uniform ideas will exist about the nature of fair solutions to conflicts. It would seem, then, that social morality, confidence, trust, and the institutional framework are all interrelated. The expenses of public education, and of motivating people, have to be viewed, in part, as contributions that bring about lesser "frictions" (transaction costs) in society and enhance economic productivity.

### 2.3. Guesstimating the Size of Transaction Costs

In recent decades, economists have come to realize that the gains from specialization and the division of labor are not a free lunch (Wallis and North 1988, 95). A voluminous literature has evolved on the topic of transaction costs, and the flow of writing testifies to the importance with which these costs are now viewed. It is true, however, that much of the discussion has focused on transaction costs as a heuristic device. Comparatively little effort has been undertaken to establish a precise empirical definition or to initiate serious measurement programs. Nevertheless, the objective of this section is to provide at least some basic ideas about the general order of magnitude of transaction costs—understood as the "costs of running the economic system." Setup costs are ignored. Further, a distinction is made between "own" transaction activities (which are not paid for) and remunerated transaction activities or "transaction services" (Wallis and North 1988, 97). Rough guesses will be hazarded only for costs in the latter category.

### 2.3.1. Market Transaction Costs

A consumer seeking to purchase a good or service has first to devote time and effort to securing information about the quality of the product. Then he must search for a price-worthy supply. Prices, of course, may differ considerably for similar products or even for the same product. For example, the price of a given type of camera can show variations of plus or minus 10 percent around the average price.[7] Even though consumers know that price differences are significant for certain products, many individuals avoid expending the time and effort

---

    7. The prices of Honeywell Pentax ES II ranged from \$360 to \$450 in the Ann Arbor–Ypsilanti market, 1974 (Maynes 1976, 4).

necessary to find the lowest cost supplier. If this were not true, we would not find such major price differences extant for identical goods.[8] It seems reasonable to say that the price differences observed relative to an average price can be interpreted as measures of the costs of the consumers' own transaction activities (search costs in this case). Note, however, that the satisfaction consumers draw from their acts of purchasing must be balanced against their transaction costs. This may be one reason for the variety of distribution systems described, for example, by Müller-Hagedorn (1995).

For the purchase of expensive objects like houses, consumers tend to hire advisers such as realtors, lawyers, and financial consultants, who supply "transaction services." The fees paid by consumers to these individuals or firms show up in the national income accounts and thus the (aggregate) magnitudes of such transaction expenditures can be inferred.

From the suppliers' side of the market, transaction costs or selling costs (Scherer 1987) consist of the outlays made in marketing a particular commodity minus the costs of transporting it from the manufacturer to the final consumer. The costs of marketing are measured by the difference between production costs and the price paid for the commodity by the final consumer (Seyffert 1966, 215). Data from West Germany in 1959 reveal that, for 116 nonfood commodity groups, the average marketing cost was 49 percent of the final consumer price (221). From this figure it is necessary to deduct 3.7 percent as the average transport cost and 7 percent as the average turnover tax burden. Thus, market transaction costs at the suppliers' end amounted to 38.3 percent of final consumer prices. This estimate represents merely an unweighted average of the respective components. Nevertheless, the broad indication is that transaction costs are significant, and one can only wonder whether such costs have not increased during the last thirty years.[9]

Next, attention must be given to *managerial transaction costs.* And here it seems permissible to use overhead costs as a basis for our attempted estimation procedure. Of course, overhead costs include both production costs (such as depreciation, repair, water, and insurance costs) and internal transaction costs. The share of overhead costs relative to total costs or total value added has

---

8. In a further example, life insurance, for example, participation straight-life policies, cost $4 to $13 per $1,000 protection (1962 data from Belth 1966, quoted in Maynes 1976, 4). Drugs such as Tetracylin, a broad-spectrum antibiotic cost $.75 to $7.45 for thirty capsules (*Consumer Reports,* May 1970, 278–79, quoted by Maynes (4), a plus or minus 74 percent difference with respect to the average price.

9. U.S. Federal Trade Commission survey data for 1975 reveal, according to Scherer (1987, 300), that in consumer foods industries manufacturers' media advertising outlays plus "other" selling costs averaged 13.4 percent (with a maximum of 29.8 percent for over the counter drug makers). For further material and sources of selling-expense data, see Weiss, Pascoe, and Martin (1983).

increased considerably during the last century. In the United States, such costs have reached a level of anywhere from 35 to 60 percent.[10] Unfortunately, we do not know precisely the share of transaction costs in total overhead costs. Assuming, however, that the transaction-cost share amounts to 50 percent, it follows that intrafirm transaction costs would lie somewhere between 18 and 30 percent (including the marketing costs of firms). Thus, the production-related transaction costs of a typical firm might amount to 10 to 20 percent of total costs. Research and development costs, which vary substantially in different branches of industry, could perhaps, on the average, represent 10 to 15 percent. The managerial transaction costs connected with production may, therefore, be about 20 to 35 percent of total cost. Further, if it is assumed that a producer's profit per unit is 20 percent of the selling price (after accounting for internal market transaction costs) and that the market transaction cost per unit is 40 percent of the final consumer price, the sum of managerial and market transaction costs may lie somewhere between 50 and 57 percent of the final price to the consumer.

Certain transaction costs take the form of "sunk costs" or "specific investments," and these must be approached differently than purely current outlays. Specifically, the objective must be to calculate the economic return on each investment made (cf. Clarkson 1977).[11]

The preceding discussion has considered transaction costs in situations in which only one production stage exists. But there are normally several stages in the production process. If it can be assumed that the transaction costs associated with the additional stages amount to 10 percent of the final consumer price, it appears that transaction costs are no less than 60 to 67 percent of the final consumer price.[12]

In an extensive study concerned with the measurement of transaction costs in the American economy, Wallis and North (1988) estimated transaction costs for the system as a whole to be 46.66 to 54.71 percent of GNP in 1970.

---

10. Jehle (1982, 61); Rayner (1987); Berliner and Brimson (1988, 27).

11. "[A]ccounting rates of return, even if properly and consistently measured, provide almost no information about economic rates of return" (Fisher and McGowan 1983, 83). This is important in industrial economics since accounting rates of return are frequently used as indices of market performance by economists and lawyers (83).

12. Assume further that the same percentage applies for investment goods (smaller market transaction costs but higher managerial transaction costs because of larger planning costs). Furthermore, assume that the total value added by the government (mainly wages and salaries paid by the public sector) are 100 percent transaction costs while the goods and services purchased by the government include also a 60 to 67 percent transaction-cost share of final market prices. If we apply the same percentage for net exports of goods and services, we calculate for western Germany in 1990 transaction costs of 64.2 to 69.5 percent of GNP. It therefore seems reasonable to say that total "payed-for" transaction costs (transaction services) amount to some 60 to 70 percent of GNP in a modern market economy like that of Western Germany.

The calculations they made do not consider the value added by government to GNP to be 100 percent transaction costs.[13] To gain historical perspective, Wallis and North calculated the GNP transaction percentages for 1870, 1880, 1890, . . . up to 1970. From 1870 to 1970, the transaction-cost percentage more than doubled, rising from 26.09 to 54.71 percent. The results are striking, and the authors conclude that the relative growth of transaction costs is a necessary part of realizing gains from increases in division of labor and specialization (122).

Wallis and North argue that there are three major reasons why transaction costs have risen over the last century.

First, the costs of specifying and enforcing contracts became more impor- tant with the expansion of the market and growing organization in the second half of nineteenth century. As the economy becomes more spe- cialized and urbanized, more and more exchanges are carried out between individuals who have no long-standing relations, that is, impersonal ex- change. . . . Rational consumers engage in more search and information- gathering activity (including purchasing information through middlemen, i.e., transaction services) as they come to know less and less about the persons from whom they buy their products. . . . The second part of our story is the effect of technological change in production and transporta- tion on transaction services. The new capital intensive production tech- niques were often more profitable to operate (i.e., lower costs) at high output levels. . . . [larger business organizations] placed a premium on the coordination of inputs and outputs and on monitoring the numerous contracts involved in production and distribution. . . . The third part of our story is the declining costs of using the political system to restructure property rights. . . . [The consequence of this change was the further development of commissions] which replaced the decision-making ability by executive departments of the government . . . [and] imposed transac- tion costs on the rest of the economy. (1988, 122–23)

It should be noted that Oi confirms these findings for the share of the econ- omy's resources devoted to distribution. There is evidence that allocation for this purpose grew steadily over time. Thus, in 1900, of the total man-hours worked to produce goods, only 11 percent were used in the U.S. distribution process. But by 1980 the figure had climbed to 61 percent (1990, 4).

---

13. They exclude from transaction costs what they call "social overhead"—education, highways, hospitals, health, fire protection, sanitation, natural resources, housing, urban renewal, and so on (115). The lower figure treats all government activities as nontransaction industry. If we were to proceed in the latter manner, we would obtain transaction costs on the order of 50 to 55 percent of GNP for western Germany in 1990—still a rather high sum.

Based on their findings concerning the magnitude of transaction costs in a modern economy, Wallis and North criticize our present system of national income accounting. Since the present conventions were developed at a time when transaction costs were assumed to be irrelevant, a recasting of the national accounts would seem to be indicated. The authors suggest that the national product should be divided into three basic categories with emphasis on activities in the spheres of production, transportation, and transactions. Only in this way is economic growth likely to be better understood. As Wallis and North argue, some fundamental questions still have to be addressed in growth economics, and transaction costs must figure prominently in any future research efforts designed to deal with these questions.

The growing size of the transaction sector poses a major explanatory challenge to economists and economic historians. What is the relationship of those inputs to their outputs? How have transaction and transformation costs interacted in the transformation of the economy? What are the implications of the growing sector for a variety of social and institutional changes? These are only a few important questions which should be explored . . . (125)

The material in this section has shown that transaction costs play an increasingly practical role in areas outside of institutional economics proper. Applications of the transaction-cost concept are found in cost accounting (checking overhead costs), in the search for an appropriate measure of capital stock, in the determination of the productivity of distribution trades, and so on. In this section, it was further shown that minimizing absolute or relative transaction costs is not an economically reasonable aim. Rather, what matters for the judgment of the economic quality ("efficiency") of an economic entity are its total economic results not its level of transaction costs. Transaction costs attract increasing attention from microeconomic theorists, economic historians, accountants, and others because of their steadily growing share of total production costs and GNP. The question of whether such costs are economically justified takes on great significance under these conditions, and there seems little doubt that transaction costs deserve the attention of the profession.

### 2.3.2.  Political Transaction Costs

What we are calling political transaction costs also deserve such attention. Indeed, transaction-cost analysis should be integrated into cost-benefit analysis. Thus, in the case of revenue-producing laws, it is essential to take into account "the costs of acquiring information about revenue sources, constituent behavior and agent behavior: and the costs of enforcing compliance with that policy" (Levi 1988, 27). This is the cost of public choice. Similar observations might be made with respect to the costs and benefits of the prohibition of tobacco smoking, alcohol consumption, or drug use. Furthermore, the costs to society of a particular law, old or new, consist not only of the government expenditures directly associated with the law but also of the transaction costs it imposes on society—for example, resource losses due to the impairment of freedom of exchange (cf. the comparative study of the effects of reduced economic freedom in Gwartney, Lawson, and Block 1995 and the effects of rent-seeking activities invited by a particular law in Buchanan 1980). Similar things, of course, can be said of public administration or public education. For example, it is arguable that the (unpaid for) transaction costs in terms of the time invested by students in public education programs may be wasteful. Social waste may exist in the sense that the younger generation remains for an unnecessarily long period of time as a net consumer of public goods instead of becoming net taxpayers at an earlier age. And, last but not least, there are the costs of setting up and running political organizations and pressure groups. Olson (1965, 46) assumes that such costs are an increasing function of the number of individuals in a group and that per capita costs remain constant or do not decrease much.

From the conclusion just noted, Olson, in the *Logic of Collective Action* (1965), goes on to say that since the benefit going to any individual member of a group diminishes with the size of the group, "the larger the group the farther it will fall short of providing an optimal supply of a collective good . . . " (48). It follows that Commons, or equal-minded political economists and political scientists like Galbraith (1952) and Bentley (1949) have built their theories around an inconsistency. "They have assumed that, if a group had some reason or incentive to organize to further its interest, the rational individuals in that group would also have a reason or an incentive to support an organization working in their mutual interest. But this is logically fallacious, at least for large . . . groups with economic interests" (Olson 1965, 127). This explains the widely observed fact that small "special interest" groups have disproportionate power (127)—another important insight achieved by use of the transaction-cost hypothesis.

### 2.4. Modeling Transaction Costs: The Activity "Transaction"

The concept of transaction costs has been considered in the literature in connection with two basic questions:

1. How can one model transaction costs given the institutional framework?

2. How can one analyze, or at least describe, organizations as transaction-cost-economizing instruments?

The second question is central to Williamson's analysis of institutions. Representatives of the New Institutional Economics have dealt with it by asking why similar activities involving transactions are often so differently organized. In their analysis, institutionalist writers are particularly interested in the details of the governance structure of contracts (e.g., the classical market contract and various types of incomplete market contracts) and other forms of organization.

By contrast, the first question posed above is approached rather differently. The literature attempts to answer it by undertaking a simple extension of neoclassical microeconomics. Transaction costs are included, for example, by Foley (1970) in the standard model of perfect competition by adding the activity "transaction" to the system as though it were analogous to the activity "production." The activity or process "transaction," according to this view, may be performed by existing economic units (consumers or manufacturing firms) or by new economic units such as wholesalers, retailers, and financial intermediaries. Extension along these lines enables one to explain, with the usual institutional superficiality of neoclassical analysis, such phenomena as the spread between the producer's price for a commodity and the final price paid by the consumer (the trade margin) or the difference between interest on bank loans and deposits (the interest margin).

As has been suggested, organizational details are not given adequate attention in the "transaction-as-activity" approach. More significant, however, is the fact that this approach disregards the link between transaction costs and the information status of decision makers. There is no persuasive reason to believe that transaction costs represent a set of relations, or constraints, that can *simply be added* to the standard neoclassical model. As noted, when an analytical jump is made to a system that assumes positive transaction costs and some form of "bounded rationality," decision makers are in a quite different position with respect to the elements that have been taken, traditionally, as the "initial data" of the neoclassical model (Furubotn 1990, 230). People are no longer "fully informed." That is, once positive transaction costs are admitted, information becomes costly to obtain, and individuals have limited ability to acquire (and process) information. The result is that each individual has only *partial* knowledge of the options offered by the system, and each person's knowledge endowment tends to be somewhat different from those of others. A general equilibrium model defined by these new conditions is obviously entirely distinct from the orthodox model.

More will be said subsequently about the way transaction costs force a reinterpretation of neoclassical economics. Given the state of the literature, however, it is still worthwhile to look briefly at "transactions as activities" in the style of conventional neoclassical analysis in which decision makers are "perfectly rational."

Suppose that a commodity (wheat) is traded in exchange for money. Two individuals are involved in the exchange—a producer and a consumer. Inevitably, however, the initiation, conclusion, monitoring, and enforcement of this purchase contract produce transaction costs, which are assumed to be established in terms of wheat.[14]

Suppose the producer intends to sell 1 kilogram of wheat to the consumer, who will, however, receive only 0.9 kilograms. The (real) transaction costs in this example amount to 0.1 kilograms, or 10 percent of 1 kilogram of the wheat produced. The general formulation of this relationship can be interpreted as follows. The activity "transaction," defined as the purchase of wheat, may, in analogy to the orthodox production function, be represented by a "transaction function"

$$Y_c = F(Y_p),$$

where the subscript $p$ denotes wheat promised to be delivered by the producer, and $c$ denotes wheat promised to be accepted by the consumer. Graphically, the transaction function is shown in figure 2.1. Its shape is reminiscent of the standard production function. The distance OA is the amount of wheat sold by the producer, the "transaction input." The distance AB is the corresponding (net) amount bought by the consumer, the "transaction output." The transaction costs, represented by the relation $K = Y_p - Y_c$, are indicated by the distance BD. It is apparent from the figure that the transaction curve must lie below the 45-degree line if there are positive transaction costs.

The slope of the transaction curve can be called the marginal productivity of the transaction process. What it shows is, roughly speaking, how many additional kilograms of wheat the consumer will receive when the producer supplies an additional increment of wheat. As drawn in figure 2.1, the marginal productivity of the transaction process declines with increases in the volume of transactions. This is a special case in which it is assumed that marginal transaction costs increase with increases in the volume of future wheat traded. The situation portrayed could exist if, from a certain point onward, buyers and sellers have to search harder for exchange possibilities and monitor transactions with increasing care as the total volume of wheat transactions increase. Increased monitoring and enforcement effort may be needed so that the parties

---

14. We assume that the quantity of wheat used up as transaction costs is necessary to pay for the labor input in the activity "transaction."

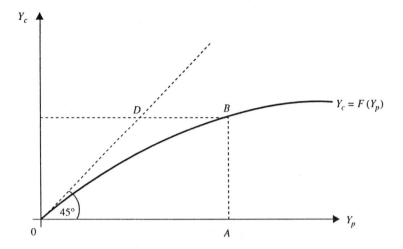

**Fig. 2.1. The transaction curve**

to the exchange can guard against opportunistic behavior, which may arise from either side of the contract.

Assume next that the "transaction" activity is taken over by a special transaction firm (a commercial enterprise). This firm buys wheat at price $P_p$ from the producer and sells it at price $P_c$ to the consumer. The transaction firm can be conceived of as maximizing its profit ($R$) subject to its transaction function:

$$\text{Max } R = P_c Y_c - P_p Y_p$$
$$\text{s.t. } Y_c = F\,(Y_p).$$

Then, the necessary condition for the profit-maximizing turnover of the transaction firm emerges as:

$$\frac{dY_c}{dY_p} = \frac{P_p}{P_c}.$$

Figure 2.2 provides a graphical representation of the situation just described. The ideal, or profit-maximizing, transaction plan Q is found at the point of tangency between the isoprofit curve (SS) and the transaction curve. On our assumptions, the slope of the transaction curve will be everywhere less than one, so that:

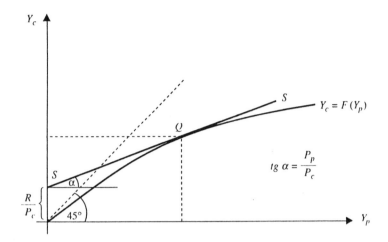

**Fig. 2.2.  The profit-maximizing transaction plan**

$$\frac{dY_c}{dY_p} < 1$$

and at the equilibrium of the transaction firm:

$$\frac{P_p}{P_c} < 1 \quad \text{or} \quad P_p < P_c.$$

It follows that the consumer (the buyer) pays more for the traded wheat than the producer (the seller) receives. The difference, of course, is due to transaction costs. Assuming that there are decreasing returns to scale of the activity "transaction," as we have, there then exists an optimal size for the individual transaction firm.

Note, however, that several things have been ignored in the preceding model in the interest of simplicity. First, the transaction costs associated with the specialized transaction firm's purchase of wheat from the producer are ignored, as are the producer's transaction costs. Second, no account is taken of the "unpaid" activities of the consumer. The consumer supplies essential services that will have to be recognized in the transaction function if accurate measurement of productivity in the distribution trade is desired (Oi 1990).

Considering other possible organizational schemes, it is clear that the activity "transaction" could also be integrated into the production firm or into the household of the consumer. To shift the transaction process to the set of

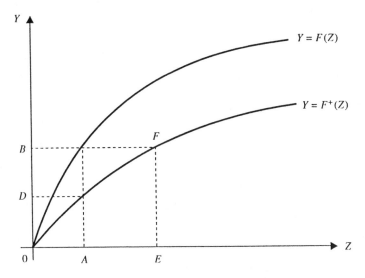

**Fig. 2.3. The gross and net production curves**

activities undertaken by the producer is quite easy. From a quantitative standpoint, the situation could be assessed by deducting the appropriate transaction
cost from the maximum gross product achieved by the firm (with given technique of production). The curve of net production would then lie below the
gross production curve, as in figure 2.3, with $Y$ denoting output of wheat and $Z$
seed input. Conventional optimizing considerations of the producer relate now
to the net production curve (or function). As the diagram suggests, the producer
who wishes to sell $OB$ units of wheat cannot achieve this goal if he produces
only $OA$ units. This is so because he has to spend $BD$ units of wheat available
as transaction costs. In other words, in order to be able to deliver $OB$ units of
wheat net of transaction costs, the producer would be required to produce $OE$
units of wheat. The curve of net production $F^+$ (i.e., the gross production curve
minus transaction costs) is always below the gross curve if transaction costs
measured in wheat are positive. The slope of the net curve, the net marginal
productivity, is, at each input $Z$, smaller than the corresponding gross marginal
productivity.

By analogy, the technical relations just discussed can be drawn upon to
interpret the aggregate production function. With a given level of technical
knowledge, the net aggregate production curve lies further below the gross
curve the less efficient the coordination of economic activities in society is. It
may happen, for example, that governmental activity, through poor legislation

or otherwise, leads to a substantially lower net production curve $F^+$ in one economy, compared with another, even though each system possesses the same technological knowledge.

In extreme cases, high transaction costs may prevent any exchange from taking place. Transaction costs, in terms of wheat, may be so high that the sum of transaction and current production costs will completely discourage consumers from demanding wheat. Wheat purchases will simply not occur. This represents a case of "market failure." Organizational arrangements other than spot markets have to be applied, for example, private firms or government organizations. Thus, the organizational side of the problem has great importance. A high level of technological knowledge may be rendered economically ineffective by bad institutional policy (Ordnungspolitik).

It follows from this understanding that if the economic development of a country is to be stimulated attention must be paid to the development of both production and organizational technique. Legislation that increases transaction costs, even if it costs "nothing" directly, may offset an improvement of productivity based on technical progress and may actually reduce the total productivity of an economy. On the other hand, legislation that reduces transaction costs may increase total productivity despite the existence of unchanged technical knowledge. Economic stagnation, then, may be caused as much by poorly designed organizational (institutional) measures as by the absence of innovation in productive technology or product development. In short, the rejuvenation of a stagnating economy does not always require the use of new engineering or technical advances. Institutional policy, in the sense of creating or recreating a more efficient market economy, so as to reduce transaction costs, or in the sense of diminishing institutional obstacles to the demand for labor or the use of capital, may in some circumstances be more effective and cheaper than quantitative economic policy. Examples of this type of economic enhancement can be found in the West German currency and economic reform of 1948 and in the deregulation and tax reduction efforts of the United States during the 1980s. The lively debate on the reorganization of the economies of the European Union, which is generally considered necessary to overcome increasing long-term unemployment ratios, provides a further example. Thus, it appears that a role exists for an "entrepreneurial politician" who, somewhat like the Schumpeterian economic entrepreneur, can discover new ways to improve the system. The need for this kind of institutional reform is, of course, crucial to the transformation of Eastern European economies into more productive systems of market capitalism.

The work of this section can be summarized as follows. It has been assumed that "transaction" activity represents a type of "production" process and can be modeled in much the same way as conventional production processes can. Thus, a convex transaction technology is posited, and analysis proceeds as a simple extension of the neoclassical theory of the firm. Some fraction of the source inputs are used up in bringing any transaction to a successful conclusion. Hence, the marginal conditions of the model look a bit different from those associated with the orthodox model that assumes zero transaction costs throughout. Apart from this, the results of standard general equilibrium analysis are said to remain the same. In particular, the argument is that a general equilibrium system, extended by the explicit introduction of "transaction" processes, remains Pareto efficient. Indeed, from a formal point of view, as Dahlman (1979, 144ff.) has pointed out, this approach would seem to yield results analogous to those produced by a general equilibrium model with transport costs included.[15]

Whether this general interpretation is correct, however, is open to serious doubt. Technically, a *first-best* equilibrium solution, and an operating position on the conventional welfare frontier, cannot be achieved once it is assumed that transaction costs are greater than zero in *any part of the system.* Insofar as real resources have to be used for transaction purposes anywhere, there must be some diversion of factors from the production of standard commodities. It follows, therefore, that, ceteris paribus, a system forced to deal with costly transactions will have what amounts to an *effectively smaller factor endowment* than an otherwise comparable system operating with zero transaction costs throughout will have. Against this view, it can be argued that, characteristically, transaction costs involve the costs of securing information and:

Information costs are no less real than production costs, and an evaluation of the efficiency of the economy must take these into account. (That is why I dislike the use of the term second best Pareto optimality or constrained Pareto optimality in analyzing the optimality properties of economies with imperfect information: we do not use the term "constrained" or second best optimality to refer to economies in which inputs are required to obtain outputs.) (Stiglitz 1985, 26)

---

15. We disregard setup costs associated with each transaction. They cause problems with the existence and uniqueness proofs of general equilibrium, which forced mathematical economists to resort to radical measures. Thus, Heller (1972), for example, showed that the resource misallocations resulting from such setup costs are small under certain conditions in relation to the size of economy. Dahlman (1979, 146), in criticizing this approach, argues that, parallel to the fixed cost in production theory, setup costs of an exchange are not really fixed at all: "Just as a firm can choose any level of its fixed costs, so may the individual transactor choose between different rates with different setup costs—that is, the fixed cost in any trade is really endogenously determined as known and adjusted costs of 'producing' the exchange." In other words, we may assume that the transaction function and its explicit version contains not just one input (the product transferred, wheat in our example) but several, factors like the various types of labor, capital, and so on necessary to "produce" a certain type of transaction. We may consider, then, that all these inputs will be variable in the long run.

The position adopted by Stiglitz is understandable but not particularly helpful. Given the nature of the real world, with its numerous constraints beyond those considered in the orthodox welfare model, it is certainly true that "technically correct," first-best solutions will never be obtained in practice (Stiglitz 1985, 28). But Stiglitz's approach would seem to lead, ultimately, to another problem, the contention that the solution reached for a system is *always* Pareto efficient if it meets all of the constraints that are imposed on the system (DeAlessi 1983, 69; Dahlman 1979, 152–54). Using this logic, all solutions can be rationalized as efficient, and the concept of inefficiency effectively disappears. To escape the dilemma what is needed is some clear distinction between those constraints that are *unavoidable* and those that can conceivably be circumvented. For example, the approach could parallel that used in defining the frontier production function. Then, in principle, both efficient and inefficient outcomes might be distinguished (Furubotn 1986). Unfortunately, however, it is very difficult to determine, on an a priori basis, which constraints are avoidable and which are not. For example, it is even difficult to decide, on empirical grounds, which production units are truly efficient and which are not. Thus, a clear-cut efficiency criterion comparable to that found in neoclassical theory does not seem to be available for a world of positive transaction costs.

The problem of how to interpret the concept of economic efficiency in the context of the New Institutional Economics will be considered in greater detail in section 3.3.2. and will be mentioned in this book time and again. For the moment, it will be sufficient to note that, even when analysis is more closely connected with the neoclassical perspective, the importance of transaction costs and institutions can be established. As the material of this section has shown, we are led, in the end, to the understanding that an economic system must seek an institutional framework that is consistent, inter alia, with a transaction-cost economizing organization of production and exchange.

## 2.5. Some Notes on the Development of the Transaction-Cost Literature

Historically, an early attempt to analyze economic institutions appeared in the area of monetary theory. Transaction costs, under the name of "frictions," were used in this context. Thus, the institution of money was said to have emerged in order to overcome the frictions of a barter economy. Money was compared with a lubricant that would reduce friction (Mill 1857). As Niehans has explained: "In a frictionless economy, therefore, monetary exchange would have no advantage over barter. An analysis of the role of money in economic equilibrium would thus require a theory of frictions" (1978, 3). Hicks (1935) also noted this point in his well-known article, "A Suggestion for Simplifying the Theory of Money" without developing the theme any further. About the same time, Coase (1937) attempted to close more fully with the issue.[16] His starting point, as he wrote later, was the "make or buy" decision of the firm:

> The solution of the puzzle was, as it turned out, very simple. All that was needed was to recognize that there were costs of carrying out market transactions and to incorporate them into the analysis, something that economists have failed to do. A firm had therefore a role to play in the economic system if it were possible for transactions to be organized within the firm at less cost than would be incurred if the same transactions were carried out through the market. (1988a, 19)

On the basis of his concept of the firm, Coase was able to explain the optimal size of firms. Rationally, an enterprise will tend to expand until the costs of organizing an extra transaction within the firm become equal to the costs of carrying out the same transaction by means of an exchange on the open market or the costs of organizing in another firm (Coase 1937, 395).

Despite these early stirrings in the literature, the concept of transaction costs remained largely dormant for more than thirty years. However, transaction costs did play a role in the second famous paper by Coase (1960) on "The Problem of Social Cost," where he showed that, regardless of whether production has negative external effects or not, "people can always (whatever the property-rights assignments) negotiate without cost to acquire, subdivide, and combine rights whenever this would increase the value of production" (1988b, 14). Here, of course, the assumption of zero transaction costs is crucial. Using the same assumption, Demsetz (1968b, 61) argued that it does not matter whether a good is supplied by a single firm (a monopolist) or by a large number of firms in a competitive industry. Optimal allocation is supposed to arise in both cases as long as perfect information holds. But this judgment seems questionable.[17]

The important point, though, is that Coase's emphasis on transaction costs caused economists to think along new lines. As a direct consequence of Coase's 1960 article, market failures could be traced to transaction-cost origins. Arrow pointed this out very clearly.

> Market failure is not absolute. It is better to consider a broader category, that of transaction costs, which in general impede and in particular cases completely block the formation of markets. . . . The identification of

---

16. The draft of this article was completed by the early summer of 1934 (Coase 1988a, 19).
17. See Arrow (1969, 52ff.); and Furubotn (1991). The latter argues that in a world of costless transactions consumers should be able to form a coalition and defeat the efforts of a "perfectly discriminating monopolist."

transaction costs in different contexts and under different systems of resource allocation should be a major item on the research agenda of the theory of public goods and indeed of the theory of resource allocation in general. (1969, 48)

It is important to recognize that so-called market failures are not absolute. Deadlocks arise only in cases in which transaction costs are so high that they prevent exchange. It is also useful to realize that not all market failures can correctly be described as externalities. Arrow has mentioned as examples of this kind of market failure the nonexistence of markets for many forms of risk bearing and for most futures transactions (1969, 59). In any event, correction of market failures is possible. Collective action but not necessarily state action is needed:

> [M]any other departures from the anonymous atomism of the price system are observed regularly. Indeed, firms of any complexity are illustrations of collective action, the internal allocation of their resources being directed by authoritative and hierarchical controls. (62)

The connection between transaction costs and market failure was also of interest to Williamson (1971). From his perspective, market failures may be seen as failures only in the limited sense "that they involve transaction costs that can be attenuated by substituting internal organization for market exchange" (114). Internalization of transactions through vertical integration represents one example of this procedure. Following this theme, Williamson then discusses three alternative options for firms: a once and for all contract, a series of short-term contracts, and vertical integration. Analysis is focused on the problems of contractual incompleteness and opportunistic behavior. In his later work, Williamson elaborated on these topics and worked the theoretical cases out more completely. He argues that the advantages of integration are "that integration harmonizes interests . . . and permits an efficient (adaptive, sequential) decision process to be utilized" (1971, 117). These early thoughts on organization represent the beginnings of Williamson's transaction-cost economics—something we will deal with in greater detail in chapter 4.

Along similar lines, Cheung's work contributed to the growing discussion of transaction costs and contracts. As he argued: "Every transaction involves a contract. . . . Why do the patterns of contractual choices differ? What determines the choice of contracts?" (1969, 25). Cheung shows that the systematic examination of contracts provides us with a set of observations from which to derive testable hypotheses to explain forms of economic organization.

Another important contributor to the early literature of transaction-cost economics was Alchian (1969). He tends to equate transaction costs with information costs. Following Stigler (1961), he recognizes that acquiring and processing information about potential exchange opportunities are costly undertakings that can be performed in various ways. Two significant questions must be answered. First, what are the means for providing the required information more efficiently? Second, given the costliness of information, what kinds of substitute arrangements can be used to economize on search costs? Alchian describes price stability as one way of reducing expenditures on market adjustment costs. Further, inventories are seen as another way of economizing on information costs. While inventories may appear to involve excess or unemployed resources, they can be understood more reasonably as means that conduce to the economical use of resources. Alchian's analysis of information problems also explains why an employee will not necessarily accept a pay cut to retain a job. Unemployment may be chosen because: "An employee correctly and sensibly believes he can, with some search and evaluation of alternatives, get approximately his old wage at some other job . . ." (1969, 117).

Later, Alchian and Demsetz (1972, 778) went on to consider the "metering" problem faced by all firms. They note that the problem of economic organization is closely connected to the need to find an economical means for metering (or measuring) productivity and rewards. Since this problem is not confronted directly in the neoclassical theory of production and distribution, they see a serious gap in the literature. What seems necessary is to view the firm as a contractual structure that arises as a means of enhancing efficient organization of team production. "The ability to detect shirking among owners of jointly used inputs in team production is enhanced (detection costs are reduced) by this arrangement and the discipline . . . of input owners is made more economic" (1972, 794).

One of the continuations of the article by Alchian and Demsetz (1972) is an article by Jensen and Meckling (1976), which is based, i.a., on the at that time newly developed principal-agent theory (see, e.g., Ross 1973). They introduce the concept of agency costs described in section 2.2. The concept of agency costs is closely related to the property-rights issue. We will return to it in chapters 3 and 4.

In the area of economic history, North (1978) suggests, among other things, that the systematic study of transaction costs offers a promising basis for explaining economic organization and institutional change. Movement in this direction is regarded as important because, as North observed, the new economic historians, despite the cliometric revolution, were still unable to explain changes in the institutional structure. By contrast, North pioneered a new path by applying the whole spectrum of the New Institutional Economics to the institutional framework of politics and showed how transaction-cost/property-rights analysis leads inevitably to an integrated model of *political economy*.

The central hypothesis of Olson's (1965) *The Logic of Collective Action* rests on the assumption of the "costs of organization," that is, a different class of transaction costs, and their changing relative importance with the increase of group size. He provides a modern institutionist explanation of the disproportionate power of "special interests."

Turning next to another aspect of transaction-cost research, we consider how transaction costs have been modeled when the institutional structure is taken as given and fixed. It should be noted that for some time transaction costs have been dealt with explicitly in the theory of money. The holding of cash balances due to transaction costs was first modeled by Baumol (1952) and Tobin (1956). The approach was later improved by Bernholz (1965, 1967) and by the work of Niehans (1969, 1971, 1975). For a simplified version, see Richter (1989a). Transaction costs, in the garb of adjustment costs, were similarly modeled in the theory of investment of the firm (see, e.g., Gould 1968). The role of transaction costs in general equilibrium theory has also been broached in the literature. In principle, two general approaches to the topic exist.

1. The situation of the economy can be conceived such that there is a *single market date* (one "day") on which all contracts are concluded for "all times to come" (as in the Arrow-Debreu world). For the fundamentals of this approach, see Foley (1970). Discussion of efficiency issues is found in Hahn (1973) and Starret (1973). The latter article takes up the role of money and gives examples of inefficient equilibrium allocation that arise in the absence of money. Ostroy and Starr (1990) provide a useful survey of work in this area.

2. Alternately, a "sequence economy" can be posited in which a series of market dates exists. In this case, the market is assumed to reopen at each new period of time. For further discussion of this model, see Hahn (1971), Grandmont (1974), and Grandmont and Younes (1972, 1973). An overview of the literature here is provided in Grandmont (1977) and Ulph and Ulph (1975). Interestingly, the benefits to monetary theory from these writings is disputed. Niehans, for example, argues that: "It is fair to say that this literature has not progressed in the subject matter of monetary theory" (1978, 19).

In considering the problem of externality, Dahlman (1979) repeats the argument of Demsetz (1969) "that it is a logical fallacy to use as a frame of reference a world in which transaction costs are zero, for that world is unattainable, given human behavior in our world (153). He urges the use, instead, of the comparative systems approach that attempts to ascertain the economic consequence of alternative ways of organizing the allocation of resources.

The analysis thus directs attention to the point that institutions fulfill an economic function by reducing transaction costs and therefore ought to be treated as variables determined inside the economic scheme of things. The question then ultimately becomes: how can economic organization be improved upon by endogenous institutional rearrangements? (161–62).

## 2.6. Suggested Readings for Chapter 2

It is always valuable to read the original literature. Therefore, in considering the concept of the "transaction" as the "smallest unit of institutional economics" it is well to begin with the relevant pages in Commons (1934, chap. 1, sec. 2) on "From Exchange to Transactions." You will discover here how he views his concept in relation to (1) neoclassical economics and (2) the German Historical School. In the former case, he finds no common ground, while in the latter he sees his work as a continuation or completion of this line of thought.

Next, the objective should be to learn something about the costs of transactions (and of transacting). Demsetz (1968a) deals with some findings on the costs of exchanging ownership titles on the New York Stock Exchange. Wallis and North (1988) consider quantitative measures of transaction costs ("the economic value of the inputs used in performing the transaction function" [97]) on the *macro* level. In a different direction, to get an idea about the practical application of the transaction concept to manufacturing overhead costs, read Miller and Vollmann (1985) on the activity-based costing approach.

For a simplified presentation of Foley's (1970) model of costly marketing, see Richter 1989a, section 3.3. Dahlman's (1979) frequently quoted critique of early attempts to interpret transaction costs in the context of the neoclassical model is also worth reading. While transaction costs were explicitly modeled by some writers, Dahlman notes that the result was to make transaction costs look essentially like transportation costs. Such a view, however, is not in keeping with what exponents of the New Institutional Economics call the "transaction cost approach." The latter deals especially with the *institutional consequences* of transaction costs.

As an economic historian, North is concerned with the change and evolution of the institutional framework at large. He provides a useful overview of his research in his Nobel Lecture (1994). Williamson, who has done much of the pioneering work in the new institutionalist movement, seeks to explain the great variety of private contracts in terms of transaction considerations and in the light of the given institutional framework. For an introduction to his thinking, read Williamson 1985, chapter 1.

CHAPTER 3

# Absolute Property Rights: Ownership of Physical Objects

Who owns what? This is a basic question, factually and morally, that has existed throughout human history, since the expulsion of Adam and Eve from paradise. The existence of physical objects and things in general requires that there be regulation among men regarding the appropriation and use of things. Indeed, sanctioned behavioral relations (e.g., allocations of property among individuals) are indispensable in a world of scarcity. While this understanding seems to be generally accepted (Radbruch 1956), the question of whether ownership should be private (individual) or social (collective) was and is a hotly debated issue that has contributed to the enormous bloodshed of this century. The recent breakdown of existing socialism does not signify the end of the struggle between exponents of the philosophies of private and social ownership. We find today that the struggle continues in various guises. Discussion of individualism versus collectivism now tends to proceed at one remove, and it involves questions of environmentalism, immigration, development policy, and war as a means to defend property rights.[1] Debate is sharp but perhaps more restrained than in the past when events were often interpreted in terms of an ongoing conflict between the socialist archangel and the capitalist devil (or vice versa).

Two major philosophies of ownership can be identified—the individualistic and the social theories of ownership. Representatives of the doctrine of natural rights, who provided the basis for classical economics, were in favor of the individualistic view. They deduced their conclusion from a rational theory of society in which man is seen as a selfish creature who "loves himself better than any other single person, and in his love of others bears the greatest affection to his relations and acquaintances" (Hume [1739–40] 1969, 539).

In this kind of social theory, it is argued that society provides the corrective for the natural limitations of individual human beings: "By the conjunction of forces, our power is augmented. By the partition of employments our ability

---

We must thank Professors John Henry Merryman and Kenneth E. Scott for their advice on Anglo-American Property Law.

    1. Human rights, for instance can be regarded as property rights (see sec. 3.2.1).

increases. And by mutual succor, we are less exposed to fortune and accidence" (Hume [1739–40] 1969, 537). It is recognized, however, that in forming a society the selfishness of human beings needs to be taken into account. We must realize that the "enjoyment of such possessions as we may have acquired by our industry and good fortune" (539) may be ended by the abuse of power. But, insofar as such corruption occurs, man will tend to be less industrious than he would otherwise be. Therefore, it appears that the instability of property rights over goods, along with their scarcity, is a major impediment to social wealth. Following this doctrine, Hume argues that "the stability of possession" is one of three fundamental laws of nature on whose strict observance the peace and security of human society depends. The other crucial laws noted are "the transference of property by consent" and "the performance of promises" (578).

Critics assert that this individualistic theory of ownership is based on the assumption of the "preestablished harmony" of social life or, in the terminology used earlier in this book, on the assumption of the inherent stability of the organization of the liberal state. According to this liberal view, the social function of ownership is inseparably connected with its individualistic nature. But exponents of social theories of ownership argue, by contrast, that the preestablished harmony of society is an illusion. Individualism is said to be the source of permanent conflict of interest, and, as a consequence, a social function of ownership, in addition to the individualistic function, needs to be strived for and secured.

Interestingly, in both old and new classical economics, ownership is considered to be given. It is not an object of analysis. In fact, general equilibrium theory is able to leave the efficiency aspects of the ownership issue completely out of its models. For the zero-transaction-cost economy of general equilibrium theory, it does not matter whether the factors of production are owned or rented by their users (Samuelson 1957, 894). The existence of costless transactions means that strict observance of Hume's three fundamental laws of nature becomes routine. This is so because any deviation from appropriate behavior can be detected instantly and dealt with costlessly. Clearly, in such a frictionless world, it is irrelevant for economic results whether resources are owned or rented under contract. Questions of distribution aside, the ownership of productive assets does not matter. Thus, we find that in the most abstract form of general equilibrium theory (i.e., the pure futures economy of Arrow-Debreu), with symmetric information and perfect foresight, markets for property in the means of production (or shares in firms) do not appear. These markets play no role because there is no control problem in the system. Consumers are able to determine in advance the stream of consumer goods they wish to enjoy at each moment of time given their economic constraints, and, by the nature of the frictionless environment, all purchase contracts will be honored perfectly. Therefore, only the possession of goods that are planned to be consumed immediately (at any period of time) is important, not ownership of various stocks of goods that are not to be consumed currently. The focus, in short, is on a flow-flow rather than a stock-flow system. Consideration is given to the services provided by durable assets (such as a house), not to the asset itself.

In the real world, where positive transaction costs are ubiquitous, the situation is quite different. Uncertainty (imperfect foresight) and asymmetrical information rule, and, as experience shows, ownership of resources matters for economic results. The reason is that, under the new conditions, economic incentives are affected by the ownership structure and behavior changes correspondingly. For example, it now becomes costly to monitor a tenant under lease, and the tenant, recognizing that he is not completely constrained, will feel greater freedom to pursue his own interests, even though his actions may affect the landlord adversely. Fortunately, the incentive effects of private property rights help to economize on transaction costs and thus contribute to the economic welfare of society. The situation, though, is not entirely favorable. As a consequence of positive transaction costs, property rights cannot be fully assigned (e.g., the right to pollute the air), perfectly enforced (e.g., thefts are not reduced to zero), or priced (e.g., parking spaces in privately owned suburban shopping centers are assigned on a first-come first-served basis).

As will be shown, the economic incentives generated under a regime of private property contribute, in general, to the efficient, nonwasteful use of scarce resources and hence to social welfare. In the case of environmental wealth, for example, it is the impossibility of making a complete assignment of property rights in resources to individuals, and not private ownership as such, that explains environmental problems. Of course, the distributive aspects of private ownership may also create social difficulties, but these difficulties are not necessarily solved by social (or collective) ownership.

## 3.1. The Property-Rights Approach: Some Basic Concepts

To understand the basic concepts of property-rights analysis, it is best to start by assuming that all activity takes place within the elementary institutional framework of the classical liberal state (see sec. 1.3). That is, we assume that property rights are assigned to individuals in accordance with the principle of private ownership and that sanctioned ownership rights are transferable by consent in accordance with the principle of freedom of contract. To simplify matters, we assume further that "property" relates only to physical objects, as in the Roman law tradition, and that the system is one in which individual rationality (see sec. 1.1) and competition prevail. However, the existence of positive transaction costs in this system means that, while decision makers are rational, rationality is imperfect. Individual knowledge and skills are taken to be limited.

In this world, the right of ownership in an asset is understood to consist of the right to use it, to change its form and substance, and to transfer all rights in the asset, or some rights, as desired. The right of ownership is an exclusive right, but ownership is not an unrestricted right. Against this background, it is clear that property gives individuals discretionary power over resources and provides a basis for competitive markets (Eucken 1952). It also follows that the economic decisions of the holder of a private property right are determined from two sides. First, there is the discretionary side by virtue of the content of ownership rights. Second, there is the (competitive) market side. What is involved is the market for property itself (durable assets such as farmland) as well as the market for the commodities produced with the aid of property (such as grain raised on the farmland). Under conditions of full private ownership, the holder of property rights has the choice of utilizing the owned asset himself, leasing the asset, or selling it to someone else. In the case of a sale, what happens effectively is the transfer of a "bundle" of property rights from one person to another. It follows, of course, that the value of any property exchanged depends, ceteris paribus, on the bundle of property rights that can be conveyed in the transaction. If, as the result of government action or otherwise, the content of property rights in an asset is changed, the value of the asset must be changed too—for the asset's owner and for any would-be buyers of the asset. And, as might be expected, changes in the exchange value of goods tend inevitably to affect the way people behave. Through this effect on behavior, then, property rights assignments influence the allocation of resources, the composition of output, the distribution of income, and so on. The interconnections here have prompted Alchian to argue that:

> In essence economics is the study of property rights over scarce resources. . . . The allocation of scarce resources in a society is the assignment of rights to uses of resources . . . [and] the question of economics, or of how prices should be determined, is the question of how property rights should be defined and exchanged, and on what terms. (Alchian 1967, 2–3)

The prevailing structure of property rights in a society can be understood as the set of economic and social relations defining the position of each individual with respect to the utilization of resources. But, from a practical standpoint, the crucial requirement for the property-rights approach is to show that the content of property rights affects the allocation and use of resources in specific and statistically predictable ways (Furubotn and Pejovich 1972a, 1139). Without such assurance, there would be no possibility for developing analytically significant and empirically refutable propositions about the effects of different property-rights configurations on the extent and character of economic activity in a society.

There is, of course, good reason to believe that systematic relationships do exist between property-rights assignments and economic choices. Technically, institutional features reflecting particular property-rights arrangements can be represented as distinct constraints in an optimization model, and we can recognize that, when such constraints change, the solution values of the model will change correspondingly. Rational decision makers, seeking their own welfare, must take cognizance of changing constraints (including transaction costs). A simple example may be used to clarify the situation envisioned here. In the socialist, labor-managed firms that existed at one time in the former Yugoslav Republic, workers in an enterprise possessed a special set of property rights in the firm. The economy was largely decentralized and workers at each production unit had substantial control over the policies of the firm to which they were attached. They were empowered to decide how the firm's assets were to be utilized, and had legal claim on the firm's residual earnings (for as long as they were employees of the firm). Moreover, current workers had the option of investing in the firm in order to enlarge its capital stock and bring about greater incomes for themselves in the future.

What was critical, however, was the fact that, as citizens of a socialist state, workers could not be granted full private ownership rights in capital (in the material means of production). Workers possessed usufruct rights but had neither permanent nor transferable claims on the assets of the labor-managed firm. This rights arrangement meant that decision makers operated with relatively short planning horizons and viewed economic choices with a somewhat distorted perspective. Workers could appropriate rewards only during the period of their active employment with the firm. Thus, one would expect that the rewards that were most meaningful to these workers were not the pleasures that come from improving the enterprise and "building socialism" but the pecuniary and nonpecuniary returns that they could actually capture during their period of tenure with the firm. Granting this bias, however, workers seeking their own narrow interests are likely to push the policies of the firm in undesirable directions. To take a dramatic case, assume the following scenario. If a majority of workers in a socialist enterprise were planning to leave the firm and retire at some future period, T, they might find it expedient to vote for durable investments that promise good payoffs to period T but disastrous results thereafter. The point is that, once retired, workers need not have any further concern with the fortunes of the firm. In principle, at least, this property-rights structure is socially inefficient. Whatever its contribution to industrial democracy, the socialist, labor-managed firm does not generate incentives that conduce to good economic performance.

It is worth noting, at this point, that the property-rights structure associated with full private ownership produces different, more efficient incentives than those found in the socialist case. In particular, perverse investment behavior of the sort possible under labor management is not likely to occur under capitalism. While mistakes in investment choice can certainly be made, each private entrepreneur has reason to try to conduct his affairs so as to maintain or enhance the projected "present value" of his firm. He acts in this way not out of altruism or regard for future generations but simply to maintain the option of selling his property for a good price. Impending retirement would not, of itself, cause an entrepreneur to disregard the long-term consequences of any current investment undertaking.

In general, a capitalist owner has an incentive to attend to his property according to its actual or expected market value. Contrary to the situation in a zero-transaction-cost world with perfect information, property rights and markets in property rights matter. In effect, the market value of an asset and its allocation are "controlled" by its supply and demand. Individuals compete on asset markets for ownership and thus make use of the society's scattered knowledge. In this sense, the competitor is the best supervisor of the use of resources a society can find. Each resource will go to the particular owner who expects the resource to yield the highest value. Moreover, the value estimates in question are backed, in each case, by the willingness of the purchaser to risk his own wealth in the transaction. Private ownership thus contributes, in an essential way, to the solution of the economic problem of society—the utilization of knowledge not given to anyone in totality (Hayek 1945).

Given our assumptions (bounded rationality and positive transaction costs), it is evident that, under ideal conditions, "all resources should be owned by someone, except resources so plentiful that everybody can consume as much of them as he wants without reducing consumption by anyone else . . . " (Posner 1972b, 29). Posner calls this the criterion of the universality of property rights. It is the first of three criteria for what he calls "an efficient system of property rights." The second criterion is exclusivity of property rights, and the third is transferability of rights. These three criteria, together with the assumption of individual rationality, are said to ensure that individuals will endeavor, through appropriate actions, to maximize the value of their property and thus also further the "wealth of nations." See also Posner's nice examples on the economic basis of individual property rights:

> Imagine a society in which all property rights have been abolished. A farmer plants corn, cultivates it etc., but his neighbor reaps and sells it. After some such experiences the cultivation of land will be abandoned [see also Demsetz, 1967]. The legal protection of individual property rights has the important economic function of creating incentives to use

resources "efficiently." Transferability ensures that if the farmer is a bad farmer, someone who is more productive will offer him a price for the land slightly higher than what he could earn himself. Thus the bad farmer is induced to sell the land to the better farmer. (27)

From what has been said so far, it should be clear that freely transferable private property plays a fundamental role in a market economy. Conditions in the economy that impede exchange have the general consequence of reducing efficiency. Private property provides both the incentive effect of ownership and the necessary control effect of competition—that is, the carrot and stick combination that tends to promote economic success. Nutter, with an eye on socialist market models, puts the issue as follows:

Markets without divisible and transferable property rights are a sheer illusion. There can be no competitive behavior, real or simulated, without dispersed power and responsibility. (1968, 144)

The same point was made earlier by Eucken, with the added warning that competition can be restricted or even abolished in a private ownership economy through monopolistic practices. Eucken, therefore, demands that the constitutional state should not only guarantee private property but also competition between private owners by means of a suitable law requiring competitive behavior ("competition order"). He writes:

As private ownership of the means of production is a precondition of a competitive order, so is in return the competition order a precondition that private ownership does not lead to economic or social abuses. (1952, 275)

Property-rights assignments in the sense of exclusive individual rights to physical objects are absolute rights, ". . . which guarantee the owner a power that he can exercise against all others (*erga omnes*) . . ." (Merryman 1985, 74). They define norms of behavior with respect to things that nonowners must observe or bear the cost of nonobservance. However, for owners themselves to protect their rights would be a relatively difficult and expensive undertaking. Costs would be high for both the owners and society. Thus, other arrangements are normally worked out, and it is widely believed that the state is much better able to enforce the absolute rights of individual owners. As Locke has noted, the preservation of property is "the end of government and for which men enter into society ([1823] 1963, 5:421).[2] This does not mean that the origin of private property is governmental. For, as Hume later argued, the legal rules of (private)

---

2. But this does not give the supreme power the right to "take from any man part of his property without own consent" (421).

property can be imagined to date back to social conventions that evolved spontaneously. Presumably, each individual is able to conclude that it will be in his interest "to leave another in the possession of his goods, provided he will act in the same manner with regard to me" ([1739–40] 1969, 541). In short, the existence of trust, reinforced with institutional safeguards, can lead to the convention of private property and its social protection.

To this point, the discussion has concerned property rights in physical goods. But, in fact, ownership includes more than rights in physical entities. It includes such rights as financial claims. The next question that must be addressed, then, is this. What precisely is meant by the term *property rights* as it is employed broadly in the property-rights approach?

## 3.2. Property Rights: Illustrations and Attempts at Definition

In legal literature, we find two meanings for the term *property rights*. First, there are property rights in the narrow sense of Continental civil law (as, e.g., German civil law, which originated from Roman law). Here, property rights are related only to physical objects or tangibles. Second, there are property rights in the wide sense of Anglo-American common law, which are related to both tangibles and intangibles, the latter including patents, copyrights, and contract rights (see, e.g., Lawson and Rudden 1982, chap. 2). This wider sense of property rights is also used in the German Constitution (Grundgesetz), Article 14, which guarantees private property in the wide sense, including not only rights in intangibles but rights to membership and social entitlements (see, e.g., Dürig 1958, 1080). Finally, a third type of property rights can be identified. Individuals have certain rights that are not covered by law but rather by conventions "supported by the force of etiquette, social custom, and ostracism" (Alchian 1977a, 129; see also Alchian 1965b) or other nonlegal instruments such as self-enforcement (Telser 1980).

Modern property-rights analysis was developed largely in the United States, and thus, naturally, it is based on common law terminology, that is, property rights in the wide sense of the word (see, e.g., Coase 1960). Still, the narrow Roman law sense of property rights, aimed only at tangibles, played an important role in the expositions of the early American property-rights literature (e.g., Alchian 1965b; and Demsetz 1967). But, since the early 1970s, contract rights have become of increasing interest to economists (see, e.g., Furubotn and Pejovich 1970b, 1972a; Williamson (1971, 1975; Jensen and Meckling 1976; and Goldberg 1976. The third type of property rights (Verhältnisse) concerns property rights in the sense of customer relationships, friendships and so on, which are guaranteed by various types of self-enforcement and are gaining increasing interest among neoinstitutionalists.

Another classification of property rights consists of the distinction between absolute and relative property rights. As mentioned previously, absolute property rights are directed against all others (as, e.g., property in land or other tangibles) but they also include intangibles such as copyrights and patents. Relative property rights, on the other hand, give the owner "a power which he can exercise only against one or more determined persons" (Merryman 1985, 74), as against the obligor in the case of obligations. Under aspects of the theory of law, the two categories of "absolute" and "relative" property rights may not be without problems.[3] Yet, for the institutional economist, who deals with property rights issues, they are, we believe, helpful. They permit the analyst to put early property-rights analysis, and later contract theory, under one roof—property rights—and they make it possible to draw a sharper picture of their similarities and differences.

This chapter is concerned with absolute property rights—in the first place, property rights in physical objects. Relative property rights are the subject of chapter 4.

### 3.2.1. Absolute Property Rights: Ownership and All That

Property rights in the narrow sense of Roman law give people discretion over tangible assets. It is useful, however, to make certain distinctions among the different categories of rights.

1. Ownership: Following Roman law, the main elements of ownership are:

The right to make physical use of physical objects (ius utendi)
The right to the income from it (ius fruendi)
The power of management, including that of alienation (ius abutendi)[4]

Full ownership comprises these three rights.

It is generally understood that the (full) owner can make unlimited use of the object he owns—provided his action does not conflict with other laws or with the rights of third parties (cf. German Civil Code Art. 903).

Of interest for students of economic property-rights analysis is the fact that property rights in land can be created

---

3. They are taken from the civil law tradition. See Merryman (1985, 74), on the fundamental division of "subjective rights" in civil law.
4. See Lawson and Rudden (1982, 6). *Ius abutendi* means literally the right to use up or destroy a physical object. It was extended to cover alienation as well (6, 8).

in such a way as to give to the owner of one piece of land rights over another piece of land in such a way as to enhance the value of the former. For example the landowners must not commit nuisance, like excessive noise, escape of fumes, smells etc., i.e., they must not do anything that interferes to an unreasonable degree with the comfort of their neighbors or the proper use of their land. If it [*sic*] does, the occupiers have to pay damages for injury they cause. (Lawson and Rudden 1982, 126)

This legal rule is debated by Coase (1960) from the standpoint of economic efficiency. We will deal with Coase's arguments later in this chapter.

For practical purposes, private property rights over physical objects are restricted to things that can, in fact, be used exclusively by their owners and can be defined clearly and unambiguously. Understandably, exclusivity of use cannot be assigned to the open air, running water in rivers or creeks, the waters of the open sea, and so on. These "open access" cases relate to public goods, and in this area the basic ownership concept, described in the preceding section, does not work. Environmental problems encountered today have their roots in the fact that clear, private ownership arrangements cannot always be established easily. Unfortunately, the criteria of universality, exclusivity, and transferability of property rights,[5] important as they are, cannot be realized for all physical objects directly—even under the conditions of the liberal state in its purest form.

The basic difference between the Romanic concept of ownership in land and the Anglo-American "estate" or "interest" is lucidly described by Merryman (1974, 927):

Romanic ownership can be thought of as a box, with the words "ownership" written on it. Whoever has the box is the "owner." In the case of complete, unencumbered ownership, the box contains certain rights, including that of use and occupancy, that to the fruits or income, and the power of alienation. The owner can, however, open the box and remove one or more such rights and transfer them to others. But, as long as he keeps the box, he still has the ownership, even if the box is empty. The contrast with the Anglo-American law of property is simple. There is no box. There are merely various sets of legal interests. One who has the fee simple absolute has the largest possible bundle of such sets of legal interests. When he conveys one or more of the sets to another person, a part of his bundle is gone.

---

5. While common ownership, for example, in a pasture, can be transferred because it is specified to a particular piece of land, public ownership of the kind illustrated above cannot be transferred.

According to the Romanic concept of ownership, a person can give away some of his rights without giving up legal ownership—a technical difference that does not concern us in this book. Important to us is the fact that full or complete ownership of land (in the Romanic sense of ownership or in the common law sense of the fee simple absolute) includes the right to sell the land, which presupposes the curtailment of restraints on the alienation of land from a feudalistic or (now) communist past (see Rheinstein 1935–36).

2. Fragmentation of ownership: Full ownership in physical objects can be fragmented or partitioned by transferring one or more of the three components of ownership (ius utendi, ius fruendi, ius abutendi) to other persons. Thus, for example, the right of use of a physical object can be leased to someone else (like leasing an apartment or a car) or the fruits of income can be transferred to another person for a period of time. Common law and civil law handle such fragmentations of ownership differently. While in common law the norms of the lease of land or any other tangible are considered to be part of property law (the lease of land being interpreted as "an instrument of conveyance of an estate in the land . . .")—that is, it is not a contract—in civil law it is a contract (Merryman 1974, 936; see also German Civil Code, Art. 585). No real rights are conveyed to the lessee in the latter case. Still, there exists also a number of fragmental real rights in civil law, called "restricted real rights" in German Civil Code (*beschränkte dingliche Rechte*). These include usufruct, residential rights, real servitude, and collatered securities such as mortgages—that is, rights that are also part of property rights in common law nations.

In this book, we shall apply the civil law classification and therefore deal with lease (or tenure) as a contract in the next chapter. Usufruct, on the other hand, is a real right in both legal traditions. It is of interest for the neoinstitutionalists and therefore will be given some closer consideration here.

The right of usufruct entitles the holder to the "fruits" or "produce" derived from an asset. Examples include the agricultural products yielded by a piece of land and the rent from the sale of the services of a house. The holder of a usufruct right has an exclusive right only to the fruits of the property, not to the asset from which the fruits spring. Moreover, the holder has to observe certain limits in the exercise of his usufruct right. According to German civil law, he has to maintain, for example, the economic integrity and character of the property. He must not convert a forest into a ploughed field, and he must carry out his operations in accordance with the principles of orderly management.

In Germany, usufruct rights are rarely used anymore in economic transactions. Rather, attention has shifted to the economically similar legal construct of the lease. From a legal standpoint, however, the lease in Germany falls under the law of obligations and is regarded as a relative property right.

3. Ownership in immaterial rights or intellectual property rights: A more

modern type of absolute property rights is classified under the heading of immaterial or intellectual property rights. Involved here are copyrights (literary, artistic, musical, etc.), trademarks, trade secrets, patents, and semiconductor chips. While Anglo-American jurists use the term *intellectual property,* German legal scholars (being used to the narrow property rights concept of Roman law) prefer to speak of "immaterial rights" because in each case the object of protection is essentially different from a well-defined physical asset or "thing." The entities covered by immaterial rights or intellectual property rights are not easily measured or monitored, and the problems that arise because of these limitations explain why such assets received legal protection only in comparatively recent times. England led the movement toward protection with the Copyright Law of 1710. France followed with similar legislation in 1791 and 1793, and Prussia joined in this effort in 1837. The U.S. Constitution of 1787 empowered Congress, in Article 1, section 8, to enact a copyright law, which Congress did.

Of special economic interest are the services provided by intellectual works—for example, works of art or science, including technical or organizational knowledge. Such services are important, and the role of immaterial property rights in maintaining incentives to produce intellectual works is evident. The purpose of rights in the nonmaterial area is the same as that of material property rights. In each situation, the intention is to protect the holder of rights against unauthorized use of his assets. Of course, insofar as nonmaterial assets are created by their owners, protection of the assets tends to ensure the continuance of creative efforts and the prompt communication of intellectual results to others in the community who are willing to pay appropriate prices to the creators for their discoveries.

Legally, ownership of immaterial property rights is limited to a certain period of time. In Germany, copyrights characteristically run for seventy years after the death of the creator; in the United States they last for the life of the creator plus fifty years. Hence, immaterial rights cannot be bequeathed in unlimited fashion to individuals of younger generations. On incentive grounds, this arrangement is understandable. An intellectual asset, such as a piece of information, is not subject to physical deterioration and requires no maintenance as physical objects do. There may be, however, some problems associated with data storage.[6] On the other hand, an intellectual asset may become inconsequential in the course of time and be forgotten, or it may become part of the culture, a public good to be utilized by the community. For an introduction to the American law and economics of intellectual property, see Besen and Raskind 1991. As usual, economists are of different opinion regarding the

---

6. There are exceptions, like paintings, sculptures, films, and photographs. Again, it is a matter of "demand" (public interest) whether they are kept up or not.

usefulness of intellectual property rights. The ruling opinion is that efficiency requires government support for innovative and creative activity (Arrow 1962). But there also exists a dissenting view, namely, that government actions of any kind, including the legal protection of copyrights and patents, is not necessary to stimulate such activity (see, e.g., Plant 1934; Frase 1966; and Hughs 1988).

The economics of intellectual property rights is a natural field of the economic analysis of law whose leading proponents, Landes and Posner, wrote studies on the economics of trademark law (Landes and Posner 1987) and copyright law (Landes and Posner 1989). Following the tradition of the economic analysis of law, these studies are specifically concerned with the question of the extent to which trademark law or copyright law can be explained as a means of promoting efficient allocation of resources. This is not the kind of problem—at least not in this straightforward sense—we are dealing with in this book on the New Institutional Economics. Therefore, and for lack of space, we leave aside issues of intellectual property rights. The basic economics of intellectual property rights together with the main literature is surveyed in Besen and Raskind 1991.

4. Property in one's own person: human rights: Human rights do not belong to the category of property rights in the legal sense of the word, not even in the wide, common law sense of the term. But for institutional economists, who are concerned with norms of behavior more in their incentive than their litigational aspects, human rights may very well be discussed using concepts of property-rights analysis. Thus, the liberal state's right of human self-determination may be, and actually was, interpreted by John Locke as "property in one's own person."[7] The similarity of this right to the right of private ownership of things is striking if one reads the relevant German laws.[8] Yet one important difference must be noted. A person is not allowed to sell his right to human self-determination, that is, a person cannot enslave himself. In the liberal state, slavery is forbidden.[9]

The right of self-determination can be interpreted as an arrangement that leads to efficiency if it is assumed that each person knows better than outsiders his own capacities and preferences. Then it follows that an individual is best able to plan his own life. In principle, each individual can draw on his knowledge of his personal capacities, his life expectancy, and the set of actual and expected market prices for goods and services in order to invest optimally and

---

7. The relevant sentence is: "Every man has a property in his own person. This nobody has the right to but himself" (Locke [1823] 1963).

8. See, for example, the text of Article 2 in combination with Article 1 of the German constitution (Grundgesetz) compared with the text of Article 903 of German Civil Code (BGB) on ownership

9. See, for example, the Thirteenth Amendment to the U.S. Constitution.

maximize the present value of his utility index. The human-capital research program, originally formulated by Schultz (1963), Becker (1975), and Mincer (1958) resulted from this view. In this connection, note that:

> Human capital refers to the productive capacities of human beings as income producing agents in the economy. (Rosen 1987, 681)

> Human-capital formation is typically conceived as being carried out by individuals acting in their own interests. This is the natural view to take in respect to job search and migration, but health care, education, information retrieval, and labor training are either wholly or in part carried out by governments in many countries. (Blaug 1976, 830)

Further, it is usually argued that certain basic social investments are necessary to establish and maintain a liberal society. These investments are the "fixed" political transaction costs described earlier (sec. 2.3)—that is, the costs of setting up, maintaining, and changing a polity.

### 3.2.2.  Relative Property Rights: Some Preliminary Remarks

Though relative property rights will be dealt with in the next chapter, a few preliminary remarks, to compare them with what we called absolute property rights, may be in place here. Relative property rights can result from either freely concluded contracts or court orders (in the case of tortuous act). They comprise, in other words, contractual property rights such as credit-debt or purchase-sale relations and legally imposed obligations. Common law jurists speak in such cases of such things as "predominant interest in funds" (Noyes 1936, 498), whereas in civil law these rights are part of the law of obligations (Schuldrecht in the German Civil Code), which—as mentioned previously—include, contrary to common law, leases in land and other physical objects. Since, in the end, the economic meaning of the norms is pretty much the same, we don't think that economists have to dwell much on that difference. Still, the difference between common law terminology and categorization, on the one hand, and that of Civil Law, on the other, is worth mentioning to improve the understanding of the property-rights literature by authors from these two legal spheres.

1. *Contractual obligations:* These are of particular interest to the institutional economist—and probably also the legal scholar—in cases in which time elapses between a promise and its execution, as in the case of exchange when both sides of a transaction are not carried out at once and simultaneously. This lack of synchronization occurs in the case of credit purchases, rental contracts,

leases (or other long-term obligations), complex long-term projects (such as the construction of an airport or a supertanker), utility contracts, loans, partnerships, and so on. Characteristically, allocational difficulties tend to arise in these cases. They are related to information, namely:

> *Lack of foresight:* The parties to a contract are unable to foresee precisely what the future will bring. Thus, insofar as contractual obligations are adaptable to new and unexpected situations, allocational efficiency is improved.
>
> *Asymmetric information:* One party knows more than the other either about the state of the world in general or his own position as it relates to the contract. For example, a seller may be better informed about the quality of the merchandise offered in a transaction than is the buyer, or an agent may know the effort level he intends to maintain in the future. Opportunism is an important issue. Lack of foresight would be no problem without the possibility, and thus the incentive, for opportunistic behavior. Asymmetric information can be responsible, then, for serious problems of contractual performance, a central issue in the economic theory of relative property rights.

   2. *Obligations as a consequence of legal liability:* The three major bodies of liability law are property, contracts, and torts. Contract law concerns broken promises, tort law deals with accidental or intentional harm to people or property, and property law considers the appropriation of ownership rights or interference with such rights (Cooter and Ulen 1988, chaps. 8, 9). Damages are assessed and regulated by law and court orders. In the case of tort law, one objective is to consider incentives and structure the legal framework (the negligence standard) so that the expected costs of accidents are as low as possible. According to Calabresi (1970), the costs of accidents tend to be minimized if the party who can avoid the accident at least cost is made liable for the cost incurred ("cheapest-cost-avoider" rule). Tort law also deals with the ex post regulation of harmful "external" effects (see chap. 4), but so does part of property law (e.g., German neighborhood law).

### 3.2.3.   Other Rights and Conventions

In addition to the more obvious property rights taken up so far, identification and feelings have a place in the panoply of rights. Love, friendship, religious faith, and patriotism all have roles to play. Furthermore, all sorts of personal and social relationships, whether protected by law or not, can imply the existence of rights—for example, "relational contracts" such as marriage, customer relationships, political associations, national affiliations, and religious affiliations. These rights were called Verhältnisse ("relationships") in the older German-language literature (Böhm-Bawerk 1881). These attachments represent specific investments that help to stabilize social relations and the resulting individual property rights. Like other specific investments, however, they also contribute to the vulnerability of the parties involved. Examples of opportunistic behavior in relationships are easily found: the abuse of a wife by her husband, of the idealistic party member by party bosses, of the patriotic citizen by his political leaders, and so on.

The property rights under consideration here influence outcomes through their incentive effects. Ideally, the arrangements in question will generate impulses that help to improve resource allocation and social welfare. Typical examples include the division of labor between family members, the way people assist each other in raising children, and the care given by family members and friends to their sick or old. In effect, part of the social safety net of an individual consists of family ties, neighbors, friends, and so on. These "assets" constitute part of his wealth. At the same time, the public social safety net, based on such things as social security provisions and public health insurance, helps to overcome deficiencies in the informal arrangements. That is, the public contributions supplement individual property rights, or the "social capital" (Coleman 1990, 300ff.).[10]

Personal and social relationships provide certain rights, but they demand commitments in return. Indeed, higher quality social relations are not normally available in exchange for money. The give and take of commitments are central to the existence of the informal system. Relations such as trust, loyalty, and honesty cannot be bought. Trade of these goods on the open market is technically impossible or simply unimaginable despite the fact that:

> They are goods, they are commodities; they have real, practical, economic value; they increase the efficiency of the system, enable you to produce more goods or more of whatever values you hold in high esteem. But they are not commodities for which trade on the open market is technically possible or even meaningful. (Arrow 1974, 23)

It is apparent that personal and social relationships in this sense contribute considerably to the final aim of economics: individual welfare. They are, therefore, economically important. Viewed as private property rights they add to an individual's effective wealth. To economists, every right may be interpreted as a property right (Fisher 1912, 12).

---

10. Ben-Porath (1980, 1) stresses: "the identity of the people engaged in a transaction is a major determinant of the institutional mode of transaction." And, he continues: "Investment in resources specific to a relationship between identified parties can save transaction costs and stimulate trade" (1).

Note in this context that Marx and Engels (1848), and subsequent radical thinkers, demanded not only the abolition of private property in the means of production but also the abolition of such social relationships as the family and national and religious affiliations. Thus, as the *Communist Manifesto* states: "The communist revolution breaks most radically with traditional property relationships" (23; our translation). Marx and Engels also insisted on restricting the right to human self-determination by demanding "equal compulsion to work for all, [and] foundation of industrial armies, in particular in agriculture" (24).

### 3.3. Property in Physical Objects: The Private Property Issue

For the remainder of this chapter, attention will be centered on absolute property rights to physical objects. As noted, these represent, both historically and conceptually, the most elementary form of property rights. In consequence, property in tangible assets presents itself as an excellent area for study. Here, it is possible to demonstrate, quite simply, the economic incentive argument for private ownership. Throughout the rest of this chapter, the term *property rights* is taken to mean property rights in physical objects.

As has been stressed in the preceding discussion, ownership is crucial to efficiency only in a world of positive transaction costs. In what follows, however, we shall consider only two types of transaction costs—notably, the costs of specifying and assigning and the costs of monitoring and enforcing full or restricted property rights. Both categories together may be called exclusion costs.

Efficiency problems arise if the costs of specifying (assigning) and/or monitoring (enforcing) property rights are prohibitively high—whatever the reason may be for such costs. The economist's suggestion for dealing with the situation is straightforward: if possible, one should avoid cases posing this problem by intelligent design of organizational structures. In this connection, note that specifying costs are sunk costs and do not affect decisions regarding output once the transfer of rights has taken place. Monitoring and enforcing costs, on the other hand, are variable and must be repeated in each successive period of time (Eggertsson 1990, 96).

We shall first discuss basic problems relating to monitoring costs and then go on to consider some important specifying cost problems.

### 3.3.1. Ownership and Control: Some Basic Observations

The essence of the monitoring-cost problem can be illustrated with the aid of a simple example drawn from the agricultural sector. Assume that a farmer has the right to the exclusive use of certain farmland and buildings for only a limited period of time (usufruct rights). He is not allowed to sell, donate, or otherwise act as though he possessed transfer rights in this property and could pass it on to others at will. As a result, the farmer is unable to capitalize the future consequences of the way he makes use of his (restricted) property rights. He cannot, for example, realize any capital gain that might accrue because his current policies are viewed as favorable to the long-run value of the assets. Moreover, if the farmer is not responsible for the state of the farm at the time he must surrender his usufruct rights, he would, as a rational, utility-maximizing individual, attempt to completely use up the soil and the buildings by the time these "assets" are surrendered. Similar results could be expected if the right to cut wood were assigned to individuals under comparable conditions. Incentives for excessive exploitation of a resource tend to be generated unless the terms of the usufruct contract include certain restrictive provisions. To avoid overuse of an asset, German usufruct law demands that the holder of the usufruct right has to maintain the economic integrity of the property and is not allowed to subvert its substance.

These restrictions are, of themselves, merely statements of conditions that should be fulfilled by the usufruct holder. For good results to be realized, the legal provisions would, of course, have to be enforced. And to ensure appropriate enforcement the definitive owner of the farm of our illustration (the landlord) would have to monitor the activities of his farmer routinely and, if necessary, would have to employ legal or other means to discipline him. The monitoring and disciplining activities would, of course, entail some cost to the landlord if he chose to proceed with this mode of enforcement. He could, however, save much of the cost if he utilized another option and entered into an appropriate contractual arrangement with the farmer. That is, the landlord could demand, at the beginning of the usufruct period, that the farmer give him a deposit equal to the current market value of the farm at that time. In addition, though, the landlord would agree to return the deposit to the farmer at the end of the usufruct period plus or minus the gains or losses in the final market value of the property. Such an agreement would approximate a situation in which the landlord sells the farm outright to the farmer but reserves for himself the right of first refusal. In these circumstances, the farmer, as the full owner of the land, is now "fully monitored" by himself. Monitoring of resource allocation would be completely "decentralized." In addition, of course, the farmer would bear the market-value risk of the farm. Given this ownership structure, the farmer will not simply attend to his farm in accordance with the set of maintenance rules required in the case of the monitored holder of a usufruct. Rather, he will adapt his resource allocation activities as quickly as possible to changes in the actual or expected market value of his farm. It follows, then, that decentralization saves not only on monitoring and enforcement costs but contributes also to a more rapid adaptation of economic behavior to actual or expected new conditions in the system. The basic requirement here is, of course, that trade in farms (durable assets) is allowed and there is a functioning market for farms, not merely for farm products.

Our example illustrates the role private ownership can play in saving on monitoring and adaptation costs. Alternatively viewed, the results obtained emerge as a by-product of decentralized decision making. The example would be misread, however, if one were to interpret it as a case against usufruct or similar legal arrangements (e.g., leasing). A risk-neutral landlord may wish to keep the farm for his family (his heirs), while the individual farmer (lessee) may wish to avoid the market risks of full ownership. In addition, the farmer may not have the money or bank credit available to buy the farm. Clearly, there may be good economic reasons for the use of usufruct or similar legal constructs, and individuals may prefer these alternatives in spite of the higher monitoring and adaptation costs they entail.

It is true, of course, that without bonding the farmer as the holder of usufruct rights needs to be monitored. But an important question that arises here is: who will monitor the monitor? Consider the following situation. Assume the farm in question is now owned by "the people" and is administered by an agricultural ministry far away in the capital city. Presumably, a long hierarchical chain of monitors is necessary to perform the desired oversight duties. Most individuals in this chain, however, cannot be expected to have target functions or objectives that are perfectly consistent with the ends of the ultimate supervisors in the capital or with the efficient use of the farm. Even if the monitors are selfless and have good intentions, it is likely that they will face a variety of unforeseen constraints and special circumstances that prevent them from operating in a completely efficient manner. In short, the "socialist" problem is inherently difficult and probably insuperable. Thus, the answer of private ownership economics to this dilemma is: let the monitor possess the title to the market value of the farm and through this device attribute to him all gains or losses in the farm's market value. Under such an arrangement, the monitor has an incentive not to shirk (Alchian and Demsetz 1972, 782). In other words, the best solution would seem to be to allow the monitor to become the full owner of the farm (like the landlord in the earlier example). Insofar as organization proceeds along the lines just suggested, limits exist to the size of a hierarchy of monitors, and strong incentives exist to structure the hierarchy in a way that is more efficient than is possible without ownership incentives.

Our example may be built into a brief and stylized version of a rational theory of the state. To begin, assume that the ruler (a benevolent dictator without rivals) owns all of the farmland in the nation. Assume further that the ruler wishes to maximize the annual output of goods and services. One solution to the organizational problem would be to have all farmland worked by farmers who would be supervised by an extensive government bureaucracy. In the latter, the ruler would serve as the ultimate authority. But this organizational arrangement would not be very effective for the reasons given previously. Another solution would be to establish a private-ownership economy with freedom of contract. This approach would permit major property rights in farmland to be placed in the hands of the ruler's subjects in accordance with the principle of private property and would allow these individuals to transfer rights by consent consistent with the principle of freedom of contract. The scheme, however, would involve some restrictions on individual property rights. The ruler would presumably wish to reserve some rights for himself— so-called prerogatives. Limitations of exclusive rights, such as zoning of land for different purposes, are often imposed by the state (such restrictions are called attenuations of property rights). And, of course, the ruler would reserve to himself the right to raise taxes on the owners of farmland. This is a highly significant power because very high taxes can come close to achieving economic expropriation of the formal owner. In any event, to maximize his income from taxes, the ruler's choice of the organization of the economy is as important as his choice of tax law. We do not have to look far into history to realize the truth of this conclusion. Thus, in England, for example, ownership in land resided in the king, "and the distribution and retention of lands throughout the kingdom was carried out according to the theory of tenure" (Merryman 1974, 927). Restraints on alienation were originally prominent and are, for the liberalist state, a problem.[11]

There exists, of course, no benevolent dictator, and, benevolent or not, no ruler is without rivals. North describes the problem as follows in his neoclassical theory of the state—which represents a simplified model of a political system comprised of a ruler and constituents:

> [T]he ruler acts like a discriminating monopolist offering to different groups of constituents protection and justice . . . in return for tax revenue. Because different constituent groups have different opportunity costs and bargaining power with the ruler, different bargains result. (1990, 48)

The division of the gains between the ruler and the public depends on the relative bargaining power of the groups that make up the public. Thus:

> property rights and hence individual contracts are specified and enforced by political decision making, but the structure of economic interests will also influence the political structure. (1990, 48)

---

11. In civil law countries, restraints on alienation were almost entirely swept away in the reforms of the nineteenth century (Rheinstein 1935–36, 625).

We return to this issue in greater detail in chapter 9.

Of particular importance for economic development, as should be evident, is the *credible commitment of the state to respect private property*. Thus, "the greater the credibility of a right to property, the greater will be the investment in improving the economic productivity of the property" (Riker and Weimer 1995, 94). Postcommunist institutional transformation makes this point clear. As Riker and Weimer (94) point out:

> The post-communist countries face severe problems in establishing the credibility of their systems of property rights for several reasons. First, their governments have yet to achieve levels of stability that make policy at least somewhat predictable. . . . Second, . . . there does not seem to be a broad and deep understanding of the role of private property in market economies. . . . David Mason (1992) found that majorities of residents of the post-communist countries supported values and policies associated with the socialist system, even though large majorities also expressed disfavor toward socialism. . . . Third, both historical and current experience of these countries undermines credibility.

This last point relates to the path-dependency argument of North.

### 3.3.2. Assigning Property Rights: The Internalization of External Effects

In the preceding section, we assumed that it is perfectly clear which person has authority (or rights) over which real assets. The problem, then, reduced to this: how well does the individual possessing rights take good economic care of the assets and how efficiently does he utilize them? In the present section we ask a different question. We should now like to consider the problems that may arise in the process of assigning property rights to individual decisions makers and to explore the consequences of incomplete specification of rights. Because of specification costs, it is clear that some property rights cannot be fully assigned. For example, there are inherent difficulties (and major costs) in any attempt to allocate rights in the atmosphere or the open seas. But, in the absence of appropriate rights specification, external effects result. In effect, the specification problem of individual property rights is directly related to the problem of "internalizing" externalities.[12]

An externality is said to appear in situations in which one individual's economic position is affected by what other individuals do with respect to

---

12. The resources necessary to "produce" private property rights are often substantial (see, e.g., Anderson and Hill 1975).

consumption or production. Insofar as benefits or disbenefits are transmitted through the price system, so-called pecuniary externalities exist. These effects, though they can be important, cause no particular problems because the effects are reflected in markets and can be dealt with in the usual way through market choices. Significant difficulties for a price-directed system do emerge, however, when benefits and disbenefits "short-circuit" markets and bear directly on the production and consumption activities of certain individuals. In short, it is the lack of markets for externalities that pushes a system away from Pareto-efficient allocation.

We say external effects may be either harmful or beneficial to an individual. But, in a private-ownership economy with freedom of contract, whether an individual has to suffer under harmful external effects or can enjoy costlessly beneficial ones depends on the specification and transfer costs of property rights. In a well-functioning capitalist system, externalities will be internalized by the transfer of the relevant property rights. The necessary conditions for the internalization of external effects include: (1) a sufficiently clear specification of property rights and (2) freedom for their exchange. Relative to the latter, Demsetz has rightly stressed that:

It is the prohibition of a property right adjustment, the prohibition of the establishment of an ownership title that can henceforth be exchanged, that precludes the internalization of external costs and benefits. (1967, 349)

The external effects problem can be explained simply in terms of an example. Thus, consider the issues raised by something as commonplace as a building plot. Its borderlines can be determined with great precision at relatively low cost. The space above (and below) the surface of the plot also belongs to the landowner, but here a more serious specification problem arises. Clearly, the air in the space above the plot cannot be assigned, molecule by molecule, to the exclusive use of the landowner. What the state can do instead, for example, is to give the owner the right to apply for an injunction to rule out the creation of smoke, noise, smells, or other external effects in his immediate neighborhood.[13] This approach is not the only possible solution, however. The state may assign rights in the opposite fashion and give the neighbors the right to pollute the air or be noisy. Nevertheless, whatever the assignment of rights turns out to be, if zero transaction costs are assumed, individuals will (ideally) trade some of their rights away until a Pareto-efficient allocation of resources has been realized (i.e., until the marginal benefit of the transfer is just equal to the marginal disbenefit). This understanding is the central message of the so-

---

13. One could also think of a general human right to clean air for everybody independent of the ownership of land. We shall treat that issue further below.

called Coase theorem in its general form (Coase 1960; see also Furubotn 1995). Another, more specialized interpretation of the theorem is that the organizational arrangement reached will be independent of the initial assignment of property rights.

The important "discovery" of Coase was to point out that the right to clean air and quiet or the right to undertake activities that generate harmful effects are property rights and are thus completely parallel with other rights that go with property ownership (such as the right to till land or cut timber). Such rights can be given away or sold to another party just as any other good can. And transfers can be anticipated. As in the case of no externalities, there is no reason why the initial endowments of rights should be Pareto efficient. In general, gains can be achieved through exchange, and thus people will often find it advantageous to trade their rights to such things as clean air and quiet for money.

The situation can be explained effectively with the aid of a diagrammatic representation involving the familiar Edgeworth Box. Thus, following Varian (1987, chap. 30), we consider a case of consumption externalities in which two roommates seek mutual accommodation. The individuals in question are A, a smoker, and B, a nonsmoker, who have preferences defined over "money" and "smoke." Both see money as a commodity (rather than a discommodity), but A likes to smoke and B likes clean air. Assume that each decision maker has an initial endowment of $100 and that the nonsmoker (person B) has the legal right to clean air. The point of departure for analysis, then, is point W in figure 3.1, where the quantity of smoke is zero and each individual has $100. As usual, the preference orderings of the two individuals are represented by indifference curves. The locus of mutual tangencies of these curves, or the contract curve EF, shows all Pareto-efficient combinations of smoke and money.

As is shown in figure 3.1, the nonsmoker, B, would be willing to trade away some of his property right to clean air for money and in this way increase his satisfaction level (relative to point W, the lines through this point represent the indifference curves of A and B). Insofar as exchange of this type is initiated, the two roommates would end up with an exchange equilibrium at some point on the contract curve between E and F. If there were an auctioneer calling out prices and asking how much each individual would be willing to buy or sell at the announced prices, the system could move to an equilibrium solution. That is, when the auctioneer manages to find a set of prices where supply equals demand, trade is possible—say, at point G. The price line intersecting points W and G establishes the equilibrium price set that permits trade to take place and Pareto-efficient consumption levels (of smoke and money) to be realized.

The outcome of the externality situation is different if the smoker (A) has the property right to create smoke and pollute the air up to the amount AD (on the "smoke" axis in fig. 3.1). If, again, A and B have initial money endowments

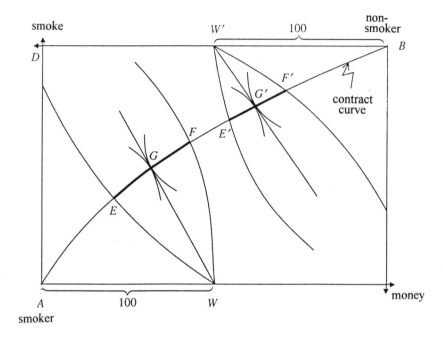

**Fig. 3.1.  The nonsmoker and the smoker exchange money for smoke**

of $100 each, then the point labeled W' in the diagram indicates the amounts of the respective "commodities" that individuals A and B possess before exchange begins. By assumption, the commodity configuration at W' is not Pareto optimal and thus trade is called for. In this case, the smoker would be willing to trade some of his rights to create smoke for money. The nonsmoker (B) could, in effect, "bribe" the smoker (A) to reduce his creation of smoke. Each party would improve his welfare by moving from point W' to some point on the contract curve between E' and F'. If an auction is held and a "competitive" solution emerges, the equilibrium point would be at G'. In general, if there is a market for smoke, a competitive equilibrium will be Pareto efficient (Arrow 1969, 49ff.).

The analysis here is the same as that used in the standard Edgeworth Box case except that we have been considering situations in which individuals possess different initial property rights in an externality. As long as there are well-defined property rights in the good representing the externality (no matter whether, e.g., the smoker or the nonsmoker possesses the right), the individuals can trade from their initial endowments to a Pareto-efficient allocation.

Problems arise, however, if the property rights are not well defined: "If A believes that he has a right to smoke and B believes that he has the right to clean air, we have difficulties. The practical problems with externalities generally arise because of poorly defined property rights" (Varian 1987, 546).

When expressed in its "strong" form, the Coase theorem asserts that the initial assignment of property rights or legal entitlements makes no difference to efficiency because identical Pareto-optimal allocations will emerge regardless of whether the party generating an adverse externality does or does not bear legal liability for the damages he causes to others. There is, of course, acknowledgment that, in order for this interesting outcome to be realized, some very far reaching assumptions have to be made. The key requirements cited in the literature are: (1) costless negotiation, (2) fully defined property rights, and (3) the absence of wealth effects. In this special environment, transaction costs are zero and the negotiating parties have quasi-linear preferences, so that the distribution of income occasioned by trade does not affect marginal valuations. If, in addition, certain problems posed by strategic behavior and free riding are ruled out, it is said that efficient bargaining can go forward and the level of an externality will be set optimally. For example, in the case of production externalities, the idea is that by following a program of joint-benefit maximization the level of the externality will be established optimally in the sense that the sum of the marginal net benefits and disbenefits produced by the externality will be zero.

Returning to the simple example of the roommates, it can be shown that allocative results are independent of the assignment of property rights if we assume individuals A and B possess quasi-linear preferences (Varian 1987, 541–43). In the circumstances envisioned, the contract curve is a line parallel to the money axis of the Edgeworth Box (fig. 3.2). The implication of this condition is that every efficient solution has the same amount of the externality. What remains, of course, is a distributional problem. Just as in the first case studied, the nonsmoker will end up with a larger amount of money than his initial endowment if the right to clean air is allocated to him and with less money if the smoker has the right to create smoke. For the smoker, the opposite would be true. In other words, it certainly matters from a distributional point of view who has the (initial) property rights in goods that cause harm to others. The amount of "property" an individual has command over affects his wealth position. But the same is true for an initial endowment in physical goods that cause no external effects—as the usual examples of the Edgeworth Box attest.

The existence of costless transactions is a sine qua non for the operation of the Coase theorem. But this is a very strong assumption because zero transaction costs must imply, inter alia, that every individual knows every other individual's tastes and opportunities (Arrow 1979). As Farrell has noted:

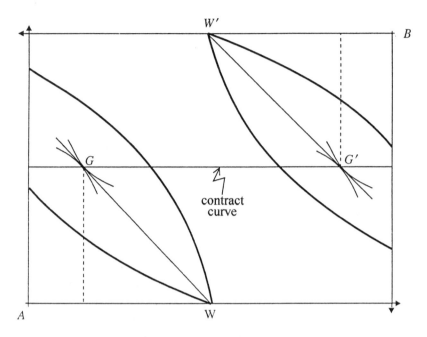

**Fig. 3.2.   The Coase Theorem in its strong form: quasilinear preferences**

. . . When people don't know one another's tastes or opportunities, then experience, theory and experimental evidence all confirm that negotiations may be protracted, costly and unsuccessful. A potential buyer may value a house more than its prospective seller does, but less than the seller believes "most" buyers do. He would then have trouble persuading the seller to lower the price enough to make the deal. Exactly the same is true if it is quiet, rather than a house, that is being bought or sold. (1987, 115)

Farrell concludes that we cannot assume that

all mutually beneficial contracts are signed, unless we assume that everyone knows everything about everyone, which they do not. The strong form of the Coase Theorem—the claim that voluntary negotiation will lead to fully efficient outcomes—is implausible unless people know one another exceptionally well. (115)

It follows from this assessment that action based on individual property rights and private bargaining can easily produce less efficient results than those generated by governmental action—even though the bureaucratic decisions may be less than optimal.[14]

Along these lines, it is worth pointing out that Arrow has described a game of incomplete information between two individuals in which no one knows for sure what the other individual's utility function is. Both parties do know, however, the various types of utility functions extant and the probability ($p_i$) of the utility function ($U_i$) being correct. Under special assumptions, one can find a set of rules of a game in which each individual is to announce his utility function. Then "the allocation of resources is a function of the announcements, and the rewards are such as to induce each to announce truly" (Arrow 1979, 32). The special assumptions of the model are: (1) income effects have to be neglected and (2) the probabilities of different possible utility functions for the agents are known and are independent of each other.

Once probabilities are introduced, the objective of each individual is to maximize expected utility according to the conventional Bernoulli or von Neumann–Morgenstern hypothesis. But: "The absence of income effects means that the utility function is linear in income and therefore, in particular, implies risk-neutrality toward income. This is a serious limitation" (Arrow 1979, 32).

Despite the possible criticisms of the idealized Coase theorem, it is arguable that in practice the general approach emphasized by Coase has interest. Indeed, there is a tendency to internalize external effects privately, without state intervention, if negotiations between parties are economically feasible. Moreover, there is reason to believe that this possibility of private negotiation should be used whenever possible (Sohmen 1976, 257ff.).

It has been suggested that the establishment of norms might help in the process of internalizing externalities (Ullmann-Margalit 1978). Thus, Coleman argues that if social issues are resolved in this way

the decision-making process will give a socially efficient outcome in a way that is precisely analogous to the market for externalities envisioned by Coase (1960) as a means by which a socially efficient outcome is achieved. (1990, 386)

Coase was not concerned with norms but with the question of how cases involving externalities imposed by one actor on another should be decided in law. Who should pay for the social costs? That problem is closer to the problem of disjoint norms than at first appearance—for law and social norms are close relatives in the family of social control mecha-

---

14. See Furubotn (1995).

nisms, and the structure of the situation examined by Coase . . . is . . .
exactly that in which a demand for a disjoint norm arises (1990, 160)

Coase's point is that there is an economic value to the activity that produces the externalities and the economic cost created by the externalities,
and if (but only if) the former exceeds the latter, the activity will continue,
independent of who pays the costs. (261)

Finally, it can be noted that, in the case of public goods, the free-rider problem
may be particularly severe when transaction costs are greater than zero. That is
"all the non-dictatorial social choice mechanisms will be subject to misrepresentation of preferences if there are privately held pieces of information"
(Green and Laffont 1979, 13). Under these circumstances, it is said that there is
a presumption that the state might usefully intervene and, for example, try to
establish optimal arrangements by either taxation or regulation. At best, however, governmental corrective action is subject to problems arising from informational limitations and administrative costs. Moreover, if we are to understand what behavior the state is actually likely to pursue, a model of the
government sector must be specified so that the motivations of the government
actors and the constraints they face can be established. And, as DeJasay (1989)
has argued, the existence of some free riders does not preclude the possibility
that other individuals in the system that is contemplating public goods provision will collaborate and secure gains. That is, if public goods promise to yield
sufficiently large benefits to some members of the community, this group may
be willing to finance the construction of public goods despite the fact that free
riders will gain benefits for which they did not pay.

Pommerehne, Feld and Hart (1994) report on a successful real-life Coase-
like bidding game in which the German community of Kleinblittersdorf
bought off the planning and operation of a waste incinerator by its French
sister community Grosbliederstroff just across the river Saar. On the basis
of a survey study of the inhabitants of Kleinblittersdorf the authors conclude that in a decentralized setting people are able to handle the free rider
problem on their own, conducted in the present case by the mayor of
Kleinblittersdorf Robert Jeanrond. His activities helped to transform the
original impersonal large group setting into a quasi private decision making framework. (512–15)[15]

---

15. The authors mention in this context a study by Isaac and Walker (1988), who also found
(experimental) evidence for the positive influence of communication on the reduction of free-
riding behavior.

Note, however, that Coase did not believe the zero-transaction-cost (ZTC) case to be a representation of the real world. He called it "a very unrealistic assumption" (1960, 15) and used it only as a convenient device to point out what would happen in the neoclassical ZTC world. He writes that "once the costs of carrying out market transactions are taken into account it is clear that such a rearrangement of rights will only be undertaken when the increase in the value of production consequent upon the rearrangement is greater than the cost which would be involved in bringing it about" (15). This approach raises the general question of alternatives to market organization such as the firm or direct government regulation. Relative to government intervention, he argues that such action is not the only, or necessarily the best, way to solve the problem of externality: "All solutions have costs and there is no reason to suppose that government regulation is called for simply because the problem is not well handled by the market or the firm" (18). The debate on the logic of the Coase theorem, interesting as it may be, obscured Coase's intention.

### 3.3.3. The Concept of Efficiency in Property-Rights Analysis

In neoclassical demand theory, the consumer is assumed to have property rights in the assets constituting his initial endowment. These assets represent the consumer's human and nonhuman wealth. For any individual, the efficient allocation of his property rights is said to occur when he maximizes his utility level subject to the given budget constraint (see, e.g., DeAlessi 1980). This is unproblematic in the case of the neoclassical, zero-transaction-cost world. With positive transaction costs, however, information becomes costly and, inter alia, the consumer's problem must be reformulated with the inclusion of additional constraints (see chaps. 5 and 10). But, unfortunately, adding constraints leads to other difficulties. If efficiency is defined simply as *constrained maximization* (with due account being taken of various real-world restrictions), any situation observed in the economy can be rationalized as "efficient." This is so because any failure to realize performance superior to that actually observed can be attributed to the existence of some troublesome constraint. In effect, then, what "is" is efficient.

To escape this problem, one might try to classify constraints as "avoidable" and "unavoidable" and argue that inefficiency holds if potentially avoidable constraints are not avoided. This approach, though, is unworkable because it is hardly possible to establish objective criteria for determining which constraints are, in fact, avoidable. As a practical matter, it seems to be preferable to do without the neoclassical efficiency criterion when judging institutions in a world of "frictions." Rather, institutions or organizations can be assessed on the basis of their comparative production of desired results—as evaluated by the individuals granted decision-making power. For the purposes of this book, however, we shall often find it convenient to follow the literature and continue to use neoclassical efficiency criteria and speak in terms of first-best or second-best Pareto optimality. The reader, though, should be aware of the limitations of the efficiency concept.

## 3.4.  Common Pool Resources

What has to be considered next is the possibility that the costs of defining, monitoring, and enforcing private property rights, or of internalizing external effects, may be too high to permit effective action to be taken against externalities. In other words, exclusion costs and integration costs may prevent trade of externalities among private individuals. Then some form of collective action may be preferable. We face the problem of governance and management of common pool resources (or CPRs).

Two variant cases of CPRs have to be distinguished: (1) The open-access CPR, in which no one has any sanctioned property rights in the asset (e.g., in the waters of the open sea, the atmosphere, or outer space) and (2) The closed-access CPR, in which a well-defined group owns property in common (e.g., communally owned alpine meadows in the Swiss, Austrian, and Bavarian Alps). Here common property rights exist.[16] By the nature of the incentives generated by these institutional arrangements, common pool resources are in danger of being overused. To illustrate the difficulty, we refer to a story by Hardin (1968). He posed the problem in the context of common grazing land.

### 3.4.1.  The Tragedy of the Commons

Varian (1987, 552) has summarized the essentials of the common property case as follows:

Consider an agricultural village in which the villagers graze their cows on a common field. We want to compare two allocation mechanisms: the first is the private ownership solution where someone owns the field and decides how many cows should graze there; the second is the solution where the field is owned in common by the villagers and access to it is free and unrestricted.

---

16. The terminology is not standardized. We use here that of Ostrom (1990, 91), who writes that "since the work of Ciriacy-Wantrup and Bishop (1975), the presence of boundaries concerning who is allowed to appropriate from the CPR has been used as the single defining characteristic of 'common-property' institutions as contrasted to 'open-access' institutions." Eggertsson (1990, 36) instead uses "common ownership" and "open access" as synonyms.

Suppose that it costs $a$ dollars to buy a cow. How much milk the cow produces will depend on how many other cows are grazed on the common land. We'll let $f(c)$ be the value of the milk produced if there are $c$ cows grazed on the common. Thus the value of the milk per cow is just the average product, $f(c)/c$.

How many cows would be grazed on the common if we wanted to maximize the total wealth of the village? To answer this question we have to solve the following problem:

$$\max_c f(c) \; - \; ac.$$

Assuming decreasing marginal returns, maximal production will occur when:

$$f'(c^*) = a.$$

If the common grazing ground were owned by someone who could restrict access to it, this is indeed the solution that would result. For in this case, the owner of the grazing grounds would purchase just the right amount of cows to maximize his profits (1987, 552–53).

But, at this point, the obvious question is: what will happen if the grazing ground is owned in common by the villagers and if each villager is free to decide whether or not to use the common field? Given the assumptions of the model and the usual understanding that decision makers are self-seeking, behavior is predictable. Specifically, it will be profitable for each villager to graze an additional cow as long as the output produced by the cow is greater than the cost of the cow. The equilibrium number of cows on the commons will then be $\hat{c}$. This point is determined by the equality of the average product (or the value of the milk per cow) with the price of a cow. Villagers will stop adding cows to the common field only when profits have been driven to zero. That is, when:

$$\frac{f(\hat{c})}{\hat{c}} \; - \; a = 0,$$

where $\hat{c} > c^*$ and $f' < 0$.

Individuals in this case ignore social cost in their calculations, namely, that each extra cow beyond $c^*$ will reduce the output of milk from all of the other cows. As a result, too many cows will be grazed on the common ground. Note that at $\hat{c}$, the marginal product of a cow is less than zero (fig. 3.3). This tendency toward the misallocation of resources is called the tragedy of the

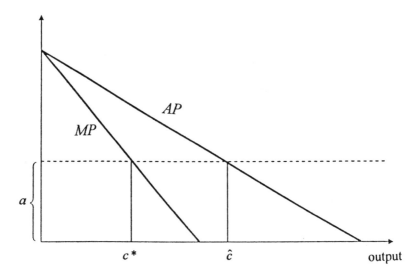

**Fig. 3.3.  The tragedy of the commons**

commons. In spite of the fact that the example refers to a closed-access CPR (only villagers are allowed to use the commons), the common property solution, without further restrictions, leads to an inefficient result (Furubotn 1987). In effect, each herder has perverse incentives. Each is motivated to add more and more animals because he receives the direct benefit of his own animals and bears only a share of the costs resulting from overgrazing. Hardin therefore concludes:

> Therein is the tragedy. Each man is locked into a system that compels him to increase his herd without limit—in a world that is limited. Ruin is the destination toward which all men rush, each pursuing his own best interest in a society that believes in the freedom of the commons. (1968, 1:244)

This account leaves out the possibility of the assignment of common pool resources to individual users through collective action. One problem involves the question:

> under what conditions can voluntary cooperation exist without the Hobbesian solution of the imposition of a coercive state to create cooperative solutions? As we know from experience, the coercive power of the state has been employed throughout most of history in ways that have been inimicable to economic growth. (North 1990, 14)

Earlier examples of the Hardin problem were given by Aristotle, who observed that "what is common to the greatest number has the least care bestowed upon it. Everyone thinks chiefly of his own, hardly at all of the common interest" (*Politics,* 2.3). In the same vein, Ostrom (1990, 2) quotes Hobbes's parable of men in a state of nature as a prototype of the tragedy of the commons. Men seek their own narrow goals and end up fighting one another. The generalization to which we are led seems clear:

> There appears then to be some truth in the conservative dictum that everybody's property is nobody's property. Wealth that is free for all is valued by no one because he who is foolhardy enough to wait for its proper time of use will only find that it has been taken by another. . . . The fish in the sea are valueless to the fisherman, because there is no assurance that they will be there for him tomorrow if they are left behind today. (Gordon 1954, 124)

The "tragedy of the commons" has come to symbolize the degradation of the environment that is to be expected whenever many individuals use a scarce resource in common. In the literature it has been used to describe, as Ostrom (1990, 3) reports, such diverse problems as the Sahelian famine of the 1970s, firewood crises throughout the Third World, the scourge of acid rain, the inability of the U.S. Congress to limit its predisposition to overspend, and the difficulties of international cooperation. Apparently we are facing two problems here: "market failure" and "government failure." Market failure suggests the difficulty of internalizing external effects that obtains because of high exclusion costs, while government failure suggests the high costs of preventing abuse of coercive state power by those who run the state.

### 3.4.2. Institutional Solutions of the CPR Problem: Design Principles

Private property is not the only social institution that can encourage efficient use of resources. If exclusion costs are comparatively high, common ownership solutions may be preferable. If the latter alternative is chosen, rules would, of course, have to be formulated about how many cows may graze on the village common. Further, there would have to be an institutional structure that could enforce the rules established. Conceivably, this approach may represent the best hope for finding a low-cost solution to the problem of ensuring efficient use of a common resource.[17] In general, then, the most efficacious institu-

---

17. Even if the definition and enforcement of private ownership rights in land were *costless,* it does not necessarily follow that privatization produces a clear gain in social output. A valid

tional solution for the CPR problem may be anything between perfect centralization (the case of the autocratic ruler who owns all resources) and perfect
realization of the principles of private property and freedom of contract. The
latter (the classic private ownership solution) would not be applicable, however, if we assume, as we do in this section, that the costs of specification and
internalization are too high to expect that externalities will be internalized
through private contracts between individuals. To overcome this "market failure" problem, collective action would be necessary.[18] The issues that have to
be dealt with are the same as before—answers must be found to the key
questions: (1) who has discretion over which resources (the specification problem) and (2) who ensures that the person in charge does not waste resources
(the monitoring problem)?

Clearly, if the specification issue remains unresolved, as in the open-
access CPRs, effective monitoring of the conditions and use of common pool
resources will be difficult and very costly. This is so because no single individual or smaller group of individuals is in a position to bear full responsibility for
the CPR in question. Thus, the economic problems of open-access CPRs can
hardly be expected to be solved efficiently. Indeed, it would seem that closed or
limited access to common pool resources, however organized, represents a
minimum requirement for even tolerably efficient management. Nevertheless,
the market failure problem of environmental economics does not necessarily
justify full state intervention. Many successful CPR institutions are mixtures of
"private-like" and "public-like" institutions (Ostrom 1990, 14). A central question, then, is: what are the design principles that produce successful arrangements of closed-access CPRs.

Apparently, self-organized and self-governed CPRs need an institutional
structure that takes care of appropriation, provision, monitoring, enforcement,
conflict resolution, and governance activities—as does the private ownership
economy. Details of different cases will, of course, show some variability and
depend on local conditions. In any event, Ostrom, in reporting on the insti-
tutional-economic analysis of a number of long-enduring, self-organized, and
self-governed CPRs, finds that private property and communal property can
exist side by side (1990, 58ff.):

> Generations of Swiss and Japanese villagers (for example) have learned
> the relative benefits and costs of private-property and communal-property

---

assessment of the net gains flowing from participation cannot be made unless all the basic welfare
issues involved in institutional restructuring are faced. See Furubotn (1987); Eggertsson (1990,
98–101); and Anderson and Hill (1983).

    18. Note that the system of a private-ownership economy with freedom of contract is itself a
public institution and as such the result of collective action (see Binger and Hoffman 1989).

institutions related to various types of land and uses of land. The villagers in both settings have chosen to retain the institution of communal property as the foundation for land use and similar important aspects of village economies. (61)

The example of high-mountain grazing meadows in the Alps (die Almwirtschaft) is well known to Europeans, and it appears that the private ownership solution would be impractical in the alpine setting. In reaching this conclusion, Ostrom relies strongly on studies by Netting (1981), who made an intensive investigation of the "Almwirtschaft" of the Swiss village of Toerbel. Ostrom notes:

Although yields are relatively low, the land in total has maintained its productivity for many centuries. Overgrazing has been prevented by tight controls. The CPR not only has been protected but also has been enhanced by investments in weeding and manuring the summer grazing areas and by the construction and maintenance of roads. (63)

Considerably more intractable problems arise in the case of open-access CPRs. The appropriation problem, in particular, is harder to solve here, but with increasing technical progress it can be, if not solved, at least tackled. Obviously, the open air cannot be assigned in fine detail to individuals, communities, or nations. Yet it is possible to restrict usage of the atmosphere so that individuals or firms cannot freely release certain chemicals into the air. In other words, access can at least be limited. One drastic way to proceed would be simply to forbid the use of particular chemicals. Alternately, it is possible to limit air pollution by demanding that appropriate technical precautions be taken by actual or potential polluters. A fundamental problem, of course, is whether the restriction of pollution leads to an "efficient" allocation of resources. It is, however, plausible that efficiency can be improved by the creation of freely tradable titles or property rights in air pollution. First, the maximum amount of allowable pollution per year would have to be determined by the state and then vouchers in this amount could be distributed (or auctioned) to potential users. The latter would, moreover, be granted the privilege of trading these rights as they deemed appropriate (Bonus 1991). The specification of such property rights would certainly entail some problems, and it could be a relatively costly process—as would be the monitoring of the observance of these rights. But quite similar problems would arise if air pollution were to be controlled by other means. The organization of a market in pollution certificates may cost no more than a purely administrative solution and, for the same outlay, may produce a more efficient allocation of resources. Another, though not market-oriented, method would be to levy fees based on the actual emissions of pollutants per year that an individual operator generates—for example, the owners of automobiles might be forced to account for their contributions to the general pollution problem. In this case, total emissions would not be limited directly, but the system would at least encourage vehicle owners to find low-cost ways of reducing their emission levels (White 1982).

Courts, in addition to administrative agencies and markets, provide another avenue that can be used for dealing with environmental risks. The United States, for one, relies heavily on courts to assign responsibility for environmental harms (Menell 1991, 93). Thus, court law in the United States remains a principal means for determining compensation for victims of environmental pollution. Further, as Menell notes, "the Federal Superfund legislation uses the court system to assign liability for the clean-up of dangerous hazardous waste sites" (93). The problem is again one of specification and monitoring. But unfortunately it is extremely costly, if not scientifically impossible, to link (legally) a particular injury or disease to a particular environmental cause. Menell therefore argues that the objective of efficient deterrence of environmental harms, and equitable compensation of victims, could be furthered by reducing the role of legal institutions and appropriately increasing the role of administrative and market institutions (111).

### 3.5. The Emergence of Property Rights

The literature dealing with the development of property rights is, in general, an optimistic one. The tendency is to view the

> design of institutions or governance structures as maximizing decisions to economize on transaction costs and to facilitate new economic activities. Market forces are argued to erode property rights institutions that are poorly suited for responding to new economic opportunities. If the existing rights structure limits or blocks reactions to changes in relative prices or technology, the existence of unexploited potential gains will lead individuals to mobilize for the adoption of more accommodating property rights. (Libecap 1989a, 6–7)

It is true, however, that since property rights define simultaneously the distribution of wealth and political power, changes in property-rights structures are likely to be influenced by more than pure efficiency considerations. Indeed, as Libecap argues, if a balanced analysis of the evolution of property rights is to be achieved, it is essential to take account of the political bargaining process that underlies the creation and modification of property rules and laws. The state, of course, plays an important part in the emergence of property rights. It is no exaggeration to say that "a theory of property rights cannot be truly complete without a theory of the state" (Furubotn and Pejovich 1972a, 1140). Unfortunately, though, despite progress in the area of property-rights theory, no generally accepted theory of the state exists (North 1990, 48).

Current research suggests that there is an important relation between rent-seeking behavior and the operations of the state. Historically, the king, as the locus of public authority, could give exclusive rights to natural resources or other assets to favored individuals or groups. The latter could then capture the established monopoly rents. What developed, therefore, was a system in which it became advantageous for people seeking government favors (e.g., aspiring monopolists) to make expenditures in order to lobby the king or other authorities and thus improve their chances of acquiring valuable rights. Such lobbying expenditures in the form of legal fees, bribes, and related expenses are, however, wasted resources from a social standpoint. In essence, rent seeking involves the expenditure of scarce resources to capture transfers (Buchanan, Tollison, and Tullock 1980). History, of course, provides a rich set of examples showing that the prerogatives of public authorities are not necessarily used in economically efficient ways.

Regardless of efficiency considerations, the emergence of property rights has to be seen as part of the evolution of polities. One often conceives of the development of governmental systems as moving from single absolute rulers to democratic arrangements, and it is assumed that this process implies movement toward greater "political efficiency" (North 1990, 51). In a sense, the creation of a constitutional state does bring about greater efficiency, but "it would be wrong to assert that the result is efficient political markets in the same sense as we mean efficient economic markets" (51). The number of parties operating in the political game is too small for that purpose. And, as North goes on to say,

> rational ignorance on the part of constituents is going to increase the role, in many situations, of incomplete subjective perceptions playing an important part in choices. . . . The point is that formal political rules, like formal economic rules, are designed to facilitate exchange but democracy in the polity is not to be equated with competitive markets in the economy. (51).

For further details, see chapter 9.

### 3.5.1. The Invisible-Hand Theory of the Emergence of Property Rights

The institution of property, like the institution of money, need not be a "creature of law" in the sense that its structure is imposed on society by exogenous civil authority. Rather, property-rights arrangements can be understood to have been determined, ultimately, by self-interest as "a form of spontaneous order" (Sugden 1989, 86). In other words, the origin of property in its various forms is, according to this view, not a governmental but a social phenomenon. The institution of property, though, has been perfected over time by a process in which the state attempts to clarify and regularize property law. Under state intervention, absolute rights become "perfected" conventions. There is, however, a problem with all this because it is by no means clear how society can ensure that the state will always behave as an impartial third party. As North, among others, has pointed out:

> Third party enforcement means the development of the state as a coercive force able to monitor property rights and enforce contracts effectively, . . . [but], if the state has coercive force, then those who run the state will use that force in their own interest at the expense of the rest of the society. (1990, 59).

Both respect for the law and the honesty and integrity of judges represent important factors that have contributed to the rise of the Western world. But the question remains as to how it is possible to create a system of formal rules and effective enforcement and encourage public behavior that is based on significant moral constraints. Writers from Hume to North have suggested that the appropriate conditions for success tend to develop only slowly over time. Nevertheless, progress toward effective social cooperation is feasible because, as people acquire experience in the world, more and more individuals come to recognize that they have common interests and that cooperative behavior leads to mutual gains. In effect, unwritten conventions and agreements make their appearance spontaneously in society.

> Two men, who pull the oars of a boat, do it by an agreement or convention, though' they have never given promises to each other. . . . In like manner are languages gradually establish'd by human conventions without any promise. In like manner do gold and silver become the common manner of exchange . . . (Hume [1739–40] 1969, 542).

Hume's general line of explanation is supported by contemporary theorizing and even has an echo in discussions of the extended prisoners' dilemma game.

To see the significance of all this, consider any convention that assigns de facto property rights in a valuable resource. Suppose the convention is well-established. Then each person has a well-grounded expectation—an expectation grounded in induction from experience—that other people will follow the convention. Given this expectation, each person finds it in his interest to follow the convention. And given that a person is following the convention himself, he not only expects the people with whom he interacts to demand no more than the convention allows them, he also wants them to behave in this way. In addition, anyone who is favored by the convention on at least some occasions is likely to regard any breach of the convention as an indirect threat to himself. (Sugden 1989, 95)

Sugden warns, though, that conventions do not necessarily favor rules that are Pareto efficient. Inefficiencies may be caused for various reasons—including the monopolization of private property by a few private decision makers or government bodies. In assessing the role private property plays in promoting economic efficiency, it is important to keep in mind that private property is a necessary but not sufficient condition for competition. Similarly, it should be clear that it is not necessary that everyone benefits from the existence of a convention or that the convention increases the overall welfare of society (Furubotn 1989a). Indeed, institutional reorganizations that bring about actual Pareto improvements must be understand as rare events. In any case, Sugden's argument is that, as far as conventions are concerned, all that matters is that breaches of the convention are harmful to all those people who follow it (Sugden, 1989, 96).

In this general context, it should be noted that sociologists emphasize the consensual character of rights (Coleman 1990, 53). It is asserted that rights are assigned on the basis of a power-weighted consensus. This position is certainly plausible, as is the further idea that no right can exist unless it is the consensus of the group that it exist (Frank 1992, 167). There also seems to be truth in the contention that "reputation" can serve as an enforcement mechanism for rights. For example, long-term benefits can be expected to flow to those individuals who are scrupulous in adhering to well-recognized principles of probity and honor in their economic transactions (Hume [1739–40] 1969, 552).

As the preceding discussion has established, a convention can be understood as a regularity in behavior. This simple interpretation, however, should not blind us to the recognition that conventions and institutions tend to become highly elaborated and complex. Lewis makes this point as follows:

At its simplest—say, among anarchists—the institution of property might be nothing more than a convention specifying who shall have the exclusive use of which goods. This seems to be Hume's theory of property. For us, the institution of property is more complicated; we have built it into an elaborate system of laws and institutions. (1969, 48)

108     Institutions and Economic Theory

It is, of course, the very complexity of contemporary property relations that makes property-rights/transaction-cost analysis so challenging.[19]

### 3.5.2. The Optimistic Theory of the Emergence of Property Rights

Another, more optimistic theory of the creation of property rights has been advanced by Demsetz (1967, 350ff.). The theory can be classified as "optimistic" because of its confidence that market forces push economic organization in the direction of efficiency. Specifically, it is believed that market forces in a capitalist system can be expected to eliminate inefficient property-rights structures and promote the introduction of new arrangements that are better suited to the exploitation of economic opportunities. All this is in contrast to Sugden (1989) who, as we have seen, argues that property rights have emerged over time by convention (or through the operation of the invisible hand) but that the structures that have evolved need not be efficient. Interestingly, both Sudgen and Demsetz fail to comment on the possible abuse of the enforcement power of the state.

From the standpoint of individual decision makers, the question of whether attempts should be made to change the existing institutional configuration reduces to one of assessing costs and benefits. That is, subjective calculations must be made concerning the potential costs and benefits of efforts to bring about change. Insofar as this behavior is followed, however, there would seem to be no necessary reason why the choices made should tend to enhance social efficiency. In any event, Demsetz emphasizes the positive. His thesis is that the emergence of new property rights takes place in response to the desires of people to adjust to the effects of new external economies or diseconomies. Expressed differently, the presumption here is that property rights develop to internalize externalities when the gains from internalization become larger than the cost of internalization. A broad range of examples is consistent with this theory—the development of rights to the atmosphere, renters' rights, rules for liabilities in automobile accidents, and so on. Demsetz himself presents a group of examples that deal with the development of property rights in land among American Indians. He refers to the fact that a close relationship existed, both historically and geographically, between the development of private rights in land and the growth of the commercial fur trade.

---

19. Cooperation becomes relevant in coordination problems for which no coordination equilibrium exists—like the well-known Prisoners' dilemma (Lewis 1969, 14ff.). It is closely allied to Olson's (1965) free-rider dilemma. The dismal aspects of these models result from the static nature of the analysis (one-shot games). In a dynamic setup (for repeated games), the dilemma may be overcome through cooperation (see North 1990, 13, for further literature). Guarantee instruments play a vital role. We shall deal with the problem of cooperation in chapter 4.

Before the fur trade became established, hunting was carried on primarily for purposes of food. . . . The externality was clearly present. Hunting could be practiced freely and was carried on without assessing its impact on other hunters. But these external effects were of such small significance that it did not pay for anyone to take them into account. (1967, 351)

As the fur trade became larger in magnitude, however, the external effects associated with free hunting increased considerably. Accordingly, the property rights system began to change in order to accommodate the new situation and, in particular, to take account of the external effects being generated by the fur trade. As a result, territorial hunting and trekking arrangements by individual families took on greater and greater importance.

This process of privatization was aided by the fact that forest animals tend to confine their territories to relatively small, well-defined areas. Thus, the cost of internalization, and the husbanding of animals, was perceived as relatively modest. The limited costs of bringing about these efficiency-enhancing changes, together with the higher commercial values associated with fur-bearing animals, provided strong incentives to establish private hunting lands.

The theory Demsetz advances has come under some criticism in the literature. Eggertsson, for example, has argued that Demsetz offers only a "naive theory of property rights." In defense of this view, he cites an article by McManus (1972), which indicates that the property-rights arrangements in Demsetz's example failed to protect the beaver population over time. The outcome in any instance would seem to turn on how effectively the internalization process is carried out. It is interesting to note that North and Thomas (1977) use the general theme of privatization to put forward a new explanation for the development of agriculture in human prehistory. These authors theorize that the first settled agricultural communities were based on exclusive communal property in land, with individual groups sharing each commons. Within each commons, taboos and custom constrained, at least in part, the incentive to overexploit the resource. Thus:

The first economic revolution was not a revolution because it shifted man's major economic activity from hunting and gathering to settled agriculture. It was a revolution because the transition created an incentive change for mankind of fundamental proportions. The incentive change stems from the different property rights under the two systems. When common property rights over resources exist, there is little incentive for the acquisition of superior technology and learning. In contrast, exclusive property rights which reward the owners provide a direct incentive to improve efficiency and productivity, or, in more fundamental terms, to acquire more knowledge and new techniques. It is this change in incentive that explains the rapid progress made by mankind in the last 10,000 years in contrast to the slow development during the long era as a primitive hunter/gatherer. (240–41)

Eggertsson has discussed a simple model by Barry Field that attempts to come to grips more fully with the various costs that have to be considered when there is movement toward privatization. The model in question identifies three types of cost functions—a neoclassical cost of production function, a cost of internal governance function, and a cost of exclusion function. Against this background, it is concluded that:

The dissipation of the rent from the shared resource can be reduced by collective action, but such measures are costly and give rise to internal governance costs, costs that are justified if the limits on overutilization increase net output. . . . Exclusion costs arise when property rights are defended against encroachment by outsiders. (1990, 257)

While it is important to distinguish among different types of costs, it must also be kept in mind that the respective cost functions are not normally independent of one another—for example, different governance arrangements may affect individual incentives and hence the neoclassical cost function. Finally, it can be reemphasized that the so-called optimistic view of the emergence of property rights disregards some important factors. Other forces that tend to affect the speed of development and actual content of property rights include monopolization of ownership, distributional conflicts, and the political process (see e.g., Oppenheimer 1922 and the rent-seeking literature).

### 3.5.3.  Contracting for Property Rights: The Role of Political Bargaining

Libecap's analysis of distributional issues in contracting for property rights represents an important way of looking at the formation of property relations, and his work on the topic can be taken as one interesting example from a large literature. The German Historical School was, of course, concerned with the interrelation of political and economic factors, and this perspective still has clear relevance for contemporary writers. In any event, Libecap considers in some detail four property-rights responses to common pool problems involving natural resources in the United States. The cases examined include nineteenth-century private mineral rights on federal land, late-nineteenth-century private rights to federal timber and agricultural land, twentieth-century fishery rights, and twentieth-century property rights to crude oil production. The contracting parties involved with these historic episodes are, characteristically, private claimants, politicians, judges, and bureaucrats. Their motivations spring from self-interest and an understanding of common pool problems (Gordon 1954; Cheung 1970). That is:

> Primary motivations for contracting for property rights are the aggregate losses of common pool conditions. A share of the expected gains from mitigating those losses encourages individuals to bargain, to establish or modify property rights to limit access and to control resource use. (Libecap 1989a, 9)

Conceptually, private claimants include current holders of property rights and those who seek rights. Politicians who are responsible for legislation regarding property rights have an obvious role to play and, among these, there are both incumbent officeholders and those who aspire to government positions. In competing for votes and the political support of influential interest groups, politicians seek to respond to the demands of private claimants. Moreover, in the general process of rights assignment, judicial rulings are critical in resolving disputes and molding property rights. Hence, efforts to influence the opinions of judges can be expected, and judicial viewpoints are likely to reflect prevailing ideas about economic and political conditions. Finally, it must be clear that bureaucrats exercise a key influence in the definition and allocation of property rights. They cannot be regarded as passive respondents to politicians because agencies have their own independent concerns. Like others in the system, bureaucrats can be conceived of as decision makers who maximize utility subject to institutional and other constraints that are in place. Thus, in bargaining, bureaucrats attempt to exchange favorable administrative rulings for political support.

Given these active participants in the bargaining process over rights, Libecap's states the thesis that:

> The intensity of political bargaining over distributional issues and the likelihood of successful property rights change will be influenced by i) The size of the aggregate expected gains from institutional change; ii, iii) the number and heterogeneity of the bargaining parties; iv) the skewness of the current and proposed share distribution; and v) information problems. (1989a, 11)

According to Libecap, the case in which mineral rights were assigned to private parties represented the most successful example of privatization. He notes that:

In response to potential common pool losses, miners quickly formed over 600 mining camp governments to devise local rules for the assignment and enforcement of private mineral rights. Allocations were made quickly with little conflict, and the mining camp rules subsequently were incorporated into State and Federal Law. (13)

Three basic reasons are given for this successful experience in establishing private mineral rights. First, it was widely believed at the time that ore deposits were extensive relative to the number of active claimants. This assessment encouraged the belief that economic gains were available to all, and that legal reorganization would be generally beneficial. Second, the ease of contracting was further promoted by the fact that the gold and silver discoveries were made on previously unclaimed land in uninhabited areas. Thus, there were no parties with vested interests whose claims would require reconciliation with those of the miners. Third, the bargaining that took place was made easier because the contracting parties in each mining camp were small in number and similar in respect to race, culture, skill, expectations, and so on. Given these auspicious conditions, Libecap concludes,

> mineral rights could be reached quickly because there were no critical information asymmetries among the contracting parties regarding the valuing and marking of individual claims. . . . Ore bodies were stationary and procedures were adopted in the mining camps for adjusting the size of allowed claims according to value expectations. Under these near laboratory conditions, distributional issues did not arise as an impediment to property rights agreements. Rights were established quickly and modified as needed to reduce uncertainty and to promote economic growth. As a result there was consensus among politicians for rapid changes in mineral rights law and the mining camp rules and State mineral right laws were routinely made part of revisions of federal land law. (16)

The situation was quite different in the case of federal land policy concerning agricultural land. Unlike mining, secure rights were never assigned to vast tracts of public land. What was evident was a reluctance to revise the law appropriately. Disputes over changes in federal land laws centered on their distributional implications and, in particular, on the size of individual shares of benefits and who should have them. Aggregate losses to the "common pool" caused by too rapid harvesting of timber and overgrazing of range land were recognized, but such losses were apparently not large enough in the late nineteenth century to force the bargaining parties to come to terms. The basis for necessary political bargains simply did not exist.

Libecap continued his empirical research on the evolution of property rights, together with Alston and Schneider, on the demand for and supply of land titles on the Brazilian frontier (cf. Alston, Libecap, and Schneider 1996). They demonstrate that governments can increase economic performance and wealth by providing clear, secure title. However, the study shows also that "the government response to the demand for property rights will be influenced by a variety of political factors, including competing constituent pressure, electoral demands, conflicting agency and government jurisdictions, and fluctuating budgets and staffing for titling agencies. All of these can have important consequences for the provision of rights institutions, and hence for the path and success of economic development programs" (58).

A more modern example of the difficulties that can arise in assigning property rights is found in the history of crude oil extraction in the United States. The common pool problem arises here because numbers of firms compete for subsurface migratory oil but under the rule of capture property rights are assigned to oil only upon extraction. At the same time, the standard solution seems elusive.

> Unitization agreements are extremely difficult to conclude because of conflicts over shares of unit revenues and costs. In negotiations two serious problems arise. First, unitization problems must assign once-and-for-all shares at the time the contract is completed. Contingent updates are not possible due to changes in reservoir dynamics after unitization. . . . Second, there is general uncertainty and asymmetrical information regarding relative lease values. Information issues therefore repeatedly stalled negotiations by compounding distributional conflicts over shares to the unit. (Libecap and Wiggins 1985, 695)

In summarizing the lessons his analysis points to, Libecap suggests that institutional change to promote rational resource use and economic growth cannot be taken for granted. Presumably, the distributional conflicts that are inherent in any property-rights arrangement can override efficiency considerations and act to block or critically constrain the institutional structure that can be adopted. And, because of such "bargaining" limitations, institutional change at any time is likely to produce only modest gains over the status quo. Insofar as this interpretation is correct, it follows that more attention must be directed to the distributional implications of property-rights arrangements. What has to be known in any given application of internalization theory is more information about the identities and preferences of the various bargaining parties. By understanding more about the motivations and strengths of the players in the privatization game, there is greater chance for predicting the side-payment scheme or schemes that might be effective in promoting agreement.[20]

A basic theme in Libecap's analysis (and in the common pool literature) is that the failure to internalize condemns a system to inefficient allocation and lesser social welfare. Libecap himself has emphasized that:

> If influential parties cannot be sufficiently compensated through share adjustment in the political process to win their support, otherwise beneficial institutional change may not occur with potential economic advance foregone. Even though society is made worse off, the distributional implications lead influential parties to oppose institutional change. (1989a, 8)

While this explanation seems plausible at first glance, there is no clear indication of what constitutes an improvement in social welfare. Mention is made of compensation to individuals who are affected by institutional change, but Libecap makes clear that in practice side payments to all those harmed by reorganization cannot be anticipated. Thus, for the historical cases examined, strict adherence to the Pareto criterion is simply not contemplated. The desire to avoid a Pareto test for social gain may be understandable, but difficulty arises because no alternative measure of "economic progress" or "rational allocation" is introduced. The point is, of course, that one cannot speak confidently of improvement through institutional change unless the standard used to determine improvement is specified.

In the end, it appears that distributional effects are significant at various levels. If the reorganization of property rights is major and exerts a substantial effect on economic activity in the system, serious welfare questions emerge. What has to be considered is the relation between income distribution and the relative valuation of commodities. Ultimately, how "large" an aggregation, or mix, of commodities is depends on the particular distribution that is used as the basis for its valuation.

### 3.6.  The Economic Analysis of Property Rights: Some Notes on the Literature

The relation between private property and "efficient incentives" is hardly a new idea. Aristotle counseled: "Property should be as a general rule private; for

---

20. Whether CPR problems can be solved or not depends on the institutional environment. For example, Rosenthal (1990) shows that in France the Old Regime failed to develop irrigation facilities because of fragmented political authority over the rights of eminent domain: "Since many groups could hold projects up, transaction costs increased dramatically. Reforms enacted during the French Revolution reduced the costs of securing rights of eminent domain" (615).

when everyone has a distinct interest, men . . . will make more progress, because everyone will be attending to his own business" (McKean 1941, 1151).

But ownership has also a strong distributional and thus moral component, and private ownership needs justification. It is systematically offered on an efficiency basis by natural law philosophers like Hume ([1739–40] 1969) with his utilitarian justification of private property—considering its incentive aspects. But Hume also offers a psychological line of argument in defense of private ownership. Specifically, he points out the psychological commitments that go with property. Schlicht (1997, sec. 11.2) elaborates both lines of Hume's argument. He criticizes the "economistic" view of the property-rights approach for "reducing the effect of private property to incentive aspects while neglecting 'ownership effects' and all kinds of psychological commitments that do go with property" (sec. 12.9).

Among the classicists, Mill ([1848] 1902) deals extensively with the economic issues of the institution of private property in book 2 ("Distribution") of his *Principles*. Mill, though, appears to have been rather skeptical regarding common views about the superiority of the incentives of individual as compared with collective ownership. Comparing private property with communism, Mill (127) concludes, for example: "To what extent . . . the energy of labor would be diminished by communism, or whether in the long run it would be diminished at all, must be considered for the present an undecided question." Even with regard to the aspect of human liberty, Mill remained very cautious in his judgment: "It remains to be discovered how far the preservation of this characteristic [human liberty] would be found incompatible with the communist organization of society" (129).

In the nineteenth century, German writers discussed efficiency aspects of property rights in their criticism of socialism. As early as 1854, Gossen criticized communism by arguing "that only through private property is the measurement found for determining the quantity of each commodity which would be best to produce under given conditions. Therefore, the central authority, proposed by the communists, for the distribution of the various tasks and their reward, would soon find that it had taken on a job the solution of which surpasses the abilities of individual men" (1889, 231, quoted in Mises [1932] 1981). Similar economic arguments against common ownership are brought to bear by German liberal-social-reformist writers such as Schäffle ([1874] 1885), Brentano (1878), and Nasse (1879), as reported by Hutchison (1953, 294–98). They anticipated the efficiency arguments for private property that in the early twentieth century were vigorously supported by Mises ([1920] 1935) and Hayek (1935, 1945) and opposed by Lange (1938) and other representatives of market socialism. The debate has extended into our day (cf. Richter 1992a).

In the older literature we find more taxonomic and social-philosophical aspects of property rights than efficiency considerations as, for example, in Wagner (1894, bk. 2) and Schmoller (1900) in his chapter on "The Nature of Property and the Principles of Its Distribution." An extensive, still readable, classification of immaterial property rights, including nonlegal rights (Verhältnisse) is provided by Böhm-Bawerk (1881). Fisher (1912) derives in a chapter on "Property" a general definition of property rights, which is similar to that applied in our book. He provides a rich interpretation of it, showing that property and wealth are each the opposite aspect of the other (22). In German literature around and after World War II, neoliberals and members of the Freiburg School such as Eucken ([1952] 1975, 270ff.) stressed the role of private ownership in productive means as an indispensable precondition of competitive markets and individual freedom.

The examples from early literature show that, even though efficiency arguments can be found in some of the debates on the distribution of property among men—material or immaterial—there are good reasons to say that these were at most loose common-sense arguments. There existed no systematic research on the economics of property rights. No wonder that the subject indexes of such comprehensive works on the history of economic thought as Schumpeter 1955 and Blaug 1985 do not contain listings for "property," "property rights," or "ownership."

Property-rights analysis as a systematic treatment of the economic incentives of ownership in scarce resources began only in the 1960s. It was initiated by Coase (1959, 1960), Alchian (1958, 1965b), Alchian and Kessel (1962), Demsetz (1964, 1966, 1967), and others, who pointed out that alternative institutional arrangements typically confront individual decision makers with different rights to the use of resources. Furubotn and Pejovich (1972a) gave a review of the early theoretical literature and DeAlessi (1980) of the early empirical work in this field. We shall comment briefly on some of this literature.

Coase, with his article of 1960, was one of the main initiators of property-rights analysis. We reported in this chapter on its central hypothesis. It is also a programmatic article, stressing toward its end the need for a change of approach. Three changes are demanded by Coase:

1. The use of an opportunity cost approach "when dealing with questions of economic policy and to compare the total product yielded by alternative social arrangements" (42).
2. Instead of discussing policy issues for an ideal world (with zero transaction costs) one should begin "analysis with a situation approximating that which actually exists, . . . examine the effects of a proposed policy change, and . . . attempt to decide whether the new situation would be, in total, better or worse than the original one" (42).

3. Instead of viewing factors of production as purely physical entities, a faulty concept that leads to the failure to develop an adequate theory of how to handle external effects, they should be thought of as items that possess rights to perform certain (physical) actions, that is, as property rights. From this, the central proposition of the early property-rights school emanates, namely, that a clear definition of property rights is in principle sufficient to ensure efficiency. Yet that is only the case if transaction costs are zero (Coase 1988b, 14ff.) or, in the language of game theory, when everyone's tastes and opportunities are common knowledge.[21] Recent studies have added still other assumptions concerning coalitional stability (Aivazian et al. 1987) and the need to abstract from interdependent preferences (Furubotn 1995).

Alchian's (1965b) article is one of the first general presentations of the economics of property rights. He defines a system of property rights as "a method of assigning to particular individuals the 'Authority' to select, for specific goods, any use from a nonprohibited class of uses" (1977a, 130). He stresses that private property rights protect private property from physical changes, not from changes in exchange value. Alchian compares the efficiency problems of private versus public ownership, stating that "under public ownership the costs of any decision or choice are less fully thrust upon the selector than under private ownership" (1977a, 146). He suggests that public and private ownership are, in some cases, used because of their different behavioral implications.

Another early representative of the property rights approach is Demsetz. In Demsetz 1964, he discusses the article of Coase (1960), pointing out the role of the assumption of zero transaction costs for what later was called the Coase theorem. Practical internalization of externalities is illustrated by a description of the emergence of hunting rights among Canadian aborigines (Demsetz 1967).

Furubotn and Pejovich (1972a) state in their review article that the property-rights approach can be understood as an attempt to formulate meaningful optimization problems.

This is so because regardless of the number, character, or diversity of the goals established by an individual decision maker, the goals can always be

---

21. Or as Arrow says: "on the . . . assumption that every player knows every other player's payoff (utility, profit, whatever) function or the strategies played" (Arrow 1979, 24). Arrow (1979) also showed that the Coase theorem may possibly hold even under conditions of incomplete information. In general, however, efficiency cannot be achieved. On this literature and for further arguments, see Schweizer 1988.

conceived as arguments in some type of utility function that can be maximized subject to appropriate constraints (1138).

They stress that most of the restrictions discussed in this context are those imposed by the state. "It follows, . . . that a theory of property rights cannot be truly complete without a theory of the state" (1140). The authors, therefore, direct readers to the work of Buchanan and Tullock (1962), Niskanen (1968), and others.

While the earlier property-rights literature, like Hardin (1968), Smith (1969), and Clark (1977), stressed private property rights in resources as the way out of the tragedy of the commons, later advocates of the property rights analysis like Ostrom (1990) realize "that many solutions exist to cope with many different problems . . . [and] that 'getting the institutions right' is a difficult, time-consuming conflict-invoking process" (14). Such institutions are rarely either private or public, Ostrom writes. Many successful common property institutions are mixtures of both. To illustrate this, Ostrom offers a variety of field studies addressing such subjects as communal tenure in meadows and forests, irrigation communities and other water rights, and fisheries. Common ownership is here "characterized by institutional arrangements which act as surrogates for at least some of the constraints that would have been enforced in the market under private ownership arrangements" (DeAlessi 1980, 7). Common ownership in capital, the worker-managed firm, has been studied, among others, by Furubotn (1974a, 1980). He examined how the availability of long-term bank credit affected the capital investment decisions of a Yugoslav firm.

DeAlessi (1980) provides an extensive overview of the evidence of the economics of property rights. He reports, inter alia, about literature *on job property rights* like the job access rights in longshoring (Martin 1972) or the job termination rights (Martin 1977) on privately owned and manager-controlled firms, franchise arrangements, mutuals, and other nonproprietary firms. Furthermore, government regulation and government ownership are thoroughly studied areas. The general findings in this field are that regulation by state commission yields higher prices and lower output, fixed capital is higher, and R&D activities are lesser. As for government ownership, the evidence is that relative to regulated private firms, for example, "municipal electric utilities in the United States generally charge lower prices; have higher operating costs; have greater capacity; . . . favor voters to nonvoters; . . . maintain managers in office longer . . . " (DeAlessi 1980, 41). DeAlessi concludes that the evidence "presents a strong case for the hypothesis that property rights matter. The effects of alternative systems of property rights on behavior, and welfare, are substantial and pervasive" (40). Many other examples could be cited.

An interesting and important field not covered in this book is the economics of intellectual property. Dissenting views exist about government support for innovative and creative activity. The central problem considered by Arrow (1962), for example, is the "conflict between the social goals of achieving efficient use of information once produced versus providing ideal motivation for production of information" (Hirshleifer and Riley 1979, 1404). Property rights in "caught" ideas may lead to the same result as property rights in caught fish with free entry in fishing (or inventing): excessive resources may be devoted to inventing (or fishing). As Hirshleifer and Riley point out in their survey of uncertainty and information, the arguments pro and con patent protection are more complex than had previously been realized (1406). Also at issue are copyrights, trade secrets, and the like. In their introductory article to a symposium on intellectual property, Besen and Raskind (1991) rightfully stress that the interest in the economics of intellectual property is timely: "The pace of technological change during the last few decades has forced intellectual property law into unknown areas and hard cases. . . . How should innovations related to semiconductor chip or computer software be protected? Should genetically engineered life forms be patented? Under what conditions should videotaping a television show for home use infringe the rights of program producers?" (25).

## 3.7. Suggested Readings for Chapter 3

Property rights have always been, and still are, a major political-philosophical issue. In view of the importance of natural law philosophy in this context, start with Hume [1739–40] 1969 (bk. 3, pt. 2, "Of Justice and Injustice"). To get an idea of definitional issues read Fisher (1912, his chapter on "Property") and continue, if you read German, with Böhm-Bawerk's (1881) clear exposition of "Rechte und Verhältnisse." The nineteenth-century criticism of socialism, mainly to be found in the German literature, is briefly reviewed by Hutchison (1953, 294–98). It is part of the ongoing debate over common versus private ownership.

As for the economics of property rights proper, start with Demsetz (1964) as an introduction to Coase (1960), which, of course, must be read, too. Proceed to Alchian (1965b) and Demsetz (1967). Continue with the review article on property rights by Furubotn and Pejovich (1972a). About the literature on the Coase theorem prior to 1972, see Whitcomb (1972). On the Coase theorem and the theory of the state, read, for example, Buchanan (1973). As for the evidence that institutions matter, read the review article of DeAlessi (1980) and some of the literature quoted there. On common ownership, read Ostrom (1990). On the law of property as dealt with in common law and civil law read, for example, the comparative legal study by Merryman (1974) on ownership in land. For an explanatory text on the common law of property, see Lawson and Rudden (1982). "Property" in the sense of civil law, is dealt with in German Sachenrecht (literally "the law of 'things'" in the sense of physical objects— the third book of the German Civil Code [Bürgerliches Gesetzbüch, BGB]); see the English review by Horn, Kötz, and Leser (1982, chap. 10).

CHAPTER 4

# Relative Property Rights:
# Contractual Obligations


People in a modern society operate within a network of legally binding and legally nonbinding obligations into which they enter either voluntarily or through compulsion. *Contractual obligations* are legally binding. There are voluntarily assumed obligations like the obligation of the seller of a commodity to deliver the appropriate merchandise to the purchaser at the agreed upon time and location and the obligation of the buyer to pay the purchase price in timely fashion. Legally nonbinding, freely assumed obligations result, for example, from agreements as to social engagements, the promise to visit one's friend, or the legally nonenforceable ("moral") obligation of a gambler to pay his gambling debts. Involuntarily incurred obligations (*noncontractual* obligations) are legal liabilities that arise because of tortuous acts. In all such cases, we are dealing with property rights, though, in contrast to the previous chapter, with *relative* property rights.

In this chapter, attention will be focused primarily on issues relating to the transfer of property rights by voluntarily assumed obligations. More concretely, what will be investigated are contracts that are freely concluded by individuals and are relatively well protected by law. Freely concluded, legally nonbinding obligations will also be considered. Noncontractual obligations resulting from broken promises, accidental or intentional harm to people and property, and so on will only be mentioned and not studied in detail.

Relative property rights, as described in chapter 3 (sec. 2.2), consist of a claim of a certain individual, the obligee, against one or more other individuals, the obligor(s), and can only be exercised against them. Thus, in the first place, relative property rights can be violated or "stolen" by the person(s) against whom claims are directed, for example, the obligors. Neoinstitutionalist writers use the term *opportunistic behavior,* instead of *stealing,* to describe such violations of obligations by the obligor.

Contractual obligations can be deduced from the second and third "funda-

We wish to thank Robert W. Gordon and Kenneth E. Scott for their advice on Anglo-American contract law.

mental laws of nature" enunciated by David Hume.[1] These laws relate to the transference of possession by consent and the fulfillment of promises—or, differently expressed, to freedom of contract and the obligation of promises. In a world of costless transactions, the observance of the two principles can, of course, be achieved without expenditure of resources. Problems arise, however, if consideration is given to the existence of positive transaction costs and limited rationality. Under the latter conditions, organization matters, and interest must center on such things as the organization of markets, firms, and legal arrangements. In this context, two distinct types of activities should be recognized—the setting up of organizations (which involves acts of collective choice) and the use of organizations by individuals (which represents matters of individual choice). In the first instance, transaction costs are fixed (sunk); in the second, they are variable (for a definition of fixed and variable transaction costs, see sec. 2.2). The economic analysis of institutions suggests that there should be a tendency for decision makers to adopt the most efficacious institutional arrangement to deal with any problem. Thus, we might expect the "best" institutional framework to be chosen on the constitutional or legal level and, within this given framework, to observe the operation of the "least-wasteful" type of voluntary contracts. The existence of transaction costs, however, makes the monitoring and enforcement of all legal and contractual obligations an ever present problem.

At the individual choice level, individuals direct their attention to the execution stage of contracts with the objective of suppressing, as much as possible, ex post opportunistic behavior on the part of their contractual partners. In this way, court ordering is complemented by "private ordering" in the form of contractual safeguards against opportunism. Williamson (1985, 29) speaks in this context of "ex post support institutions of contract." This conception of contractual arrangements represents a central theme in Williamson's transaction-cost approach.

At the collective choice level, where individuals decide about institutional frameworks, particular concern tends to exist with the development of institutional structures that will enable certain types of business transactions to avoid market failure problems. Clearly, such institutional adaptation is important to practical economic outcomes. Nevertheless, this and the next chapter will deal with behavior at the individual choice level while assuming that the fundamental institutional framework is given. Problems relating to collective choice of institutions will be introduced in chapter 9.

---

1. The three fundamental laws of nature are, according to Hume ([1739–40] 1969, 578), "that of the stability of possession, of its transference by consent, and of the performance of promises." Hume continues that it is "on the strict observance of those three laws, that the peace and security of human society entirely depend . . ." (578).

## 4.1.  Basic Principles of Contractual Obligations

Contractual obligations can be prepared, concluded, and exercised within various institutional frameworks. In neoclassical economics, the crucial institutions are taken to be the market and the firm. More precisely, the focus is on the ideal types of the "perfect market" and the idealized, profit-maximizing, neoclassical firm. Under perfect markets, contractual obligations are completely controlled by competition in a world of full information. Similarly, in the neoclassical firm, contractual obligations are flawlessly directed by an efficient hierarchy (Hess 1983, chap. 1), which can acquire and process information instantly and costlessly. In other words, in the zero-transaction-cost world, it does not matter which "governance structure" (Williamson 1985) we choose—market or hierarchy. Supposedly, the efficiency results will be the same whether the economy is organized as a wholly free-market economy without any hierarchically organized firms or as a centrally planned economy in which the bureaucratic hierarchy performs all of the necessary functions. Moreover, any mixed system falling between these two extremes will also generate an efficient solution.

Even at the theoretical level, there is reason to question the correctness of this interpretation of a "frictionless" system (Furubotn 1991), but we also know, as a practical matter, that frictionless economies do not exist in the real world. Indeed, experience tells us that governance structure, or institutional arrangements, play a crucial role in determining the behavior and efficiency of an economic unit (Williamson 1979, 235). There is reason, therefore, to consider carefully the conditions under which the difficulties imposed by positive transaction costs can be offset, at least in part, by appropriate organization. A prime question here concerns the contribution that a laissez faire system can make to economic efficiency.

Two principles of contractual obligation, together with the principle of private ownership, form the core of the constituent principles of a free market economy: (1) liberty of contract and (2) liability from contract.[2]

### 4.1.1.  Freedom of Contract

The principle of freedom of contract is central to the efficacious use of resources. Such freedom enables the private owner of a property right (which in general is a bundle of rights) to transfer his right, and the asset to which the right refers, to the locus where it is valued most highly. Since property rights

---

2. Eucken (1952, 254) speaks of the "constituent principles of the policy of a competition order," to which he adds four more principles: Ordnungspolitik instead of direct intervention by the state, sound money, open markets, and stability of economic policy (see Schmidtchen 1984, 59).

can be partitioned in various ways, transfer arrangements can be quite flexible. For example, an individual can transfer his rights either completely (as in the sale of a house) or make only a limited transfer (as when a house is leased for a finite period of time). Note further that the transfer of private ownership rights concerns both absolute and relative property rights—for example, property rights to land as well as legal obligations arising from an employment contract. In summary, liberty of contract comprises the freedom to: (1) conclude a contract or not, (2) choose one's partner or partners to a contract, (3) determine the contract's content (i.e., the contractual parties are not forced to choose from among a closed number of legal contract types but may invent new types), and (4) choose the form of the contract.

The general idea animating the principle of freedom of contract is that each individual is free to regulate the circumstances of his life himself. Since contracts can be legally enforced, individuals create law on the microlevel by concluding particular contracts within the framework of the existing contract law of the system. Freedom of contract, and the resulting private autonomy, may, therefore, be regarded as the legal counterpart of the principle of de-centralization of economic decision making. Eucken ([1952] 1975, 275) has argued that this principle is "apparently a precondition for the realization of competition." But he hastens to add that "the freedom of contract served also to abolish competition with the aim of creating a monopolistic position . . . " (275). Thus, the freedom of contract principle, if left entirely to itself, can create conditions under which the principle can no longer be sustained. For this reason, Eucken demands that freedom of contract be protected by the state through its creation of a suitable competitive order. It seems true, however, that in a world characterized by decreasing information and transport costs, Eucken's monopoly problem may become less dangerous than he originally feared. In principle, at least, free trade and other forces conducing to open markets may be of substantial help in maintaining workable competition.

There are other elementary preconditions and limits needed to ensure that freedom of contract will function properly. In particular, the principle requires the freedom of will of the contractual parties and the protection of third-party interests (Larenz 1982, 41ff.). Analogously to the full right of ownership, individuals may, in the contractual case, use their freedom to conclude con-tracts with each other as they wish, *provided* their agreements do not conflict with the law (and with boni mores) or with the rights of third parties.

The principle of freedom of contract is restricted by law for various reasons, and not all of the reasons advanced are good ones from the standpoint of the best interests of society as a whole. For example, the restrictions arising from the demands of European and American agricultural policy cannot be said to contribute to the growth of wealth. Contractual liberty is also restricted increasingly in the area of employment. In Germany and elsewhere, conditions are such that the parties are only free to determine the content of an employment contract within the limits of an increasingly elaborate body of labor law and the norms of collective agreements.

### 4.1.2. Liability from Contract

Freedom of contract does not preclude state activity. As noted, the principle of contractual liberty works well only if the freely reached obligations (to perform promises, deliver goods, etc.) can, as a last resort, be enforced by the state when the occasion demands. In fact, a free market economy is characterized by the strict observance of this kind of state intervention. The role of "liquidity" (the ability to fulfill one's payment obligations) becomes clear in this general context. It can be seen that the obligation of individuals or firms to remain liquid by their own efforts may be made less crucial if the state is willing to intervene in business affairs (Stützel 1959, 625). That is, the state may undertake, through official or unofficial pledges, to come to the aid of private entities in need of liquidity. But use of this "soft-budgeting" approach amounts to a basic deviation of the economic system from the requirements of a pure market system. This is so because with potential intervention the allocation of resources is not determined exclusively by market forces. Rather, public agencies supplement, or even replace, private markets as directors of the allocative process.

The obligation to keep one's promises (the "sanctity of promise") concerns, of course, all kinds of contractual obligations. Still, the financial side of longer-term contractual arrangements is of particular interest to the economist. It is here, where financial capital enters the organization of the economy, that the need for an "advocate of capital" becomes relevant (Hinds 1990). Control of the financial means by banks or other financial intermediaries having direct stakes in the outcome of the allocative process appears to be unavoidable. The problem can be seen with particular clarity in the case of current attempts by Central and Eastern European countries to transform their economies. Thus, Hinds writes:

> In the absence of central planning, the financial system becomes the center piece of the allocation of resources. However, the financial system is essentially a capitalist mechanism. To allocate resources efficiently at the margin, it relies on modifying incentives to owners of capital, i.e., raising or lowering the marginal productivity of real capital accruing to them through modifying the cost of its financing. (20)

The lack of an "advocate of capital" became evident in socialist countries that tried the most progressive market-oriented reform programs: Hungary, Poland,

and Yugoslavia. These countries soon suffered from the greatest economic instabilities. Poland and Yugoslavia had hyperinflation and, together with Hungary, experienced the worst foreign debt crises. Without question, the reform effort failed there thoroughly. These "market reforms" put an end to central planning but did not introduce real markets with competition and free pricing. Significantly, private firms played only a minor role in these economies. The nationalized firms kept their monopoly positions and were protected from foreign competition through import restrictions and foreign exchange controls. They were aware that the government would keep them alive at any cost through subsidies, cheap loans, and tax exemptions. Their managements behaved accordingly. With increasing decentralization, workers and managers found new ways to use their firms (and the assets of their firms) for their own purposes. Workers, for example, demanded ever higher wages, and these demands were routinely granted by management. Both parties knew that the government would act to sustain the existing industrial structure and therefore would finance higher wage costs. Similarly, any problems with foreign debts could be expected to be dealt with in comparable fashion, with the government shouldering ultimate responsibility. In the worst case, the government was prepared to take over the foreign debts of firms completely and relieve management of the penalties normally resulting from bad decision making. The behavior observed in Central and Eastern Europe suggests that halfway measures of market reform do not work in economies still dominated by socialist institutions. This conclusion is, of course, fully consistent with the understandings provided by modern property-rights analysis.

Before we continue, a few general remarks may be appropriate concerning some of the similarities and differences of Anglo-American common law and Continental civil law regarding contractual obligations. In both legal traditions, contract law deals with rules that permit resource owners to enter into a planned relationships for the use of their separate resources (see Mehren and Gordley 1977, 784: "Obligations arising from these relationships are ordinarily said to arise ex contractu"). A contract seeks to secure "cooperation to achieve social purposes by the use of promises given in exchanges arrived at through bargain . . . " (Farnsworth 1990, 576, 578, quoted in Mehren and Gordley 1977, 785). These are, to be precise, bilateral contracts.

As for the formation of a contract, the legal concepts of promise and agreement play vital roles in common law while in German civil law the concept of declaration of will (Willenserklärung) is central. According to this concept, a contract consists normally of two declarations of will, an offer and an acceptance. Unlike the case in England, the offeror is bound in Germany by his offer for a reasonable period of time (German Civil Code, Art. 145). But these are merely technical details of the two legal systems and are not of concern to us in this book.

In the United States, common law, embodied in court decisions, is (still) the primary source of general contract principles. Quantitatively, however, the general common law of contract has become residual—the law that regulates only what has not yet become subject of more specialized statutory and administrative regulation (e.g., employment, insurance, consumer contracts, lending transactions, sale and lease of goods, and professional services).[3] Of particular relevance in recent legislation is Article 2 of the Uniform Commercial Code," which governs the sale of goods (Calamari and Perillo 1987, 13). In German private law, contractual issues are distributed through all five books of the German Civil Code. As for contractual and noncontractual obligations, the German legal literature distinguishes between the General Law of Obligations (Schuldrecht I, Allgemeiner Teil) and the Special Law of Obligations (Schuldrecht II, Besonderer Teil). The latter deals with the type of contracts that are regulated specifically in the German Civil Code such as sale, loan, and employment (but also lease), as was mentioned in chapter 3.

Both legal systems have to regulate the same basic transactions and thus must deal with the same set of problems. From the economist's viewpoint, they do this (de facto) in a quite similar fashion, and since codified law is more systematic and easier to report on than the court decisions of common law we are following in the next section the classification of contracts in the German Civil Code extended by and compared with some American legal provisions.

## 4.2. Diverse Types of Contractual Obligations

Economists have an interest in bilateral, or *synallagmatique,* contracts. These are agreements in which the parties to the contract pledge to exchange performances that both sides view as adequate or commensurate. The basic principle underlying the bilateral agreement is the age-old concept of "do, ut des," in which each gives something to the other and receives something in return. In other words, economists are interested in contracts that arrange the allocation of resources by direct bilateral exchange through bargaining between individuals. These are, by the way, also the types of contracts with which the law of contract is primarily concerned.

Exchange may occur instantly ("Zug um Zug"—a present exchange—say, when a newspaper is exchanged for money) or may take place so that a period of time elapses between the formation of contract and the actual fulfillment of promises. Furthermore, the parties to an exchange may fulfill their

---

3. It should also be mentioned that in the modern commercial world most contractual obligations are specified on *standard forms* that the parties adopt to govern their relationships. Thus, in the United States, for instance, almost all construction contracts are governed by a single set of standard form documents drafted by the American Institute of Architects.

commitments at different points in time. In this latter case, which is of particular interest to institutional economists, the "order of performance" is specified explicitly or implicitly in the contract. For example, the restaurant owner delivers on his promise and serves a meal before the customer completes the transaction and pays for the meal. Similarly, an employee performs work in advance of securing his salary from the employer (Wiggins 1991, 640ff.).

Institutional economics is to a large degree concerned with deferred exchanges or exchanges that provide for a definite order of performance and thus involve the passage of time for their completion. This is the case with contracts in the common law sense, wherein the law of contracts is confined to the concept of "promise," that is, a commitment by a person as to future behavior (Farnsworth 1990, 5). But note that the Uniform Commercial Code, Article 2A–106(1), defines a "contract for sale" as "both a present sale of goods and a contract to sell goods at a future time." The reason for this is that even in a simultaneous exchange (e.g., of goods for cash) some future promises (like a warranty, a promise that the goods will live up to some standard of quality) may also be transferred.

Of course, transaction costs play a major role in any exchange process. Among the most important economic problems that arise because of transaction costs, and because of the passage of time between the formation of a contract and its performance, are those associated with: (1) asymmetric information and (2) transaction-specific investments. In the latter case, there is a need for investments to begin delivering services before they receive their full reward, and this circumstance makes possible the appearance of opportunistic behavior. The difficulties encountered in these areas represent central issues of the new institutional economics. The problems rooted in (1) and (2) can arise both before and after the conclusion of a contract, causing ex ante and ex post transaction costs, respectively. What is involved, essentially, is the allocation of the risk of contingencies.

Asset specificity is of particular concern for ex post transaction costs. Williamson (1985, 95ff.) distinguishes among four types of specific investments and this interpretation has been accepted by economists generally.

1. *Site specificity:* "[B]uyer and seller are in a cheek by jowl relation with one another, reflecting ex ante decisions to minimize inventory and transportation expense" (Joskow 1985a, 38). An example of this situation is found in the close relationship of a coal mine and a coal-burning electricity-generating plant.
2. *Physical asset specificity:* "[O]ne or both parties to the transaction make investments in equipment and machinery that involve design characteristics specific to the transaction and which have lower values in alternative uses" (38).

3. *Human capital specificity:* This arises "as a consequence of learning-by-doing, investment, transfer of skills specific to a particular relationship" (38).
4. *Dedicated assets:* These comprise "general investments that would not take place but for the prospect of selling a significant amount of product to a particular customer. If the contract is terminated prematurely, it would leave the supplier with significant excess capacity" (38).

The next step is to illustrate the problems of pre- and postcontractual opportunism for four different types of *synallagmatique* agreements: sales contract, lease contract, employment contract, and loan contract.

### 4.2.1.  Sales Contract

A sales contract provides for the permanent transfer of property rights in an asset from one party to another by agreement. Under the Uniform Commercial Code ([ULA] Pr. 2–106[1]), a "sale" consists in the passing of title to goods from the seller to the buyer for a price. According to Art. 433 of the German Civil Code, a sales contract requires the seller of a good to deliver the good and transfer ownership in it, while the buyer must pay the price and take delivery of the good (Horn, Kötz, and Leser 1982, 118).

Note that in German law the sales contract and the (abstract) legal act of the transfer of ownership are separated from each other (Trennungsprinzip), while under common law and French law the transfer of ownership is part of the sales contract (Einheitsprinzip) (Larenz 1982, 2:16; Horn, Kötz, and Leser, 1982, 119). According to common law, it is therefore possible to describe the general equilibrium model as a clearing system of titles of ownership and to write, as Hicks did: "Actual trading need involve nothing more than exchange of titles" (1967, 7).

It is not difficult to see that the sales contract, certainly in the common law sense, in which time is involved in an essential way, leaves ample room for problems to arise. Both precontractual and postcontractual opportunism are possible due to asymmetrical information in particular in combination with transaction-specific investments. Williamson's well-known definition of *opportunism* is worth repeating at this point. It is

self-interest seeking with guile. This includes but is scarcely limited to more blatant forms, such as lying, stealing and cheating. Opportunism more often involves subtle forms of deceit . . . more generally, opportunism refers to the incomplete or distorted disclosure of information, especially to calculated effort to mislead, distort, disguise, obfuscate, or otherwise confuse. It is responsible for real or contrived conditions of information asymmetry. (1985, 47)

1. *Precontractual opportunism* related to sales contracts is largely the result of asymmetric information. That is, the seller usually knows more about his merchandise than the buyer does, and as a result "bad" merchandise may drive out "good" merchandise. Akerlof (1970) explained the basis of this phenomenon in his famous "lemon" model (which is discussed briefly in the next chapter). For the present, it is sufficient to note that "bad" (or lower quality) used cars will tend to displace "good" ones in the secondhand market. They sell at the same price as good cars do because, given asymmetric information, "it is impossible for the buyer to tell the difference between a good and bad car; only the seller knows (490). Sellers of high-quality used cars have reason, then, to withdraw their vehicles from the market, and the used car market tends to break down. Under these assumptions, "trust" becomes important. "Informal unwritten guarantees are pre-conditions for trade and production. Where these guarantees are indefinite, business will suffer . . . " (490). Sellers will undertake efforts to inform potential buyers about their products and therefore change the initial asymmetric information structure of the market.

Inter alia, what has to be investigated in a world of positive transaction costs is the effectiveness of signaling or screening devices.

All signaling devices involve self-selection. . . . For a signal to be effective, it must be unprofitable for sellers of low quality products to imitate it. . . . Product guarantees can tell consumers about products because the expected cost of a guarantee is negatively correlated with the durability of the product. (Spence 1976, 592)

Looking at the problem from a somewhat different standpoint, measurement (or sorting) costs play a role.

When a buyer receives subpar units, he can never tell with certainty whether he was unlucky or whether he was cheated. Repeat purchase . . . reduces the severity of the problem but does not eliminate it. Thus the seller can get away with some cheating, and given maximization, cheating will occur. Under competition, price will adjust to the cheating. What is costly, however, is not the cheating per se; rather, resources are devoted to cheating and to its prevention which sharply distinguishes the outcome from that obtained in the Walrasian world. (Barzel 1985, 8)

Precontractual specific investments generally play a role in the sellers' side of consumer-goods markets. Such outlays are made as part of the process of organizing the market. When negotiations are involved in a major way, precontractual specific investments may be associated with opportunistic behavior, though this outcome is not encountered so frequently in practice (Shell 1991).

2. *Postcontractual opportunism* related to sales contracts becomes a problem in such cases as physical asset specificity, dedicated assets, purchases involving products requiring servicing over time, and repeat purchases involving site specificity or human-capital specificity. The difficulty here is not so much asymmetric information but the presence of transaction-specific investments, which creates incentives for opportunistic behavior.

An open form of opportunism occurs in the case of the so-called holdup. This phenomenon occurs when some or all of the quasi rent of the party with the greater specific investment is captured by the other party or parties to the business venture.[4] By contrast, a hidden form of opportunism is found in the moral-hazard phenomenon—as in the case of the principal-agent problem. Information of the parties here is asymmetric. Uncertainty plays a part in the sense that it "is assumed to be present in sufficient degree to pose an adaptive, sequential decision problem" (Williamson 1985, 79). But both parties may be risk neutral; risk aversion plays no vital role in incomplete contract theory.[5]

Problems of the general type just described cannot be dealt with fully by *court orderings*. Consequently, they may lead to "contract failure," or the failure of individuals to regulate the circumstances of their lives by themselves on a private basis. Contract failure includes "market failure" as well as the failure of private organizations (such as firms). Characteristically, writers in the neoinstitutionalist tradition ask the question: what private institutions arise to counteract market or contract failure? On the other hand, those interested in the economic analysis of law focus on the question: what constitutes efficient design (or juridical application) of statutory or common law?

In the case of the sales contract, the literature takes up such topics as coercion, incapacity or incompetence, mistake, disclosure, misrepresentation and fraud, and commercial impracticability. For a survey, see Cooter and Ulen 1988, chap. 7. Another interesting field considered by the economic analysis of

---

4. An example would be a steel mill which located beside a power station in order to buy electricity cheaply. "Once the steel mill incurs costs that become sunk, the power company would raise power prices" etc. (Alchian and Woodward 1988, 67). "The owner of a unique resource will be more tempted to exploit the situation as the composite quasirent grows large and as the unique resource's flow of services becomes more controlled (for example, by failing to pay the rent, or to show up to work)" (68).

5. On the assumption of risk aversion as a "conversation stopper," see Goldberg (1990).

law concerns the economics of remedies for breach of contract. Of special importance currently is the so-called efficient breach debate (288ff.).

## 4.2.2.  Lease Contract

There are generally, in common law and civil law, two types of lease:

Of real property (an agreement between landlord and tenant)
Of personal property (an agreement between lessor and lessee)

The German Civil Code speaks in the first case of "Pacht" in the second of "Miete."

In the English literature, one finds the distinctive terms *lease* and *hire* (Lawson and Rudden 1982, chap. 11), though in general the term *lease* seems to be used for both types of contracts (Black 1990, 879). In the first case, both, usus and usus fructus, are leased, in the second only usus. In both cases, the relevant rights are leased for a specified period of time in exchange for periodic payments of a stipulated price, the rent. In the case of modern-style *operating leasing,* which embraces the renting of industrial machinery, office equipment, and even complete industrial installations, both usus and usus fructus are leased and the old distinction between Miete and Pacht no longer applies.[6] Still, the differences between the types of lease contracts remain, even though the objects have changed. For explanatory purposes, we consider old-style Miete and Pacht and use the descriptions given in the German Civil Code.

As already mentioned, the German Civil Code views a lease (in both senses) as a contractual obligation, a point of interest to us only insofar as it justifies our decision to deal with leases in the present chapter on contractual obligations. The German Civil Code describes the nature of lease of real property (Pacht) as follows:

By the lease contract the landlord is obliged to grant, for the period of the lease, the tenant the use of the leased object [Gegenstand] as well as the enjoyment of its fruits, insofar as they can be regarded, in accordance with the rules of orderly management, as its yield. The tenant is obliged to pay the landlord the stipulated rent. (German Civil Code, Art. 581, sec. 1)

Relative to the lease of personal property, the German Civil Code describes the nature of a lease (Miete) as follows:

---

6. The Uniform Commercial Code has a new article, Article 2A, which governs leases (of goods). Article 2A–103(j) defines a lease as "a transfer of the right to possession and use of goods for a term in return for consideration . . ."

The lease contract obliges the lessor to grant the lessee the use of the rented object [Sache] for the duration of the lease. The lessee is obliged to pay the lessor the stipulated rent. (German Civil Code, Art. 535)

The lease of real and personal property is of interest because of its relation to risk allocation. The tenant, who has to pay a fixed rent, carries the risk of the yields of the object, while the market value risk remains with the landlord. The lessee of an apartment, who rents only the right of use, carries the risk of changes in his opportunity costs while the market risk is the lessor's.

Many leases provide lessees with the option to buy the property for a fixed price during, or at the end of, the lease term. This option, called a fixed price purchase option, shifts at least part of the risk of residual value fluctuations away from the lessor. As long as the property's fair market value remains above the option price, it should be presumed that the lessee will exercise the option; therefore, the risk of fluctuations in fair market value above the option price is borne solely by the lessee. The only risk the lessor retains is that the asset's value on the exercise date will fall below the option price. (Auerbach 1985, 327)

Precontractual and postcontractual opportunism may occur in connection with the lease contract. Again, postcontractual opportunism is likely to be of greater practical importance and will tend to arise because of the existence of contract-specific investments or asymmetric information.[7] Consider, for example, the lease of an apartment. Contract-specific investments are typically higher for the lessee than for the owner of the apartment. They result from such things as moving expenses, neighborhood connections, and specifically designed furnishings. After the lessee has moved into the apartment and settled down, he will tend to find himself "locked in" to the contractual relation—as contrasted with the period of time before he bargained with the owner of the apartment about the conditions of the contract. The lessor, who now has a relatively stronger position relative to the lessee, may seek to exploit the situation and raise the rent just enough to capture some of the lessee's quasi rent (or "returns") on his sunk cost. From the standpoint of the apartment owner, it would be optimal to raise the rent enough to secure some gains but not so high as to cause the lessee to move.

On the other hand, the asymmetric information problem normally works to the disadvantage of the apartment owner. As is well known, the tenant or lessee does not have the same incentive as a full owner to use the property with

---

7. To be sure, in certain leasing cases precontractual opportunism is a big issue—as in the case of the one-night lease of a hotel room.

care and show serious concern over its maintenance. Thus, maintenance has to be required in the contract, and monitoring costs arise for the owner. What exists here is a typical moral hazard (or hidden action) problem that is a subject of principal-agent theory.

Both of these problems belong to the contract-execution stage of transactions. And, fortunately, this area has been analyzed with particular thoroughness by Williamson. A key question posed is this: which "ex-post-support institutions of contract" are likely to be developed by individuals seeking stable business relations? In other words, how do private decision makers help themselves through special contractual arrangements when the problem is to devise a scheme that will provide each party to a transaction a sufficient guarantee against opportunistic behavior on the part of the other?

Government intervention can, of course, be used in an attempt to achieve "suitable" commercial relations. In Germany, for example, a large percentage of the population lives in rented apartments, and housing has been subject to significant regulation by the state since World War I. This predisposition to interventionist policy is probably one of the reasons why Germany and the many other countries that apply similar policies experience housing problems. A strong belief exists that tenants need state protection regarding the rents charged and that limitations must also be placed on the owner's right to give notice to vacate rented premises. In consequence, an owner's freedom to price his property and his right to control the terms of its use have been severely attenuated by government. The climate is such that market forces cannot fully perform their normal function in the rental housing market and, inter alia, considerable government support is necessary to stimulate the supply of apartments (Eekhof 1981; Schlicht 1983; Börsch-Supan 1986).

### 4.2.3. Employment Contract

The employment contract has outgrown conventional private law in both the common law and civil law systems. It now forms the core of labor law. Basically it deals with the same kind of exchange, personal services for remuneration, in both legal systems. The services may be subject to direction, as in case of the employment contract proper, or not, like the services of a doctor or a lawyer. The German Civil Code gives the following general description of the "contract of service" (Dienstvertrag), seen again as a set of contractual obligations:

The contract of service obliges the party who pledged services to perform the promised services. The other party is obliged to grant the stipulated compensation. (German Civil Code, Art. 611, sec. 1)

The nature of the employment or labor contract is more specific. It deals with services that are subject to instructions, that is, a relationship in which one side, the employer, has the power or right to control and direct the other party, the employee, in the material details of how the work is to be performed (Black 1990, 525). The employer in return must grant the agreed wage. Simon (1951, 293) speaks in this case of an "authority relationship" between employee and employer. Kreps (1990a, 111) refers to the same relationship as a "hierarchical transaction." The right to give directions is important to the employer because he is then free, within certain limits, to adjust the work patterns of his employees to conform to changing external conditions (states of nature). In the absence of the right to give instructions to employees, employment contracts would have to be written so as to take account, in advance, of all conceivable states of nature. But, of course, in a world of positive transaction costs, such "complete" contracts would be prohibitively expensive and impossible to formulate.

The sales and lease contracts just described are concerned with control over nonhuman resources. The employment contract, with its right to give instructions, deals with control over people. There are qualitative differences between leasing a machine and hiring, directing, and possibly firing an employee. One important difference is that employees can form coalitions rather easily. Thus, political processes may be released—a possibility that the economist cannot avoid taking into consideration. The principle of freedom of contract in the case of the employment contract is, therefore, seriously compromised by collective action and government regulation (labor law). The debate on the organization of work illustrates the problem (Williamson 1980).[8] For example, questions exist about the role of hierarchy in the firm and the extent to which decision-making power should be allocated to rank-and-file workers (Furubotn 1988).

Precontractual and postcontractual opportunism strongly condition behavior in labor markets, and as a result institutional arrangements to avoid opportunism have to be considered.

1. *Precontractual opportunism* in connection with an employment contract is tied to asymmetric information. Workers looking for jobs know their abilities better than most prospective employers do. Would-be employees may, therefore, misrepresent their capabilities to potential employers, and hence adverse selection is a problem. To overcome the measurement problem, signaling devices can be of help—for example, the educational level achieved by a worker may provide some useful information about his likely productivity on the job. As Spence says: "Education can signal productive potential if its costs

---

8. Sale of rights, namely, the ownership of a firm, raises similar problems. Takeovers in Germany illustrate the point, as do sales of firms through the Treuhandanstalt.

are negatively correlated with that potential" (1976, 592). Spence argues that there are two qualitatively different types of signaling or screening devices. The first class is associated with what may be termed "contingent contracts." An example here would be a firm's guarantee of product quality. The second class involves what Spence calls "exogenously costly signals." These devices rely on a negative correlation of signaling costs with quality—as in the education example (Spence 1974).

2. *Postcontractual opportunism* occurs in the employment relation due to both asymmetric information and specific investments. Moreover, adding to the complications in this area is the fact that information relevant to any contractual dispute may not be verifiable by the courts.

Since employee performance on the job is only imperfectly observable, the problem of moral hazard is raised. Monitoring of workers is possible, but because of its cost the procedure can be carried only so far. Other approaches can, of course, be used to induce labor to supply appropriate levels of effort. Efficiency-wage models deal with some of the issues here (Akerlof and Yellen 1986), as do models of profit sharing. Principal-agent theory can also come into play. The latter approach is often applied in the analysis of service contracts with corporate managers (Holmstrom and Tirole 1989).

The lock-in effect, which arises when one party to a contract has made a much larger transaction-specific investment than the other, is of particular importance in the case of the employment contract. Both parties to a contract have some concern about its effective realization, but in practice one side is often more vulnerable to serious welfare loss than is the other. Labor unions can, through collective action, protect workers' firm-dependent values: "This is a major defense of unions, and if this were their only function, firms would not object to them . . . [but] firms fear the reverse risk of employees expropriating employers' quasi rents (Alchian and Woodward 1987, 131). Labor representation on boards of directors can also be mentioned in this context (Furubotn and Wiggins 1984). Still another way in which to safeguard specific investments in human capital is to allow labor to secure partial or complete ownership rights in the firm, as in the case of law firms (Furubotn 1988).

As noted earlier, verifiability of information by the courts may be costly or even impossible. This situation has important consequences for contractual arrangements.

> For example, even if a firm can monitor a worker's effort at very little cost, a contract contingent upon effort cannot be easily enforced, since, unless the court can directly monitor effort, the firm will always have an incentive to say the monitored effort was low and to pay a low wage. (Worrall 1989, 339)

### 4.2.4.  Loan Contract

A loan contract of the type we are interested in pertains to money or other fungibles. If we take again the formulation of the German Civil Code as an example, the nature of a loan (Darlehen) is defined as follows:

> Who received money or other fungible things as a loan is obliged to return the received assets in equal kind, quality, and quantity to the creditor. (German Civil Code, Art. 607, sec. 1)

Common law, by its nature, contains no legal definition of *loan.* Further, there exists no distinction between "Darlehen" (relating to money) and other fungible items (such as wheat), which have to be returned in kind with or without compensation, and "Leihe" (a specific physical object such as an armchair), which is loaned out for a period of time free of charge. For common law examples, see the quotations from court decisions in Black 1990, 936.

As was explained in our other three examples, the loan contract regulates the transfer of control over resources—either directly in the case of a loan in kind (e.g., a bushel of wheat) or indirectly in the case of a money loan. Note, though, that in both legal systems (cf. Noyes 1936, 524–34) the recipient of the loan (the debtor) acquires ownership of the object of the loan. Therefore, in contrast to the lessee, the debtor may use the received asset at his pleasure (e.g., he may sow, eat, or burn the wheat). He is not obligated to return the identical asset received, merely an equivalent quantum (e.g., of wheat). This arrangement, of course, represents a change from the requirements of a lease contract—wherein the lessee must return the asset originally secured.

From what has been said, it is clear that the flexibility, or "plasticity," of this kind of temporary transfer of resources to the debtor is considerable. For example, in the case of a money loan, the debtor is free to commit the proceeds of the loan in any economic direction he deems appropriate (Alchian and Woodward 1987). But this situation creates a major information problem for the creditor. Because of the greater plasticity of the loan, as compared with leased goods, the creditor faces quite serious problems of precontractual and postcontractual opportunism.

1. *Precontractual opportunism* is an ever present possibility in a loan contract. Asymmetry in information between potential creditors and debtors can obviously be considerable. In general, a potential debtor knows his own economic prospects and his integrity better than his potential creditor does. Moreover, measurement or sorting costs tend to be high in this area. Such costs can be partly overcome by the development of financial intermediaries (Diamond (1984; S. Williamson 1986, 1987; Schmidt-Mohr 1992). Signaling

devices, and thus self-selecting mechanisms, may also help (as was shown in our labor market example). Baltensperger has noted that creditors can offer

> different types of contracts (combinations of credit volumes and interest rates, possibly also of collateral levels and equity requirements) to different types of customers. . . . Under certain conditions it may be possible, by exploring the differences between high and low quality customers, to offer different types of contracts, so that each potential debtor has an incentive to choose of his own will the appropriate offer designed for his quality class. (1987, 716)

Still another approach is to try to overcome the information deficiencies underlying the problem of adverse selection directly through the use of information technologies. Then, insofar as the kind of information needed is customer specific, creditors would be encouraged to develop long-term customer relationships. In short, specific investments play an important role in this area.

2. *Postcontractual opportunism* in loan contract relationships is generally a result of the presence of both specific investments and asymmetric information. The fact that money loans have high "plasticity" makes the monitoring of debtors a costly process. Thus, moral hazard is a particularly serious problem here. Safeguards such as collateral requirements are not always feasible. What can be attempted, however, is movement toward long-term business relationships between creditor and debtor. Such monitoring as takes place should be performed by reliable individuals who can act as informed "advocates of capital" (Hinds 1990). Without objective analysis of risk levels and investment alternatives, there is good reason to fear that money loans will be misallocated, dissipated, and/or expropriated. It seems clear that capital market controls must exist and that they must involve the strict application of the principle of liability from contract (see sec. 4.1). Fortunately, the New Institutional Economics has been able to shed new light on the problems in this area, as the subsequent exposition will reveal.

In summary, we can begin by asking what the four examples of the preceding pages actually show. Although various specific points were made, what stands out is the fact that transaction costs play a central role in the analysis of contracts. Neoclassical economics, with its emphasis on the functioning of a frictionless system, bypassed many practical problems connected with the transfer of property rights in resources, and thus a new perspective is essential. To understand behavior in the real world, we must be concerned with frictional forces and the way contracts are established to mitigate such forces and facilitate exchange.

As noted, some contracting problems arise because of asymmetric information on the part of decision makers. And this special condition may influence economic behavior both before and after the conclusion of a contract. The relevant phenomena are considered under the heading of "adverse selection" if events occur in the period before the conclusion of the contract and under the heading of "moral hazard" if events occur during the execution stage of the contract. In each case, behavior cannot be accounted for adequately by the orthodox neoclassical theory of the price mechanism. Thus, in practice, it is possible that the actions of decision makers may lead to the breakdown of markets (market failure) or contractual arrangements (contractual failure).[9] Furthermore, contract-specific investments can play a role here. Depending on the level of specific investments (or sunk costs) made by the different parties cooperating in an activity, individuals are, in general, "locked in" in different degrees after the conclusion of a contract. Then, expropriation of the quasi rent of one party by another is quite conceivable. Such "holdups" represent a danger that must be guarded against, to the greatest extent possible, by skillful contract formulation.

The possibility of both precontractual and postcontractual opportunism has to be dealt with on the two levels mentioned at the beginning of this chapter. That is:

1. The individual choice level, which concerns the establishment of the content (the governance structure) of a contract between two or more parties
2. The collective choice level, which concerns the formation and content of conventions, laws, and constitutions by associations, corporations, communities, and so on

Both absolute and relative property rights deal with the control of economic resources. As for the latter rights, as we have seen, opportunistic behavior represents a central problem. Furthermore, as in the case of the loan contract, absolute and relative property rights have to be seen in relation to each other. Thus, full ownership of a bushel of wheat may be acquired with funds paid out of one's own pocket or by means of a money loan (or a loan in kind). In the first case, we would have no moral hazard problem; in the second, we have one. In fact, the moral hazard risk in loan contracts is large, compared with lease and employment contracts, because of the "plasticity" (or employment alternatives) of the object of, for example, a money loan. The lessee of a house, an apartment, a machine, and so on is in general much more restricted in his future choices than the recipient of a loan is. This condition is understood

---

9. The problem in this case is that in a world with transaction costs complete contingent contracts are impossible or too expensive. Salaries of managers, for example, cannot be precisely agreed upon (or paid) according to a specific result.

by, and reflected in the organization of, financial markets in a free market economy. Indeed, both individual and collective actions are influenced by the potential for the moral hazard problem in loan contracts, and governance structures are shaped accordingly.

A market economy is perhaps best viewed as a network of rights and obligations based on contracts and legal requirements. The network in question is organized, or "woven," in such a manner as to secure "economic efficiency"—insofar as this is feasible in a system fraught with Knightian uncertainty. That is, systematic attempts are made within a competitive capitalist economy to structure contractual and institutional arrangements so as to: (1) avoid the waste of resources, (2) promote the responsiveness of production to consumer desires, and (3) stimulate innovation in the system. Organization matters, and it is this theme that we shall try to develop further in the following pages.

## 4.3.  Some Elements of Contract Theory from the Economist's Viewpoint

Contracts and the contracting process play vital roles in modern institutional economics. There is particular interest in analyzing contractual provisions and finding rational explanations for the multiplicity of contractual arrangements observed in the business world. This approach represents a new theoretical departure because traditional microeconomics has all but ignored contractual matters. As Klein (1985) has said of earlier practice:

> The standard economic view of contracting differs substantially from common commercial practice. Economists consider contracts as the means by which transacting parties fully define future performance and allocate risks of future contingencies. Within this narrow framework it is difficult, if not impossible, for economists to explain the flexibility that is present in the contracts that govern real world business relationships. (594)

In contrast with the traditional approach, then, the following sections seek to explain the behavioral consequences of different contractual structures and, in particular, to show the importance of incomplete or relational contract theory for economic analysis.

### 4.3.1.  The Ambiguity of the Term *Contract*

The literature suggests that the word *contract* describes a somewhat ambiguous concept, not only in economics but in the legal sciences. Thus, for example, the American legal scholar Llewellyn (1931–32, 708) distinguishes between four usages of the term *contract:*

1. "business agreements-in-fact, as such, irrespective of their legal consequences—irrespective indeed of whether they have legal consequences." This use may overlap the nonbusiness field.
2. "agreements-in-fact with legal consequences."
3. "the legal effects . . . of promises."
4. "the writing, embodying an agreement (commonly assumed to be one with legal consequences)." (707–8)

Llewellyn adds that no discussion of the meaning of *contract* in society can be confined to a single one of the concepts just mentioned. As for the law of contract, he adds that it takes its beginning "in the notion that legal officials should enforce, or should at least draw into reckoning, certain of men's bargains or promises" (708).

If we add the language of the German Civil Code, we get a fifth usage of the term *contract:*

5. "a juristic act [Rechtsgeschäft], normally consisting of two declarations of will [Willenserklärungen]" (Horn, Kötz, and Leser 1982, 74).

The difference between the concepts of promise and declaration of will is that in the first case time is involved in an essential way. Since legal theories of contract are not our concern, and since the economics of contracts deals only with contractual issues in which time plays a role, we are going to use, in the rest of this chapter, only the common law concept of promise in our contractual theoretic observations. We are following Llewellyn, who uses the word *contract* in the sense of the legal effects of a "promise" (above, point 3). A promise is in this context understood as a commitment to act later. It invokes trust in future actions of the promisor. It commits the promisor. From an evolutionary viewpoint, promising (and thus commitment) may be considered as a convention.

> The convention of promising (like that of language) has a very general purpose under which we may bring an infinite set of particular purposes. . . . By doing this (promising) I can facilitate the projects of others, because I can make it possible for others to count on my future conduct. . . . (Fried 1981, 13)

Economic theory deals mainly with exchange situations in which the gain is reciprocal for the parties engaged in the transaction. In simultaneous exchange, there is no need for commitment. But when trade is to take place over time the situation is different. Conditions must be such as

> to allow me to do A for you when you need it, in the confident belief that you will do B for me when I need it. Your commitment puts your future performance into my hands in the present just as my commitment puts my future performance into your hands. A future exchange is transformed into a present exchange. And in order to accomplish this all we need is a conventional device which we both invoke. . . . (Fried 1981, 13)

There are conventions, like language, that are in each person's interest to observe if everyone else observes them (Lewis 1969). Moreover, these conventions will tend to be observed without the need for any special mechanisms of commitment or enforcement to be invoked. Yet "promising" is different because, unlike language, it will often be in the promisor's interest not to conform to the convention when the time comes to deliver on his promise. In the language of Llewellyn, contracts are legally enforceable promises.

Clearly, legal enforcement poses no problem if the terms of a contract are completely stated and verifiable for all possible contingencies as is assumed, for example, in the time-state-preference theory of Arrow-Debreu. This is the ideal type of the *complete* contract, which may be understood as a legal corollary of the model of perfect markets in which personal relationships play no role whatsoever. Such "discrete transactions" are also, according to Macneil (1974), the model of traditional or "classical" legal contract doctrines—the contract to sell a horse, a house, a plot of land, short-term services, and so on. "In today's world such transactions continue but are overshadowed by long-term relational contracts: franchises, collective bargains, long-term supply contracts . . ." (Calamari and Perillo 1987, 13). We may add that long-term business relationships played a role throughout economic history, not only in today's world but in real life where contracts are *incomplete,* that is, incomplete beyond the kinds of elementary incompleteness covered by the default terms supplied by the legal system.[10] The parties to a contract do not know all possible contingencies, and in any event it would be too costly to try to write provisions for all contingencies into a contract. Thus, decision makers can find it advantageous to enter into cooperative exchange relationships and will seek specially adapted contractual devices. The resulting "relational contracts" (the term was introduced in Macneil 1978) are relevant to most generic agency relationships—including distributorships, franchises, joint ventures, and employment contracts.

---

10. That is, the terms that supply gaps in the agreement, that will govern if the parties don't displace them by specific terms of their own.

A contract is relational to the extent that the parties are incapable of reducing important terms of the arrangement to well-defined obligations. . . . Long-term contracts are more likely than short-term agreements to fit into this conceptualization . . . (Goetz and Scott 1981, 1091)

It is possible to think in terms of a whole spectrum of different types of contracts as defined from a legal standpoint (Macneil 1974, 738). At one extreme, we have the "classical" contract, while at the other end of the spectrum we find relations or arrangements such as marriage and employment relations (fig. 4.1).

Contracts at the extreme "relational" pole entail strong personal involvement, are long term, and anticipate the possibility of trouble as a normal part of the ongoing association between the parties to the contract. Any difficulties that do, in fact, arise are to be dealt with by means of cooperation and other restorational techniques (Macneil 1974, 738–40).

For economists, the term *contract* also applies to legally nonbinding promises—which may be guaranteed by some form of social pressure (Weber 1968, 34) or by "self enforcement." Macneil's spectrum of relational contracts can be extended by this branch of contracts in the nonlegal sense. The older Austrian literature speaks in this case of "relations" (Verhältnisse) that result from promises without legal effects, or of nonpromissory projections (such as friendship, political relations, and family relations) that are not covered by law (Böhm-Bawerk 1881, 103–26). These relations comprise legally unprotected, or only weakly protected, expectations. Thus, for example, one might expect help from friends in an emergency situation. Such expectations may be based on moral commitments made by other parties, but they do not rest on any *legal* obligation. Conceivably, though, the expectations may turn into legal commitments. For example, during a period of gas rationing, a steady customer of a gas station may be legally entitled to receive a certain percentage of his former gas purchases per week.

Unfortunately, there seems to be no clear and clean separation between contracts in the legal sense and contracts in the nonlegal sense. More concretely, what is revealed is that the legal effects of a promise may be ill defined in a broad area around Macneil's "relational pole" of legal contracts. The region beyond the legal contract part of the spectrum includes the previously described "Verhältnisse," private relations like friendship and public relations like the famous "*contrat social.*"

Figure 4.1 illustrates our generalization of Macneil's argument. Contractual relations in the legal sense are shown as a subset of the voluntarily incurred social relationships extant. On the "extreme transactional pole" at the left of the figure, contracts are perfectly guaranteed by law. However, as contracts show an increasing degree of "relationality" in their makeup, they are less and less

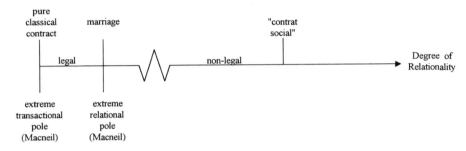

**Fig. 4.1. The spectrum of relational contracts**

protected by law and depend more and more on convention or internal instruments of enforcement. Indeed, self-enforcement is likely to become progressively more important the further one moves from the extreme transactional pole. Further, the voluntary character of the "contract" may become less and less significant with increases in the degree of relationality—as, for example, in the case of the *"contrat social."*

In the real world, actual contractual behavior is oriented much more toward the "relational" approach than toward the "transactional," as Macaulay (1963) showed in his famous study "Non-Contractual Relations in Business." Inter alia, he points out that:

Businessmen often prefer to rely on a "man's word" in a brief letter, a handshake, or "common honesty and decency"—even when the transaction involves exposures to serious risks.

[M]any, if not most, exchanges reflect no planning, or only a minimal amount of it, especially concerning legal sanctions and the effect of defective performances. As a result, the opportunity for good faith disputes during the life of the exchange relationship often is present.

Disputes are frequently settled without reference to the contract or potential or actual legal sanctions. There is a hesitancy to speak of legal rights or to threaten to sue in these negotiations. . . . One purchasing agent expressed a common business attitude when he said: ". . . if something comes up, you get the other man on the telephone and deal with the problem. You don't read legalistic contract clauses at each other if you ever want to do business again. One doesn't run to lawyers if he wants to stay in business because one must behave decently."

Or as one businessman put it. "You can settle any dispute if you keep the lawyers and accountants out of it. They just don't understand the give-and-take needed in business" (61).[11]

Once economists recognized that "contracts" posed problems of interest and importance to themselves, as well as to legal scholars, they began to develop their own specialized terminology for the field. As a result, new terms were introduced into the literature to define different concepts of the contract and its attributes. Not surprisingly, considerable attention was given to the discussion of opposing interpretations. Thus, economists speak of contracts as being:

Complete or incomplete
Classical or relational
Explicit or implicit
Binding or nonbinding
Formal or informal
Short-term or long-term
Standard or complex
Third-party enforced or self-enforced
Individual or collective

There is also concern with:

Symmetric or asymmetric information contracts
Contracts whose relevant information is or is not verifiable by the courts
Contracts concluded in one's own name, or (by an agent) in someone else's name

These and other terms infuse the literature of institutional economics. Many reflect a certain ambiguity, just as does the basic concept of the contract itself. Nevertheless, in what follows, we shall try to clarify this area of technical jargon as fully as possible.

First, it is important to note that the contract-theoretic terminology frequently encountered applies only to the fully contingent contract of the Arrow-Debreu world. This "complete" contract can be understood as follows. Complete contracts are explicitly agreed-upon symmetric information contracts. They are binding in an ex ante clearly defined sense, independently of whether they are formal ("written") or informal ("verbal") agreements. They may be short term or long term, standard or complex. They are third-party enforced,

---

11. Tempora mutantur, these things have somewhat changed in recent years, at least in the United States, with litigation having become a new pastime.

that is, their relevant information is verifiable by the courts. Whether they are individual or collective and whether they are agency contracts or not does not matter. From the standpoint of institutional economics, then, complete contracts are not very interesting. We find that in the Arrow-Debreu world risk allocation is perfect and so is the execution of contracts. No special contractual provisions are necessary to correct for failures of the insurance or futures markets or to secure protection for oneself against postcontractual opportunism on the part of other individuals involved in the contract. Given this high level of abstraction, it seems fair to say that the Arrow-Debreu model does not have great practical relevance.

### 4.3.2.  The Raison d'Être of Economic Contract Theories

Contracts, whether in the legal or the nonlegal sense of the term, become a problem for the economist as soon as there is movement away from the perfect-contingent-claims model just described. For reasons already explained, the formulation of a contract and its performance over time are affected by positive transaction costs and the relation of such costs to (1) asymmetric information between parties (including third parties such as courts) and (2) the need for transaction-specific investments. In effect, transaction costs cause a mix of information and contract enforcement problems. But, during the last few decades, various contract-theoretic concepts have been developed by economists to deal with these problems. The writings here fall into three partly overlapping groups:

Agency-contract theory, which is concerned particularly with the problem of asymmetric information possessed by the parties to the contract

Self-enforcing agreement or implicit-contract theories, which deal with the difficulties that arise because agreements are not enforceable or are not perfectly enforceable

Relational contract or incomplete-contract theories, which focus on the postcontractual opportunism that results from differences in the transaction-specific investments made by the cooperating parties and the difficulties courts and other third parties face in verifying the execution of contractual obligations (this is the main topic of Williamson's [1985] transaction cost economics)

These three types of contract theory have roots in traditional economic analysis. In each case, what is envisioned, ultimately, is a constrained optimization problem. Of course, since the environment considered is one in which transaction costs are positive, first-best solutions cannot be anticipated. Nevertheless, economic incentives play an essential role in the analysis, and contract theory becomes another way to explain differences between ideal and actual outcomes—for example, between marginal costs and prices.

In standard microeconomic theory, these differences were thought to result from monopolistic or monopsonistic practice. And, consistent with this interpretation, the suggested policy for improved performance was to ensure the existence of "more competition." Contract theory, by contrast, attributes departures from the ideal marginal conditions to unavoidable frictions in the system. Presumably, departures result from individually rational behavior in a world where transaction costs and imperfect information rule. The remedy, according to contract theory, is not necessarily "more competition" or "more market" but rather the possible need for "more hierarchy." What may be essential to greater efficiency are organizational improvement, measures that decrease transaction costs and/or improve incentives, arrangements that reduce risk and promote confidence, and so on. All this does not imply that competition policy is obsolete but that the competitive approach may require considerable refinement.

Even in its present formulation, contract theory is able to offer explanations of such diverse phenomena as real-wage rigidity, sticky prices, vertical integration, public and private regulation, separation of ownership and control in firms, credit rationing by commercial banks, corporate culture, and new forms of conducting business such as leasing, franchising, and other nonstandard forms of contracting. Moreover, contract theory has special interest today because it can contribute to a better understanding of the enormous organizational task facing Eastern European nations as they attempt the transformation of failed socialist economies into free market systems.

## 4.4.  Three Types of Contract Theory

The next objective is to describe and briefly discuss each of the three economic contract theories—agency-contract theory, self-enforcing agreements theory, and relational-contract theory. Economists from different schools of thought have contributed to the development of these theories, and as a consequence different methodological perspectives are reflected as well as different substantive contents. Those writers favoring a more literary or verbal approach to economics have tended to incorporate substantial descriptive detail when analyzing contractual relationships. On the other side, there are scholars who operate at a more abstract theoretical level, and these writers have tended to make extensive use of mathematical and logical tools in reaching conclusions. Given the differences between groups, it is understandable that their constructs show certain distinctive characteristics. Verbal theorists, avoiding the rigidity of mathematical models, have had greater freedom for developing and applying their ideas to real-world cases. But this flexibility has been secured at the cost of working with less precisely defined concepts and, at times, reaching conclusions with only limited regard for rigorous derivation. Mathematical model builders, on the other hand, may achieve clarity and precision in exposition, but they pay the price of having a rather narrow analytical focus and of being somewhat restricted in their capacity to pursue broad new themes (DeAlessi 1990; Furubotn 1990). In this connection, Williamson (1993a) has warned of the dangers of "prematurely formal theory."[12] However, in what follows, this book is going to touch on both of the contending methodological approaches—the more verbal one in the remainder of this chapter and the more formal variant in the following chapter.

### 4.4.1. Agency Theory

The so-called agency relationship is a pervasive fact of economic life. What is understood by the concept can be summarized simply as follows. There are at least two economic actors present in each case—the principal and the agent. The principal engages the agent to perform some service on his behalf, and to facilitate the achievement of the activity he delegates some decision-making authority to the agent. Information (after contract conclusion) is taken to be asymmetric in the sense that (1) the agent's action is not directly observable by the principal (e.g., the effort level put forth by a worker) or (2) the agent has made some observation that the principal has not made (e.g., accurate assessment of the output of a Soviet-type firm—where the agent [the Soviet enterprise manager] knows the output but the principal [the Soviet planning authorities] does not). Further, it is too costly for the principal to either directly monitor the agent's actions or acquire full knowledge of the agent's unique observational information directly. In the first case, one speaks of hidden action, in the second of hidden information (Arrow 1985b, 38). Both are subsumptions of *moral hazard,* a term borrowed from insurance theory. Information is asymmetric after contract conclusion. In addition to the assumption that the agent's action or information cannot be observed directly by the principal, principal-agent analysis presupposes that the outcome is determined not only by the agent's action but also by some outside shocks. "In technical terms, the outcome is a random variable whose distribution depends on the action taken" (Arrow 1985b, 37). Under these conditions, of course, the agent can always argue that a poor result was attributable to forces beyond his control and, thus, not his fault. Needless to say, cases of this general type are of central interest for practical policy. The model suggests that, characteristically, the

---

12. "Prematurely formal theory purports to deal with real phenomena without doing the hard work of making serious contact with the issues" (Williamson 1993a, 43).

agent will not act in the best interest of the principal. The question that emerges is how this situation can be moderated or overcome.

Examples of principal-agent problems are plentiful. In the case of *hidden action,* Arrow mentions, in addition to the employee's effort question, the physician-patient relation, with the physician being the agent who chooses actions affecting the welfare of the principal (in this case the patient): "The very basis of the relation is the superior knowledge of the physician. Hence, the patient cannot check to see if the actions of the physicians are as diligent as they could be" (1985b, 38).

Another, less obvious example is that of torts. "One individual takes an action which results in damage to another—for example, an automobile collision. The care taken by the first driver cannot easily be observed, but the outcome is very visible indeed. Although it may be an odd use of language, one has to consider the damager as the agent and the one damaged as the principal" (Arrow 1985b 38–39). Furthermore, the relation between stockholders and management, the problem of the separation of ownership and control, should be mentioned.

The stockholders are principals, who certainly cannot observe in detail whether the management, their agent, is making appropriate decisions. The principal agent theory provides an instrument to discuss the rationale of the "separation of ownership and control" problem which Adam Smith focused on and which Berle and Means (1932) popularized 157 years later. (Jensen and Meckling 1976, 327)

Other examples abound. Thus, sharecropping represents a formally similar principal-agent relation. It is in the interest of a landlord, as the principal, to offer an agricultural worker (the agent) a share of the crop the latter produces on the landlord's acreage. Such an arrangement is preferable to the paying of straight wages because it gives the worker an incentive to push for greater production, and the landlord gains from this. Insofar as the landlord cannot monitor the worker's effort level, some inducement for hard work is necessary. True, if the landlord charged a fixed rent, the worker would have even greater incentive for exerting effort and producing a good crop. But then the worker, who has limited wealth, would bear all the risks of weather, price, and so on. Finally, insurance problems can be considered from the principal-agent perspective. Fire insurance dulls incentives for caution and even creates an incentive for arson. Similarly, health insurance creates an incentive to use excessive medical care. The term *moral hazard* has its origins in precisely these insurance situations.

The nature of the hidden information problem is well illustrated, as has been mentioned, by the case of a command economy (Furubotn and Pejovich 1972a). Arrow has stated the issue as follows:

> Because the knowledge of productivity cannot be centralized, the individual productive units have information about the possibilities of production not available to central planning unit. The productive unit may well have incentives not to reveal their potentiality, because it will be easier to operate with less taxing requirements. The problem for the central planning unit (the principal) is how to tap the agent's information. A similar problem occurs in decentralization within a firm. (1985b, 39)

Another type of principal-agent relationship is known as adverse selection. It deals with problems of asymmetric information before contract conclusion. This term also originated in the insurance industry. In the case of life insurance, for example, it is known that some individuals have a higher probability of dying young than do others. But quite possibly some of those seeking insurance coverage can estimate the probable time of their own deaths more accurately than can the insurance company. Asymmetric information exists. It follows, then, that if the *same premium* is charged to all persons in the market, the high-risk individuals will tend to purchase more insurance while the low-risk people will tend to purchase less. The policyholders mix that emerges from this selection procedure will not represent faithfully the characteristics of the population as a whole (in any age group). And, insofar as the insurance company bases its premium charge on expectations about death rates in the general population, it will find that its payouts will be excessive. In short, inefficient allocation of risk bearing will hold (Rothschild and Stiglitz 1976). From a terminological standpoint, the case is one in which the insurance company is the principal and the customer possessed of superior knowledge of his own health status is the agent (Spence 1977).

In this chapter, however, we deal only with moral hazard examples. In the next, both moral hazard and adverse selection cases will be taken up.

The literature indicates that there are two dominant styles of principal-agent analysis currently in vogue. First, there is a normative principal-agent approach that follows conventional microeconomics and focuses on problems in which individual utility functions are subject to constrained maximization. Second, there is a "positive agency" approach that is concerned with "the technology of monitoring and bonding on the form of . . . contracts and organizations" (Jensen 1983, 334). This type of analysis proceeds without any explicit formal microfoundation. In brief, the first approach is mathematical and not empirically oriented, while the positive agency writings are generally nonmathematical and empirically oriented. Note that the examples used earlier to introduce the principal-agent position were all characteristic of the norma- tive mathematical principal-agent theory, which we shall take up in greater detail in the next chapter. In the present chapter, the positive agency approach, which is much richer in institutional input but more informal in presentation, will be the center of attention. The theory here is probably best illustrated in its application to the familiar problem of ownership-control separation. A general overview of the approach follows—with particular reference to the contribu- tions of Jensen and Meckling (1976), Fama (1980), and Fama and Jensen (1983).

The concept of agency cost plays a major role in the positive agency literature and can be understood in these terms:

> The *principal* can limit divergences from his interest by establishing appropriate incentives for the agent and by incurring monitoring costs designed to limit the aberrant activities of the agent. In addition in some situations it will pay the *agent* to expend resources (bonding costs) to guarantee that he will not take certain actions which would harm the principal or insure that the principal will be compensated if he does take such actions. . . . In most agency relationships the principal and the agent will incur positive monitoring and bonding costs (non-pecuniary as well as pecuniary). And in all there will be some divergence between the agent's decisions and those decisions which would maximize the welfare of the principal. (Jensen and Meckling 1976, 308)

In essence, then, Jensen and Meckling define agency costs as the sum of: (1) the monitoring expenditures by the principal, (2) the bonding expenditures by the agent, and (3) the residual loss, which may be defined as the difference between the hypothetical profit that would accrue to the principal in a classic "first-best" solution and the profit that is actually available when transaction costs are positive and the welfare of the principal is not truly maximized by the actions of the agents. This situation is often described as one in which there is a divergence between the (idealized) first-best solution and a second-best solu- tion that reflects the presence of at least one constraint in addition to those considered in the standard welfare model. In the context of our present discus- sion, the difference between the first- and second-best solutions is said to be the gross agency costs. These are said to be the costs of the "separation of owner- ship and control" and represent a special type of transaction costs.

The magnitude of agency costs varies from firm to firm. It depends on the tastes of managers (or, more generally, on the attitudes of agents), the ease with which they can exercise their own preferences as opposed to adopting behavior that conduces to the maximization of the owners' residual, their degree of risk aversion, and the costs of monitoring and bonding activities.

The agency costs will also depend upon the cost of measuring the manager's (agent's) performance and evaluating it, the cost of devising and enforcing specific behavioral rules or policies. Where the manager has less than a controlling interest in the firm it will also depend upon the market for managers. (Jensen and Meckling 1976, 328)

From the standpoint of the New Institutional Economics, the firm is seen as a nexus of contracts. Moreover, in the case of large corporations, the separation of ownership and control can be interpreted as an efficient form of economic organization. That is, the two functions of the classic entrepreneur, risk bearing and management, are treated as naturally separate areas within the set of contracts called a firm (Fama 1980, 288).

The way in which decisions are arrived at and carried out within the firm has obvious importance. Fama and Jensen, in considering the decision process, conceive of it as involving four basic steps:

1. Initiation: generation of proposals for resource utilization and structuring of contracts
2. Ratification: choice of the decision initiative to be implemented
3. Implementation: execution of ratified decision
4. Monitoring: measurement of the performance of decision agents and implementation of rewards (1983, 303).

Fama and Jensen call the first two functions decision management and the second two decision control. Then, they argue, the most significant and interesting problem of positive agency theory is to explain how the respective functions of decision management, decision control, and residual risk bearing should be allocated among agents in order to ensure economic efficiency. In other words, the organizational structure of the firm is at issue, and the general conclusion on this matter is that whether the three functions should be placed in the hands of the same individuals or dispersed among different individuals depends on the degree of complexity of the optimal firm.

A combination of decision management, decision control, and residual risk bearing in one or a few decision agents is said to be preferable if the optimal organizational form is noncomplex. In this case, specific information (i.e., detailed information that is costly to transfer between agents) is concentrated in one or a few individuals.[13] In effect, restriction of residual claims to one or a few important individuals substitutes for costly control devices

---

13. "Information impactedness" (Williamson 1975, 305) is a closely related notion.

designed to limit the discretionary behavior of decision agents. Examples are the residual claims arrangements in proprietorships and partnerships, which tend to be small, noncomplex organizations. While agency problems between residual claimants and decision agents may be reduced by the approach just described, the solution is not ideal because it sacrifices the benefits of specialization in risk-bearing and decision functions. When residual claims are concentrated in a few hands, those making decisions for the firm must be selected on the basis of wealth and the willingness to bear risk, and these individuals may or may not have outstanding decision-making skills. In general, then, the costs and benefits of alternative decision systems and alternative risk-allocation schemes have to be assessed carefully before an organizational structure is chosen. Enterprise survival indicates that this is the case.

> The proprietorships, partnerships, and closed corporations observed in small scale production and service activities are the best examples of classical entrepreneurial firms in which the major decision makers are also the major residual risk bearers. (Fama and Jensen 1983, 307)

The issue concerning the separation of ownership and control is normally associated with large, open corporations, but the problem may also come up in connection with large professional partnerships, financial mutuals, and non-profits. Fama and Jensen assert that all such organizations tend to separate decision management from residual risk bearing by separating the management of decisions and the control of decisions. Insofar as specific knowledge in complex organizations tends to be distributed among numbers of agents, the diffusion of decision management can reduce costs by delegating power to the agents possessing relevant knowledge. At the same time, the agency problems of diffuse decision management can be limited by separating the management and control of decisions. For example, an agent who is in charge of billing should not have responsibility for receiving or recording customer payments (Fama and Jensen 1983, 310).

If residual claims are diffused among many different individuals, the organization can capture the benefits of such widespread risk sharing. One the other hand, when there are many residual claimants, it is costly for all of them to be engaged in decision control. Efficiency requires that decision control be delegated. Moreover:

> When residual claimants have no role in decision control, we expect to observe separation of the management and control of important decisions at all levels of the organization. (Fama and Jensen 1983, 309)

The reason is, of course, that separation of decision management and decision control serves to limit the ability of individual decision makers to expropriate the assets of the residual claimants.

Summing up, we see that the positive agency approach results in two complementary hypotheses about the relation of decision systems and residual claims:

1. Separation of residual risk bearing from decision management leads to decision systems that separate decision management from decision control.
2. Combination of decision management and decision control in a few agents leads to residual claims that are largely restricted to these agents (Fama and Jensen 1983, 322).

It appears, from this line of argument, that it is quite possible to use positive agency theory to establish a rational economic interpretation and defense of the observed corporate practice of separating ownership from control.

The limiting case of the so-called classical firm, in which the major decision makers are also the major residual risk bearers, was analyzed in a famous article by Alchian and Demsetz (1972). The authors begin by discussing team production and the means available for monitoring such production. Given the technical condition of superadditivity, the gross output of a team can be larger than the sum of the separable productions of its members. There are, however, costs of organizing and disciplining the team members. It is not easy to observe the individual contributions of team members to output, and thus the costs of determining the marginal products of individuals becomes an important problem. Indeed, new organizations and procedures are normally required to deal with this problem.

The Alchian-Demsetz model represents less a contract theory than a property-rights analysis, but is important for a better understanding of the further development of contract theory. What is revealed is that, because detection, policing, monitoring, and measuring or metering activities are necessary (and costly), a free-rider problem exists. That is, part of the effects of one person's shirking will be borne by other team members. Fortunately, though, there are various methods available to limit such behavior. One method for reducing shirking involves the use of a specialized monitor to check on the actual performance of team members. The difficulty here is that the monitor himself may shirk. Alternately, market competition among individual factor owners is, in principle, another way to solve the problem. But this approach has its difficulties, too, because the costs of using the market effectively can rule out this option. A more promising solution is to have firms organized so as to give the monitor of the "team" title to the firm's residual earnings.

> If owners of cooperating inputs agree with the monitor that he is to receive any residual product above prescribed amounts . . . the monitor will have an added incentive not to shirk as a monitor. . . . To discipline the members and reduce shirking, the residual claimant must have power to revise the contract terms and incentives of individual members without having to terminate or alter every other input's contract. Hence, team members who seek to increase their productivity will assign to the monitor not only the residual claimant right but also the right to alter individual membership and performance on the team. (Alchian and Demsetz 1972, 782)

As a result of this line of thought, Alchian and Demsetz come to the conclusion that ownership of the classical capitalist firm is defined by an individual's possession of the following rights:

1. To be a residual claimant
2. To observe input behavior
3. To be the central party common to all contracts with inputs
4. To alter the membership of the teams
5. To sell these rights (1972, 783)

In effect, the organization implied by this rights structure is one in which there is an *owner-manager* who has full responsibility for determining the firm's policies and running it on a daily basis. Complete income, control, and transfer rights are in the hands of the "owner" because he is also the individual who has arranged for the firm's capital endowment. While this "classic" organizational form is consistent with efficiency, it is also quite specialized. Specifically, the important, real-life problem of the separation of ownership from control is not broached.

  Miller (1992) is highly critical of the Principal-Agent (PA) literature with its "mechanistic" use of rewards and punishments to shape subordinate behavior. He notes further that the PA approach contrasts sharply with the more organic view of organizations, "which is centered primarily in political science and organizational psychology." This "literature regards the manager's primary job to be one of leadership . . . " (2). Such a view may help to explain the empirical "anomalies" discussed by Baker, Jensen, and Murphy (1988). These writers found that in many organizations the performance of managers is not, as PA theory suggests, closely correlated with payments. Miller proposes to answer this puzzle, noting that "a hierarchy that can induce the right kind of cooperation—defined as voluntary deviation from self-interested behavior—will have an important competitive edge over other firms" (1992, 12). Considerations of this sort lead us directly to the theory of self-enforcing agreements as a way to explain cooperation among self-interested individuals (see also chapter 8).

### 4.4.2. Self-Enforcing Agreements or Implicit Contract Theory

Agency contracts of the kind just described are by assumption legally enforceable agreements. But not all agency relationships or other exchange relations are of this type. The legal system may be imperfect or the relevant information may not be verifiable by the courts. Still, there exist various ways to reach trade and other types of agreements. One possibility for long-term business relationships is found in the self-enforcing agreement. Under this approach, the only recourse of the party who discovers a violation of the contract terms by the other side is to terminate the agreement. No third party intervenes, no public reaction of disapproval is necessary. A self-enforcing agreement is designed so that the benefits from defaulting are always less than the long-term benefits of honoring the contract. People are, by assumption, strict individual utility maximizers—that is, "someone is honest only if honesty, or the appearance of honesty, pays more than dishonesty" (Telser 1980, 29).

The theory of self-enforcing agreements will be exemplified by a simple formal model in the next chapter (sec. 5.6). We shall also return to this important theory in section 4.4.3. Using this theory one can explain, for example, the existence of higher than market clearing prices in the case of repeat purchase of experience goods. As Klein and Leffler (1981) showed:

> A necessary and sufficient condition for performance is the existence of prices sufficiently above salvageable production costs so that the non-performing firm looses a discounted stream of rents on future sales which is greater than the wealth increase from non-performance. (615)

Coleman (1990) employs a similar cost-benefit argument in analyzing the decision of whether to trust someone, as does Frank (1992), who notes that:

> individuals will rationally place trust if the ratio of the probability that the trustee will keep the trust to the probability that he will not is greater than the ratio of the potential loss to the potential gain . . . (152)

It also follows that, in matters of trust, bilateral relationships tend to show greater stability and productivity than unilateral ones do. Mutual trust makes it easier to agree on mutual sanctions. As will be shown in the next chapter, these general considerations lend themselves to mathematical treatment. Instead of the term *self-enforcing agreements* we also find in the literature, as a synonymous expression, the term *implicit contracts,* though the latter notion is used in a different sense in formal contract theory (see sec. 5.5). Okun's work (1981) represents an example of the first version of "implicit contracts." He speaks of an implicit employment contract in the sense that firms, in addition to committing themselves to binding obligations,

> try to influence the expectations of willing applicants and potential quitters by various types of statements about the future that are not binding. They can have some force and some credibility by putting the firm's reputation on line. (89)

Okun goes on to argue that employers rely heavily on the "invisible handshake" as a substitute for the invisible hand, which does not operate very effectively in the career labor market. Nonbinding statements about opportunities within a firm can influence the long-term expectations of workers favorably without unduly restricting the firm's flexibility. Firms compete not only with other firms on the labor market but also with their own past efforts to develop favorable job expectations (90).

Another informal discussion concerning the microfoundations of implicit contracts is offered by Akerlof (1982):

> Its emphasis is sociological. It focuses on the gift-exchange nature of employment arrangements, where the exchange is based partially on norms of behavior that are endogenously determined. (544)

The implicit contract covers norms of behavior rather than risk sharing. In this view, the difference between capital and labor inputs is that in the case of labor the willingness to cooperate (e.g., to exert effort) plays a decisive role. Workers' effort is determined, inter alia, by norms of behavior. Akerlof argues that wages are determined, at least in part, by the norms of workers' effort, and at the same time wages also influence the norms of workers' effort. The idea of "gift exchange" is used to explain the situation. This concept rests on the presumption that part of workers' effort is a gift and therefore part of the wages paid should be a gift.

> In pure market exchange, the maximum price at which a buyer is willing to purchase a commodity or factor service is the minimum at which the respective commodity or factor is obtainable. Obversely, the minimum price at which a seller is willing to sell a commodity or factor service is

the maximum at which the respective commodity or factor service can be sold. In gift exchange buyers may be willing to pay more than the minimum at which they can purchase a commodity or factor service because of the effect of the terms of exchange on the norms. Similarly, sellers may be willing to accept less than the maximum at which they can sell a commodity or factor service because of the effects of the terms of exchange on the norms. (1982, 567–68)

A major problem with self-enforcement agreements exists because of the possibility of multiple equilibria among them—some "good," others "bad" (see sec. 5.6). To achieve a "good" equilibrium, a coordination problem has to be solved.[14] In the case of hierarchies, an answer to the coordination problem is suggested by Miller (1992). A "good" equilibrium requires that a particular set of norms of cooperation be present. But, ideally, a manager can inspire trust among employees and bring about other conditions that induce appropriate norms to appear. An example of this type of solution is found in the high-commitment work system at the Volvo Kalmar plant in Sweden (Miller 1992, 179). Trust and communication represent key elements in any program intended to realize cooperation. This issue will be considered subsequently.

### 4.4.3. Relational Contract Theory

Relational contracts can be understood as contracts that do not try to take account of all future contingencies but are nevertheless long-term arrangements in which past, present, and expected future personal relations among the contractual parties matter (Macneil 1974, 753). Therefore, such contracts are, to a degree, *implicit, informal, and nonbinding.* Self-enforcement plays an important role here. Actually, most transactions concluded under relational contracting are more or less firmly embedded in a structure of relations that transcends the discrete transaction. Transactions are normally part of ongoing and long-term business associations. As such, they play an important role in modern economic life (as was suggested in sec. 4.3.1).

Often contracts are necessarily and intentionally incomplete because mutual desires for flexible but bounded responses to uncertain future conditions that limit the scope and precision of verifiable terms. Moreover, incomplete contracts often exist deeply embedded in an ongoing relationship. The parties are not strangers; much of their interaction takes place "off the contract," mediated not by visible terms enforceable by a court,

---

14. This point has been made clear by Calvert (1995, 243ff.).

but by a particular balance of cooperation and coercion, communication and strategy. (Hadfield 1990, 927)

Relational contract theory has direct applicability to situations in which there is bilateral dependence of the contractual parties because of the existence of transaction-specific investments. Williamson speaks of the "fundamental transformation" that takes place, for example, in the area of labor relations when initially unskilled workers are forced to acquire firm-specific human capital over time and when the firm is increasingly dependent on the availability of workers possessing such capital. Then, "what was a large-numbers bidding condition at the outset is effectively transformed into one of bilateral supply thereafter. This fundamental transformation has pervasive contracting consequences" (Williamson 1985, 61).[15]

The literature shows that the analysis of relational contracting can be approached in two ways. First, following standard microeconomic theory, a formal optimization model can be utilized to show where rational behavior leads. Or, alternately, discussion can proceed in a nonmathematical, descriptive style under the assumption of boundedly rational behavior by the parties to the agreement. The first approach is known as "incomplete contract" theory, and it will be taken up in the next chapter. The second approach is spoken of as "relational contract" theory. It was illustrated in section 4.3.1 and will be investigated further in this section. The concept of relational contracting is central to the New Institutional Economics. The approach is very general and includes, suitably interpreted, the positive principal-agent theory and the theory of self-enforcing agreements.

To repeat, we have said that the relational contract allows for gaps in an agreement because there is recognition that bounded or limited rationality and high transaction costs make it impossible to agree ex ante on all future eventualities that may affect the business relationship or to verify all of the relevant information to outsiders such as courts. The gaps are not closed by the law of contract. In fact, the relationship may be, to a degree, a "noncontractual" agreement (i.e., a nonlegal contract). Characteristically, the relational contract is embedded in a social system of relationships whose beginning and end cannot be determined precisely (Macneil 1974, 753). The parties to the contract agree in one phase of development, either explicitly or implicitly, about

---

15. In a footnote, Williamson (1985, 63) asks why this condition was so long ignored in the literature. He gives three reasons: (1) such transactions do not occur in the context of comprehensive, once and for all contracting, assuming hyperrationality; (2) it does not arise in the absence of opportunism; and (3) even if bounded rationality and opportunism are conceded, the "fundamental transformation appears only in conjunction with an asset specificity condition, which is a contracting feature that has only recently been explicated."

the procedure (the "constitution") that will be employed to deal with any problems that may arise in the future. In other words, the general basis on which they intend to come to new arrangements from case to case will be spelled out in advance or exists implicitly. Moreover, as part of the desire for flexibility in the relational contract, it is accepted that negotiations on matters of concern will be undertaken more or less continuously.

Relational contracts have no more than limited guarantees by law. As a consequence, opportunism has to be deterred largely by means of nonlegal sanctions or, as Williamson (1985) calls it, "private ordering." Note, however, that in this context "private ordering" may also be understood as "ordering through contract" or "autonomous ordering" (Mehren and Gordley 1977, chap. 11), as opposed to collective ordering. In fact, a considerable portion of Williamson's "private orderings" consists of contractual arrangements, which are protected by law and are designed as governance structures to protect each party against ex post opportunism of the other side. In addition, "private orderings," like self-enforcing agreements, as instruments working against ex ante opportunism, are not enforceable by law.

*Types of Private Ordering*
1. *Self-enforcing agreements* with brand-name capital (and/or "hostages") play an important role in protecting against ex ante and ex post opportunism on the part of contractual partners. As was described in section 4.4.2, the credibility of commitments and mutual trust are crucial to the outcome in this case. An appropriate environment for contracting, then, can be created by precontractual and postcontractual specific investments. These expenditures may range from symbolic, low-cost investments such as gift giving, exchanges of food and drink, and visits (Haas and Deseran 1981; Shell 1991, 259) to expensive investments in brand-name capital such as the design and use of a firm logo or large outlays on advertising to promote the firm's name (Klein and Leffler 1981, 626). In addition, following Williamson (1983), we may note that an ex post bonding effect can be generated through the giving of "hostages."

The cultivation of the business "relation" becomes, to a degree, an end in itself. Thus Macneil (1983, 362) has argued that "peace is valued in its own right." Solidarity plays a part in this context, yet, as Lindenberg (1988) cautions, "strong solidarity" would be counterproductive to exchange.[16] "Weak solidarity" is different. It may well contribute to a favorable climate for contracting. In his writings, Lindenberg has explained that weak solidarity is characterized by four conditions:

---

16. Close social ties are known to prevent the making of efficient contracts. "For example, when City Hall gives construction contracts to loyal party friends rather than to the bidder with the lowest offer, most people would call it corruption" (Lindenberg, 1988, 41).

(a) no premium is put on the importance of the group vis-à-vis the individual and thus no premium is put on the redistribution as against what
Sahlins (1972, 219ff.) calls "balanced reciprocity" or "equity"; an individual's claim for a share that is proportional to his input is thus perfectly
compatible with weak solidarity; (b) it eliminates some alternatives
(namely those that are a clear sign of the lack of operative solidarity
norms, such as open opportunistic behavior); (c) it selects some alternatives (namely those that are a clear sign that solidarity norms are operative, such as gift giving); and d) it affects the terms of contracting by
rendering "going all out" less likely. (48)

This line of argument presumes that there must be an extensive "solidarity
industry" woven into the markets of the system, and that substantial resources
must be allocated here in order to provide the gifts, favors, or special attention
needed to keep business relations in good form. Feelings and emotions are
important in this context (Frank 1990). Indeed, the exchange of hostages in the
form of investments in feelings may be understood as a device to make commitments credible.

The best insurance against a change in future material incentives is a
strong bond of love. If ten years from now one partner falls victim to a
lasting illness, the other's material incentives will be to find a new partner.
But a deep bond of affection will render this change in the incentives
irrelevant, which opens the door for current investments in the relationship which might otherwise be too risky. (76)

Note that Frank distinguishes between *commitment models* and *self-interest
models*. The former type is concerned with situations in which seemingly
irrational behavior can be explained by the existence of emotional predispositions that serve to solve commitment problems, while the latter type considers
cases in which people always act narrowly and straightforwardly in the pursuit
of self-interest. The concept of "loyalty" may be assessed from this general
perspective. That is, loyalty can be understood as the identification of an
individual with corporate goals, and feelings or emotions are involved in such
an association. As Simon has emphasized:

Pride in work and organizational loyalty are widespread phenomena in
organizations. . . . Willingness of employees at all levels to assume responsibility for producing results—not simply "following rules"—is
generally believed to be a major determinant of organizational success.
(1991, 34–37)

The theory of self-enforcing agreements described so far is based on the assumption that any deliberate violation of an agreement will be met with extreme action by the injured party. In effect, there is the danger or threat that the party who discovers a breach of the terms will act precipitously and *terminate the agreement* forever. Real life, of course, knows more subtle forms of reaction and punishment.

2. *Tit-for-tat strategy* represents one possible form that retaliatory behavior can take. This approach is discussed in connection with the iterated prisoner's dilemma game, but it is normally not applied in the mainline institutionalist literature (Axelrod 1984). A crucial part of this strategy is a willingness to make a cooperative first move and therefore risk exploitation during the initial round of interaction with the opposition—that is, the "never be the first to defect" rule (Axelrod 1984, 27ff.; Shell 1991, 258). Of course, if such concessive behavior by one side (say, A) is ignored by the other player (B), retaliation (or defection) is the appropriate move for A in the next round of the game. What A should not do, however, is punish B for more than one round if rapid convergence to mutual cooperation is to be encouraged.

3. *Private third-party-enforced contracts* are included in the category of "private orderings." That is, independent arbitrators may be used to resolve disputes and evaluate performance (Williamson 1985, 75). Such a procedure has been used in the diamond industry to settle disputes. An important reason for the prevalence of this form of private ordering seems to be the inefficiency of the legal system.

The sources of this inefficiency are the uncertainty of recovery, the way courts calculate damages, the length of time it takes to obtain a judgment, and, in some instances, the fact that many diamontairs do not have ready access to capital markets (Bernstein 1992, 135).

Another example is franchising. Disputes are not brought to court but are dealt with by means of mechanisms within the franchise system. These cases illustrate a central point made by Williamson, who disputes that court orderings are efficacious (1985, 29). Nevertheless, pure extralegal enforcement of relational contracts is extreme. In general, one may argue with Mnookin and Kornhauser (1979) that private ordering operates in "the shadow of the law." The important issue for Williamson is that "the incentive of private parties to devise bilateral contractual safeguards is a function of the efficiency of court adjudication, and that this varies with the attributes of transactions" (1983, 521).

The conclusion would seem to be that the parties must establish some form of governance mechanism for the relationship (Goldberg 1980, 341). In general, the agreement will not be completely self-enforcing, and relational contracts may be improved by some kind of third-party administration.

4. *Regulation,* either private or public, is characteristic of third-party administration of a relational contract. For example, the regulator, in the case

of a public utility, acts as an agent of the suppliers and consumers of electricity. He monitors, enforces, and revises the rules of the (implicit) "constitution" defining the long-term relationship among the individual electricity producers and users.[17]

5. A *"union" of parties* such as exists in vertical integration or marriage is a strong, perhaps the strongest, form of protection against ex post opportunism. Moreover, this arrangement establishes a high level of legal protection for a relationship between individuals. Williamson speaks of "unified governance." The advantage of vertical integration is said to be that adaptation can be made in a sequential way without the need to consult, complete, or revise interfirm agreements. There are, of course, limits to firm size in a world of transaction costs. But then, as Williamson has asked, why is a large firm never comparable to a collection of small firms, and why can't such a composite firm do everything a collection of small firms can do and more (1985, 131)? In its simplest terms, the answer is that, if the status of a small, independent firm is changed and it becomes merely a "branch" of a large enterprise, the property-rights structure is changed. Inter alia, former entrepreneurs (and residual claimants) become managers, and so economic incentives are changed and behavior is altered.

*Organizational Culture*
A self-enforcing agreement, whether "pure" or "in the shadow of the law," presupposes that it is possible for the parties involved to recognize immediately (and in a simple manner) what a breach of contract is. That is possible if the parties can foresee all possible contingencies at the outset. But the lack of knowledge of what the future will bring (unforeseen contingencies) is precisely the reason why relational contracts come about in the first place. In this general connection, Kreps argues that "while a particular contingency may be unforeseen, provision for it is not completely impossible" (1990a, 117). After all, it should be feasible to establish some sort of principle or rule that has both wide applicability and sufficient simplicity to be interpretable readily by all affected parties. Such a rule, or, more broadly, such a set of rules for defining appropriate behavior, can provide the basis for a principal's action in a relational agency contract. This structure of understandings is what Kreps considers to be "corporate culture." The area can be interpreted, more generally, as "organizational culture."

> The organization will be characterized by the principle it selects. . . . In order to protect its reputation for applying the principle in all cases, it will apply the principle even when its application might not be optimal in the short run. (93)

---

17. See Goldberg's "case against the case against regulation" (1976).

In his writing, Kreps applies the "principle" logic only to a hierarchical organization and argues that the principle selected "gives hierarchical inferiors an idea ex ante how the organization will react to circumstances as they arise" (1990a, 126). But the concept of a guiding principle can just as well be applied to cooperation among equals such as the partners in a law firm or the members of a university faculty. A crucial task of any organization is "to communicate the general decision rule it applies to all those who undertake the actual application" (126).

Interestingly, the focal point interpretation of corporate culture is able to give some indication of when an agreement will be broken as a consequence of unforseeable contingencies. This makes it possible to apply self-enforcement under conditions of imperfect foresight. In a hierarchy, at least, it also helps to overcome, through coordination of activities, the problem of multiple cooperative equilibria of self-enforcement (see sec. 5.6). As Calvert has noted: "Recognizing or creating focal points is one important way in which the players can successfully coordinate" (1995, 244).

The theory of corporate culture can also be used to explain the optimal size of an organization. The problem with an increase in the size of an organization (in the sense of more types of contingencies that must be dealt with) is that one must either employ a wider range of principles/contracts or keep the same clear focal principle and apply it to an increasingly large number of phenomena. Difficulties lie on both sides. If the first option is chosen, it may become harder for participants to determine ex post whether a contract was applied faithfully or not. On the other hand, as the range of coverage of a single principle is stretched, the consequence is that the principle is being applied to contingencies for which it is less and less appropriate. Thus, it follows that at some point the benefits from widening the scope of an organization are more than offset by the inefficiencies that result from such widening. The appearance of net inefficiency is, of course, a signal for the organization to shun any further enlargement. And this argument may be applied to the limits of all kinds of organizations—markets, firms, unions, and so on. Finally, it is worth mentioning that from a different perspective, organizational culture can be interpreted as a means for specifying more fully the property-rights structure extant within an organization.

*Bounded Rationality*
The concept of bounded rationality, which was first introduced by Simon (1957), plays an important role in relational contract theory. As noted earlier, bounded rationality does not mean nonrationality or irrationality. However, some advocates of the concept of bounded rationality, such as Selten, oppose the view that "human behavior is guided by a few abstract principles" (1990, 653). Selten argues, therefore, that bounded rationality "is not just another kind

of utility maximization or something close to it" (657). He makes the point that we do not yet fully understand the limits of rationality, and as a consequence much more experimental research is needed to improve our knowledge. It is true, of course, that some definite hypotheses are required for an experimental program to go forward. Selten advances the hypothesis of the *casuistic structure of boundedly rationality strategies.*[18] He says:

> The empirical evidence suggests that the typical strategy is casuistic in the following sense: a system of case distinctions based on simple criteria determines which simple decision rules are employed. (653)

Existing systems of rules, such as legal systems and service regulations, are believed to have casuistic structures and thus invite researchers to give more attention to this new hypothesis. Denzau and North (1994) argue that in order to understand decision making under conditions of strong uncertainty we must understand the relationship between the mental models that individuals construct to make sense of the world around them, the ideologies that evolve from such constructions, and the institutions that develop in a society to order interpersonal relationships. Thus:

> Mental models, institutions and ideologies all contribute to the process by which human beings interpret and order environment. Mental models are, to some degree, unique to each individual. Ideologies and institutions are created and provide more closely shared perceptions and ordering of the environment. (21)

Finally, it can be noted that Conlisk (1996, 692) concludes his review article on bounded rationality by remarking that economists who include bounds on rationality in their models have excellent success in describing economic behavior beyond the coverage of standard theory.

### Transaction-Cost Economics

When it is recognized that courts are not always able to settle contractual disputes efficiently, it follows that

> the study of contract is appropriately extended, from legal rules, to include an assessment of alternative governance structures, of which the courts are only one. (Williamson 1983, 537)

---

18. In this context, "casuistic" means that typical cases are identified and studied—as, e.g., study is conducted in case law.

Concern with governance structures, however, leads logically to the trans-action-cost economics that has been explored extensively by Williamson. Departing from the frictionless neoclassical model, Williamson assumes that bounded rationality and opportunism are characteristic features of the real world, and these two behavioral assumptions form the foundation on which transaction-cost economics is built.

Williamson (1993b, 107) describes the procedure of transaction-cost economics as follows:

It (1) examines alternative forms of organization that differ in kind (that is, in discrete structural rather than marginal respects), [and] (2) ascribes farsightedness, but not hyperrationality, to economic actors and employees assessed comparatively. . . . Whereas neoclassical optimization models typically (1) employ maximization and minimization techniques, (2) either ascribe hyperrationality to economic actors or work out of strong-form selection, and (3) include and are sometimes preoccupied with hypothetical forms of organization in which interesting institutional features are ignored or excised . . . " (italics in the original)

Williamson classifies transactions by certain major properties they possess: specificity (of investments) and uncertainty and frequency (of transactions). In the subsequent analysis, he assumes that a sufficient degree of uncertainty exists in the system to justify an adaptive and sequential decision-making process on the part of individuals or firms. To answer the further question of how firms are likely to organize their business relationships, he points to asset specificity and the frequency of transactions as major factors influencing choice.

Organizational solutions are achieved through "private orderings." The contracting parties, who can be understood as boundedly rational, discuss matters and agree on a suitable organizational vehicle for their relationship. The hypothesis is that the parties will formulate a constitution for their contractual association in such a way as to minimize the cost of adapting to the constantly changing conditions of the economic environment. Technically, the objective is to find an efficiency constitution for a relational contract, a constitution that promises to reach the desired end with the lowest possible total of production and transaction costs. While the basic objective may be stated simply, actual realization of an appropriate organizational form can pose serious difficulties. In effect, the property-rights structure of an organization must be established so as to provide efficient incentives for the various participants. But, in determining such structure, transaction costs must be economized on, and sufficient flexibility must exist in arrangements so as to limit ex post costs of maladaption, haggling, subsequent disputes, bonding, and so on. Because

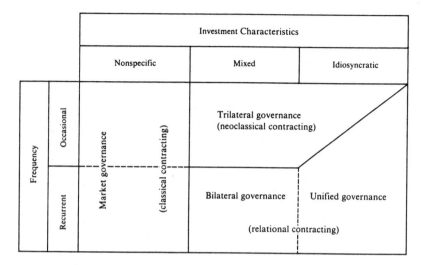

**Fig. 4.2. Efficient governance. (Reprinted with the permission of The Free Press, a division of Simon and Schuster, from *The Economic Institutions of Capitalism*, by Oliver E. Williamson [1985, 79]. Copyright © 1985 by Oliver E. Williamson.)**

the achievement of any given subgoal (as transaction-cost minimization) may require action that is adverse to the achievement of another subgoal, difficult problems of tradeoff appear. Of course, the existence of collective decision making on organizational policy and uncertainty about future economic conditions add to the difficulties of attaining an optimal solution (Furubotn and Richter 1991, 24–28).

In his analysis, Williamson (1985) argues that much can be learned about organization and governance structure by considering the frequency of transactions between parties and the level of specific investment undertaken by them. Then, depending on the particular frequency-investment configuration extant, four distinct types of governance structure can be distinguished (see fig. 4.2). The four types have the following characteristics.

a. *Market governance:* This approach, relying on impersonal transactions across well-functioning markets, is regarded by Williamson as the main governance arrangement for nonspecific transactions of both occasional and recurrent contracting.

The assumptions of the discrete contracting paradigm are rather well satisfied for transactions where markets serve as a main governance mode. Thus the specific identity of the parties is of negligible importance. . . . Market alternatives are mainly what protect each party against opportunism by his opposite. Litigation is strictly for selling claims; concentrated efforts to sustain the relation are not made, because the relation is not independently valued. (1985, 74)

Despite this, there is reason to believe that "relatively noncontractual practices" are common (Macaulay 1963). Business units want not only to deal with each other again but "to deal with other business units in the future. And the way one behaves in a particular transaction, or a series of transactions, will color his general business reputation. Blacklisting can be formal and informal" (64). Macaulay adds that "a breach of contract law suit may settle a particular dispute, but such action often results in 'divorce' ending the 'marriage' between the two businesses . . . " (65).

    b. *Trilateral governance:* What is termed trilateral governance becomes desirable when transactions are occasional and of the "mixed" or "highly specific" types. In these situations, reliance on markets alone is unsatisfactory because substantial costs are associated with the switching of business partners. Third-party assistance, in the manner of neoclassical contracting, is used instead for resolving disputes and evaluating performance.

    c. *Bilateral governance:* The basis of bilateral governance has been explained as follows:

The two types of transactions for which specialized governance structures are commonly devised are recurring transactions supported by investments of the mixed and highly specific kinds. The fundamental transformation applies because of the nonstandarized nature of the transactions. Continuity of the trading relation is thus valued. The transactions' recurrent nature potentially permits the cost of specialized governance structure to be recovered. (Williamson 1985, 75)

Under the bilateral arrangement, the autonomy of the respective trading partners is maintained, and thus independent organizations are not merged into one entity. Relational contracting, in this setting, is relied upon to achieve the "optimal" solution.

    d. *Unified governance:* This is the case of vertical integration in which individual units give up their autonomy in order to make it more likely that joint profit maximization will take place and adaptation to changing economic conditions will be swift.

The advantage of vertical integration is that adaptations can be made in a sequential way without the need to consult, complete, or revise interfirm agreements. (Williamson 1985, 78)

What has to be understood here is that the incentives for trading across markets become progressively weaker as transactions take on a more and more specialized character. That is, as human and physical assets become more specialized to a single use, they become more vulnerable to opportunism and require the special protection that integration can supply. It is also true, of course, that integration may be attractive because economies of scale can be as fully used by the buyer as by an outside supplier (Williamson 1985, 78).

Finally, it should be noted that the list of governance structures can be expanded to take account of various institutional arrangements that reflect special mixtures of markets and hierarchies like franchising, leasing, factoring and other nonstandard contractual relationships. As we have seen, the general principle guiding organization is this: the greater the specificity of investments, the further away is the chosen organizational structure from market governance.

The conditions described in Williamson's "fundamental transformation" raise problems, but they also help to further cooperation between self-interested individuals, as Kranton (1996) shows. She investigates the process by which individuals forge and maintain cooperative relationships when there is always the possibility of starting again with a new partner:

The analysis shows that an ever-present opportunity to form new relationships need not destroy cooperation. Simple strategies achieve the (constrained) optimal level of cooperation. These strategies involve a "bond" in the form of reduced utility at the beginning of the relationship. Two newly matched agents may have an incentive to forgo paying this bond, given that everyone else in the population requires payment of a bond to start a new relationship. This incentive disappears, however, if there is enough initial uncertainty about a new partner's valuation of future utility. Accounts from the sociological and anthropological literature indicate that individuals may indeed pay bonds to form cooperative relationships. (214)

## 4.5. Resume

This chapter is concerned with the attributes of contractual obligations as relative property rights. In contrast to absolute property rights, these rights can only be "stolen" by the obligor, not by just anybody. Institutional economists speak in this connection of (ex post) opportunistic behavior. Ex ante measures designed to guard against ex post opportunism are, therefore, one of the central theoretical interests of the New Institutional Economics. Such measures, of course, necessarily play a prominent role in cases in which the parties to a contract are locked into a relationship because of transaction-specific investments. Then a contract has to be supplemented with arrangements that can be termed "private orderings." In short, the governance structure of a contractual relationship matters. Reputation, which affects the credibility of commitments, is important under these general conditions, and the cultivation of a business "relation" becomes, to a degree, an objective in its own right.

Economists of the New Institutionalist School view an organization as a nexus of contracts involving the various individuals who participate in the organization. Economic theories of contract and organization are thus closely connected for these writers.

Positive agency theory comes to the conclusion that agency costs, which result from the asymmetric information held by the respective parties, are influenced by the pattern of residual-claim holding and the allocation of decision-making rights. In the case of small, noncomplex firms, the restriction of residual claims to "owners" (decision makers) substitutes for costly control devices to limit the discretion of agents. The price of this arrangement, though, is that the benefits of unrestricted risk sharing cannot be reaped. On the other hand, in the case of large, complex firms, residual risk bearing and decision making should be separated, and, in addition, decision making should be separated in the management and control of decisions. Such separation and diffusion of decision management and decision control limits the power of individual agents to infringe upon the interests of the residual claimants.

Third-party enforcement of contracts becomes a problem under conditions of constrained information. An extreme case of legally nonbinding agreements is dealt with in the theory of self-enforcing agreements. The carrot that substitutes for the stick of legal enforcement must be, in this situation, the conviction that honesty pays better than dishonesty. This approach is closely connected with the theory of hostages. Hostages, in this context, take the form of specific investments in brand-name or reputation capital (i.e., advertisement expenditures and other sunk costs). In some of the literature, the term *implicit contract* is applied for self-enforcing agreements guaranteed by reputation. The term is used, in particular, in labor market theory for the "invisible handshake" of employers with their employees. What are at issue here are nonbinding statements that affect the long-term expectations of workers favorably without overly restricting the firm's flexibility.

Relational contract theory, as far as it is of interest to the economist, deals with complex long-term relationships between buyers and sellers who are encumbered with transaction-specific investments and are subject to the possibility of ex post opportunism. Because of information costs (verification costs), court ordering is not efficacious and private ordering techniques have to be applied. Again, it must be emphasized that the governance structure of a contractual relationship matters. This is the focus of Williamson's transaction-cost approach—which represents one of the central elements of the New

Institutional Economics. Purely self-enforced agreements and purely third-party enforced contracts are the two extreme poles of the whole spectrum of contract-enforcement techniques. Unforeseen contingencies can arise, of course, and they can make it difficult for the parties to a relationship to determine whether a true breach of promise has occurred. The possible difficulties here can be understood as the main reason for the existence of relational contracts. In any event, the problem is solved practically by the adoption of a "principle" that gives all participants in the relation (organization) an idea of how adjustments will be made to the appearance of unexpected circumstances. The concept of "organizational culture" is best interpreted as the set of "rules" or procedures that defines the "principle" to be applied in resolving conflicts.

Relational contract theory has clear connections with sociology. Thus, for example, the concept of "weak solidarity" has applicability. Similarly, feelings and emotions have roles to play in the analysis of contractual arrangements. Viewed from this perspective, specific investments include such activities as gift giving, exchanges of food and drink, love tokens, and visits. The latter represent relatively low cost investments, but major outlays may be made in social capital and the brand-name capital of firms.

The concept of "bounded rationality," although somewhat ill defined, cannot be omitted from any serious discussion of relational contract theory. In its simplest interpretation, bounded rationality is said to suggest merely that, in a world of "frictions," a decision maker cannot acquire and process information costlessly and instantly. In this view, individuals may try to act, more or less, like rational utility maximizers, but they face a variety of constraints that prevent "classical" maximization from being achieved. Indeed, it is often noted that as uncertainty about economic conditions increases there is increasing reliance placed on the use of "rules of thumb" for decision making. The possibility of "satisficing" behavior is also recognized as a practice that can lead away from simple utility maximization. In the case of complex organizations, collective decision making tends to be the norm, and when this arrangement exists the model of individual utility maximization is clearly inappropriate. Thus, in the New Institutional Economics, there is a growing consensus that bounded rationality involves more than constrained maximization. Selten, for example, has advanced the empirical hypothesis of a casuistic structure of boundedly rational strategies and Williamson's catalogue of efficient governance structures for contractual relations can be interpreted in this way.[19]

Inter alia, what emerges from the logic of the New Institutional Eco-

19. The diversity of possible interpretations of rationality is considerable. See, for example, Singer (1994, table 2).

nomics is that organizations (which represent institutions together with the people participating in them) are networks of relational contracts. Moreover, this understanding is applicable to all types of organizations, small and large. That is, effective relational contracts can be said to hold in market relationships, firms, nonprofit institutions, governmental bodies, governmental enterprises, and so on. (Jensen and Meckling 1976, 310). Some of these organizations, seen as networks of relational contracts, will be discussed in chapters 6–9. On the term *organization,* see section 6.2.

### 4.6. The Economics of Contract Law and Contractual Behavior: Some Notes on the Literature

Certainly "the propensity to truck, barter, and exchange one thing for another" (Smith 1776, chap. 2) and, in this context, to conclude exchange contracts, is systematically analysed by economists and the Edgeworth Box, with its contract curve, represents one of the most widely used results of economic theory. Yet the economics of the norms underlying bilateral contracts and of actual contractual behavior was practically neglected in the economic literature before the second half of this century. This is even true for the old institutional economics, as represented by the books of Wagner (1894), Schmoller (1900), and Commons (1934). They discussed elements of contract such as debt and obligation (e.g., Commons 1934, chap. 9) but not the economic rationale for the differences in debt contracts, sales contracts, employment and lease contracts, and their variants. As in the case of property rights, such terms as *contract rights, economics of contract,* and so on, are not mentioned in the subject indexes of the history of economic analysis books by Schumpeter (1955) or Blaug (1985). The field was left to legal scholars and sociologists. In his *Economy and Society* (1968), Weber describes the evolution of contracts, among them the "purposive contract" (Zweckkontrakt), that is peculiar to the market economy, though without direct use of economic arguments (672). The role of contract in the social order, that is, the part that contract plays in the life of men, fascinated the legal scholar Llewellyn whose article "What Price of Contract? An Essay in Perspective" (1931–32) was quoted extensively in this chapter. As opposed to the doctrine of classical contract theory (Cooter and Ulen 1988, 223), Llewellyn stressed the need for greater attention to the purposes to be served by contracts, a point later emphasized by Williamson (1985, 4).

Today, the economics of contract rights and remedies is dealt with intensively by the economic analysis of law as surveyed in books such as those of Posner (1972b) and Cooter and Ulen (1988). Topics of discussion that receive special attention include the economics of formation and performance defenses and the economics of remedies for breach of contract. These topics will not be taken up in the present book because our focus is on contractual problems that belong to the New Institutional Economics as defined in chapter 1. Thus, in this chapter, attention was directed to the positive theory of agency, self-enforcing agreements (briefly here, more extensively in chap. 5), and relational contracts. The more important contributions were illustrated in the text. Nevertheless, some bibliographical remarks may be added.

### 4.6.1. Positive Agency Theory

The term *positive agency theory* was introduced by Jensen (1983) to distinguish his work, and that of other economists pursuing a similar approach, from what he called "normative agency theory." He criticized the latter for its abstract nature and its attachment to mathematical modeling. True agency theory, in Jensen's view, aimed at explaining the contract structures and actual practices of organizations and necessarily employed qualitative data that cannot be dealt with through the use of inference techniques. Given this situation, Jensen argued that it would be "unwise to ignore important institutional evidence while paying great attention to unimportant quantitative evidence simply because its dimensions are more familiar" (333).

One of the first articles on positive agency theory was that of Jensen and Meckling (1976). That work was reported on in this chapter together with follow-up articles by Fama (1980) and Fama and Jensen (1983). The theory of the classical capitalist firm advanced by Alchian and Demsetz (1972) was also treated, and this can be understood as a higher-level answer to the agency problem.

Also deserving mention is the work of Baker, Jensen, and Murphy (1988), which considers the role financial incentives play in organizations. Using empirical information, these writers find that, contrary to some theoretical hypotheses, financial rewards are used to only a limited extent to shape behavior. Miller (1992) takes up this point in exploring the rational choice literature of social institutions as expounded, for example, by Calvert (1995a) and North (1990). Miller seeks a theoretical bridge between the PA and organizational psychology literature (e.g., Schein 1986, on *Organizational Culture and Leadership*).

### 4.6.2. Self-Enforcing Agreements or Implicit Contract Theory

It is an old wisdom that "honesty pays"—given certain circumstances. When this dictum is interpreted in a relative sense, it suggests that honesty is the expedient course of action if it pays better than dishonesty (Telser 1980). However, custom and morality in the straightforward, "absolute" sense play important roles in older institutional constributions such as those of Schmoller (1900, 41–48) and Commons (1934, 40–52). Weber (1968, 637), on the other hand, gives an economic explanation of the advantages of honesty in the case of repeat purchases. He notes that because of the interest of trading partners "in the future continuation of the exchange relationship, be it with this particular partner or some other," a basis exists for making honesty the best policy. Telser's (1980) model of self-enforcing agreements, which will be presented in the next chapter, is predicated on the belief that people behave honorably and honestly only if it pays better to be honest than to be dishonest. Of course, a question that immediately arises here is: how is "payment" defined? If purely material rewards are considered (as Telser assumed), behavior is one thing. If other, "higher-level" satisfactions are considered as rewards, the answer is different. It should also be pointed out here that the idea of "hostage giving" discussed by Williamson (1983), and also taken up in the articles of Klein, Crawford, and Alchian (1978) and Klein and Leffler (1981), belongs to the category of self-enforcing agreements. The concept is widely applied—as in labor market theory. Also well known in this general area are contributions by Lazear (1979), who formulated a life-cycle incentive model, and Shapiro and Stiglitz (1984), who introduced a shirking model. Carmichael (1989) reviews this literature.

Krep's interpretation of *corporate culture* in terms of the so-called focal principle (1990a) has importance in the general area of implicit contract theory. As noted earlier, the focal principle provides hierarchical inferiors with an instrument that can be used to determine, under conditions of imperfect foresight, whether their superiors' behavior will lead to broken promises or not. Calvert (1995, 244) says in his review article: "Recognizing or creating focal points is one important way in which players can successfully coordinate." These views are expanded on by Miller (1992), who gives an explanation for the success of high-involvement management. Miller bases his analysis on the prisoners' dilemma game, in which individual rationality leads to group irrationality. That is, by attempting to maximize their individual benefits, decision makers can, under certain conditions, end up greatly reducing their joint benefits. In principle, joint-benefit maximization represents a policy that will make everyone better off. What has to be achieved, however, is cooperation to ensure realization of the maximum solution and trust that the benefits secured will be shared fairly among the cooperators. Miller sees skilled and attentive leadership by managers as the element that will permit the necessary cooperation to be effected. He goes on to say that the gap between economics and sociology has "shrunk dramatically as economists have learned to accept the possibility that individual choices in coordination games are rationally constrained by social conventions and norms" (1992, 206).

### 4.6.3. Relational Contract Theory

1. *Relational contracts:* This theory developed as an outgrowth of the criticism of classical contract theory. Discussion in its present form began with a widely quoted article by the American sociologist of law Macauly (1963). He describes the results of an empirical analysis that indicated that (at least in "the old days") many exchanges were not neatly rationalized and disputes were frequently settled without reference to contracts and potential or actual legal sanctions. Legal aspects of these findings were soon taken up by Macneil (1974, 1978, 1983). Subsequently, the concept of relational contracts was "discovered" for economics by Goldberg (1976) and Williamson (1976). The latter writer uses the term *incomplete long-term contracts* instead of *relational contracts* (1976, 79). One of the most intriguing examples of what can be achieved by highly incomplete, long-term contracts to structure a complex set of relations is the franchise contract. There is a dual commitment problem, so typical for relational contracts, worked out clearly by Hadfield (1990): the franchisor's interest in quality control, on the one hand, and the franchisee's interest in protecting its sunk costs from opportunism on the other (for further literature, see sec. 7.6.3).

2. *Bounded rationality:* Simon introduced this analytical concept in a 1957 article. It inspired early oligopoly experiments by Sauermann and Selten (1959) on the European side of the Atlantic. Selten continued work on this theme in a series of writings (1965, 1967, 1970), and other former associates of Sauermann also made contributions. For a review, see Tietz (1990). Cyert and March (1963), in the United States, put forward a "behavioral theory of the firm" that described empirical models of boundedly rational pricing behavior. The book by Nelson and Winter (1982) on an "evolutionary theory of economic change" also draws on the concept of bounded rationality. Finally, it must be noted that the transaction-cost approach pioneered by Williamson (1975, 1985), and the New Institutional Economics writings (as interpreted in the present book) have close connections with the concept of bounded rationality (see Conlisk 1996).

There are, however, at least two understandings of boundedly rational behavior. According to one view, bounded rationality represents nothing more than the inability of decision makers to acquire and process information instantly and costlessly. What is conceived is a process of optimization under constraints—where the constraints relate particularly to cognitive limitations such as those on memory size and computational capabilities. Articles sympathetic to this position include those on repeated games (e.g., Aumann and Sorin 1990; Binmore and Samuelson 1992; and Rubinstein 1986). Another approach to bounded rationality is found in the work of Selten. He strongly opposes the ideas of the "constrained optimization" school and argues that "there is no reason to suppose that human behavior is guided by a few abstract principles" (1990, 653). Experimental work tends to support this view (e.g., Kahneman 1994). In any event, increasing interest is being shown in the concept of bounded rationality. Conlisk (1996) has surveyed recent developments in the literature and states the case for bounded rationality succinctly as follows:

> In this survey, four reasons are given for incorporating bounded rationality in economic models. First, there is abundant empirical evidence that it is important. Second, models of bounded rationality have proved themselves in a wide range of impressive work. Third, the standard justifications for assuming unbounded rationality are unconvincing; their logic cuts both ways. Fourth, deliberation about an economic decision is a costly activity, and good economics requires that we entertain all costs. (669)

3. *Transaction-cost economics:* As noted, this area builds on the concepts of relational contract and bounded rationality. Transaction-cost economics is the original centerpiece of what Williamson (1975, 1) called the New Institutional Economics. The leading contributions to this literature are found in a series of articles and books by Williamson (1971, 1973, 1975, 1983, 1985). His more recent articles with a fresh overview of transaction-cost economics are published in Williamson (1996). Other important writings in this theoretical line include those of Goldberg (1976); Klein, Crawford, and Alchian (1978); Klein (1980); and Klein and Leffler (1981). Discussion of these articles was presented in this chapter. For a review of Williamson 1985, see Alchian and Woodward 1988. For a general debate on Williamson's approach and the New Institutional Economics, see the exchange between Posner (1993a) on one side and Coase (1993) and Williamson (1993c) on the other in the *Journal of Institutional and Theoretical Economics*. Empirical support for the validity of the transaction-cost approach is substantial (e.g., Joskow 1985a). There is much empirical work being done on transaction-cost economics. Shelanski and Klein (1995) survey and assess some one hundred references on empirical research in transaction-cost economics published prior to 1993.

### 4.7. Suggested Readings for Chapter 4

1. On the concept of contract, it is unavoidable for economists to read some legal literature. For an introductory text on contract in common law, see, for example, the work of Calamari and Perillo (1987, chap. 1) or the longer treatment by Farnsworth (1990, chap. 1). On contract in a civil law system (Germany), read Horn, Kötz, and Leser (1982, chap.

5). As a general introduction to the civil law tradition from a common law viewpoint, see Merryman (1985). For a systematic analysis of the English law of obligations in the comparative context of a civil law system (the Netherlands' Civil Law Code), see Rinkes and Samuel (1992).

2. Relational contract theory is central to the New Institutional Economics. Reading should begin with Macaulay (1963) and Macneil (1974). The latter is a quite extensive, but it provides an excellent description of the problem. Then continue with the work of Goldberg (1976, 1980) and Williamson (1971, 1973). In the same line, consider the thesis of Klein, Crawford, and Alchian (1978), who stress the issue of quasi rents and their ex post expropriations. The first three chapters of Williamson (1985) provide the best introduction to his transaction-cost approach. Joskow (1985a) gives a brief summary of this approach and some detailed empirical support of it.

3. Self-enforcing agreements, and in this connection credible commitments, are an important issue for the New Institutional Economics. Suggested readings on self-enforcing agreements can be found at the end of the next chapter in which this issue is more intensively considered. On the sociological aspects of commitments, see Coleman (1990) and Frank (1990). Relative to the basic problems of the enforcement of contracts in the absence of the state, read Kronman (1985).

4. Principal-agent theory is nicely introduced by Arrow (1985b). An illustrative explanation of the formal side of the issue is given in chapter 5. For the more verbal, "positive agency" approach, read Jensen and Meckling (1976) or Fama and Jensen (1983). Both articles are intended to follow up the work of Alchian and Demsetz (1972). On the criticism of the "mechanistic view" of optimization taken in PA theory, read Miller (1992).

5. Bounded rationality is widely assumed in institutional economics. Simon (1987) gives a survey of theories of bounded rationality. The debate over whether decision makers are rational or boundedly rational is no longer very controversial. A summary of empirical research is provided by Eisenhardt and Zbaracki (1992). On the usefulness of the concept of bounded rationality in theoretical work, read some of the contributions in Richter (1990) and Conlisk (1996).

# CHAPTER 5

# Contract Theory

This chapter deals with the formal modeling of some basic problems of the New Institutional Economics. As has been pointed out over and over again in this book, transaction costs play a prominent role in the analysis of the representatives of the New Institutional Economics. At first sight, therefore, a natural question for model builders would seem to be: how should transaction costs be formally modeled? One possible answer was given in section 2.4. Transaction costs were introduced into general equilibrium theory by adding the activity "transaction," understood as the activity of middlemen between buyers and sellers without any further changes in the assumptions. In particular, individuals were assumed to behave, in spite of transaction costs, as if they were living in a zero-transaction-cost world with perfect information. In models of this type, individuals continue to maximize their utilities (or their profits), given a set of competitive prices, as if markets were efficient. In other words, they act as if prices reflected all relevant information. Exactly this is questioned by the representatives of the NIE.

Another approach to dealing formally with transaction costs (information costs to be precise) is not to model them at all but to look at their effects, assuming that they are prohibitively high for certain (but not all) domains. In formal contract theory, two types of informal constraints are considered. Specifically, the situation is assumed to be such that it is too costly or impossible to find out:

What the future will bring (*imperfect foresight*)
What others know more or better than I know (*asymmetric information*)

*Asymmetric information* is the basic assumption of the principal-agent approach in which the agent enjoys some informational advantage over the principal. The principal may be, for example, the owner of a firm and the agent his manager. More generally, the principal may be the employer, the agent the employee, and so on. Two types of asymmetric information are distinguished

Peter Mathis assisted us in preparing this chapter. Eva Boessmann, Bettina Mohr, Udo Schmidt-Mohr, and Urs Schweizer read it and made helpful comments. Any remaining errors are our own.

in this connection, depending on whether the parties are asymmetrically in-formed before and up to the moment of contract conclusion or thereafter. In the literature, the two types are referred to as *adverse selection* (precontractual asymmetric information) and *moral hazard* (postcontractual asymmetric infor-mation). The better-informed party is tempted to engage in *precontractual opportunism* in the first case and *postcontractual opportunism* in the second. Furthermore, in the latter, the moral hazard case, one distinguishes between *hidden information* (the agent has acquired some information that the principal has not) and *hidden action* (e.g., the effort level of the agent, which is unob-servable by the principal).[1]

Imperfect foresight has the effect of making it impossible to enumerate and contract upon all conceivable contingencies that the future will bring. In other words, Arrow's time-state-preference theory does not work in practice. In the real world, there exists only a very small number of futures and insurance markets. One extreme way out of this problem was Hicks's (1946) pure spot-market model, that is, temporary equilibrium theory. This is a neoclassical general equilibrium model for one period only (the present), given each state of the world. In this model, markets (spot markets) are equilibrated anew by supply and demand in each period and spot prices or wages will fluctuate according to the variations of the state of the world (expressed by a shock variable). As an alternative, risk-neutral employers may offer risk-averse workers a contract one period in advance. This reduces wage variability in return for, for example, a lower average wage level. Differently expressed, firms offer workers, for a price, a kind of insurance contract against variations in real wages.

Another effect of imperfect foresight is that enforcement can be difficult or impossible. The reason may be that some payoff-relevant activities or infor-mation are not verifiable by courts or that the contingencies are too complex to allow a contract to be written. As a result, parties leave gaps in their contracts with the understanding that the gaps will be closed when the time comes for adjustment. Incomplete contract theory deals with these and similar issues.

Finally, there are agreements that cannot be enforced by courts at all, that is, noncontractual agreements like the customer relation that exists between a seller and his clientele. The theory of self-enforcing agreements deals with this problem. Its subject is to show under which conditions honesty is the best policy for self-interested individuals.

We start with models dealing with the asymmetric information problem and consider, first, the *moral hazard* issue. The separation of ownership and

---

1. The terms *hidden action* and *hidden information* were introduced by Arrow (1985b), though he does not use them as systematically as we do here. We follow the form employed by Rasmusen (1989).

control issue serves as an example. It will be demonstrated by use of a managerial theory of the firm model. A simple principal-agent model follows, together with some further thoughts on the formal principal-agent approach. Next, the *adverse selection* issue will be dealt with by the use of models that show how rational individuals may overcome the adverse-selection problem through signaling or screening devices and how institutions can be designed to counteract it.

We continue with models that tackle the imperfect foresight problem. A particularly simple version of this type is the implicit contract model. Here, information is symmetric, but, for reasons such as incomplete foresight, individual human wealth, unlike nonhuman wealth, cannot be diversified. We then deal with incomplete contract theory, in which the assumption of costly contracting plays a central role. Finally, we demonstrate the theory of self-enforcing agreements with the aid of a simple model. An evaluation of the various formal approaches, and some bibliographical notes on formal contract theory, will close this chapter.

## 5.1. Overview of the Types of Contract Theory to Be Discussed

Contract theory is a complex, and often confusing, area of study. Thus, there is reason to present a brief overview of the formal contract models that will be taken up in this chapter. By considering the types of problems analyzed and resolved by these models, it may be possible to help the reader see the field with improved perspective.

1. *The expense-preference model of the managerial theory* of the firm may be seen as a forerunner of principal-agent theory (with the owner being the principal and the manager the agent). The owner has limited information about operations and cannot observe (fully) the actions of his managers. Owners demand the realization of "satisfactory profits," where the amount in question is determined, for example, by the relative performance of rival firms. Subject to this constraint, a manager is free to realize his expense preferences—such as those for staff expenditures. Then it is true, in general, that the first-best optimum of the firm, its profit-maximizing output, will not be achieved. The problem is seen as the result of "ex post opportunism" by management (i.e., opportunistic behavior *after* contract conclusion between firm owners and managers).

2. *The principal-agent model of the moral hazard type* also deals with ex post opportunism of agents (e.g., managers). The principal operates subject to limited information and cannot observe (fully) his agent's actions. The principal, however, is not satisfied, as above, by some exogenously determined profit payment. Rather he tries actively to come as close as possible to his first-best

utility maximum. For that purpose, the principal offers the agent, on a take it or leave it basis, a contract that requires the agent to maximize, nolens volens, the principal's utility together with his own. Granted certain assumptions, the principal can realize in this manner his first-best optimum when no uncertainty surrounds the agent's activities. In the case of uncertain results, a second-best optimum obtains. This is unquestionably a richer model than the one offered by the managerial theory of the firm. Nevertheless, it does rely on some specialized assumptions, which can be challenged.

3. *The principal-agent model of the adverse selection type* deals with ex ante opportunism of agents. Here, the principal (e.g., the employer) cannot observe (fully) the qualities of the individual agent (e.g., a job applicant) *before* contract conclusion. The agent, in these circumstances, is tempted to misrepresent his qualifications. To avoid this outcome, the principal proposes a menu of contracts that leads the individual agent, under certain conditions, to reveal his type (qualities) and at the same time promote the principal's welfare. However, the behavior induced brings about only a second-best utility optimum for the principal.

4. *The theory of implicit contracts* deals, inter alia, with the phenomenon of sticky wages. It assumes, in its simplest version, a combination of risk and (contrary to Principal-Agent [PA] theory) symmetric information. Employers are assumed to be risk neutral. Workers, however, are taken to be risk averse because they are unable to diversify the main part of their capital stock: human capital. At a price, employers offer workers a long-term (fixed) wage contract instead of a series of fluctuating spot contracts. Workers can find this arrangement attractive. The theory here, which differs from disequilibrium theory, provides an economic explanation for sticky wages and the divergence between a worker's wage and his marginal revenue product.

5. *The incomplete contract model* represents an attempt to formalize Williamson's transaction-cost approach. Key assumptions of the model are (1) symmetric information between decision makers and (2) incomplete foresight of what the future will bring (Knightian uncertainty). Given these conditions, it is impossible to take all future contingencies into account when writing a contract. It follows that the gains from specific investments are not only subject to serious risk but also in such a position that they cannot secure sufficient protection by law. Nevertheless, under certain assumptions, a second-best level of specific investments can be realized if the contracting parties agree to integrate and give one party certain decision rights over the other.

6. *Self-enforcing agreements* are contracts that are in no way enforceable by the courts. The situation is such that only the parties involved can determine whether the agreement has been violated, and only they can enforce the performance of promises—by means of the threat to discontinue the agreement. Information is assumed to be perfect, with one exception. Specifically, the

parties do not know whether the other side is reliable (honest). A reputation for honesty is important. It may be achieved by making credible commitments (such as specific investments). Ideally, a reputation equilibrium will be attained. This equilibrium is a steady state in which the seller maintains his promises over time and the buyer's expectations are always fulfilled. The case can, however, yield multiple equilibria.

### 5.2. Managerial Theory of the Firm: The Expense-Preference Model

Given the fact that managers' and shareholders' interests are not necessarily the same, the divorce of ownership from control permits managers to pursue their own interests rather than those of shareholders within the limits of what the shareholders are unable to observe and prevent. This is a typical example of moral hazard of the hidden action type and possibly also of the hidden information type. Opportunistic behavior on the part of management becomes possible. We begin with a forerunner of principal-agent theory, the expense-preference model of Williamson (1963).

In Williamson's account of this model, opportunism[2] among firms' managements may take two forms:

"Emoluments" ($M$) such as expense accounts, executive services, and office suites. These "are economic rents and have associated with them zero productivities" (Williamson 1963, 1035).

"Discretionary profits" as a source of funds "whose allocation may be importantly determined by managerial, in addition to economic, considerations" (Williamson 1963, 1036). Examples are expenditures on staff as a source of power, status, prestige, or professional achievement. Williamson assumes in this context that staff expenditures have an influence not on production but on sales, and thus they affect the level of profits.

The more emoluments (which in effect have to be paid out of actual profits) the better for management. Thus, profit maximization and emolument maximization go together. This is not necessarily the case, however, with staff expenditures. Assume now, as Williamson did, that the firm's management has an *expense preference* for staff expenditures. Then, in general, utility maximization of management and profit maximization of the firm will be contradictory. Utility-maximizing management will, in general, not maximize profits, that is,

---

2. Williamson did not use this term at that time.

it will not act in the interest of shareholders. This is the point of the managerial theory of the firm, a forerunner of the principal-agent theory.

Williamson goes on to argue that, in order to keep shareholders happy, management tries to realize and pay out, in the form of dividends, "satisfactory profits" ($Q_0$) whose level is determined by the relative performance of rival firms, the historical performance of the firm, and special current conditions that affect the firm's performance (1963, 1035).

To simplify matters let us assume that $Q_0 = 0$ and that actual profits $Q$ are completely used up for emoluments $M$. The utility $U$ of the managers depends, then, on the two variables, $Q$ ($=M$) and $S$, the staff expenditures. Management's target function is then an ordinal utility function

$$U = U(Q, S),$$

which management wants to maximize. The usual assumptions about utility functions apply. Management has to solve the following problem:

$$\max_{X,S} U = U(Q, S)$$

subject to

$$Q = R - C - S,$$

$$C = C(X) \quad \ldots \text{ production costs depending on output } X,$$

$$R = R(X, S) \quad \ldots \text{ revenue function with } R_S > 0.$$

The (short run) production cost function is assumed to possess the usual properties. The revenue function is assumed to have the usual inverted U-shape as in monopoly theory. For a given level of $X$, it is assumed that increasing staff expenditures $S$ increases revenue $R$, though at a diminishing rate.

The utility maximization problem can now be rewritten as

$$U = U(R(X, S) - C(X) - S, S).$$

The necessary conditions for a maximum of $U$ are:

$$U_X = U_1(R_X - C_X) = 0$$

$$U_S = U_1(R_S - 1) + U_2 = 0$$

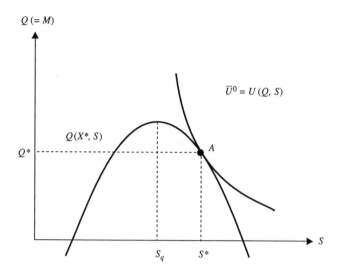

**Fig. 5.1. Profit and staff-expenditure levels that maximize the manager's utility function**

or

$$R_X = C_X \tag{1}$$

$$R_S = 1 - \frac{U_2}{U_1} < 1. \tag{2}$$

In words, (1) marginal revenue equals marginal production costs (both with respect to output $X$), (2) marginal revenue with respect to staff expenditures equals 1 minus the marginal rate of substitution between emoluments and staff expenditures. By assumption, both ($U_2$ and $U_1$) are positive, implying that $R_S < 1$.

The graphical representation of the maximization problem, given the utility-maximizing output $X^*$, is demonstrated in figure 5.1. In the figure, Point A determines the utility-maximizing level of staff expenditures $S^*$, and profits equal emoluments (given the profit function $Q(X^*, S)$ and the utility function $U(Q, S)$. $\overline{U}^0$ determines the maximum achievable utility level of management. The rate of increase of profits at point A equals $Q_S = R_S - 1$, where $R_S < 1$. The rate of increase of the indifference curve, the marginal rate of substitution, equals $-U_2/U_1$. As a result, we obtain $R_S = 1 - U_2/U_1$ at point A in equation (2).

As the figure shows, utility-maximizing management will, under our conditions, always spend more on staff than the profit-maximizing expenditures

$S_q$. This is so because it is implicitly assumed that the owners are unable to monitor their management's staff expenditures and the owners don't care about what management does as long as they receive their promised reward (i.e., their "satisfactory profits" $Q_0$). Management, on the other hand, receives the residuum, here described as "emoluments" $M$. The resulting optimal output, or (here) staff expenditure level $S$, is now only a second-best and not a first-best optimum. This can be interpreted as a special kind of incentive contract, as shall be seen in the next section.

Even though the managerial theory of the firm points in an interesting new direction—toward the moral hazard problem—it remains unsatisfactory. First, it leaves the contractual structure underlying the assumed behavior of owners and management in the dark. In particular, there are no answers to questions such as:

What are the postcontractual states of information of owners and managers, and what role do the uncertainties of economic life play in the problem?

What are the precise incentive schemes of the contract between owners and management given the assumptions noted previously?

What is the time structure of the conclusion and execution of such contracts?

Second, the managerial theory of the firm disregards the owners' utility function completely and "cheats" (analytically) by introducing, ad hoc, an argument into management's utility function that seems to have little rational basis (i.e., staff expenditures). As we shall see, however, the reason for our concern with staff expenditures, as well as the size of such expenditures, can be explained by means of economic theory.

The principal-agent approach took up these issues, at least partly, and it has helped explain such questions as the economic problems of the divorce of ownership and control.

### 5.3. The Principal-Agent Model: Moral Hazard

The principal-agent models, in which the agent enjoys some informational advantage over the principal, offer a natural framework for investigating the thesis that informational constraints are economically significant in many trading relationships and should therefore be treated on par with standard resource constraints. (Holmstrom and Milgrom 1987, 303)

A general remark on terminology: the basic studies of behavior under asymmetric information, in particular the principal-agent problem, are also

called "*information economics*" or, the "*economics of information*" in some of
the literature (see, e.g., Kreps 1990b, pt. 5; or Varian 1992, chap. 25). Stigler
(1961) used the latter title for a different problem (search cost). That may be
the reason why Stiglitz and other writers on issues of asymmetric information
sometimes speak of the *New Informational Economics* (Stiglitz 1985).

With an eye on the ownership-control problem discussed in the previous
section, we begin our presentation with a single-period Principal-Agent model
of the moral hazard type with hidden actions but certain results.

### 5.3.1.  The Case of Certain Results

An agent (the management) controls a firm owned by a principal (the shareholders). The profits, $Q$, of the firm depend, on the effort, $e$, exerted by the
agent, $Q(e)$. In the deterministic case, the relation $Q(e)$ is taken to be certain.
Thus, profit increases proportionally with effort, for example,

$$Q = e. \tag{1}$$

Both $Q$ and $e$ are expressed in dollars.[3]

The principal is unable to observe directly what effort level the agent is
supplying. Information is, in short, asymmetric. Yet, because the agent's effort
always produces definite, quantifiable results on the level of profit, the actual
effort exerted by the agent can always be inferred by the principal from realized profits $Q$.

We assume that effort causes the agent (subjective) costs, $c$, which, expressed in terms of money, are

$$c = \frac{k}{2}e^2, \tag{2}$$

with $k > 0$ as the rate of increase of the marginal cost of effort ($c' = ke$). The
principal offers the agent a wage or incentive schedule $w$. The difference
between the agent's wage and his effort cost, $A = w - c(e)$, expresses the
agent's utility level, $A$, in money terms. Because of (2), the agent's utility
function is

$$A = w - \frac{k}{2}e^2. \tag{3}$$

---

3. Note that equations are numbered anew from (1) onward for each section of this chapter.

We assume further that the principal offers the agent a *linear incentive schedule*[4]

$$w = r + \alpha Q, \tag{4}$$

with $r$ designating a fixum, or *fee,* and $\alpha$ a *profit share* ($0 \le \alpha \le 1$).
The *agent's decision problem* can thus be formulated as follows:

$$\max_{e} A = r + \alpha Q - \frac{k}{2} e^2$$

$$s.t. \ Q = e.$$

The first-order condition is, after substitution for $Q$,

$$\alpha - ke = 0$$

or

$$e = \frac{\alpha}{k}. \tag{5}$$

Equation (5) is the agent's *response function* to the principal's incentive scheme $w = r + \alpha Q$.

In our example, the first-order condition is also sufficient for the utility maximum of the agent.

Assume now that the principal knows his agent's response function. He then can induce some effort level $e_1^*$ from the agent by offering him, as an incentive, a certain profit share $\alpha^*$. Equation (5), therefore, is also called the *incentive constraint* (IC) of the principal with regard to the agent's decisions.[5]

Furthermore, assume that the agent is free to decide whether he will accept the principal's offer or not. He will accept if the principal offers him at least his reservation utility $\overline{A}$, which is determined, for example, by his next best employment possibility. This is the *participation constraint* (PC). Accord-

---

4. This is a restrictive assumption intended to simplify calculation. The precise problem is to determine an optimal compensation *function,* that is, a function that brings us as close as possible to the first-best result. By assuming a *linear* incentive schedule, the result may diverge more from the first-best optimum than it would need to otherwise.

5. Replacing the agent's maximization problem with the first-order condition when solving the principal's problem is not always feasible. For the limitations of this so-called first-order approach, see, for example, Laffont (1989, chap. 11).

ing to equations (1), (3), and (4) of this section, the participation constraint is

$$r + \alpha e - \frac{k}{2}e^2 \geq \overline{A}. \tag{6}$$

The principal's target function are his net profits

$$Q^n = Q - w$$

or

$$Q^n = (1 - \alpha)e - r. \tag{7}$$

The *principal's decision problem* can thus be formulated as follows:

$$\max_{r,\alpha} Q^n = (1 - \alpha)e - r$$

$$s.t. \ \ e = \frac{\alpha}{k} \ \ (IC)$$

$$r + \alpha e - \frac{k}{2}e^2 \geq \overline{A} \ \ (PC).$$

The principal maximizes his net profits subject to his agent's incentive and participation constraints.

The net-profit-maximizing principal, of course, will offer his agent as little as possible to win his services. That is, the participation constraint (6) will become "binding" in the sense of

$$r + \alpha e - \frac{k}{2}e^2 = \overline{A}$$

or, solved for $r$ and assuming $\overline{A} = 0$,

$$r = \frac{k}{2}e^2 - \alpha e. \tag{8}$$

The principal's decision problem then becomes

$$\max_{r,\alpha} Q^n = (1 - \alpha)e - r$$

$$s.t. \ \ e = \frac{\alpha}{k} \ \ (IC)$$

$$r = \frac{k}{2} e^2 - \alpha e \quad \text{(PC)}.$$

By substituting (IC) and (PC) into the target function, the principal's decision problem reduces to

$$\max_{\alpha} \ Q^n = \frac{\alpha}{k} - \frac{\alpha^2}{2k}.$$

The first-order condition is

$$\frac{1}{k} - \frac{\alpha}{k} = 0 \qquad (9)$$

or

$$\alpha^* = 1.$$

In words, the agent gets 100 percent of the firm's profits, $Q$, and he becomes, in effect, the *residual claimant* of the firm's profits.

Substituting (5) and (9) into (8) gives for $\alpha = 1$

$$r^* = -(2k)^{-1}. \qquad (10)$$

In words, the agent must pay a lump-sum fee, $-r^*$ (or "franchise"), to the principal. What emerges is a "franchise contract."

Renting the firm to the agent for a fee, $-r^*$, and allowing the agent to keep all the profits, or selling the firm to the agent serves to ensure the optimal effort level $e^*$ and the profit maximum $Q^*$ (Lazear 1987, 745).

The optimal effort level is in our example

$$e^* = \frac{1}{k}, \qquad (11)$$

and the profit maximum is, because of (1),

$$Q^* = \frac{1}{k}. \qquad (12)$$

The optimal wage, $w^*$, to be offered by the principal to the agent is then

$$w^* = r^* + \alpha^* Q^* = \frac{1}{2k}. \tag{13}$$

It is equal to the agent's *reservation price,* that is, the sum of the reservation utility $\overline{A}$, which in our example equals zero, and the compensation for his effort costs $c(e^*) = 1/(2k)$:

$$w^* = \overline{A} + c(e^*) = \frac{1}{2k} \qquad (\text{for } \overline{A} = 0). \tag{14}$$

According to the optimal compensation level $w^*$, the agent receives, in effect, because of (12), 50 percent of maximal profits $Q^*$. The other 50 percent is paid to the principal.

The principal's maximal net profits are

$$Q^{n*} = (1 - \alpha^*)e^* - r^* = \frac{1}{2k}. \tag{15}$$

This is not the only way to implement the optimal effort level of $e^*$.

In the case in which results are certain, the principal can always infer from the results of (1) the agent's effort level. He knows the agent's reservation utility $\overline{A}$ (in our case zero) and the cost-of-effort function $c(e)$, that is, the agent's reservation price $\overline{w} = \overline{A} + c(e)$.

The optimization problem of the principal can therefore be reduced to

$$\max_{e} Q^n = e - \overline{A} - c(e)$$

or, for our example,

$$\max_{e} Q^n = e - \frac{k}{2}e^2. \tag{16}$$

The incentive constraint (IC) is superfluous, as will be seen immediately. The first-order condition is again the optimal effort level

$$e^* = \frac{1}{k}, \tag{17}$$

and the maximal gross profit is, as before,

$$Q^* = \frac{1}{k}. \tag{18}$$

The principal can therefore set $Q^*$ as a target profit and offer to pay the agent his reservation price

$$w^* = \overline{A} + c(e^*) = (2k)^{-1} \tag{19}$$

if he reaches the target. If the agent fails to reach the target, the principal can demand that he pay a sufficiently large conventional fine (Varian 1992, 443). Equation (16) corresponds to the *bilateral-monopoly* model. Its solution assumes that the principal (the buyer) dominates the agent (the seller) and forces him to accept the price he sets.

This *target profit scheme* is another way to make $e^*$ the optimal choice for the agent. That is, the agent can be induced to choose a function, $w(Q)$, such that

$$w(Q^*) = \begin{cases} \overline{A} + c(e^*) & \text{if } e = e^*(=\frac{1}{k}) \\ -\infty & \text{otherwise.} \end{cases}$$

Effort cannot be observed directly but can be inferred from $Q(Q^* = e^*)$.

The effort level $e^*$ (eq. (11)) is the *first-best* level, that is, the level that would also be chosen if effort were directly observable.

In the case in which results are certain ("full information") the divorce of ownership from control is no problem. Specifically, no losses arise due to asymmetric information because the principal can always conclude from the result what the actual efficiency level exerted by the agent was.[6]

The situation is, of course, different as soon as we assume that the results of the agent's effort are uncertain. In our example, this would mean that the profit level $Q$ is uncertain.

### 5.3.2. Uncertain Results

Consideration will now be given to the case in which results are uncertain. In this version of the $PA-$ problem, profits, $Q$, are not only determined by the effort, $e$, of the agent but also by some kind of exogenous shock, $\tilde{\theta}$, the

---

6. The special features of this "canonical model" are described in Sappington (1991, 48ff.).

probability of which neither principal nor agent can control. This means, in a sequential description, that the agent moves first by choosing his effort level, $e$, and then "nature" moves, that is, chooses a particular value of the random variable $\tilde{\theta}$. The gross profit function is assumed to be

$$\tilde{Q} = e + \tilde{\theta}. \tag{20}$$

We assume that the random variable $\tilde{\theta}$ is normally distributed with zero mean value and variance $\sigma^2$. While the effort level $e$ exerted by the agent and the manifestation of $\tilde{\theta}$ cannot be observed by the principal, the actual result $Q$ (the realization of (20)) can be observed by both, the principal and the agent, correctly and without costs. Hence, the principal can offer the agent an incentive schedule, which we assume to be:

$$w = r + \alpha Q, \qquad \text{where } 0 \leq \alpha \leq 1.$$

But now the utility levels of the principal and the agent are uncertain because profit $\tilde{Q}$ is uncertain. Therefore, the principal's and the agent's attitudes toward risk have to be taken into account. If both are risk neutral (i.e., "uncertainty" $\sigma^2$ does not matter for them), their decision problem under uncertainty is very simple: the principal maximizes the expected value of his uncertain net profits $E(\tilde{Q}^n)$, and the agent maximizes the expected value of his uncertain utility $E(\tilde{A})$. We obtain the same results as we did in subsection 5.2.1, that is, the agent bears all the risk. (For an illustration of this, see Sappington 1991, 46–49.)

Yet risk neutrality is a rather special assumption. Let us assume that the agent is risk averse while the principal remains risk neutral. The usual explanation for this presumption is that the agent, for example, the manager (who invested his human wealth in the firm), does not have the same opportunities to diversify his investments that the principal does. That is, it is reasonable to assume that the "principal" is, in fact, an aggregation of a large number of homogeneous shareholders (acting as one decision maker)—with each shareholder having only a few shares. Thus, these individuals are able to diversify their assets perfectly. In this case, we have to apply a different utility function for the agent to allow for his risk-averse attitude.

An elegant way to do so is to apply the von Neumann-Morgenstern utility $u(\cdot)$ approach and maximize the expected value $E(u(\cdot))$. To continue our algebraic example in as simple a fashion as possible, we assume a von Neumann-Morgenstern utility function of the constant absolute risk-aversion type

$$u(\tilde{A}) = -\exp(-a\tilde{A}), \qquad a > 0. \tag{21}$$

The agent's von Neumann-Morgenstern utility of his uncertain $\tilde{A}$ can be expressed by the corresponding certainty equivalent

$$C(\tilde{A}) = E(\tilde{A}) - R, \quad (R > 0) \tag{22}$$

where $R$ denotes the *risk premium*. This is the difference between the expected value $E\ (\tilde{A})$ and the amount of money the agent would be willing to pay for the "lottery" $(\tilde{A})$, that is, its certainty equivalent $C(\tilde{A})$. Given our special von Neumann-Morgenstern utility function (eq. 21) and a normally distributed random term $\tilde{\theta}$ we have

$$R = \frac{a}{2}\alpha^2\sigma^2, \quad a > 0. \tag{23}$$

(Bamberg and Spreman 1981).
   Assuming a linear payment schedule (4) and a gross profit function (20), we can substitute these two equations in (3) to obtain

$$\tilde{A} = r + \alpha e + \alpha\tilde{\theta} - \frac{k}{2}e^2. \tag{24}$$

Substituting (23) and (24) in (22) gives

$$C(\tilde{A}) = r + \alpha e - \frac{k}{2}e^2 - \alpha^2\frac{a}{2}\sigma^2. \tag{25}$$

First, it will be useful to determine the first-best solution, which can then serve as a benchmark. It can be obtained for the case of uncertain results if we assume symmetric information—that is, if we assume that the principal is able to observe directly the effort level being supplied by the agent. Assume further that the effort level is contractible. Then, the principal's decision problem becomes

$$\max_{e,\alpha,r} E(\tilde{Q}^n) = (1 - \alpha)e - r \tag{26}$$

$$s.t.\ C(\tilde{A}) = r + \alpha e - \alpha^2\frac{a}{2}\sigma^2 - \frac{k}{2}e^2 \geq \overline{C} \quad (PC).$$

The principal maximizes the expected value of his net profits subject to his agent's participation constraint and does this in full knowledge of the effort level $e$ supplied by the agent. As before, the participation constraint is binding, so that

$$r = -\alpha e + \alpha^2 \frac{a}{2}\sigma^2 + \frac{k}{2}e^2, \qquad (27)$$

where $\overline{C} = 0$. Next, substitute (27) in (26) in order to establish the principal's reduced decision problem:

$$\max_{e,\alpha} E(\tilde{Q}^n) = e - \alpha^2 \frac{a}{2}\sigma^2 - \frac{k}{2}e^2. \qquad (28)$$

Since the expected net profit is decreasing with the profit share $\alpha$, and since $0 \leq \alpha \leq 1$, we can immediately obtain the optimal profit share

$$\alpha^* = 0.$$

Then we maximize $E(\tilde{Q}^n)$ with respect to $e$. The necessary and sufficient condition for an optimum emerges as

$$e^* = \frac{1}{k}.$$

Substituting $\alpha^*$ and $e^*$ into the participation constraint yields

$$r^* = \frac{1}{2k}.$$

Thus, the first-best solution for our principal-agent example (with symmetric information and uncertain results) is

$$w^* = \frac{1}{2k} \quad \text{and} \quad e^* = \frac{1}{k}. \qquad (29)$$

The agent gets a fixed wage payment. The risk-neutral principal bears all the risk.

We now return to the principal-agent model with uncertain results and asymmetric information. Under these new conditions, the principal can no longer observe the agent's effort level directly. But, since he knows the agent's utility function, he can at least control the agent's effort level indirectly. As we shall see, the first-best contract $(w^*, e^*)$ is now unfeasible.

From the participation constraint, it follows immediately that unvarying compensation ($\alpha = 0$, $r = \bar{r}$) would cause the agent to cease effort (i.e., to select $e = 0$). Consequently, profit sharing ($\alpha > 0$) is now necessary to induce the agent to exert some positive level of effort ($e > 0$). The result that appears, however, is only second best.

To determine the optimal value of the profit share that is to be offered to the agent, the principal must now consider the *agent's decision problem,* which can be formulated as follows:

$$\max_{e} C(\tilde{A}) = r + \alpha e - \frac{k}{2}e^2 - \alpha^2\frac{a}{2}\sigma^2.$$

From the first-order condition, there follows

$$e = \frac{\alpha}{k}.$$

This equation will again serve as the principal's incentive constraint (IC). The participation constraint (PC) is now secured from the certainty equivalent (25) as

$$r + \alpha e - \frac{k}{2}e^2 - \alpha^2\frac{a}{2}\sigma^2 \geq \bar{C}. \tag{30}$$

As before, we assume that $\bar{C} = 0$.

The *principal's decision problem* in the asymmetric information case with uncertain results then becomes

$$\max_{r,\alpha} \quad E(\tilde{Q}^n) = (1 - \alpha)e - r$$

$$s.t. \quad e = \frac{\alpha}{k} \quad (IC) \tag{31}$$

$$r + \alpha e - \frac{k}{2}e^2 - \alpha^2\frac{a}{2}\sigma^2 \geq 0 \quad (PC).$$

Or again, since PC is binding under our conditions and

$$r = -\alpha e + \frac{k}{2}e^2 + \alpha^2\frac{a}{2}\sigma^2,$$

we can substitute $e$ and $r$ into (31) to obtain the principal's reduced decision problem

$$\max_{\alpha} E(\tilde{Q}) = \frac{\alpha}{k} - \frac{1}{2}\frac{\alpha^2}{k} - \alpha^2 \frac{a}{2}\sigma^2.$$

From the first-order condition of this maximization problem, we find the optimal profit share

$$\alpha^{**} = \frac{1}{1 + ka\sigma^2} < 1; \tag{32}$$

and it is positive since $ka\sigma^2 > 0$, which under our assumptions is also a sufficient condition for a maximum of $E(\tilde{Q}^n)$. The share $\alpha^{**} < 1$ means that the risk-averse agent does not bear all of the risk. We secure a "sharing contract."

The corresponding optimal effort level is then

$$e^{**} = \frac{1}{k(1 + ka\sigma^2)} < \frac{1}{k}. \tag{33}$$

That is, the agent will exert less effort than in the case of certain results. The optimal lump-sum fee amounts to

$$r^{**} = \frac{ka\sigma^2 - 1}{2k(1 + ka\sigma^2)^2} > -\frac{1}{2k}. \tag{34}$$

The term $r^{**} > 0$ if $ka\sigma^2 > 1$. In other words, the principal has to *pay* the agent a fixed fee, $r^{**}$, to induce him to accept the contract if the agent's degree of risk aversion, $a$, or the uncertainty of the result (the variance of $\tilde{\theta}$) are sufficiently high:

$$a\sigma^2 > \frac{1}{k}.$$

Since the risk is shared between principal and agent, the optimal profit share $\alpha^{**}$ decreases with increasing risk aversion $a$ or variance $\sigma^2$ given $k$, while the optimal value of $r^{**}$ first increases and becomes positive and then decreases toward zero (figure 5.2).

If $\tilde{Q}^n$ has a great variance $\sigma^2$ (is highly uncertain), or if the degree of risk aversion of the agent is very large (great coefficient $a$), or the marginal cost of effort is very steep (large $k$), the agent will demand a positive fixum, $r^{**}$,

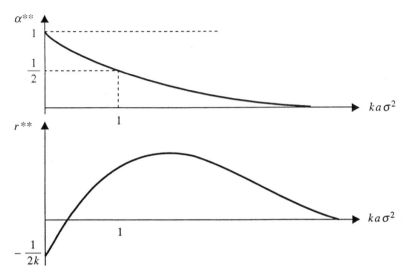

**Fig. 5.2.   The Moral Hazard Case: Optimal Profit Shares and Lump Sum Fees**

combined with a comparatively small profit share, $\alpha^{**}(<1/2)$. The optimal effort level $e^{**}$ will decrease because it becomes too costly to give incentives.

The principal-agent problem combines two inextricable elements, risk sharing and differential information. Even if there were no problem of differential information, there would be some sharing of the outcome if both parties are risk-averse. Indeed, if the agent were risk neutral, the principal-agent problem would have a trivial solution: the agent would bear all the risks, and then the differential information would not matter (as in sec. 5.2.1). That is, the principal would retain a fixed amount $[r^* = -(2k)^{-1}$ in our example] and pay all the remainder to the agent, who therefore would have no dilution of incentives (Shavell 1979). . . . Thus the landlord renting land to a tenant farmer would simply charge a fixed rent independent of output, which in general depends on both the tenant's effort, unobservable to the landlord, and the vagaries of the weather. However, this solution is not optimal if the agent is risk averse. Since all individuals are averse to sufficiently large risks, the simple solution of preserving incentives by assigning all risks to the agent fails as soon as the risks are large compared with the agent's wealth. The president of a large corporation can hardly be held responsible for its income fluctuations" (Arrow 1985b, 44–45).

We finally ask what the value of the principal's maximal expected net profit is if the results are uncertain. Using the target equation (26), we have to calculate

$$E(\tilde{Q}^n)^{**} = (1 - \alpha^{**})e^{**} - r^{**} \tag{35}$$

and receive, by substituting (27) and (29) in (31),

$$E(\tilde{Q}^n)^{**} = (2k)^{-1}(1 + ak\sigma^2)^{-1}. \tag{36}$$

As indicated above, the result is only second best because

$$(1 + ak\sigma^2)^{-1} < 1.$$

The maximal (expected) net profit of the principal $E(\tilde{Q}^n)^{**}$, is, under uncertainty, ($\sigma^2 > 0$), and the risk aversion of the agent ($a > 0$) is smaller than the first-best net profit $E(\tilde{Q}^n)^* = (2k)^{-1}$.

The (expected) welfare loss, *WL,* of the principal amounts to

$$WL = E(\tilde{Q}^n)^* - E(\tilde{Q}^n)^{**} = \frac{a\sigma^2}{2(1 + ak\sigma^2)}.$$

In the present example, *WL* is equal to the total welfare loss since the agent receives in this model his constant reservation utility $\overline{C}$.[7] Thus, a small degree of risk aversion (small *a*), or uncertainty (small $\sigma^2$), or a flat marginal cost of effort (small *k*) will allow a solution close to the first best. "All of this accords well with intuition" (Holmstrom and Milgrom 1987, 323).

Additional information is valuable for the solution of the agency problem, which, in the case of a normal distribution, implies that a reduction in the variance $\sigma^2$ will benefit the principal. This is confirmed by the formulae of the preceding example (Holmstrom and Milgrom 1987). The welfare loss arises because of the unobservability of effort and the agent's risk aversion.

The principal, if it is only one person, could avoid the welfare loss by taking over the agent's tasks himself, for example, by managing his own firm. He will do so if his reservation price (not considered in this model) is not greater than his welfare loss *WL*. That could be possible if we assume sufficiently equal skills among individuals. If that is not the case, if the agent is more skilled for a certain task than is the principal himself, delegation of the task (and in this sense division of labor) would be advantageous to the principal

---

7. Note that this is a special case.

even if he faces a bigger "welfare loss." Note the Demsetzian nirvana character of the welfare loss concept!
The welfare loss is part of the *agency costs,* which Jensen and Meckling (1976) defined as the sum of

> The monitoring expenditures of the principal
> The bonding expenditures of the agent
> Welfare loss

Monitoring and bonding expenditures are assumed to be zero in our example. The welfare loss, *WL,* provides an upper boundary for monitoring costs.

Principal-agent problems are, in general, treated mathematically in *static* terms. Still, they are usually discussed as a sequence of actions of the principal and the agent. The model exemplified here can be interpreted by the following sequence of steps following Rasmusen (1989, 135):

> The principal (P) offers the agent (A) a contract which he accepts or rejects. After the agent accepts, he invests a certain level of effort, and nature (N) adds noise to the task being performed. It is assumed here that the agent moves before nature. The final result depends on both, the applied effort and the exogenous risk: $\tilde{Q}^n = Q(e, \tilde{\theta})$.

See figure 5.3.

The model just described is of the *moral hazard type with hidden action.* Another case of moral hazard occurs when, after the conclusion of the contract, nature moves *before* the agent and the agent conveys a "message" (in the sense of additional information) to the principal about nature's move. This is the model of the *moral hazard type with hidden information* (Rasmusen 1989). We are not dealing with this version here.[8]

### 5.3.3. Comments on the PA Approach of the Moral Hazard Type with Hidden Action

At this point, it will be useful to make some general comments on the basic principal-agent model of the moral hazard type with hidden action.

---

8. As an example of a moral hazard case with hidden information, Arrow (1985b, 39) gives the case of a decentralized socialist economy: "Because the knowledge of productivity cannot be centralized, the individual productive units have information about the possibilities of production not available to the central planning unit. The productive units may well have incentives not to reveal their full potentiality, because it will be easier to operate with less taxing requirements." See also Furubotn and Pejovich (1972b).

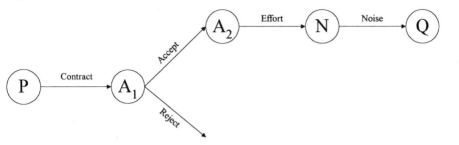

**Fig. 5.3. The moral hazard case: sequence of actions**

1. The asymmetric information assumption implies that acquiring information requires the use of resources. As a result, welfare losses due to informational constraints are generally unavoidable. The resulting agency costs may be regarded as some type of transaction cost. In this respect, the model differs from the neoclassical contingent-claims contract literature.
2. The informational constraints do not concern the future. Rather, perfect foresight is assumed in the PA approach in the sense that, as in the neoclassical contingent-claims contracting theory, all the relevant contracting issues are resolved in a comprehensive ex ante bargain. Both assume that court ordering is efficacious (Williamson 1985, 28) and can be had at zero cost. Contracts once concluded are executed as agreed upon. No problems arise that were unknown to the parties before they concluded the contract. Disappointments will not occur.
3. In the PA approach (and not only in its basic versions), the mix of informational constraints, on the one hand, and perfect information, on the other, is quite striking. The principal knows perfectly his agent's preferences and reservation utility. Both know perfectly the profit or result function with the stochastic properties of the influences of nature on the results. On the other hand, the principal is blind with respect to the effort exerted by his agent and the actual moves of nature. In this case, information costs are extremely high in one respect while they are zero in all the rest.
4. Perfect rationality on the part of both the principal and the agent is assumed. In most of the PA analyses, the principal and agent are omniscient in an important sense (as described previously).
5. Contracts are complete in the sense that, once concluded, they are (and can be) executed as agreed upon. Nothing is left open for later decisions, and no recontracting occurs.

6. "The main insight of the basic Hidden Action Model is that the optimal incentive scheme looks like one based on an inference about the agent's action from observable signals" (Hart and Holmstrom 1987, 105). This statement implies that the optimal incentive schedule, $w$, is highly sensitive to the information content of the observable signals (to the principal's knowledge about his agent's utility function, etc.). "Consequently, fiddling with the information technology will accommodate almost any form of incentive schedule and the theory is really without predictive content in this regard" (105). "The common Hidden Action Models are rather weak predictively" (106).

7. The extreme sensitivity of the incentive schedule to information variables is at odds with reality. "Real world schemes are simpler than the theory would dictate and surprisingly uniform across a wide range of circumstances. . . . The conclusion is that something other than informational issues drive whatever regularities one might observe" (Hart and Holmstrom 1987, 105). Recent empirical studies show that the link between the performance of corporations and the rewards received, directly or indirectly, by their corporate executive officers (CEOs) is extremely weak (Jensen and Murphy 1990). One answer may be that the contract terms tend to be regulated by regularities in behavior, social norms like custom or professional ethics.

Arrow (1985b, 48ff.) also argues along these lines but concludes that the limiting elements of the PA theory go beyond the usual boundaries of economic analysis: "It may ultimately be one of the greatest accomplishments of the principal-agent literature to provide some structure for the much-sought goal of integrating these elements with the impressive structure of economic analysis" (50).

### 5.4. The Principal-Agent Model: Adverse Selection

Another type of PA problem is one in which the parties are asymmetrically informed before and up to the moment of contract conclusion. Afterward, they are symmetrically informed. That is, the principal (e.g., the employer) cannot observe the subjective cost functions of each individual agent (e.g., the job applicant). But again it is assumed that he has some information, namely, which kinds of subjective cost functions exist and how the cost functions are distributed among agents. He knows the probability, $\pi_j$, that an agent has a cost function of type $j$. But the principal does not know which agent is of which type. The agents, on the other hand, know their individual cost functions before the contract is concluded.

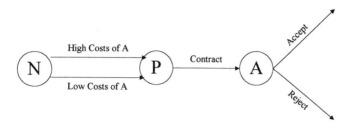

**Fig. 5.4. The adverse selection case: sequence of actions**

The adverse selection case presented here can be interpreted by the following sequence of steps (following Rasmusen (1989, 134ff.): nature (*N*) moves first and picks the agent's cost function (high or low costs), which only the agent learns. The principal (*P*) moves next and offers the agent a contract. The agent (*A*) accepts or rejects it (fig. 5.4).

We can continue with our owner-manager example, assuming that the owner now wishes to employ several managers. Yet it seems advisable to follow the usual style and use instead an employer-worker story. Now the asymmetric information problem concerns the period before the contract is concluded. Up to that point, the employer (principal) does not know the worker's subjective cost function

$$c_j(e_j). \tag{1}$$

The effort level, $e_j$, which each individual worker supplies after contract conclusion, is perfectly observable by the employer.

As for the rest, we apply the same profit or output function as before, assuming that the agents' contributions to $Q$ are *separable*. If $Q_j$ is the output of one worker of type $j$, and if there is only one worker of each type, then total output is

$$Q = \sum_j Q_j, \quad Q_j = e_j, \quad j = 1, \ldots, n, \tag{2}$$

where $n$ is the number of agents as well as (here) the number of different types. The payment or incentive schedule offered by the principal to agent $j$ is a function of the observable effort level $e_j$:

$$w_j = w_j(e_j). \tag{3}$$

The agent's utility level is, like that described previously,

$$A_j = w_j(e_j) - c_j(e_j). \tag{4}$$

As before, an agent participates only if he receives at least his reservation utility, $\overline{A}_j$, which we assume again to be zero. Again, the cost functions of the agents are of the type

$$c_j = \frac{k_j}{2} e_j^2.$$

There are two agents, $j = 1, 2$. Agent number 1 has a smaller subjective cost of effort for any given level of effort than does number 2:

$$k_1 < k_2.$$

The principal's problem is now to find the profit-maximizing payment schedules $w_1$, $w_2$.

### 5.4.1.  The Case of Symmetric Information before and after Contract Conclusion

Let us assume first that the principal knows the agents' cost functions before contract conclusion. He then would simply have to maximize his total net profit, $Q^n$, subject to the participation constraints of agents 1 and 2:

$$\max_{w_1, w_2, e_1, e_2} Q^n = e_1 + e_2 - (w_1 + w_2)$$

subject to

$$w_1 - \frac{k_1}{2} e_1^2 = 0 \qquad (PC_1)$$

$$w_2 - \frac{k_2}{2} e_2^2 = 0 \qquad (PC_2)$$

Substituting the two participation constraints into the target function of the principal, we can establish the optimization problem

$$\max_{e_1, e_2} Q^n = e_1 + e_2 - \frac{k_1}{2} e_1^2 - \frac{k_2}{2} e_2^2.$$

The first-order conditions are

$$e_1^* = \frac{1}{k_1},$$ (5)

$$e_2^* = \frac{1}{k_2}.$$ (6)

Under the assumptions of our model, the first-order conditions are sufficient for a profit maximum. The optimal payment schedules are then

$$w_1^* = \frac{1}{2k_1},$$ (7)

$$w_2^* = \frac{1}{2k_2}.$$ (8)

Because $k_1 < k_2$, the agent with the lower subjective cost of effort is offered the higher payments and will invest more effort:

$$w_1^* > w_2^*, \quad e_1^* > e_2^*.$$

This is represented graphically in figure 5.5 (after Varian 1992). Agent 1 invests effort $e_1^*$ and produces output $Q_1^* = e_1^* = 1/k_1$; agent 2 behaves similarly. Agent 1 would receive a payment $A + B$, agent 2 a payment of $A + D$. Both payments are equal to their total costs of effort. To achieve this result, the principal would simply have to set a target profit (or output) scheme for each agent ($j = 1,2$) of the same kind as that presented in subsection 5.2.1:

$$w_j(Q_j^*) = \begin{cases} c_j(e_j^*) & \text{if } e_j = e_j^*(=\frac{1}{k_j}), \text{ assuming } \overline{A}_j = 0 \\ -\infty & \text{otherwise.} \end{cases}$$

The maximum total net profit of the principal is in our example

$$Q^{n*} = \frac{1}{k_1} + \frac{1}{k_2} - \frac{1}{2k_1} - \frac{1}{2k_2} = \frac{1}{2k_1} + \frac{1}{2k_2}.$$

For $k_1 = 1, k_2 = 2$, we receive

$$e_1^* = 1, \quad e_2^* = \frac{1}{2}$$

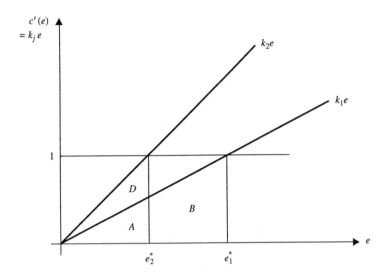

**Fig. 5.5.   Effort levels of agents in the symmetric information case**

$$w_1^* = \frac{1}{2}, \ w_2^* = \frac{1}{4}$$

$$Q^{n*} = \frac{3}{4}.$$

This is the first-best optimum of our exercise.

### 5.4.2.   Adverse Selection: Asymmetric Information until the Contract is Concluded

In the case of informational asymmetry before the contract is concluded, the principal does not know which agent belongs to which cost type. As a result, the low cost-agent, no. 1, could pretend to be high cost and produce only $e$, receiving a surplus of $D$ (fig. 5.5). In other words, in the case of adverse selection, this payment scheme tempts the agents to misrepresent their types. The scheme is not incentive compatible.

This result can be avoided if the principal restructures his payment or incentive schedules so that agent 1's utility from choosing $(w_1, e_1)$ is higher than his utility from choosing $(w_2, e_2)$ and similarly for agent 2. These are the incentive compatibility conditions that in this context are called *self-selection constraints* or *truth-telling constraints* (Varian 1992, 460).

Under the assumption that the agents will cheat only if it pays, they will tell the truth (will realize their type's effort) if they are indifferent about choosing $(w_1, e_1)$ or $(w_2, e_2)$. The incentive constraints are

$$w_1 - c_1(e_1) \geq w_2 - c_1(e_2) \quad (\text{IC}_1)$$

$$w_2 - c_2(e_2) \geq w_1 - c_2(e_1) \quad (\text{IC}_2)$$

or, for $c_j = (k_j/2)e_j^2$,

$$w_1 - \frac{k_1}{2}e_1^2 \geq w_2 - \frac{k_1}{2}e_2^2 \quad (\text{IC}_1)$$

$$w_2 - \frac{k_2}{2}e_2^2 \geq w_1 - \frac{k_2}{2}e_1^2 \quad (\text{IC}_2).$$

Unlike the moral hazard case, the agents do not act under uncertainty. Each knows his type before he enters an employment contract. Only the principal decides under uncertainty. Hitherto, we have assumed that there exists only one agent per type. From now on, however, we analyze the more general case. That is, the number of workers of type $j$ is $m_j$. The principal does not know which agent is of which type, but he knows the probability, $\pi_j$, that an agent has a cost function of type $j$ for all $j$; $\pi_j$ is equal to the number of workers of type $j$ relative to the total number, $m$, of workers:

$$\pi_j = \frac{m_j}{m}, \quad \sum_j m_j = m.$$

We assume again that the principal is risk neutral, that is, the principal maximizes his average net profit $\hat{Q}^n$. The constraints are now the two incentive constraints noted previously plus the aforementioned participation constraints. Rearranging the four inequalities somewhat, the *principal's optimization problem* can be written as follows (cf. Varian 1992, 460):

$$\max_{e_1,e_2,w_1,w_2} \hat{Q}^n = \pi_1(e_1 - w_1) + \pi_2(e_2 - w_2)$$

subject to

$$w_1 \geq \frac{k_1}{2} e_1^2 + \left( w_2 - \frac{k_1}{2} e_2^2 \right) \quad (\text{IC}_1)$$

$$w_1 \geq \frac{k_1}{2} \ e_1^2 \qquad\qquad\qquad (\text{PC}_1)$$

$$\left. \vphantom{\begin{array}{c} a \\ b \end{array}} \right\} \qquad (9)$$

$$w_2 \geq \frac{k_2}{2} e_2^2 + \left( w_1 - \frac{k_2}{2} e_1^2 \right) \quad (\text{IC}_2)$$

$$w_2 \geq \frac{k_2}{2} \ e_2^2 \qquad\qquad\qquad (\text{PC}_2).$$

$$\left. \vphantom{\begin{array}{c} a \\ b \end{array}} \right\} \qquad (10)$$

Only one equation from each of the pairs (eq. 9) and (eq. 10) has to be used in the optimization procedure. The other inequality is automatically fulfilled also. The relevant constraint will be "binding" (i.e., used as an equality) because the optimizing principal will keep his wage offer, $w_j$, as small as possible.

Taking first the constraints (eq. 9) for the agents of type 1, we conclude from (PC$_2$) and $k_1 < k_2$ that

$$w_2 - \frac{k_1}{2} e_2^2 > w_2 - \frac{k_2}{2} e_2^2 \geq 0.$$

Therefore, $(w_2 - (k_1/2)e_2^2)$ in (IC$_1$) is positive and (IC$_1$) is the relevant constraint, and it will be used as "binding" by the profit-maximizing principal

$$w_1 = \frac{k_1}{2} e_1^2 + (w_2 - \frac{k_1}{2} e_2^2). \quad (\text{IC}_1). \qquad (11)$$

Similarly, only one of the constraints (10) will be binding. As for (IC$_2$) and the fact that (IC$_1$) binds, substitution of (11) in (IC$_2$) leads to the expression

$$\frac{k_2}{2} e_1^2 - \frac{k_2}{2} e_2^2 \geq \frac{k_1}{2} e_1^2 - \frac{k_1}{2} e_2^2.$$

Whenever $e_1^2 > e_2^2$, this is a strict inequality because of $k_2 > k_1$. Therefore, (IC$_2$) does not bind in this case. Only (PC$_2$) is binding, that is,

$$w_2 = \frac{k_2}{2} e_2^2 \quad (\text{PC}_2). \qquad (12)$$

The optimization problem of the principal, using our special subjective cost functions, becomes

$$\max_{e_1, e_2, w_1, w_2} \hat{Q}^n = \pi_1(e_1 - w_1) + \pi_2(e_2 - w_2)$$

subject to

$$w_1 - \frac{k_1}{2}e_1^2 = w_2 - \frac{k_1}{2}e_2^2 \quad (\text{IC}_1)$$

$$w_2 - \frac{k_2}{2}e_2^2 = 0 \quad\quad\quad (\text{PC}_2)$$

$$e_1^2 > e_2^2.$$

Substituting (11) and (12) into the target function, the optimization problem reduces to

$$\max_{e_1, e_2} \hat{Q}^n = \pi_1\left(e_1 - \frac{k_1}{2}e_1^2 - \frac{k_2 - k_1}{2}e_2^2\right) + \pi_2\left(e_2 - \frac{k_2}{2}e_2^2\right)$$

$$e_1^2 > e_2^2.$$

Let us ignore the remaining inequality and solve the unrestricted optimization problem. Later, we will verify that the solution of the unrestricted problem automatically satisfies the ignored inequality $(e_1^2 > e_2^2)$. Therefore, the solution thus obtained is also the solution of the restricted problem.

The first-order conditions for the unrestricted optimization problem are

$$\pi_1(1 - k_1 e_1) = 0$$

$$\pi_1[(k_1 - k_2)e_2] + \pi_2 [1 - k_2 e_2] = 0$$

or

$$e_1^{**} = \frac{1}{k_1}(=e_1^*), \tag{13}$$

$$e_2^{**} = \frac{1}{k_2 + \frac{\pi_1}{\pi_2}(k_2 - k_1)} \left(< \frac{1}{k_2} = e_2^*\right). \tag{14}$$

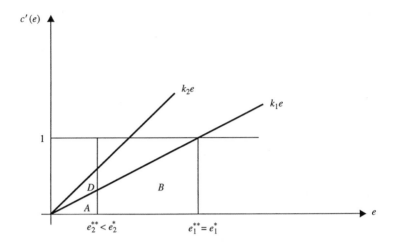

**Fig. 5.6.    Effort levels of agents in the asymmetric information case**

It is easy to verify that $e_1^{**2} > e_2^{**2}$ holds. This is graphically represented in figure 5.6.

Next we determine the optimal wage offers. As for $w_1^{**}$, substitute (12) in (11) to secure

$$w_1 - \frac{k_1}{2}e_1^2 = \frac{k_2}{2}e_2^2 - \frac{k_1}{2}e_2^2 \tag{15}$$

and (13) and (14) in (15) to secure

$$w_1^{**} = \frac{1}{2k_1} + \frac{k_2 - k_1}{2\left[k_2 + \frac{\pi_1}{\pi_2}(k_2 - k_1)\right]^2}\left(> w_1^* = \frac{1}{2k_1}\right). \tag{16}$$

The low-cost agent, no. 1, now receives an "information rent" in addition to his costs (in fig. 5.6, the area $D$ in addition to the area $A + B$). The surplus is just big enough to make it uninteresting for him to pretend to be the high-cost agent, no. 2.

As for $w_2^{**}$, we see that high-cost agent no. 2 receives just his costs (in fig. 5.6 the area $A + D$), that is,

$$w_2^{**} = \frac{k_2}{2}\left(\frac{1}{\left[k_2 + \frac{\pi_1}{\pi_2}(k_2 - k_1)\right]^2}\right)\left(< w_2^* = \frac{1}{2k_2}\right). \tag{17}$$

*Numerical Example.* For $k_1 = 1$, $k_2 = 2$, and $\pi_1 = \pi_2 = 1/2$ we obtain:

$$e_1^{**} = 1 \quad (= \text{first-best optimum } e_1^*) \tag{18}$$

$$e_2^{**} = \frac{1}{3} < \frac{1}{2} \quad (\text{less than first-best optimum } e_2^*) \tag{19}$$

$$w_1^{**} = \frac{1}{2} + \frac{1}{18} > w_1^* = \frac{1}{2} \tag{20}$$

(the low-cost agent's rent amounts to 1/18)

$$w_2^{**} = \frac{1}{9} < w_2^* = \frac{1}{4}. \tag{21}$$

The average profit of the principal is now

$$\hat{Q}^{n**} = \pi_1(e_1^{**} - w_1^{**}) - \pi_2(e_2^{**} - w_2^{**})$$

or

$$\hat{Q}^{n**} = \frac{1}{3}. \tag{22}$$

Note that to compare the average profit $\hat{Q}^{n**}$ with the total profit $Q^{n*}$ we have to recognize that

$$\hat{Q}^{n**} = \frac{Q^{n**}}{2}$$

or

$$2\hat{Q}^{n**} = Q^{n**} = \frac{2}{3} < Q^{n*}\left(=\frac{3}{4}\right).$$

This is a second-best result. The welfare loss of the principal is due to the inefficiency of the high-cost worker ($e_2^{**} < e_2^*$) and the information rent paid to the low-cost worker ($w_1^{**} > w_1^*$). It amounts in this case to

$$WLP = \frac{3}{4} - \frac{2}{3} = \frac{1}{12}.$$

To calculate the community's welfare loss ($WL$), we have to subtract the welfare gain of no. 1, his rent of $1/18$:

$$WL = \frac{1}{12} - \frac{1}{18} = \frac{1}{36}.$$

### 5.4.3. Adverse Selection: Two Generalizations

We assume next that the agents have different utility functions (different marginal costs $k_j$) *and* different marginal productivities, $v_j$. Their productive contributions per agent (worker) are represented by

$$Q_j = v_j e_j; \qquad j = 1, 2.$$

Suppose that $v_1 > v_2$ and $k_1 < k_2$. Furthermore, let us *first* continue to assume that the reservation utilities $\overline{A}_j$ are both equal to zero. Then the *principal's optimization problem* becomes

$$\max_{e_1, e_2, w_1, w_2} \hat{Q}^n = \pi_1(v_1 e_1 - w_1) + \pi_2(v_2 e_2 - w_2)$$

*s.t.* equations (11) and (12) and $e_1^2 > e_2^2$

or

$$\max_{e_1, e_2} \hat{Q}^n = \pi_1\left(v_1 e_1 - \frac{k_1}{2} e_1^2 - \frac{k_2 - k_1}{2} e_2^2\right) + \pi_2\left(v_2 e_2 - \frac{k_2}{2} e_2^2\right) \qquad (23)$$

*s.t.* $e_1^2 > e_2^2$.

The first-order conditions of the unrestricted maximization problem are now

$$\pi_1(v_1 - k_1 e_1) = 0$$

$$\pi_1[(k_1 - k_2)e_2] + \pi_2[v_2 - k_2 e_2] = 0$$

or

$$e_1^{**} = \frac{v_1}{k_1} \qquad (24)$$

$$e_2^{**} = \frac{v_2}{k_2 - \frac{\pi_1}{\pi_2}(k_1 - k_2)}. \tag{25}$$

Note that $e_1^{**}$, $e_2^{**}$ satisfy the ignored inequality.
The optimal wage offers are

$$w_1^{**} = \frac{v_1^2}{2k_1} + \frac{(k_2 - k_1)v_2^2}{2\left[k_2 - \frac{\pi_1}{\pi_2}(k_2 - k_1)\right]^2} \tag{26}$$

$$w_2^{**} = \frac{k_2 v_2^2}{2\left[k_2 + \frac{\pi_1}{\pi_2}(k_2 - k_1)\right]^2}. \tag{27}$$

In the present case, with different marginal costs and marginal productivities, the first-best results can easily be calculated as follows:

$$e_1^* = \frac{v_1}{k_1}, \quad e_2^* = \frac{v_2}{k_2}$$

$$w_1^* = \frac{v_1^2}{2k_1}, \quad w_2^* = \frac{v_2^2}{2k_2}.$$

*Numerical example.* For $k_1 = 1$, $k_2 = 2$, $v_1 = 2$, $v_2 = 1$, and $\pi_1 = \pi_2 = 1/2$, we obtain:

$$e_1^* = 2, \quad e_2^* = \frac{1}{2}; \quad w_1^* = 2, \quad w_2^* = \frac{1}{4};$$

$$e_1^{**} = 2, \quad e_2^{**} = \frac{1}{3}; \quad w_1^{**} = 2 + \frac{1}{18}, \quad w_2^{**} = \frac{1}{9}.$$

From the first-order conditions (24) and (25), one can easily see that, in the case of equal marginal costs ($k_1 = k_2$), the first-best solution is incentive compatible if we assume, as before, reservation utilities $\overline{A}_1 = \overline{A}_2 = 0$. Cheating does not pay. Agents (workers) will tell the truth by assumption (see fig. 5.7).

So far, it does not pay for the high-cost agent to pretend to be the low-cost one. The opposite may be the case, though, if we generalize further and include cases of different individual reservation utilities $\overline{A}_j$. The *principal's optimization problem* is then, in extenso,

$$\max_{e_1,e_2,w_1,w_2} \hat{Q}^n = \pi_1(v_1 e_1 - w_1) + \pi_2(v_2 e_2 - w_2)$$

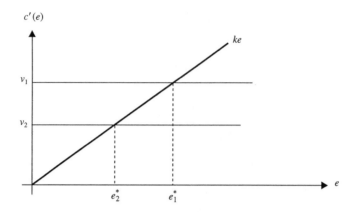

**Fig. 5.7. Effort levels of agents in the symmetric information case with different marginal productivities $v_j$ and equal marginal costs $k_j$**

subject to

$$\left. \begin{array}{ll} w_1 - \dfrac{k_1}{2}e_1^2 \geq w_2 - \dfrac{k_1}{2}e_2^2 & (\text{IC}_1) \\[2em] w_1 - \dfrac{k_1}{2}e_1^2 \geq \overline{A}_1 & (\text{PC}_1) \end{array} \right\} \tag{28}$$

$$\left. \begin{array}{ll} w_2 - \dfrac{k_2}{2}e_2^2 \geq w_1 - \dfrac{k_2}{2}e_1^2 & (\text{IC}_2) \\[2em] w_2 - \dfrac{k_2}{2}e_2^2 \geq \overline{A}_2 & (\text{PC}_2). \end{array} \right\} \tag{29}$$

The first-best solutions are in this case

$$\begin{aligned} e_1^* &= \frac{v_1}{k_1} \\[1.5em] w_1^* &= \overline{A}_1 + \frac{v_1^2}{2k_1} \end{aligned} \tag{30}$$

$$e_2^* = \frac{v_2}{k_2}$$

(31)

$$w_2^* = \overline{A}_2 + \frac{v_2^2}{2k_2}$$

CASE 1

Agent 1 will cheat if he achieves a higher utility level pretending to be agent 2. That is, if for (30) and (31) the incentive constraint ($IC_1$) is *not* fulfilled (the contract pair $(e_1^*, w_1^*)$, $(e_2^*, w_2^*)$ is not incentive compatible), then

$$w_1^* - \frac{k_1}{2} e_1^{*2} < w_2^* - \frac{k_1}{2} e_2^{*2}$$

or

$$\frac{(k_2 - k_1)v_2^2}{2k_2^2} > \overline{A}_1 - \overline{A}_2.$$

(32)

CASE 2

Agent 2 will cheat if it pays to cheat. That is, if for (30), (31)

$$w_2^* - \frac{k_2}{2} e_2^{*2} < w_1^* - \frac{k_2}{2} e_1^{*2}$$

or

$$\frac{(k_2 - k_1)v_1^2}{2k_1^2} < \overline{A}_1 - \overline{A}_2.$$

(33)

If $k_1 < k_2$ and $\overline{A}_1 > \overline{A}_2$, it may be advantageous for the high-cost agent to assert that he is the low-cost one.

### 5.4.4. Many Principals: Market Screening

We now turn the optimization problem on its head and assume that the principal (the representative firm under perfect competition) has a given reservation utility. The principal's net profits are assumed to be zero. At the same time, the agents maximize their utilities given the zero-net-profit constraint.

We continue to assume two types of workers ($j = 1, 2$). Each firm (principal) competes for workers. Each worker will choose the most attractive offer

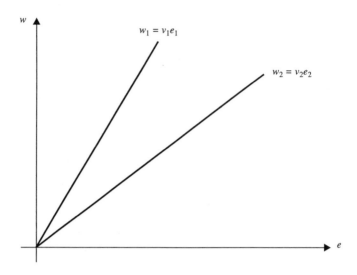

**Fig. 5.8. The zero-profit lines**

$(w, e)$, the one that maximizes his utility. In a competitive equilibrium, the net profits of the representative firm per type of worker will equal zero:

$$\hat{Q}_1^n = v_1 e_1 - w_1 = 0$$

$$\hat{Q}_2^n = v_2 e_2 - w_2 = 0$$

or

$$w_1 = v_1 e_1 \tag{34}$$

$$w_2 = v_2 e_2. \tag{35}$$

Equations 34 and 35 are represented for $v_1 > v_2$ in figure 5.8. Note that positive profits of the firm per type of worker $j$ are represented by points below the respective isoprofit line.

The utility functions are again

$$A_1 = w_1 - \frac{k_1}{2} e_1^2 \tag{36}$$

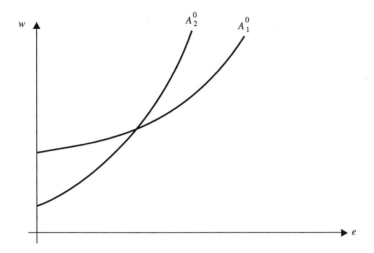

**Fig. 5.9.** **The indifference curves of individual workers intersect at only one point**

$$A_2 = w_2 - \frac{k_2}{2} e_2^2 \qquad (37)$$

We can now construct indifference maps of the individual workers that show the ranking of their preferences between wages paid and effort levels. Each indifference curve shows various combinations of wage and effort levels that yield the same level of satisfaction (utility) to the individual worker. The indifference curves are upward, open parabolas. The indifference curves of the more able (more productive) worker no. 1 are flatter than those of the less able worker no. 2 (since $k_1 < k_2$). Therefore, if we graph the indifference curves in the same diagram, any two indifference curves $A_1^0$, $A_2^0$ of the two workers will intersect, but only once (fig. 5.9). This is known as the *single-crossing property*.

We continue to assume that there is one agent of each type. In the case of full information, the equilibrium $(w, e)$ combinations can be determined by the following optimization programs

For type 1:

$$\max_{w_1, e_1} A_1 = w_1 - \frac{k_1}{2} e_1^2$$

$$s.t. \quad w_1 = v_1 e_1,$$

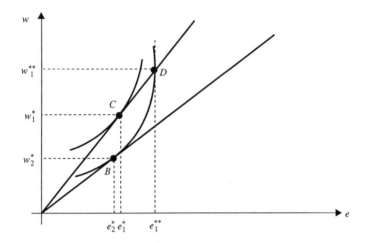

**Fig. 5.10.   The separation equilibrium BD implies a second-best outcome**

for type 2:

$$\max_{w_2, e_2} A_2 = w_2 - \frac{k_2}{2} e_2^2$$

$s.t.\quad w_2 = v_2 e_2.$

The constraints $w_j = v_j e_j$ represent the *wage schedules* for each type of worker. The first-order conditions are as follows.

For type 1:

$$e_1^* = \frac{v_1}{k_1}, \quad w_1^* = \frac{v_1^2}{k_1},$$

for type 2:

$$e_2^* = \frac{v_2}{k_2}, \quad w_2^* = \frac{v_2^2}{k_2}.$$

They are represented by points $C$, $B$ in figure 5.10.

In the case of full information, firms would offer the contracts $B$ and $C$. The low-ability worker, no. 2, would choose contract $B$, the high-ability worker contract $C$. But $B$ and $C$ are only equilibrium points as long as we assume that

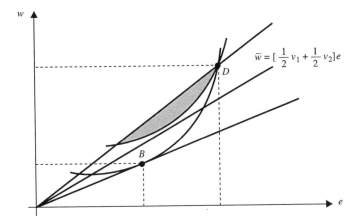

**Fig. 5.11. If a separation equilibrium exists it is uniquely characterized by BD**

workers' abilities and costs (their $v_j$, $k_j$) are *observable*. As soon as this is no longer the case, firms will experience adverse selection. Specifically, the less able workers will prefer the contract targeted for the high-ability workers. They will find it worthwhile to apply for the better-paid job (in which they have to invest more effort while their productivity or ability remains at the low level). In other words, the full information pair of equilibrium contracts $B$, $C$ does not satisfy the self-selection constraints. Firms would incur losses if they were to offer these contracts under asymmetric information; they would experience adverse selection.

Firms could solve this adverse selection problem by offering the contract pair $B$, $D$. Both contracts lie on the indifference curve of the low-ability worker, who is, therefore, indifferent between his contract and that of the high-ability worker. The low-ability worker remains on his first-best utility level (point $B$), the high-ability worker's utility level is now somewhat lower than his first-best (point $D$). The price of asymmetric information is again some welfare loss. The separation equilibrium $BD$ is a second-best equilibrium.

Furthermore, if a separating equilibrium exists, it is uniquely characterized by $BD$. To see this, consider figures 5.11 and 5.12.

1. Even though there is an area that is preferred by both, the firms and the high-ability workers (the shaded region in fig. 5.11), no contracts are offered in this region because they would also attract the low-ability workers.

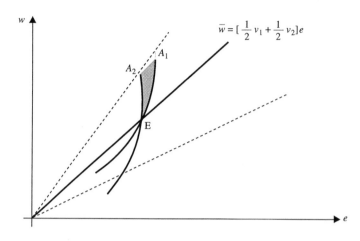

**Fig. 5.12.  No pooling equilibrium exists**

2. A pooling equilibrium, if it were to exist, would lie on the zero-profit line $\overline{w}$. All workers would get the same wage, $\overline{w}$, which in our example, with an equal number of worker types, is

$$\overline{w} = \left( \frac{1}{2}v_1 + \frac{1}{2}v_2 \right) e.$$

A pooling equilibrium would be a point (e.g., point $E$) on the zero-profit line $\overline{w}$. Because of the single-crossing property of the indifference curves of type 1 and type 2, two indifference curves intersect in $E$. Since the less-productive workers have steeper indifference curves, it is possible for a deviant firm to offer a contract in the shaded area that attracts only highly productive workers and therefore results in a positive profit (Varian 1992, 467). This construction can be carried out at any point on the zero-profit line $\overline{w}$. Consequently, there is always a profitable alternative to the pooling contract, which is equivalent to saying that no pooling *equilibrium* exists.

It can also be the case, however, that no separating equilibrium exists. Assume that the proportion of high productivity workers is very large and that therefore the $\overline{w}$ line of figure 5.11 is much steeper and intersects the shaded area. It would now be profitable for the firms to offer a pooled contract. Hence, the proposed separating equilibrium would be broken. But, since pooling cannot be an equilibrium (fig. 5.12), no equilibrium would exist. Thus, unless the proportion of high productivity workers is sufficiently small, no separating equilibrium exists. This was first shown by Rothschild and Stiglitz (1976) whose presentation we were following here in the simplified interpretation of Varian (1992).

*Summing Up So Far*
It is assumed in the underlying story that even under perfect competition firms behave as option fixers. In other words, they determine a set of contracts that workers can either accept or reject. Knowing that they will end up on their zero-profit lines, and knowing also the $v_j$, $k_j$, but being uninformed about which worker is of which type, they offer a pair of contracts $BD$. With such a self-selection device, workers are forced to reveal truthful information about themselves by means of their market behavior. As a result, there exists either one separating equilibrium or none. A pooling contract is incompatible with equilibrium.

The model under consideration can also be interpreted differently by understanding $e_j$ as educational level of agent $j$ and

$$c_j(e) = \frac{k_j}{2} e^2$$

as an education-costs function. Education causes higher costs (e.g., time) for the less able (less productive) worker no. 2 than for the more productive worker no. 1: $k_1 < k_2$. If this is the case, the educational level can be understood as a *signal* of each worker's ability (productivity).[9] The signal (education) is easier to acquire by the more productive workers than by the less productive workers. In our example, firms offer a menu of two contracts $(w_j, e_j)$. Then workers consider this menu, sign the contract they like best, and go off to school. No ex post surprises occur. Workers acquire the promised educational level, $e$ (e.g., measured by the number of years at school), and then join their firms as active employees. Keeping their part of the bargain, firms pay the promised wages, $w$ (Kreps 1990b, 638; look there for comments). Note that in this model education has no effect on productivity. Education costs may be considered as a substitute for information costs. Education's only role is to enable firms to distinguish more productive from less productive workers.

In another theory, proposed by Spence (1974), it is assumed that both parties are price takers. The workers move first, and "with no guarantees except that they expect the market mechanism to work when the time comes, workers choose how many years to go to school. They do so anticipating some wage

9. See in this connection Spence's (1973, 357) definition of the term *signal:* a signal is an observable attribute of an individual (or good, title, etc.) that is alterable. For example, education is a signal in this sense, while age is not. Spence calls the latter type indices. Observable attributes may be used as screening devices.

function $w(e)$ that gives wages for every level of education. After they spend their time in school, they present themselves to a competitive labor market, and the firms in that market bid for their services" (Kreps 1990b, 632). In this case, many signaling equilibria are possible.[10] The somewhat disturbing difference of the results arises from the different notions of equilibrium. We will not present the Spence model since it suffices for our purpose to give one example of a self-selection mechanism (for a more complete description, see Kreps 1990b, chap. 7).

Finally, some remarks on terminology. The terms *signaling, self-selection,* and *screening* are used confusingly in the literature. Spence (1974, 14) speaks of "education as a signal," while for Stiglitz (1975, 285) "one of the functions of education is to screen individuals."

We are following Kreps (1990b, 651): "If the informed side takes the active role as in Spence's analysis, this is known as *market signaling.* If the side without information proposes a menu of contracts among which the informed side selects, this is conventionally called *market screening*" (italics in the original).

### 5.4.5. The Lemons Principle

The adverse selection problem suggested by the phrase "the lemons principle" underlies a famous article by Akerlof (1970). His example is the used car market on which "good" and "bad" used cars or, as the Americans say, "peaches" and "lemons," are traded. There is again information asymmetry. Characteristically, the sellers have more knowledge about the quality of the cars they are selling than do the buyers. But, since the buyers cannot tell the difference, both good and bad cars must sell at the same price. Under the given circumstances, Akerlof argues, Gresham's law makes a modified reappearance.

For most cars traded will be the "lemons," and good cars may not be traded at all. The "bad" cars tend to drive out the good. (Akerlof 1970, 489).[11]

---

10. In the context of signaling games, one is often confronted with the problem that a plethora of Nash equilibria exists. These equilibria are in general characterized by different amounts of signaling activities and thus by different degrees of inefficiency. This, in turn, leads us to a critical remark concerning a measure of transaction costs, if defined as the difference between social welfare with and without any information asymmetries. Thus, whenever there are multiple equilibria, there is no unique measure of this kind of transaction cost. For further consequences, see Hellwig 1988b, 200.

11. The analogy with Gresham's law is not quite complete: "Bad cars drive out the good because they sell at the same price as good cars; similarly, bad money drives out good because the

Even though Akerlof did not develop a contract-theoretic model, we will deal briefly here with his theory because of its general interest and importance.

Akerlof argues that, under certain conditions, it is possible for trade in used cars to collapse completely. Assume that the demand for used automobiles, $D$, depends on the price of the automobile, $p$, and on the average quality of the used cars traded, $\mu$:

$$D = D(p, \mu),$$

with first partial derivatives $D_1 < 0$, $D_2 > 0$. The average quality is positively related to the price:

$$\mu = \mu(p), \quad \mu' > 0.$$

As the price falls, the quality of the cars traded will also fall. The supply of used cars, $S$, depends on price alone:

$$S = S(p), \quad S' > 0.$$

In equilibrium, supply must equal demand:

$$S(p) = D(p, \mu(p)).$$

Because of $\mu(p)$, the demand curve may rise and then fall again with $p$ (see fig. 5.13). Under certain conditions, there may be no intersection between the supply and the demand curve.

To get the slope of the demand curve $D(p, \mu(p))$, compute

$$\frac{dD}{dp} = \frac{\partial D}{\partial p} + \frac{\partial D}{\partial \mu} \frac{d\mu}{dp}.$$
$$(-) + (+)(+)$$

If the second term is large enough relative to the first term, the demand curve may have a positive slope.

---

exchange rate is even. But the bad cars sell at the same price as good cars since it is impossible for a buyer to tell the difference between a good car and a bad car; only the seller knows. In Gresham's law, however, presumably both buyer and seller can tell the difference between good and bad money. So the analogy is instructive, but not complete" (Akerlof 1970, 490).

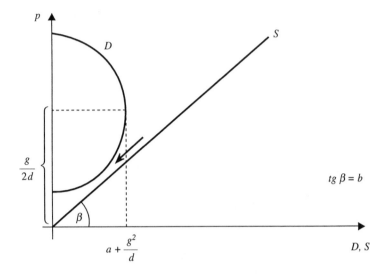

**Fig. 5.13. Supply is greater than demand for any price _p_**

To illustrate the general observations just noted, we make the following special assumptions. The supply function is

$$S = bp, \quad b > 0.$$

The demand function is

$$D = a + \mu - dp^2; \quad a, d > 0$$

$$\mu = gp; \quad g > 0.$$

Substituting the $\mu$-equation into the demand function $D = a + \mu - dp^2$, we obtain

$$D = a + gp - dp^2.$$

The demand curve is a parabola. For a low $p(p < g/2d)$, the slope of the demand curve is positive, but for larger $p$s it is negative.

The graphical representations of the demand and supply functions may then look like those shown in fig. 5.13. Supply is always greater than demand. Consequently, price will drop to zero and the used car market will collapse.

Akerlof (1970) gives various examples for such extreme cases of adverse selection.

*Insurance.* "It is a well-known fact that people over 65 years have great difficulty in buying medical insurance. The natural question arises: why doesn't the price rise to match the risk? Our answer is that as the price level rises the people who insure themselves will be those who are increasingly certain that they will need the insurance. . . . The result is that the average medical condition of insurance applicants deteriorates as the price level rises— with the result that no insurance sales may take place at any price" (Akerlof 1970, 492). Akerlof argues that this adds one major argument in favor of medicare: "On a cost-benefit basis medicare may pay off: for it is quite possible that every individual in the market could be willing to pay the expected cost of his medicare and buy insurance, yet no insurance company can afford to sell him a policy—for at any price it will attract too many 'lemons.' The welfare economics of medicare, in this view, is *exactly* analogous to the usual class-room argument for public expenditure on roads" (494).

*The employment of minorities.* "The Lemons Principle also casts light on the employment of minorities. Employers may refuse to hire members of minority groups for certain types of jobs. This decision may not reflect irra-tionality or prejudice—but profit maximization. For race may serve as a good *statistic* for the applicant's social background, quality or schooling, and general job capabilities" (Akerlof 1970, 494). Good quality schooling could serve as a substitute for this statistic. But the certifying establishment must be credible.

> The unreliability of slum schools decreases the economic possibilities of their students. . . . This lack may be particularly disadvantageous to members of already disadvantaged minority groups. For an employer may make a rational decision not to hire any members of these groups in responsible positions—because it is difficult to distinguish those with good job qualifications from those with bad qualifications. (494–95)

*Credit markets in underdeveloped countries.* As one example of the oper-ation of the lemons principle, Akerlof mentions the extortionate rate that local moneylenders charge their clients in underdeveloped countries such as India (1970, 498).

The welfare loss due to asymmetric information may be regarded as the *cost of dishonesty.* Akerlof (1970, 495) writes: "The presence of people in the market who are willing to offer inferior goods tends to drive the market out of existence—as in the case of our automobile 'lemons.' It is this possibility that represents the major cost of dishonesty—for dishonest dealings tend to drive honest dealings out of the market. . . . The cost of dishonesty, there-fore, lies not only in the amount by which the purchaser is cheated; the cost also must include the loss incurred from driving legitimate business out of existence. Dishonesty in business is a serious problem in underdeveloped countries."

## Counteracting Institutions

Dishonesty is unquestionably costly, and, as Arrow (1974, 23) puts it:

> Trust is an important lubricant of a social system. It is extremely efficient; it saves a lot of trouble to have a fair degree of reliance on other people's word.

Trust, though, cannot be bought over the counter. It can be achieved only in a roundabout way with the help of institutions such as guarantees, reputation ("brand-name capital"), diplomas or licenses given by someone who is known to be trustworthy, and so on. The establishment and cultivation of such institutional arrangements, of course, costs resources (and time), but it is the level of these costs that *signals* to the buyer that the seller offers a good product (that his promises are *credible*). In other words, the quality of the signal depends on the resources invested in it. Consider the following illustrations:

> "Offering a *warranty* is a costly activity for the seller of lemons, but not very costly for the seller of good cars. Hence, this signal allows the buyers to discriminate between the two types of cars" (Varian 1992, 469). Provided it is sufficiently costly, the seller of the good product can afford to apply the signal "guarantee," while the seller of bad ones cannot.

> Investment in *brand-name capital* through, for example, advertising expenditures, requires considerable resources, and these are "sunk." Nevertheless, they serve as an indicator for the buyer of the quality level of the product and act in a sense as "hostages" in the hands of the firm's customers. In this sense, one may say: "Advertising . . . supplies valuable information for the consumer—namely that the firm is advertising" (Klein and Leffler 1981, 630).

> *Educational diplomas* or certificates signal to the employer the quality level of the prospective employee (Spence 1974, 14). Productivity on the job is positively correlated with performance in school. Therefore, the higher-productivity worker has, on average, a lower personal cost of obtaining a given set of educational credentials. Since the more productive employee can earn more than the less productive, the more productive individual has an incentive to invest in education as a "signal."

These cases relate to rather obvious, real-world examples. Of interest to the economist is that signaling involves the use of resources and prompts the not quite obvious question: what is the optimal level of investment in signaling, from the viewpoint of both the buyer and the seller?

### 5.4.6. Some Comments on the Principal-Agent Approach with Adverse Selection

In summary, the following points can be made.

1. In both the moral hazard and adverse selection cases, the PA approach incorporates *incentives* explicitly into economic analysis. The idea is to induce self-seeking agents operating with asymmetric information to behave with greater efficiency by employing suitable incentives that are built into contractual arrangements ex ante. In this way, individuals acting in their own interest do things that are, if only in a second-best sense, also in the interest of the principal. In the moral hazard case, the incentives consist of some kind of risk-sharing scheme (sharing of risky results), while in the adverse selection case, incentives are used to ensure that honesty is the agents' best policy. Cheating becomes too expensive. That is how the self-selection or truth-telling constraints operated in the cases considered earlier. Still, welfare losses are the unavoidable consequence in situations in which asymmetric information is present.
2. The principal's blind spot is again quite limited. There is only one hidden characteristic. In our examples, the principal does not know which agent is of which type. Otherwise, he knows everything, including such private things as his prospective agents' utility functions. The problem of unforeseeable events is left aside. As a result, we get the usual neoclassical equilibria, provided any exist. That is, we get states in which individual expectations are perfectly fulfilled, and, after the music stops, nobody experiences surprises. Individual plans, and thus contracts between individuals, do not have to be changed during the period of their execution.
3. Perfect rationality of the principal and agents, perfect foresight, and complete contracts enforceable by courts at no cost are assumed throughout the PA analysis.

### 5.5. Implicit Contracts

Implicit contract theory deals, inter alia, with the phenomenon of sticky wages. It suggests that these may be the outcome of jointly optimizing behavior of employers and employees under conditions where opportunities to shed risk are limited for employees (as opposed to employers). Such conditions arise because of the impossibility (or the difficulties) of diversifying the main part of their capital stock: human capital. It is here that transaction costs enter the picture by creating imperfections in the market for contingent claims.

While owners of firms are able to diversify their portfolios, workers, who do not own much more than themselves, cannot do so because of the existence of market imperfections. "This difference suggests that there may be gains from trade," between firm owners and workers (Taylor 1987, 126). "By agreeing to accept some of the risk of wage variation, employers implicitly offer an insurance service to workers. This is attractive to workers because of their risk aversion, and is relatively costless to the firm because of risk neutrality" (127). Risk-reducing policies are thus a profitable way to attract workers. Therefore, "the theory of implicit labor contracts models the labor market not as a spot auction but as one where employers and workers enter into mutually advantageous, unwritten, long-term contracts" (126).

A growing literature has developed in this field. It began with articles by Bailey (1974), Gordon (1974) and Azariadis (1975), which were written under the assumption of *symmetric information*.[12] Issues of asymmetric information were added later with the growth of the PA approach in the 1980's. In this section we limit ourselves to the simpler case of symmetric information. We shall illustrate implicit contract theory by assuming, as in Section 5.2, two decision units. Specifically, we consider a firm and a worker. Production is again affected by exogenous shocks, $\tilde{\theta}$, which now, unlike the case in section 5.2, influence the marginal productivity of labor. For that purpose, we define the firm's production function as

$$y = f(n), \quad f' > 0, \quad f'' < 0,$$

with $n$ designating hours of work. The random variable $\tilde{\theta}$ has the mean value 1. Both, the firm and the worker, observe the realization of $\tilde{\theta}$ at any period and know the number of hours actually worked. In other words, information is symmetric. In a particular state of nature, $\theta$, the (real) profit of the firm is defined as

$$Q^n = \theta f(n) - wn,$$

where $w$ denotes the wage rate in real terms.

---

12. Hart and Holmstrom (1987, 106) speak, therefore, of the Azariadis-Bailey-Gordon (ABG) model.

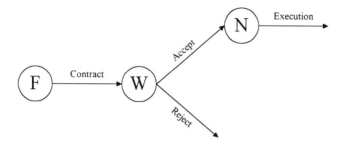

**Fig. 5.14. Implicit contract theory: sequence of actions**

First, we ask what the equilibrium wage would be if the labor market were organized like an impersonal *competitive spot market*. In this case, the firm maximizes $Q^n$, given $w$, while the worker in our simplified example supplies a fixed amount of labor, $n$. The labor demand equation is for a particular state of nature, $\theta$:

$$\theta f'(n) = w.$$

For a fixed labor supply, $n$, this equation determines also the equilibrium wage of the competitive spot labor market. It varies with the realization of the state of nature, $\tilde{\theta}$. An increase/decrease in $\theta$ will increase/decrease wages. In other words a particular equilibrium wage level, $w^0$, of the competitive spot market is also a function of a particular state of nature, $\theta$: $w^0(\theta)$.

We next ask, assuming again a fixed labor supply, $n$, what wages would be if the labor market were organized like a *contract market,* where the latter is understood as a bilateral monopoly with the firm dominating the worker. By assumption, the firm ($F$) moves first by offering a labor contract consisting of a set of wages for each $\theta$. That is, in the case being considered here, the employment level, $n$, remains constant and the wage is contingent on each state of nature: $w(\theta)$. For simplicity, we use the normalization $n = 1$. The worker ($W$) accepts or rejects. After that, nature ($N$) moves and production occurs. If the worker accepts (on date 1), the contract is executed as agreed upon (on date 2) (fig. 5.14). The relationship is long term in the sense that it lasts for two periods.

In this case, the individual's attitude toward risk plays a role. The firm is again assumed to be risk neutral and the worker to be risk averse. As before, we express risk aversion by use of a concave von Neumann-Morgenstern utility function $u(w(\theta))$:

$$u = u(w(\theta)), \quad u' > 0, \quad u'' < 0.$$

Note that in our present example $n = 1$. Thus, utility can only vary with real wages, $w$.

The firm offers a set of wages for each state, $\theta$, $w(\theta)$, that maximizes its expected profits

$$E(\tilde{Q}^n) = f(1) - E(w(\tilde{\theta}))$$

(since $E\tilde{\theta} = 1$). The worker accepts if he gets at least his reservation utility $\overline{C}$, which, under the given assumption, is equal to the expected utility of the "spot market lottery" $w^0(\tilde{\theta})$, $Eu(w^0(\tilde{\theta}))$. If the agent is risk averse, there always exists a $C^0$ such that the worker is indifferent between the deterministic return, $C^0$, his certainty equivalent, and the lottery $w^0(\tilde{\theta})$: $u(C^0) = Eu(w^0(\tilde{\theta})) = \overline{C}$. Since the worker is assumed to be risk averse, $C^0 < Ew^0(\tilde{\theta})$ holds. The expected value of the worker's von Neumann-Morgenstern utility would therefore have to fulfill the participation constraint (PC):

$$E(u(w^0(\tilde{\theta}))) \geq \overline{C} \text{ (PC)}$$

The profit-maximizing firm knows the worker's utility function and his reservation utility $\overline{C}$. It offers, therefore, a contingent labor contract, $w(\theta)$, for each $\theta$, such that (PC) is just fulfilled. Thus, the *firm's complete decision problem* is to maximize its expected profits subject to the binding worker's participation constraint, with respect to a set of contingent wage offers $w(\theta)$. In other words, the optimal contract is defined as the set of values of real wages, $w$, for each $\theta$, that fulfills:

$$\max_{w(\cdot)} E(\tilde{Q}^n) = f(1) - E(w(\tilde{\theta}))$$
$$s.t. \quad Eu(w(\tilde{\theta})) - \overline{C} = 0$$

or

$$\max_{w} f(1) - E(w(\tilde{\theta})) + \lambda \, [E(u(w(\tilde{\theta})) - \overline{C}], \quad \lambda > 0.$$

Maximization w.r.t. $w$ in each state $\theta$ (pointwise maximization) leads to the following first-order condition for each state $\theta$:

$$-1 + \lambda u'(w(\theta)) = 0$$

or

$$u^*(w(\theta)) = \frac{1}{\lambda} = \text{const. for each } \theta.$$

This implies that the risk-neutral firm offers a set of wages for which the worker's marginal utility is constant or, under our special conditions, real wages $w$ offered by the firm are equal across states of nature. The quantity produced, though, still fluctuates with $\theta$ because of $y = \theta f(n)$, $n$ = const.

Compared with the spot market model, we see "that the pattern of output is exactly the same as it would be if there were a competitive spot labor market, while the real wage" would in our example remain constant (Blanchard and Fischer 1989, 431).

Now, the certainty equivalent, $C$, of a particular set of real wages, $w^0(\tilde{\theta})$, is some real wage $\overline{\overline{w}}$. The worker is indifferent between $\overline{\overline{w}}$ and the lottery $w^0(\tilde{\theta})$. Furthermore, $\overline{\overline{w}}$ is smaller than the expected wage level $E(w^0(\tilde{\theta})) = \overline{w}$. The worker will prefer the firm's contract offer, $\hat{w}$, to the spot market results if $\hat{w} > \overline{\overline{w}}$. On the other hand, the risk-neutral firm, which is indifferent to paying a constant wage $E((w^0(\tilde{\theta})) = \overline{w}$, or the set of wages $w^0(\tilde{\theta})$ under the condition of a competitive spot market, is better off paying $\hat{w} < \overline{w}$. Thus, for a $\hat{w}$ for which

$$\overline{\overline{w}} < \hat{w} < \overline{w},$$

both parties prefer the institution "contract market" to the institution "competitive spot market." There are gains from trade for both, the firm as well as the worker, from organizing the labor market in the described contract style instead of as an auction market. The wage $\hat{w}$ is "sticky," and there is a rational explanation of why this is so.

An immediate consequence of this framework is that wages are disengaged from the marginal revenue-product of labor. Part of the risk of the uncertain labor income stream is shifted to third parties . . . by the tacit or open commitment of the firm to guarantee its personnel that their wage rates, hours worked, employment status, or a combination of all such factors, will be in some degree independent of the vicissitudes of the business cycle. The risk is thereby transferred from wages to profits and, via the capital market, to the income streams of the firm's owners and creditors (Azariadis 1975, 1184).

The term *implicit contract* was introduced by Azariadis in this context. He writes that "in uncertainty, labor services are not auctioned off in quite the same way fresh fruit is. Rather, they are exchanged for some implicit set of commitments, hereinafter called an *implicit labor contract,* on the part of the firm to employ the owner of those labor services for a 'reasonable' period of time and on terms mutually agreed upon in advance" (Azariadis 1975, 1185). Not only the firm but also the worker has to agree implicitly to stick to the "implicit contract" once the state of nature $\theta$ actually appears. Firms don't pay less than $\hat{w}$ if $w^0(\theta) < \hat{w}$; workers don't quit if $w^0(\theta) > \hat{w}$. But this is merely an interpretation that is not justified by explicit modeling.[13] We might as well argue (and prefer to do so) that in implicit contract theory it is assumed that the described contract is explicitly agreed upon and perfectly enforceable with no costs. In this respect, implicit contract theory does not differ from the PA approach. The execution phase of contract in both types of models is assumed to work out perfectly, and at zero cost, whether the terms of the contract were agreed upon explicitly or implicitly. Contract execution is not part of this type of analysis.[14] Furthermore, the alleged "reasonable period" of time is not modeled either. Implicit contract theory of the type illustrated here is in fact a "one shot game."

We conclude, with Hart and Holmstrom (1987, 109), that:

> The ability to explain the divergence between workers' wages and their marginal (revenue) product of labor is the principal achievement of the ABG model. In fact, the model provides a striking explanation of sticky (real) wages or incomes, which is in notable contrast to that provided by, say, disequilibrium theory.

For further critical remarks see Hart and Holmstrom (1987).[15]

### 5.6.  The Incomplete Contract Model

In principal-agent theory and implicit labor contract theory, it is assumed that contracts are concluded once and for all. The phase of contract execution is considered to be unproblematic. Contracts are "complete" in this sense as well as in the sense that all contingencies are known in advance.

These theories were criticized heavily by Williamson (1975, 1985) and others for failing to consider relation-specific investments and the resulting incentives for opportunistic behavior of parties. Relation-specific investments imply that once made they have a higher value inside the relationship than outside.

---

13. For the "quit model," see Hart and Holmstrom 1987, 110 ff.

14. Rosen (1985, 1149) rightly stresses that "the economic analysis of implicit contracts amounts to working out the details of an explicit contract concerning wages and employment under uncertainty. Hence, an implicit contract must be interpreted in the 'as if' sense of an explicit one, as a mutual understanding between worker and employer that the invisible handshake Okun (1981, 89) implies, as in commercial contracts."

15. Various attempts have been made to enrich the Azariadis-Bailey-Gordon model. An important development of asymmetric information is given by Grossman and Hart (1981, 1983b) and Azariadis and Stiglitz (1983). For a review, see Hart and Holmstrom (1987, 112–28).

Given this "lock-in" effect each party will have some monopoly power ex post, although there may be plenty of competition ex ante, before investments are sunk. Since the parties cannot rely on the market once their relationship is underway, a *long-term contract* is an important way for them to regulate, and divide up the gains from, their trade. (Hart 1987, 752; italics added)

Due to transaction costs, such long-term contracts will be *incomplete* in important respects. "The parties will quite rationally leave out many contingencies, taking the point of view that it is better 'to wait and see what happens' than to try to cover a large number of individually unlikely eventualities" (Hart 1987, 753). It would be too costly to write down in advance all the possible contingencies (imperfect foresight).

Another problem is that contingencies, even though they may be foreseeable by the parties, cannot be *verified* by outsiders such as courts, with the result that such contracts will be practically not enforceable. "To use the jargon, incompleteness arises because states of the world, quality and actions are *observable* (to the contractual parties) but not *verifiable* (to outsiders)" (Hart 1987,754). Unlike principal-agent theory, there is no asymmetry of information between the parties, but there is between both parties and outsiders (e.g., the courts).

The next objective is to present an incomplete contract model with incompleteness due to both lack of foresight and verifiability of actions to outsiders. It is a simplified version of the model developed by Grossman and Hart (1986) as presented by Tirole (1988, 31ff.).

There are, as in our other contract theory examples, two decision units—in this case two firms, a buyer and a seller. We assume that they have agreed to trade a certain quantity of a some good of a basic design for some price at date 1. All of this is given and not analyzed. Now comes the story that leads us to the incomplete contract model. The two parties know that an opportunity to improve the quality of the good may arise at date 2, but they don't know at date 1 what the quality improvement will be. That is, at date 1 the parties cannot make the contract contingent on a change in design at date 2. They learn this quality improvement only at date 2 (i.e., at date 2 the improvement can be contracted on). To carry out the quality improvement costs the seller a certain amount, $c >$ 0, in period 2; $c$ is noncontractible. The buyer, on the other hand, can increase the probability, $\pi$, that the improvement comes about by a relation-specific investment in period 1. For example, the buyer can invest in flexibility, for example, by training his employees to adjust to changing technology. For simplicity, it is assumed that $c$ is known to both parties at date 1 and is independent of the particular improvement. The buyer's value for the improvement in period 2 is $\tilde{v}$. For simplicity, we assume that there are only two possible

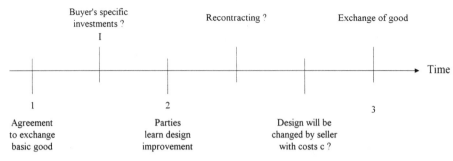

Fig. 5.15.  Incomplete contract theory: sequence of actions

outcomes for $\tilde{v}$: $\tilde{v} = v > c$ with probability $\pi$ (i.e., the improvement should be carried out) and $\tilde{v} = 0$ with $(1 - \pi)$ (the improvement should not be carried out). The possible outcomes of $\tilde{v}$ are also known to both parties in $t = 1$ (as is $c$), but they are too costly to contract for (Grossman and Hart; 1986, 703, n.14). To preclude the possibility of contracting for the realization of the value of the improvement, it is assumed that the values of $\tilde{v}$ and $c$ cannot be verified by a third party. The cost of the specific investment is assumed to be $I = \pi^2/2$. The seller can observe the specific investments of the buyer, with the result that their level is also known to both parties at date 2, but these investments cannot be verified to outsiders (such as courts). Hence, the parties cannot contract on this matter. Finally, we assume that the two firms are risk neutral.

The time structure of the incomplete contract is represented in fig. 5.15. Let us calculate first the social optimum, that is, the maximum of the expected value of the joint additional profit of the two firms without considering its distribution:

$$\max_{\pi} E(\Delta \tilde{Q}^n) = \pi(v - c) + (1 - \pi)(0 - 0) - \frac{\pi^2}{2}. \tag{1}$$

The first-order condition is

$$\pi^* = v - c.$$

The optimal specific investments in period 1 are then[16]

$$I^* = \frac{\pi^{*2}}{2} = \frac{(v - c)^2}{2}, \tag{2}$$

---

16. For simplicity, we assume that the optimal investment level never violates $0 \leq \pi \leq 1$.

and the maximum of expected joint profits is

$$\Delta \overline{Q}^{n*} = \frac{(v - c)^2}{2} > 0, \quad \Delta \overline{Q}^n \equiv E(\Delta \tilde{Q}^n). \tag{3}$$

This is the first-best optimum.

Now assume that the parties act *independently,* as *self-interested* firms, and that the quality improvement, although not specifiable at date 1, becomes known at date 2 and therefore can be contracted for.

Before we continue, remember that

$c$ is incurred by the seller, while

$\left.\begin{array}{c} v \\ I \end{array}\right\}$ relate to the buyer.

The two independent parties know in advance that in case of $v > c$ a design improvement will be implemented. We will consider the following three institutions:

CASE I. *Nonintegration: both sides can block a change in design.*

Buyer and seller are nonintegrated. They are free to "bargain in the second period over whether to make the improvement; if they cannot agree, the improvement is not made because it was not specified in the contract" (Tirole 1988, 32).

We apply the Nash-bargaining solution. The additional profits of the agreement are split in equal parts between the two firms. The buyer anticipates this bargaining result and maximizes ex ante his expected profit:

$$\max_{\pi} \Delta \overline{Q}_b^n = \frac{1}{2}[\pi(v - c)] - \frac{\pi^2}{2}. \tag{4}$$

From the first-order condition, it follows that

$$\pi^{**} = \frac{1}{2}(v - c)$$

and the resulting specific investments are

$$I^{**} = \frac{(v - c)^2}{8} < I^*,$$

that is, he "underinvests" in specific assets compared with the first-best solution. The expected profit of the buyer is accordingly

$$\Delta \overline{Q}_b^{n**} = \frac{(v - c)^2}{8} \tag{5}$$

and of the seller is

$$\Delta \overline{Q}_s^{n**} = \frac{(v - c)^2}{4}. \tag{6}$$

The expected joint surplus is then

$$\Delta \overline{Q}^{n**} = \frac{3}{8}(v - c)^2 < \Delta \overline{Q}^{n*}, \tag{7}$$

that is, the joint surplus is smaller than in the social optimum (3).

CASE 2. *Seller control: the seller can implement a change by fiat.*

The two firms agree to integrate and give the seller the right to decide whether to make the improvement. If the parties disagree, the seller chooses not to make the improvement since this is the less costly action for him. The buyer calculates as in the unconstrained bargaining case. Again, we get $\pi^{**}$ and $\Delta \overline{Q}^{n**}$, that is, less than optimal specific investments.

CASE 3. *Buyer control: the buyer can implement a change by fiat.*

The parties agree to integrate and give the buyer the right to decide whether to make the improvement without compensation being paid to the seller. For that privilege, the buyer pays the seller a certain price at date 1. Under these circumstances, the buyer will decide to make the improvement under all conditions (even when $\tilde{v} = 0$). This is so because a change in design will never leave him worse off. The seller, though, is interested in avoiding, if possible, the improvement costs $c$. He will, therefore, be interested in renegotiating ex post (at date 2) his original promise to spend $c$ at date 2 if $\tilde{v} = 0$.

Clearly, if at date 2 the value of the improvement is $v$, "the *status quo* is efficient and no renegotiating occurs. The buyer gets $v$ by imposing the improvement on the seller" (Tirole 1988, 32).

The status quo is inefficient and recontracting takes place if the value of the improvement is zero. We assume again the Nash-bargaining solution, that is, the buyer asks the seller to pay him half of $c$ and forget about the rest. The buyer can then determine the optimal level of his specific investments by maximizing his expected profit $\Delta\overline{Q}_b^n$ w.r.t. $\pi$:

$$\max_{\pi} \Delta\overline{Q}_b^n = \pi v + (1 - \pi)\frac{c}{2} - \frac{\pi^2}{2}. \tag{8}$$

The first-order condition is

$$v - \frac{c}{2} = \pi^0 > \pi^*.$$

Optimal specific investments of the buyer are now

$$I^0 = \frac{(\pi^0)^2}{2} = \frac{\left(v - \frac{c}{2}\right)^2}{2} > I^*. \tag{9}$$

The buyer now "overinvests." That is, his specific investments are larger than under joint surplus maximization because the buyer's authority "will allow him not to pay the production cost $c$ if his value is $v$. Because he does not internalize this production cost, he overinvests in the activity that makes production more likely" (Tirole 1988, 33).

The expected profit $\Delta\overline{Q}_s^{n0}$ of the seller will then be

$$\Delta\overline{Q}_s^{n0} = -\pi^0 c - (1 - \pi^0)\frac{c}{2}, \tag{10}$$

which is a negative number. The expected additional joint surplus is

$$\Delta\overline{Q}^{n0} = \Delta\overline{Q}_s^{n0} + \Delta\overline{Q}_b^{n0}$$

or

$$\Delta\overline{Q}^{n0} = \pi^0(v - c) - \frac{(\pi^0)^2}{2} \tag{11}$$

$$\Rightarrow \Delta\overline{Q}^{n0} = \frac{1}{2}(v - c)^2 - \frac{1}{8}c^2 < \Delta\overline{Q}^{n*}. \tag{12}$$

It can be shown that

$$\Delta\overline{Q}^{n0} \geq \Delta\overline{Q}^{n**} \quad \text{if } v \geq 2c. \tag{13}$$

As a result, we see that if the gains from the improvement $v$ are great enough buyer control is optimal relative to nonintegration or seller control. The reason is that buyer control encourages specific investments. At the same time, though, the buyer overinvests (relative to the first-best solution) because he does not consider the costs, $c$, properly. In the case of $v > 2c$, the buyer will be able to pay (and interested in paying) the seller a fixed sum to secure the authority for the decision.

The seller would demand at least a sum equal to the difference of his expected profits

$$\Delta \overline{Q}_s^{n**} - \Delta \overline{Q}_s^{n0} = \frac{v^2 + 2c}{4}$$

for leaving to the buyer the final decision to improve the product or not.

The buyer, in this case, gets the residual decision rights of the seller. In the sense of Grossman and Hart (1986), this means that the buyer becomes the *owner* of the seller's firm (buyer integration). The residual decision right, though, is limited to the decision about whether the improvement is to be made or not. In other words, the seller's improvement costs, $c$, are not internalized, as they were in equation 1. Therefore, in spite of the fact that the two firms are integrated, the expected joint profits are smaller than the first-best optimum $\Delta \overline{Q}_s^{n*}$. The reason is, besides the assumed asymmetric information between insiders and outsiders regarding specific investments, the noncontractibility of the cost $c$ and the value $\tilde{v}$ of the improvement. In fact, the noncontractibility of $c$ and $\tilde{v}$ is a crucial assumption for the "incompleteness" of the incomplete contract model just presented. If, by contrast, we assume that $c$ or $\tilde{v}$ can be contracted for, the parties would be able, in spite of the nonverifiability of specific investments, to write a complete contingent contract for $\tilde{v}$ and $c$. Then they would realize the first-best optimum (2) by giving the buyer the right to demand a design change whenever he pays for the production costs.

Contractual incompleteness results in distortions vis à vis the first-best optimum, as did asymmetric information in the PA models. In both cases, these distortions are to be read with quotation marks. They result from the existence of transaction costs.

*Some Comments on Incomplete Contract Theory*

1. As described previously, we find that incomplete contract theory is designed to give economically rational explanations of how the relationship between two contractual parties can be organized so that uncontractable actions, such as transaction-specific investments and complex production decisions, can become part of a binding bundle of agreements. Such explicit agreements, when formed, can then be enforced by outsiders such as courts. In the model just

explored, the critical consideration was to determine in advance which party was to have residual decision rights, that is, which party was to be the owner. Ownership can be perfectly and costlessly enforced in this model. Then there remains no contract incompleteness in the legal sense.

2. The assignment of ownership affects specific investments and thus efficiency (see Holmstrom and Tirole 1989, 71).

3. In a sense, unforeseeable events are given attention in this type of theorizing. Since the parties are unable to describe completely in advance the possible improvement of the buyer's product, they prefer to wait and see what happens and thus allow for recontracting. This represents progress compared with PA theory. Nevertheless, the interacting parties have blind spots with respect to the future, and the contractual contents are rather limited relative to the complexities of the outside world.

4. On the other hand, the parties are assumed to know many things in advance. For example, they know tomorrow's costs, $c$, the possible gains, $\tilde{v}$, and the precise way in which to influence $\pi$. Moreover, they know the probability, $\pi$, of success. Accordingly, they are able to act with perfect rationality just as the decision units in PA analysis did. They do so by assumption for the analyst's convenience because there does not exist, and probably will never exist, an axiomatic theory of bounded rationality.

5. Crucial for the incomplete contract model presented here is the assumption that the parties know in advance cost $c$ and the possible values $\tilde{v}$ of the ex ante unknown design improvement. At the same time, however, they are also assumed to know that $c$ and $\tilde{v}$ are not verifiable and cannot be contracted. Such an information status is not very plausible, at least not under the conditions of our simple model. Chung (1991), for example, shows that nonverifiability does not prevent efficient relation-specific investments if agents are risk neutral. (Contracts have, in this case, to specify a quantity and a payment together with an ex post revision.)

### 5.7. Self-Enforcing Agreements

The previous models dealt with contracts that in effect were legally binding and enforceable by courts. As we have seen, the implicit contract model was explicit, and the incomplete contract model solved its incompleteness problem by transforming the agreement into a complete contract. They all were, or became, contracts in the legal sense of the term.

We shall now deal with the question of modeling contracts in the nonlegal sense, that is, noncontractual agreements or "relations" (as defined in section 4.3). In the literature, these kinds of arrangements are called "self-policing" or "self-enforcing agreements," "self-enforcing implicit contracts" (Carmichael 1989, 81), or simply "implicit contracts" (understood in a different sense than in section 5.4). Hart (1987) deals with such arrangements under the title *incomplete contracts*. In this section, we are going to use the term *self-enforcing agreements*.

In a self-enforcing agreement model, it is assumed that the government or other third parties are unable:

To determine whether the agreement was violated
To enforce the performance of promises

Rather, it is left to the judgment of the parties concerned to determine whether or not there has been a violation of the agreement, and the performance is "enforced" by the explicit or implicit threat to discontinue the agreement Telser (1980, 27).

Information is perfect except for one asymmetry. It is assumed that the parties to an agreement do not know whether the other side is reliable (honest) or not. This, of course, represents an important departure from the assumption of the PA models. In the circumstances described, people seek information about the reliability of those with whom they deal. Experience plays a role, that is, the history of the behavior of the other side (and its resulting *reputation* in "completing" an agreement) has significance. In short, the theory of self-enforcing agreements builds on the concept of reputation (e.g., the "goodwill" value of a firm's brand name). Time also plays an essential role since reputation is fundamentally a dynamic concept.

Of course, reputation works only as an enforcement mechanism if a sufficient number of individuals can observe when an actor reneges. We are going to assume that whether an actor fulfills or reneges is observed by *everyone else*. Furthermore, reliability (honesty) is not considered to be an inherent personality trait. Instead, a person is assumed to act in a responsible and reliable way only if it is more advantageous to him than being unreliable is. As was quoted in section 4.4.2:

The basic hypothesis of this approach is that someone is honest only if honesty, or appearance of honesty, pays more than dishonesty. (Telser 1980, 29)

To achieve a good reputation requires investments. That is, firm-specific assets must be acquired, and investment in these assets will be undertaken only if appropriate market returns can be made on them. High-quality products, therefore, have to earn a premium, which can be viewed either as a return to reputation or an incentive payment to induce quality maintenance.

Without premiums for high-quality items, sellers would find that a *fly-by-night* strategy of quality reduction would be profit maximizing. The reason is that, in markets with reputations, sellers can always increase profits in the short-run by reducing the quality of their products. (Shapiro 1983, 660)

We shall consider a simplified version of the Klein and Leffler (1981) and Shapiro (1983) model following Tirole (1988, 122ff.). Assume a monopoly situation: one seller (a firm) and a large number of buyers (consumers). The seller offers one product of two potential qualities: low ($q = 0$) and high ($q = 1$).[17] The buyer cannot observe the quality (he cannot distinguish between low and high quality) at the date of purchase, $t$. He learns the quality of the good purchased only one period later, at date $t + 1$. Thus, the seller can, at least for one period, surprise his customers with lower quality than was expected.

In order to focus on the monopolist's quality choice, we assume that he produces a fixed number of goods in each period. For simplicity, we set this number at unity. The cost of producing an item of quality $q$ is denoted by $c_q$. The unit cost of producing the low-quality variant is $c_0$, while $c_1$ is the cost associated with the high-quality variant. As would be expected, $c_1 > c_0$. Consumers are identical. Their net benefit function (utility minus cost) is:

$$B^n = \tau q - p_q$$

if they buy at price $p_q$ a good with quality $q$. The symbol $\tau$ designates taste. $B^n = 0$ if consumers do not buy. The seller is free to choose quality in each period. The price of a high-quality product is $p_1 > 0$, and that of a low quality product is $p_0 = 0$. As noted, time plays an essential role in a reputation model. With time, we have also to consider the role of interest. The market interest rate $i$ per period is given and constant over time, and so is the discount factor $\delta = 1/(1 + i)$.

A *reputation equilibrium* of the model is a steady state in which the seller maintains quality over time and the buyers' expectations are always fulfilled. The price, $p_q$, remains constant. There can be a high- or a low-quality equilibrium. In the latter case, we would have an extreme lemons situation, and under our conditions no trade would occur. (To be precise, the buyer would be indifferent between buying and not buying the low-quality good.)

In order to consider the general trade situation here, it will be useful to assume the following strategies of the seller and the consumer:

---

17. Shapiro (1983, 663), for example, assumes the low-quality good to meet some minimum legal standards to limit the extent to which suppliers can reduce quality if following a fly-by-night strategy of quality deterioration.

Consumers base their expectations of quality in $t$ on the seller's reputation, that is, quality chosen by the seller at $t - 1$. We assume that consumers start with the belief that the producer offers high quality ($q = 1$) in the first period and that this is known to the seller.

The seller starts with $p_1$ and high quality ($q = 1$) in the first period. Deviation to low quality leads to the provision of low quality from that point on and to the price $p_0 = 0$. Consumers would then stop buying. Consumers know the seller's strategy.

Note that information is perfect with the exception of one massive blind spot. That is, the buyer does not know the quality of the product at the moment of its purchase. Otherwise, he knows the other side's selling strategies. Crucial for the result is the assumption that the seller knows the consumers' initial beliefs and the consumers know the seller's strategy.[18]

Following Tirole (1988, 122), we will show that these strategies, together with the seller's choice of $(q_1, p_1)$ at the start, lead to an equilibrium if $p_1$ is chosen appropriately. Specifically, conditions make it worthwhile for the seller to maintain his high reputation. We have to prove that under the given restrictions both sides make their best choices in the sense that they act rationally by repeating $(q_1, p_1)$ for all $t$. We proceed as follows.

For the *consumers* in our model, there is only one decision left open: to buy or not to buy. This decision depends on consumers' expectations about the seller's behavior. Utility-maximizing consumers have to make their best possible forecasts. In other words, they have to form rational expectations. This is what is required for equilibrium. In such a state, consumer expectations are fully rational; they predict exactly what follows from the known strategy of the seller.

As for the *seller*, it must be more profitable for him to sell the high-quality product for an unlimited number of periods of time. He must find it expedient to choose $(q_1, p_1)$ for all $t$. The seller must do this instead of "milking his reputation" by going to $(q_0, p_1)$ at some period and then selling nothing afterward. Sales would cease, of course, because of the inevitable reaction of buyers who recognize that they have been cheated.

In the first case, in which the seller offers high quality at $p_1$ forever, the present value of the seller's profit, including todays profits, would be

$$(p_1 - c_1)(1 + \delta + \delta^2 \ldots) = \frac{p_1 - c_1}{1 - \delta}$$

---

18. If consumers start with $q = 0$ at $t = 1$, the seller would choose $q = 0$ and charge $p_0 = 0$ forever!

$$= \left(\frac{1+i}{i}\right)(p_1 - c_1).$$

In the second case, in which the seller deviates and sells a low-quality good at price $p_1$, he would obtain $p_1 - c_0$ in the deviation period and zero thereafter. Hence, a necessary condition for a reputation equilibrium is that honesty pays:

$$\left(\frac{1+i}{i}\right)(p_1 - c_1) \geq p_1 - c_0$$

or

$$p_1 - c_1 \geq i(c_1 - c_0). \tag{1}$$

Shapiro (1983) calls this the *no-milking condition*. In order for the supplier not to cut quality, the high-quality price must exceed marginal cost by at least $i(c_1 - c_0)$. This is because short-run profits can always be earned by milking one's reputation. If the seller cuts quality now (at date $t$), he saves on production costs $(c_1 - c_0)$. However, he loses the present value of all future profits (from date $t + 1$ onward), that is, his reputation rent:

$$(p_1 - c_1)(\delta + \delta^2 + \dots) = \frac{(p_1 - c_1)}{i}.$$

The no-milking condition puts a lower bound on the price at which high quality can be sold at equilibrium:

$$c_1 + i(c_1 - c_0) \leq p_1. \tag{2}$$

If $p_1$ is below its lower bound (2), it pays for the seller to cut quality, that is, to produce at cost $c_0$ and thus to increase his profits by $c_1 - c_0$ (the amount saved in production costs). This extra profit would now be larger than his reputation rent $(p_1 - c_1)/i$.

There also has to be an upper bound on the price $p_1$ to ensure that the seller remains a monopolist. Assume, with Shapiro (1983, 666), a richer model with $n$ firms, one for each quality level. The firm offering quality level 1 remains a monopolist, given free entry, if a potential entrant into quality-level segment 1, who sells at a very low price (here $p_1 = 0$, i.e., the low-quality price) in one period, makes nonpositive profits.

This would cost him $c_1$ and would bring him a reputation rent of $(p_1 - c_1)/i$. The upper bound of $p_1$ is therefore determined by

$$p_1 \leq (1 + i)c_1. \tag{3}$$

Shapiro calls this the *free entry* condition.

The range of prices $p_1$ at a reputation equilibrium is, using (2) and (3),

$$(1 + i)c_1 - ic_0 \leq p_1 \leq (1 + i)c_1.$$

If we assume $c_0 = 0$, the reputation equilibrium price is

$$p_1 = (1 + i)c_1.$$

(Under our special conditions, we also have to assume that $p_1 \leq \tau$ to make sure that the net benefit of a consumer is positive, i.e., that the consumer will purchase the good.)

The model shows that "the producer has an incentive to produce a high-quality item only if high quality implies a rent that the producer is afraid of losing if he cuts quality" (Tirole 1988, 123). Or, as Klein and Leffler (1981, 617) put it: "Cheating will be prevented and high quality products will be supplied only if firms are earning a continual stream of rental income that will be lost if low quality output is deceptively produced."

The rent has to be the higher the more expensive it is to produce high quality. In other words, assuming that $c_1$ increases with quality, rent also must increase with quality. The difference $c_1 - c_0$ in equation (1) can be also interpreted as *information cost:* "The information cost is the cost of establishing a reputation for quality $q$. A seller incurs this cost in the initial period, given our simple dynamic structure" (Shapiro 1983, 668). The price $p_1$ reflects not only the production cost $c_1$ but also the rate of return on information cost $i(c_1 - c_0)$. If buyers could observe quality at the date of purchase, that is, if information were completely symmetric, reputation and reputation rent would be irrelevant. Then consumers would get the high quality product at a lower price.

*Some Comments on Self-Enforcing Agreements*

1. A self-enforcing agreement has to be long term and can be understood as a noncontractual skeleton agreement between, for example, a seller and his clientele. Within this framework a series of legally enforceable contracts, for example, repeat purchase contracts, are concluded. If the seller cheats, the relationship is discontinued forever under the rather strong conditions of our model.

2. Information is assumed to be asymmetric in the special sense that only the party that offers a product or service is informed about the quality of the product or service at date $t$ of its exchange. The other side (e.g., the buyer of the product) learns the quality of the exchanged item only one period after the purchase. Apart from this, information is symmetric and knowledge is perfect. In particular, the history of the seller's behavior is known to the buyers and

from it they infer the seller's reliability or reputation. Further, the strategies available to the respective parties are also common knowledge.

3. Reliability of the seller is not assumed to result from internalized moral standards (norms) but exclusively from a seller's profit calculation. The seller will only be reliable if reliability is the most profitable policy for him.

4. In the reputation equilibrium described previously, quality items sell for a premium above market cost. The premium (i.e., the higher price) would vanish if information were perfectly symmetric from the beginning. Given such ideal conditions, a first-best solution would emerge.

5. There exists no reputation equilibrium if the threat of losing one's investments in reputation disappears (or never existed) Gibbons (1992, 112). Similarly, no reputation equilibrium would exist if sunk investments were paid by a third party such as the state. This might occur if the planning bureau of a socialist market economy allowed firms to operate with "soft budget" constraints.

6. The model shows only that repeat purchases *may* offer an incentive to supply quality, not that they necessarily will. The reason is that the reputation equilibrium relies heavily on the consumers' *beliefs*. "Reputation matters only because consumers believe it matters. If they did not, and if they believed instead that whatever the past qualities, the monopolist would supply low quality in the future, the monopolist would have no incentive to sustain quality, and the consumers' expectations would again be fulfilled. Thus, we have another equilibrium with an extreme lemons effect . . . " (Tirole 1988, 123). Consumers would not buy the product at all under our conditions. Thus, low-quality production would be permanent.

7. This second ("bad") equilibrium would result if the long-term agreement were established so that it would end, with certainty, at some future period $T$. This weakness of the model disappears if we assume that the exact date of the final period is unknown to the parties. This seems to be quite a reasonable assumption for many cases.

To elaborate on this argument, we note that a sequence has no last term if there is always a positive probability of continuing it. Assume that the series of purchases will be discontinued at any date $t$ with probability $\pi$ (e.g., because the firm's market "disappears"). The discount factor to be used in computing the equilibrium would then have to be modified as follows:

$$\delta = \left(\frac{1}{1+i}\right)(1 - \pi).$$

8. Nevertheless, in a case with a known final period, a reputation equilibrium can still exist if one of two possible types of monopolist is "crazy" and always provides high quality (Kreps and Wilson 1982).

9. The concept of "bounded rationality" is again ignored, together with the fact that decision makers do not know what the future will bring (e.g., that $\pi$ is objectively unknown).

10. Self-enforcing contracts, as described in our model, are incomplete noncontractual agreements as far as quality is concerned. On the other hand, it is perfectly clear to both parties to the agreement, though with a brief delay for the buyer, whether the agreement has been broken or not. The consequences of such an action are also perfectly clear to both sides from the beginning. There exist no excuses for errors, pretended errors or not. Therefore, the situation envisioned is one in which there will be no repair if something goes wrong, no forgiving, no mutual trust, no (weak) solidarity. In other words, the self-enforcing contract is tough as tough can be. It has little in common with the concept of relational contracts described in chapter 4.

11. In a sense, the model of self-enforcing agreements deals with a problem similar to that of the incomplete contract model. In both cases, the assumption is that there is no possibility of having the execution of the agreement enforced by the courts. But, since the self-enforcing agreement deals from the beginning with a noncontractual relation, such as the relation between the seller and his clientele, the problem cannot be solved by transforming the ongoing relationship into some kind of a complete *contract*. Rather, the only course of action open is to transform the relationship into a complete noncontractual *agreement*.

## 5.8.  Looking Back

The contract theory models presented in this chapter explain (rationalize) differences between marginal cost and price not as the result of monopolistic practices, as models of imperfect competition argue, but as the unavoidable result of transaction costs. In particular, the costs of information, verification, and contract formulation are emphasized. The resulting welfare losses in the system are, therefore, not interpreted as the price of monopolistic misbehavior, which could be ruled out by means of a stern competition policy, but as the outcome of transaction costs. This last understanding, of course, is based on the assumption that men are purely self-interested individuals (just as in the orthodox model of perfect competition). Good manners and moral norms (honesty) are by assumption only applied as long as such behavior is expected to pay more than misbehavior (dishonesty) does. Therefore, in this world pre- and postcontractual opportunism are of central interest to the model builder. The concept of the homo oeconomicus, with its presumption of perfect rationality, underlies the models of contract theory. The assumption of bounded rationality might be expected to lead to richer results. Yet it is not applied because it does not lend itself, so far at least, to satisfactory formalization ("satisfactory" in the sense of conventional-style neoclassical model building).

Basically, contract theory is an extension of monopoly or bilateral monopoly theory. Prices are not determined by an impersonal auctioneer but by the parties themselves, as are quantities and other conditions. Characteristically, two individual parties, a seller and a buyer (or a principal and an agent), deal with each other. Sometimes, however, one party may be on one side and many parties on the other. In any event, the sequence of moves is explicitly stated. Usually the monopolist (principal, employer, or seller) moves first by fixing the price or wage and the other conditions of the contract. The other side follows (the agent[s], employee[s], or buyer[s]).

Both (or all) parties are perfectly informed about each other with the exception of "blindness" presupposed in models with asymmetric information on the part of the traders (in the PA models and the model of self-enforcing agreements). The inability of individuals to make direct observations is compensated for in these models through the use of economic incentives. Hence, one can speak of *incentive contracts* (Lazear 1987). In the PA model with moral hazard, the incentives are embodied in the *incentive schedule* offered by the principal to the agent. In the adverse selection PA model, incentives are reflected in the *self-selection constraints,* which also constitute an incentive schedule for the principal. In the self-enforcing contract model, the *reputation premium* may offer an incentive to supply quality. Further, in the incomplete contract model, in which information is perfectly symmetric between the parties, the incompleteness concerns the protection of transaction-specific investments and the noncontractibility of the value $\bar{v}$ of a future improvement. And here the incentive for sufficient investments in specific assets consists of giving the *residual decision rights* over the use of specific assets to a particular party. Normally, this would mean giving ownership authority to the party that provides the specific investment if, in our model, the gains, $\bar{v}$, from the improvement of the product are high enough. As for implicit contract theory in its original form, informational problems do not arise. Transaction costs are represented only indirectly by market imperfections (e.g., in the market for human wealth).

Relative to the distinction between complete and incomplete contracts, it is understood that "a complete contract is one that specifies each party's obligations in every conceivable eventuality, rather than a contract that is fully contingent in the Arrow-Debreu sense" (Hart and Holmstrom 1987, 147). According to this terminology, the PA contracts and the implicit contract described previously are complete contracts, while the models of incomplete contracts and self-enforcing agreements represent cases of incomplete contracts.

In all the contract models described, the usual target functions of neo-classical economic theory (utility and profits) are maximized under certain constraints by the parties to the contract.

In the moral hazard model, the principal knows from the beginning the agent's reaction function (response function) as well as his reservation utility, and the principal behaves like a Stackelberg leader. In the adverse selection model, the principal knows the utility functions and abilities of the agents but cannot tell which individual agent is of which type. He includes this knowledge in his optimization calculation to determine the appropriate (expected profit-maximizing) self-selection constraints. As noted, the parties in the incomplete contract model are able to calculate their profit maxima under the three possible cases (nonintegration, seller control, and buyer control) and to choose the most profitable of the three governance structures. The consumers of the self enforcing agreement model form their expectations rationally. Similarly, the seller calculates his expected profits to determine his lower and upper bound on the price at which high quality can be sold in a reputation equilibrium.

All of these equilibria are only *second best*. The resulting welfare loss (the difference between first-best and second-best equilibrium profits) may be interpreted as the result of the existence of transaction costs (or even as their measure?). Yet, since the first-best solution can only be achieved in a world of zero transaction costs and complete information, it is misleading to use the term *welfare loss*. Any constraints that are *unavoidable* cannot be regarded as causing the economic system to lose welfare. If this were not so, production costs would have to be interpreted as phenomena that lead to "welfare losses." Still, with this remark in mind, we continue to apply the term.

Having determined equilibrium plans, the next step is to undertake comparative static analysis. For our simple moral hazard case, we have found that the size of the welfare loss depends on the degree of risk aversion, the uncertainty level of the environment, and the marginal cost of effort. The smaller these three qualities, the smaller the welfare loss (or transaction costs). In the adverse selection case, comparative static results will depend on assumptions about market structure, knowledge, and the distribution of uncertainty.

In the incomplete contract model, the welfare loss depends on the proportions in which the profits are distributed to the respective parties and on the magnitude of the costs, $c$, incurred in carrying out the quality improvement. The difference between marginal cost and price in the self-enforcing agreement model is the consequence of transaction or information costs. Stability is a problem. In particular, the reputation equilibrium will not be achieved again once it is disturbed. In fact, it need not to be achieved at all since it depends heavily on consumers' beliefs. Low-quality production could be permanent. This fragility is, of course, the result of our rather extreme assumptions. There are other assumptions such as the "tit-for-tat" strategy, described by Axelrod

(1984), for playing the iterated prisoner's dilemma game. Here, defection of the opponent is punished by the other player in the following period by the same "bad" behavior. If afterward the opponent returns to cooperative behavior, the first player will match this by resuming cooperative play see, e.g., Myerson (1991, 323ff.). Another possible assumption is that the rules of behavior can evolve spontaneously so that conventions tend to become norms that people believe they *ought* to follow. This point about maintaining certain social patterns was made by Sugden (1989), who follows the theory originally put forward by David Hume ([1739–40] 1969). Note, however, that neither of these examples is an extension of the neoclassical approach to modeling described in this chapter.

The intention of this chapter is to show that contractual arrangements ("governance structures"), and in this sense "institutions," can be analyzed through the use of the basic behavioral hypothesis of neoclassical economics: self-interest as expressed by homo oeconomicus. The analytical technique of constrained utility or profit maximization is applied ingeniously in the formal branch of modern institutional economics called contract theory. The result is a genuine extension of the neoclassical standard model. Such an advance was not made in the case in which the activity "transaction" was added to the general equilibrium model of perfect competition (sec. 2.4). From this standpoint, then, contract theory is an improvement, a move in the right direction. On the other hand, though, it has definite shortcomings. Some of them can be, and in fact are, modified by extending or blending the various contract theory models. In this chapter, we illustrated the various models only in their simplest and most basic versions. In any event, a large specialized literature has been developing in this field during the last ten to fifteen years, and we shall report on this literature briefly in the next section.

Other, more serious, difficulties with the neoclassical approach result from the limits of the assumption of perfect rationality and from the fact that the orthodox neoclassical model is changed in some fundamental ways once positive transaction costs and bounded rationality concepts are introduced into the analytical scheme. More will be said about these problems in chapter ten, but, with respect to the question of human motivation, there is increasing skepticism that it is possible to model man's behavior in terms of a few abstract axioms and without any significant reference to empirical evidence. A shift to the use of "bounded rationality" in some form seems essential. Moreover, empirical research seems destined to play a larger role in the construction of "models of man" (see Selten 1990; and Williamson 1985). Much has been done in this respect since the early work on experimental game theory by Sauermann and Selten (1959) and Siegel and Fouraker (1960). For a review of the early German work, see Tietz (1990); for the largely American work, see Roth 1995.

Arrow's remarks on PA theory, quoted earlier, can be applied to contract theory in general: the variety and vagueness of monitoring devices and the role of socially mediated rewards are not modeled in formal contract theory. Nevertheless, contract theory is a step in the direction of the much-sought goal of integrating the "impressive structure of economic analysis" with other social sciences and thus introducing a new style of social research.

### 5.9. Bibliographic Notes on Formal Contract Theory

Formal contract theory in its present form was developed largely during the last twenty years. It shows that managerial discretion can be limited efficiently in a second-best sense, though, by the owners of firms.

### 5.9.1. Managerial Theory of the Firm

The separation of ownership from control issue raised by Berle and Means (1932) led to the managerial theory of the firm by Baumol (1959) and Williamson (1963). The latter is briefly described in this chapter. Marris (1964) expanded this view to what he first calls an economic theory of "managerial" capitalism; later he speaks of "the corporate economy" (Marris and Wood 1971) and "the corporate society" (Marris 1974). Other representatives of this broader philosophy are Aron (1967), Galbraith (1967), and Nichols (1969). The general hypothesis is that managerial pursuit of self-interest need not lead to maximum present values of investment streams (Marris and Mueller 1980).

### 5.9.2. Principal-Agent Theory: Moral Hazard

The first steps of what became the (formal) principal-agent theory can be found in the analysis of insurance market contracts (e.g., Spence and Zeckhauser 1971). These studies focused on the moral hazard problem (the problem that the insured individual may influence the probability of the insured event to his advantage). The term *principal-agent problem* derives from Ross (1973), who also provides one of the first clear expositions of the canonical principal-agent problem. Other early contributions are by Mirrlees (1974, 1976) and Stiglitz (1974). The basic principal-agent model was further analyzed by Holmstrom (1979), Shavell (1979), and Grossman and Hart (1983a), in three frequently quoted articles.

A large number of variations and extensions of the basic model of the Principal-Agent approach have been published since the beginning of the 1980s. For lack of space, we can mention here only a few variations.

1. *Alternative incentives:* The basic idea behind an incentive contract is that individuals love leisure and dislike putting forth effort. "In a managerial context, however, effort is only part of the overall incentive problem. It is likely

that many executives believe their managers are industrious enough; what they worry about more is how effective these managers are at making decisions" (Holmstrom and Ricart i Costa 1986, 835). Examples are as follows.

Grossman and Hart (1982), whose article is an extension of the managerial theory of the firm, is described in section 5.1 in the style of the Principal-Agent approach. The assumed incentive problem here is that managers tend to invest resources to secure "emoluments" instead of investing fruitfully. The disincentive in the Grossman and Hart model is that managers are concerned about losing their incomes and perquisites in case of bankruptcy.

Holmstrom and Ricart i Costa (1986) are not concerned with the effort aversion of managers but with their unwillingness to take risks. "To the extent that these incentive problems cannot be fully removed by monitoring (as marginalist thinking would readily suggest), they have allocational consequences . . . " (836). The (investment) incentives in this model are based on the simple idea that managers are concerned about the impact of decisions on their future careers. Baron (1989) surveys incentive issues in regulated industries. The natural incentive of the firm is to overstate its costs in order to obtain a higher price and thereby higher profits.

2. *Many agents and relative performance evaluation:* Suppose that there is one principal and several agents whose effectiveness in production depends on how well they work together, for example, several workers unloading a truck. In addition to the moral hazard problem described in the basic PA model, there is now a free-rider problem. In fact, in contrast to the single-agent case, moral hazard problems may now occur even if there is no uncertainty in output. "The reason is that agents who cheat cannot be identified if joint output is the only observable indicator of inputs" (Holmstrom 1982, 325).

Holmstrom (1982) shows that noncooperative behavior will always yield an inefficient outcome if joint output is fully shared among the agents. The paper relates to the well-known article by Alchian and Demsetz (1972), who argue that efficiency can (and will) be restored by bringing in a principal who monitors the agents' inputs. Holmstrom shows that, under certainty, incentives alone can remove the free-rider problem. The primary role of the principal, in Holmstrom's model, is to administer incentive schemes that police agents in a credible way rather than monitoring agents as in Alchian and Demsetz's story.

Mookherjee (1984) analyzes further a number of multiple agents issues in connection with the use of the concept of relative performance in incentive contracting. Rank-order tournaments play an important role in this context.

Lazear and Rosen (1981) showed earlier the importance of rank-order tournaments in an article that also relates to the work of Alchian and Demsetz (1972). When monitoring is difficult, so that workers can alter their input with less than perfect detection, input-wage schemes invite shirking.

Nalebuff and Stiglitz (1983), in a follow-up article, explain the central role that competition plays. It allows the development of compensation schemes in which pay is based on relative performance. "This provides an additional reason that competitive economies perform better than monopolies, a reason which is quite distinct from the loss in consumer's surplus arising from the monopolist's reduction in output" (283).

Shleifer (1985) applies the relative performance concept to public regulation. He speaks of "yardstick competition," a concept that describes simultaneous regulation of identical or similar firms (e.g., hospitals). "Under this scheme the rewards of a given firm depend on its stand *vis-à-vis* a shadow firm constructed from suitable averaging the choices of other firms in the group. Each firm is thus forced to compete with its shadow" (319).

Lazear (1989) points out that in all of these articles the central idea is that competition encourages increased effort, which has positive effects on output. But competition also discourages cooperation among contestants and can lead to outright sabotage. Lazear shows that some pay compression is efficient. The results of his study suggest that:

1. Firms rationally take personality into account when deciding which workers to hire. Ignoring personality may result in excessively competitive behavior.
2. Pay by relative performance is more of a problem at the higher levels of the job hierarchies. Those jobs tend to have an abnormally high proportion of competitive individuals . . . [but] rivals can be separated [so] that they do not damage one another. (579)

Rey and Tirole (1986) argue that competition may also act as a tournament between sellers (retailers) in a product market when informational problems prevent the manufacturers from using contracts based on relative performance. Manufacturers may always prefer competition to resale-price maintenance.

3. *Multitasks principal-agent analyses:* Baker, Jensen, and Murphy (1988) criticized formal PA models for not explaining the fact that in real life pay is not very closely related to performance in many organizations. The question is whether pay is always an effective motivator. Holmstrom and Milgrom (1991) show, by use of a linear multitask PA model that in a multitask PA problem,

> *job design is an important instrument for the control of incentives.* In the standard model, when each agent can engage in only one task, the grouping of tasks into jobs is not a relevant issue. (1991, 25, emphasis in the original)

While in much of the older PA literature the organizational structure has been determined exogenously, separately from the explicit incentive contract, Holmstrom and Milgrom started a branch of PA research in which the organizational structure is used as an optimizing instrument. Contributions of this type are Melumad, Mookherjee, and Reichelstein (1992); Itoh (1992); and Hemmer (1995).

Itoh (1992), for example, questions whether cooperation among some but not all members of an organization is good for an organization as a whole and, if so, when? The answer is, as Itoh shows, not simply: "yes" and "always."

Hemmer (1995) tries to give a rational explanation for why in the automobile industry the assembly-line approach has been supplemented, from a certain point on, by a team approach. He provides an integrated analysis of the optimal investment in production technology, the optimal use of alternative organizational forms, and the optimal explicit incentive using a multitask PA model of the kind introduced by Holmstrom and Milgrom (1991).

4. *Common agency:* Instances of "common agency" describe situations with one individual agent and several principals.

Bernheim and Whinston (1985) took the first step toward developing a coherent, abstract framework for analyzing instances of common agency. This was further developed by Stole (1991).

5. *Hierarchies:* In this area, two problems are of particular interest. First, it is important to understand how organizational slack can trickle down in a hierarchy. Second, there is interest in knowing what role coalitions between agents and their supervisors play in hierarchies.

Calvo and Wellisz (1979) addressed the first problem. They give an endogenous explanation for the hierarchic differentials in worker quality, wages, and the degree of supervision. Their results help to explain the skewness of income distribution and the wage differentials across layers that are inexplicable in terms of differences in labor quality and difficulty of tasks.

Tirole (1986) tackled the second problem of the hierarchy literature. His article views an organization as a network of coalitions and contracts and recognizes that covert transfers of a diverse nature take place in the organization. He also emphasizes, in the manner of the sociological literature, that behavior is often best predicted by the analysis of group incentives. Finally, an attempt is made to give precise definitions to such concepts as "power," "cliques," "corporate politics," and "bureaucracy" and to incorporate these terms into the general analysis. In this respect, the article is a continuation of the work of Cyert and March (1963).

6. *Dynamic models:* The principal-agent problem exists because uncertainty prevents the principal from using observed results to determine unambiguously the agent's action. The uncertainty will be reduced if the same

situation repeats itself. It can be shown that in a repeated principal-agent model, where the principal is risk neutral and there is no discounting, the first-best solution can be arbitrarily closely achieved as the number of periods goes to infinity. This result has been proved in a game-theoretic way by Radner (1981) and Rubinstein and Yaari (1980).

Townsend (1982) and Lambert (1983) show that, in this case, the principal can diversify and reduce some of the uncertainty surrounding the agent's actions by compensating him in one period on the basis of performances in prior periods as well as the current period. Memory plays a strong role, but the duration of the contract is also important.

Rey and Salanie (1987) are concerned with the consequences of limited commitment. Their question is: can long-term efficiency be achieved through a succession of renegotiated short-term contracts? Their analysis shows that, if information is symmetric, renegotiated short-term contracts permit the achievement of long-term efficiency if the objectives are conflicting and the transfers are not too limited. In the presence of asymmetric information, dynamic consistency is more difficult to achieve.

Fudenberg, Holmstrom, and Milgrom (1990) investigate the renegotiation question. What has to be determined is when a series of short-term contracts can be part of an efficient incentive scheme and when parties would do better by signing a long-term contract that cannot be renegotiated. Relative to the employer-employee relationship, the authors are concerned with finding the conditions under which short-term contracts are sufficient for good performance.

### 5.9.3. Principal-Agent Theory: Adverse Selection

The modern theoretical treatment of *adverse selection,* a well-known problem in the insurance business as well as in other markets, was initiated by Akerlof (1970) with his article "The Market for 'Lemons.'" His result, which showed the possibility of complete market failure, is of course extreme. As he indicated, however, numerous devices or institutions arise to counteract the effects of quality uncertainty. Among these are information-producing devices such as market signaling. A brief, selective report on the literature follows.

1. *The theory of markets with adverse selection—the general approach:* Spence (1973, 1974) provided the first formal discussion of Akerlof's lemons problem by use of what Spence called a signaling device. He examines markets (labor markets) in which sellers (workers) have private information about the quality of their products (their marginal productivity). Since sellers of higher-quality products can achieve a higher than average price (or wage), they have an incentive to undertake some activity (education in the case of labor) that is

less costly to them than to sellers with lower-quality products. Recognizing that this activity is a potential "signal" of product quality, buyers are willing to pay higher premiums for higher levels of signals (e.g., higher levels of education).

Under Spence's assumption, *signaling equilibria* exist, but they are multiple and often continuous spectra of equilibria: "Resiliency is lost. If a signaling equilibrium is exogenously upset, a return to the original equilibrium is at best problematic" (Spence 1974, 108).

Signaling costs resources (transaction costs). For example, there are the costs of education in our example in section 5.3.6. Note that, in this context, education is only a signal. It does not increase the workers' marginal productivity and therefore leads to only second-best optima.

Rothschild and Stiglitz (1976) (and independently Riley 1975) make it clear that Spence's result is critically linked to the assumption that all individuals are price takers. Therefore, most of the following literature on competition with adverse selection "is based on the Bertrand paradigm of price-setting firms with constant marginal and average costs which offer to serve an arbitrary number of customers at the prices they set" Hellwig (1987). In the Rothschild and Stiglitz model, individuals bargain on prices, and an informational equilibrium may not exist (we provided a simplified version of this model in sec. 5.3.6). There have been several attempts to overcome this failure by use of different types of equilibria. They all build on an article by Wilson (1977), who introduces the notion of an *anticipatory* equilibrium. Firms can adjust not only their policy offers but also their expectations in response to their market experience. Wilson is able to show that an information equilibrium in this sense does exist. Pooling equilibria are possible and sometimes there is more than one equilibrium.

Riley (1979a) introduced the concept of a *reactive* equilibrium in which potential price-searching agents take account of possible reactions by other agents. In contrast to Wilson, he shows that a "reactive" informational equilibrium is always a unique and separating equilibrium under the usual assumptions.

Dasgupta and Maskin (1986) show that mixed-strategy Nash equilibria do exist in the class of models considered earlier even if a pure strategy equilibrium does not exist.

The concept of equilibrium that should be used in this context is still unsettled. Kreps (1990b, 645) argues that the most preferable of the three approaches (Rothschild and Stiglitz, Wilson, or Riley) depends on what one thinks are reasonable assumptions under given circumstances. The fact that most results are sensitive to the precise structure of the underlying model is methodologically unsatisfactory. "Explaining everything, explaining nothing?" asks Sutton (1990) with regard to the new theoretical developments in the field of industrial organization. Sutton denies it, but readers may have their doubts.

2. *Some applications of the theory of markets with adverse selection:* The signaling and screening devices just described are applied to a great variety of fields. Some examples follow.

Labor markets, for example, education as a signal (Spence 1974) or wage level as a signal (Greenwald 1986; Stiglitz 1987)

Insurance markets, for example, offering an optimal menu of contracts (Rothschild and Stiglitz 1976)

Commodity markets, for example, warranties (Grossman 1981), product failure, and producer liability (Spence 1977)

Litigation, for example, a demand for high pretrial settlements as a signal that the plaintiff's case is strong (Reinganum and Wilde 1986)

The stability of the banking system, for example, banks competing for the deposits of two types of agents with different withdrawal probabilities (Smith 1984)

Public regulation, for example, contract menus offered by governments to firms (Laffont and Tirole 1986; Baron and Besanko 1987)

Credit markets, for example, the capital share of the firm held by the entrepreneur as a signal (Leland and Pyle 1977) or credit rationing as a screening device (Stiglitz and Weiss 1981)

There are many other applications. We shall limit our attention, however, to a few early applications of the adverse selection principle to the *credit-rationing issue* and dynamic models of *public regulation.*

a. *On credit rationing:* Jaffee and Russel (1976) were the first to explain credit-rationing behavior through the use of a self-selection device. They analyzed lender and market behavior in a simplified system in which two types of borrowers, honest and dishonest, are known to exist. Individuals can be identified, though, only by actual defaults. The authors demonstrate, in particular, how credit rationing arises as a means of market response to adverse selection.

In the following discussion, borrowers are distinguished by the riskiness of the economic undertakings in which they invest their loans. In this sense, different borrowers have different probabilities of repaying their loan.

Stiglitz and Weiss (1981) contributed a key article to this literature. They proved the existence of a rationing equilibrium by using the concept of a Nash-Bertrand equilibrium. Credit restrictions take the form of limiting the *number* of loans a bank will make. Some potential borrowers will not receive loans, and would not be able to borrow "even if they indicated a willingness to pay more than the market interest rate, or to put up more collateral than is demanded of recipients of loans" (Stiglitz and Weiss 1981, 408).

Besanko and Thakor (1987) and Hellwig (1988a) worked on credit rationing under the assumption of a monopoly bank.

Milde and Riley (1988) derive, in contrast to Stiglitz and Weiss (1981), a credit market equilibrium that is characterized by separation and no rationing. And, contrary to Jaffee and Russel (1976), they find that the multiple-contract solution is a stable equilibrium.

b. *On the dynamics of public regulation:* Freixas, Guesnerie, and Tirole (1985) employ a dynamic principal-agent model in order to discuss the effect of the "ratchet principle,"[19] which is universally used in centrally planned economies. The central planner revises his incentive schemes over time to take into account the information provided by a firm's actual performance. Managers of centrally planned firms therefore underproduce in order to avoid "ratcheting up" future targets. This is called the *ratchet effect* by the authors. They show that the *ratchet effect* exists "in the sense that the planner may choose a scheme that is suboptimal from a static viewpoint in order to induce revelation, with the marginal price of output exceeding its optimal static value" (173). See also Furubotn and Pejovich (1972a).

There is a *commitment problem* of the principal involved. The decisive assumption of the model is that the central planner (the principal) cannot credibly commit himself to an intertemporal sequence of incentive schemes. If he could, he would be able to announce the current scheme as well as the revision procedure, such that the firm could solve its dynamic programming problem given the central planners' plans. Weitzman (1980) and Holmstrom (1982) make this strong assumption in their articles.

Laffont and Tirole (1988) apply the ratchet effect resulting from noncommitment of the principal to a general two-period model that is applicable, for example, to public regulation problems. Ex ante efficiency is reduced when the regulator cannot credibly commit himself to multiperiod policy.

Baron and Besanko (1987) continue this line of discussion by asking if some limited form of commitment, institutionalized as rules or procedures, could arise in a regulatory relationship. They propose a "fairness" arrangement to allow, for example, a public utility some nonnegative return on its assets, and they study the properties of such arrangements.

---

19. The term *ratchet principle* was coined in this context by Berliner (1957). Current performance acts like a notched gear wheel in fixing the point of departure for the next period's target.

*Final Remarks*
Stiglitz (1985), on the theory of adverse selection in his overview of information and economics, argues that we have learned "that the traditional competitive equilibrium analysis, though having the superficial appearance of generality . . . is indeed not very general" (21). The more general approach of
informational economies, though, results in "a myriad of special cases and few
general principles" instead (21), a not very encouraging result. In addition,
Stiglitz (1987) surveys the literature dealing with the causes and consequences
of the dependence of quality on price and, in particular, considers the microfoundations of the efficiency wage theory, which he discusses at length. He
argues that efficiency-wage theory provides a far better explanation of unemployment than do the standard implicit contract theories, which at best would
provide an explanation for work sharing (33, n.60).

### 5.9.4. Implicit Contract Theory

Implicit contract theory, in the sense of section 5.4, became known as the
formal theory of the employment contract. It started with three independently
developed formal models by Bailey (1974), Gordon (1974), and Azariadis
(1975) that were motivated by the seeming puzzle of sticky wages and layoffs.
Azariadis describes the paradox as follows: "Competitive wage theory predicts
that firms will adjust to contraction in product demand by lowering both
employment and the real wage rate, in contradiction to the normal industrial
practice of laying off unneeded workers and paying unchanged wages to the
rest of the work force" (Azariadis 1975, 1183).

The term *implicit labor contracts* was coined by Azariadis (1975). It has
entered the economics vocabulary with amazing speed, but there are strong
differences of opinion on the meaning of the term and its applications (Rosen
1985, 1144).

Akerlof and Miyazaki (1980) demonstrate that implicit contract theory
can explain only half of the above paradox. The ability to share risk will lead
risk-averse firms to offer more risk-averse workers low wage variability contracts. But if workers' labor supply is inelastic (as in the example in section
5.4), the optimal contract will also involve low variability in employment.

Grossman and Hart (1981, 1983b) show that once we drop the assumption
that workers can observe an increase in profit associated with hiring additional
labor the analysis is affected significantly. Then the optimal contract may
involve high variability of employment, even though the workers' labor supply
is inelastic. This type of research belongs to the application of the principal-
agent approach with moral hazard.

Hart (1983a) provides a review of these newer insights by pointing out
that if only the firm, and not the workers, can observe the state of the world,

wages cannot be made dependent on the state of the world directly: "For if the contract says that wages should fall in bad times, then it is in the interest of the firm to always claim that times are bad. Instead wages can only depend on variables such as employment within the firm which are observable to both the firm and the workers. Thus the contract will specify that the firm can reduce total wages, but only if it reduces employment. As a consequence, in bad states, employment will fall by more than it should from an efficient point of view, simply because this is the only way the firm can get wages down" (3).

In their introduction to a symposium issue of the *Quarterly Journal of Economics*, Azariadis and Stiglitz (1983) write about the role of information and the implementability of the implicit labor contract hypothesis. Seen from a Keynesian viewpoint, the problem with this kind of analysis is, apparently, that it explains only the real wage and not nominal wage stickiness.

Azariadis and Cooper (1985) address the problem of nominal wage stickiness without reaching the desired outcome—a coherent story of money-wage rigidity. Typically macroeconomic models like Fischer 1977, Barro 1977, and Okun 1981 do not give a full microeconomic derivation of sticky nominal wages.

### 5.9.5. Incomplete Contract Theory

While in the principal-agent approach the focus of the analysis is on asymmetries of information *between* contractors, incomplete contract models of the type described previously devote their attention to cases in which private information is *shared* by the contracting parties but unavailable to outsiders like courts. The situation is one of observable but *unverifiable* information. The central issue is the lock-in effect due to transaction-specific investments. The first scholars to investigate this sort of incompleteness were Grossman and Hart (1986) and Hart and Moore (1988). There are other early articles on incomplete contracts. In most of them, it is assumed that certain contingent statements have fixed costs associated with them. In extreme cases, the costs are infinite and therefore cannot be included in the contract at all. See, for example, Crawford 1988, Dye 1985, Grout 1984, Hall and Lazear 1984, Rogerson 1984, Shavell 1980, and Weitzman 1981. The next objective is to report briefly on the line of incomplete contract research put forward by Hart and Moore, Grossman and Hart, and others.

Grossman and Hart (1986, 1987) developed the model illustrated in section 5.5. They developed a theory of vertical integration and ownership based on the concept of contractual incompleteness in the sense of asymmetric information between the parties to the contract and outsiders. Certain variables (the cost of a quality improvement, its value, and the amount of specific investments) are *observable* to the contractual parties but are *not verifiable* to out-siders. Grossman and Hart do not distinguish between ownership and control and virtually define ownership as a power to exercise control. For them, owner-ship is the purchase of the residual rights of control, that is, rights that are too costly to be specified: "Vertical integration is the purchase of the assets of a supplier (or of a purchaser) for the purpose of acquiring the residual rights of control" (1986, 716).

According to Hart and Moore (1988), the incompleteness of the initial contract is understood in this paper, as above in section 5.5. The principle concern, though, is to provide for the possibility of revising and/or renegotiat-ing the contract once the unknown future becomes the present. The information problem here concerns the act of delivery of the good. The contractual parties can observe, but cannot demonstrate to outsiders, whether the good has in fact been delivered or whether its acceptance was refused. The authors deal with the problem of designing an optimal revision game to be played once the unknown state of the world is realized. The purpose of this is to yield final quantities and prices that are appropriately sensitive to the parties' benefits and costs. As in Grossman and Hart 1986, the optimal incomplete contract is, at least, second-best. Aghion, Dewatripont, and Rey (1990, 1991) argue that unverifiability by third parties is not sufficient to explain underinvestment in specific assets (second-best solutions). They show that the problem can often be overcome by contractual *renegotiation design.* That is, problems can be overcome by the design of rules that govern the process of renegotiation.

> Such rules, while overlooked in contract theory, are commonly observed in practice. For instance, joint venture contracts, which typically require specific investments, usually outline a procedure to be followed in case one of the parent firms wants to quit the joint venture. Construction contracts sometimes include *per diem* penalties when some pre-specified dead-lines are not met. For office building projects, some contracts stress that only the architect can make new price proposals in case a contracting party wishes to modify the initial project. If the base-ball player wants to quit his team before the end of his contract, he must abide by bargaining rules which, although not formally written, are thoroughly followed. Fi-nally, severance payments and no-strike provisions typically influence the outcome of labor contract renegotiations. (1991, 2)

Chung (1991) shows that nonverifiability does not prevent efficient relation-specific investments if agents are risk neutral. "Specifically, when the parties are risk neutral, efficient investments and outcomes can be induced by a contract that specifies a quantity and a payment together with an ex post revision via a take-it-or-leave-it offer, regardless of the identity of the party who makes such an offer" (1991, 1032).

Aghion and Bolton (1992) depart from the models of Grossman and Hart and Hart and Moore by introducing explicit wealth constraints into their framework. The owner of a firm will choose its financial structure by weighing the marginal costs of diluting his control rights to new shareholders against the marginal costs of debt and default.

Hart and Moore (1989) consider a dynamic model with incomplete contracts that takes account of situations in which issues of control and ownership arise. They deal, in particular, with the question of how to get the borrower to transfer nonverifiable revenues to the lender. The problem is solved by giving the lender liquidation rights in the event of default.

Zender (1991) considers an agency model with wealth constraints in which the limited wealth of both the entrepreneur and the investor prevents one of them from becoming a full residual claimant. Unlike Aghion and Bolton (1992), Zender shows that bankruptcy induces efficient investment decisions rather than providing a framework for renegotiation.

Holmstrom and Tirole (1991) developed a model that may be interpreted as a generalization of the model originated by Grossman and Hart (1986). Contrary to the latter, however, Holmstrom and Tirole incorporate explicitly the separation of ownership and control and analyze how different levels of decentralization influence the determination of transfer prices and the design of managerial incentives.

For a comprehensive overview of the incomplete contract issue, see Hart and Holmstrom 1987 and Holmstrom and Tirole 1989. On the state of the debate, see Jean Tirole's Walras-Bowley lecture of 1994 (Tirole 1994). Hart (1995, chap. 2) establishes what he calls a "property-rights approach" to the theory of the firm through the use of incomplete contract theory. According to this view, the owner of an asset has the *residual property rights* over that asset, "the right to decide all usages of the asset in any way not inconsistent with a prior contract, custom, or law" (30). For a general, easy to read description of his ideas, see also Hart (1989).

### 5.9.6. Self-Enforcing Agreements

Among the first formal articles on self-enforcing agreements are those of Telser (1980) and Klein and Leffler (1981). The basic hypothesis of the two articles is, as Telser formulates it, "that someone is honest only if honesty, or the appearance of honesty, pays more than dishonesty" (29). Klein and Leffler stress the role of *reputation* in this context. The function of sunk cost in production capital or in advertising expenditures etc. is to ensure the supply of quality.

Shapiro (1983) builds on the Klein and Leffler article by developing more precisely the concept of a reputation equilibrium. He includes in his analysis perfect competition, free entry, and quality choices by firms under imperfect information.

An important hypothesis contained within models of this general type is that quality depends on price. This has some fundamental implications such as the idea that demand curves may not be downward sloping, demand and supply may not be neatly separable, and markets may be thin (Stiglitz 1987).

Bull (1987) deals with the issue of implicit labor contracts and the role of reputation in "completing" a contract. He speaks of "implicit contracts," which he describes as nontrivial Nash equilibria in the posthiring trading game between a worker and an employer. These are supported by intrafirm, rather than labor market, reputations. The existence of an implicit contract that supports efficient trade is proved in a simple model.

Kreps (1990a) describes a theory of the firm (or other organizations) on the basis of the concept of a relational or incomplete contract between the employer and his employees. The firm or organization is characterized by its reputation: "The way an organization adapts to an unforeseen contingency can add to or detract from that reputation, with consequences for the amount of faith future employees . . . will have. This faith is the glue that permits mutually beneficial transactions to take place . . . " (92). The role of corporate culture is developed on the basis of the concept of reputation.

Reputation effects play a role in the theory of repeated games. Bull (1987) and Kreps (1990a) follow this literature by assuming infinite repetition in order to avoid unraveling problems. Trading relationships of finite length with asymmetric information, though, are studied by Kreps and Wilson (1982) and Milgrom and Roberts (1982).

Carmichael (1989) points out that self-enforcing implicit contracts are quickly taking over in the theory of labor markets. The main reason is that they seem to capture explicitly the idea that a firm's promises to its workers can be reliable even though they are not legally enforceable. He illustrates in his article some of the important ideas in the context of a very simple incentive model and outlines some of the accomplishments and limitations of the life cycle incentives explanation for wage growth and mandatory retirement provided, for example, by Lazear (1979, 1981).

### 5.10.  Suggested Readings for Chapter 5

Contract theory is not particularly easy to understand. Thus, to help the reader find his way into this field, we provide a few suggestions for first readings. For further studies, one should make use of our bibliographical notes in section 5.9.

1. *Managerial theory of the firm:* For a good textbook presentation of the managerial theory of the firm, see Gravelle and Rees (1987, chap. 13).

Williamson's expense-preference theory is explained there. The reader is advised to read also the article by Williamson (1963). For an extreme view of the "managerial capitalism" hypothesis, see the survey by Hughes (1987).

2. *The theory of contracts—general overviews:* The complete field of contract theory (principal-agent theory, theories of implicit contracts, incomplete contracts, and self-enforcing contracts) is reviewed briefly and quite readably by Worrall (1989) and more extensively by Hart and Holmstrom (1987). Don't mind the mathematics. The articles are interesting to read even without mastering the formal analysis briefly mentioned in them.

3. *The principal-agent model:* A general introduction into the two types of the principal-agent approach is provided by Arrow (1985b, chap. 2). Sappington (1991) gives an excellent exposition of the principal-agent approach and its various applications.

For the formal approach of the moral hazard type of the principal-agent theory, see Varian (1992, chap. 25); or Kreps (1990b, chap. 16). The latter shows the connection of the PA approach with game theory. For an algebraic calculation similar to the one presented in section 5.2, see Holmstrom and Milgrom (1987, 323 ff.); and Spremann (1987).

A readable presentation of formal approaches to the hidden information (adverse selection) type of the principal-agent theory can be found in Varian (1992, chap. 25); or Kreps (1990b, chap. 17). For a more detailed presentation, see Philips (1988, chaps. 3 and 6). It is essential to read the first description of the lemons problem by Akerlof (1970). It is also important to read Spence (1974), who introduced the market-signaling concept.

Stiglitz (1985) provides an interesting evaluation of the "new informational economics," as some authors call this approach. For the implications of information economics for macroeconomics, see Stiglitz (1987) or Akerlof and Yellen (1986).

4. *Implicit contracts:* A good introductory overview is given by Azariadis (1987). An extensive, and not very formal, survey of implicit contract theory is provided by Rosen (1985). More demanding to read is the survey by Hart (1983a). The mathematical example given in our text was inspired by Blanchard and Fischer (1989, 429ff.).

5. *Incomplete contracts:* For an introduction to incomplete contract theory of the kind presented here, read Hart (1987) plus Holmstrom and Tirole (1989, 66 ff.). The formal approach to incomplete contract theory presented earlier is from Tirole (1988, 29 ff.). As far as the article by Grossman and Hart (1986) is concerned, one should read the first pages for general information on their interpretation of ownership. The relationship between the transaction-cost approach of Williamson (1975, 1985) and Klein, Crawford, and Alchian (1978) is expounded in part 1 of Hart (1995), a very readable book.

6. *Self-enforcing agreements:* It is best to start with Telser (1980) and

Klein and Leffler (1981). The mathematical model on reputation presented in our text is from Tirole (1988, 121). The model follows a very readable article by Shapiro (1983), who provided a clear exposition of the issues involved. For a game-theoretic interpretation of efficiency wages, see Gibbons (1992, 107 ff.).

An interesting application of the reputation effect is given in Kreps's (1990a) interpretation of corporate culture.

See the overview by Carmichael (1989) for a discussion of the application of the hypothesis of self-enforcing agreements in the theory of labor markets.

CHAPTER 6

# The New Institutional Economics
# Applied to Markets, Firms, and the
# State: General Remarks

Having described and briefly illustrated the analytical methods of the New
Institutional Economics, we are now in a position to illustrate more systematically the application of this new research style. We shall do this for three basic
types of institutions (organizations): markets, firms, and states. Before proceeding with this plan, however, we wish to remind the reader of several
fundamental points. First, it must be recognized that central to modern institutional economics is the solution of the coordination problem of economic
transactions between individuals by mutual agreement. The concept of the
*relational contract* is used to explain cooperation between individuals in a
world with unforeseeable events. Second, depending on circumstances, relational contracts are "administered," "organized," or "governed" by different
"governance structures," "orders," or "constitutions" which are explicitly or
implicitly developed through the activities of cooperating individuals. Markets
and "hierarchies" are the two extremes. The economic problem for neoinstitutionalists is then to determine which institutional arrangement (governance
structure, order, or constitution) is "rational," or economically preferable, under which detailed circumstances. In principle, the institutional solution
adopted can be one of the two extreme forms (markets or hierarchies) or
anything in between.

Relational contracts between individuals may be bilateral or multilateral—such as bilateral cooperation between buyer and seller in a market
exchange or multilateral cooperation between all buyers and sellers forming a
market or a firm. These are joint actions between two or more individuals. In
the latter case, the term *collective action* is used in the literature. Collective
action can be private (the market, the firm) or public (the community, the state,
etc.). As a result, the New Institutional Economics works at two levels of
analysis. There is a macroscopic level that deals with what Davis and North
(1971, 6) call the *institutional environment* and a microscopic level that the
same authors call *institutional arrangements.* Williamson (1993a, 53) speaks
of the institutions of governance. Williamson's transaction-cost economics

deals with the latter. The institutional framework—"the customs, norms, politics, judiciary, property, and contract laws—are considered as shift parameters that change the competitive costs of governance" (1993a, 74). North (1990), on the other hand, uses the concept of transaction costs to analyze the institutional environment.

In the following chapter we wish to consider the application of the NIE to the analysis of both the institutional environment and institutional arrangements. Unlike North, we shall argue that the concept of relational contracts can be applied, as in transaction-cost economics, to the analysis of the institutional environment.

Thus, the elementary legal framework of the classic liberalist state described in section 1.3 can be interpreted as the governance structure of a multilateral or collective relational contract among its constituents. In a similar manner, it is possible to understand the organizational or institutional framework of a market or a firm. In this way, institutions or organizations can be explained as the result of contractual activities (intended or not) of the individuals who use them.

The present chapter therefore begins with a general description and interpretation of the elements of the institutional environment of a private ownership economy, that is, its elementary order or rules, which we use as a benchmark for the analysis in the following chapters.

## 6.1. The Elementary Rules of a Private Ownership Economy

The institution of a private ownership economy is not to be understood as a structure having a dome comprised of the rules of civil law and its relevant judgments, a floor, far below, where competing individuals negotiate and conclude exchange contracts, and nothing in between but thin air. Rather, the space between the external institutional hull (the constitutional rules) and the "floor" of the economy is filled with special private or public organizations that are established and extended by individuals through private or public collective actions and corresponding working rules. In fact, the everyday transactions between buyers and sellers on markets or between members of a firm are carried out within specific organizational structures that grow from below and in which personal relationships play an important role. In other words, markets and firms are networks of more or less relational contracts between individuals who act in their own names or in someone else's. They are social constructs that involve, besides their rules, investments in the cultivation of the "relation" between individuals ("Verhältnisse"). For example, strengthening the organizational culture (or mutual trust) represents an important goal of such investments.

It is important to realize that the concept of relational contracts is applicable to *all* relationships of an economy and thus to the institutional hull itself, the "dome" of constitutional rules "far above." In a general sense, a private ownership economy is a system of self-enforcing relational contracts of different duration and plasticity that support each other and sustain the outer hull, that is, the economy's (formal and informal) constitution. The system is held together by convention (Binmore 1994). In fact, our entire political-economic life can be understood as a system of multilateral relational contracts in which bargaining is pervasive. What interests us in this section is the elementary *constitutional* and *operational rules* of the private ownership economy, which steer individual behavior—that is, the institutional framework of a private ownership economy.

Essential for the institution of a private ownership economy is the fact that the transfer of individual property rights is, in principle, voluntary. The elementary *constitutional rules,* therefore, have to be based on the principle of the inviolability of individual property rights. This demands, as was shown in section 1.3, an elementary legal order plus its enforcement apparatus, which regulates:

1. The *property* of individuals (according to the principle of private property)
2. The *transfer* of these property rights by mutual consent (according to the principle of freedom of contract)
3. The individual's *liability* in cases of tortious acts or for contractual obligations (according to the principles of neminem laede and pacta sunt servanda)

The principle of the inviolability of private property, that is, its voluntary transfer, implies that contracts are not to become a dictate of the more powerful. This condition can be achieved (to a degree) by competition within collectively set limits. That is, agreement must exist in society concerning the use of violence and other illicit activities such as industrial spying. In economics, as in sports, the rules of the game of competition must be characterized by the principle of fair play. Old institutional economists like Schmoller (1900, 58) criticized adherents of free competition for demanding the abolishment of legal barriers. He did not accept the argument that morality would develop by itself, that "legal rule would be too mechanical, would create harm here and there," or that "free rearrangement would be sufficient, would be preferable, because the inner moral forces would be sufficient." Rather, Schmoller believed that social institutions and organizations, among them the state, are the most important result of our moral life. They are its "cristallization" (61). The New Institutional Economics does not, as yet, analyze ethical questions, but it comes pretty close to it (cf. Richter 1994). Business ethics has become an issue in business education in the United States since the 1980s (cf., e.g., DeGeorge 1990), and it has received increasing interest in Germany (cf. Homann and Blome-Drees 1992).

To enforce the rules of the game of competition, or of business in general, a large modern society cannot do without the help of the state. Competition as a control mechanism needs to be supplemented by the authority of the courts or the state in general.

The problem is, though, that the state not only has the power to protect private property but the power to take it away. The basic condition for a market economy to work, therefore, is, besides the elementary legal order just described, a credible commitment by the state to respect private property as well (North 1994). "Thriving markets require not only the appropriate system of property rights and a law of contracts, but a secure political foundation that places strong limits on the ability of the state to confiscate wealth" (Weingast 1993, 1).

The elementary constitutional rules of the private ownership economy are complemented by a number of elementary *operational rules* or regulations whose primary purpose is to lower transaction costs, that is, the costs of resource allocation. Some of them are general in character while others are more transaction specific. Among the operational rules of *general character* are those concerning common:

1. Language and writing
2. Ethical values
3. Numerical systems
4. Measures and weights
5. Division of time (hours, days, weeks)
6. Units of account and means of exchange (money)

Evidently, these six operational rules are indispensable to furthering production and trade, and the first two are indispensable for human social life in general. All six rules can, and probably did, develop by means of some invisible hand process. Yet, as we have learned from experience, they can be considerably improved and cultivated through private or public collective actions concerning the supply of

7. General education
8. Communication
9. Transportation
10. Money (e.g., mints of money and banks of issue)

For an organization—that is, the institutional rules plus the people applying them properly—*education* is vital. Its task is to build up and cultivate ethical and moral codes of the economy, a point aptly stressed by Max Weber (1905, 1930) in his famous article "The Protestant Ethic and the Spirit of Capitalism." Some of his views can be translated into the concept of "organizational culture" in the sense of Kreps (1990a).[1] Education—the way to learn how to learn—is of vital importance in a world of strong uncertainty and complex problems, as becomes clear in reading the exploratory study by Denzau and North (1994).

To set up, apply, and protect the constitutional and operational rules, and to train the users of these rules correspondingly, requires the input of resources—that is, *political transaction costs* as described in section 2.2.3.

Finally, there are operational rules that deal with the allocation of specific resources (wheat, labor, etc.) through exchange contracts. These *specific operational rules* regulate transaction activities of:

11. The precontractual phase (with search and inspection)
12. The conclusion of contracts
13. The postcontractual phase (with execution, control, and enforcement)

They comprise six types of *transaction activities;* namely, search, inspection, contracting, execution, control, and enforcement.

In effect, these six transaction activities are concerned with the handling of information. They can be organized, in a private ownership economy, either within markets (by market transaction) or within firms (by hierarchical transaction). Their organization may be the result of bilateral or multilateral cooperation. In the latter case, public or private collective action may occur. That is, market orders can be set up and administered by the state, private individuals, or both. Examples are medieval or modern fairs, stock exchanges, public regulation of trade, and informal market organizations.

In the next two chapters, on markets (chap. 7) and firms (chap. 8), we assume, following the style of reasoning of the NIE, that the constitutional and general operational rules are given. In the chapter on states (chap. 9) we shall deal instead with NIE aspects of the general institutional framework of society.

## 6.2. General Remarks on Organizations: The Firm, the Market, and the State

As was mentioned in section 1.1, organizations are generally understood as structured groups of individuals who seek to achieve common goals. Firms,

---

1. On the role of the focal principle in a monetary economy, see, for example, Richter (1994).

markets, and states are organizations in this sense. In case of the firm, such common goals are, for example, to secure the parties' transaction-specific investments, to maximize the firm's residual gains (i.e., the owners' income), and so on. In the case of the market, a number of common goals of potential buyers and sellers can be identified. In general, a market represents a means for increasing the utility of those who participate in it. Thus, an increase in the size of a market is desired because of the economies of scale and scope that size can bring about. Similarly, other goals can be the optimization of the market's locations, the easing of exchange (by, e.g., the use of particular contracting techniques), payment practices, and so on. As for a state, a major common goal in a private ownership economy is to supply a certain level of public goods and to raise enough taxes for this purpose.

The individual members of an organization have their own objectives, which partly coincide with the common target and partly do not. Externality problems are solved by an explicitly or implicitly agreed upon limitation of the range of feasible individual decisions, a formal or informal "constitution."

One important reason for the formation (evolution) of organizations is that *information* is not a free good. It needs to be produced (discovered, invented, searched, or found out by bargaining) and, under certain conditions, can be exchanged. Inter alia, it needs to be made credible or trustworthy. In fact, the way information is produced, transferred, and made credible are characteristic features of an organization. Property rights in information (e.g., property rights to price quotes; see Mulherin, Netter, and Overdahl (1991) and other types of economic incentives play an important role in this context.

Following the viewpoint of the New Economics of Organizations (Moe 1984; Williamson 1993a; and sec. 1.1),[2] we regard an organization (in the economic sense) to be a network of (more or less) relational contracts between individuals whose purpose is to regulate economic transactions (including transactions in information) between individual members of the organization. The organization's "governance structure" or "constitution" depends inter alia on the degree of asset specificity and the frequency of said transactions. Time plays an essential role. The relational contracts may be multilateral, as, for example, in the contract between the partners of a law firm or the owner-traders of a stock exchange, or they may be bilateral, as between the employer and the employees of a firm. The transaction-cost approach of Williamson (1985) and its variants deal only with bilateral relationships. The property rights approach in its old garb, dealing with *absolute* property rights like ownership in things, is

---

2. Vanberg (1992, 238ff.) speaks in this context of the *constitutional paradigm* of organization theory. The "nexus of contracts approach" of the New Economics of Organizations falls, according to his classification, under either the constitutional or the exchange paradigm (the Alchian and Demsetz [1972] view of the firm), depending on how it is specified (239).

a technique for handling multilateral coordination. Property rights define the economic or material position of each individual relative to the rest of society. They make decentralization of decisions possible. Its order constitution can be viewed as the result of a multilateral agreement (e.g., a convention in the sense of Hume or Sugden) meant to facilitate multilateral coordination. The other extreme is to completely centralize decision making. In its pure form, it is practically never done, not even in a Soviet-type economy or in the army.

The concept of an international regime, suggested by political scientists such as Keohane (1984), presupposes the existence of a mixture of centralization and decentralization of decision making. Keohane uses the transaction-cost approach in his analysis, which deals with the structure of relative property rights. With the aid of the regime concept, political scientists explain the voluntary cooperation between sovereign states (see in chap. 9). The question we have to deal with in this context is: how should the contractual relationship between many parties be organized to save on transaction costs? The simplest answer is to have a central party common to all contracts, that is, the *hegemon* (in case of international regimes) or the *entrepreneur* (in case of a firm).[3] This answer was already given by Coase (1937). We are back again to bilateral agreements, understood as the "cheapest" way to solve the multilateral contract problem (i.e., to save on bargaining and influence costs; see Milgrom and Roberts 1990a). In other cases, though, this may be impractical, and direct multilateral contractual relationships between the members of the organization may be economically preferable or politically unavoidable (the United Nations Organization [UNO], EC, etc.—see Keohane 1984). In a way, we can say that all organizations are characterized by the assignment of absolute property rights in combination with a regulation indicating how these property rights can be used or transferred. And this arrangement can be interpreted as the governance structure or constitution of an explicit or implicit relational contract.

Note that the relational contract concept deals with all sorts of transactions: market transactions, managerial transactions, and political transactions (as described in chap. 2). In addition, there are social transactions that play a more or less important role in all social relationships, namely, the exchange of symbols of approval or prestige (Homans 1958, 606; Blau 1964). Social transactions engender feelings of unspecified, diffuse, future personal obligations, trust, and gratitude (Blau 1964, quoted in Starr and MacMillan 1990, 80). They are, of course, also valuable vehicles of information. "Social capital" (Schlicht 1984; Coleman 1990) is built up by both economic and social transactions. It

---

3. This could also be the hegemon of a market organization, which may be understood as the agent of the prospective trading partners (his principals). The concept of the administered contract (Goldberg 1976) as a long-term relational PA contract becomes applicable here.

consists of a set of obligations, expectations, and mutually developed norms and sanctions that evolve from prior social interactions (Starr and MacMillan 1990, 80). Friendship is an example (Ben-Porath 1980). The role of the concept of organizational culture, as a method to transfer information and help guarantee its content (sec. 4.4.3), is to be seen in this context. The "relation" becomes, within limits, an objective of its own. Weak solidarity (Lindenberg 1988) and loyalty (Hirschman 1969; Simon 1991) are important norms for the functioning of social relations. The need to educate the members of an organization accordingly becomes understandable. As Popper (1957, 66) puts it, institutions are like fortresses: "They must be well designed *and* properly manned." *General education and professional training* are important means to this end (the "training and drilling process," as Schmoller [1900, 61] explains).

We shall now introduce basic definitions of the three organizations we are going to examine: firms, markets, and states.

A *firm* is understood in this book as a network of relational contracts between individuals[4] (generally the resource owners) with the purpose of efficiently organizing production. Characteristically, what is involved is the giving of orders through *managerial or hierarchical transactions.*[5] The relational contracts are based largely on freely concluded long-term contracts protected by law (e.g., employment contracts), given an institutional framework of the kind described in the previous section (the constitutional and general operational rules). Relational contracts' governance structure determines the production and transfer of information and the methods that help to make information credible. Differently expressed, they determine the firm-specific property-rights assignments of each member of the firm and regulate how these property rights can be used or transferred. The organization firm deals, in the first place, with the transaction activities of the postcontractual phase (execution, control, and enforcement).

Contrary to most of the economics literature, in which markets are simply assumed to be "there," we argue that not only the firm but also the market, even the primitive market, is an organization in the sense we have described. Note, however, that the terms *market* and *organization* are generally regarded as opposite terms in the literature—see, for example, Albert (1967, 393), who defines an organization as a social structure "for which a central leadership exists, while a market is structure, for which this is not the case." Vanberg

---

4. Self-employment without employees is here understood as a limiting case of the firm.

5. Kreps (1990a, 99) uses the term *hierarchical transactions* for transactions in which certain terms are left unspecified in advance ("what is specified is that one of the two parties has, within broad limits, the contractual right to specify how the contract will be fulfilled"). This is opposed to the concept of "specified transactions" (Macneil's discrete transactions) in which all terms are spelled out in advance.

(1982, 76) speaks of two types of patterns of relational networks. One is the exchange model, which is the characteristic feature of markets, and the other is the centrally coordinated network of corporate membership relations, which is the characteristic feature of organizations. Such a clear distinction between the two is appropriate, though, only for the neoclassical world of costless transactions, and we are not considering that case here. Interestingly, Williamson (1975), in his transaction-cost approach, does distinguish between markets and hierarchies. This inconsistency is possibly the result of Williamson's disregard of the precontractual phase of operations. What must be emphasized is that, in a world of positive transaction costs, there exists a difference between occasional exchange and exchange through the use of a market as a social *arrangement for repeated exchange among a plurality of potential market participants*.[6] Personal contacts, cooperation, "relationships," and social ties between potential buyers and sellers (including hierarchical relationships and relationships arising from organized groups)[7] all play roles in the "personal side" of the institution (see sec. 1.1). In other words, a market does not function in a social vacuum (Hamilton and Feenstra 1995, 61). The problem of costly transactions and their relation to social structure has to be faced.[8] This goes for the "commodity" as well as the "financial" side of the market.

Thus, a *market* is understood in this book as a network of (more or less) relational contracts among individuals who are potential buyers and sellers and may be engaged in vertical business relationships or those based on cartels, trade organizations, and so on. The arrangement reached is intended to promote an efficacious institutional environment for trade in the sense of providing for (1) "competition . . . for opportunities of exchange among a plurality of potential parties" (Weber 1968, 635), and (2) the exchange itself, that is, *market transactions*. The relational contracts are concerned with, or based on, all types of exchange contracts (sales, lease, employment, or loan contracts), given an institutional framework of the kind just described. The governance structure of relational contracts determines the production and transfer of information and the methods that help to make information credible. Differently expressed, governance structure helps to define the market-specific property-rights assignments of each potential trader and to indicate how these property rights can be used or transferred. The organization market deals, in the first place, with the transaction activities of the precontractual phase (search, inspection) and contract conclusion itself, but in many instances it also influences postcontractual activities. Note that relational contracts among (actual or

---

6. This follows Weber (1968, 635). However, Weber does not deal with the problem of the social structure of markets and its relation to transaction costs.
7. This is in the sense of Olson (1965) (see sec. 2.2.3).
8. This issue is treated more extensively in Richter 1996b.

potential) market participants can be quite loose or limited for some participants. Examples of this approach are found in the case of spontaneously organized markets such as the "Polish Market" in East Berlin after the elimination of the Wall in 1989 or the various black markets around the Kaiserstrasse in Frankfurt am Main after 1945. On the other hand, the relational contract in operation may be very strict in its provisions, as in the New York Diamond Dealers Club or the New York Stock Exchange. There is, in short, a wide spectrum of possible relationships among potential market participants, relationships that can be more or less narrow with a perfectly "invisible hand pole" on the one end and a perfectly "visible hand pole" on the other. Our point is that there always exists some organization that characterizes a particular market and has to be developed. No market is simply "there."

There is no sharp and clear difference between a hierarchical and a market transaction (or between a firm and a market). Time plays a role, yet deferred exchanges also occur on markets, for example, the purchase of a good now to be delivered tomorrow and paid for a week later. Specific investments and the resulting lock-in effects can be found in both types of organizations, markets and firms. Also, as in the firm, the right to determine how the contract is to be completed can be left to one party in the case of an agreed-upon market exchange. For example, a relational purchasing contract that determines only in very general terms what types of goods are to be exchanged during a period of time of considerable length (say, a year), may leave the actual specifications to the buyer. In a general sense, we may say that, in case of market transactions, the parties are less locked in, or "closer" to other opportunities, than in the case of hierarchical transactions.

Note further that hierarchical transactions of a sort can be found also in lease and loan contracts—not only in the employment contracts of a firm. There are markets for loans, leases, and employment just as there are sales markets. A loan, lease, or employment contract is typically a long-term contract, though sales contracts may also be long term. The distinction between the organizations "firm" and "market" are therefore not always helpful. It might be better to distinguish between the organization of search, inspection, and contracting of *any* kind of deferred or nondeferred exchange contract on a market and the organization of the completion of the contractual relations thereafter. The first would then be called a "market" organization and the second (for want of a better term) a "nonmarket" organization—including the firm as a special case. This distinction relates to a great part of a modern market economy (Simon 1991).

The organizations "firm" and "market," considered in this book, are special cases of private collective actions, in the sense of individuals cooperating on the basis of freely concluded *formal* contracts protected by law, and *infor-*

*mal,* self-enforcing, or otherwise protected relational contracts, given the constitutional[9] and the general operational rules.

Entrepreneurial activities play a role in both markets and firms. Market making is also an economic activity (Gould 1980). The incentive in this case is the establishment of property rights in market organizations. Note that organizational capital, which is protected by public or private barriers to entry, can be exchanged for a price (Prescott and Visscher 1980). An example here would be the right to trade on the New York Stock Exchange. As in the case of the firm, the entrepreneur as a market maker does not need to invest his own money (does not need to be a financial risk bearer), though capital is necessary to establish or extend markets. Cases of this type exist currently in eastern Germany as that region seeks to build institutions appropriate to a market economy. Both in firms and in markets, what the entrepreneur needs to do is to establish and lead "private collective actions" to create the necessary structures. For this he needs to acquire and use information (as Hayek 1937 and Kirzner 1973 stress) and show an ability to form voluntary coalitions, networks of relational contracts, between many resource owners, including capital owners. Note, however, that the figure of the entrepreneur (or hegemon) is typically not analyzed by the representatives of the transaction-cost approach.

For many transactions, it is not clear a priori whether they are better organized within a market (through market transactions) or within a firm (through hierarchical transactions). Outsourcing of, say, the production of car doors may be relatively more efficient for automobile production than own production is. Furthermore, the boundaries between markets and firms are blurred, as a closer look at such things as marketing procedures illustrates: the choice of "marketing channels" may be organized via independent wholesale and retail firms, directly by the producer, through franchisees, and so on. And industries such as the automobile industry, sportswear and equipment, and the computer industry consist of more or less widely knitted networks of complex relational contracts between firms and markets: product markets, financial markets, advertising markets, on down to actual consumer markets. In some cases, markets and firms coexist within the same organization (e.g., stock exchanges and auction houses). Simon (1991) speaks in this context of the ambiguity of organizations (meaning firms and the like) in a capitalist market economy.

An important insight of the institutional economic approach is that market failure may be dealt with by privately owned firms. As Arrow (1969) points out, transaction costs can be regarded as being the general reason for the

---

9. Instead of constitutional rules one can also use the term "economic constitution," as understood by the German Freiburg School (see Böhm, Eucken, and Grossmann-Doerth 1936).

nonexistence or failure of markets. Collective actions are necessary to over-come market failures, but they do not need to be state actions. "Indeed firms of any complexity are illustrations of collective action, the internal allocation of their resources being directed by authoritative and hierarchical controls" (62).

In this context, it may be worthwhile to have a look at the employment problem as it is considered in macroeconomics. A large group of markets, which generally "fail" in actual life, is that of future goods. Keynes (1936) illustrates this point with the well-known opening remarks of chapter 16 of his "General Theory":

An act of individual saving means—so to speak—a decision to have dinner or to buy a pair of boots a week hence. . . . [A]n individual deci-sion to save does not, in actual fact, involve the placing of any specific forward order for consumption. (210–11)

For this reason, Keynes demands a greater responsibility of the state for directly organizing investment (1936, 164). But, as we have argued, collective action to overcome market failure can also be a private collective action such as the founding of a privately owned firm. Also the establishment of long-term business relationships (of "intimate business relations" as Jevons calls them) as they occur in many market transactions helps to overcome the failing or miss-ing markets for future goods. The Industrial Revolution illustrates best how networks of privately owned firms, coordinated via markets by relational con-tracts, solved this problem successfully. Besides private firms, there are coor-dination mechanisms such as long-term business relationships and "hybrid" forms between markets and hierarchies such as franchises and political coali-tions (pressure groups, political parties, public authorities, etc.).

In considering the ways society can react to overcome market failure, Arrow (1969, 62) also draws attention to the "less visible form of social action: norms of social behavior, including ethical and moral codes. . . . It is useful for individuals to have some trust in each other's word. In the absence of trust it would become very costly to arrange for alternative sanctions and guarantees, and many opportunities for mutually beneficial cooperation would have to be foregone." To make promises trustworthy, *credible commitments* need to be established. This is unproblematic if agreements can be made binding by the courts, but such court-assured solutions are difficult to bring off in many relational contracts. Judicial solutions have to be substituted for by private ordering. This is where representatives of the NIE like Klein and Leffler (1981) and in particular Williamson (1983) contribute important insights (see chap. 4). In a sense, credible commitments (credibility) are the "cement" of relational contracts between individuals.

Thus, networks of relational contracts between individuals and firms (coalitions of individuals) and political groups and organizations characterize a market economy. Inter alia, they can be used to overcome the difficulties posed by the absence, or the limitations, of the markets for future goods. They extend into the future and help to reduce uncertainty regarding future spot markets. They facilitate adaptation to unforeseen events in a world driven by changes such as those arising from the appearance of new products, new markets, new production techniques, new forms of organization, and the results of political or natural events. They contribute to the rational formation of expectations (Simon 1991), and they help decision makers to overcome problems arising from informational asymmetries (like the lemons problem).

In fact, not only firms and markets but also the *economy* as a whole—the state in general—can be understood as a nexus of long-term relational contracts between individuals. So let us attempt a definition of the organization "state," understood as a constitutional democracy, in the sense of the New Institutional Economics.

A *state* is understood in this book as a network of relational principal-agent contracts between the constituents (the principals) and their representatives (their agents) with the objective of optimizing the public weal through a suitable organization of the use of force (coercion), that is, by the suitable allocation, administration, and transaction of political property rights. The governance structure (constitution) determines the flow of information and the methods that help make information credible (e.g., promises by the government or single politicians). Differently expressed, the constitution determines the nation-specific property-rights assignments of each constituent and indicates how these property rights can be used or transferred.

The division of powers among the various branches of government (legislative, administrative, and judicial), together with periodic democratic elections of lawmakers, provide a certain amount of control over the activities of lawmakers. These individuals, the members of governments and their administrators, are the agents, while the voters are the principals in this PA relationship. Yet, as in the cases discussed earlier, information between the agents and the principals is not only asymmetric but also incomplete regarding future events. Thus, the control of politicians and public administrators is similar to the control of managers of private firms. The constitutional state was certainly an achievement in political life, but, as in the case of economic relations, court ordering alone does not provide sufficient control of political relations and does not sufficiently protect the principals against the "bad behavior" of their agents. In the end, the political system has to be self-enforcing. Credible commitments, the reputation of individuals and institutions, play as important a role in political life as they do in economic life. Political institutions, from the constitution of a state downward, can be analyzed from this standpoint in a *constructive* way. That is, unlike the rent-seeking approach, which focuses on the deficiencies of governmental actions, the use of principal-agent concepts permits more positive suggestions to be made. An example of the constructive approach is found in the argument for the independence of the central bank of a state (in combination with the legal requirement to secure the purchasing power of money) as a method to make the government's commitment to sound money credible.

The open-endedness of relational contracts, as well as their system of formal and informal norms and enforcement mechanisms, are decisive for their success. So is the "training" of their participants, the development of their organizational culture. Appropriately structured, relational contracts between educated individuals offer an efficacious (relative efficient) solution to what Hayek (1945) called the main economic problem of society: rapid adaptation to change.[10] Yet, while Hayek thought only of market transactions, the representatives of the New Institutional Economics include also hierarchical transactions as an answer to the problem of rapid adaptation to change. In many cases, it is the preferable answer.

### 6.3. A Brief Guide to the Literature on Order and Organization

*On the Elementary Order of a Private Ownership Economy.* The concept of *order,* understood as a set of formal and informal rules that steer individual behavior in a particular direction, was not much analyzed by economists after Adam Smith. We find interest in an explanation of the *evolution* of order (or institutions) among Austrian economists like Carl Menger ([1883] 1963) or later Friedrich A. Hayek (1978), who support, as David Hume ([1739–40] 1969) did, an invisible hand theorem of the evolution of institutions like markets, money, private property, and states. A game-theoretic extension of this type of reasoning was later provided by Sugden (1986, 1989). This literature typically favors a laissez-faire policy toward the formation and further development of institutions—a view not shared by representatives of the German Historical School such as Schmoller (1900). For him, custom developed, from the recurrence of equal or similar situations in human life, through usage. Custom is formed by the complete set of human instincts or motives, not only

---

10. Hayek demands for that purpose that the ultimate decisions must be left to the people who are familiar with the circumstances of time and place, who know directly the relevant changes and the resources immediately available to respond to them. For him, it is the price system, the mechanism for communicating information, that is the "market" and not a "hierarchy." But, where the market fails, as in our example, the private firm may be the most efficient kind of organizational alternative.

by self-interest (Schmoller avoids the term *self-interest;* he speaks of *Erwerbstrieb*). Moral concerns (ethical forces) develop in the course of time and control our instincts (the natural forces). Both forces play an important role in the economy.[11]

Out of the German Historical School grew a comparative institutional style of reasoning (Werner Sombart's "economic systems" or Arthur Spiethoff's "economic style"), which, in combination with the fundamental laws of nature, leads to the theory of *economic order* or economic constitution developed by Böhm (1937), Eucken (1950), and other representatives of the Freiburg School.[12] These authors concentrated on the detailed study of the appropriate legal framework, or "order," of a free market economy. Thus, Eucken (1952, 25) suggested the development of an economic morphology to enable economists to "exactly ascertain" the forms of economic order realized since the Industrial Revolution and to determine how the economic process was controlled by these orders: "Perhaps one is able to succeed in this manner to find the searched for, useful forms of economic order." That is, unlike the work of the representatives of the New Institutional Economics, Eucken did not ask for an economic analysis of the historic forms of economic order. Rather, he assumed them as given "data." And, unlike Hayek, Eucken did not favor laissez faire because he was afraid that such a policy would concede too much power to monopoly. He therefore concluded: "The economic system has to be consciously shaped" (1950, 314). But he is against state intervention into the economic process: "The State has to influence the *forms,* within which economic activities are carried out, not the economic *process* itself" (1951, 71). This view became the basis of German Ordnungspolitik.[13]

In a very general sense any order or institution has to answer the same basic elementary needs independent of whether it evolves spontaneously or was constructed. For example: the use of money, any kind of money, requires an explicit or implicit *elementary currency order* (see Richter 1989a, 99–135).

The formal or informal *rules* of an order can be understood as *constraints* on individual behavior. Formal rules make up a small (although very important) part of the sum of constraints that shape individual choices. Informal rules develop spontaneously "determined by self-interest" (Weber 1968, 29); they are *conventions* in the sense of Lewis (1969), Sugden (1986, 1989), and Binmore (1992, chap. 9). Furthermore, informal rules are complemented and improved in their effectiveness by formal rules, which help lower information,

---

11. "One can view the economy as a system of natural forces or of ethical forces; it is both at the same time . . ." (Schmoller 1900, 59).
12. See Möller (1940) for a comparison of the work of Eucken with that of Sombart and Spiethoff.
13. For a brief description of Eucken's views, see Hutchison (1979).

monitoring, and enforcement costs (cf. North 1990, 46). The transaction-cost approach developed by North (1981, 1984b, 1990), Cheung (1969, 1983), Barzel (1982, 1989), and others deals with the evolution of the institutional framework from the standpoint of transaction costs without explicitly dealing with ex post opportunism (the subject of Williamson's transaction-cost economics). *Constitutional economics* (Buchanan 1990), a field that grew out of public choice theory with Buchanan and Tullock as its leading pioneers, is an Anglo-Saxon continuation of the early German work at Freiburg. Finally, a social order, or a social structure, is, of course, a central field of sociological research (see, e.g., Weber 1968, Blau 1964, Coleman 1990, and Elster 1989). The idea of *coercive force* (and the opposition to such force) has been neglected by economists, but the issue is at least considered in the sociological literature (e.g., in Blau 1964).

On the other hand, Williamson's transaction-cost economics assumes the constitutional and legal framework to be given. He concentrates on the analysis of the governance structure within private contracts (1994).

*On the Economics of Organizations.* There are, roughly speaking, two general strands in the economic theory of organization—a strongly formal axiomatic approach and an informal or semiformal, approach.

The first formal approach to the theory of organization is represented by the work of J. Marschak (1971, 1979), T. Marschak and Radner (1971), and Hurwicz (1960, 1973). It deals with questions of the *efficient design of organizations,* partly by assuming that the members of an organization are programmable robots (T. Marschak 1986) and partly by taking the incentive aspects of decentralization into account (Hurwicz 1986). Information processing is taken explicitly into account (Arrow 1985a). The latter work deals with the resource allocation mechanism in general, and it introduced what later became principal-agent theory. Among German mathematical economists who work in this line, Beckmann is to be mentioned. Concerned with organization theory, his studies explain the allocation and utilization of personnel in hierarchical organizations. Among other things, he points out the need for rank in organizing the division of labor (1978, 1988).

The second, informal or semiformal, approach focuses more on practical problems. This is the New Economics of Organization, which emerged during the last twenty-five years. This field overlaps the New Institutional Economics and is characterized by a contractual perspective on organizational relationships, a theoretical focus on hierarchical control, and formal analysis via incomplete contract models. Information is also regarded as an important issue. Contrary to the first approach, though, major interest is on the problem of sending false signals (a euphemism for cheating) and its avoidance through private efforts. For a review, see Moe 1984, and Williamson 1993a. Transaction costs play an important role here, too, and thus informational asymmetries are considered. "Trust" among people, as an "important lubricant of social system" (Arrow 1974), becomes an issue.

To make promises trustworthy, *credible commitments* need to be established (Schelling 1960). This is unproblematic if agreements can be made binding through the courts. But such a result is difficult or even impossible to achieve in certain situations. The credibility problem became a serious issue for economists after the rational expectations revolution in the 1970s.

Particularly interesting from our viewpoint is the literature on self-enforcing contracts mentioned in chapter 5, (see, e.g., Telser (1980), Klein and Leffler (1981), and Williamson (1983). In macroeconomics, the credibility problem became known as the "time-inconsistency problem," first noted by Kydland and Prescott (1977). It deals with the conflict of interest between the policymaker and his voters. For a broad survey of this important issue of today's theory of macroeconomic policy, see Persson (1988). The formal game-theoretic background was investigated by Rogoff (1987). Problems concerning the credibility of threats and promises are also considered by game theorists. Selten (1965, 1975) provides the basic machinery for examining the credibility of threats and promises. On this literature, see the bibliographical notes in Kreps (1990c, 543ff.).

Finally, we should mention that we do not make explicit use of game theory in our book. The reason is that, in the work of the representatives of the NIE, decisions made under lack of knowledge of what the future will bring are a central issue. On the other hand, game theory, in its present form, is a language in which one describes possible strategic interactions, and it requires (again in its current form) very detailed information about what can happen. It should be mentioned, though, that work has been done on boundedly rational behavior by game theorists such as Ken Binmore, David Kreps, and Reinhard Selten. The concept of organizational culture developed by Kreps (1990a) and the concept of casuistic structure of boundedly rational strategies of Selten (1990) are described in chapter 4).

## 6.4  Suggested Readings to Chapter 6

*The Elementary Order of a Private Ownership Economy.* It is best to begin by reading some sociological literature concerning the rational-action-based approach to sociological analysis (e.g., Coleman 1990). Continue with Hayek (1960, e.g., chaps. 4, 9–11) and (Hume [1739–40] 1969, bk. 3, pt. 2, secs. 1–6). Eucken [1952] 1975 (chap. 16) is strongly suggested for readers who understand German.

*On the Economics of Organizations.* First, read Arrow (1974), which provides an excellent survey of general organizational issues. Continue with Williamson (1993a), which describes how the New Theory of Organization, a version of the New Institutional Economics, has evolved from informal to increasingly formal analysis in the form of a combined analysis of law, economics, and organization.

On the various meanings of the term *trust* from the viewpoint of the economic theory of organization, see Williamson (1993e).

CHAPTER 7

# The New Institutional Economics
# of the Market

Coase (1988b, 7) argues that "although economists claim to study the working of the market, in modern economic theory the market itself has an even more shadowy role than the firm." And he goes on to say that "in the modern microeconomic textbook, the analysis deals with the determination of market prices, but discussion of the market itself has entirely disappeared." Coase is certainly right with respect to neoclassical microeconomic textbooks that deal with models of the zero-transaction-cost type. Henderson and Quandt (1958), for example, say only that in the market, "where consumers and entrepreneurs meet and exchange commodities," prices are determined.[1] German economists, too, like Eucken, a devotee of the "Ordo" analysis (Ordnungsdenken), write only that the market consists of the "meeting of supply and demand" (Eucken 1947, 175). Eucken adds that what we find in neoclassical microeconomics since Cournot (1838) is the importance of the number of suppliers and sellers and the entry conditions. Equilibrium market prices and quantities depend on the number of market participants. This is the famous structure-conduct-performance hypothesis of Bain (1956), which became the core of the field of industrial organization for a number of years (for an overview, see Schmalensee 1987).

Only during the last twenty or so years have information constraints and other transaction-cost issues been added to the agenda of scholars of industrial organization, among them the representatives of the NIE, in their research on the functioning of markets. As a result, "market imperfections" appeared in a new light, not necessarily as forms of monopolistic behavior but as efficient solutions of the problem of market organization related to transaction costs. The competition issue came to be seen in a more realistic light, that of organizing exchange in a transaction-cost-saving manner.

---

1. Marshall (1920, bk. 5, chap. 1) has a chapter on markets which is, however, general and does not deal with institutional detail. He argues that "the organization of markets is intimately connected both as cause and effect with money, credit, and foreign trade; a full study of it must therefore be deferred to a later volume, where it will be taken into connection with commercial and industrial fluctuations, and with combinations of producers and of merchants, of employers and employed" (270). To our knowledge, this volume was never written by Marshall.

## 7.1. The Market as Organization

In a world of costless transactions, a market without any kind of cooperation (or personal relations) between traders is imaginable. But in the real world of positive transaction costs and bounded rationality, perfect competition would consist of individuals playing blind-man's bluff, drifting around suspicious of each other, and avoiding trade (or much of it) for lack of the resources needed to find suitable and trustworthy trading partners. At the same time, the individuals who found it feasible to engage in some trade would be concerned with protecting themselves against ex post opportunism because of the shortcomings of court ordering and other enforcement mechanisms. The market, then, is best understood as a social arrangement that facilitates *repeated* exchange among a plurality of parties (as opposed to occasional exchange between individuals). The organization "market" consists of a set of institutional rules (an institution) plus the people who create and apply such rules to trade in special types of goods. The objective is to achieve, in this manner, higher utility levels than would be possible if operations took the form of completely unorganized exchange between strangers.

As noted, the organization "market" is understood tin this book as a network of (more or less) relational contracts among individuals or organized groups of individuals (in the sense of Olson 1965). These are the potential buyers and sellers. Characteristically, a relational contract exists between at least some of the parties, and it may take the form of anything from a loose, hardly visible arrangement to an extremely strict arrangement. Organization makes a "market." The objective of the organization of a market is, of course, to organize exchange efficiently, that is, to facilitate market transactions (including the production, transfer, and guarantee of the reliability of information). The relational contracts are governed by a set of formal and informal operational rules concerning the transaction activities of search, inspection, contracting, execution, control, and enforcement. These rules are formed and implemented partly through collective (multilateral) action, partly through bilateral actions. They determine the market-specific (explicit or implicit) property-rights assignments of each trader. The multilateral or bilateral actions also require specific investments and current expenditures (fixed and variable transaction costs) by the trading partners. These are the costs of setting up, maintaining, and changing the organization "market." Such costs include the costs of setting up, maintaining, and changing organized groups of individuals (e.g., pressure or special interest groups, as described in Olson 1965).[2] In this respect, the transaction-cost approach applies with a mix of both market and political transaction costs. The relation-specific investments tend to lock investors into the existing situation, and this may invite opportunistic behavior in its

---

2. Miller (1993) speaks of private "third-realm" organizations. See section 9.3.

various forms. Hierarchical structures play a role, though, in the Weberian sense of "domination by virtue of a constellation of interests," not "by authority" (Hamilton and Feenstra 1995, 61). It can be noted, however, that so far transaction-cost economics has focused most attention on bilateral transactions, even though applications to multilateral action would also be possible (as, e.g., within or between pressure groups). In what follows, the discussion will be limited to actually existing applications of the property-rights or the transaction-cost approach to the analysis of the organization "market." Consideration will be given to the six basic transaction activities (search, inspection, contracting, execution, control, and enforcement) on the assumption that the constitutional and general operational rules are known.

## 7.2. On Price Rigidity

The functioning of a market is to a large degree characterized by its price behavior. In this respect, neoclassical theory diverges remarkably from reality. According to neoclassical theory, including monopoly theory and numerous oligopoly models like the one by Cournot, equilibrium prices react immediately to demand or cost shock. In reality, that is not the case. Prices for large numbers of goods are rigid. Indeed, the findings of one of the earliest studies on price flexibility (Mills 1927) demonstrates this (fig. 7.1).

Certainly, there are many products whose prices change frequently, but there are also many others whose prices change infrequently. Carlton (1989, 917ff.) writes that he is unaware of any attempts by economists to explain empirically the U-shape of the frequencies of price changes discovered by Mills.

From the 1890s to the mid-1920s it is interesting to see that the frequency of price changes did not change much. In fact, the phenomenon of rigid prices characterizes advanced economies like those of the United States and Germany. Carlton (1986), for example, calculated for the period of January 1, 1957, through December 31, 1966, the average duration of price rigidity for individual associations between buyers and sellers. Table 7.1 presents a summary of some of his findings: "It shows that the degree of price rigidity differs greatly across industries. In some industries the average price does not change for periods well over one year while in other industries the price changes quite frequently. . . . Some markets are apparently not cleared by prices alone but by quantity adjustments like delivery lags in addition to price changes" (Carlton 1989, 921). Table 7.2 (from Carlton 1983) shows that the variability of delivery lag swamps the variability in price for many industries.

There are many more studies on price rigidity. Blinder (1991, 93) reports about survey research in progress in which some twenty-five thousand U.S. firms are asked: "How often do the prices of your most important products

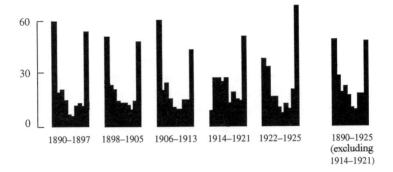

|  | 1890–1897 | 1898–1905 | 1906–1913 | 1914–1921 | 1922–1925 | 1890–1925 (excluding 1914–1921) |
|---|---|---|---|---|---|---|

**Fig. 7.1. Frequency of price change. (Reprinted with the permission of the National Bureau of Economic Research from *The Behavior of Prices*, by Frederick C. Mills [1927, 371]. Copyright 1927 by Frederick C. Mills.)**

**TABLE 7.1  Price Rigidity by Industry**

| Product Group | Average Duration of Price Rigidity (months) |
|---|---|
| Steel | 17.9 |
| Nonferrous metals | 7.5 |
| Petroleum | 8.3 |
| Rubber tires | 11.5 |
| Paper | 11.8 |
| Chemicals | 19.2 |
| Cement | 17.2 |
| Glass | 13.3 |
| Truck motors | 8.3 |
| Plywood | 7.5 |
| Household appliances | 5.9 |

*Source:* Reprinted from Carlton (1986, p. 641, table 1), with the permission of the *American Economic Review.*

**TABLE 7.2.  Price and Delivery Lag Fluctuations**

| Industry | Standard Deviation of Log of Price | Standard Deviation of Log of Delivery Lag | Median Delivery Lag (months) |
|---|---|---|---|
| Textile mill products | 0.06 | 0.17 | 1.26 |
| Paper and allied products | 0.05 | 0.08 | 0.46 |
| Steel | 0.03 | 0.25 | 1.95 |
| Fabricated metals | 0.03 | 0.18 | 3.06 |
| Nonelectrical machinery | 0.04 | 0.25 | 3.63 |
| Electrical machinery | 0.05 | 0.10 | 3.86 |

*Source:* Reprinted from Carlton (1983, p. 563, table 1), with the permission of *Rand Journal of Economics.*

**TABLE 7.3. Measures of Price Stickiness**

| Frequency of Price Change[a] | Percentage of Companies |
|---|---|
| More than 12 | 10.1 |
| 4.01 to 12 | 4.3 |
| 2.01 to 4 | 10.1 |
| 1.01 to 2 | 20.3 |
| 1.0 | 37.7 |
| Less than 1.0 | 17.4 |

*Source:* Reprinted from Blinder (1991, 93, table 1), with the permission of *The American Economic Review.*
*Note:* Based on seventy-two interviews completed as of mid-November 1990.
[a]Times per year.

change in a typical year?" The distribution is shown in table 7.3. According to these data, less than 15 percent of the companies change prices more frequently than quarterly, and 55 percent change their prices no more often than once per year.

These examples illustrate that in many cases market transactions do not rely on price alone. Thus, the simple model of price clearing is inapplicable to a number of markets. Simon (1991) rightly remarks:

Actual contracts negotiated between business firms—putting consumer products aside, for the moment—usually specify far more than prices and quantities. Contracts for construction of a building or of a product of engineering (like a generator or an airplane) specify in enormous detail the specifics of the product to be delivered. They require a massive exchange of information in both negotiation and execution.

The assertion that markets permit each firm to do business with little knowledge of its partners is a fiction. (41)

Thus, the organization of markets concerns much more than price formation and contract conclusion.

### 7.3. Market Organization as a Result of Market Cooperation

As we have argued, economic agents are less locked in in the case of market transactions (in a "market relationship") than in the case of hierarchical transactions (in a "nonmarket relationship"). In this sense, competition (the possibility of choosing among opportunities) plays a more prominent role in the organization "market" than in the organization "firm." As Williamson (1985, 90) puts it:

> The main differences between market and internal organization are these: (1) Markets promote high-powered incentives and restrain bureaucratic distortions more effectively than internal organization; (2) markets can sometimes aggregate demands to advantage, thereby to realize economies of scale and scope; and (3) internal organization has access to distinctive governance instruments.

Yet, as indicated, competition is not the economic equivalent of Hobbes's state of nature. It is not anarchy or war of all against all. Competition, like any mode of conflict, can be preserved only within some collectively set limits. A great part of the debate on market organization is about regulating competition to safeguard it against monopolistic practices. The elementary constitutional and general operational rules (inclusive of their enforcement mechanism), described in section 6.1, apply together with the specific operational rules concerning the transaction activities of search, inspection, contracting, execution, control, and enforcement. We are dealing here only with the latter. They are not simply "there." They have to be developed and cultivated explicitly or implicitly through public or private collective actions either in terms of *conventions,* that is, regularities of behavior (Lewis 1969) as explained by the invisible hand theorem (Hayek 1960), or *formal rules* prescribed and enforced by a visible hand (Chandler 1977). The contents of these rules and the way they are enforced and actually applied depend on the types of goods traded, the general state of the art (especially of information techniques), the general institutional environment (the constitutional and general operational rules of the polity), and the ethical norms of society. Depending on these circumstances, market organizations develop into such types as:

Auction or customer markets
Markets in experience or search goods
"Organized" or "nonorganized" markets

The development and cultivation of market organizations requires explicit or implicit cooperation among potential traders. The identity of potential traders matters (Ben-Porath 1980). Market development necessitates specific investments, which may invite opportunistic behavior on the part of members of a cooperative arrangement or of outsiders wishing to free ride on the market organization, a public good. Barriers to entry are therefore not necessarily social waste. Quite the opposite, they may be necessary to provide sufficient incentives for the creation or improvement of market organization (given an evolutionary setting).[3]

Cooperation between potential traders can be arranged between pairs of buyers and sellers. For want of better terminology, we shall speak of "vertical cooperation" when only sellers are involved in a cooperative arrangement and of "horizontal cooperation" when only buyers are involved. However, a mix of vertical and horizontal cooperation (i.e., cooperation between potential traders on both the supply and the demand side of the market) is possible. An example of the latter situation is found in the case of the stock exchange, which economists such as Walras (1954, 84) used as an illustration of real-life market organization and which supposedly comes closest to the concept of a *perfect market*. But the ideal type of the perfect market is an open market where faceless buyers and sellers[4] trade homogeneous products. By contrast, the stock exchange is a strictly closed market in which the identity of traders matters (see Coase 1988b, 8ff.). Furthermore, contract formation (price negotiation) is organized according to strict rules—and so are the terms of payments and the transaction of the objects of trade. As a result, there is not much room left for misbehavior (opportunism) before, during, or after trade. Insofar as problems arise, they are preferably settled by private arbitrators instead of the courts. Apparently, the organization of a perfect market in real life is a complicated and costly task.

Most markets are organized differently than a stock exchange or an auction market. Their organization depends on the type of goods or titles traded. Transaction costs apparently play a role. Thus, the instruments of the New Institutional Economics (i.e., property-rights theory, the transaction-cost approach, and relational contracting) can be applied to explain the operation of markets more fully. Yet, so far, representatives of the NIE have dealt with only a few aspects of market organization. Exponents of property-rights analysis, like Alchian, Barzel, and Klein, have done more in this respect than Williamson, whose transaction-cost approach deals almost exclusively with problems of vertical cooperation between producers, that is, the markets for intermediate products. Furthermore, the property-rights or transaction-cost analysis of forms of horizontal cooperation between firms, such as formal conventions or alliances (joint ventures), are only beginning to be analyzed.[5]

Both horizontal and vertical cooperation can be *incomplete* in the sense

---

3. Contrary to Baumol and Willig's (1981) view, sunk cost (e.g., in advertising) may have no undesirable welfare consequences.

4. The irrelevance of identity in the perfect market results from the zero-transaction-cost assumption of neoclassical theory.

5. On the transaction-cost theory of joint ventures, see, for example, Hennart (1988; 1991).

that cooperation is limited to single transactions or to transaction activities such as search, inspection, and pricing techniques without infringing upon competition in general. On the other hand it can be *complete* in the sense that the cooperating units stop competing with each other and form a hierarchically organized firm. Incomplete cooperation in the form of quasi agreements (Fellner 1949) between competitors can be found, for example, in the agreement to engage in qualitative competition (advertising, R&D) instead of price competition. This, too, is a wide open field of research.

Similarly, a problem largely neglected by the NIE is that of choosing "marketing channels." Industrial products, for example, can be distributed to consumers either directly, by the producing firm itself or through its agents, or indirectly on someone's own account. Examples of the organization of direct distribution are factory outlets, regional branch shops, and traveling salesmen employed by the producer. In a sense, syndicates and franchising arrangements also belong to this category. Indirectly organized distribution is accomplished with the aid of different kinds of middlemen or intermediaries such as wholesale or retail firms. The examples illustrate the close relationship between the organization of markets and distribution.

The increasing returns to scale resulting from cooperation can be interpreted in the sense of positive external effects. An example of external effects in market organizations is found in network externalities (Tirole 1988, 405).[6] We know that numerous modern products demand the setting up of service networks as in the case of automobiles, television sets, personal computers, household machines, telephones, and cameras. But, to a degree, these networks can also be used by consumers of rival products. The Volkswagen repair shop can be used to repair a tire or the exhaust system of a Ford. The creation of open standards is a big issue. Explicit horizontal cooperation may help to create standards, though in the new computer industry the widespread adoption of a single firm's product has, so far, been the only way that truly open multifirm standards have been established (see *Economist*, "Do it my Way," Feb. 27, 1993, 14).

---

6. "Positive network externalities arise when a good is more valuable to a user the more users adopt the same good or compatible ones. The externality can be direct (a telephone user benefits from others being connected to the same network . . . ). It can also be indirect; because of increasing returns to scale in production, a greater number of complementary products can be supplied—and at a lower price—when the network grows (more programs are written for a popular computer; there are more video-cassettes compatible with a dominant video system . . . ). Note also that the size of the network is either firm specific (as is often the case with automobiles) or industry-wide (an extreme example is that of phonographs, because of the standardization of records)" (Tirole 1988, 405; see also Farrell and Saloner 1985, quoted in Tirole).

## 7.4.  Some Views of Neoinstitutionalists on Market Organization

Traditional economics ascribes departures of actual market organizations from the ideal type of *perfect markets* to monopolistic practices.[7] The approach of neoinstitutionalist writers, on the other hand, holds that because of transaction costs, and thus informational problems, such departures *may* serve economizing purposes (see, e.g., Williamson 1985, 23). In this section, we present some informal arguments of neoinstitutionalists that support an "efficiency" explanation of deviations of actual market organizations from perfect markets (26). To structure our presentation, we are using, as far as possible, the distinction between vertical and horizontal cooperation among potential traders with regard to the six transaction activities (search, inspection, contracting, execution, control, and enforcement). The latter can be reduced to the following three categories:

Precontractual activities (search, inspection)
Contract formation (bargaining) activities
Postcontractual activities (execution, control, enforcement)

Only a few examples from the literature need be given to provide an idea of how neoinstitutionalists try to rationalize actual market organizations.[8] Note, however, that in addition to the exponents of the NIE, an increasing number of modern economic theorists now work on economic explanations of nonstandard contracts (deviations of the organization of actual markets from the ideal type of perfect market). These include game theorists, informational economists, and contract theorists. What defines a "typical" representative of the NIE is his strong reliance on the application of the concepts of property rights, transaction costs (ex ante and ex post), and relational contracts in combination with the attempt to come closer to reality by using less formal methods of analysis.

---

7. Coase (1972, 59), discussing the emphasis on monopoly in research on industrial organization, states: "One important result of this preoccupation with monopoly is that if an economist finds something—a business practice of one sort or other—that he does not understand, he looks for a monopoly explanation" (quoted in Mulherin, Netter, and Overdahl 1991, 630).

8. The "efficiency approach" to deviations of market organizations from perfect markets is not to be understood as the other extreme of the monopoly approach, explaining existing market organizations in a Panglossian style as the best of all possible worlds. The arguments of Goldberg (1976) and Williamson (1976) on public regulation make this clear.

## 7.4.1. Precontractual Transaction Activities: Search and Inspection

*Search* and inspection are specific informational problems. Search as a buyer's activity was first analyzed theoretically by Stigler (1961) in his fundamental article "The Economics of Information." In his article, though, search was exclusively directed toward commodity prices of a certain good, not toward product quality (and prefrences were assumed to be given).

1. Nelson (1970) extended Stigler's article to the search for information about product quality.[9] Information about product quality can not only be achieved by way of search but also by way of experience: "Experience will be used when search becomes too expensive" (318). Nelson correspondingly distinguishes between "search goods" and "experience goods." Typical search goods are, according to his classification, cameras, furniture, china, glassware, and floor coverings. Typical experience goods are radios, televisions, tires, batteries, automobiles, and bicycles.

Advertising as a vehicle for information plays a role in the case of search goods, but personal inspection is also important (search for an apartment, a suit, a dress, etc.). Misleading advertising results in costs to the advertiser, for "he suffers a decline in his credibility for future advertisements and pays the costs of processing non-buying customers" (Nelson 1974, 730). Therefore, "consumers can have some confidence that the advertising of search qualities bears a close relation to the truth" (730). This is much less so in case of experience goods: "The major control that consumers have over the market for experience qualities is whether they repeat the purchase of a brand or not" (730). Therefore, consumers cannot expect much direct information from advertising concerning experience qualities. What they get is important indirect information: "The consumer can learn that the brand advertises. I contend that this is the useful information that the consumer absorbs from the endorsement of announcers, actors, and others who are paid for their encomiums. These and other advertisements for experience goods have no informational content. Their total informational role—beyond the relation of brand to function—is simply contained in their existence" (732). It is advertisement for experience goods that is of particular interest to neoinstitutionalists such as Williamson, Klein, and Leffler. They are concerned with cases in which inspection plays only a minor role. Here advertising is not (necessarily) socially wasteful.[10]

---

9. Nelson assumes that consumers already know where they can obtain each of the options open to them. Their information problem is to evaluate the utility of each option. He defines search to include any way of evaluating these options subject to two restrictions: (1) the consumer must inspect the option, and (2) the inspection must occur prior to purchasing the brand (1970, 312).

10. A formalization of Nelson's idea on the informational role of advertising is provided in Milgrom and Roberts (1986).

For more on this issue, see Tirole (1988, 289–95), which presents two interesting models: those of Butters (1977) and Grossman and Shapiro (1984). Interesting are the findings by Schmalensee (1986) quoted in Tirole (1988, 294), who found that "in broad samples of manufacturing industries, especially those producing consumer goods, advertising intensity is positively related to industry-average profitability." As for our view, advertising expenditures may be regarded (to a point) as an overall resource-saving technique of running the organization "market."

Relative to the question of inspection, we note two contributions from the informal New Institutional Economics literature: a paper by Barzel (1982) and one by Kenney and Klein (1983). Both papers appeared in the *Journal of Law and Economics.*

2. Barzel argues in his article "Measurement Cost and the Organization of Markets" (1982) that the problems and costs of measurement pervade and significantly affect all economic transactions. Errors in measurement are too costly to eliminate entirely. The value of equally priced items will differ, then, and people will spend resources to acquire the difference. Such resource expenditure is wasteful, and it is hypothesized that exchange parties will form contracts and engage in activities that will reduce this kind of resource use. The customer's random selection from an already optimally sorted commodity will avoid the excessive expense. Thus, for example, it is expected that some readily obtainable information will be suppressed to preempt opportunities for excessive measurement (Barzel 1982, 48)

In practice, various methods are applied to lower measurement costs. Thus, we have product warranties, share contracts, brand names, and vertical integration. Barzel gives the following examples.

*Product warranties.* In this case, measuring is left to the buyer to be performed at the time of consumption. Measurement costs may be saved in this manner because the consumer can detect defects in the product at the time of consumption more cheaply than the seller can (see also sec. 5.3.5 on adverse selection and counteracting institutions).

*Share contracts.* Share contracts, such as royalty contracts between authors and publishers, have importance too. Barzel explains such contracts as follows: instead of a lump-sum payment, only a share formula is set in advance. The absolute amounts the two parties will receive are contingent on consumers' actual demand subsequent to publication. What are saved here are the costs of finding out the ultimate success of the venture, which may or may not be considerable. A sharing contract reduces the need for market research. Error is limited largely to the setting of the sharing rule, and this condition tends to make the expected value of the contract larger than the value of an agreement calling for a lump-sum payment.

*Brand name.* If the buyer is to buy without measuring every item, and thus to save on measurement costs, he has to be persuaded to rely on the seller's assertion of the prior measurement. This can he achieved through the use of a "brand name." This requires, on the other hand, extensive measurement by the seller. The seller, however, can choose the measure at the cheapest point in the production process rather than at the time of exchange, as would be necessary if the buyer were to insist on verification of the measurement. As Barzel notes,

> to gain the buyer's patronage the seller must persuade him that he himself will suffer a substantial loss if his product is found deficient. By backing the quality of the item with a brand name, a bad item sold under that name will tarnish the entire brand. (1982, 37)

The "hostage" argument of Williamson (1983) should be mentioned in this context. The customer can destroy the "hostage" by no longer buying the brand (see sec. 5.6 and our subsequent presentation of the ideas in Klein and Leffler 1981).

*Suppression of information.* To avoid search among equally priced units of heterogeneous products, a costly activity, information about the detailed quality of each product may be suppressed (e.g., oranges sold in sealed bundles). To do this successfully, the seller would have to persuade the buyer that he is offering a random selection. "The buyer will have to submit to the choice effected by the seller, but the resource expense of duplicated sorting is bypassed. Thus, abstracting from risk aversion, he will be willing to bid up to his expected valuation" (Barzel 1982, 37).

Provided the consumer trusts the seller, he may be willing to pay a higher average price for the entire batch when inspection is not allowed because he saves excessive inspection costs.

Another example of information suppression is found in the case of patients selecting physicians.

> Comparison among physicians also is discouraged. Physicians are constrained from criticizing one another, and until recently (in the U.S.A.) were not allowed to advertise and were severely restricted with respect to office signs, yellow-page entries, and the like . . . (Barzel 1982, 39)

In this case, large amounts of resources are spent by medical schools to attain a high uniformity of skills among physicians so as to create a situation in which random choice of graduates seems reasonable.

*Vertical integration.* An argument for efficient vertical integration is that the policy economizes on measurement costs. Barzel argues that firms integrate so that difficult to measure steps are performed within the firm, while distinct firms will form and trade with each other at junctures where output can be readily measured.

Between the time that a commodity such as canned salmon leaves the manufacturer and the time it reaches the consumer, its physical properties and its value will have changed only slightly. Other goods such as produce and bread may change a great deal. . . . It is predicted that ownership will change more frequently (between production and consumption) the less the commodity is subject to change. Thus, canned salmon is expected to change ownership more times than fresh salmon, powdered milk more than fresh milk, cookies more than fresh bread, and so on. (Barzel 1982, 42)

3. Kenney and Klein (1983) provide an interesting example showing how oversearching can be avoided. The case comes from the experience of the Central Selling Organization (CSO) of the De Beers Group, which markets most of the world's gem-quality uncut diamonds. The authors suggest that the cartel's selling organization contributes to a reduction of search cost by minimizing buyers' oversearching for information.

Stones are sorted according to shape, quality, color, and weight in more than two thousand categories. Still, the variants in the value of stones within each category are substantial. To avoid oversearching, stones of each category are sold in preselected blocks (or "sights"), which the CSO assembles for each individual customer according to his preannounced wishes.

Each buyer examines his sight before deciding whether to buy. . . . There is no negotiation over the price or composition of the sight. In rare cases where a buyer claims that a stone has been miscategorised by the CSO, and the sales staff agrees, the sight will be adjusted. If a buyer rejects the sight, he is offered no alternative box. Rejection is extremely rare, however, because buyers who reject the diamonds offered then are deleted from the list of invited customers. (Kenney and Klein 1983, 502)

To sum up: "stones (a) are sorted by De Beers into imperfectly homogeneous categories (b) to be sold in preselected blocks, (c) to preselected buyers, (d) at non-negotiable prices, with (e) buyers' rejection of the sales offer leading to the withdrawal by De Beers of future invitations to purchase stones." (502)

This policy is advantageous also to buyers, who, since they have a long-term business relationship with De Beers, are earning rents the present value of which is greater than they would earn if they rejected sights of lower than average quality. "Since these rents are lost if the buyer decides to reject a sight and is terminated from the list of invited buyers, a wealth-maximizing buyer will not generally reject sights . . . " (Kenney and Klein 1983, 506). This is a self-enforcing arrangement similar to that found in Klein and Leffler 1981.

These examples deal with what is called "vertical cooperation," the cooperation that takes place before contract conclusion. The next topic concerns horizontal cooperation.

Horizontal cooperation (or integration) occurs in various types of bilateral or multilateral agreements: the formation of implicit or explicit agreements between competitors (conventions, quasi agreements, alliances, joint ventures, marketing agreements, cartels, etc.), the establishment of local markets or fairs, the foundation of trading firms or financial intermediaries (like wholesale or retail businesses, supermarkets, department stores, shopping malls, banks, and leasing firms), the establishment of associations (employers' associations, labor unions) or cooperatives, and the formation of lobbying alliances that influence the passing of legal regulations or of strategic alliances between competitors. All these activities influence the organization of markets: labor, commodity, service, financial, etc. They help make search and inspection easier ("cheaper"). We are interested in this section only in types of *horizontal cooperation* short of hierarchies.

4. Of particular interest here are *implicit agreements*—for example, the quasi agreement between competing sellers or buyers described by Fellner (1949) in his book on oligopoly theory. Unlike Williamson (1975), we interpret Fellner's quasi agreement between monopolists as a relational contract, an implicit long-term agreement open to change according to rules that are enforced by such things as "tit-for-tat" strategies. Consider an oligopolistic industry with high advertising outlays such as the American cigarette industry. We may interpret this case in the sense of Klein and Leffler (1981) as one based on investments in brand-name capital that are only profitable if product prices are sufficiently above salvageable production costs. Price competition (or a price war) becomes unlikely in this case. Instead, one can expect price changes in the same direction (as is the case with gasoline stations) or price leadership, possibly in combination with stable prices over long periods, as in the case of the American cigarette industry between 1923 and 1939.[11] Under these conditions, the relational contract among the oligopolists can possibly be described as being renegotiation-proof. The ex ante measures against ex post opportunism by the oligopolists are their considerable advertising outlays. Because of the high depreciation rate of the effects of current and past advertisement outlays,[12] advertisers run the risk of losing brand-name capital if they decrease their advertising expenditures to make up for competitive price cuts. The high advertising expenditures also serve as a barrier to entry for newcomers and thus

---

11. During this period, the four great suppliers changed their prices only seven times. Four price increases were led by Reynolds. Three price decreases occurred, with Reynolds leading one and American Tobacco leading two (Nicholls 1951, 181).

12. According to Thomas (1989), the durability of advertising is quite brief. He estimated an annual depreciation rate in excess of 80 percent.

help to protect the incumbents' quasi rents from their specific investments in market organization. This may represent a socially desirable incentive.

Note the parallel between the concept of hegemonial leadership that is discussed in political science and the dominant firm or—possibly—price leadership. Note also the possibility of applying the concept of "hegemonial cooperation" (Snidal 1985) to explain the role of the big three or four in the U.S. automobile or cigarette industry.[13]

Of interest in this context is the fact that advertising outlays are interpreted by representatives of the New Institutional Economics such as Klein and Leffler (1981) and Williamson (1983) (and modern game theorists?) quite differently from what one can read in the earlier literature (as reviewed, e.g., in Schmalensee 1972, 4ff.).[14]

5. *Strategic alliances,* which are considered a "hot" issue today, can be understood as explicit bilateral horizontal agreements. They have increased in frequency in recent years and are particularly characteristic of high-technology industries, such as the computer industry (see *Economist,* "Do it my Way," Feb. 27, 1993, 6). Yet, so far, they have not been analyzed in the transaction-cost style and need, as Williamson (1993e, 293) writes, an "added apparatus" to deal with the full set of issues raised. For a definition, see Teece (1992b, 189), who writes:

---

13. We did not assume (as, e.g., Fellner [1949] did) joint-profit maximization by the oligopolists. Williamson (1975, 234ff.) rightly criticizes this assumption. It would be more realistic to assume a common desire of the actors to avoid a price war. Williamson criticizes the joint profit maximization hypothesis by arguing that, even if firms were allowed to agree explicitly, it would be impossible to conclude a complete (classical) comprehensive joint profit maximizing contract due to the lack of foresight. Even if that could be done, the monitoring expenses that profit pooling entails would invite opportunistic behavior by oligopolists. Firms foresee this and decline from the outset to accept a full-blown pooling arrangement. Williamson concludes that it is "naive to regard oligopolists as shared monopolists *in any comprehensive sense*—especially if they have differentiated products, have different cost experiences, are differently situated with respect to the market in terms of size, [and] plainly lack the machinery by which oligopolistic coordination, except of the most primitive sort, is accomplished and enforced. . . . In the usual oligopoly situation, efforts to achieve collusion are unlikely to be successful or, if they are, will require sufficient explicit communication that *normal remedies* against price fixing, including injunctions not to collude, will suffice" (264).

14. The main criticisms of advertising are:

(1) The content and presentation of some advertisements are annoying or offensive.
(2) Too much advertising is produced from a welfare economics point of view (Kaldor, 1950).
(3) There is socially wastefeul competition for market shares: if all firms in most oligopolistic industries would drastically reduce their advertising budgets, no firm's sales would be altered, the society would be better off.
(4) Advertising influences the formation of consumers' tastes (hidden persuaders thesis).
(5) Advertising is a source of monopoly power (Bain, 1956).

For a neoclassical exposition on optimal advertising see Dorfman and Steiner (1954, 826ff.) and Nerlove and Arrow (1962).

A strategic alliance can be defined as a bilateral relationship characterized by the commitment of the two or more partners of the firms to reach a common goal, and which entails the pooling of specialized assets and capabilities. Thus a strategic alliance might include one or more of the following: technological swaps, joint R&D or co-development, and the sharing of complementary assets (for example, when one party does manufacturing, the other distribution, for a codeveloped product).

For further comments, see Porter 1990 or Mody 1993.

So much for the two precontractual activities: search and inspection. Our presentation has attempted to provide some idea of the arguments advanced by neoinstitutionalist writers when they assert that deviations from the ideal type of perfect market may offer efficient solutions to distributive problems. In a world with transaction costs, advertising without any direct informational content may be a way to save on search costs. Block booking, or the suppression of information, may be a technique to save inspection costs. Quasi agreements between competitors (such as price leadership) may help to channel competitive control into a socially desirable direction. That is, such behavior may help guarantee high product quality and avoid price wars. Long-term relationships (implicit or explicit relational contracts) vertically between buyers and sellers, or horizontally between competitors, play a role.

The problem is, as everywhere in modern institutional economics, the lack of a general theory concerning the organization of precontractual activities that is comparable to the reasoning we are used to from general equilibrium theory. Though the analytical methods are rather general (the property-rights approach, the transaction-cost approach, and the principal-agent approach), the explanations given by the analysts are able to throw light on only some parts of the whole field of market organization.

### 7.4.2. Contract Formation

Economic interest attaches to the organization of price negotiations (bargaining). Things are perfectly clear in this respect in the case of an auction. The auctioneer "administers" price negotiations between the seller and the many potential buyers according to an agreed upon rule (e.g., the English auction rule). Here, the price of a good or title is used so as to clear the market perfectly. On most other markets, though, the organizational problem of price negotiation between potential sellers and (many) potential buyers is solved quite differently, with the result that prices are comparatively rigid.

1. Representatives of the New Institutional Economics such as Armen A. Alchian argue that rigid prices are the result of the organization of price negotiations between sellers and buyers (e.g., the convention, or law, of *posted prices*). Thus, Alchian and Woodward (1987) explain posted prices as follows:

Posted prices, announced publicly and maintained until publicly revised, are prices at which the posting party will transact any amount. All parties obtain the same price; the price to a particular party could not be changed while all others were getting better prices. Posting and stability of the price indicates reliability as a non-opportunistic buyer (seller) to all dependent sellers (buyers). An implication is that posted prices that are stable be more commonly present where there is "dependency," i.e., reliance investments. (127)

The authors give as examples tuna and salmon fishing, "where the fishing boats are reliant on a unique buyer-processor. Similarly, a fixed price guarantee occurs in many agricultural product markets where farmers plant crops relying on a unique buyer-processor" (127).

Another reason for price rigidity is that, in long-term business relationships that require relationship-specific investments, "opportunistic price changes (intended to effect a hold-up) are not clearly or cheaply distinguishable from price changes to which the parties would have agreed had the demand and supply environment been mutual foreseen" (Alchian and Woodward 1987, 128).

All this draws upon neoinstitutionalist reasoning. That is, relational contracts develop between suppliers and their customers. Customer relationships play a role, that is, a vertical type of cooperation appears. Given the specific investments on both sides, and the resulting lock-in effect, quantity adjustments have much better incentive compatibility properties than do price adjustments. As Williamson (1985) argues:

Price adjustments have an unfortunate zero-sum quality, whereas proposals to increase, decrease, or delay delivery do not. Also, price adjustment proposals involve the risk that one's opposite is contriving to alter the terms within the bilateral monopoly trading gap to his advantage. By contrast, a presumption that exogenous events, rather than strategic purposes, are responsible for quantity adjustments is ordinarily warranted. (76)

This is not only true for bilateral relationships between buyers and sellers. The argument could also be applied to the relationship between a seller and his (many) customers (the seller's clientele) previously described. Both parties make specific investments. Both are locked in to a degree and (now) price inflexibility may be interpreted as a "protection of the expropriable composite quasi-rent of dependent resources" (Alchian and Woodward 1987, 128). Furthermore, the seller in such a market relationship can also be seen as the agent of his clientele whose task it is not only to actually supply the product quality he offered but also to charge a fair price (however understood). In addition, the seller may be a member of some horizontal cooperative arrangement among competitors (a quasi agreement like price leadership) who determine or influence the rules of competition (price formation) in a particular product market. Similar arguments may be applied to explain wage rigidities, the employment relationship being a strongly relational contract with specific investments (in human and physical capital on both sides). Alchian and Woodward (1987) give an extreme example to illustrate this point:

> Imagine an employer and employee. Will they renegotiate price every hour, or with every perceived change in circumstances? If the employee were a waiter in a restaurant, would the waiter's wage be renegotiated with every new customer? Would it be renegotiated to virtually zero when no customers were present and then back to a high level that would extract the entire customer value when a queue appeared? Obviously, prices and wages do not vary at every moment at which there is a change in the monetary demand or supply, as with the unimaginable waiter. But what is the right interval for renegotiation or change of price? The usual answer, 'as soon as demand or supply changes,' is uninformative. (128)

2. Relative to the determination of prices in long-term contracts, Joskow (1985a) has provided an interesting empirical study explaining the nature of price formation in markets in which long-term contracts are used extensively, a problem that has received little attention to date. There exists, of course, the possibility of fixed prices, but there are good reasons to expect that they won't be used. In actual experience, in the coal contracts examined by Joskow, prices tended to be changed over time. Such contracts "generally have fairly complicated pricing provisions based on various combinations of actual costs, input price indices and prevailing market prices" (1985b, 591). Joskow observed wide variations in transaction prices for coal (properly adjusted for quality differences) within particular geographical supply and demand regions at any point in time. "Spot prices and contract prices often differ substantially. . . . This type of price diversity and price rigidity raises important questions about the nature of price adjustment and market equilibrium, the meaning of efficient pricing in individual markets and necessarily raises issues of macroeconomic importance as well" (101). (For more on this study, see sec. 7.4.3.)

3. What is to be seen in this context is that, contrary to legal doctrines, contract negotiation is far from being a clocklike mechanism. It is "a complex commercial institution that marks the preliminary stage in all business relations" (Shell 1991, 223).

In fact, the costs of contract formation are to a large degree bargaining costs. They are increasingly considered by game theorists, or other formal analysts, in combination with incomplete contracting. We are not reporting on this work here. An overview of *bargaining with private information* is given by Kennan and Wilson (1993). They argue, in a similar fashion to neoinstitutionalists, that

> delay may be required to convey private information credibly. For instance willingness to endure a strike might be the only convincing evidence that the firm is unable to pay a high wage . . . (46)[15]

4. Next, let us return to a typical organized market and consider the (private) stock exchange as a limiting case. It is, as has been mentioned, a rather closed market[16] and in fact may be better considered as a firm that has successfully established a market in financial products. Mulherin, Netter, and Overdahl (1991) present this view. They argue that financial exchanges create markets and actually "produce" prices. In effect, they create property rights in prices. To support their view, the authors draw attention to U.S. court decisions. In a long series of cases,

> the courts came to view financial exchanges as organizations that created property rights through contracting among exchange members and between the exchanges and external parties such as telecommunication companies. A central feature of the exchanges' contracts were rules limiting when members could trade. The prohibition against off-exchange trading was enforced by the threat of expulsion. . . . By allowing the exchanges to establish rights to such property, they enabled the exchanges to reap the gains from technological innovation and thereby promoted the growth of exchanges in the United States. (626)

While economic theorists view stock exchanges as an ideal case of perfect competition, applied economists interested in economic policy see things quite differently when observing the tight regulations of exchanges. They assume that these regulations represent an attempt to exercise monopoly power and aim to restrain competition.[17] Coase points out, however,

> that for anything approaching perfect competition to exist, an intricate system of rules and regulations would normally be needed . . . in order to

---

15. See also Milgrom and Roberts (1988, 452); Sutton (1986); and Rubinstein (1987) for surveys. Introductory texts can be found in game-theoretic books like Fudenberg and Tirole (1991 chap. 10); Kreps (1990c); and Myerson (1991). See also Milgrom and Roberts (1990a).

16. The degree of closedness of stock exchanges increased in the course of time and became quite extreme, for example, in case of the New York Stock exchange (cf. Bindseil 1994).

17. For example, the U.S. Congress called for the creation of a National Market System, which would effectively make prices of financial instruments a common pool (Mulherin, Netter, and Overdahl 1991, 643).

reduce transaction costs and therefore to increase the volume of trade. (1986, 9)

To summarize our discussion of behavior at the contract formation stage, we can note the following. Consideration has been given to neoinstitutionalist explanations of why there are deviations from the idealized markets of pure theory. The literature suggests that, contrary to traditional thinking, *price rigidity* and *barriers to entry* can play useful economic roles.

Under certain circumstances, price inflexibility may be interpreted as some kind of protection of the expropriable composite quasi rent from the specific investments of the traders. Posted prices, as applied in many markets, can be understood in this manner—as can qualitative competition (including advertising) that arises instead of price competition. On the other hand, explicit long-term contracts can hardly be based on permanently fixed prices. Relational contract theory may help to throw some light on the variety of pricing provisions in long-term contracts.

The actual organization of the stock exchange, the typical example of the perfect market, may illustrate efficiency reasons for barriers to entry. Barriers are, here and possibly elsewhere, a device to further the development of efficacious market organizations. Other legal protections such as trademarks, patents, and licenses may be interpreted similarly—and possibly also nonlegal barriers to entry. This is not to say that barriers to entry have desirable welfare consequences in general. It is one of the problems of the "discovery" of the costs of using the market that their integration into microeconomics does not make things easier for the analyst. In fact, one important insight of the New Institutional Economics is that there are no ready-made conclusions about what constitutes a welfare-increasing (or welfare-decreasing) institutional arrangement. Each individual case has to be analyzed carefully, and the arguments for and against the desirability of a certain institutional setup have to be weighed carefully against each other.

It can be noted, for example, that a stock exchange performs more services than is sometimes recognized. The exchange organizes not only the conclusion of contracts but also all associated transaction activities (from search to enforcement) through all-embracing, self-enforcing, institutional arrangements. On a macro scale, the same point can be made concerning the evolution of "privately ordered" medieval trade organizations. Two illustrations of the process follow—the first by Greif (1989), the second by Milgrom, North, and Weingast (1990).

Greif (1989) examined the organization of a group of Jewish traders, the *Maghribi,* who pursued complex, long-distance trade in the Mediterranean during the eleventh century. The Maghribi had organized an informal principal-agent relationship—with the traders being the principals and their employed "overseas agents" being the agents. The latter accompanied the sea transport of the goods, searched for buyers, negotiated and concluded purchasing contracts, monitored the transfer of the goods, and secured payments. Complete contingent contracts between principals and agents were impossible because of lack of foresight. Also impossible was a direct monitoring of the agents by the principals. Similarly, court ordering against fraudulent agents was not feasible. Despite these difficult conditions, the Maghribi merchants were still able to help themselves by establishing the following agreement. The agents were, or became, members of a coalition, the group of traders of the Maghribi. They earned premiums for good behavior. But, if any agent deceived his principal just once, he got no more assignments for the rest of his life from the merchants of the Maghribi group. If a fraudulent agent tried to become a principal (a merchant) himself, his Maghribi agent was free to deceive him in the sense that he was not punished in the usual manner by the Maghribi tradesmen or merchants.

In effect, the Maghribi formed an "organized group" or coalition that represented a nonanonymous organizational framework of people of the same cultural background. They enforced the agency relationships between traders and their agents through a self-enforcing mechanism based on valuable reputation. Within the coalition, an informal information-transmission system served to deal with the existence of asymmetric information. "This reputation mechanism explains the observed 'trust' relations among traders." The trust did not constitute a social control system. "Rather, the Maghribi traders established a relationship between past conduct and future economic rewards. As a result, agents resisted the short-term gains attainable through deception . . . " (Greif 1989, 881).

Along somewhat similar lines, Milgrom, North, and Weingast (1990) analyzed the law merchant system of the Champaign Fairs of the twelfth and thirteenth centuries. This was a private enforcement mechanism of contracts. The institution of the fairs provided information about the previous behavior of participants by closely controlling entry and exit. That is: "A merchant could not enter the Fair without being in good standing with those who controlled entry, and any merchant caught cheating at the Fair would be incarcerated and brought to justice under the rules of the Fair. So anyone a merchant met at the Fair could be presumed to have a 'good reputation' . . . " (20). The authors explain the meaning of "good reputation" by use of a prisoner's dilemma game model. They conclude that their approach suggests the following understanding. The significance of the state taking on the role of enforcer of contracts was not that such action provided a means for enforcing contracts where one previously did not exist. Other means were available, as the law merchant story shows. "Rather, it was to reduce the transaction costs of policing exchange" (21).

### 7.4.3. Postcontractual Transaction Activities: Execution, Control, and Enforcement

From the standpoint of transaction costs, the three postcontractual activities (execution, control, and enforcement) can be dealt with comparatively cheaply by means of simultaneous exchange. There remain, of course, problems such as product liability (manufacturer's liability in tort to people injured by a defect in his product) and dissatisfaction of the consumer with the purchased good. The first problem is dealt with economically by the economic theory of tort law, a special field of the economic analysis of law, the second by the economic theory of self-enforcing agreements described previously (and in chap. 5): the disappointed consumer retaliates by discontinuing his purchase of the particular brand of the good.

Simultaneous exchange, though, does not dominate a market economy. Of particular interest for institutional economics are cases in which time elapses between the conclusion of a contract and the single steps of its execution. Thus, the literature of the New Institutional Economics concentrates on control and enforcement activities and disregards contract execution.

Williamson's (1979, 1985) transaction-cost approach, which we described in section 4.4.3, is probably the most detailed informal analysis of the control and enforcement problems of transaction activities in which transaction-specific investments play a role. It deals, though, mostly with vertical cooperation between manufacturers. Without repeating his arguments here in full, let us state that in such cases the ex ante competition between several sellers and/or buyers is transformed into some kind of a bilateral monopoly: the parties to the contract are to a degree locked in ex post, a situation Williamson (1985, 61) calls the Fundamental Transformation. Protection against postcontractual opportunism becomes a problem. Court ordering alone may be either impossible (for lack of verifiability) or too expensive, time consuming, and uncertain to be relied upon. "Private ordering" may therefore be preferable. The problem of the contractual parties is to organize ex ante its transactions so "as to economize on bounded rationality while simultaneously safeguarding against opportunism" (Williamson 1985, 32, see also chap. 4).

In this subsection, we illustrate some neoinstitutional arguments concerning the efficiency (social-welfare-increasing abilities) of the following five phenomena:

Market prices above competitive prices
Franchising

Vertical and lateral integration
Public regulation
Private third-party resolution of disputes

The first two examples deal with what we have called vertical cooperation; the last three are concerned with either vertical or horizontal cooperation or a mix of both.

1. Are there efficiency reasons for *market prices being above competitive prices?* The answer to this question is given by the theory of self-enforcing agreements described in sections 4.4.2 and 5.6. We are going to report briefly about the argument of Klein and Leffler (1981) that, under certain circumstances, self-enforcing contracts are the cheapest way to assure quality supply. The authors write:

> When quality characteristics can be specified cheaply and measured by a third party, and hence contract-enforcement costs are anticipated to be low, explicit contractual solutions with governmentally enforced penalties (including warranties) may be a less costly solution. When explicit contract costs are high and the extent of short-run profit from deceptively low quality supply and hence the quality-assuring price premium is also high, governmental specification and enforcement of minimum quality standards may be an alternative method of reducing the cost of reducing the costs of assuring the supply of high-quality products. And, finally, vertical integration, which in this consumer-product context may consist of home production or consumer cooperatives, may be a possible alternative arrangement. (634–35)

The article examines the nongovernmental, repeat-purchase, contract-enforcement mechanism. The authors assume that contracts are not enforceable by the government or any other third party. Transactors rely solely on the threat of termination of the business relationship for enforcement of contractual promises, an assumption realistic for contractual terms concerning hard to measure product characteristics such as the "taste" of a hamburger (Klein and Leffler 1981, 616).

However, even when it is possible, third-party enforcement may be rather expensive and time consuming. "Market arrangements such as the value of lost purchases which motivate transactors to honor their promises may be the cheapest method of guaranteeing the guarantee" (Klein and Leffler 1981, 616). We gave a mathematical illustration of this point in section 5.6.

The fundamental theoretical result of the article by Klein and Leffler is that market prices above the competitive level and the presence of nonsalvageable capital are means of enforcing quality promises. The role of brand-name capital investments, which are "sunk investments," becomes understandable. "What assures high-quality supply is the capital loss due to the loss of future business if low quality is produced" (1981, 627). The role for advertising is also to be seen in this context, for,

> when consumers do not know the minimum quality guaranteeing price, the larger is the firm's brand-name capital investment relative to sales, [and] the more likely its price premium is sufficient to motivate high quality production. Competitive investment in brand-name capital is now no longer constrained to assets which yield direct consumer service flows. . . . For example: Luxurious storefronts and ornate displays or signs may be supplied by a firm even if yielding no direct consumer service flows. Such firm-specific assets inform consumers of the magnitude of sunk capital costs and their supply of information about the quasi-rent price-premium stream being earned by the firm and hence the opportunity cost to the firm if it cheats. (630)

The authors repeat the argument by Nelson (1974) that advertising, by definition, supplies valuable information to the consumer—namely, information that the firm is advertising (1981, 631ff.).

The paper by Klein and Leffler implies "that consumers can successfully use the price as an indicator of quality" (1981, 634). The authors refer in this context to the informed buyers who know of a gap between firm price and salvageable costs. In other words, there is knowledge of the existence of a price premium that supplies buyers' quality assurance.

2. *Franchising* as a hybrid form of market and hierarchy is explained by Klein, Crawford, and Alchian (1978) in an article that deals with the protection of what the authors call the "appropriable *quasi-rent value*" of a specific asset. It is defined as follows:

> The quasi-rent of an asset is "the excess of its value over its salvage value, that is, its value in its next best *use* to another renter. The potentially appropriable specialized portion of the quasi rent is that portion, if any, in excess of its value to the second highest-valuing *user*. . . . An appropriable quasi-rent is not a monopoly rent in the usual sense. . . . It can occur with no market closure . . . (298–99)

Opportunistic behavior of the parties to the contract relates to an ex post redistribution of the appropriable quasi rent (a holdup) to the disadvantage of one side of the specific investors. In view of this possibility, lack of protection against ex post opportunism would result in less-specific investments being made so as to avoid being "locked in." Therefore, ex post opportunism not only consists of wealth distribution but also of a loss of efficiency.

The authors provide various examples. The problem is, of course, to take ex ante measures against ex post opportunism. They use this concept to explain various actual phenomena, among them franchising. They propose, interestingly, to interpret the franchise contract as a lease contract of the brand-name capital (the trade name or the logo) of a firm. Brand-name capital is a highly specific asset that is particularly problematic to lease. If it were to be rented (without special precautions), the renter of the brand-name capital "would be very hesitant to build up its good will, for example, by advertising or by successful performance, because such investments are highly specific to that 'name'" (Klein, Crawford, and Alchian 1978, 321). He might not only stop investing in the brand name, but in addition he might take action to depreciate the valuable rented brand name by selling poorer quality. Still, rental of the capital input of a firm's brand name is not entirely unknown. "A franchisee is fundamentally a renter of the brand-name capital (and logo) owned by the franchisor. Because of the specific capital problem noted above, direct controls are placed on franchisee behavior. The rental payment is usually some form of profit sharing arrangement and, although the franchisee is legally considered to be an independent firm, the situation is in reality much closer to vertical integration than to the standard contractual relationship of the independent market" (321).

3. *Vertical and lateral integration* can be defended on efficiency grounds, as was mentioned in sections 4.4.3 and 5.5. Vertical integration becomes especially attractive when long-lived, transaction-specific, sunk investments represent a large fraction of total costs, where uncertainty is important, and where reputational constraints are not likely to constrain "bad behavior." A frequently quoted early informal study was presented by Klein, Crawford, and Alchian (1978, 308), using as an illustrative example the ownership by automobile-producing companies of the giant presses used for stamping body parts. Dies for stamping are highly specific investments. Therefore, the die owner would not want to be separated from the automobile producer. An independent die owner may have no comparable demanders other than the automobile producer that ordered the particular body parts. The incentive for the automobile producer

to opportunistically renegotiate a lower price at which it will accept body parts from the independent die owner may be large. Similarly, if there is a large cost to (the automobile producer) from the production delay of obtaining an alternative supplier of specific body parts, the independent die owner may be able to capture quasi rents by demanding a revised higher price for the parts. Since the opportunity to lose the specialized quasi rent of assets is a debilitating prospect, neither party would invest in such equipment. Joint ownership of designs and dies removes this incentive to attempt appropriation. (308)

In this general context, Klein, Crawford and Alchian discuss the merger that occurred in 1926 of General Motors and Fisher Body. Cooperation between the two firms had become a problem by 1919 when the original wooden automobile bodies began to be displaced by large closed metal bodies for which specific stamping machines were important. The basic facts of this *lateral integration* process are summarized by Williamson (1985) as follows:

1. In 1919 General Motors entered a ten-year contractual agreement with Fisher Body whereby General Motors agreed to purchase substantially all its closed bodies from Fisher.
2. The price of delivery was set on a cost-plus basis and included provisions that General Motors would not be charged more than rival automobile manufacturers. Price disputes were to be settled by compulsory arbitration.
3. The demand for General Motors' production of closed body cars increased substantially above that which had been forecast. As a consequence General Motors became dissatisfied with the terms under which prices were to be adjusted. It furthermore urged Fisher to locate its body plants adjacent to GM assembly plants, thereby to realize transportation and inventory economies. Fisher Body resisted.
4. General Motors began acquiring Fisher stock in 1924 and completed a merger agreement in 1926. (1985, 114–15)

Williamson concludes that transaction cost reasoning does not forecast this sequence in detail (115). Nonetheless, the observed succession of changes is consistent with the transaction-cost argument for vertical integration when, as has been argued, long-lived transaction-specific investment represents a large fraction of total costs, when uncertainty is important, and when reputational constraints are not likely to constrain ex post opportunism.

Systematic hypothesis testings confirm the special importance of transaction-specific sunk investments for an explanation of the extent to which firms prefer the acquisition of certain inputs. See, for example, the article by Monteverde and Teece (1982), who statistically tested the hypothesis that assemblers will integrate vertically when the production process, broadly defined, generates specialized, nonpatentable know-how. "When production processes are of this kind both assembler and supplier are exposed to the possibility of opportunistic recontracting. . . . The existence of transaction-specific know-how and skills and the difficulties of skill transfer mean that it will be costly to switch to an alternative supplier. . . . An assembler will tend to choose vertically integrated component production when high switching costs would otherwise lock the assembler into dependence upon a supplier and thereby expose that assembler to opportunistic recontracting or to the loss of transaction-specific know-how" (206).

The hypothesis is tested with data from General Motors and Ford for their U.S. production in 1976. The results confirm that transaction-cost considerations "have important ramifications for vertical integration in the automobile industry . . . " (Monteverde and Teece 1982, 212) and thus support the view that the vertical structure, in this case of General Motors and Ford, is based on efficiency considerations.

4. *Public regulation* is traditionally defended by the argument of market failure in the case of natural monopolies. Demsetz (1968b) opposed this view in his article "Why Regulate Utilities?" The efficiency argument that there should be only one supplier in the case of a natural monopoly does not necessarily result in supply prices in excess of per unit cost of the natural monopoly good in question. Basically, Demsetz argues as follows (using Williamson's [1976, 76ff.] summary): "Conventional analysis is flawed by the failure to distinguish between the number of ex ante bidders and the condition of ex post supply. Even though scale economies may dictate that there be a single ex post supplier, large-numbers competition may nevertheless be feasible at the initial bidding stage. Where large numbers of qualified parties enter noncollusive bids to become the supplier of the decreasing cost activity, the resulting price need not reflect monopoly power. The defect with conventional analysis is that it ignores this initial franchise bidding stage."

What should be done in such a situation is to auction off the franchise by awarding it to the bidder who promises the lowest per unit price. Provided that there are many qualified and noncollusive bidders for the contract, and that the contract is awarded to the party that offers to supply the good at the lowest per-unit price, "the winning price will differ insignificantly from the per-unit cost of producing" the good in question (Demsetz 1968b, 61).

Demsetz is convinced that long-term contracts for the supply of natural monopoly goods can be "concluded satisfactorily in the market place without the aid of regulation" (1968b, 64). He therefore believes that "rivalry of the open market place disciplines more effectively than do the regulatory processes of the commission" (65).

As the reader will realize immediately, this is a typical example of Williamson's "fundamental transformation." A major problem is the unavoidable incompleteness of a long-term contract between the franchisee (the supplier) and the franchisor (e.g., the community). Unanticipated developments demand that the parties agree at the outset to a renegotiation procedure with a rule indicating how the gains of the resulting adaptation are to be shared. General agreements to this effect are not necessarily self-enforcing. Williamson argues that among the problems to be anticipated when incomplete long-term contracts are negotiated under conditions of uncertainty are the following:

> (1) The initial award criterion is apt to be artificial or obscure; (2) execution problems in price-cost, in other performance, and in political aspects are apt to develop; and (3) bidding parity between the incumbent and prospective rivals at the contract renewal interval is unlikely to be realized. (1976, 80)

He discusses these three conditions in detail and later illustrates the difficulties with experiences from the franchise bidding for the Oakland cable television franchise in 1969–70.

Goldberg (1976) writes in a similar vein. He also stresses the incompleteness of long-term contracts, using the term *administered contracts* for what we have called relational contracts. One central point of his article is that Demsetz's arguments work only if prices can either be perfectly fixed or fixed according to a strict redetermination provision for a sufficiently long period. This is not possible in the face of unknown future events. The necessary price changes invite opportunism on both sides of the franchising contract. Goldberg (430) interprets the regulator as the agent of both parties whom he assumes throughout to be a faithful representative of his principals' interests. He concedes that the institution of regulation is subject to political abuse. Yet, this is true for all institutions. Like Williamson, he does not defend regulation under all circumstances. Rather, he views his article "as the case against the case against regulation" (443). Regulation is not justified on narrow natural monopoly grounds but because of the unavoidable long-term relation in the face of uncertainty in the future.

5. *Private third-party determination of performance* can be found in occasional as well as recurrent transactions. As for the first, Williamson (1985, 74ff.) argues that trilateral governance will be applied in cases in which not only specific investments are high "but the transfer of those assets to a successor supplier would pose inordinate difficulties in asset valuation." A direct third-party determination of performance may be agreed upon. Macneil (1978, 866) mentions as a good example the role of the architect under firm construction contracts of the American Institute of Architects (AIA). Another important technique for third-party determination of performance content is arbitration. It is best known for its utilization in resolving "rights disputes" (866ff.).

Arbitration procedures can also be found in cases of recurrent transactions, as, for example, in the New York Diamond Dealers Club (DDC), which functions as a bourse. Bernstein (1992) gives an interesting description and analysis of this market. Business disputes are not brought to the courts or resolved through the application of legal rules announced and enforced by the state. The reasons why this is the case are, according to Bernstein:

The extraordinary difficulties of calculating lost profit of a buyer if the seller fails to deliver a stone.

The narrow financial side of the diamond industry. Since diamond dealers have no ready access to capital markets or excess cash on hand, disputes have to be solved and enforced quickly.

The extremely important role reputation plays for dealers in the diamond trade. Thus, to contain damage to a dealer's reputation the existence of a dispute and its resolution are kept secret "as long as the arbitrators' judgment is paid promptly" (149).

Bernstein summarizes: "By a variety of reputational bonds, customary business practices, and arbitration proceedings, the diamond industry has developed a set of rules and institutions that its participants find clearly superior to the legal system. . . . The market is organized to promote the low cost and rapid intraindustry dissemination of information about reputation, which enables it to use reputation bonds to create intraindustry norms that function as a deterrent to breach of contract and a private sanctioning system whose judgments can always be enforced completely outside the legal system" (1992, 157).

The diamond industry, which has long been dominated by Orthodox Jews (Bernstein 1992, 140), is a special case of "homogeneous middlemen groups" that are very successful in providing middleman activities, including private ordering, at a lower cost than members of the surrounding society could achieve. "Success stems from the small number of group members, their shared characteristics, and substantial remoteness from the surrounding society" (La Croix 1989, 220).[18]

To summarize our presentation on postcontractual activities: the efficiency arguments for deviations from perfect markets are here extended to cases of market prices above competitive prices, vertical and lateral integration, the limits of public regulation, and the extreme dependence of the franchisee on the conditions of the franchisor. Furthermore, private third-party resolution of disputes, unexplainable under standard neoclassical theory, is described as an efficient institutional arrangement. The first three examples

---

18. "In a series of articles Landa (1981), Carr and Landa (1983), and Cooter and Landa (1984) have creatively used economic theory to explain why middlemen often share a single attribute—for example, they are kinsmen, clansmen, or members of the same religious or ethnic groups" (La Croix 1989, 211). See also Ben-Porath (1980).

illustrate again the conclusion of the last section: there are no ready-made conclusions about what constitutes a welfare-increasing institutional arrangement. To derive a judgment, the individual case has to be analyzed carefully using the analytical techniques of modern (not necessarily only "new") institutional economics, as described, in part at least, in this book. This is an important insight from the viewpoint of both antitrust judgments and competition policy. All examples, and in particular the last one concerning the New York Diamond Dealers Club, illustrate Ben-Porath's point "that the identity of the people engaged in transaction is a major determinant of the institutional mode of transaction" (1980, 1). This is the consequence of the fact that in the real world we have neither free information nor free enforcement, as is assumed in standard neoclassical theory. See also the recent collection of empirical studies on contracting, vertical integration, and hybrid organizational forms edited by Masten (1996).

## 7.5.  Markets: Conclusion and Outlook

We have tried to illustrate in this section the role of market organization as conceived by the New Institutional Economics. In doing so, we relied on the elementary order of a private ownership economy and its general operational rules (described in section 6.1). We concentrated on what we called "special operational rules," that is, the rules regarding the basic transactional activities of search, inspection, contracting, execution, control, and enforcement. These six activities are organized through private bilateral, or through private or public multilateral (collective), agreements between market participants or their political representatives. Coordination or cooperation occurs in two directions: vertically and horizontally. In the latter case, cooperation exists between actual or potential competitors. The concept of relational contracts is applied to analyze these relationships. Market organization is seen as the governance structure of horizontal and vertical relational contracts among market participants. In effect, relational contracts determine the property rights structure of the market participants and how these property rights can be used.

In a strict sense, the organization "market" deals with the organization of transaction activities only at the moment of contract conclusion—which is the "happy ending" of the story of neoclassical economics. In the case of perfect markets with zero information and enforcement costs, the elementary constitutional and general operational rules described in section 6.1 would be sufficient. The identity of the people engaged in exchange would not matter. Yet this is not true (at least not in general) in the world in which we live. The examples we presented of the views of neoinstitutionalists on market organizations illustrate the importance of social relationships and of implicit or explicit cooperation, both vertically and horizontally, including ethical and moral codes, as arrangements that permit potential trading partners to deal with the possibility of market failure. The examples illustrate that it is difficult to analyze the activities of search, inspection, and contract conclusion completely independent of the postcontractual activities of execution, control, and enforcement. It is therefore advisable to view the organization market in a wider sense, that is, by including the organization of the postcontractual phase, as we did. As a result, an overlap with the organization "firm" becomes unavoidable, as was shown in our presentation on vertical integration.

Some of the market transaction activities considered here (search, inspection, control) are dealt with by formal contract theories: adverse selection, self-enforcing agreements, and moral hazard models. The results of these formal models (described in chap. 5) should be considered together with the results of informal theories presented in this chapter. Both formal and informal neo-institutional analyses contribute to our understanding of why complete realization of the conditions of the perfect market is only feasible under very restrictive regulations and is, in general, hardly socially desirable. The theoretically ideal market would, in a world with transaction costs, probably lead to devastating results: lost bearings, mistrust, large costs in time for potential traders, and so on. Thus, competition policy appears in a new light. Departures from the conditions of the ideal type of the perfect market, depending on circumstances, may ease informational problems and thus serve economizing purposes. Block booking, the suppression of information, price leadership, advertising, sticky prices, barriers to entry, market prices above competitive prices, vertical and lateral integration, the extreme dependence of the franchisee on the regulations of his franchisor, and private third-party enforcements—these all may be efficient institutional arrangements. Whether this is so or not has to be analyzed carefully case by case using the analytical techniques of modern institutional economics described, at least in part, in this book.

Market organization, as understood here, is the result of bilateral or multilateral cooperation to overcome informational problems. Private ownership in market organization plays a role in some of our examples (e.g., the price of the right to become a dealer at a stock exchange). It provides an incentive in the setting up and maintaining of such market organizations.

The analysis of private or public horizontal relationships between competitors, such as associations or unions, leads us into the field of public choice theory and, in the end, into the analysis of the role of interest groups in the lawmaking process. Market organization should be discussed together with political decision making. The roles played by pressure groups, special interests, and "third-realm" interests are relevant and should be included. But, surprisingly, very little has happened in this area so far, and virtually nothing within the NIE literature.[19] The approach of the New Institutional Economics (property rights, transaction costs, relational contracting), together with the more formal approaches described in chapter 5, would have to be combined with the theory of public choice for that purpose. A combination of the analytical techniques of the NIE and public choice to further the understanding of private and public collective action is desirable. Constitutional economics is a step in this direction.

### 7.6.  A Brief Guide to the Literature on Market Organization

*Market organization matters.* Coase (1988b, 7), whom we quote at the beginning of this section, mentions Marshall, who had a chapter "On Markets" in his *Principles of Economics* (1920), "but it was general in character and did not probe . . . " Marshall quotes in this chapter Jevon's theory of political economy. Jevons remarks that, while originally the term *market* described a public place where trade took place, "the word has been generalized, so as to mean any body of persons who are in intimate business relations and carry on extensive transactions in any commodity" (quoted in Marshall 1920, 270). This old description comes closer to the modern departure from impersonal economics (described, e.g., by Ben-Porath [1980] than Weber does in his fragment of chapter 7 in *Economy and Society* ("The Market: Its Impersonality and Ethic"). Weber writes: "The market community as such is the most impersonal relationship of practical life into which humans can enter with one another. . . . "The reason for the impersonality of the market is its matter-of-factness, its orientation to the commodity and only on that . . . there are no obligations of brotherliness or reverence, and none of those spontaneous human relations that are sustained by personal unions. . . . Market behavior is influenced by rational, purposeful pursuit of interests" (1968, 636). What follows is a verbal description of what later became known as the theory of self-enforcing agreements. Weber's description comes rather close to the concept of perfect markets, which is, strictly speaking, applicable only to a zero-transaction-cost world. In the real world, where information is a scarce and therefore valuable resource, "the identity of the people engaged in a transaction is a major determination of the institutional mode of transaction" (Ben-Porath 1980, 1). Hamilton and Feenstra (1995) use Weber's *Economy and Society* to develop a synthesis between Coase's and Williamson's conceptions of the dichotomy

---

19. Little work has been done in the field of the economics of organized groups since Olson (1965) made his contribution. The representatives of the NIE disregard the area almost completely. Public choice writers, for their part, concentrate on a special aspect of organized groups—rent-seeking activities (see, e.g., Tollison 1982, 1988).

between market and hierarchy and Weber's distinction between economic power and authority. They hold that certain aspects of hierarchies exert independent effects on the formation of market economies. Then, on the basis of empirical analysis relating to the economies of South Korea and Taiwan, Hamilton and Feenstra demonstrate the practical relevance of their new conceptual approach.

The informational problem is at the center of market organization. Stigler (1961) and Nelson (1970, 1974) provide early contributions to what later became informational economics—reviewed by Stiglitz (1985). It is part of modern contract theory, described in chapter 5, including the lemons problem and other adverse selection issues as well as implicit contract theory and self-enforcing contracts (see secs. 5.3, 5.4, and 5.6).

Besides economic contracting, economists increasingly are considering "social contracting," which has been taken up by such strategic management theorists as Starr and Macmillan (1990). The theory goes back to Homans (1950, 1958) and Blau (1964). According to this view, markets are to be understood as networks governing economic and social transactions. While this approach still consists of a straightforward application of the assumption of individual rationality (utility maximization), Etzioni (1988), with his socioeconomic paradigm, argues that constraints on rational choice are not only attributable to bounded rationality but also that "individual choice is characterized by tension between rational choice factors and moral commitment." He suggests that in most cases the strictly self-interested "rational" decision is inhibited by moral commitments of the individual to what seems "fair," "right," or "appropriate" (quoted in Starr and Macmillan 1990, 80). A comparison of this style of reasoning with Schmoller (1900, 60) suggests itself.

The role of norms of social behavior, including ethical and moral codes (which are not simply "there"), are also mentioned by Arrow (1969, 62) as a reaction of society "to compensate for market failure. It is useful for individuals to have some trust in each other's word." The concept of organizational culture as applied by Kreps (1990a) to the organization of the firm may possibly also be applied to the organization of the market or the "market community" in the sense of Weber (1968).

Also note in this context Brennan and Buchanan (1985), who rightly stress that to understand the market one must pay attention to the rules that govern its operation: "Economists, themselves, have been notoriously negligent in this respect. Complex analytical exercises on the workings of the market are often carried out without so much as passing reference to the rules within which individual behavior in those markets takes place" (13).

*Price rigidity.* Sticky prices and wages play a central role in Keynesian macroeconomics. The microtheories of sticky wages, though, account mostly for real rather than nominal wage rigidity. The implicit contract theory described in chapter 5, to take one example, dates back to the work of Bailey (1974) and Azariadis (1975). On this literature, see section 5.8.4. Another explanation for sticky real wages, coming close to the neoinstitutionalist approach, is the hypothesis of efficiency wages, which was introduced by Schlicht (1978), Solow (1979), Akerlof (1982), and others. These models assume realistically that it would be too costly for firms to specify (and monitor) all aspects of a worker's performance. If labor productivity depends on the real wage paid, it may be an effective way for the firm to pay a wage above the market-clearing wage. This can provide an incentive for workers to work rather than shirk (see, e.g., Shapiro and Stiglitz 1984). In equilibrium, all firms will pay a real wage above the hypothetical market wage. "Unemployed workers cannot bid for jobs by offering to work at lower wages. If the firm were to hire a worker at a lower wage it would be in the worker's interest to shirk on the job" (Akerlof and Yellen 1986, 5—a review of this literature).

As for rigid nominal prices, the standard explanation is of the oligopolistic or monopolistic type like the kinked demand curve concept (Negishi 1979) or monopolistic power (e.g., Bils 1989). These theories belong to the "monopoly branch" of contract theory and are not of our concern in this book. The "efficiency branch" of contract-price rigidity has often been attributed to the costs of nominal price adjustments. Barro (1972), Mussa (1981), and Okun (1981) introduced for this purpose the distinction between auction and customer markets. In the latter, customer relationships, and thus reputation, play a role. For more on this literature, see section 7.7.

*Market organization as a result of market cooperation.* The invisible hand evolution of markets is nicely described by ethnologists such as Fröhlich (1940), who writes on the evolution of marketplaces in Africa. Interestingly though, some visible hands seem also to be involved, like the elders or chieftains representing their tribes, who develop (and own) a marketplace. Garvy (1944) describes the evolution of the New York Stock Exchange. This market traces its ancestry to a small group of brokers who at the end of the eighteenth century began to deal in securities. See also Mulherin, Netter, and Overdahl (1991), who analyze the nature of financial exchanges such as the New York Stock Exchange and the Chicago Board of Trade. They report about firms that have successfully established markets in financial products and argue that the establishment of property rights to "price quotes" is a central function of financial exchanges. Another interesting article provided by Telser (1981), who presents an explanation of the existence of organized futures markets, showing that futures contracts on organized futures markets acquire the same advantages over forward contracts as does trade conducted with the aid of money over barter. Fellner's (1949) idea of quasi agreements between competitors is an early example of relational contracting.

The organization of markets is also closely connected with the development of intermediaries as trading firms. Chandler (1977) examines the evolution of modern mass retailers in the 1870s and 1880s: the department store, the mail order house, and the chain store. These firms improved the productivity of the American distribution system considerably. Furthermore, the organization of markets is influenced by the development of modern contractual arrangements such as joint ventures, franchising, leasing, factoring, know-how contracts, credit card contracts, and so on. On legal aspects, see, as a German reader, Martinek (1991, 1992, 1993). For an institutional economic discussion of joint ventures, see Hennart 1988, 1991). Among the early institutionalist contributions on leasing are Klein, Crawford, and Alchian (1978, 319ff.) and Flath (1980). The latter deals with the operating lease and tries to show, in particular, that leasing economizes upon transaction costs. He also provides a useful survey of the various reasons for leasing mentioned in the earlier literature. Krahnen and Meran (1989) and Krahnen (1990) apply agency theory to rationalize the financial lease. As for franchising, a particularly interesting topic, we would like to mention Rubin (1978), who uses the institutional economics theory of the firm to explain the nature of the franchise contract. Klein, Crawford, and Alchian (1978) stress the protection of the franchisor's interest in quality control. On this basis, Klein (1980) defends the termination-at-will clause of franchise contracts. Hadfield (1990) points out the dual aspect of the commitment problem of a franchise contract, namely, that the franchisee has an interest in protecting his specific investment. She also provides an overview of the U.S. franchising industry, the American legal structure of franchising, the relational aspects of franchising, and its economic structure. This protection of franchisees and franchisors from each other's opportunistic behavior is exemplified by Dnes (1992a). His exposition includes a considerable number of real-life cases. In another study by Dnes (1992b), it is argued that the asset specificity at the retail end of business forces a would-be franchisor to select those who are profit motivated and likely to be vigorous in pursuing new business for the franchisor. For a more recent review article on franchising, see Dnes 1996. The German legal franchising situation is touched upon by Müller-Graff (1988). For a detailed monograph (in German) on this issue, see Martinek (1987).

Search costs play an important role in modeling the evolution of markets. Market making as a profitable action is modeled, for example, by Gould (1980), who develops a simple model involving two traders. The traders must expend resources to find each other so that trade can take place. Contractual arrangements taking search costs into consideration were dealt with in sections 5.3 and 5.6.

*On the economics of market organization.* The economics of market organization, as understood in this chapter, is closely associated with the field of industrial organization (IO). Broadly defined, IO is "the field of economics concerned with markets that cannot easily be analyzed using the standard textbook competitive model" (Schmalensee 1987, 803). While traditional IO argues that complex forms of contracting are a consequence of monopolistic activities, the NIE approach holds that the departures serve economizing purposes instead (Williamson 1985, 23). Bibliographical notes on the NIE approach are in effect provided in the text of section 7.4. There are, of course, many other examples. Since the 1970s, industrial economics has become a field of increasing interest to formal theorists. They deal with the monopoly argument and use noncooperative game theory as the standard tool for the analysis of strategic conflict (for an overview, see Tirole 1988, pt. 2). It can be argued, though, that these new theoretical models "merely formalize long standing intuitive arguments which can be found in the traditional literature" (Sutton 1990, 506). Sutton adds that "this formalization has, at the very least, sharpened the focus of debate and has provided for extending and elaborating the arguments involved" (506). Since neoinstitutionalism is concerned with the efficiency branch of contract theory, not the monopoly branch, we did not discuss these other theoretical developments. A complete analysis of market organization would have to include these developments, with the work of Sutton (1992) coming relatively close to our interests.

An important issue in industrial organization is the problem of *regulation*—government actions to control price, sales, and production decisions of firms in the "public interest." Among the arguments against regulation is Demsetz's (1968b) famous article "Why Regulate Utilities?" Demsetz suggests the possibility of auctioning off the franchise rights of a monopolist. Thus, even though scale economies may suggest that there be a single ex post supplier, "large number competition may nevertheless be feasible at the initial bidding stage." This is an argument that Stigler (1968, 1974), among others, finds persuasive. Yet, as Williamson (1976) has shown, this is a typical example of the fundamental transformation and thus of ex post opportunism by the winner of the franchise bidding. Goldberg (1976) argues in a similar fashion. Relational contract theory comes into play (see sec. 4.4.3). Also interesting in this case are the activities of market participants seeking to escape the regulatory rules in a legal way. As Schanze (1995) observes: "At the border of important markets we observe the creation of new markets escaping regulation. And, indeed, diligent evasion will be tolerated" (165). In the name of private autonomy, courts concede what Schanze terms a *regulatory bifurcation*. Lawmakers, in their desire to close loopholes they did not foresee, extend regulatory laws—which may be an explanation for the increase (rather than the decrease) in public regulation (Hax 1995).

## 7.7. Suggested Readings for Chapter 7

*Market organization matters.* The problem of this section is posed by Coase (1988b), chap. 1. Read also the classic sociological text on the market as an organization by Weber (1968, chap. 2.8, 7).

*Price rigidity.* For empirical examples, read Carlton (1989) and Blinder (1991). For the theoretical explanation by neoinstitutionalists, see section 7.4.2.

*Market organization as a result of market cooperation.* Market organization as a result of implicit or explicit collective action is best illustrated by ethnologists like Fröhlich (1940; in German).

Economic historians such as Garvy (1944) provide interesting examples like the history of the New York Stock Exchange. Entrepreneurial activity may play a role: read Coase (1988b, 8) and, for example, Pease and Chitty (1958) on fairs and markets in medieval England, which were organized by individuals under a franchise from the king. In modern times, public collective actions by governments play a central role in setting up markets. Public choice issues, and particularly the influence of pressure groups, are discussed in the context of trade-policy decisions (see, e.g., Baldwin 1985).

*Views of neoinstitutionalists on market organization.* It is advisable to read the articles discussed in section 7.4 in order to become fully acquainted with the neoinstitutionalists' style of reasoning, its advantages, and its shortcomings. We suggest particularly that Barzel (1982) be read on measurement cost and the organization of markets. Similarly, read Acheson (1985), whom we did not mention, on the peculiarities of the Maine lobster market, Alchian and Woodward (1987) on posted prices, and Joskow (1985a), who tests Williamson's transaction-cost hypothesis empirically for the American coal-burning electricity-generating plants. Further, Klein, Crawford, and Alchian (1978) and Klein and Leffler (1981), two path-breaking articles, are obligatory reading to supplement the work of Williamson (1985). Williamson's chapters 7 and 8 (on credible commitments) and 13 (on regulation) are particularly important.

Stock or commodity exchanges provide illustrations of the kinds of problems a market organization has to solve. We suggest that the detailed studies of such exchanges by Mulherin, Netter and Overdahl (1991) and Bernstein (1992) be read. To compare neoinstitutionalists' views on market organization with mainstream industrial organization, read Williamson (1985, 23–42) together with a survey of the work on orthodox industrial organization such as that written by Schmalensee (1987).

CHAPTER 8

# The New Institutional Economics
# of the Firm

Like other areas of microeconomics, the theory of the firm has been undergo-
ing substantial rethinking and revision during the last few decades. Traditional
neoclassical analysis has been challenged by a variety of new approaches that
seek to explain the basis of the firm, its structure, and its significance for a
modern economic system. The literature suggests that, while there is not as yet
anything like complete agreement on what form the new enterprise model
should take, there is general recognition that the artificial assumptions of
neoclassical theory have to be relaxed. In one fashion or another, new ideas
drawn from such fields as game theory, evolutionary economics, principal-
agent theory, and mechanism design will have to be dealt with and reflected in
any revised construct. This section focuses on the theoretical contributions
associated with the New Institutional Economics and considers what can be
called transaction-cost/property-rights analysis. The interpretation of the firm
emphasized here has, however, much in common with other new approaches
and may be said to offer a relatively comprehensive view of current thinking on
organizational questions.

This chapter is divided into two parts. The first part embraces sections 8.1
through 8.4 and discusses the general conception of the firm advanced in the
literature of the New Institutional Economics. The second part considers special applications of the new approach and is found in sections 8.5 through 8.8.
The chapter ends, like the others, with detailed suggestions for additional
readings.

## 8.1. The Orthodox Neoclassical Firm

In order to proceed systematically, it will be desirable to begin with a brief
discussion of the orthodox neoclassical conception of the capitalist, owner-
managed enterprise. Characteristically, profit is assumed to be the sole dimension of the firm's objective function, and in formal terms the problem is seen as
one of profit maximization undertaken against a background of given market
and technological conditions. Thus, in the simple static case in which only one
commodity is produced, we have

$$\max \ \pi = p^o q \ - \ \sum_{i=1}^{n} r_i^o x_i \tag{1}$$

$$s.t. \quad q = f(x_1, x_2, \ldots, x_n). \tag{2}$$

Here, profit ($\pi$) is the difference between the total revenue from the sale of the output ($q$) at the market price ($p^o$) and the total expenditure on all inputs ($x_i$), whose known parametric prices are $r_1^o, r_2^o, \ldots r_n^o$. The entrepreneur, who possesses an exclusive right to the firm's residual, seeks to maximize $\pi$ subject to the engineering or technical conditions reflected in the production function ($f$). Then, the first-order conditions resulting from the constrained maximization of the profit equation (1), subject to the production function (eq. 2), represent the *marginal rules* that must be followed to achieve optimal factor utilization and commodity output. Specifically, the indication is that either the value of the marginal product of each input should be equated with its price or, equivalently, the marginal cost of output should be equated with the ruling commodity price. On the basis of this type of reasoning, Henderson and Quandt (1958, 42) are able to say:

> A firm is a technical unit in which commodities are produced. Its entrepreneur (owner and manager) decides how much of and how one or more commodities will be produced, and gains the profit or bears the loss which results from his decision. An entrepreneur transforms inputs into outputs, subject to the technical rules specified by his production function. The difference between his revenue from the sale of outputs and the cost of inputs is his profit, if positive, or his loss, if negative.

All this seems straightforward enough, but, from the standpoint of the New Institutional Economics, the neoclassical model of the firm is quite disappointing.

Questions about the neoclassical position arise at various levels and are not easily answered. If, as is assumed, events take place in a "frictionless" world where each decision maker is able to acquire and process any information desired instantly and costlessly, we must wonder how much scope exists for entrepreneurship. For example, to solve the static, one-period problem represented by equations (1) and (2), the firm's "fully informed" owner need only follow the requisite marginal rules to achieve success. And what is involved in following these rules is at best the exercise of low-level managerial skills. Indeed, in the environment posited, the entrepreneur remains a ghost— as does the Walrasian auctioneer. It is clear that the role of information and its use in an economic system has to be reassessed. Such study has, of course, been going on steadily in recent decades and has prompted Stiglitz (1985, 21) to note that

we have learned that much of what we believed before is of only limited validity; that the traditional competitive equilibrium analysis, though having the superficial appearance of generality—in terms of superscripts and subscripts—is indeed not very general; the theory is not robust to slight alterations in the informational assumptions. It is but a special—and not very plausible—"example" among the possible set of informational assumptions which can be employed to characterize an economy.

This line of criticism is very potent because it contradicts, in good part, the fundamental notion introduced by Samuelson (1947) that the analysis of maximizing behavior is the key to understanding a wide range of economic phenomena.

Even the logic of the contention that individual and firm behavior can be thought of as the solution to a maximization problem has been questioned: for how is the individual to resolve the infinite regress of whether it is worthwhile to obtain information concerning whether it is worthwhile to obtain information . . . (Stiglitz 1985, 23; see also Winter 1964).

When positive transaction costs exist, straightforward evaluation of the marginal costs and marginal benefits of information is not possible except under very special conditions. Of course, the assumption that transaction costs are greater than zero violates the neoclassical presumption of a frictionless world. At the same time, however, it is abundantly clear that real-world problems cannot be addressed very meaningfully if we assume that everyone is completely and accurately informed.

More will be said subsequently about the significance of positive transaction costs, but before leaving the elementary enterprise model summarized in equations (1) and (2) it will be useful to explore the case more fully. First, it is obvious that the production function (2) plays a dominant role in this theory of the firm. But, as conceived in neoclassical thought, the production function is an abstract and highly specialized construct. It is viewed essentially as a technological relation and thus takes little or no account of institutional arrangements or the internal organization of the firm. Realistically, however, a firm's institutional structure is important to a proper understanding of its production function. The arrangements in existence affect the incentives offered input suppliers and hence the effective flows of productive services going to the firm. Ceteris paribus, the output obtainable from the factors contracted for will vary with the firm's institutional and organizational configuration (see

Jensen and Meckling 1979; and Furubotn, 1996). Another difficulty is that the production function, in its characteristic form as (2), is a one-period concept that relates flows of productive services to a flow of output. While durable capital stocks are recognized, they appear only dimly in the background of the theory. Questions about investment and finance tend to be avoided because it is assumed that the services supplied by any piece of capital equipment can always be rented at the going market price ($r_i$). But, even on its own terms, this analysis does not go far enough. The difficulty is that a whole array of rental prices must exist—with a different price associated with each possible leasing period. Presumably, the entrepreneur must choose the time interval during which he is to be "locked in" with a particular input at a particular price. And ultimately the issue of whether to lease or buy must arise.

It is true, of course, that multiperiod or dynamic investment models of the firm can be substituted for the simple static model based on equations (1) and (2). There is no great difficulty in conceiving of a stock-flow production function that possesses neoclassical properties and can be used to consider the problem of optimization over time. Assuming, for example, a point-input/ continuous-output case, the objective of the firm can be established as one of maximizing net present value rather than one-period profit. The shift to an explicitly dynamic formulation, however, makes it much harder to avoid dealing with the kinds of questions that concern the New Institutional Economics. Under the changed conditions, it seems natural to recognize the existence of uncertainty and the corresponding need of the entrepreneur to forecast future economic conditions. Expected values take center stage. But this approach leads inevitably to the problems of how the marginal (expected) benefit of information is to be estimated at any point and how far search should be pressed. Further complications are suggested here if the calculations for the firm are to be made by a decision maker who is boundedly rational.

While the maximization of net present value may seem to be a plausible objective for a firm operating over time, this criterion does present a problem because it permits a decision maker to rationalize virtually any action or policy as one that contributes to optimization. If the meaning of one-period profit maximization is in any doubt, the meaning of net present-value maximization is in greater doubt. Further, once attention is directed to the behavior of an ongoing firm operating subject to uncertainty, the number of potential policy options expands and the firm's decision-making process must come under greater scrutiny. Institutional structure cannot be ignored. If the firm is not a simple owner-managed entity, the actual property-rights arrangement in existence plays a crucial role in shaping outcomes. For example, the hired managers of a dispersed-ownership corporation may seek their own personal objectives, pursue goals other than profit, and trade off potential profits for nonpecuniary and other benefits that they can appropriate at the expense of stockholders. The separation of ownership from control thus becomes an issue here. Alternately, a codetermined firm can be expected to show a somewhat different pattern of behavior based on its special property-rights structure. Neoclassical analysis, which is institutionally neutral, is unable to deal effectively with such variant cases.

When the firm is understood to possess stocks of durable capital, certain problems become evident that would tend to be overlooked in the service flow model (1) and (2). One important matter that has received considerable attention in the new institutionalist literature concerns asset specificity. Insofar as an individual owns durable capital that is *firm specific,* he has reason to insist on contractual safeguards against opportunism that would not be necessary for an individual who supplied a "general" or nonspecific input to the firm. In other words, the owner of firm-specific capital must seek protection because otherwise he is vulnerable to the "hold up" and can have his quasi rents expropriated by other members of the coalition of factor owners constituting the firm (Furubotn, 1988). Conventional neoclassical theory does not place much emphasis on the details of contracting and in general takes a rather superficial view of contractual activity. For example, in the basic model of the firm sketched earlier, equations (1) and (2) suggest that all of the input flows contracted for and paid for in (1) will be supplied in *full measure* when introduced into productive operations via (2). The model makes no provisions for outlays by the firm on monitoring and enforcement procedures. Presumably, in a world of costless transactions, all contracts can be enforced fully, automatically, and instantly—with no messy economic calculations intervening to disturb the process.

This simplistic view of the firm has, of course, been challenged by writers in the New Institutional Economics tradition. Thus, it can be said:

At the heart of modern theories of the firm lies a puzzle. If we view the firm from the outside and ignore the details of its operation, we see the firm to be an enterprise fundamentally characterized by cooperation. If we view it from the inside, however, we are unsure as to how cooperative a venture the firm really is. (Eaton and Eaton 1988, 147)

Clearly, a firm depends on "cooperation" in the sense that the production of goods requires the joint effort of all those who work in the firm. Moreover, the efficiency and success of the firm will be greater or lesser depending on how well its members (those who supply inputs and are within the enterprise) are able to blend their efforts and cooperate effectively.

The usual assumption is that self-interest prompts at least some willingness on the part of individuals to accept the authority of the firm and cooperate within its boundaries. The rationale here is that by combining in an organization people can produce relatively greater output than they could if they operated as independent agents coordinated only by a series of transactions across markets. But the attractions of cooperation go only so far. It remains true that individuals have *private objectives* that are often in conflict with what may be regarded as the wider, collective interests of the firm. Thus, a key problem for organizational economics is to determine how to motivate individuals so that they will, in fact, work toward collective interests and make the firm successful. Broadly speaking, two approaches are open. On the one hand, monitoring and enforcement activities can be undertaken in an attempt to force individuals to honor contractual obligations. On the other hand, efforts can be made to motivate people by giving them material rewards and recognition for good performance. Following these general lines, various specific devices may be employed to enhance enterprise efficiency. Nevertheless, there is always a question as to how to proceed. Some writers, such as Simon (1991), argue that material incentives alone are insufficient to provide adequate motivation for all firm members to work wholeheartedly toward firm goals; but, even if a more optimistic assessment is made of material incentives and disincentives, it is not obvious precisely how the firm's penalty-reward structure should be established. Organizational structure, like technology, is open ended and can be changed and improved over time as innovation takes place.

The preceding discussion has suggested some of the limitations of the orthodox theory of the firm and indicated the general direction in which new, institutionally oriented research is moving. As things have developed, it appears that the firm is now viewed as a nexus of contracts that regulate the nonmarket transactions between resource owners who form, under conditions of asymmetric information and imperfect foresight, a private enterprise. As Jensen and Meckling (1976, 311) put it:

> The private enterprise or firm is simply one form of legal fiction which serves as a nexus for contracting relationships and which is also characterized by the existence of divisible residual claims on the assets and cash flows of the organization which can generally be sold without permission of the other contracting individuals.

As noted earlier, the modern theory of the firm has grown rapidly during the last twenty years. For a review, see, for example, Holmstrom and Tirole 1989 and the bibliographical material at the end of this chapter. Many questions are open. In what follows, however, attention will be limited to a few key issues that are closely associated with major themes of the New Institutional Economics. Specifically, we shall focus on applications of (1) the property-rights approach, (2) transaction-cost economics, and (3) contract theory to questions of (a) firm size, (b) ownership and control, and (c) capital structure.

Insights drawn from this general line of analysis will then be used to explore and interpret the labor-owned firm, the socialist labor-managed firm, the codetermined firm, and the Soviet-type firm.

The new institutional analysis of the firm began with the famous article by Coase (1937), which forced economists to think more systematically about a pervasive organization that previously had been more or less taken for granted. Coase asks two basic questions: (1) Why are firms necessary if economic activities can be conducted and coordinated through market transactions? and (2) What limits the size of the firm? His answers to these questions are simple but illuminating.

"The main reason why it is profitable to establish a firm would seem to be that there is a cost of using the price mechanism" Coase (1937, 390). Two types of transaction costs are identified as significant. These are search costs—"the costs of discovering what the relevant prices are"—and contracting costs— "the costs of negotiating and concluding a separate contract for each transaction which takes place on a market" (390–91). In other words, the message is that, if a firm is formed, the number of contracts that have to be concluded between parties is greatly reduced. The owner of a productive factor is not required to make a separate contract with each of the factor owners with whom he is cooperating in the firm. Rather, he concludes only one contract with the entrepreneur, whose directions he agrees to obey in exchange for a stipulated reward. Characteristically, the contract between a factor owner and the entrepreneur (or central party) is established in rather general terms. This is so because the future cannot be foreseen perfectly, and provision for some flexibility in contract terms is beneficial to enterprise productivity and hence to both parties. It appears, then, that even at this early stage Coase was thinking about relational or incomplete contracts. Specifically, he asserts: "A firm is likely therefore to emerge in those cases where a very short term contract would be unsatisfactory" (391).

Coase's answer to the second question builds essentially on the assumption of diminishing returns to management. Thus,

> a firm will tend to expand until the costs of organizing an extra transaction within the firm become equal to the costs of carrying out the same transaction by means of an exchange on the open market or the costs of organizing another firm. (1937, 395)

This can be interpreted also as an application of the principle of marginal substitution applied to the activity "organization." In general, one might say that, although Coase's argument is plausible, it is only another view of the drive for profit maximization and it remains empty as long as the activity transaction and the concept of transaction costs are not explained more fully

(Bössmann 1981, 671ff.). Coase provides no detailed reasons for the existence of the firm, even though he argues that it is a particular type of contract (the employment contract) that makes a firm. Moreover, he hardly discusses post-contractual issues. Control and enforcement costs are not mentioned as reasons for or against the establishment of a firm. Only some thirty years later, with the development of the property-rights approach, transaction-cost economics, and contract theory, was more elaborate microeconomic analysis put forward to explain such deeper problems of the firm as enterprise size, capital structure, and ownership.

## 8.2. The Incentive to Integrate

One of the first attempts to establish a more detailed institutional description of the firm, and to relate structural considerations to the economic nature of the firm, was made by Alchian and Demsetz (1972). These writers stress the postcontractual phase of transactions and give attention to the problems associated with execution and control. In particular, the so-called metering problem is analyzed. The latter becomes important in the widely encountered cases of team production. By working together in teams, individuals are often able to secure increasing returns to scale (superadditivity effects), but "it is difficult solely by observing total output, to either define or determine each individual's contribution to this output of the cooperating inputs" (778). Alchian and Demsetz then argue that: "The costs of metering or ascertaining the marginal products of the team's members is what calls forth new organizations and procedures" (780). Viewed from this perspective, the "classical" capitalist firm represents an organizational form that is well adapted to deal with the need for efficient metering. That is, the property-rights arrangements here permit the entrepreneur (or owner-manager) to specialize as a monitor. His position in the firm (which has legal sanction) gives him both the right to check the input performance of team members and the incentive not to shirk in carrying out this duty. The entrepreneur has the right motivation because he is the exclusive claimant to the firm's residual. Thus, the more effectively he monitors perfor-mance, and eliminates team members who shirk, the greater is his reward via the residual. To be able to discipline team members, the residual claimant must, of course, have the right to revise contract terms and influence the incentives of individual members without having to terminate or alter every other input's contract (Alchian and Demsetz 1972, 782). For Alchian and Demsetz as was shown in Section 4.4.1, the classical firm is a unique organization headed by an entrepreneur whose ownership of the firm is defined by his possession of the following rights: (1) to be a residual claimant, (2) to observe input behavior, (3) to be the central party common to all contracts with inputs, (4) to alter the membership of the team, and (5) to sell these rights (783).

This approach, which stresses the conditions of "ownership" extant, is characteristic of the property-rights theory of the firm (Furubotn and Pejovich 1972a, 1148). In general, the various members of a firm have certain rights in the firm—as specified by the formal and informal contractual arrangements agreed upon by the input owners. The particular rights possessed by any individual are significant, though, because they affect his incentives and hence his economic behavior. Over time, of course, the rights structure of a firm can be altered either by private parties within the firm or by the state. For example, in the case of the classical firm described by Alchian and Demsetz (1972), the original rights of the entrepreneur may be partitioned so that workers can be given some claim on the firm's residual. Insofar as members of the firm are involved in the restructuring of rights, it can perhaps be assumed that the restructuring is intended to improve incentives and/or lower transaction costs with a view to making the firm a more efficient producer. However, the goal of efficiency need not always dominate—for example, if unionized workers have great bargaining power, they may be able to push through changes in rights that are beneficial to them but detrimental to other members of the coalition of factor owners and to productive efficiency. Similarly, rights changes dictated by government may reflect the power of political pressure groups and need not result in improved conditions of production. Whatever the effects of property-rights assignments may be in a given case, the theory here suggests that it is important to know what the rights structure of the firm is at any time in order to predict the firm's behavior.

The metering problem can also be interpreted as one that arises from the activity "inspection," where inspection is one of the six transaction activities noted in chapter 7. Barzel (1982, 39ff.) argues, as was pointed out in section 7.4.1, that vertical integration may also be undertaken in order to economize on inspection costs.

The last of our six transaction activities, "enforcement," became a central issue of the modern theory of the firm through the work of Williamson (1975, 1979, 1985), who introduced the concepts of ex post opportunism and bounded rationality into popular discussion (see sec. 4.4.3). He suggests that these assumptions about the behavior of decision makers go a long way in explaining why incomplete contracts present problems. That is, given small-numbers exchange and transaction-specific investments, individuals who are pre-disposed to take advantage of others have considerable opportunity to cheat when engaged in market transactions. Thus, according to Williamson (1975, 29), the incentive to integrate, under the general circumstances noted, is due to three advantages of internal organization over market modes of contracting:

> First, in relation to autonomous contractors, the parties to an internal exchange are less able to appropriate subgroup gains, at the expense of the

overall organization (system), as a result of opportunistic representations. . . . Second, and related, internal organization can be more effectively audited. Finally, when differences do arise, internal organization realizes an advantage over market mediated exchange in dispute settling respects.

In later work, Williamson (1979; 1985, 71ff.) speaks of *unified governance* as the organizational structure of rational contracting.

In discussing asset specificity, Williamson (1985, 95ff.), as was shown in section 4.2, identifies four different types of specificities, or transaction-specific sunk investments Joskow (1985a, 38), namely, site specificity, physical asset specificity, human capital specificity, and dedicated assets.

For a discussion of Williamson's general approach to questions in the New Institutional Economics and his transaction-cost approach, see chapter 4. It can be pointed out at this point, however, that there is some empirical confirmation of Williamson's analysis of the role of transaction costs. Joskow (1985a) supplies an interesting example in the case of coalburning electricity-generating plants. His findings show that "mine-mouth" operations, which demand highly specific investments, are much more likely to lead to vertical integration.

Specifically, while mine-mouth operations only account for fifteen percent of electricity output, they account for more than fifty percent of vertical integration between mining operations and electricity plants. Hence a much higher portion of mine-mouth operations are integrated, confirming the role of specific investments in integration. (Wiggins 1991, 619)

Williamson's theory concerning the incentives to integrate leaves the ownership question open. This is significant because, as the property-rights literature has emphasized, the allocation of rights in an organization has an influence on behavior. Property rights can be viewed as ownership conditions that are supplemented by particular guarantee instruments, including private guarantees. In effect, then, both transaction costs and property-rights must be considered. Williamson is correct in pointing out that, in a world of positive transaction costs, the actual costs attaching to guarantee instruments affect the governance structure used by a firm. Nevertheless, the impact of property-rights assignments cannot be neglected. When numbers of independent decision makers, characterized by diverse and conflicting objectives, are forced to interact within a firm, group maximization of utility seems to be an inappropriate concept. Similarly, the idea that an organization's policies are guided by one individual, or "as if" by one individual, cannot be sustained. In other words, depending on the manner in which property rights in the firm are allocated (i.e., how contracts are written), the nature of the optimization problem will be of one form or another. At any moment of time, the existing property-rights arrangements establish the identities of those individuals who are in effective control of the organization and indicate the standpoint from which policies of the organization will be framed. The property-rights arrangements extant affect not only transaction costs and productive efficiency but also the distribution of income and power among the different factor owners associated in the coalition. Thus, any (voluntary) changes in the rights structure over time will tend to be made in such a way as to improve the welfare of those in control of policy. Assuming self-seeking behavior, what matters to the different participants in the firm is their ability to appropriate rewards—in the form of pecuniary and nonpecuniary income. Under these conditions, however, there can be no assurance that either profit maximization or cost minimization will be the principle guiding the firm's behavior. While there may be limits to how far a firm can go in sacrificing productive efficiency to other goals, decision making (based on internal "political" realities) can still place preponderant emphasis on policies that are especially rewarding to those having major influence and bargaining strength in the firm.

Thinking in terms of property rights and the problems of contracting, Grossman and Hart (1986) developed a theory of organizational integration that represented one of the first models of incomplete contract theory. A simplified version of the model was described in section 5.5. As noted, the authors distinguish between two types of contractual rights: specific rights and residual rights.

When it is too costly for one party to specify a long list of the particular rights it desires over another party's assets, it may be optimal for that party to purchase all the rights except those specifically mentioned in the contract. Ownership is the purchase of these residual rights of control. (1986, 692)

In essence, the question raised by Grossman and Hart is this: how do we identify the precise differences between the credible contracts available within a firm and those available between firms? We know, first, that if two separate firms own sets of transaction-specific assets then distinct parties will own residual rights to control these assets. On the other hand, if the same firm owns all of the assets, then just one party will possess the residual right of control. This difference is significant because when unforeseen contingencies arise (as they will inevitably) transactions within the firm can be decided by the single owner, while transactions between firms must be negotiated. Such a difference in the way solutions are reached affects the ex post division of surplus and therefore must affect the ex ante decision to invest.

On the basis of this reasoning, it is arguable that the limits to firm size are linked to the residual right to control assets. Experience suggests that, if an integrated firm is established as one large unit embracing numerous subunits, transaction costs and coordination problems will set limits on firm size because of growing costs and inefficiency. At the same time, if the integrated firm tries to avoid these costs of centralization by operating the subunits just as they were before integration except for an occasional central directive, a different problem appears. Specifically, the managers of the subunits will have what amounts to *residual control rights* over the assets of the subunits. And then these units will tend to behave in ways that are not fully in the interest of the integrated firm. Inter alia, ex post division of the surplus will be different. The point to be emphasized here is that a contract can delegate only a *limited set* of rights of control to another party.

We know that modern institutional economics views the firm as a nexus of contracts. The contracts in question relate to the supply of productive services or other inputs to the firms and are established between an authority (the "entrepreneur") and the owners of factors of production. Because the future is unforseeable, contracts are formulated in very general terms (Coase, 1937, 391). Thus, within the limits that are understood to exist, the entrepreneur is free to direct the factors associated with the firm as he thinks appropriate. The power to direct activity is especially important in the case of the employment contract. Simon (1951) speaks of an "authority relationship" between the employer and the employee. Before taking up Simon's discussion, however, it should be clear that an employer can use a variety of approaches to maintain or enlarge his authority over workers. For example, the efficiency wage can be adopted as a device to "enforce higher productivity standards on individual workers, without simply increasing turnover" (Miller 1992, 68). See Miller's explanation of "employer authority" (1992, 67–74).

Simon has pointed out that it is the entrepreneur, as the central party to the firm's contracts, who is normally better informed than others about the actual environment in which the firm is operating. His position as firm leader and controller gives the entrepreneur both the incentive and the opportunity to acquire knowledge about the current "state of nature." From this it is argued that the entrepreneur is the one who should have the power to determine how contracts are to be interpreted and how factors should be employed. Nevertheless, the entrepreneur must proceed with some care. In particular, he must not attempt to go beyond the limits of his authority or deal capriciously with his employees. Here Kreps's (1990a) observations about the employment relation as a centerpiece of the theory of the firm becomes relevant. He writes: "If employees . . . are to grant such authority to a firm . . . they must believe that it will be used fairly" (92). The source of this faith must be the firm's reputation, particularly its reputation concerning how it responds to unforeseen contingencies. Kreps goes as far as to say that faith in the firm's willingness to use its authority wisely is the "glue that permits mutually beneficial transactions to take place" (93).

It is true, however, that reputation works as an enforcement mechanism only if it is possible to observe whether an actor reneges on his responsibilities. In our model in section 5.6, we assumed that everyone was able to observe whether an actor fulfilled his promises or reneged. In general, the requirements for efficacy of the reputational mechanism are these: (1) it must be clear to everyone from the beginning precisely what has been promised, and (2) it must be immediately observable to everyone what the promisor actually did. Given (1) and (2), it follows that relational contracts cannot be enforced very effectively through the use of reputation. The first condition can hardly be met by a relational contract! This is so because relational contracts are characterized by the need to deal with unforeseen contingencies and therefore, by definition, cannot be clear ex ante about what is called for in a contingency that cannot be foreseen ex ante.

Granting the existence of limited information and uncertainty, reputation can still play a role, as was briefly pointed out in Section 4.4.3, provided conditions such as those described by Kreps (1990a, 124) hold:

What is needed is (i) the ability, after observing a particular contingency, to know what should be done and (ii) a belief ex ante by the hierarchical inferiors that application of what should be done will be good enough to warrant undertaking the transaction.

The problem, though, is that it seems unlikely that unambiguous and general rules can be found to cover most situations. In any event, Kreps's analysis adds to transaction-cost economics and the study of hierarchical authority a theory of reputation that emerges from noncooperative game theory. He argues that Schelling's theory of focal points supports the view that general rules or principles can in fact exist. What is stressed is the need for reasonable interpretation. Thus,

the rule is to act in some specified manner (or according to some principle) in most cases, but is not meant to be applied in a few others. Here it will only be necessary that we can agree, ex post, that a particular contingency was one in which the rule was meant to be applied. "We do XYZ as long as it makes sense can be quite effective as long as it makes sense" most of the time and everyone can agree on cases where it doesn't. (125)

Having selected some principle, the task of the firm's management is to communicate that principle to potential and actual employees. This is the role of *corporate culture,* which was briefly introduced in section 4.4.3. Kreps identifies corporate culture "with the principle and with the means by which it is communicated" (126). His conception is that corporate culture serves to give hierarchical inferiors an idea in advance of how the organization will react to changing conditions as they arise. In a real sense, then, the approach taken, whatever it may be, gives identity to the organization.

In this book, we use the more general term *organizational culture* and argue that the concept applies to all kinds of organizations—among them markets, firms, and states. In the case of markets, "culture" relates to the specifics of what "one does" in a sequential contract facing the unforeseeable. In other words, in cases of long-term customer relationships, individual "cultures" can develop to supplement the purely legal clauses of contracts. Under certain conditions (e.g., long-term multilateral labors contracts), hierarchical transactions within the firm may be considered preferable to market transactions by one or both parties for the formation and cultivation of organizational culture. It can be concluded from this that incentives may exist to integrate in order to build up a more efficient and attractive organizational culture. Such improvement, of course, may bring about, in turn, an enhanced reputation for the firm and a more stable structure of (relational) employment contracts. Note that another reputation model of interest has been advanced by Cremer (1986). Critical remarks on the reputational approach to the theory of the firm can be found in Holmstrom and Tirole 1989, 77.

The general theme of corporate culture has also been taken up by Miller (1992), who stresses the importance of what can be termed the cooperative culture of a firm. It is well known, of course, that the efficiency and success of any business organization will be greater the more effectively the various members of the unit cooperate in the process of production. But wholehearted cooperation among the individuals who constitute the coalition of resource owners representing the firm is by no means assured. Rather, difficulties can be expected because individual firm members normally have private objectives that are in conflict with the collective or social interests of the coalition as a whole. A basic problem for organizational theory, then, is to explain how individuals can be motivated so that they will cooperate fully in trying to achieve the collective interests and ensure enterprise efficiency. The usual approach to this question, as exemplified in the organizational economics literature, is to assume that the manager of a hierarchical firm will make every effort to devise an optimal system of incentives and sanctions to induce appropriate behavior.

Miller, however, argues that, in the context of the capitalist firm, it is impossible to find an incentive system that will overcome all obstacles to cooperation and achieve a Pareto-optimal outcome. In his view, the focus has to be shifted from incentive systems to the role of the manager as a leader and shaper of attitudes within the organization. This new conception of how to proceed is said to be superior to principal-agent theory because, as political scientists and behaviorists have noted, organizational economics is based on an extremely narrow view of the possibilities of leadership and is politically naive. Along these lines, Miller points out that the literature on principal-agent theory contrasts sharply with

> the more organic view of organizations, which is centered primarily in political science and organizational psychology. From this perspective, resource allocation results from the decisions of individual leaders. The literature regards the manager's primary job to be one of leadership—that is, inspiring a willingness to cooperate, to take risks, to innovate, to go beyond the level of effort that a narrow, self-interested analysis of incentives would summon. (1992, 2)

It can also be observed here that the leadership hypothesis is generally consistent with the idea that rational choice maximization procedures become less and less appropriate for model building as information about economic variables becomes more and more uncertain and difficult for decision makers to obtain and as human motivations are recognized as extremely varied and complex.

In developing his argument, Miller emphasizes that, under some economic conditions, individuals single-mindedly seeking their own self-interest can bring about efficient social outcomes. This is, of course, Adam Smith's invisible hand case in which self-interested behavior is sufficient to guarantee a Pareto-optimal solution. At the same time, however, Miller knows that there are other circumstances, such as those outlined in the prisoners' dilemma game, in which individual self-interest is simply a trap rather than a sufficient mechanism for group efficiency (1992, 24). Given the latter situation, some arrangement other than pure, self-seeking conduct must be accepted by decision makers if they are to achieve an efficient group outcome.

What is interesting is not simply that conflicts can exist between individual interests and group interests, but that such conflicts are typical of activity within modern business firms (Miller 1992, 236–37). Once analysis begins to move beyond the frictionless world of neoclassical theory and recognizes that firm members have to seek advantage within a corporate environment characterized by firm-specific assets, positive transaction costs, bounded rationality, asymmetrical information, and so on it becomes obvious that self-seeking activities will tend to create forces that are counterproductive from a social standpoint. That is, individually rational behavior is likely to involve such things as complex coalition formation, conflict over property rights and decision-making authority, and strategic misrepresentation. There is a true social dilemma here because in principle all members of the firm could be made better off if only a way could be found to induce meaningful cooperation.

Actually, resolution of the corporate dilemma would seem to be feasible provided each decision maker in the firm could somehow be persuaded, or forced, to abandon strictly self-interested policies and contribute to the group welfare. Pursuing this theme, Miller's suggestion is to turn to leadership. He says that the role of the hierarchical leader is to

> shape expectations among subordinates about cooperation among employees, and between employees and their hierarchical superiors. This is done through a set of activities that have traditionally been in the realm of politics rather than economics: communication, exhortation, symbolic position taking. Most important perhaps, the leader has a central role in committing the organization to what is in effect the constitution of the hierarchy—the allocation of generally accepted responsibilities, rules of the game, and property rights that provide the long-run incentives for investment in the firm. (1992, 217)

There is no doubt that Miller's discussion takes the theory of the firm in an interesting new direction. What is more problematic is the matter of precisely how effective leadership operations can be in overcoming the insistence some firm members may show in continuing to seek individual autonomy and personal advantage. In practice, all plans that seek to advance enterprise efficiency will tend to be imperfect. Whether skilled leadership can accomplish more than incentive restructuring, or bring about greater improvement than may occur spontaneously through evolutionary adjustments (DeVany 1996), would seem to be an open question. In any event, Pareto optimality is not a realistic possibility for a firm operating in the real world.

### 8.3.  The Limits of Integration

Thinking along lines similar to those of Coase (1937, 394), Williamson (1985, 131) was moved to ask a fundamental question: "Why can't a large firm do everything that a collection of small firms can do and more?" This became known in the literature as the Williamson Puzzle (Tirole 1988). What has to be determined is the factor (or factors) that is responsible for the limitation of firm size. Williamson's answer to the puzzle is less abstract than Coase's. He undertakes a detailed comparative institutional analysis to demonstrate that "selective intervention, whereby integration realizes adaptive gains but experiences no losses, is not feasible. Instead, the transfer of a transaction out of the market into the firm is regularly attended by an impairment of incentives" (1985, 161).

The conclusion that selective intervention is not feasible is not really surprising. Williamson explains this at some length by pointing out a number of difficulties that stand in the way of implementing a merger agreement "that is attended by high-powered incentives" (1985, 137). His list of complicating factors is illuminating and will be taken up later. Before turning to these points, however, it is worth noting that a merger necessarily involves some change in property-rights assignments. Individual agents within the affected firms will possess somewhat different rights before and after consolidation occurs. And, when property rights change, incentives and economic behavior must change in turn. Thus, the quick answer as to why selective intervention is not feasible runs in terms of shifting property-rights structures.

Williamson's discussion of the problems that attend merger can be reduced to the following main points.

1.  If we assume that the former owner-manager of a firm absorbed into a new, larger unit becomes the manager of a supply division, he then no longer has the same incentive to utilize equipment "with equivalent care and incur identical preventive maintenance." Insofar as the manager has no firm-specific assets at stake, "the manager behaves myopically with respect to the enterprise. The object being to maximize immediate net receipts, labor costs will be saved by utilizing equipment intensively, and maintenance expenses will be deferred to a successor management" (1985, 138).

2.  A supplier who sells his assets to a buyer faces a hazard because promises made at the outset concerning the seller's future net receipt stream may not be kept. Moreover, if the seller believes the promises made and on that basis accepts a low price for transferring asset ownership, he loses even more. Indeed, the seller may even be dismissed from the new consolidated firm. The seller may, of course, demand and receive a guarantee of continued employment. But this accomplishes little since the net receipts of the seller's division in the organization can be manipulated through the exercise of accounting discretion. In effect, expropriation of the seller's promised reward can be accomplished by indirect means, and normally the seller has no feasible way of reacting to such tactics.

3.  High-powered incentives provided by markets cannot be duplicated by firms without substantial added costs. Even when lower-powered incentives are used by firms, there are additional costs to be reckoned

with. Such developments are significant because the added costs of internal organization are not necessarily offset by comparative adaptability gains.

4. Williamson (1985, 141) points out that an obvious advantage of integration is "that research and development cooperation between stages may be easier to elicit. But there are at least two incentive-impairing effects." These are: "causal ambiguity" and "general office intrusion." The first problem may be understood as follows. Assume that the supply division of an integrated firm is largely responsible for the success or failure of a particular research program. But, given the organizational structure extant, it may be difficult for the supply division not to share the gains of successful innovation with other divisions of the firm. The result, then, is that the supply division has lesser incentive for innovation than it would have if it possessed full property rights in the innovations it generates. Next, in the case of "general office intrusion," Williamson's (142) argument is that, even if the first problem can be avoided, another difficulty looms. That is, the possibility exists that the gains attributable to the operating division that successfully carried out the innovation will be appropriated, in whole or part, by ownership interests. Given the power relations within the firm, "a redistribution away from operating parts in favor of the ownership is apt to be effected by manipulation of the transfer pricing and cost accounting rules."

Insofar as the merger problem is analyzed in terms of the "costs of acquisitions," such well-known matters as agency costs and the costs of bureaucracy have to be considered. Relative to the latter, Williamson speaks of the tendency of management in a large organization to go beyond its real capacities and place faith in the unrealistic hope "that the most intractable problems would give way before the resolute assault of intelligent, committed people" (Morris 1980, 23, quoted in Williamson 1985, 149). While it is useful to recognize the various costs that arise when smaller production units are incorporated into a larger whole, one should not lose sight of the fact that it is the changed structure of property rights (implicit in the integration process) that accounts for the new economic environment. Thus, as the New Institutional Economics emphasizes, it is important to consider the roles played by both transaction costs and property rights when studying institutional questions.

    In asserting that the management factor is partially responsible for limiting firm size, Williamson is, of course, repeating an old argument that has appeared recurrently in the literature. One variant of this line of analysis has the peak coordinator as a fixed input in the firm's production function. This approach, which accords well with orthodox neoclassical theory, then suggests that expansion of the firm leads to diminishing returns with respect to the fixed factor and that this phenomenon ultimately puts an end to firm growth. A more sophisticated explanation focuses on the control-loss phenomenon that is known from bureaucratic theory (Williamson 1967). This phenomenon is observed in all hierarchically structured organizations. The approach taken to the problem in the standard literature, however, has little in common with new institutionalist perspectives and will not be reported on here.

Recently, Kreps (1990a) has applied aspects of the control-loss argument to his organizational culture theory of the firm. He writes: "The theory sketched in this chapter has a natural extension into considerations of the optimal size of organization, when we recast that as the optimal span of the implicit contract" (129). What is recognized is that an increase in the span may increase efficiency but will also increase the range of contingencies that the contract must cover. Under such circumstances, several problems are likely to arise. It will be harder for participants to determine ex post whether the contract was applied appropriately. And, at the same time, the contract may well be applied to contingencies for which it is not suited. Thus, Kreps (130) summarizes his position on firm size as follows.

The point is simple: Wider scope, in the sense of more types of contingencies that must be dealt with, can be dealt with in one of two ways. One could employ a wider range of principles/contracts, but then one may increase ambiguity about how any single contingency should be handled. Increased ambiguity is bad for maintaining reputation. Alternatively, one can keep (in a larger and larger span) the same quite clear focal principles/ implicit contract/corporate culture. But then as the span or type of contingencies encountered increases, that principle/contract/culture is being applied in contingencies to which it will be less and less appropriate. At some point the benefits from widening the scope of the organization are outweighed by the inefficiencies engendered, and will have a natural place to break between organizations.

According to Milgrom and Roberts (1990), what is characteristic of any large, bureaucratic organization is the unique authority and autonomy possessed by its top decision makers or management. These leading individuals have broad rights to intervene in lower-level decisions, and normally their judgments cannot be overturned by others in the organization. Milgrom and Roberts argue that the consequences of this concentrated power are not good. The very existence of such sweeping authority makes possible its inappropriate use. Indeed, whenever a central authority has discretion to intervene in the affairs of an organization, certain costs are incurred. So-called influence costs can be said to exist.

These include (1) a tendency for the authority to intervene excessively, both because intervening is that authority's job and because the authority may have a personal interest . . . in certain decisions; (2) increased time devoted to influence activities and corresponding reduction in organizational productivity, as interested parties seek to have the authority intervene in particular ways or to adopt their favored alternatives; (3) poorer decision making resulting from the distortion of information associated with influence activities; and (4) a loss of efficiency as the organization adapts its structure and policies to control influence activities and their costs. (1990, 89)

On an abstract level, the economic arguments that seek to explain the limits of firm size are based on comparisons of transaction costs—either without or inclusive of production costs. Thus, Coase (1937, 395) in his pioneering work writes that "firms will tend to expand until the costs of organizing an extra transaction within the firm are equal to the costs of carrying out the same transaction by means of exchange on the open market or the costs of organizing in another firm." This represents a rather general argument. Subsequently, Williamson (1985, 161) tries to build on this basic understanding by giving the transaction-cost concept some empirical content. He illustrates with a number of examples that: "Selective intervention, whereby integration realizes adaptive gains but experiences no losses, is not feasible. The conclusion must be that transactions out of the market and into a firm are regularly attended by an impairment of incentives, and this type of difficulty will tend to be particularly severe where innovations are important." These manifestations are, of course, precisely what one would expect on the basis of property-rights analysis. As changes in the effective allocation of rights occur with integration (with institutional change), the opportunities for different individuals to appropriate rewards changes correspondingly. As a consequence, incentives and motivations are restructured—with inevitable change in behavior (and costs).

From a somewhat different standpoint, it can be said that any attempt to change institutional arrangements while at the same time holding incentives constant is likely to fail. Certainly, in the case of enterprise merger, incentive neutrality cannot be achieved. The problem is that none of the following is costlessly enforceable:

promises by division managers to utilize assets with "due care"; promises by owners to reset transfer prices and exercise accounting discretion "responsibly"; promises to reward innovation in "full measure"; promises to preserve promotion prospects "without change"; and agreements by managers to "eschew politics." Internalizing the incremented transaction leads to incentive disabilities in all those respects, and as a consequence transactions are apt to be organized in an altogether different way upon merger. (Williamson 1985, 161)

The question of optimal firm size is not simply an academic issue and, thus, in concluding this section, it seems worthwhile to add a few remarks about actual developments in the contemporary business world. We find that currently the limits to firm size are a topical issue. Public attention has been drawn to the area as a result of spectacular failures at General Motors, IBM, and Phillips and difficulties experienced at Japan's Matsushita and Germany's Daimler Benz. The *Economist* (April 17, 1993, 13–14) stresses that today managements recognize the costs involved with the expansion of businesses. The *Economist* notes that today, with falling trade barriers, the largest multinational firms are open to attack.

> Difficulties of operating in dozens of countries may have annoyed big firms, but they were often the only companies to surmount such obstacles [trade barriers]. . . . The opening of markets is removing many of these barriers and making it easier for smaller firms to sell their products all over the world. (13)

Interestingly, the advantages of size are diminishing in manufacturing and distribution today because of the increasing use of computers by business firms.

> Factory automation is making it possible to produce goods cheaply in much smaller firms [and] to employ the same logistical techniques, sophisticated financial models, and automated payrolls and other administrative tasks that were available only to big firms in the past. (13)

Moreover, still other forces at work in the world economic system are making it possible for smaller firms to compete with or even surpass large organizations.

> The growing efficiency and internationalization of capital markets is allowing medium-sized firms to raise money in much the same way as the world's biggest companies. . . . And the quality-control techniques pioneered in Japan are being applied almost everywhere by big and small firms alike, eliminating any variation in the quality of many products. . . . similarly, bigger firms can still spend bigger sums on R&D, but in an embarrassing number of industries, from computer to biotechnology, small and medium sized firms are proving the most innovative. (13)

In general, then, existing trends seem to be running against the giant corporation; its advantages are seen to diminish while its long-ignored costs are becoming all too evident.

## 8.4.  Ownership and Control

Granting the existence of a firm, we may ask such questions as: (1) who owns the firm? (2) what does ownership of a firm mean? and (3) does it matter whether the firm is owned by those who invested capital in it, by its workers, by the state? The answers to these questions are not necessarily easy, but it should be apparent immediately that, from the standpoint of neoinstitutionalist theory, ownership is extremely important. The structure of property rights in the firm is significant because it affects both transaction costs and incentives and therefore economic behavior.

Within a capitalist system, a firm's owners are understood to be those persons who share certain legally sanctioned rights. Briefly stated, the rights in question are: (1) the right to control the firm, (2) the right to appropriate the firm's residual earnings, and (3) the right to transfer the first two rights to others as desired. These rights are formal rights, and, as Hansmann (1988, 269), has noted:

> The reference here to formal right is important. Often the persons who have the formal right to control the firm . . . in fact exercise little effective authority by this means over the firm's management. It is sometimes said that the owners of such firms do not control them—hence the familiar references to the separation of ownership and control.

It is true, of course, that ownership rights in the firm, as elsewhere, have to be enforced if they are to be effective. But enforcement is costly, and consequently the level of enforcement may vary. In general, the institutional arrangements of the firm are influenced by the need of its owners to protect their rights from expropriation by other firm members. What complicates the situation, though, is the fact that the rights described in (1) through (3) can be partitioned among various factor owners who are participants in the coalition known as the firm. The objective of organizational design is to establish a property-rights structure that will minimize conflict between the private interests of individual firm members and the collective interests of the coalition.

Ownership of human capital requires some discussion. Characteristically, both human and nonhuman assets cooperate in a firm's production effort. In a world without slavery, individuals own their human capital and services, but this does not mean that such assets are unencumbered. There can exist obligations from labor contracts to a firm and these obligations can be traded. Similarly, a firm may use only leased nonhuman assets, even a leased brand name (as in franchising). Thus, in the limit, ownership in a firm may consist only of ownership of *contractual obligations,* including the obligations of management and workers.

The issue concerning the separation of ownership and control was introduced in section 4.4.1, and we shall continue with it here. The problem can be seen as a special case of the principal-agent model, with the owners of the firm being the principals and its management the agents. In a world of positive transaction costs, the agents do not necessarily act in the principals' best interest. Thus, if the owners of the firm are not their own managers, "agency costs" diminish their residual earnings. Relative to our six types of transaction activities, the concern here is with the activities of control and enforcement of discipline on the managers (the agents) by the firm's owners (the principals).

Using a property-rights approach, Manne (1965) developed a response to the separation of ownership and control issue. His idea was that takeover threats represented the most efficient instrument for disciplining management. As he put it: "A fundamental premise underlying the market for corporate control is the existence of a high positive correlation between corporate managerial efficiency and the market price of shares of that company" (112). In a badly run company, the market price of shares would be comparatively low. But a low current price for shares suggests the possibility of a more profitable future for the company provided its existing assets were managed more efficiently. Thus, the company becomes an attractive target for a takeover by those individuals who believe that they could improve its performance. If the system were characterized by zero transaction costs, the takeover threat would work perfectly because of the law of one price. Then, the possibility of a takeover (as the possibility of any other arbitrage transaction) would be sufficient to "solve" the agency problem. Unfortunately, however, in a world of positive transaction costs, the efficacy of the takeover threat is more questionable, and the mechanism may even produce counterproductive effects (as in "greenmail").[1] The agency problem is not so easily addressed (Scherer 1980). If the owners of a firm are not their own managers and if transaction costs are operative, "agency costs" have to be considered.

The agency-cost issue is central to the so-called positive principal-agent theory put forward in the work of Jensen and Meckling (1976) described in

---

1. *Greenmail,* a term coined by the *Wall Street Journal,* designates the following operation: a hostile investor buys a sizable portion of a company's stock and then threatens a takeover if the company doesn't buy back the investor's shares for more than the going market rate. The operation is also known in the literature under the names "targeted share repurchases" and "privately negotiated stock repurchases." See, for example, Dann and DeAngelo (1983) or Bradley and Wakeman (1983). Note that, unlike the American corporation, the German Aktiengesellschaft is not allowed to buy back its own shares.

Section 4.4.1. They define *agency costs,* one may remember, as the sum of three cost elements: (1) the monitoring expenditures of the principal, (2) the bonding expenditures of the agent, and (3) the residual loss (308). The meaning of monitoring expenditures is self-evident. Bonding expenditures of the agent relate to the expenses incurred by him in order to guarantee "that he will not take certain actions which would harm the principal or to ensure that the principal will be compensated if he does take such actions" (309). Finally, the residual loss (or welfare loss) is the loss that results from divergences between the agent's actual decisions and the decisions that would maximize the welfare of the principal. The authors go on to say:

> Note also that agency costs arise in any situation involving cooperative effort . . . by two or more people even though there is no clear cut principal-agent relationship. Viewed in this light it is clear that our definition of agency costs and their importance to the theory of the firm bears a close relationship to the problem of shirking and monitoring of team production which Alchian and Demsetz (1972) raise in their paper on the theory of the firm. (309)

In their paper, Jensen and Meckling (1976, 342) distinguish between two types of agency costs: (1) the agency costs of outside equity and (2) the agency costs of debt. The first category relates to the costs arising from monitoring and control activities plus those established by residual loss. On the other side, the agency costs associated with debt consist of: "the opportunity wealth loss caused by the impact on the investment decision of the firm, the monitoring and bonding expenditures by bondholders and the owner-manager (the firm), the bankruptcy and reorganization costs" (342). The point made here is that both types of agency costs are functions of the fraction ($E$) of outside financing obtained from equity. The optimal fraction $E$ is the one at which total agency costs (i.e., the sum of outside equity and debt agency costs) is minimized. As a result, and contrary to the findings of Modigliani and Miller (1958), there can be an *optimal* capital structure. The authors' general hypothesis here is that agency costs are as real as any other costs faced by the firm. Institutions are involved in the problem because the level of agency costs depends, among other things, on statutory and common law, as well as on human ingenuity in devising contracts. Both the law and the sophistication of contracts relevant to the modern corporation are the products of a historical process in which there were strong incentives for individuals to minimize agency costs (Jensen and Meckling 1976, 357).

Jensen and Meckling (1976, 312) argue their case in these terms: "If a wholly owned firm is managed by the owner, he will make operating decisions which maximize his utility. These decisions will involve not only the benefits he derives from pecuniary returns but also the utility generated by various non-pecuniary aspects of his entrepreneurial activities." It is true, however, that if the owner-manager sells equity claims on the corporation to outside share-holders, agency costs will be generated because the behavior of the (fractional) owner-manager cannot be observed readily by the outside stockholders. The difficulty is that the (uncertain) residual gains of the firm, which depend on the effort put forth by the owner-manager, will tend to change after the sale of shares to outsiders. The reason is that the owner-manager finds himself in a new economic position. Having sold $x$ percent of his shares to outside inves-tors, he now receives only a fraction of the residual (i.e., $[100 - x]$ percent), but he has to bear, as before, the full private cost of his effort level. Conse-quently, it can be expected that the owner-manager will decrease his efforts to some degree. But, of course, the equity market will anticipate this reaction and correct for it.

On the other hand, the creditors of a firm have to face a moral hazard problem with respect to investment risks. If the manager does not suffer a loss of utility in case of enterprise bankruptcy, he will have a strong incentive to engage in activities (investments) that promise very high payoffs if successful even if they have a very low probability of success. If such investments turn out well, he will capture most of the gains; if they turn out badly, the creditors bear most of the costs. Potential creditors, however, will take this situation into account by formulating conditions for participation that provide them with certain safeguards. For example, they can demand that the entrepreneur-manager make an investment in the firm of some minimum size. But in doing this the creditors will experience an "opportunity wealth loss." Furthermore, there are monitoring and bonding costs and bankruptcy and reorganization costs to be faced. By considering the magnitudes of the different types of agency costs (i.e., outside equity and debt agency costs), Jensen and Meckling (1976, 344ff.) are able to calculate an optimal ratio of outside equity to debt.

Fama (1980) criticizes Alchian and Demsetz (1972) and Jensen and Meckling (1976) for attributing the task of disciplining management primarily to the risk bearers (the residual claimants). Along these same lines, he says:

Of all of the authors in property-rights literature, Manne (1965, 1967) is most concerned with the market for corporate control. . . . For him, disciplining management is an 'entrepreneurial job' which in the first instance falls on a firm's organizers and later on specialists on the process of outside takeover. (295)

In Fama's estimation, the approach taken should be quite different. He views management and risk bearing as two naturally separate factors of production. If the market for risk bearing is looked at from the standpoint of portfolio theory,

we are told that risk bearers are likely to spread their wealth across many firms
and therefore will not be interested in directly controlling the management of
any individual firm. The conclusion is that

> the viability of the large corporation with diffuse security ownership is
> better explained in terms of a model where the primary disciplining of
> managers comes through managerial labor markets, both within and out-
> side the firm, with assistance from the panoply of internal and external
> monitoring devices that evolve to stimulate the ongoing efficiency of the
> corporate firm, and with the market for outside takeovers providing
> discipline of last resort. (295)

Fama's argument concerning managerial discipline was described in section 5.2.1 for the case in which results were certain but effort was not directly
observable and could only be inferred from profits. The same logic can be
applied to a situation in which results are uncertain if it is assumed that a sufficiently large number of repeat periods are possible. In such an environment,
the principal-agent problem with uncertain results is reduced to a problem of
"certain" *expected values* of the results—that is, the manager's expected marginal product in each period. This approach contrasts with principal-agent
theory, which assumes a one-period world or a one-shot game.

> Since the managerial labor market is presumed to understand the weight
> of the wage revision process . . . any potential managerial incentive prob-
> lem in the separation of risk bearing, of security ownership, from control
> is resolved. The manager can contract for and take an optimal amount of
> consumption on the job. The wage set ex ante need not include any
> allowance for ex post incentives to deviate from the contract since the
> wage revision process neutralizes any such incentives. (Fama 1980, 301)

The theme concerning the separate roles of decision making and risk
bearing is developed further in an article by Fama and Jensen (1983), as was
pointed out in section 4.4.1. They distinguish, as may be remembered, between
decision management, decision control, and residual risk bearing. These three
functions are concentrated in one or a few agents in cases of *noncomplex*
organizations.

Most small organizations tend to be noncomplex. By contrast, most large
organizations tend to be *complex,* but this is not always so. When the same
agents manage and control important decisions, an agency problem appears. A
feasible solution to the problem is to restrict residual claims to the important
decision agents—as is done in the case of proprietorships, partnerships, and

closely held corporations. These are all examples of classical entrepreneurial firms in which the major decision makers are also the major risk bearers. Similar conclusions were, of course, reached by Alchian and Demsetz (1972). On the other hand, as was also shown in section 4.4.1, organizations such as large open corporations tend to be set up so that there is a separation of decision management, decision control, and residual risk bearing. This is the "separation of ownership and control" case. Here, decision management is kept apart from residual risk bearing, and the resulting agency problems are solved by means of an arrangement that separates decision management from decision control (Fama and Jensen 1983, 308). A formal decision hierarchy is created with higher-level agents ratifying and monitoring the decision initiatives of lower-level agents. The higher-level functionaries are also charged with the responsibility of evaluating the performance of those agents who lie below them in the hierarchy. It is argued, therefore, that: "Such hierarchical partitioning of the decision process makes it more difficult for decision agents at all levels of the organization to take actions that benefit themselves at the expense of the residual claimants" (310). The formal hierarchies of complex organizations are also buttressed by information from less formal *mutual monitoring* among agents. "When agents interact to produce outputs, they acquire low-cost information about colleagues, information not directly available to higher-level agents. Mutual monitoring systems tap this information for use in the control process" (310).

The Fama-Jensen hypothesis concerning the separation of residual risk bearing from decision management gets support from the fact that the major mechanisms for separating decision management and decision control are much the same across organizations. Nevertheless, Williamson remarks critically that the agency-cost approach limits attention to ex ante incentive alignments. And, in general, writers concerned with transaction cost economics emphasize the role of ex post transaction costs (Williamson 1975, 1979, 1985; Klein 1980; Klein and Leffler 1981). These ex post transaction costs can be understood to include:

1. The maladaptation costs incurred when transactions drift out of alignment in relation to what Masahiko Aoki refers to as the "shifting contract curve"
2. the haggling costs incurred if bilateral efforts are made to correct ex post misalignments
3. the setup and running costs associated with the governance structures or with institutions (often not the courts) to which disputes are referred
4. the bonding costs of effecting secure commitments. (Williamson 1988, 572)

In Williamson's judgment, the maladaptation costs are the key feature. He notes that: "Such costs occur only in an intertemporal, incomplete-contracting context. Reducing these costs through judicious choice of governance structure (market, hierarchy, or hybrid), rather than merely realigning incentives and pricing them out, is the distinctive TCE (transaction cost economics) orientation" (1988, 572). After discussing earlier treatments questioning the Modigliani-Miller theorem, Williamson (579ff.) describes the TCE rationale applied to corporate finance.

The TCE approach to corporate finance examines individual investment projects and distinguishes among them in terms of their asset-specificity characteristics. It also regards debt and equity principally as governance structures rather than financial instruments.

> By contrast with the earlier literature, which began with an equity-financed firm and sought a special rational for debt, the TCE approach postulates that debt (the market form) is the natural instrument. Equity (the administrative form) appears as the financial instrument of last resort. (Williamson 1988, 581)

Williamson goes on to argue: "Debt is a governance structure that works out of rules and is well suited to projects where the assets are highly redeployable. Equity is a governance structure that allows discretion and is used for projects where assets are less redeployable" (581). This line of discussion leads to a position that is summarized as follows:

> The TCE approach maintains that some projects are easy to finance by debt and ought to be financed by debt. These are projects for which physical asset specificity is low to moderate. As asset specificity becomes great, however, the preemptive claims of the bond holders against the investment afford limited protection—because the assets in question have limited redeployability. Not only does the cost of debt financing therefore increase, but the benefits of closer oversight also grow. The upshot is that equity finance, which affords more intrusive oversight and involvement through the board of directors and, in publicly held firms, permits share ownership to be concentrated, is the preferred financial instrument for projects where asset specificity is great. (589)

Williamson's emphasis on the importance of asset specificity has been criticized by Milgrom and Roberts (1990). They claim

> that the key to evaluating the efficacy of market transactions is the costs of negotiating suitably detailed short-term contracts. If these costs were

always zero, then organizing economic activity through market exchange would always be efficient. On the other hand, when the costs of negotiating periodic exchange agreements are sufficiently high, then regardless of other factors, such as the presence or absence of specialized assets, potentially important savings are to be realized by placing the activity under a central authority, which can quickly settle potentially costly disputes. (65)

To illustrate their thinking on this issue Milgrom and Roberts consider a hypothetical relationship between Fisher Body (the supplier) and General Motors (the customer), and examine the interaction between these firms over two periods of time. In the first period, the respective parties negotiate and reach agreement about investment in certain specialized assets and how the costs of this investment will be shared. Specifically, the design and site of a manufacturing plant, and the contribution each firm will make toward the cost of its construction, can be established. Then, in the second period, the parties negotiate prices, quality standards, and a delivery schedule in full knowledge of the circumstances that exist in the second period. If bargaining is costless, the agreement reached in the second period will be efficient given the conditions that prevail then. In particular, the argument is that an efficient solution will be attained in period two *regardless* of the specifics of the first-period agreement (Milgrom and Roberts 1990, 68).

To reach their conclusion, Milgrom and Roberts must assume that specific investments are verifiable in the courts. They admit this indirectly in the continuation of their illustrative case. The supplier (Fisher Body) can be compensated, they write, for the risk that the customer (General Motors) will behave opportunistically "by having General Motors bear part of the plant's cost" (1990a, 69). In other words, if General Motors behaves "badly," Fisher Body will sue and win a court order under conditions of certainty and zero costs. Bargaining costs, in the sense of Milgrom and Roberts, must, therefore, include the cost of enforcing contractual obligations. From the standpoint of these authors, however, bargaining costs include:

1. The costs of coordination failures, which "arise in situations where individuals could adopt several different patterns of mutually consistent, self-interested behavior and market institutions fail to ensure that only efficient patterns actually emerge" (74). It is said that under the usual assumptions of perfect competition such market coordination problems cannot necessarily be overcome.

2. Measurement costs (based on information acquisition), as discussed by Barzel (1982) and Kenney and Klein (1983). See also section 6.2.

3. Costs due to asymmetric information about preferences: "Unless the parties' valuations of a good being traded are common knowledge, the

parties may be delayed in reaching an agreement or may even fail to agree at all, because they strategically misrepresent the good's value." (Milgrim and Roberts 1990a, 77)

Translated into the terminology used in the book so far, bargaining costs consist of the costs of search, inspection, contracting, execution, monitoring, and enforcement, that is, the costs of all of the transactions mentioned at the beginning of the applied part of this book (sec. 6.1). In a world with zero bargaining costs (zero transaction costs), specific investments are irrelevant from an efficiency point of view—even when knowledge of what the future will bring is limited. It is a world like that of the Hicksian temporary equilibrium model in which individuals act rationally and efficiently given their symmetric knowledge about the present and their common beliefs about future events. On the other hand, the world of transaction-cost economics is one in which, because of "frictions" and constraints, individuals can only act in boundedly rational fashion.

Holmstrom and Tirole in their survey article (1989) distinguish between four types of solutions to the agency problem in the case of separation of ownership and control. These are as follows.

1. *Internal discipline:* the design of executive compensation plans. It is said that "a good plan should support the strategic objectives of the firm as well as motivate the manager to excell." What is suggested here is really an application of the principal-agent model with moral hazard. Basic discussion of this kind of case is given in section 5.2.

2. *Labor market discipline:* as discussed by Fama (1980), and Holmstrom (1982).

3. *Product market discipline:* for which it is argued that the real costs of monopoly may derive more from organizational slack than from price distortions (Leibenstein 1966). Thus, as in the case of (2), interest attaches to the use of competition to bring about improved efficiency. The idea is that competition will reduce slack since competition drives price down. "If the manager were to slack the same amount as without competition he would not be able to reach a sufficiently high profit level to collect the minimum reward that he needs. Hence he needs to work harder" (Holmstrom and Tirole 1989, 87). For the complete argument, see Hart 1983b.

4. *Capital market discipline:* under which, insofar as managers pursue their own objectives at the expense of enterprise efficiency, enterprise profits must tend to fall and the price of the company's shares can also be expected to fall. Such developments mean that the firm will find it more difficult to raise capital on acceptable terms from the financial

markets, and the possibility of a takeover attempt must be faced. In effect, the takeover represents the ultimate weapon against managerial misconduct (Manne 1965). Pressures from the capital market side, therefore, should be able to set limits on the freedom of managers to shirk and engage in discretionary behavior.

The preceding discussion has considered some leading theories concerning the ownership and control of the firm. It is clear from this review that the examination of the firm in the neoinstitutionalist literature addresses questions that have not received much attention in standard neoclassical analysis. In what follows, a number of specific enterprise models will be presented in order to show how the developing institutionalist logic has been applied to analyze different types of firms. The models, though simple, suggest some of the power and flexibility of the new approach.

### The General Part of this Chapter in Retrospect

In describing some of the best-known Coasian and post-Coasian arguments explaining why hierarchical firms rather than markets are used to undertake production, we found that they deal ultimately with some of our six transaction activities—that is, search and contracting (Coase); inspection (Barzel); execution and control (Alchian and Demsetz); and execution, control, and (especially) enforcement (Williamson, Grossman, Hart, and Kreps). Although private ownership is assumed throughout and underlies all of the arguments presented, it plays a central role only in the theories of Alchian, Demsetz, Grossman, and Hart. Williamson, in emphasizing transaction costs, tends to avoid detailed analysis of property-rights effects but puts forward the important proposition "that ex post support institutions of contract matter." In other words, Williamson avoids the trap of discussing the firm in terms of the one-period equilibrium model of elementary neoclassical theory and, in effect, considers an ongoing dynamic model of the stock-flow type. From this perspective, the firm is an institution, or governance structure, that is designed especially to maintain appropriate contract enforcement (1985, 29). A question arises, however, as to which ex post guaranteeing device is really applied within a firm. Kreps points out in this context that reputation has a role to play (the theory of self-enforcing agreements). Reputation with respect to the way the authority relationship of the employment contract is handled is, for him, the soul of the firm, controlled through corporate culture.

By contrast, Grossman and Hart focus on property rights as the necessary guaranteeing device. Specifically, concern is with the control rights or residual decision rights of the individuals who supply firm-specific, nonhuman assets to the firm. The argument is similar to that made by Alchian and centers on the fact that, without certain rights in their possession, these individuals would leave their assets open to exploitation by other members of the coalition. The issue implicitly raised here is whether a particular structure of property rights is sufficient to afford the affected parties adequate protection over time. Williamson would agree that ownership matters but would argue that ownership rights have to be supplemented by ex post support institutions of contract. In Kreps's model, ownership may be conceived as providing a mechanism for transferring reputation from one owner generation to the next. As a result of these alternative themes, we receive quite a colorful picture. Properly interpreted, the new institutional economics does not lead to simple general conclusions such as "ownership matters." Property rights are indeed important, but institutional economics is more detailed and complex. Thus, ownership rights in the firm may be partitioned and assigned to different parties in order to reduce transaction costs or improve incentives. Guarantees of contract enforcement may be established by means of mechanisms maintained within the firm or broader institutional structures in place outside the firm.

Forces exist that promote integration, but there are also forces that have an adverse effect on the process. Thus, profitable enterprises cannot grow in unlimited fashion and achieve ever larger size. Coase (1937) explains integration in rather abstract terms by an imagined comparison of market and managerial transaction costs. In later discussions, more concrete reasons are given, in particular by Williamson (1985). The argument is, essentially, that changes in institutional arrangements lead to changes in the structure of incentives. Incentive neutrality of mergers is, therefore, not to be expected. Another interesting reason for the limits to integration is found in the effect an increase in the span of the hierarchical order has on corporate culture. While the same focal principal can operate with an increasing span, the increased uncertainty that the change generates among hierarchical inferiors becomes an issue. That is, the inferiors become unsure about what management may do and have concerns about whether it will keep its implicit contract with them. Still another explanation for the limits of integration, as given by Milgrom and Roberts (1990a), is that influence costs are increased. The larger a firm becomes the greater the power of its top decision makers, and one result is that the hierarchical inferiors tend to devote an increasing amount of time and resources to activities designed to affect the decisions of their superiors. The size of a firm is also related to the problem of ownership and control. But management can be disciplined in various ways, for example:

*Internal discipline:* that is, by the design of the executive compensation plan (a topic of principal-agent theory)

*Labor market discipline:* based on the understanding that managerial behavior on the job is assessed in the market for managers and that such market evaluations have direct influence on the value of the human capital possessed by managers

*Product market discipline:* to the extent that effective competition exists in the markets for the firm's products, there will be corresponding pressure to lower prices and reduce slack

*Capital market discipline:* efficient incentives are created because agency costs can be reduced by finding a suitable mix of equity and debt (i.e., by adjusting the capital structure of the firm), and, in addition, the takeover threat remains as the ultimate weapon against managerial misconduct

In a field that is still in the process of development, it is not surprising to find that existing institutional models of the firm tend to be somewhat specialized and tentative. Characteristically, major attention is given only to particular aspects of a highly complex reality. One consequence of this situation, of course, is that institutional economics offers a large open flank for critical attacks. This should not be a matter of great concern. While there is clearly more work to be done, it remains true that a good start has been made in isolating some of the main factors that explain the nature and basis of the firm.

In the sections that follow, the development of the neoinstitutional conception of the firm will be illustrated through the presentation of a series of enterprise models that seek to deal with various real-life issues of interest to society. The starting point here is the neoclassical theory of the firm. Despite its abstract quality, the theory can be modified so that it can begin to analyze organizations that diverge from the classical firm. For example, applications can be made to study the behavior of single proprietorships or not-for-profit organizations. One has to be aware, however, that the attractive mathematical results of such models fit only imperfectly into a world polluted by transaction costs and bounded rationality. Subsequently, it is demonstrated how the property-rights theory of the firm can be applied, with rather good prognostic results, to the traditional Soviet firm. Property-rights analysis is then applied to the much discussed model of the socialist labor-managed firm. And, in this context, the shortcomings of the mainstream (neoclassical) analysis of the socialist firm are elaborated. Finally, attention is given to the matter of codetermination in business firms. This program, which has been developed elaborately in Germany, is also discussed in terms of modern property-rights theory. In particular, the economic problems of mandatory codetermination, as opposed to voluntary codetermination, are considered.

These expositions underscore the fact that the institutional economic analyst has to use his technical tools with circumspection, and a light hand, if he wishes to grasp the incentive effects, and thus the economic results, of different organizational forms. Success does not come easily, and all of the models considered reveal certain limitations because of the relatively primitive methodology employed in their construction.

## 8.5. Institutional Models in the Tradition of the Neoclassical Theory of the Firm

Since the neoclassical paradigm has long dominated thinking in mainstream economics, it is not surprising to find that, when new theoretical ideas appear, attempts are usually made to incorporate them into the standard analytical framework as mere modifications. Thus, it is urged, for example, that transaction costs represent additional constraints that can simply be added to the neoclassical structure. Whether this general approach is justified is a major question that must be confronted, and more will be said on the topic later. For the moment, however, it will be convenient to consider some models of the firm that might be termed hybrid—in the sense that they incorporate certain concepts drawn from the New Institutional Economics while remaining basically neoclassical in style and assumptions.

1. The first example is concerned with the behavior of a *one-man firm* run by its owner, the self-employed, and is designed to show that the incentive structure generated by this form of ownership and control is consistent with the owner-manager putting forth optimal effort. This model, and the next two, follow the outline established by Eaton and Eaton in their recent textbook (1988, 147ff.). The point of departure here is the usual one—notably, that the individual running the firm derives satisfaction from both income ($Y$) and leisure ($L$). Hence, the utility function is

$$U = \Phi(Y, L). \tag{3}$$

Any work performed ($w$) requires the sacrifice of time that could otherwise be devoted to leisure, since, by definition, we have

$$L = T - w, \tag{4}$$

where the parameter $T$ is the total amount of time available per period for all activities of the owner-manager. Finally, the firm's production function takes the simplified form:

$$Y = \alpha w. \tag{5}$$

Over the range of operation considered, the owner secures constant returns to his input of effort ($w$).

Given substitution of (4) and (5) in (3), it is apparent that the owner's utility level is ultimately a function of the effort or work input he supplies to the firm. Consequently, in order to serve his own interests, the proprietor must determine the optimal, or utility-maximizing, level of work. In formal terms, the first-order condition for the maximum requires that $dU/dw = 0$, and hence the expression

$$-\frac{dY}{dL} = \alpha \qquad (6)$$

emerges. The indication here is that the owner-manager should work up to the point at which his marginal product from the firm ($\alpha$) is just sufficient to compensate him for giving up an increment of leisure. Alternatively stated, the owner's (subjective) marginal rate of substitution ($-(dY/dL)$) must be equal to the (objective) marginal rate of transformation ($\alpha$). This is, of course, one of the standard Pareto conditions for optimality.

Since the individual supplying effort is the owner of the firm and has unchallenged control of its activities, the argument is that he is in a position to adjust his effort level *optimally*. In a formal sense, the conclusion is correct, but the approach taken in this type of analysis is, nevertheless, somewhat misleading. If it is assumed that transaction costs are positive and all decision makers operate subject to bounded rationality, problems arise for neoclassical theory. More is involved here than the idea that information, like other inputs, is costly and must be economized. When a jump is made to a world in which the costs of acquiring and processing information are nonzero, decision makers are placed in quite a different position with respect to the elements taken as data in orthodox theory. Each individual has only partial knowledge of, for example, the technological options known to society as a whole, and at each cross section of time each person's knowledge endowment tends to be somewhat *different* from that possessed by others.

In the previous example, therefore, there can be no assurance that the owner-manager has employed the best available technical arrangement for his productive operations (Furubotn 1996). He may well be producing less efficiently than are some of his rivals in the industry. But he can stay in business as a marginal producer while others receive rents based on their superior information status. In any event, his "optimal" effort solution in equation 6 is quite different (quantitatively) from the optimal solution that would be attained in a frictionless neoclassical world where all producers are aware of the best technology at the same moment and (in theory) all range in quickly on the ideal competitive equilibrium. Characteristically, when decision makers operate subject to positive transaction costs and have, at any moment, only partial and unequal knowledge of the system's technological base, the process of reaching long-run equilibrium is at best slower and more complex. Needed reorganization of the system will, of course, tend to occur over time. *Specifically,* diffusion of information can be expected to take place so that, for example, production functions (and production sets) will be reconstituted continually as new information is received and absorbed by the various decision makers in the system. However, the hypothetical long-run equilibrium position is unlikely ever to be reached by the industry. This is so because human action designed to adjust to present knowledge tends to affect future outcomes and targets, and thus, before any initial diffusion process is complete, changes in society's data will tend to set in motion a new diffusion process and new adjustment.

What this line of discussion makes clear is that there is some danger in constructing models that incorporate certain ideas drawn from the New Institutional Economics while neglecting others. Unfortunately, once transaction costs are introduced and the existence of incomplete and asymmetric information is recognized, the economic problem changes fundamentally. Mere modification of the neoclassical model does not seem possible; in particular, it is not appropriate to assume that transaction costs are (simultaneously) positive in some areas of the firm's operations and zero in others. Ideally, transition to a new mode of analysis is needed. But, in fact, hybrid models do exist in the literature, and, despite their structural inconsistencies, they may be able to illuminate concepts that are important to the New Institutional Economics.

2. Given this understanding, the initial enterprise model can now be changed to take account of behavior when the one-man firm is transformed into a *partnership* in which revenue is shared (i.e., we consider a two-man firm run by its owners). From the standpoint of the original owner-manager (individual no. 1), who is now a partner in the firm, the situation is as follows. His utility function is, as before,

$$U_1 = \Phi(L_1, Y_1). \tag{7}$$

Similarly, the constraint

$$L_1 = T - w_1 \tag{8}$$

holds. The real difference appears in the equation defining individual no. 1's share of the valuable output produced. Previously, he had the exclusive right to all of the output, while now he secures only half. The new partner, of course, receives the remaining half. Both individuals can be assumed to have identical preferences:

$$Y_1 = \frac{\alpha(w_1 + w_2^o)}{2}. \tag{9}$$

By assumption, there is no change in the technical conditions of production, but total output now depends on the hours of work ($w_1$) supplied by no. 1 plus whatever work input ($w_2^o$) individual no. 2 supplies.

Under the conditions noted, individual no. 1's optimization problem is much the same as in the first example. His utility-maximizing level of work is found at the point where $dU/dw_1 = 0$, and where

$$-\frac{dY_1}{dL_1} = \frac{\alpha}{2}. \tag{10}$$

The sharing arrangement in effect leads to a lesser incentive for no. 1 to exert effort. His reward here is based on the parameter $\alpha/2$, and, with this more modest compensation for an increment of work, he finds it undesirable to surrender as much leisure as he did in the single-proprietorship case (where the reward was $\alpha$).

The conclusion suggested is that the organization of the firm is inefficient. That is, the partnership structure described is shown to have an adverse effect on the incentive (of either partner) to choose work over leisure. What is not made clear, though, is the position of the model with respect to transaction costs. Presumably, the relevant transactions costs are large. This is so because the model assumes that individual no. 1 is not able to establish a reliable estimate of the effort level put forth by individual no. 2 or of understanding the significance of the sharing rule. But in a frictionless neoclassical world of unbounded rationality these difficulties would not exist. That is, the partners would be aware of each other's effort contributions and would also recognize that the partnership arrangement does nothing to increase the technical parameter $\alpha$, which determines the return per unit of effort expended. Under such conditions, if the two individuals did wish to operate out of a single firm, they would see the advantage of keeping their accounts separate and of having their rewards proportionate to the hours they actually work. Then individual no. 1's share would be

$$Y_1 = \alpha w_1 \tag{9'}$$

and we are back to the efficiency condition of the single proprietorship.

3. The preceding example secured its initial result by assuming implicitly that transaction costs were positive and decision makers were boundedly rational. By contrast, the next case works in the way indicated only if transaction costs are zero and people are highly rational. What is considered is an *owner-managed firm with one employee* in which team production leads to superadditivity in the sense that the total output of the team (consisting of the owner-manager and the employee) is greater than the sum of what would be produced

by the same individuals working independently. Specifically, the assumption about technology is

$$Y = A(w_1 + w_2), \quad \text{if} \quad w_1 > 0 \quad \text{and} \quad w_2 > 0$$
$$Y = \alpha(w_1 + w_2), \quad \text{if} \quad w_1 = 0 \quad \text{or} \quad w_2 = 0, \tag{11}$$

and where $A > \alpha$. In (11), $Y$ represents the total output of the firm, and this output will be shared by the owner (individual no. 1) and his employee (individual no. 2) so that $Y = Y_1 + Y_2$.

The reward to the employee $(Y_2)$ is determined in the following way:

$$Y_2 = 0, \quad \text{if} \quad w_2 < w^*$$
$$Y_2 = Y^*, \quad \text{if} \quad w_2 \geq w^*. \tag{12}$$

In other words, if the employee shirks, he receives no pay, while, if he puts forth at least the stipulated level of work $(w^*)$, he receives the fixed wage $Y^*$. Since this is a zero-transaction-cost universe, the owner-manager is able to monitor the employee with complete accuracy and take appropriate action in holding him to the terms of his wage contract. For simplicity, both individuals are taken to have the same preferences. And, in the case of the owner, the optimization problem can be stated, as before, as one of discovering the ideal level of effort:

$$\max U_1 = \Phi(L_1, Y_1)$$
$$s.t. \ L_1 = T - w_1 \tag{13}$$
$$Y_1 = A(w_1 + w^*) - Y^*.$$

The owner's reward $(Y_1)$ is given as the total product minus the wage payment to the employee. However, since the wage $Y^*$ is equal to $Aw^*$ when contractual obligations are fulfilled, the owner's reward expression reduces to

$$Y_1 = Aw_1. \tag{14}$$

This share definition, together with the first two lines of (13), leads to the familiar utility-maximizing condition

$$-\frac{dY_1}{dL_1} = A. \tag{15}$$

Assuming (15) requires an effort level $w_1 = w^*$ from the owner-manager, his reward is

$$Y_1 = Aw^* = Y^*. \tag{16}$$

In short, he receives the same reward as his employee, and since the two individuals have identical preferences optimal effort is supplied by both parties. The institutional arrangement, as described, is consistent with efficiency because the structure does not produce nonoptimal incentives.

What must be recognized, however, is that this ideal outcome depends on the existence of an economic environment that permits the owner to determine, instantly and costlessly, whether the employee is shirking. However, given positive transaction costs and bounded rationality, conditions that are characteristic of the real world, the optimal solution vanishes and the familiar principal-agent problem appears. Then the owner must expend time and resources on monitoring individual no. 2, devise an incentive scheme such as profit sharing that will induce no. 2 to cooperate more fully, or take some other action to deal with opportunistic behavior. Of course, under the new circumstances, the problems the firm faces go well beyond those that arise in dealing with employees. Once frictions are posited, all contracting is affected. In each case, a distinction must be made between, for example, the amount of any productive input that is contracted for (and paid for) and the amount of the input actually supplied for production. Similarly, the owner-manager is unable to know about all technological options available, and, even worse, he is not normally in a position to make an informed decision concerning the amount of resources he should devote to searching. In general, then, actual productive arrangements in the real world can be expected to be quite different and less efficient than those implied by the neoclassical production function.

4. The next model attempts to portray some of the characteristics of the *not-for-profit organization* and to show how its special institutional structure affects its behavior. Although the focus here is on property-rights arrangements that are significantly different from those normally ascribed to the competitive firm, the analysis follows the conventional neoclassical approach in many respects. What is envisioned is an organization, such as a museum, that provides the public with a useful output but does not conduct its operations in order to make a profit or please stockholders. By assumption, the organization is run by a director who acts as peak coordinator and establishes policy. The director is responsible to a board of overseers who are supposed to monitor his activities and assess the policies the organization is pursuing. The members of the board, however, have no direct financial stake in the organization.

The organization is able to charge a fee ($p$) for the services it produces, but the fee is nominal and the proceeds go to the organization's endowment fund as they are collected. The costs of the organization's "productive" operations in each period have to be met by a budgeted sum ($S$) that is made available to the director by the board of overseers. The money in question ($S$) comes from endowment income and current donations from benefactors. The outlays made by the "firm" on productive factors include a fixed salary ($M$) that is paid to the director (and, of course, $S > M$). By assumption, the utility of the manager depends not only on his salary but on the types of factor inputs used. That is, he enjoys the use of certain inputs ($y$, $z$) and is repelled by the use of others ($x$).

Since the economic behavior of the organization is determined in an immediate sense by the director, the problem of the not-for-profit firm can be conceived, in traditional terms, as one of constrained optimization. Specifically, the director is assumed to maximize his utility function subject to a budget constraint and an output constraint:

$$\max U = \Phi(x, y, z, M^o) \tag{17}$$

$$s.t. \ S^o = rx + sy + mz + M^o \tag{18}$$

$$q^o = f(x, z) + g(y, z). \tag{19}$$

In other words, the behavior of the organization is assumed to emerge as a by-product of the director's efforts to secure the greatest personal satisfaction consistent with his meeting the effective constraints (18, 19) that limit his options.

As (17) is formulated, the director secures greater satisfaction the greater his salary ($\partial U/\partial M > 0$), the greater the magnitudes of inputs $y$ and $z$, and the smaller the magnitude of input $x$. Some inputs he finds pleasing to employ in production because they yield him nonpecuniary benefits ($\partial U/\partial y > 0$, $\partial U/\partial z > 0$). Input $z$, however, produces only modest satisfaction, and input $x$ acts to diminish his welfare ($\partial U/\partial x < 0$). The budget constraint (18) indicates that the inputs $x$, $y$, and $z$ can be secured from competitive factor markets at per unit prices $r$, $s$, and $m$, respectively. By assumption, price $s$ is substantially higher than price $r$, even though $x$ and $y$ are technically substitutes for one another in producing the organization's output.

Equation (19) shows that the not-for-profit firm is set up so that output can be produced with the use of either one or both of two technical processes: $f(x, z)$ and $g(y, z)$. For analytical convenience, the situation envisioned is analogous to that of a firm having two plants. Both $f$ and $g$ are concave functions reflecting diminishing marginal productivity, but the total product generated by process $f$ (with inputs $x$, $z$) is always greater than the total product generated by $g$ (with inputs $y$, $z$) for equivalent input levels (where each input level is measured in physical units). The presence of process $g$ in the firm is explained, of course, by the director's attraction to $y$, and aversion to $x$, and by his possession of some discretionary power. For example, $y$ and $x$ could represent two distinct groups of people.

Since (19) suggests that the firm's output level can, within certain limits, be set arbitrarily, some discussion of the firm's position in its "market" is required. In effect, the model says that the organization is able to "sell" virtually any amount of output it wishes at the fixed price $p$ (the nominal fee noted earlier). This condition, however, does not result because the organization is competitive and is charging a competitive price. Rather, the not-for-profit firm deliberately maintains the fee it charges at a "socially desirable" low level and produces only a modest output relative to the great demand at that price. No close competitors exist. Hence, a disequilibrium situation persists. Of course, it appears to outside observers that the nonprofit organization could provide greater benefits to the public, and would fulfill its public service objective more completely, if it had greater resources. The greater resources, of course, would have to come largely from an increase in the budget, or subsidy $S$, that is made available to the organization by its patrons and benefactors.

In any given period, the budget is fixed, but the director has a clear incentive to press for greater financial resources. Ceteris paribus, the larger $S$ is, the more fully the director can indulge his predilection for nonpecuniary rewards (inputs $y, z$). Moreover, his salary $(M)$ is likely to be correlated with the size of the total budget at the disposal of the firm in each period. In any event, the director has a persuasive argument to continue his quest for greater financial support because, as noted, he can always argue that the organization could bring its benefits to a wider audience provided the scale of its operations were greater.

If the director had very wide discretionary power and was actually free to maximize his utility function subject only to the budget constraint (18), he would produce output exclusively with the aid of inputs $y, z$ and shun the use of $x$ completely. In the context of our simplified model, the problem would be analogous to that of an individual consumer choosing between two commodities—where one of the commodities is, in fact, a "bad" (i.e., $\partial U/\partial x < 0$). The solution that emerges here would be highly desirable from the standpoint of the director but at variance with the supposed goals of the not-for-profit firm and its financial backers. That is, by choosing the relatively inefficient technical option, merely a minimal output $(\hat{q})$ would be produced with the available resources:

$$\hat{q} = g(y, z)$$
$$S^o = sy + mz + M^o. \tag{20}$$

This socially unfavorable outcome, however, would appear only in the extreme case in which the board of overseers failed to act responsibly.

A principal-agent problem exists. The director is, after all, the agent of the board of overseers, and the board is supposed to protect the interests of the organization and the public. In theory, at least, the board has power because it has ultimate authority over the level of the budget ($S$) going to production, and it can, in the limit, fire the director or reduce his salary. At the same time, board members must be assumed to possess only limited and imperfect information about activities going on within the firm. Nevertheless, while they may operate at some disadvantage, they can recognize the possibility of deviant behavior on the part of the director. And, to counter or reduce such behavior, they might choose to set a target level of output ($q^o$), which the firm would be expected to reach. The magnitude ($q^o$) could perhaps be established by using the so-called yardstick approach, which takes into consideration the standards observed in comparable, well-run organizations in the same line of activity. In any case, the imposition of an additional constraint such as that stipulated in (19) should be anticipated.

Obviously, once (19) is introduced, the director's optimization problem becomes somewhat more difficult. Indeed, the higher the target level of output ($q^o$) is set by the board, the less room there is for the director to depart from technically efficient input combinations. Nevertheless, unless $q^o$ is placed so high as to preclude completely discretionary behavior by the director, he will try to gain some advantage for himself. In technical terms, he can be conceived of as deriving rules for utility-maximizing behavior from the Lagrangian expression based on (17) through (19). Specifically,

$$L = \Phi(x, y, z, M^o) + \lambda_1(S^o - rx - sy - mz - M^o)$$
$$+ \lambda_2(pq^o - pf(x, z) - pg(y, z)). \tag{21}$$

Here, the respective multipliers are $\lambda_1 = \partial U/\partial S > 0$ and $\lambda_2 = \partial U/\partial q < 0$. The latter is *negative* in sign because, over the likely range of variation of $q$, the higher $q^o$ is set the lower will be the director's utility level. That is, as $q^o$ increases, he will have progressively less scope to indulge himself in the use of input $y$, and the absolute magnitude of $\lambda_2$ will become greater and greater. In general, the director's actions will not lead to the first-best conditions for allocative efficiency specified by neoclassical theory. For example, in deciding on the employment of the favored input $y$, he will be disposed to follow the first-order condition

$$\frac{\partial U}{\partial y} = \lambda_1 s + \lambda_2 p \frac{\partial q}{\partial y}. \tag{22}$$

The price $p$ appears here because both sides of (19) can be translated into value terms by multiplying by $p$ the fee charged consumers. Relative to (22), we know that $\partial U/\partial y$ is positive because we have assumed that $y$ is desirable to the director. Further, all of the elements on the right-hand side of (22) are positive with the exception of $\lambda_2$. These considerations suggest that if equation (22) is to be consistent with respect to signs, we must have the condition $\lambda_1 s >$ $\lambda_2 p(\partial q/\partial y)$. Given the importance of the output constraint (19) for the director, the absolute magnitude of $\lambda_2$ cannot be expected to be less than that of $\lambda_1$, and thus price $s$ will be *greater than* the value of the marginal product $p(\partial q/\partial y)$. This situation means, in turn, that at equilibrium more of input $y$ will be employed than is justified by the standard rule for efficient allocation, which requires: $s = p(\partial q/\partial y)$. Similarly, there will be underutilization of the cheaper and superior input $x$. These results are hardly surprising and merely reflect the distortion caused by the director's assumed insistence on choosing inputs on the basis of their appeal to him rather than purely on the basis of their ability to contribute to low-cost output.

The board of overseers, by insisting on a comparatively high level of output relative to the resources made available to the firm, can push the system in the direction of greater efficiency. In short, the director's ability to appropriate nonpecuniary benefits will be greater or smaller depending on how effectively the monitoring function is performed by the board. But how far can we expect effective supervision to go? If this were a true neoclassical model, the principals would operate with unbounded rationality and would be able to acquire any information desired instantly and costlessly. The overseers would know everything about the organization and would presumably establish production so that there was no shirking and only the most efficient technical processes would be used. There would be no place for $g(y, z)$ in the makeup of the firm. Insofar as multiple "plants" were required, operation would be arranged so that appropriate marginal rules would be followed and first-best efficiency achieved. In other words, all sorts of real-life problems are ruled out by unreconstructed neoclassical theory, and we are left with the question of whether the neoclassical approach can be modified to consider a wider range of problems and still maintain its internal consistency.

There is little room for optimism about the question. In the case of what we have termed "hybrid" models, a consistent point of view is not maintained. For example, decision makers are routinely taken to have split economic personalities. They are perfectly informed about some matters and ignorant about others. Thus, ignorance exists despite the fact that they are supposed to be operating in an essentially frictionless world or, alternately, different economic actors in the same model show different motivations and capabilities. The director of the not-for-profit firm is highly rational and knows precisely how to pursue his own interests (i.e., he is able to solve the constrained maximization problem posed by (17) through (19). On the other hand, the members of the board operate with a lack of accurate information about the firm and its policies. Of course, it can be objected at this point that the special behavior of board members is explained by more than their restricted knowledge of events within the firm. Following the line of the New Institutional

Economics, one may argue that their motivations are different because of the institutional setting of the problem.

By definition, the not-for-profit organization has objectives that are distinct from those of the normal business enterprise, and we know that the overseers have no prospect of financial gain whether the efficiency level of the organization is high or low. It has been pointed out in the literature that the crucial determining characteristic of different types of not-for-profit firms is that: "*No one can claim the right to appropriate the residual*" (Alchian and Demsetz 1972). In other words, the future consequences of current managerial decisions cannot be capitalized. Thus, managerial decisions are costly to evaluate, and economic theory suggests that, under such conditions, the managers will use potential profits to obtain more nonpecuniary sources of utility" (Furubotn and Pejovich, 1972a, 1154). Thus, insofar as board members take up their duties to secure social prestige or the esteem of the public, it can be rational for them to limit the effort they put into supervising the behavior of the director. Similarly, since there is no profit motive operative, and since the activities of the organization are financed largely by donations, certain corrective mechanisms that function in the business world are missing and thus cannot promote efficiency. Specifically, in the absence of profit possibilities, there is no reason for takeover threats to appear and put pressure on the director, nor can there be much fear that financial markets will deny needed monies to the organization if it does not perform well. It is not even clear that the market for professional managers in this area is particularly competitive or that it places much emphasis on personal qualities that are important to the efficient management of an organization. For example, a director may be more prized for his ability to deal with organization publicity and fund-raising than for his capacity to find solutions to day-to-day administrative problems.

The picture that emerges is not encouraging. If the organization's director is chosen primarily for his personal magnetism, if the organization's objectives are not well defined for all areas of its activity, if soft budget constraints are characteristic, and so on, there can be little reason to suppose that efficient operation in either the Pareto or the normal business sense will take place. All this may be true and reasonable, but we are left with the uneasy feeling that in approaching a model we can secure any results we wish merely by introducing series of special structural and motivational assumptions. Questions arise concerning how far, and in what directions, the search for special institutional or other features should be pushed. For example, in the case of the not-for-profit firm, the conclusions about efficiency might be different if it were found that institutional arrangements within the organization made it easier and less costly for board members to determine how funds were allocated by the director. It is also possible that institutional conditions external to the firm could affect its mode of operation. Investigative reporters in the media, pursuing their own professional interests, might find it advantageous from time to time to provide more information to the public about how well a nonprofit organization is run. Then, board members who were concerned with their "images" would perhaps put more effort into supervisory activity for fear of looking foolish. In short, various factors at work in a complex system may be drawn upon to explain economic behavior, and institutional models are, in effect, open-ended constructs.

What the preceding discussion suggests is that hybrid models, reflecting themes emphasized in the New Institutional Economics, are not completely satisfying in a scientific sense. This is so because of the ad hoc character of the analysis associated with such models. By contrast, orthodox neoclassical theory may seem more appealing. After all, it rests on a limited number of axioms and appears to proceed rigorously to definite, testable conclusions. But, realistically, there can be no going back to this approach. As has been indicated in earlier chapters, neoclassical precision is achieved at a very high price in terms of realism and relevance. In a world of positive transaction costs and bounded rationality, we can never expect first-best solutions to be reached. Indeed, even as a benchmark, the Pareto conditions are arguably of little use because they are tied to such extreme assumptions. As Stiglitz has argued:

> Just as one of the great contributions of twentieth-century neoclassical economics was to make clear why considerations which they had excluded from their analyses—such as information and transaction costs— simply *had* to be brought into the analysis, so too one of the central contributions of game theory has been to make it clear that the "rational" actor model is not only descriptively inaccurate (as earlier economists had charged), but internally incomplete and/or inconsistent, (see Binmore [1987], [1988] and Reny [1985]). The hope of game theory that some simple version of rationality could lead to well-defined, let alone reasonable, prediction of behavior has been dashed. (1991, 138)

While there is, as yet, no neoinstitutionalist theory that can fill the void left by the movement away from neoclassicism, there do seem to be some early indications of the way progress will be made in the future (see, for example, Stiglitz 1991, Wiseman 1991, and North 1994). With respect to models of the firm, it would seem to be true that *partial reformulation* of neoclassical theory in the manner of the so-called hybrid, or principal-agent, models is not really satisfactory. To ensure a consistent point of view, it is necessary to make a complete break with the neoclassical universe. Analysis cannot be "half" neoclassical and "half" neoinstitutional. It is inappropriate to assume, for example, that transaction costs can be simultaneously positive in some sectors of the economy and zero in all others. Rather, the firm or organization must be understood to be embedded in an environment in which costly transactions, incomplete information, and limited rationality rule everywhere. Moreover, in this new universe, continuing adjustment of firms is likely to be the norm; if equilibrium solutions are ever reached, they will presumably not come about quickly.

## 8.6. The Traditional Soviet Firm

As modern property-rights theory developed with the writings of Alchian, Demsetz, Cheung, and others, increased attention was given to the effects of different possible property-rights assignments on penalty-reward structures, and it became possible to study the interrelationships between institutional arrangements and economic behavior more systematically. Indeed, since many economists in the decade of the 1960s believed that the new property-rights/ transaction-cost analysis could be integrated into the dominant neoclassical mode, there was faith that traditional methods could be used with minimal modification. Thus, in describing the approach to be taken, it was said:

> The usual procedure is to formulate an optimization model that is analogous to, but in general distinct from, the traditional profit maximization case. In each instance, it is necessary to define the particular utility function that reflects the decision maker's preferences, and to determine the actual set of options (penalties-rewards) that is attainable by the decision maker. Then, the formal problem emerges as one of maximizing the utility function subject to the constraint imposed by the opportunity set. (Furubotn and Pejovich 1972a, 1138)

Of course, we now know, with the wisdom of hindsight, that optimization models of this type have serious limitations. Nevertheless, such models are worth considering because they illustrate the ways in which some parts of neoinstitutionalist thinking evolved. And it is also true that, despite their simplicity, they can often provide some basic insights into the ways particular organizations can be expected to function.

Once property-rights considerations were broached, a natural area of application for neoinstitutionlist logic was found in the field of comparative economic systems (see, for example, Nutter 1968; Pejovich 1969, 1972; Furubotn 1971a, 1976a; and Furubotn and Pejovich 1970a, 1970b, 1971, 1972a). Since the new mode of analysis, based on the maximizing behavior of individual decision makers, possessed great flexibility, the same technique could be used to explore what seemed to be, at first sight, quite disparate organizations. For example, despite their differences in certain obvious respects, there existed a significant degree of similarity in the content of the bundle of property rights that defined ownership of the Soviet firm, on the one hand, and the content of the bundle defining ownership of the modern capitalist corporation on the other. In the latter organization, just as in the case of the not-for-profit firm of section 8.5, we know that hired managers have some freedom to pursue their own interests at the expense of the ostensible "principals." That is, given the relatively high detection, policing, and enforcement costs in existence, the manager of a dispersed-ownership capitalist firm soon discovers that the "prices" of various types of utility-producing behaviors are comparatively low. While the manager's willingness to assume risk may be a factor in his decision-making process, he is, in general, interested in "purchasing" certain of these behaviors. Positive transaction costs and asymmetric information ensure that results diverge from those predicted by orthodox neoclassical theory. From the new perspective, however, knowledge of the institutional structure makes it possible to anticipate such specific practices as managerial consumption of nonpecuniary income, maintenance of a ratio of retained earnings to profits in excess of stockholders' time preference, and so on (see also sec. 5.1).

When the manager's position in the capitalist firm is viewed in these terms, it is but a short step to the recognition that the Soviet manager, in the former scheme of things, occupied an essentially similar position in his firm. That is, in the traditional Soviet firm of the early 1960s, the relationship between the Soviet manager and the state was analogous to that between the capitalist manager and the corporation's stockholders. The costs to the state of monitoring the firm's policies and enforcing a desired pattern of behavior in the manager were clearly large. Moreover, at best, the central authorities faced difficulties in securing a reliable, truthful, and easily interpretable flow of information from their sources at lower levels. What has to be kept in mind is that self-seeking behavior was not limited to firm managers; everyone in the system had reason to shape his behavior so as to secure personal advantage. Conflicting objectives, general uncertainty, collective decision making, and other factors conspired to make taut, consistent, clear-cut control from the center an unrealizable goal. In any event, in this environment, the manager of the Soviet firm was able, within his own estimate of the transaction costs faced by higher authorities, to *attenuate* the state's ownership of the firm. Quite simply, the manager was in a position to use some of the firm's resources in ways that contributed to his personal satisfaction (utility) and to do this contrary to the law and at the expense of government objectives.

The model that follows (Furubotn and Pejovich 1972a) presents an explanation of how the Soviet manager might proceed in his drive for greater personal security and utility. As in all optimization models of this type, its usefulness depends on how skillfully the specification is made of the objective function and the opportunity set. A first requirement, then, is to provide a very brief sketch of the forces with which the manager has to contend in carrying out his duties. Only with knowledge of this background is it possible to introduce specific and relevant content into the utility and constraint functions of the model. To begin, we can note that historically the Soviet government controlled and evaluated the performance of firms through the use of certain success indicators. The two objectives that were regarded by the administrative planners as most important were (1) the achievement of the gross output target and (2) the realization of average planned costs and average planned profit. The Soviet manager's tenure in the job, promotions, and monetary rewards depended on his ability to produce at least the planned output quota. At the same time, given the governmental allocation of planned supplies (including the wage fund) and the officially established product and input prices, production of any output in excess of the quota implied average costs lower than those planned and average profit higher than the planned level. Such a favorable outcome was significant when it occurred because a percentage of the excess profit could be allocated for monetary rewards to the manager and other employees of the firm.

By law, the Soviet government owned the nonhuman means of production and had the final authority over their use. Thus, the state, at its discretion, allocated new capital goods to the firm, transferred existing ones, and determined the use of depreciation funds. The Soviet firm has correspondingly limited powers; in theory, the firm could only utilize its available capital stocks for producing the planned output. On the positive side, though, the firm was not required to pay rent or interest on its fixed assets. As noted, the supplies of most variable inputs going to the firm were decided by the production plan, while the associated financial plan provided the means for their purchase. It was required, however, that the firm purchase most of these inputs from the particular suppliers specified in the plan and at the stated prices. Even in the case of labor, which the firm purchased in the market, the relative wages for different types of skills were set administratively, and the plan established a limit on the size of the firm's wage fund. In short, the state tried to exercise the right of *unattenuated* ownership of the firm and its resources; the state allocated the various supplies to the firm, determined their sources, and stipulated their monetary values.

Given the nature of the property-rights relations that existed between the state and the Soviet firm, and the importance that was attached to quota fulfillment, certain inferences can be made about the probable attitudes and motivation of the manager. Specifically, it is arguable that, in this type of command economy, the manager will tend to view capital goods as a free reserve and concentrate on developing arguments that will convince the state of his firm's urgent need for more fixed assets to achieve efficient production. On the other hand, the planned supplies of variable inputs do not appear to be free. Such inputs are reflected in the firm's official cost of production, and the manager who wishes to receive more current supplies must have the planning authorities believe that the firm's cost of production is relatively high given the required output.

In general, then, if the manager is concerned about being able to meet his quota obligation on time and consistently, he will be desirous of accumulating both fixed assets and stocks of the variable input. By having excess plant capacity and abundant variable supplies, the manager is able to protect himself against unforeseen production difficulties and increase the probability of his always fulfilling the official quota. Moreover, the behavior the manager must adopt in order to achieve his ends is clear. To accumulate fixed assets, he must be vocal about his firm's need for additional physical capital. To accumulate variable inputs, he must convince the state that the firm's production function has *less* technical efficiency than it actually possesses.

On the basis of the rationale just presented, the Soviet manager's utility function can be specified as:

$$U_t = \Phi(q_t, S_t, Q_t), \tag{23}$$

where $q_t$ is the output of the firm in period $t$ and the parameter $Q_t$ represents the firm's planned output quota for period $t$ (as determined by the state authorities). For simplicity, $S_t$ is assumed to be a general measure of the stocks or inventories of the variable inputs (including labor) that have been accumulated by the manager over time through informal means and held back from active production in period $t$. Equation (23) implies that, at any period $t$, the manager's level of satisfaction depends on the magnitudes of the variables $q_t$ and $S_t$ and the parameter $Q_t$. Given the crucial significance of meeting the quota, the manager will always prefer more production $(q_t)$ to less up to the level $Q_t$. But beyond output $q_t = Q_t$, further current production will be valued in greater or lesser degree depending on the state of the firm's stocks $(S_t)$ and the manager's attitude toward risk.

At any given period, output in excess of the quota implies greater material rewards and prestige for the manager. The activities of the firm, however, extend over time, and the wise manager must also consider his ability to meet future quotas. The justification for including the stock variable $(S_t)$ in the utility function rests on the fact that there was substantial uncertainty in the Soviet economy. Since Soviet managers understood that input allocations were frequently delivered late or not at all, the firm's possession of unplanned reserve stocks of variable factors was seen as a way to alleviate production crises. Precautionary stocks, then, contribute to satisfaction by giving the manager added assurance that he will be able to meet future output targets even when planned resource allocations are not received.

Turning next to the constraints to which the firm is subject, we assume that the manager sees the condition of input supply and use in terms of certain technical relations. Thus,

$$S_t = V_t + S_{t-1} - v_t \qquad (24)$$

defines the firm's stock level at period $t$. For convenience, only one variable input $(V_t)$ is identified. The centrally planned factor allocation $(V_t)$ plus the previously accumulated stock of this input $(S_{t-1})$ minus the current use of the input in production $(v_t)$ equals the current stock of the variable input held for next period's operations $(S_t)$. It might be asked, at this point, how the manager is able to accumulate units of the variable input when the flow of the input to the firm is legally controlled and the official allocation $(V_t)$ is based on the planned output $(Q_t)$. In a world of positive transaction costs, however, the answer in not hard to find. Asymmetric information rules, and the manager is able to gain a certain amount of stock for his operation by convincing the state that his (short-run) production function shows relatively low technical efficiency. Thus, the *reported* production function is specified to the state as

$$q_t = F(v_t, K^o, m), \qquad (25)$$

while the *true* relation, characterized by greater efficiency, is

$$q_t = f(v_t, K^o, n). \qquad (26)$$

The manager is assumed to know the capabilities of his plant more accurately than the state does because of his hands-on experience with its operation. In any event, (25) and (26) show that the flow of output per period $(q_t)$ depends on the contemporaneous use of the variable input flow $(v_t)$ in conjunction with the fixed capital stock $(K^o)$ that has been made available to the firm by the state. The two stock-flow functions differ because the technological parameter $n$ implies greater overall productive efficiency than $m$ does.

The Soviet manager of our model controls the magnitude of the gap between parameters $m$ and $n$ by means of his power to falsify his reports on the true production capabilities of the firm. There are, of course, risks associated with any policy of deliberate misinformation because the planning authorities have sources other than the manager's testimony for estimating a firm's technological efficiency. Thus, the manager has to reach a decision about the reported production function (25) in the light of his assessment of the costs and difficulties that the state must face in order to monitor the firm more accurately, his willingness to take risks, his own knowledge of the true technological relation, and so on. While different managers will tend to reach different solutions for reported efficiency, the potential gains from falsification of the production function make it unlikely that the true function (26) will be revealed by anyone.

Assuming that the reported production relation (25) is approved by the state, the central authorities can then determine the official allocation of the variable input $(V_t)$ that will be earmarked for the firm in period $t$. This calculation will be made in conformity with the system of regulated prices and the planned profit requirement as well as with the technological data. What emerges is the understanding that if the output quota is $Q_t$, the firm's input allocation must be $V_t$. Of course, if the planned allocation $V_t$ is actually delivered to the firm, the manager will be in a position to produce more output than is called for by the quota $Q_t$. This so because, by assumption, the firm's true production function is (26) not (25). A successful falsification policy means that the firm is no longer tied to the centrally planned operating point $(V_t, Q_t)$. The Soviet manager is able to create for himself a set of opportunity choices. At one extreme, the manager can commit all of the input $V_t$ to current operations and produce a maximum output of $Q_t'$ (via (26)). Since $Q_t'$ is greater than $Q_t$, the firm overfills its quota. But this production strategy also has the effect of reducing the costs of the firm and increasing its profit per unit over the required level. These outcomes are, ceteris paribus, favorable from the manager's standpoint.

Nevertheless, the production of output $Q_t'$ has a down side. Specifically, the firm will completely use up the $t$th period's input allocation and thus will add nothing to accumulated stocks. By contrast, if the manager chooses to produce merely the planned output $Q_t$, not all of the current input allocation will be used (say, only $V$). Then, the firm will be able to accumulate $(V_t - V_t')$ units of the variable input to add to stocks in period $t$. The sacrifice implied here is, of course, that the quota is not overfilled, and this means, in turn, that no special bonuses or other rewards can be appropriated in the *current* period. In any case, the set of opportunity choices open to the manager includes the two extreme output/factor-use programs $(Q_t', V_t)$, $(Q_t, V_t')$ described previously and all intermediate points lying between these extremes.

As a utility maximizer, the manager will select an operating position from the set of feasible alternatives just noted. The critical factor limiting his potential satisfaction is the availability of the variable input—that is, accumulated stocks $S_{t-1}$ and the state allocation $V_t$. The size of $S_{t-1}$ is known and can easily be verified by the manager, but the effective size of $V_t$ is open to some doubt even after it has been established by the state. That is, the manager knows from experience that the official input allocation in any period will not necessarily be delivered in total or in time for current use. Hence, the manager is likely to calculate an *expected input delivery* (as $V_t^*$) on the basis of a subjectively determined probability distribution. If the expected delivery is considered equivalent to the same number of input units possessed with certainty, the manager's optimization problem can be established as follows:

$$\max U = \Phi(q_t, S_t, Q_t^o)$$
$$s.t. \ S_t = V_t^* + S_{t-1}^o - v_t \tag{27}$$
$$q_t = f(v_t, K^o, n).$$

The first-order condition for the maximum then appears as

$$-\frac{dS_t}{dq_t} = \frac{1}{(\partial q_t / \partial v_t)}. \tag{28}$$

Equation (28) indicates that, at equilibrium, the manager's subjective marginal rate of substitution of stock for output ($-dS_t/dq_t$) has to equal the ratio of certain "shadow" prices (or $1/(\partial q_t/\partial v_t)$). The latter, the shadow price of output (1) and the shadow price of stock ($\partial q_t/\partial v_t$) are, in effect, opportunity costs with which the firm's manager must reckon. We know that the alternative uses to which the input $v_t$ can be put are *mutually exclusive;* the manager can utilize the available input either to produce commodity output ($q_t$) or to add to existing stocks ($S_t$). It follows, then, that the "cost" or "price" of diverting a unit of $v_t$ from output to stock is the marginal product foregone ($\partial q_t/\partial v_t$), and similarly the "price" of shifting a unit of the input from stock to output is the loss of one unit of inventory. Note that equation (28) can be interpreted as saying that the Soviet manager, in order to maximize his utility, will arrange things in a manner comparable to the actions of the neoclassical consumer. Thus, at equilibrium, the marginal utility of output ($\partial U/\partial q_t$) is to the "price" of output (1) as the marginal utility of stock ($\partial U/\partial S_t$) is to the "price" of stock ($\partial q_t/\partial v_t$).

At any cross section of time, the manager will reach a solution for the optimal values $\hat{v}_t, \hat{q}_t, \hat{S}_t$, and his solution will maximize his utility at $t$ while weighing both present and future benefits. An inevitable difficulty arises, however, because insofar as he exceeds the initial quota and claims greater productive efficiency, his quota for the *next period* will be raised by the state. Then, ceteris paribus, the manager's output choices will be more restricted in period

$t + 1$ than in the original situation. Indeed, as long as the firm *overproduces,* a ratchet effect will occur. As time goes on, the *reported* production function must show progressive improvement and must approach the true production function more and more closely. Thus, the scope for independent output policy will grow smaller and smaller. Such disappearance of choice is important to the manager because it implies the end of stock accumulation and signals potential difficulties. That is, the firm is left vulnerable to the behavior of external suppliers of the variable input.

To avoid the problem just described, it might be thought that the manager could adopt a purely defensive policy, shun bonuses, and never produce more than the quota (i.e., $\hat{q}_t = Q_t^o$). Then, storage of surplus amounts of the variable input could continue. But, since such accumulation could go on period after period as long as actual and planned output are equal, the stock could in theory become extremely large. Practically, of course, there is a physical limit to storage and to the amount of the input that can be laid away without arousing the attention of the state. Thus, it appears that the manager must ultimately use some of the surplus input in active production if he is to stay within the storage limit. Ceteris paribus, periodic overfilling of the quota is inevitable, and in the end the firm's true production function must be revealed to the state.

As has been explained, if the background conditions of the problem are truly fixed, the range of the manager's policy options must tend to shrink over time and ultimately disappear. But, because this pattern holds, the utility-maximizing manager has a strong incentive to undertake action that changes his economic environment. Indeed, the manager can preserve a range of policy choices for himself by pursuing one or more of the following actions: (1) acquiring additional fixed assets from the state, (2) discovering and implementing cost-saving innovations to increase firm efficiency, and (3) introducing new or modified products. Note, however, that the manager's success in gaining room for maneuver depends on his ability to conceal from the state authorities the true implications of any reorganization based on (1) through (3). While no single act of reorganization will be sufficient to solve the manager's problems permanently, continual change in the data can help to sustain his area of freedom and can even contribute somewhat to greater efficiency in the command economy in which the firm operates.

The model of the firm presented earlier is typical of early neoinstitutionalist constructs in its use of basic neoclassical methodology and its emphasis on the details of institutional structure. Since there was confidence, in the period of the 1960s and 1970s, that the standard neoclassical framework could be extended to accommodate new institutionalist ideas, there was little hesitation in accepting familiar concepts such as those of the production or utility function without much reevaluation and in assuming that the firm's problem could be represented in terms of a constrained maximization model. Methodological individualism dictated that major attention be given to the decision maker's utility function and to the particular institutional arrangements that constrained him. The objective was to formulate empirically meaningful optimization problems by recognizing that business decisions are made by individuals rather than by faceless "organizations," and that specific empirical content must be introduced into the utility function and the opportunity set. The latter requirement meant, of course, that considerable discussion had to be devoted to the unique institutional features of the firm, bureau, labor union, or other organization being studied. Reduced to its simplest terms, then, the rationale underlying these New Institutional Economics models was that the property-rights/transaction-cost configuration extant shaped incentives and hence behavior.

In the case of the model of the Soviet firm, it would seem that its predictions about behavior were reasonably accurate. Historically, observers of the Soviet economy have called attention to the tendency of managers to violate Soviet regulations to protect their own interests and gain some room for independent policy making (Bornstein 1979; Prybyla 1969; Zaleski 1967). These so-called informal activities are easily understood as strategies that a utility-maximizing manager would be likely to adopt. Nevertheless, as indicated earlier, it must be appreciated that the conclusions reached by any neoinstitutionalist model are sensitive to the particular institutional features that are included in or excluded from the model. We must proceed cautiously in this area, for, despite the progress that has been made in clarifying some positions and concepts of the NIE, there is still no generally recognized theory of the firm grounded in the new thinking.

Today, although opinion is far from uniform, there seems to be some recognition that the NIE cannot be developed as a mere extension of the neoclassical model. Neoclassical assumptions concerning rationality and perfect information are especially ill adapted to the type of analysis that neo-institutionalist writers are attempting. Thus, in considering the firm, current research is likely to be more skeptical about the usefulness of the constrained maximization approach (e.g., Aoki 1983; Stiglitz 1985) and more willing to devote time to determining the extent and basis of the information endowments possessed by decision makers (e.g., Nelson 1981; Wiseman 1991). It should also be pointed out that there has long been a group of scholars who believe that institutional questions cannot be dealt with very effectively through the medium of formal economic models and that the focus should be on careful empirical study. Given the existing diversity of thinking, then, we have to expect that a variety of enterprise models will be with us for the foreseeable future.

## 8.7. The Socialist Labor-Managed Firm

Despite the fact that neoclassical theory proceeds as though institutions, such as that of private ownership, do not matter, neoclassical analysis was routinely applied to problems in the field of comparative economics. Thus, when considering firms operating in different economic systems, the approach usually taken was to associate each type of firm with what was supposed to be its characteristic maximand. In this interpretation, the objective of the capitalist firm must be seen as *profit maximization* while the objective of the socialist labor-managed firm is taken to be *wage maximization* (more precisely, maximization of the wage rate). Insofar as labor management schemes did allow the workers' collective running a firm to retain at least some of the firm's "profits" and distribute these among its members, the idea of wage maximization has surface plausibility. But since most orthodox analysis is purely static and ignores virtually all of the institutional features that make labor management distinctive, the approach has little to commend it.

The failure to understand the true nature of the labor-managed firm was unfortunate because this socialist innovation commanded a great deal of public attention in the 1960s and 1970s. As developed in the Yugoslavia of that period, the labor-managed firm seemed to promise an enticing combination of industrial democracy, productive efficiency, and economic growth within the framework of a wholly decentralized economy. Indeed, the Yugoslav "model" was often seen as the means to the fabled "third way" that would avoid the pitfalls of a command economy while capturing the dynamism of free enterprise in a system that has rejected the evils of private property. Conventional theory in the West contributed to this picture by suggesting that, under appropriate theoretical conditions, a labor-managed economy could achieve all of the Pareto equivalences for first-best allocational efficiency and thus could duplicate the performance of an idealized capitalist system.

The image of the labor-managed firm changes significantly, however, when it is viewed from the standpoint of the New Institutional Economics. That is, once the institutional structure of the labor-managed firm is considered in greater detail, and the organization is understood as more than a technical production function, oversimplified notions about its objectives and efficiency level are soon banished. To proceed along these lines and develop criticism of the orthodox literature systematically, it will be necessary to establish a basic outline of the socialist labor-managed enterprise as it was conceived in Yugoslavia (Furubotn and Pejovich 1970b). We find that as early as 1950–51 the right to manage the firm was, within certain legal limits, in the hands of its employees. The workers' collective, through its elected body, the Workers' Council, was empowered to make all major decisions concerning such matters as the rate and quality of output and investment, the level of employment, and the hiring and firing of workers. Moreover, the collective was given sufficient power to ask for the removal of the firm's director if that action was thought desirable.

The director of the labor-managed firm was to be selected in a public contest by a commission appointed jointly by the Workers' Council and local government. When appointed, he was expected to implement decisions made by the collective, organize and control production, and, in general, be responsible directly to the Workers' Council. Given his special position, the director could not afford to be either a dictator or a paternalistic supervisor. For success, he had to show some evidence of good management by generating acceptable wages. He also had to be able to persuade the collective at all times that his ideas on enterprise policy were wise.

The legal provisions for the distribution of the firm's total revenue gave the labor-managed organization its unique character. Significantly, the wage bill was excluded from the firm's costs of production. This situation meant that the actual pay of a worker depended on (1) the profits realized by the firm after the costs of supplies, depreciation, taxation, and so on were met; (2) the distribution of the profits between the Wage Fund and the Business Fund; and (3) the criteria used to distribute the Wage Fund among the different employees of the firm. By 1965 in Yugoslavia, the Workers' Council had been permitted direct control over (2) and (3) and had indirect control over (1) through its power to make business decisions. Insofar as there was concern by workers with the profit position of the firm and its implications for rewards to labor, attention had to be given to the quality and quantity of its capital stock. Hence, the Business Fund was important because allocations to it could be used to acquire additional capital.

In a socialist regime, of course, a firm cannot legally own capital goods. In Yugoslavia, however, the law did establish that the collective had the *right of use* of its firm's capital. The law allowed the firm to produce, buy, and/or sell capital goods subject to only two major constraints: (1) the firm had to maintain the book value of its assets via depreciation allowances or otherwise;[2] and (2) the firm was required to pay interest on the value of its capital to the state. The purpose of this latter obligation was, in addition to asserting the state's ownership of the capital stock, to provide funds for administratively planned investment projects and to induce the profit-oriented firm to use capital goods efficiently.

The preceding outline of the institutional arrangements under which the socialist firm was required to function in Yugoslavia suggest, at first blush, two

---

2. For example, if the firm sold assets to another firm for less than their book value, the difference had to be deducted from the firm's profit during that period and earmarked for investment.

general behavioral goals—*wage maximization* per worker and *wealth maximization* per worker. In the standard literature, the pure theory of the labor-managed firm, as developed by Ward (1958), Domar (1966), and Vanek (1969, 1970), is based on the first assumption. Presumably, the collective agrees completely on policy and seeks the best wage attainable. Apart from this special behavioral postulate, however, the analysis runs parallel with conventional neoclassical theory (Vanek 1969, 1006–7). When the firm's objective is simple "wage" maximization, a straightforward optimization problem can be formulated. Then, by following familiar technical procedures, it is possible to determine the equilibrium levels of factor usage in the long and short run, the response of the firm to price changes, and so on. But, as noted earlier, the real question is whether this interpretation of the case leads to any significant understanding of the behavior of the labor-managed enterprise.

To gain some insight into the kind of worker behavior that wage maximization implies, it will be useful to consider the following model. Thus, assume that the firm operates subject to the production function

$$q = f(L, K),\qquad(29)$$

where $q$ is commodity output per period, $L$ is a homogeneous labor input, and $K$ is the flow of capital services drawn per period from the capital equipment at the disposal of the firm. At any moment, the firm has the use of a definite quantity of capital goods and hence the availability of a certain flow of services from these goods. For the initial period, this flow can be designated as $K^o$. If it is assumed that any incremental capital equipment acquired in the first period will not be integrated into the firm's productive organization until the next period, the available flow of capital services will be fixed at $K^o$ until the beginning of period two. By contrast, the labor input is taken to be effective immediately (i.e., without any lag). Under these conditions, we have a type of short-run situation in the initial period and at each cross-section of time thereafter.

Given the "short run" situation of the initial period, variations of the labor input in that period are crucial, and the firm's profit function for period one takes the following form:

$$\pi = pf(L, K^o) - Z(K^o).\qquad(30)$$

Granting that the firm is able to sell any output it can produce at the official state price $p$, profit $\pi$ is equal to price times output minus cost $Z$. The latter represents the production expenses of the firm that must be paid because of contractual or other obligations. Note again, however, that labor costs do not appear in $Z$. For convenience, the magnitude of cost $Z$ is taken to be a function of the flow of capital services (which are $K^o$ in the first period). By law, the collective is free to allocate the firm's profit between the Wage Fund and the Business Fund. The Workers' Council decides on the proportions of the division and in so doing influences the level of wage rate $w$. The accounting relation is

$$\pi = wL + I, \tag{31}$$

where $I$ is the monetary value of the Business Fund. In the absence of any governmental interference, $I$ can assume any value from zero to some limit established by the need to maintain a minimally acceptable wage per unit of labor $w^*$.

If the (homogeneous) workers in the collective insist on maximizing the average wage rate with respect to $L$, the Business Fund will be set at zero, and acquisition of incremental capital will be nil. Of course, with $I = 0$, the expression for the wage rate reduces, via (31), to

$$w = \frac{pf(L, K^o) - Z(K^o)}{L}, \tag{32}$$

and the employment level $\hat{L}$ that maximizes the wage rate is easily found through differentiation. In textbook terms, the first-order condition can be written as

$$pAP_L - Z/L = pMP_L. \tag{33}$$

At the wage-maximizing equilibrium, the value of labor's average physical product minus average fixed cost per unit of labor must be equal to the value of labor's marginal product. It is apparent from (33) that if outlays for supplies, depreciation, interest on capital, taxes, and so on are zero, the term $Z/L$ will disappear and the optimal operating position $(\hat{L})$ appears at the point where $AP_L = MP_L$, or the point where the average product of labor is at a maximum. However, on the more reasonable assumption of a positive value for $Z$, the ideal labor solution changes. Specifically, the larger the cost $Z$ the more the operating point for the maximum attainable wage rate is pushed in the direction of larger labor employment (i.e., $AP_L > MP_L$).

The first-order condition for the maximization of wage rate $w$ involves the variable $L$ and a number of parameters relating to commodity price, production function, and so on. Thus, the equation for the wage-maximizing employment level $(\hat{L})$ can be established as

$$\hat{L} = g(p, Z, K), \tag{34}$$

and the direction of influence of certain key factors can be suggested by the signs of the partial derivatives

$$\frac{\partial \hat{L}}{\partial p} < 0, \frac{\partial \hat{L}}{\partial Z} > 0, \frac{\partial \hat{L}}{\partial K} \gtreqless 0. \tag{35}$$

For example, an increase in the price of the commodity or a *decrease* in firm costs $Z$ leads to a decrease in the equilibrium volume of employment. Further, consistent with Ward's findings (1958, 574–75), similar relations hold with respect to output in the simple model being considered. As in Ward's model, output and price are inversely related over the relevant range of the production function. In other words, the labor-managed firm's supply curve, as opposed to the standard neoclassical theory of the firm, has a negative slope. As indicated, though, it is not possible to make any simple generalizations about the effect of a change in the flow of capital services on employment. The outcome in any given case hinges on the mathematical forms ascribed to the production function (29) and the cost function $[Z = Z(K)]$.[3]

As noted above, when the firm's expenses, $Z = Z(K^o)$, are subtracted from the value of the total product, $pf(L, K^o)$, the firm's profit function is obtainable. This function (30) relates profit ($\pi$) to different possible levels of employment. If the collective opts for one-period wage maximization, the equilibrium labor input, say, $\hat{L}_1$ will be at the point where $\pi/L = d\pi/dL$. However, in socialist practice, a government interested in promoting capital investment might establish administrative guidelines that would force the collective to earmark a particular sum, say, $I^o$, for the Business Fund. Then the result would be an adjustment that would bring about an increase in the labor input and a reduction in the wage rate (relative to the $I = 0, \hat{L}_1$ case). As far as the labor input is concerned, the hypothetical limiting case is found where $I = \pi, \hat{L} = \hat{L}_n$, and the wage rate is zero. Since the marginal physical product of labor is zero at $\hat{L}_n$, the solution implies that profits are being maximized while labor's compensation is ignored completely. In summary, then, we can note that tradeoffs between $I$ and $w$ can proceed continuously over the effective operating range $\hat{L}_1$ to $\hat{L}_n$.

Under the policy of strict wage maximization, which is emphasized in much of the conventional theory of the socialist labor-managed firm, the presumption is that workers never see any reason to limit wage rewards and invest some portion of the firm's profits in capital goods. From the standpoint of the New Institutional Economics, however, this position seems to require some

---

3. Depending on the nature of the production function, the ideal labor solution may also be affected by the magnitude of the change in the capital service flow. Thus, for small increases in $K$, a decrease in the level of employment might be indicated, while for large increases an increase in employment could be required.

modification. It has already been observed that the state may place greater or lesser pressure on the firm to save and invest. In such a campaign, government authorities may well use *informal* means to secure their objectives, and it is in this connection that the role of the firm director takes on special importance. Indeed, when the director is seen as a central figure in the formulation of enterprise policy, it is possible to explain why the collective is unlikely to pursue a pure wage-maximization program. The director occupies a middle ground between the local workers and higher government officials. He must be sensitive to the desires of both groups and take actions that are at least broadly acceptable, if not pleasing, to both. At the same time, the director, as a type of entrepreneur in the relatively free labor-managed system, is extremely important to the success of his firm. His superior education and experience give him the ability to exert considerable influence over the workers in the collective. Moreover, by virtue of his key position as organizer and controller of production, he tends to possess greater information and perspective on the alternatives confronting the firm. Workers, even if they tend to oppose his policy suggestions, must recognize the director's special knowledge of the firm and be amenable to persuasion.

The director himself may have mixed feelings about the desirability of pushing for greater enterprise investment. On the one hand, he may recognize that his own salary could be increased, along with the basic wage rate paid to workers, as the Business Fund is reduced and made to approach zero. Further, his good relations with the Workers' Council and rank-and-file employees might be jeopardized by his strong advocacy of investment. On the other hand, the director is necessarily concerned with the economic growth achieved by his firm. And, since he represents the central government,[4] he is particularly aware of national purposes and priorities. He is aware, too, that his long-term career is likely to be influenced by the degree to which his guidance of the firm contributes to the realization of national goals.

Even without departing very far from the structure of the standard wage-maximization model of the labor-managed firm, it is possible to construct a more institutionally oriented enterprise model based on the role of the firm's director. For analytical purposes, the director's conflicting motivations can be reflected by a simple, ordinal preference function:

$$U = \Phi(w, I). \tag{36}$$

---

4. In Yugoslavia, for example, the Basic Law on Commercial Enterprises of April 1965 indicated that the director's duty was to monitor the Workers' Council decisions and inform the state whenever he believed that the collective's action was contrary to the intent of the positive laws and regulations of the land.

Here the director's satisfaction is assumed to depend on the level of the wage rate, $w$, and the magnitude of the allocation of profit to the Business Fund, $I$. Then, knowing the technical conditions of production and the other factors that determine the tradeoffs that can actually be made between the wage rate and the investment allocation, one major constraint, representing the set of theoretically feasible $(w, I)$ policies, can be established. But behavioral considerations also enter. Thus, supplementary constraints must be added that reflect the director's estimates of the policy views of the central authorities and local workers. Against this background, an optimization problem of the usual neoclassical type emerges. That is, the director can be conceived of as maximizing his utility function subject to the set of constraints established. The solution, which yields him the greatest satisfaction consistent with the existing limitations, is given in terms of the "ideal" $(w, I)$ combination (see Furubotn and Pejovich 1970b, fig. 3). Thus, when the director is assumed to be the central figure in the formulation of enterprise policy, we see that labor management no longer leads inevitably to simple wage-maximizing behavior.

It is not necessary, however, to assume that the workers' collective is a passive constituency pulled along by a director with strong leadership qualities. There need not be any conflict between the desires of workers for higher wages and the insistence of the director on greater retained earnings and investment. In shaping the opinions of the collective, the director can emphasize, quite logically, that high rates of net investment by the firm $(I > 0)$ may be advantageous to the local workers as well as to the economy as a whole. Indeed, once workers recognize the implications of additional capital for physical productivity, they can appreciate that the best income stream *over time* may depend on the firm's investment in a growing capital stock. In short, a worker concerned with his *wealth position,* as opposed to his income level in a single period, may well vote for policies that require a positive allocation to the Business Fund and a wage rate less than the maximum attainable one.

Considering optimization over time, then, we can assume that the workers' goal is to maximize the present value of their expected earnings subject to their time preferences and expected periods of employment with the firm. Then the problem of choosing the ideal $(w, I)$ value at each period would seem to be the familiar one of balancing the attractions of current and future consumption. What makes the choice process of the labor-managed firm distinctive, however, is the fact that, under socialism, the exchange of current for future consumption is influenced by an important limitation not found in a capitalist system. Capital goods cannot be privately owned in a socialist state, and therefore workers have neither permanent nor transferable property rights in the capital increments they add to the firm's endowment through self-financed investment (via the Business Fund). Not surprisingly, this special property-rights arrangement exerts an important distorting effect on investment decisions.

Workers in a socialist labor-managed system have two major wealth-increasing alternatives.[5] First, they can invest in what may be termed "nonowned" assets. If the collective, through the Workers' Council, decides to allocate some of the firm's profits in any period to investment $I$, contemporaneous wages and consumption become lower than they would otherwise be, but additional capital goods can be purchased in which the employees have certain limited rights (by law). Specifically, the workers can expect to benefit from the enhanced future revenues and profits that the added capital should make possible. As long as the workers *remain employed by the firm*, they are in a position to realize gains through greater wage payments. Should they leave the firm, though, they lose all claims on the organization (and have no responsibilities to it). The behavioral implications of this quasi-ownership status must clearly be a shortened time horizon and a higher time preference relative to that which would prevail if the workers were granted the full right of ownership over the assets acquired by the firm during the period of their employment.

Second, investment in owned assets has to be considered as a possible alternative to enterprise-based investment. Even in a socialist economy, there are some limited opportunities for private individuals to own property and financial assets. The most significant option here lies in the area of individual savings accounts. Such accounts permit fully owned deposits to be held at state banks and to earn a positive rate of interest. It follows, then, that the collective could choose to place all of its profits each period into the Wage Fund and allow each worker to establish his own savings plan. Insofar as savings accounts are owned by depositors, it would be advantageous for the collective to concentrate on a policy of strict wage maximization unless some investment opportunities in *nonowned assets* that promised to yield returns at least as large as the return on savings accounts were available. From a theoretical viewpoint, then, what is needed is an understanding of how the returns from owned and nonowned assets can be compared in a systematic and meaningful way.

Consider a highly simplified model of the socialist labor-managed firm. We assume that all workers in the collective have identical (homogeneous degree one) preference functions and identical planning horizons. Then, if an individual expects to leave the firm in one year, the following situation holds. One dollar invested in owned assets (i.e., in a savings account) at 5 percent would yield 5 cents in interest at the end of the year. The investor would, of course, also be free to withdraw his original deposit of one dollar from the

---

5. We leave aside, at this point, the possibility of individual investment in human capital. Such investment may be subsidized heavily by the state and in any event cannot be completely controlled by government authorities or removed from the possession of the individual.

savings bank at the end of the year. Thus, considering both interest and principal, the individual can withdraw $1.05 from his account after one year. On the other hand, the same one dollar left with the firm (i.e., invested in *nonowned* assets) would have to promise the worker at least a 105 percent return in order to induce him to forego higher current wage payments and invest in the firm. Such a high rate of return on the firm's capital investment is necessary because, in a socialist economy, it is illegal to pay out capital shares.[6] The $1.05 would have to be paid out in the form of higher wage earnings—which the dollar investment in nonowned assets would, ideally, make possible. The two types of investments, the "owned" and the "nonowned," have the same present value if, for an investment period of one year and a savings bank interest rate of 5 percent (or $i = 0.05$), the rate of return $r$ on nonowned assets fulfills the equation $(1 + i) = r$, that is, if $r = 1.05$. In general, for a planning horizon of $n$ periods, the condition required for the equivalence of present values is

$$(1 + i)^n = (1 + r)^n - 1.$$

Since the interest rate $i$ prevailing at the savings bank is a known parameter, the appropriate value of $r$ can easily be found. For example, with the rate of interest on savings deposits fixed at 5 percent, the required rate of return on nonowned assets becomes roughly 18 percent, 15 percent, 10 percent, and 7 percent for planning horizons of five, six, ten, and twenty years (see Furubotn 1971b).

What is apparent is that when the planning horizon is short a very great difference is required between the rate of return on physical capital at the firm, $r$, and the interest rate, $i$, at the banks to make a worker-investor indifferent as to which type of asset he chooses. The property-rights structure established by the socialist state obviously has an impact on economic behavior. In fact, the existence of distinct types of investment alternatives, owned and nonowned, influences the collective's decisions on employment, output, the wage rate, and the rate of enterprise growth. Nevertheless, the collective can still be conceived of as making its choices, within the constraint set, so as to produce the best attainable time stream of consumption (utility) for its members.

Models of the general type just sketched are able to reach relatively straightforward conclusions because they make sweeping assumptions about the identical character of decision makers and about the information endowments of these individuals. Such simplifications may be understandable, but they do raise questions concerning the relevance of the analysis. In particular, the notion that workers have identical preferences and horizons seems to undercut one of the basic reasons advanced to justify the desirability of labor

6. Recall that the labor-managed firm has a legal obligation to maintain the value of its assets indefinitely.

management. That is, general discussions of the program often stress that this form of business organization is designed to promote industrial democracy and end labor alienation. If these latter objectives are crucial, however, it would seem that the literature should pay more attention to the internal governance system of the labor-managed firm. While the topic has not been neglected completely, there is much more to know about the way in which collective decision making proceeds within the firm and how group welfare policies are formed (see Benham and Keefer, 1991).

In an organizational setting such as the labor-managed firm, the idea that the organization's decisions are guided by one individual, or "as if" by one individual, cannot be sustained. Rather, we know that the firm's director, the Workers' Council, and the general work force all interact, to some extent, in generating policy. Once group decision making is considered, however, various questions appear. How heterogeneous is the group? Do groups decide in the same way that individuals do? What meaning can be given to the concept of maximizing group welfare? The problems here are as clear as they are extensive. From the perspective of the New Institutional Economics, though, Jensen's (1983, 327) comments on organizational objectives are probably representative of much current thinking:

Organizations do not have preferences, and they do not choose in the conscious and rational sense that we attribute to people. Anyone who has served on committees understands this fact. Usually no single person on a committee has the power to choose the outcome, and the choices that result from committee processes seldom resemble anything like the reasoned choice of a single individual.

When numbers of independent decision makers, characterized by diverse and conflicting objectives, are forced to interact (as in the Workers' Council), group maximization of utility seems to be an inappropriate concept. Indeed, pure utility maximization by any single member of the group may be impossible because under collective decision making the outcome for any one person depends on how others choose. It follows that if a stable goal function does not exist for the labor-managed firm any consistent and clear-cut objective, such as wage maximization, may simply not be attainable. The firm's behavior is perhaps best understood, then, as a reflection of the successive compromise solutions reached by the contending parties who collectively decide policy. This view of decision making under labor management may be too extreme, but there is certainly reason to believe that political processes of a sort are going to take place within the firm and affect its economic behavior. The philosophy of labor management presupposes self-government by the workers and assumes that each firm will be guided by the desires of its employees

(Horvat 1971, 99). Whether effective democratic procedures are actually implemented and sustained, however, is another matter. Given positive transaction costs, asymmetrical information, worker apathy, and other possible problems, it is not clear that voting by the collective will always be meaningful. What we can say is that an adequate theory of the self-managed firm must consider the preferences and wealth-increasing opportunities of *those individuals who are actually making economic decisions.* Note, however, that the latter group need not be the same as the total membership of the collective. Thus, if we assume that in period one a relatively homogenous majority can be formed, it is this group that will determine the policies of the firm for period two. All current members of the collective are free to vote, but individual differences among workers in respect to such characteristics as age, risk preference, time preference, length of planning horizon, and desire for on-the-job amenities must lead to different views on what actions the firm should take. It need not be easy to bring together a core group of workers whose attitudes are sufficiently similar to allow them to agree on policy. If a band of such like-minded people can coalesce, though, and if they show solidarity, the basis of political control of the firm is present.

The "original majority," as this core group of period one can be called, has an incentive to *perpetuate* its domination of policy and in this way preserve the best possible economic and "environmental" conditions for its membership. The precise set of policy alternatives open to the firm depends on various factors such as the technical conditions of production and the existing capital endowment, but, whatever the alternatives available, policies will presumably be evaluated in light of their probable consequences for the dominant decision-making group. The worker-voters who actually determine the firm's behavior are not concerned primarily with the position of workers in general but with their own welfare. This change of perspective is significant. For clearly a policy that maximizes income per worker (without regard to the particular workers involved) need not be optimal from the standpoint of the "original majority." The situation carries direct implications for the theory of the firm. The behavior predicted for the labor-managed enterprise will take one form when the maximand is income per laborer and an entirely different form when the maximand is the welfare index of a particular group of workers.

If the possibility of a dominant political group is accepted, a variant model of the labor-managed firm can be constructed readily. Under the new condition, the firm will be guided by a criterion function reflecting the preferences of the employees constituting the original majority (Furubotn 1976a). For things to go smoothly, the individuals in question will have to be in basic agreement on (1) the length of the planning horizon, (2) the general time shape of the disposable income stream that is to be generated, and (3) the economic and social environment that is to be maintained within the firm during the period of its planned operations. Many factors, of course, influence the firm's working atmosphere or environment, so consensus with respect to (3) may be difficult to achieve. At best, a delicate balancing of policy options will be required. For example, there are technical reasons why it may be desirable for the firm's labor force to expand or contract over time. From the standpoint of the original majority, however, the decision on an ideal employment level presents some difficulty. Any movement from the initial position must be considered carefully because change in the size of the collective brings about effects simultaneously in three quite different areas. For each change, then, the original majority has to assess the *costs* and *benefits* associated with (1) a production effect, (2) an environmental effect, and (3) a political effect.

In the case of an expansion of the firm's labor force, the decision makers must estimate not only the physical productivity of the labor increment but its impact on the firm's working environment (e.g., "crowding" effects) and its internal political structure. The last consideration is particularly important because change in the membership of the collective may well imply some danger to the interests of the original majority. New workers are not just factors of production but potential policymakers as well. If the new workers have different policy objectives than the original majority does, a transfer of political power and influence may occur. Voting patterns can be shifted because of the added workers and new policy directions established for the firm that are contrary to the desires of the original majority. What has to be emphasized here is that, inter alia, the labor-managed firm (like labor unions) is an arena in which political games can be played.

The multiperiod welfare function, which represents the criterion function of the original majority group, has to be maximized while the group takes account of environmental and political effects, and, of course, the maximization also has to proceed in conformity with the usual technical, economic, and institutional constraints that impose limits on the rewards the socialist labor-managed firm can provide for its members. Inevitably, there are problems. Insofar as capital increments for the firms have to be financed *exclusively* by the collective's voluntary contributions to the Business Fund, we know that some allocative distortion must occur. Moreover, the choices that the decision makers are required to make are inherently complex, and it can be questioned whether boundedly rational individuals are capable of achieving the fine policy discrimination necessary for success. In any event, the model points to the conclusion that a labor-managed firm, conducting its operations in the general way suggested earlier, will not seize all of the opportunities open for increasing wealth. The indication is that both labor and capital inputs will be restricted to levels lower than those that objective efficiency considerations would demand.

While it may seem anomalous, at first, that wealth-seeking individuals would deliberately choose to operate with factor combinations that promise lesser output per worker rather than with alternatives having greater productivity, the policy is easily explained. The choices made by the dominant majority group of the model are perfectly understandable when the role of *appropriability* is recognized. The rewards that are meaningful to these workers are the pecuniary and nonpecuniary returns that they can actually capture during their period of tenure with the firm. Having neither permanent nor transferable claims on the assets of the socialist labor-managed firm, decision makers operate with relatively short planning horizons and view economic choices in a somewhat distorted perspective.

As we have seen, the collective is free to allocate some of its profits to the Business Fund at any period in order to undertake capital accumulation. But, if such self-financing activity is inefficient because of the property-rights structure extant and if self-financing is regarded as ideologically unacceptable because it seems to move in the direction of profit and private property (Vanek 1970), it follows that the burden of financing capital investment must fall on external credit sources and, in particular, on bank credit. Such a shift to outside sources is not viewed as a bad thing, however. Various writers, including Vanek, believe that efficiency would be improved in the labor-managed system if there were exclusive reliance on bank financing of investment. It is arguable, though, that bank financing, even financing with perpetual bonds, would change nothing with respect to efficiency (Furubotn 1980).

One problem arises because a socialist government can be expected to require that each collective be scrupulous in maintaining, in perpetuity, the book value of the firm's initial capital stock and the value of any additions to it. Of course, given socialist thought and the overriding desire for economic decentralization of the labor-managed system, the rationale for the stock-maintenance rule is understandable. Specifically, it can be argued that, since the state, or society, normally endows the collective with its original capital stock and generally assists in the process of capital accumulation, the state has the right to insist that capital not be dissipated or transformed into abnormally high incomes for certain groups of workers. Moreover, basic to the ideology of the system is hostility toward nonlabor income. The belief is that, if a group of persons is earning nonlabor income, the group is exploiting others and effectively transforming social into private property (Horvat 1971, 108).

This interpretation of exploitation means, of course, that workers, as individuals or as a collective, cannot be allowed to increase their personal incomes by trading in capital goods and realizing speculative profits.[7] But,

---

7. Since workers have legal claims on the residual of the labor-managed firm, there is always a possibility that nonlabor income will be secured. Further, if the state endows a firm with capital and does not charge the collective an economic rent on this capital, nonlabor income will be realized even under conditions of long-run equilibrium.

ceteris paribus, such nonlabor income would be attainable if there were no obligation imposed on the collective to maintain the firm's capital stock. In other words, if the firm were free to vary the capital stock at will, it could use its power to borrow from the banking system to acquire capital assets for subsequent resale and thus transform itself into a type of "capitalist" enterprise. Effectively, any small group of individuals (exerting little obvious labor effort) could draw upon the savings of society for personal gain and subvert the intentions of socialist labor management.

All this may be true, but the capital-stock maintenance rule is ill designed to promote overall efficiency. Decentralized firms have freedom to buy or sell capital goods. Nevertheless, the stock-maintenance requirement, if adhered to rigorously, creates an incentive structure that militates against investment. Just as in the case of self-financed investment, voter-workers must envision quite high rates of return on potential investment projects if they are to have good economic reason to support the use of bank credit. In short, one can expect that voluntary investment in the socialist labor-managed system will be relatively restricted regardless of whether the retained earnings of the collective or bank credit is used as the means for financing capital accumulation.

In opposition to the view just expressed, it has been suggested that a central government agency might supply funds to firms via *perpetual* bonds and charge (ideally) a scarcity-reflecting interest rate for the use of such funds. Then the collective would never undertake self-financed investment, and all capital funds would be borrowed on a permanent basis from, for example, a national labor-managed agency (Vanek 1977). In principle, this approach would offset the effect of the stock-maintenance rule because the collective could always borrow rather than sacrifice current income to maintain its capital stock. Of course, to the extent that this plan functioned as desired, the system would be back to conditions that were previously condemned as conducive to "capitalist" or exploitative behavior. But the problems with the perpetual credit scheme run deeper than this. In a world of positive transaction costs, it does not seem possible for a central agency to make certain that labor-managed firms will use loan funds appropriately or ensure that they will all operate consistently with legal regulations. Certainly, any collective can have reason to use borrowed funds inefficiently. For example, if the policy-making group within a labor-managed firm has a relatively *short* planning horizon, it can be in the group's interest to invest in projects that have good near-term payoffs even though their longer-term outlook is bleak. The group in question will be gone from the firm by the time the bad economic conditions arrive, and since former employees have no obligations to the firm the investment difficulties can be left for other members of the firm to resolve.

While other questions could be raised about the role of the "national labor-management agency" in promoting sound investment, enough has perhaps been said to suggest that no easy solutions exist to the problems of a socialist labor-managed economy. We find that the property-rights structure in the system is a fundamental cause of difficulty. This is so because the ownership conditions in existence have the effect of foreshortening the planning horizons of decision makers and thus of distorting economic incentives. For self-seeking individuals, there is always advantage to be gained by shifting costs to the future and revenues to the present (Jensen and Meckling 1979; Richter 1992a). Similarly, there is reason to reconsider some of the simpler interpretations of how "industrial democracy" is implemented. Better understanding is needed of the way in which the internal politics of the labor-managed firm are played out. Ideal democratic outcomes are certainly not inevitable, and the tyranny of the majority can be real.

Even cursory study of the labor-managed firm demonstrates how great the distance is between neoinstitutionalist constructs and the traditional neoclassical models. While the latter assert that first-best Pareto efficiency can be achieved by a labor-managed system (Vanek 1970; Meade 1972; Drèze 1976), the New Institutional Economics emphasizes that results turn on the particular institutional arrangements that are in place. Moreover, the argument is that the existence of transaction costs, bounded rationality, asymmetrical information, and other factors means that, in the real world, efficiency in the sense of Pareto optimality will never be realized. It seems fair to say, then, that although improved institutional theories of labor management are needed the analysis already available provides more depth and insight into the problems of the system than do existing neoclassical theories.

### 8.8. Codetermination

During the postwar period, state-sponsored codetermination programs, designed to ensure industrial democracy and active labor participation in business decision making, have become increasingly important in Western Europe.[8] While Germany has had the most experience with this form of industrial organization, other European states have enacted codetermination legislation,[9]

---

8. Since 1970, the Commission of the European Community has prepared a number of drafts of legal regulations for a proposed new entity—the European Corportation or Societas Europea (SE). In the arrangements suggested so far, codetermination would have a prominent role. However, there has been some controversy over the form codetermination provisions should take, and no final agreement on the structure of the European Corporation has yet been reached.

9. There is considerable variety in the provisions of codetermination legislation enacted in European countries. Thus, for example, the supervisory board of a corporation must have as much as half of its membership composed of labor representatives in Germany, while the requirement in Austria and Denmark is only one-third. Moreover, in the Netherlands, France, and Sweden, the requirement for labor participation is met when just a few worker-representatives sit on the board.

and even in the United States some interest has been shown in participatory arrangements—for example, the Corporate Democracy Act of 1980 was discussed in Congress but failed to gain approval.[10] Given the significance of the "codetermined firm," then, it is not surprising that a substantial literature has grown up around the topic.[11] The objective of this section, however, is not to attempt a general survey of existing writings on codetermination but rather to show how the analytical techniques associated with the New Institutional Economics can be used to explore the nature and behavior of the codetermined enterprise.

What has to be emphasized at the outset, of course, is that a number of different models of the codetermined firm are conceivable, with each variant linked to a different set of assumptions concerning the technical, economic, and political environment in which the firm operates. Thus, before any assessment can be made of the "efficiency" or other characteristics of a codetermined firm, it is essential to define *codetermination* and specify precisely what type of codetermined firm is being studied. In a fundamental sense, codetermination can be defined as an organizational mode that ensures labor of having legally sanctioned control rights in the firm. Since ultimate decision-making power within a capitalist firm is supposed to reside at the board level, codetermination means that workers must be given at least some seats on the firm's board of directors (or supervisory board). It is true, of course, that the codetermined firm tends to be a complex entity and possesses other characteristics in addition to labor representation. Nevertheless, the essential and determining feature of the codetermined firm is its provision for the partitioning of control rights among different groups of resource owners. If the representatives of both labor and capital take part in the firm's decision-making processes at the board level, the firm is codetermined. If this joint participation does not occur, the firm is not codetermined. It is clear, therefore, that the scheme goes beyond potentially inconsequential forms of labor involvement or the use of participation as a personnel management technique.

Insofar as control rights in the firm are allocated to both labor and capital under codetermination, it is apparent that the traditional pattern of rights, as found in the "classical" capitalist firm, is violated. Thus, a question of interest to economists is whether the changed organizational structure would ever be selected voluntarily by decision makers concerned with wealth maximization

---

For a comprehensive report on the different institutional arrangements of codetermination in Europe, see EIRR (1990).

    10. See Green et al. (1979) for a discussion of the Corporate Democracy Act of 1980.

    11. Some early works assessing the codetermination movement in Europe includes Backhaus (1979), Batstone and Davies (1976), and Pejovich (1978). A more recent report on the state of industrial democracy in Europe is found in IDE (1993).

or whether codetermination is an organizational form that must be imposed by government. This topic has been considered by writers of the New Institutionalist School, and we now know that even in a free system there are circumstances in which codetermination may emerge as the choice of individuals seeking efficient organizational structure. The case for labor participation at the board level rests ultimately on the understanding that conditions in the contemporary world differ significantly from those assumed in the standard neoclassical model. As a practical matter, it is obvious that workers normally do not enjoy costless or near-costless mobility. Consequently, an ordinary "at will" employment contract may no longer be sufficient to induce workers to join a firm. If, in order to function productively within an enterprise, workers have to accumulate, and pay for, firm-specific capital assets, the simple neoclassical logic fails. A different organizational structure than that of the "classical" capitalist firm (Alchian and Demsetz 1972, 782–83) would seem to be needed.

An alternative institutional arrangement, which could deal with the problems noted, would have to take into consideration the fact that there are often two types of capital owners of a corporation—namely, the owners of firm-specific real capital and the owners of firm-specific human capital (the employees of the organization). It is arguable that the latter, the worker-investors who have supplied one part of the total capital stock needed by the firm for production, should also be regarded as equity holders and thus be granted control and income rights in the enterprise. This would be the case of voluntary codetermination in which "industrial democracy" is freely chosen on efficiency grounds.

We know, of course, that codetermination may also be established through legislation that is enacted in order to achieve certain social goals. In this case, all or most firms are required by law to maintain codetermined organization, as in Germany.[12] Certainly, the type of codetermined firm encountered most frequently in practice is this legally mandated variant. From the standpoint of the New Institutional Economics, though, the most important matter is to understand the differences between the incentive structure of the legally mandated and the voluntary codetermined firm. The following pages will deal with this question. In the first section, we describe a model of an idealized voluntary codetermined firm and in the second a stylized model of a legally mandated codetermined enterprise. These two sections follow closely Furubotn (1988). The last section deals with the so-called labor-owned firm. Here, consideration is given to the problems of a voluntary organization of workers, such as the modern law firm.

---

12. See the German Codetermination Law of 1976 (Gesetz über die Mitbestimmung der Arbeitnehmer [Mitbestimmungsgesetz—Mitbest G] May 4, 1976, BGB1.IS.1153).

## 8.8.1. The Voluntary Codetermined Firm

It is essential to recognize that workers who undertake durable, firm-specific investments commit themselves to the firm for a relatively lengthy period into the future and are therefore vulnerable. The distribution of the firm's quasi rents and the value of labor assets can be affected by the behavior of other members of the coalition. Hence, the possibility exists that worker-investors, if unprotected by institutional or contractual safeguards, may be exploited and suffer serious economic injury. It follows, moreover, that precisely how worker-investors choose to protect their investments can influence the efficiency with which the firm operates.

The modern theory of the firm indicates that all resource owners holding firm-specific assets bear risk and can experience uncompensated loss. It is for this reason that these owners have a particular desire to possess control rights in the firm. Alchian has explained the situation as follows:

The people who direct and manage a coalition are those who own the resources specific to the coalition. Owners of those resources have the most to lose by failure of the coalition. They have a greater incentive to manage or be responsible for the management of the coalition. The so-called stockholders are not less risk averse than (other coalition members); instead owners of the coalition-specific resources want to be the managers more than do owners of the general resources. While it is true that uncertainty and risk are present, stockholders or managers do not bear that risk in order to be motivated. Instead risk is inevitable, and those who bear it have the greater incentives to control and manage. (1984, 42–43)

Under this logic, the argument for labor participation is straightforward. Since worker-investors provide part of the total stock of firm-specific capital, there is reason to accept them as equity holders and give them income and control rights in the firm. In short, such workers should be viewed as "partners" and treated in the same general way as any other owners of firm-specific assets.

Codetermination represents a type of governance structure that is capable of dealing with maximizing agents who have conflicting objectives. In consequence, it appears that such an organization may be useful in resolving the problems that arise when not all of the coalition-specific resources are owned by a single party. And, clearly, common ownership is not possible in cases in which firm-specific human capital is involved. But, if firm-specific human capital is subject to different treatment than that accorded to firm-specific physical capital, serious disputes can easily occur about the apportioning of the coalition's gains or losses and about the long-term policies to be pursued by the enterprise. These considerations are important because they relate directly to the rationale for the voluntary codetermined firm. By allowing each worker undertaking reliance investment to join the firm as a "partner" and residual risk bearer, all owners of firm-specific capital are placed on the same footing. In effect, the firm assumes "ownership" of the firm-specific human capital and gives each worker-investor a share in the firm's net cash flows according to a definite formula. That is, residual reward is proportional to the amount of firm-specific investment made. Moreover, by allocating control rights to labor on the same proportional basis, information about the firm is shared equally among all coalition members, and all interests can be protected to some extent in the firm's decision-making process. The general result is that in the voluntary codetermined firm certain agency costs that would otherwise exist are obviated, and incentives for cooperation and productivity tend to be enhanced.

Optimal contracting may require the firm to "own," rather than lease, firm-specific human capital. We know, however, that contracts calling for the leasing of labor services are routine in industry. More concretely, it should be understood that if a hired worker bears the cost of accumulating firm-specific human capital, he places himself in the position of one who leases an asset to a firm. Then, any reward for the investment must be secured from a contractual wage that is paid over the lease interval or paid as long as the worker is employed by the firm. The wage stream paid by the firm compensates the worker for the time he spends on the job each period and, under ideal (and unlikely) conditions, provides, over time, for principal recovery and an appropriate rate of return on the worker's capital investment. The important thing to be noted for organizational choice, however, is that, under this type of (human) capital-leasing arrangement, transaction costs need not be low. That is, there are significant costs that will be incurred by the worker if he acts to protect his investment and attempts to ensure a proper return on sunk capital. In practice, of course, a trade union may be the main instrument used by workers to monitor and enforce contractual agreements and to guard against opportunistic behavior by other members of the coalition of resource owners. It is no secret, though, that the operation of a union involves costs. Time and resources must be committed to its activities, and insofar as strikes take place production losses and third-party losses are inevitable.

The significance of human-capital leasing will be considered further in the next section (8.8.2), where the efficiency characteristics of the mandatory codetermined firm and the voluntary codetermined firm will be compared. But, before proceeding to this analysis, it will be useful to review, in some detail, the main organizational features of the voluntary, or "joint investment," type of codetermined enterprise. Thus:

1. Workers will be granted control rights and income rights in proportion to their total investment in firm-specific assets. The objective is to treat

such workers in much the same way as any other investors. Some difficulties will exist, however, in deciding the terms on which investment in human capital is translated into shares going to labor. Valuation will be especially troublesome when there is no general market for the shares of the corporation. Moreover, because of the changing significance of marginal contributions of capital, workers joining the firm at later dates (i.e., after the firm is a going concern) may have to receive relatively fewer shares of stock per dollar invested in firm-specific assets than those who joined the firm earlier.

2. The joint investment firm will employ workers with the understanding that they will be retained over a specified contract interval $T$ unless unforeseen events make layoffs absolutely unavoidable. The interval $T$ may be quite long, but beyond horizon $T$ new contracts have to be established.

3. During the period of the contract, mutual obligations exist between the firm and a worker. Thus, a worker is expected to supply labor services to the firm over the contract interval while simultaneously investing in firm-specific human capital. On the other side, the worker can anticipate certain rewards through period $T$. In theory, labor compensation can be separated into three distinct streams. (a) the contractual wage payments $(w_t, t = 1, 2, \ldots , T)$ that must go to a worker, without fail, during each period because of the opportunity he has to be employed as a "general" input in other sectors of the economy (the wage rate, $w_t$, represents the opportunity cost of the worker's time); (b) the per period payments that take account of the depreciation of the worker's firm-specific assets and permit the principal invested by the worker to be recovered over time; (c) the per period payments representing the worker's share of the normal and extranormal profits that may accrue to the firm in each period. Only the reward component noted in (a) must be forthcoming each period. Since the worker in a joint investment firm is an equity holder and residual risk bearer, rewards via components (b) and (c) cannot be assured.

4. A worker who voluntarily leaves the firm before the end of period $T$ forfeits all claims under (a), (b), and (c) because he (necessarily) takes his human capital with him when he departs. For its part, the firm may lay off a worker if conditions force it to do so. However, any dismissed worker retains his rights to rewards under points (b) and (c). The rationale here is that, as an investor who acted in good faith, the displaced worker should retain his investment claim on the firm. The effect of this provision is to make the firm consider layoffs very carefully.

5. A worker in the joint investment firm is denied transfer rights in the

property rights he holds in the firm. The reasons for this provision are straightforward. First, if a worker were allowed to sell his control rights in the firm to outsiders, all workers could do the same thing, and the firm would no longer be codetermined in the sense that its employees provide input for decision making. Even if only some workers were willing or able to sell their control rights to others, an unfavorable situation would be created. Since control rights permit their holders to have access to sensitive information about the firm, and to influence policy, control rights in the hands of outsiders could lead to difficulties. Second, a worker is prohibited from selling his income rights under (b) and (c) to others because such a sale would tend to reduce the worker's incentive to cooperate in the activities of the firm. In general, if many workers transferred their income rights to outsiders, a serious change in atmosphere would be likely to emerge. That is, workers with no further hope of profit sharing would have much less incentive to avoid shirking, refrain from seeking nonpecuniary benefits, accept existing work rules and the work environment, and so on.

In summary, then, we can say the following about the joint investment type of codetermined firm. Such an organizational form presupposes that labor will undertake significant investment in firm-specific human capital. In return for this sacrifice on the part of labor, the firm (or coalition of resource owners) is willing to grant labor (1) finite, nonmarketable shares in the enterprise in numbers commensurate with the magnitude of labor's investment and (2) the right to representation on the firm's board of directors and the opportunity to help shape the policies of the firm. Finally, it can be noted that if there is no self-financed investment by labor the joint investment model turns into something akin to the classical capitalist firm.

### 8.8.2. Mandatory and Voluntary Codetermination: A Comparison

Having described the essential characteristics of the voluntary or joint investment firm, this type of codetermined business organization can now be compared with a stylized model of the mandatory codetermined firm. There is interest in such a comparison, of course, because of the growing importance of codetermination programs in the Western world. Inter alia, we should like to know in what way, if any, the voluntary firm's organizational structure is superior to that of the legally mandated codetermined firm. And, following the neoinstitutional approach, it is feasible to use comparative institutional analysis to shed some light on the matter. To proceed, then, what is needed is a basic characterization of the mandatory firm.

For simplicity, we say that the structure of such a firm can be summarized as follows: (1) major control rights are assigned to labor regardless of whether workers have undertaken any coalition-specific investments; (2) workers receive compensation in the form of wages, are given no formal income rights in the firm, and normally do not share directly in the firm's residual; (3) workers are not free to transfer any of their property rights in the firm to others; (4) the rights allocated to labor under this form of codetermination go on indefinitely (no specific contract period exists); (5) while long-term job security may be a desideratum of the program, the law provides only for advance warning of job termination and for severance pay; and (6) workers who leave a firm voluntarily can expect to suffer losses in the value of any investments they have made in coalition-specific assets. Given the content of (1) through (6), it seems reasonable to say that mandatory codetermination is concerned primarily with corporate governance and the maintenance of an environment conducive to industrial democracy.

This sketch of the mandatory codetermined firm is satisfactory for purposes of general discussion, but it should be understood that applied institutional analysis normally requires a more precise description of institutional structure. The type of detailed information needed is suggested by the following account of key legal provisions in the German Codetermination Law of 1976 (MitbestG). Section 7 of the MitbestG determines that the Supervisory Board (Aufsichtsrat) of a corporation[13] has to include the same number of workers' representatives as shareholders'—excluding the chairman of the board who may serve, if need be, as a tiebreaker. Thus, for example, the supervisory board of a corporation of no more than ten thousand employees consists as a rule of six representatives of equity holders and workers each, plus the chairman. Note that the German corporation (Aktiengesellschaft) has a two-tiered structure with a supervisory board (Aufsichtsrat) and a managing board (Vorstand). Members of the managing board cannot also be members of the supervisory board.[14]

Returning to the stylized model, we note that the codetermined firm being studied is a more or less conventional corporation subject to the legal require-

---

13. Besides *Aktiengesellschaften* also *Kommanditgesellschaften auf Aktien, Gesellschaften mit beschraenkter Haftung, bergrechtliche Gewerkschaften mit eigener Rechtspersoenlichkeit, Erwerbs-und Wirtschaftsgenossenschaften* (sec. 29 MitbestG)—though as a rule, with more than two thousand employees (sec. 1, MitbestG).

14. Initially, the rules pertaining to codetermination in the regulation drafts for the European Corporation followed existing German codetermination law closely. These rules were later modified and "defused," though, because of the apparent impossibility of gaining acceptance for them by the Council of Ministers. Thus, the draft of 1989 provides for three different codetermination models. The first of these comes closest to replicating German law, and according to this model at least one-third, or at most one-half, of the board members must be employees of the European Corporation or their representatives (COM [89]268–SYN 219).

ment of maintaining labor participation. Significantly, it hires labor at a wage rate arrived at through industry-union bargaining and thus is a form of business organization that requires the firm to rent, rather than own, the firm-specific assets associated with labor. In other words, the reward going to a worker for his labor services and his investment in human capital is all contained in the contractual wage rate $(r_t)$ that is established through bargaining. But, as suggested earlier, this arrangement seems to be inefficient. Compared with the legally imposed form of codetermination found in Europe, the joint investment firm shows certain preferable features. Arguably, the voluntary codetermined firm tends to promote (1) productivity-enhancing incentives, (2) relatively low transaction costs, and (3) rational allocation of risk. The justification for these claims rests on the following considerations:

1.  When workers have an investment stake in the firm, there is at least some likelihood that they will have common interest with conventional stockholders in increasing the firm's profitability during its operations to the contract horizon $T$. In this type of firm, workers acquiring firm-specific human capital are well aware that they are making long-term investment decisions. Moreover, labor has, via their representatives on the board, full information about the economic position and policies of the firm. Indeed, control rights even permit labor to affect the policies of the firm. Therefore, reasons exist for workers to display attitudes that are favorable to enterprise productivity. Specifically, the incentive structure extant conduces to greater work effort, lower monitoring costs, improved communication between labor and management within the firm, reduced labor turnover and absenteeism, lesser insistence on costly nonpecuniary benefits and work rules, and so on.
2.  Insofar as workers secure all of their pecuniary rewards through a multiperiod wage agreement $(r_t, t = 1, 2, \ldots, H)$ reached within the firm via union bargaining, there are inevitably recurrent costs attached to renewing, adjusting, monitoring, and enforcing the agreement. With this type of contractual arrangement, which is characteristic of mandatory codetermination, conflict and bargaining can be anticipated over time. Since no definite formula exists to define the extent of labor's compensation for making firm-specific investments in a world of uncertainty, opportunistic behavior must be expected. Each party has motivation to secure the most favorable division of the firm's residual that it can. Thus, workers are not assured of obtaining a normal return on their investment (even if economic conditions for the firm are good) unless they pursue their interests aggressively. In short, pecuniary rewards to labor at any cross section of time need not be tied closely to the actual market success or failure of the firm. Rewards can be smaller

or larger than investment warrants and do not change synchronously with changes in the general economic environment.

What is being discussed here are the usual problems encountered in long-term contracting and in the absence of effective relational exchange. That is, decisions must be taken under conditions of incomplete initial information. Further, new information emerges asymmetrically over time and the contracting agents display self-interested, opportunistic behavior. Difficulties exist both for the original formulation of contracts and for contract-adjustment rules. It follows that mandatory codetermination schemes relying on such wage agreements will tend to have relatively high transaction costs (including third-party costs).[15] By contrast, the joint investment firm can avoid the consequences of repeated rounds of strategic bargaining. Thus, total transaction costs associated with employment, while not zero, should be comparatively low in the joint investment case.

3. In the joint investment firm, all resource owners share the risks of production for an uncertain market in a rational and equitable fashion. The sharing rule used for the division of the firm's residual is definite and based on the magnitude of the investment an individual has made in the firm. This arrangement seems appropriate because only individuals who take investment risks in the firm, and are affected significantly by the firm's economic performance, have good reason to be guaranteed a share in the firm's residual or granted authority in decision making. The argument here is not related simply to the issue of "fairness" but to the likely behavior that will be undertaken if this reward principle is violated. For example, when workers are free to influence enterprise decisions but have no investment in the firm, they are in a position to disregard profit maximization (or productive efficiency) and are able to appropriate a greater or lesser portion of stockholders' wealth.

In general, one can say that there are significant advantages to having worker-investors participate in the firm's residual on a systematic basis. However, the typical codetermination program operative today (e.g., German codetermination) ignores this arrangement. Legally imposed programs, as we know them, do not provide consistent and clearly defined guidelines for rewarding labor for making firm-specific investments. Costly ad hoc solutions tend to emerge instead as conventional stockholders and workers effectively contend for shares in the residual. Moreover, apart from other deficiencies, this

---

15. Various dimensions of the employment contract other than the wage rate may require adjustment. Thus, controversy (and transaction costs) can be generated by a number of factors and the wage rate cannot be the only focus of attention (see Furubotn 1985).

procedure leads to more employment instability than is necessary. By contrast, the joint investment firm has certain advantages in maintaining even employment because outlays on labor fall in depressed times and rise in prosperous times. The sharing rule makes sense at several levels.

The obvious question that arises at this point is why the voluntary or "joint investment" firm, if it is so efficient, is not a more widely used form of business organization in the industrial sectors of modern economies. No definitive answer can be given here, but one factor that would seem to be significant relates to labor's motivations. Thus, a possible theoretical argument is that workers regard income variability as unattractive and believe that by accepting contractually defined wage payments they can insure themselves (for a price) against income fluctuations that the firm's equity holders assume completely (see sec. 5.4 on implicit contracts). This reasoning, however, is only partially correct. Any contractual wage program is likely to lead to at least some variation in labor income over time (via contractual changes and such devices as "givebacks"). Moreover, in the absence of strong job security arrangements, variations in employment can occur.

Another explanation for the dearth of "joint investment" firms is this: organized workers may assume that effort and resources devoted to rent-seeking behavior designed to affect government policy will yield them greater benefits than will private negotiations over property-rights allocations with a joint investment firm. If successful, interest group pressure on government can bring about changes in the law that grant concessions to the petitioning group. Reliance on strong national unions can play a role here, of course. Historically, labor has been able to secure via statute various advantages without any corresponding obligation to show worker investment in firm-specific assets. By contrast, the situation is quite different in the voluntary codetermined firm. Control and income rights are allocated only in proportion to the value of the self-financed investments undertaken by labor. Therefore, unless such investment is large, labor's influence will be relatively modest, and workers may find it expedient to rely more on political and union activities.

### 8.8.3. The Labor-Owned Firm

Close approximations to the idealized joint investment firm are actually found in a few professional fields such as law and engineering. In the literature, these kinds of organizations are often referred to as "labor-owned" firms. Thus, a typical labor-owned firm is the modern law firm. Such an organization is in many ways the quintessential high-quality service firm, a firm in which the only significant input is human capital. As Gilson and Mnookin say: "It is the dominance of human capital, we believe, that is the major determinant of law firm organization" (1989, 594). But a complete explanation of the labor-owned firm in the service sector has to involve more than a discussion of capital. Certain window- and room-cleaning companies are service firms with low capital intensity. Presumably, it is the employment of highly skilled, difficult to monitor labor that has significance. As was pointed out earlier, resource owners with firm-specific investments should have control or residual decision rights and be the "owners" of the firm. However, the skills of lawyers are, in general, not highly firm specific. What is firm specific is the lawyers' investment in the brand-name capital of the firm. A good reputation for the firm derives from high-quality advice to clients, and this, in turn, can be assured by good monitoring.

Brand-name capital serves as a signal that ex post collusive agreements between monitors (the senior owners of the law firm) and legal specialists (the young associates and employees) to the disadvantage of clients are uneconomic (Carr and Mathewson 1990, 308). Since the senior partners of the law firm have the greatest stake in the firm-specific, brand-name capital, compensation is understandably tied to seniority. In general, the institutional arrangements of the labor-owned firm are explained in terms of two themes that have been given much attention in the New Institutional Economics—namely, the incentives for efficient monitoring and the role of firm-specific investment in determining property-rights structure. Relative to the modern law firm, Carr and Mathewson (328) offer the following conclusions:

> Moral hazard issues arise when suppliers of the service are more knowledgeable than their clients. Monitoring, coupled with an appropriate distribution of ownership rights on a firm's reputational capital, can create lower-price services to clients and efficient dissonance between the objectives of the firm's owners to guarantee protection of client's interests. By creating joint specific or brand-name capital that is at risk, lawyers in partnerships bond themselves to deliver honestly their professional services. What is critical is that monitors' self-interest coincide with client's. This may require monitors to own substantial portions of their firm's brand-name capital. In this case senior law partners who hold a proportionally greater interest in firms should also serve as principal managers of clients' accounts (the case for most large law firms).

More could be said about the labor-owned firm and the way that its particular institutional arrangements influence outcomes. Enough has been done, however, to suggest that, while this type of business organization is similar to the joint investment firm examined earlier, it has its own distinctive properties. This point concerning differences has importance for institutional analysis generally. We find that economic behavior is often quite sensitive to smallish changes in institutional structure. Normally, no single model, but a number of variant models, explain events in a given area such as codetermination or the professional services firm. If a given organization is to be analyzed, it is necessary to establish the precise structure of the organization and the implications of that structure for transaction costs, incentives, information flows, risk allocation, and so on. With some ingenuity, it is possible to demonstrate how the institutional arrangements of a firm affect its economic behavior and to assess how well the arrangements are able to solve the problems faced by the firm. Nevertheless, since the New Institutional Economics does not provide us with a clearly defined efficiency standard comparable to that found in neoclassical theory, comparative institutional analysis is essentially an open-ended exercise. Diversity in the economic realm is recognized, and thus it should not be surprising to discover that multiple solutions may exist for any given problem. All this may not represent the most satisfying situation for theory, but it seems inevitable once we move away from the oversimplified neoclassical construct.

Before concluding the discussion of the firm, it will be useful to consider a number of novel technical themes that have been introduced into the NIE literature in recent years. These contributions suggest that economic analysis will have to move even further from the traditional neoclassical model of the firm if truly satisfactory explanations of enterprise behavior are to be achieved. It has been noted, for example, that in the manufacturing sector, technological developments, especially those related to modern computing procedures, have forced major changes in the way that firms undertake production. Thus, as Milgrom and Roberts say:

> Manufacturing is undergoing a revolution. The mass production model is being replaced by a vision of a flexible multiproduct firm that emphasizes quality and speedy response to market conditions while utilizing technologically advanced equipment and new forms of organization. (1990, 511)

What is pointed out is that the new production technology permits firms to use very short production runs and allows quick shifts in production from one product to another. Further, the possibility of employing computers in designing and manufacturing commodities leads to integrated production arrangements and tends to reduce the time cycle of commodity development. The consequences of computer-aided operations within the firm even spill over into the marketing area. The new economic conditions in the world require firms to be nimble and responsive to demand shifts. Therefore, it is important that information be available quickly about the success of a firm's products in the market. To the extent that sales can be monitored and assessed accurately by computers, the firm is able to modify both the design of its commodities and the composition of its product line. Ideally, the result of such action will be production that is very closely geared to demand. Then, the firm's inventory levels can be minimized and something akin to customized products can be purveyed to the public.

From the standpoint of the New Institutional Economics, the existence of high-speed computational capabilities in a system suggests that some transaction costs in that system will be relatively low. And, in such an environment, the real-life behavior of a firm can supposedly approach more closely the hypothetical behavior envisioned for the pure rental firm. That is, in a frictionless neoclassical economy, an entrepreneur is able to undertake production while operating merely as a contract monitor and coordinator of activity. But some writers argue that, in the modern world of the computer, the contemporary businessman will soon be in a similar position (if he is not already in one). Thus, the concept of the virtual firm is broached. Presumably, the modern entrepreneur is free to contract for whatever services he needs (or wishes to sell) via the information net. He can, for example, secure financial and marketing services as required or sell off any excess plant capacity or material stocks he may have available. Moreover, he is able to carry out all such transactions quickly and drift into and out of the production of a commodity almost at will.

Based on this line of reasoning, Milgrom and Roberts (1990b) assert that production decisions today are best made *across systems of organizations* or suboperations. The argument is that the efficient firm chooses organizational form, technology, and input quantities *simultaneously*. In particular, the firm does not take enterprise organization and technology as given and then select appropriate factor inputs in the manner suggested by neoclassical theory. This conclusion is interesting, in part, because it is generally consistent with recent criticism of the neoclassical production function (Furubotn 1996). The orthodox production function is said to have severe limitations because it is derived on the assumption that the determination of the best, or most efficient, utilization of any specified input combination is a *technical,* not an economic, problem. In other words, the focus is exclusively on finding those technical processes or organizational modes that can secure the *maximum* commodity output from any given input mix. Thus, while the neoclassical approach recognizes that any input combination can be utilized with many different technological arrangements and operated at many different intensity levels, the selection procedure for the production function is such that only the output-maximizing technical alternatives are retained for consideration. But this derivation procedure is defensible if and only if the prices of inputs are completely independent of the technical process employed—that is, of the way in which the inputs are utilized in production. If input prices vary systematically with the firm's actual technical and social organization, as industrial experience indicates that they do, the production function is in general an inadequate guide to profit maximization.

The explanation here is straightforward. If input prices change when inputs are subjected to different technical or organizational treatment within the firm, it can no longer be true that the firm's best interests are always served by trying to secure the maximum commodity output from given inputs. Insofar as the firm's objective is *profit maximization,* it will frequently be advantageous for the firm to choose a technical or organizational arrangement that produces *less than maximum output.* Since effective input prices tend to be highest when they are utilized in a forced-draft production situation designed to achieve maximum output, it can be profitable for the firm to accept somewhat lesser physical output (and potential revenue) in order to secure *comparatively greater* savings on the outlays for inputs. In other words, given the kind of input price variation noted, the orthodox production function is unsatisfactory. What is needed for optimization (profit maximization) is information about *all of the options represented in the production set.*

As we have seen, Milgrom and Roberts argue that the new technological conditions in manufacturing require the firm to choose organizational form and technology simultaneously. This idea is consistent with the analysis just presented because, inter alia, organizational form affects input costs, and the options specified in the production set reflect all of the different technical/organizational arrangements that exist for utilizing inputs. Thus, it might be found that a particular organizational mode that gives substantial control rights in the firm to labor reduces productivity but leads to even greater reduction in effective labor costs. Further, by determining the most profitable organizational arrangement at every point in input space and then selecting from among these solutions the optimum optimorum, the ideal *input levels* could be found along with the best technical process and best enterprise organization. This approach seems to broadly parallel the one Milgrom and Roberts have in mind when they discuss how the virtual firm might operate (1990b), but it is much simpler and does not involve the lattice-theoretic optimization mathematics called for by the Milgrom-Roberts model.

In any case, it should be emphasized that in assessing the usefulness of any theory of the firm, due consideration has to be given to all of the information requirements implied by the theory. Thus, to the extent that an optimal decision can be reached at all in a neoinstitutionalist world, we know that it can only be determined after the costs of reaching the decision have been fully taken into account. It must also be recognized, of course, that once the question of optimization costs is brought up, further questions appear about what modes of information-gathering and decision-making behavior should be used to discover options and choose among them. Section 10.2 will take up this and other issues connected with the evaluation of enterprise models, but it can be observed at this point that neither the standard neoclassical model nor the emerging theory of the virtual firm appears to have given adequate attention to information and decision problems.

Finally, to sum up the approach taken in this chapter, we should say this: no attempt has been made to present a comprehensive view of contemporary theories of the firm—or even to present all of the leading neoinstitutionalist models. The particular examples singled out for discussion have not been chosen because they reflect unexceptionable analysis or are necessarily superior to other existing alternatives. Rather, the models were selected because they seemed to be capable of showing how New Institutional Economics ideas can be applied to questions of the firm and of giving some sense of how neoinstitutional analysis has developed over time. Insofar as a great variety of enterprise models are conceivable, the important thing is to understand how basic neoinstitutionalist themes can be put together in different ways to explain behavior. Hopefully, the chapter contributes to this objective.

## 8.9.  The New Institutional Economics of the Firm: Forerunners and First Steps

Classical theory proper had no theory of the firm (Blaug 1958, 226). Consequently, the appearance of the neoclassical theory of the firm (precisely described by Debreu (1959)) represented some progress. Yet the neoclassical approach, with its focus on purely technical relationships, proceeded on a highly abstract plane, and thus ignored many of the most important aspects of firm behavior.

Early studies in which the firm is understood as a transactional structure involving individual agents were made by Commons (1934) and Knight (1922). As mentioned in chapter 3, the "transaction" represented for Commons the basic unit of economic analysis. For him, a transaction was a two-sided, joint action of individuals, the terms of which were freely agreed upon by the participants (1934, 21). Knight (1922) emphasized, in addition to the two-sidedness of transactions, the possibility of "slippages" in commitments and performance. The term used by Knight represents a nice circumlocution for opportunism, and the basic idea was amplified in his famous remark:

With human nature as we know it, it would be impractical or very unusual for one man to guarantee to another a definite result of the latter's action without given power to direct his work. On the other hand the second party would not place itself under the direction of the first without such a guarantee. The result is a "double contract" . . . (270)

Coase's work on the firm (1937) really began what has come to be known as the New Institutional Economics or its sibling the New Economics of Organization. An early and important contributor to this line of investigation was Barnard, whose book *The Functions of the Executive* (1938, 1962) had a considerable influence on organization theory. Barnard's conclusions in chapter 18 of his volume include a list of basic organizational problems that, to date, remain to be solved. He complained: "There is no science of organization or cooperative systems . . . " (290). Interestingly, the New Economics of Organization tries to meet Barnard's ambitious objective (Williamson 1993a, 36).

Chandler (1977) studied the history of the modern multiunit enterprise, administered by a set of salaried middle and top managers, in an effort to understand the role of business organization. He traces the development of the modern corporate firm and gives an interpretation of "why the visible hand of management replaced the invisible hand of market mechanism" (6). In Chandler's view, organizational capabilities, and the possibility of learning by doing, provide the basis for the continuing growth of firms in the new capital-intensive oligopolistic industries. As he says, the

> swift and dramatic success of the German and American integrated companies or their less integrated British rivals in the last decades before World War I demonstrates how the creation of organizational capabilities through the initial investment in production and distribution permitted first-movers in the new and transformed industries of this Second Industrial Revolution—chemicals, electrical equipment, light and heavy machinery and metals—to conquer world markets quickly and to raise powerful barriers to subsequent entrance. (90)

Among the authors who are dissatisfied with the neoclassical theory of the firm, besides neoinstitutionalists proper, are Simon (1957) who introduced the concept of bounded rationality and satisficing, and Cyert and March (1963), who worked on intrafirm coalitions in hierarchical structures. Also to be mentioned is the early work on the managerial theory of the firm by Baumol (1959) and Williamson (1963) in which management is assumed to pursue nonpecuniary rewards (see chap. 5). For a historic review of the theory of the modern corporation, see, for example, the survey by Williamson (1981); for a broader, more inclusive review, see, Archibald (1987).

### 8.10.  The New Institutional Economics of the Firm: Summary and Main Literature beyond Coase

There are various ways to classify the main literature on the firm that came after Coase (1937) and extended the basic neoinstitutionalist analysis of productive organizations. One possibility is to distinguish between the firm as a network of contracts when (1) it utilizes no firm-specific assets and (2) when firm-specific assets do exist. Asymmetric information can play a role in both situations.

1. In an important article, Alchian and Demsetz (1972) presented a theory of the owner-monitor. That is, for the classical capitalist firm, wherein the owner-manager has exclusive claim on the firm's residual, the owner-manager has strong incentive to monitor the performance of inputs accurately, and in a world of costless transactions he can do just that. Of course, the problem becomes more complicated when asymmetrical information is present. Jensen and Meckling (1976) emphasized the nexus of contract view of organizations and introduced what Jensen (1983, 334) called the "positive theory of agency." Here, team members are monitored by management, which is separated from the owners. The central problem is then the separation of ownership and control, and the concept of agency costs becomes significant. This strand of the literature was continued by Fama (1980). The main points made in his article are that the separation of security ownership and enterprise control can be explained as an efficient form of economic organization, and mechanisms exist in a capitalist economy to prevent agents from greatly exploiting principals. This view was taken further by Fama and Jensen (1983), who argued that the separation of ownership and control via agency had the effect of separating the risk-bearing and decision functions of business. Moreover, such an arrangement was deemed desirable on efficiency grounds. It survives, in part at least, because of the benefits inherent in specialization—with management specializing in decision making (and monitoring) and owners focusing on risk bearing.

2. The literature, of course, recognized that the presence of specific assets plays a crucial role in determining organization. Williamson early mentioned the "idiosyncratic attributes of transactions" and noted that asset specificity may represent a reason for vertical integration (1971). Later, Williamson, Wachter, and Harris (1975) discussed the problem of job idiosyncracy as a special problem affecting employment relations within the firm. As a practical matter, relational contracting tends to occur in situations in which specific asset problems are encountered. Williamson (1979, 244) noted: "The general argument is that special governance structures supplant standard market-cum-classical contract exchange when transaction-specific values are great. Idiosyncratic, commercial, labor and family relationships are specific examples." In a subsequent work, Williamson (1985, 52) establishes what he regards as the principal dimensions of transactions: specificity, uncertainty, and frequency. Then, he adds: "The first is the most important and most distinguishes transaction-cost economics from other treatments of economic organization, but the other two play significant roles."

Klein, Crawford, and Alchian (1978) argue in similar fashion and point out that the owners of firm-specific assets must protect themselves against opportunism by other team members by adopting appropriate forms of governance (or other measures). The argument is general and, as the authors show, applies to specific human capital, leasing, franchising, and social institutions. Joskow (1985a) offers support to Williamson's specificity hypothesis by presenting pertinent empirical examples.

Grossmann and Hart (1986) introduced a formal theory of incomplete contracts (see sec. 5.5) that applies to the firm. This was conceived as a "property-rights approach to the firm" (Hart 1989, 1765), and, indeed, the ideas contained were analogous to those developed by Alchian and the literary property-rights school. The Grossman-Hart argument turns on the notion of residual decision rights. Ownership is understood in the sense of the possession of these rights—rights that make possible efficient behavior not attainable with other structures.

The approach is related to the *game theoretic* treatment of the theory of the firm. Commitment strategies and reputation effects are of the greatest interest for the purposes of the New Instiutional Economics, but the book does not deal with this line of analysis. For its application to the new theory of industrial organization see Tirole (1988). The development of the theory of sequential games with imperfect information was important to the area. Such material dates back to the work of Selten (1965) and Harsanyi (1967), but the field really started to grow in importance with Kreps, Milgrom, Roberts, and Wilson (1982). It is in this context that the article by Kreps (1990a) is to be seen. The work placed the reputation argument into the theory of the firm. What is stressed is that the soul of a firm is its reputation in the eyes of its trading partners, in particular its employees. Corporate culture can then be identified as the main vehicle for sustaining and advancing reputation. It offers also, as Miller (1992) shows, an explanation of the success of modern *high involvement management,* which in its most advanced state is represented by the self-managed work teams of, for example, the automotive industry (like the Kalmar plant of Volvo). Experience shows that, given some "corporate culture," cooperation between employees and between employees and their hierarchical superiors increases efficiency. To create and tend corporate culture, argues Miller (1992), is the task of the management, whose function, according to his view, is more that of a political leader than an economic supervisor in the sense of Alchian and Demsetz (1972). The management ("leader") has to shape expectations among subordinates about cooperation and commit the members of the organization to the "constitution" of the hierarchy understood as a (relational) contract between supervisors and subordinates. As Miller says:

> Rather than relying only on a mechanical incentive system to align individual interest and group efficiency, hierarchical leaders must create appropriate cooperation norms, . . . and create institutions that will credibly

commit the leader to the nonexploitation of employee "ownership rights" in the organization. (1992, 232)

There are a number of general surveys on the theory of the firm. Prominent is Holmstrom and Tirole 1989, which reviews more than the neoinstitutionalist literature. These authors discuss in their survey such central topics as the limits of integration, capital structure, separation of ownership and control, and informal hierarchies. Another useful essay that seeks to trace the impact of the growing literature on the nature of the firm and its organization is Putterman (1986a).

It is important to realize that there is no new "theory of the firm" waiting to replace the traditional neoclassical theory of the firm. All that we can say is that the older model is in the process of being destroyed by modern institutional economics, which is developing on a broad front. Such specialties as property-rights analysis, transaction-cost economics, agency theory, game theory applied to industrial organization, and evolutionary economics are all involved in the search for superior explanations of enterprise structure and behavior. Broadly speaking, it appears that modern microeconomics consists of a heterogeneous collection of models that deal with special problems by taking account of uncertainty, information asymmetry, bounded rationality, opportunism, asset specificity, and so on. What makes these new approaches significant is, of course, the fact that they are based on assumptions that are at odds with the crucial axioms of the neoclassical model. The problem now is not to drown in details or special cases while remaining aware of the interconnections that exist between the various elements within the firm, between the firm and the economy as a whole, and between the firm and the general society.

Traditionally, literature in the field of comparative economic systems tended to fall into two main categories. On the one hand, there were largely descriptive studies that explained, in some detail, the economic organization of the system being considered. On the other, there were analytical models that differed somewhat from conventional constructs but were strongly anchored in standard neoclassical theory. In the case of the theory of the firm, the usual approach was to posit an objective function for the organization under review that was distinct from the objective function assumed for the capitalist enterprise. Then, the question was raised as to whether the noncapitalist firm (e.g., the socialist labor-managed firm) would behave in a way that was consistent with its reaching a Pareto optimum and first-best allocative efficiency. Since the notion of institutional neutrality ran deep in neoclassical thinking, it was generally concluded that, under certain idealized conditions, the decentralized socialist firm, the socialist firm in a command economy, and the capitalist firm could all perform with equal efficiency.

The advent of neoinstitutionalist writings made this conventional line of analysis harder to sustain. Articles that reveal the essential character of the new approach and indicate why different conclusions about the role of organization emerged include Furubotn and Pejovich (1970b, 1972b); Alchian and Demsetz (1972); Furubotn (1976a); and Jensen and Meckling (1979). The investigation of problems in the area of comparative economics represented merely another application of the New Institutional Economics logic and in effect drew upon many of the earlier writings mentioned in this book. Fortunately, the procedure used here was relatively straightforward. The first step was to define the basic institutional features of the type of firm being studied. Then, in light of this institutional structure, which gave information about transaction costs and the pattern of property rights present, it was possible to infer something about the penalty-reward system extant. And from such knowledge the likely behavior of the firm (and its various members) could be adduced.

Many of these early models of the firm maintained close connections with neoclassical theory despite their slant toward property-rights/transaction-cost analysis. In other words, they were examples of the class of hybrid models discussed in chapter 8. Notwithstanding this, however, they were able to reveal some essential differences that exist between socialist and capitalist firms and underscore the fact that institutional arrangements matter. One important point relates to the so-called horizon effect (Ireland and Law 1982, 43–49). Under conditions of state ownership of the material means of production, individuals have neither permanent nor transferable rights in the capital assets of a firm. And, because this is so, incentives are warped in such a way that inefficient or wasteful use of capital is likely to occur. Ceteris paribus, the same deficiency is not to be found in a capitalist system in which full ownership rights hold.

The range of questions arising in comparative economic systems is very great indeed, and, not surprisingly, we find that different methodological approaches are employed in the argumentation that goes on regarding outstanding issues. However, as volumes such as that of Ireland and Law (1982) and the series edited by Jones and Svejnar (1989–92, vols. 1–4) suggest, the perspectives of the New Institutional Economics are only gradually being introduced into the discussion, and much reliance is still placed on orthodox neoclassical theory. For example, in considering the position of labor in the modern industrial firm, contemporary writers have put forward a variety of interpretations— see Furubotn (1976b), Williamson (1980), Putterman (1984), and Bowles (1985). Clearly, there is far from unanimous agreement on the need for neo-institutionalist concepts in the explanations offered. This outcome is perhaps inevitable as long as New Institutional Economic theory is still evolving and no generally accepted neoinstitutionalist model of the firm exists (see chapter 10).

Although a decision about the adoption of mandatory codetermination is not as fundamental as one concerning public ownership of the material means of production, both problem areas can be approached within the basic framework of ideas associated with the New Institutional Economics. But, again, just as in the case of socialist labor management or the command economy, neo-institutionalist writings on codetermination represent only a small part of the voluminous literature extant. Generally, the New Institutional Economics analysis, with its emphasis on contractual freedom, is critical of codetermination schemes that are imposed by government—see, for example, Alchian (1984), Jensen and Meckling (1979), and Furubotn (1978). The basic point made is that mandatory plans emphasize the "political" aspect of the firm and the importance of corporate governance while failing to give much attention to broader economic issues and the relation between the firm's total property-rights structure and its performance. Thus, it is said:

> By granting workers major control rights without regard to their actual investment position in the firm, state programs have violated an important rule for ensuring rational allocation—namely, the rule that those making decisions should bear the full consequences of the decisions they make. This defect, together with the costly system used to apportion the firm's quasi rents between workers and stockholders, means that the orthodox codetermined firm does not possess a truly efficient organizational structure. (Furubotn 1988, 178)

It also seems apparent that full understanding of national codetermination programs requires analysis that goes beyond a narrow focus on the economics of the business enterprise itself. Interest group pressure on government may force changes in legislation and yield better employment terms to labor than would be attainable through private bargaining. Thus, interdisciplinary studies, involving both sociology and political science, in addition to economics, are likely to be part of future neoinstitutionalist efforts to explain contemporary movements toward "industrial democracy."

## 8.11. Suggested Readings for Chapter 8

To gain insight into how the movement away from the orthodox neoclassical theory of the firm began, read Coase (1937) and Barnard ([1938] 1962)). Chandler (1977) provides a good discussion of the organizational development of the modern corporation. The readings volume edited by Putterman (1986a) is useful because it reproduces a number of key articles that have contributed to neoinstitutionalist thought. It also offers an extensive bibliography of related material.

Reviews of the institutional economics of the firm, such as those of Hart (1989) and Eggertsson (1990, chap. 6) can also be recommended. Hart's article is written for outsiders of the field (e.g., legal scholars) while Eggertsson's chapter is written for economists. Eggertsson summarizes the general thrust of the less formal theorizing on the firm that has developed in the neoinstitutional-ist tradition. Consideration is given to the works of such authors as Alchian, Barzel, Coase, Demsetz, Furubotn, Jensen, Meckling, and Williamson. It is advisable to read some of the original literature according to your interests in order to get the full flavor of the new approach to the firm. Of particular importance are the articles by Alchian and Demsetz (1972), Jensen and Meck-ling (1976), and Alchian (1984). Under all circumstances, read Williamson (1985 chaps. 1–3).

Ownership issues of the firm are reviewed by Hansmann (1988). A survey article embracing both branches of the modern institutional economics of the firm, both the formal and the less formal variants, is provided by Holmstrom and Tirole (1989). Along the same lines, Wiggins (1991) gives a selective review that integrates the early work of Williamson, Goldberg, Klein, and Alchian with the later, more formal literature by Holmstrom, Hart, Milgrom, and others and with the empirical research of Crocker, Joskow, and Libecap. For business students interested in the interrelation between the New Institu-tional Economics and research in "strategic management" or business policy, the survey by Rumelt, Schendel, and Teece (1991) is of value.

As general background reading on the problems of a socialist economy, the book by Hoff (1981) is recommended. Quite useful for basic orientation are works by Buck (1982), and Pejovich (1990). Articles by Bajt (1968), Nutter (1968), and Richter (1992a) might also be read with profit. Managerial be-havior in a Soviet-type economy has been examined by a number of writers. Two examples of this literature are Furubotn and Pejovich (1971) and Bain, Miller, Thornton, and Keren (1987). Property-rights issues are discussed by Pejovich (1969, 1972).

The Yugoslav experiment with the labor-managed firm attracted wide attention in the West. For a discussion of the structure and objectives of the Yugoslav plan, see Horvat (1971) and Horvat, Markovic, and Supek (1975, vol. 2). An interesting discussion of how neoclassical analysis can be adapted to treat the problems of the labor-managed enterprise is found in Meade (1986). A more general survey of the theory of labor-managed and participatory enter-prises is provided by Ireland and Law (1982). This volume, although anchored in neoclassical theory, gives attention to some of the themes emphasized by the New Institutional Economics. Hybrid models of the neoinstitutionalist type are examined in readings volumes edited by Furubotn and Pejovich (1974) and Pejovich (1973).

The codetermined firm represents a variant type of capitalist enterprise possessing a property-rights structure that differs from the structure of the conventional privately owned firm. Controversy exists over the desirability of this organizational form. To gain some understanding of the arguments pro and con, read Hodgson (1982); McCain (1980); Sertel (1982); and Steinherr (1977), on the one hand, and Williamson (1985 302–3); (1984); Furubotn (1978, 1985, 1988, 1989b); and Jensen and Meckling (1979) on the other. While conflicting value judgments affect the discussion of codetermination, the readings suggest that at least some of the controversy arises because of the tendency of writers to formulate different models based on quite different assumptions about the nature of the codetermined firm.

CHAPTER 9

# The New Institutional Economics
# of the State


The state can be, and sometimes is, interpreted as a firm ("Japan Incorporated,"
"Standort Deutschland"), as a revenue or social product-maximizing organization owned by a single ruler, a ruling class, or the people represented by its
deputies. Both the state and the firm can be portrayed as political systems "in
which strategic decision makers have partially conflicting objectives and limited cognitive capability" (Eisenhardt and Zbaracki 1992, 35). And, of course,
both can be seen as social systems in which individuals invest their time and
energy in building social relationships (Homans 1958;, Starr and MacMillan
1990). There is, though, an important difference between a firm and a state. The
state is the supreme authority; it can make its own laws. By contrast, the firm
cannot; it has to obey the law of the state to which it belongs. Still, the
analytical concepts of the property-rights approach, the transaction-cost approach, and contract theory can be applied usefully to the state and its organizations, as has been done by political scientists like Moe (1990), economic
historians like North (1981, 1990), and economists like Weingast (1988, 1989).
These authors use the name New Economics of Organization (Moe 1984) for
what we call the New Institutional Economics.

   Community life without a minimum degree of voluntary cooperation
among its members is impractical. One hundred percent dictatorship, a perfect
command community, would be too expensive. Thus, implicit (or explicit)
political agreements among individuals play an important role in society, even
under dictatorships. Yet this system of agreements will be tolerably stable only
if at least some of the agreements are self-enforcing. This is the theoretically
fascinating part of the economic theory of the state—in particular, the theory of
the modern representative democracy. It can be understood as an application of
the theory of self-enforcing agreements to an especially complex, long-term
network of relationships between and among individuals. The advantage of the
New Economics of Organization approach is that self-enforcement is de-

James Alt read this chapter. We thank him for his comments and critical remarks.

scribed by concrete organizational structures, not by abstract cybernetic models or interpretations such as the autopoietic concept of Luhmann (1984).[1]

## 9.1. A Simple Neoclassical Theory of the State

As is well known, there exist various types of explanations for the state, which may be grouped into contract theories and predatory or exploitation theories (North 1981, 21). North (23) develops a simple "neoclassical theory of the state." Based on the idea of a contract between the ruler (the "king")[2] and his constituents, it has the following characteristics:

1. The ruler trades protection and justice (including the protection of property rights and contract rights) for revenue. "Since there are economies of scale in providing these services, total income in society is higher as a result of an organization specializing in these services than it would be if each individual in society protected his own property" (23).
2. Because of (1), the ruler becomes the supreme authority for his constituents. The state has the right to command and the right to be obeyed, and thus the ability to raise compulsory contributions. A revenue-maximizing government will do so "like a discriminating monopolist, separating each group of constituents and devising the rights for each so as to maximize state revenue" (23). This is another, not so nice, explanation of progressive income taxes that is distinct from the "fair distribution" argument.
3. The ruler is constrained in his activities, to a greater or lesser degree, depending on the difficulties faced by his constituents with respect to:
   a. The costs of emigrating to another state with more favorable living conditions ("exit").
   b. The costs required to depose the current ruler and install a rival who promises better services to the constituents ("voice"). There always exist potential rivals to a ruler who can provide similar services to the incumbent.

North (1981) elaborates on these three hypotheses in more depth as follows.
*Ad 1.* The basic service that the state (the ruler) provides consists in the development and enforcement of a constitution—be it an unwritten or written

---

1. It is true, however, that many of the formal models of self-enforcing agreements suffer from a "multiple equilibria" problem.
2. The "ruler," of course, normally consists of a group of people. North disregards this fact in his simple model. As a representative of the New Institutional Economics, he knows, naturally, that methodological individualism demands a more detailed analysis (1990, 48ff.).

one. The constitution specifies the structure of property rights of the constituents in a manner that (in North's neoclassical theory) maximizes the rents accruing to the ruler subject to political and economic transaction costs. To achieve this, it is necessary to provide a set of public (or semipublic) goods and services "designed to lower the costs of specifying, negotiating and enforcing contracts which underly economic exchange" (24).

*Ad 2.* Property rights are, according to North, specified by the state in such a way as to permit the maximization of its monopoly rents. The distribution of private ownership and common property may be explained from this standpoint. To collect taxes, the ruler needs tax collectors (i.e., agents). Principal-agent problems arise, and the monopoly rents of the ruler will be dissipated to some extent by his agents (26), for example, the public bureaucracy in a constitutional state.

*Ad 3.* Since there are always rivals, the ruler either competes with other states or with potential rulers in his own state. "The closer the substitutes, the fewer degrees of freedom the ruler possesses and the greater the percentage of incremental income that will be retained by the constituents" (27). The constituents' opportunity costs of changing the government or leaving the country play an important role in this context. Notice that the costs of leaving the country for good are considerable even in a modern, Western-type society. Specific investments of citizens (sunk costs) are, in general, much higher than, for example, those of the employees of a firm. They are intensified by the fact that individuals are born into and grow up in a particular state. Among the sunk costs are the years of their youth spent in their home country learning its language, its formal and informal rules of behavior, its religion, its culture in general, and so on. Specific investments are, furthermore, the costs they have sunk into their families, their friendships, and their business relationships. The constituents of a state find themselves, therefore, locked into their homeland in a much more general and deeper sense than are the employees of a firm—a situation that may inspire a government, any kind of government, to behave opportunistically.

A variation of North's neoclassical theory of the state is found in the work of Margaret Levi (1988). She argues that rulers are predatory because they try to extract as much revenue as they can from the population (3). They mazimize their personal objectives, which requires them to maximize state revenue, and they do this "subject to the *constraints* of their relative bargaining power vis-à-vis agents and constituents (for what they provide in exchange for revenue), their transaction costs, and their discount rates." Transaction costs are in this context bargaining costs (which are of special importance) and such things as the costs of measuring revenue sources, monitoring compliance, and punishing noncompliance (23).

North (1981, 28) notes that in his simple static model there are two constraints that the ruler has to observe: the degree of political competition with rivals and other states and the transaction-cost constraints. For both reasons, the property-rights structure, which maximizes the social product, may not maximize the ruler's (long-term) monopoly rents. Generally speaking, the maximal value of the target function of the ruler need not coincide with that of the constituents. North's judgment is rather pessimistic. He says that to stabilize his power the ruler will agree to a property-rights structure that is favorable to groups with close access to alternative rulers, regardless of its effects upon efficiency. And, because of the costs of determining and collecting taxes, a less efficient property-rights structure may be more favorable to the revenue-maximizing ruler.

> This phenomenon of institutional development goes by the name of "path dependence." Levi (1988), a political scientist, examines in detail the incentives of governments in creating economic institutions, demonstrating for the case of France how those incentives can work against efficiency even for long periods of time. (Calvert 1995, 220)

North's simple neoclassical theory of the state can be extended from the vision of an ancient kingdom to a modern representative democracy with its representatives who, following public choice theory, maximize their individual utility at the expense of their constituents. Here the development of multiple interest groups would have to be modeled, which complicates the analysis. Conceivably, though, the insights into interest group relationships provided by Olson (1965) could be utilized. In any event, it would also have to be recognized that rule makers act under bounded rationality (Hax 1995). We shall mention some of the problems that arise subsequently.

Note that even in the simple neoclassical theory of the state described here, property rights, besides transaction costs, play an important role. Nationhood is a property right. The claim of protection that the individual citizen has against his state (described in chap. 3) is of considerable material value. This becomes apparent in wars, particularly in civil wars. Bare cosmopolitism is an insecure position, as refugees and stateless persons well know. Furthermore, the economic value of citizenship depends on national wealth. The general welfare of a nation, therefore, is of considerable importance to its citizens. This is demonstrated by the long lines of people from poor nations observed in front of the immigration offices of the richer ones.

Note further that the price paid for protection is high. To offer protection necessitates the existence of public means. For such means to be available, contributions must come from the citizens in the form of money and personal services of various kinds (including the offering of life). Free riding and other opportunistic activities are likely to appear in this connection. North (1981,

31ff.) argues, though, that free riding also has its "advantages." It prevents large-group activities and therefore accounts for stability (though not the efficiency) of states throughout history. Institutional innovations, therefore, come from the ruler rather than the constituents. Revolutions will generally be palace revolutions or revolutions undertaken by small Leninist groups. Generally, disruptive changes are avoided by some rules of succession. These are the reasons, according to North, for the stability of, and change in, the structure of states throughout history.

So much for the simple neoclassical theory of the state of North. By contrast, McGuire and Olson (1996) argue that the outcome from the rulers' self-interested actions need not be as bad as has often been supposed. They demonstrate rigorously for the special cases of autocracy and democracy "that there is a hidden hand that leads encompassing and stable interests with unquestioned coercive power to act, to a significant and surprising degree, in the interests of the entire society including those who are subject to their power" (94).

## 9.2. The Role of Political Institutions

The democratic constitutional state may be conceived of as a relational (and implicit) principal-agent contract between the constituents and their ruler (their representatives). Principals are the constituents (citizens), as the original "owners" of supreme authority (sovereignty). They authorize, via a voting procedure, some of their compatriots to adminster their sovereignty as their agents. As a result, though, it is the agents who exercise public authority and who, backed by the police powers of the state, can tell their principals what to do. This is fundamentally unlike private principal-agent relationships (Moe 1990). Still, theoretically we have the same problems as in transaction cost economics: asymmetric information before and after contract conclusion. This situation results in ex ante and ex post opportunism, including, because of the constituents' high specific investments, open holdups. It follows, then, that "*ex post* support *institutions* of contract *matter*" (Williamson 1985, 29; italics in the original). They are reflected here by the principles of the separation of powers and the constitutional state (Rechtsstaatprinzip). Yet, as we know, information is not only asymmetrically distributed, it is unavoidably incomplete—in particular with respect to what the future will bring. Therefore, the decisions of lawmakers, government, public administrators, and judges cannot be perfectly bound by rules. There has to remain some room for discretionary action of the agents, whom their principals (the constituents) have to trust to a degree. Thus, the problem of credibility of government commitments vis à vis its constituents arises.

A second commitment problem arises from the fact that political exchange occurs between representatives of different interest groups in society.

Vote trading and logrolling between parliamentarians play a role, as was ana-lyzed by Buchanan and Tullock (1962), who originated public choice theory. The problem with such an exchange in general is that it has a time dimension. In many cases, "today's legislation can only be enacted by commitments made for a future date" (North 1990, 50). Commitments have therefore to be made credible, as with economic exchange, by means of suitable institutional arrangements.

In both cases, in the principal-agent relationship between voters and poli-ticians, on the one hand, and the political exchange between interest groups, on the other, Williamson's transaction-cost approach applies. Uncertainty, the bounded rationality of rule makers, imperfect legal enforcement, and opportu-nism (rule breakers) are all present (see, e.g., Schanze 1995). Commitments are made credible by political institutions. Weingast and Marshall (1988), North and Weingast (1989), Shepsle and Weingast (1987), and Moe (1990, 1991) argue in this direction.

Institutional arrangements have tremendous impact on the ability of agents to make political commitments credible. Examples are:

The Fifth Amendment to the U.S. Constitution states, in part: "Nor shall private property be taken for public use, without just compensation." Known as the taking clause, this imperative allows the government to commit itself against expropriation and uncompensated exercises of eminent domain. This, in turn, functions to assure property owners of security from government predation.[3]

The division of labor committee system of the U.S. Congress enables credible commitments because it disables the discretion of momentary majorities (Shepsle 1978; Weingast and Marshall 1988).

North and Weingast (1989) showed that the five significant institutional changes of the Glorious Revolution of 1688 allowed the British gov-ernment to commit credibly to upholding property rights.

First, it removed the underlying source of the expediency. . . . Second, by limiting the Crown's legislative and judicial powers, it limited the Crown's ability to alter rules after the fact without parliamentary con-sent. Third, parliamentary interests reassert their dominance of taxation issues, removing the ability of the Crown to alter tax levels unilaterally. Fourth, they assured their own role in allocation funds and in monitor-

---

3. See, for example, Miller (1989) on the effect of progressive reforms in the United States that "allowed thousands of entrepreneurs to invest in businesses in urban areas across the United States without having to worry that the next change in party control in their city government would result in a new round of extortion or an elimination of their property rights in favor of rivals associated with the newly successful political cliques" (91).

ing their expenditures. The Crown now had to deal with the Parliament on equal footing. . . . Fifth, by creating a balance between Parliament and the monarchy—rather than eliminating the latter as occured after the Civil War—parliamentary interests insured limits on their own tendencies towards arbitrary actions. In combination, these changes greatly enhanced the predictability of governmental decisions." (North and Weingast 1989, 829)

More recently, Weingast (1995) has reemphasized that federalism is an important political institution to credibly commit the state to preserving markets. That is, by setting limits on the discretionary powers of the government, economic freedom can be enhanced. Attention is given in this line of discussion to what makes the restrictions of federalism self-enforcing. Weingast shows how these mechanisms work "in three contexts where federalism has underpinned rapid economic development: England during the 18th century, the United States during the 19th century, and modern China" (3). As for the latter, see also Montinola, Qian, and Weingast (1995).[4]

Not only neoinstitutionalists but also macroeconomists are increasingly interested in the problem of credible commitments. They use a different approach, but reach the same conclusion: that institutions matter. For a review of this literature, see, for example, Persson and Tabellini (1990).

The credible commitments through institutions argument is also a good argument against the basic instability argument of public choice literature. It explains, as Moe (1990) points out, why, in real life, social choices are not chaotic. In fact, "they are quite stable. Its explanation is that social choices are not simply governed by majority rule, but rather by all sorts of institutions that constrain how majority rule operates. . . . Politics is stable because of the distinctive roles that institutions play." (216).

Another concept of the New Economics of Organization, the concept of organizational culture as understood by Kreps (1990a), can also be applied in the present context, namely, to the hierarchical transactions between political officeholders and their constitutents.

As was shown in sections 4.4.3 and 8.2, organizational culture is an indispensable part of the theory of self-enforcing agreements with unknown future events. Related to the principal-agent approach applied here (in the sense of a self-enforcing agreement), the argument is that agents (lawmakers, government agents, bureaucrats, etc.) have to give their principals (their constituents) ex ante an idea of the ways in which they will react to unforseeable

4. Credibility of property rights is an important condition of a successful economic transformation of Eastern Europe. Riker and Weimer (1995, 94) hypothesize, for example, that "the greater the credibility of a right to property, the greater will be the investment in improving the economic productivity of the property" (see also chap. 3, this volume).

circumstances ex post. As was explained earlier, the idea must be embodied in a clear, sufficiently general principle, a focal point in the sense of Schelling (1960), which is generally accepted by the principals. It must satisfy two conditions. The principals (citizens) must:

1. Be able to check ex post the degree to which the principle (the focal point) has been satisfied
2. Be convinced that what the agent intends to do also stands a sufficient chance of being successful

The chosen principle needs, therefore, some persuasion or educational effort ex ante to be accepted. Morality and ideology, the latter in the sense of North or Schmoller (see sec. 1.13), play important roles in this context.

As was described above, Kreps (1990a) identifies the concept of "corporate culture" with the principle as just defined together with the way it is transmitted to the members of the organization (here, from general education down to political propaganda). He writes that in a strict sense corporate culture gives members a feeling of identification with "their" organization (here, their state, community, party, etc.). Solidarity plays a role but (hopefully) only "weak solidarity" (Lindenberg 1988) among constituents and between them and their political leaders. The "relation" as such takes on a value of its own for the members of the organization (here, the state, etc.). In the end, it is the politicians' adherence to "principle" that results in the acceptance of particular government actions and the state in general. The concepts of morality and ideology have, without a doubt, something to do with the organizational culture of a society.[5]

### 9.3.  Political Markets

In a sense, votes are exchanged for promises between representatives and their constitutents, as described earlier. Democratic politics therefore has been described since Schumpeter (1942) as a *competitive struggle* for office in an analogy to economic competition. As Demsetz (1982, 68) puts it: "Competition subjects politicians and political parties to the filter of the polling place, much as competition subjects managers to the filter of the market place." Yet, North (1990, 51) warns, "democracy in the polity cannot be equated with competitive markets in the economy." This is an argument that needs serious consideration.

The decisive difference between economic and political competition is that economic competition is the struggle for economic advantages through

---

5. What made the Roman Empire possible? The classical answer to the question is: "Moribus plus quam legibus stat res Romana."

economic exchange. It occurs on the basis of secure property rights. Political competition, on the other hand, is the struggle for authority, that is, the power to change exactly these property rights—unilaterally, without any economic quid pro quo. Thus, in politics, property rights are "up for grabs," not only economic rights but also what Moe (1990, 227) calls "political property rights," the rights to exercise public authority. As a result, institutional frameworks may change frequently in a democracy and thus may be quite unstable.[6]

As has been mentioned, political actors try therefore to fashion structures that insulate their favored agencies and programs from the future exercise of public authority. That makes structures more stable but at the price of efficiency. The struggle is about who will have the rights, formal and informal, to make authoritative decisions for society, a struggle that never ends and influences the shape of institutions.[7] "The 'firms' in the public and private sectors, therefore, are likely to be structured very differently" (Moe 1990, 228). It has been argued, however, that no structure of detailed formal requirements will necessarily protect the enacting evolution if there is a subsequent political change. There is also reason to believe that greater bureaucratic autonomy ( or the insulation of bureaucrats from politics) may actually preserve the original legislators' intentions more completely when they lose office than does the policy of limiting bureaucratic autonomy. Such a result is particularly likely if the original legislators can influence the choice of regulator in a way that supports their preferences.

Moe applies his hypothesis to the organization of the bureaucracy. To protect their "political property rights" political actors will limit bureaucratic autonomy ex ante through detailed formal requirements—criteria, standards, rules, deadlines—that are written into the law instead of trying to control how rights are exercised over time. "This structural maneuver helps to control the activities, though not necessarily efficiently (oriented towards success), and at the same time protects the originator of this particular political product against problems of political uncertainty." (Moe 1990, 235).

As a result, political competition does not, in general, lead to efficient solutions. Characteristically, there are no efficient political markets. "Such

---

6. "The core ideas are that individuals enter a poltiical process with preferences and resources, and that each individual uses personal resources to pursue personal gain measured in terms of personal preferences" (March and Olsen 1989, 9).

7. "In democratic polities (and most others), public authority does not belong to anyone. It is simply 'out there,' attached to various public offices . . ." While the right to exercise public policy happens to belong to a particular group of politicians today, "other political actors with different and perhaps opposing interests may gain that right tomorrow, along with legitimate control over the policies and structures that their predecessors put in place. Whatever today's authorities create, therefore, stands to be subverted or perhaps completely destroyed—quite legally and without any compensation—by tomorrow's authorities." (Moe 1990, 227).

markets are scarce enough in the economic world and even scarcer in the political world" (North 1990, 51). Distributional conflicts, collective action programs, and free-rider problems are likely to prevent the establishment of what might be viewed as economically efficient political systems. Still, as North argues, a move toward greater political efficiency goes together with the evolution of the democratic constitutional state. Unfortunately, the process is quite slow and cumbersome.

In a very general sense, though, economic and political market systems show similarities. Both have to organize coordination through bilateral and multilateral bargaining. Thus, the same basic activities have to be undertaken before and after the conclusion of a contract. That is, there is concern with search and inspection, the bargaining procedure as such, execution, control, and enforcement—in this case of *political transactions.* Strategic decisions play an important role (Eisenhardt and Zbaracki 1992). Furthermore, in analogy to the market economy, political exchange in a democratic state can be understood to occur within a network of long-term relational contracts among individuals (its citizens and foreign inhabitants) with the purpose of organizing competition efficiently for public offices (political property rights) and for political transactions themselves. The "monopoly of organized violence" is far from perfect. There exist many ways an individual inhabitant of a state can influence political decision making, including the formation of pressure groups, strikes, sit-ins, and so on. Constituents do not need to be members of the parliament or the government or even citizens for that purpose. This is also true for the democratic constitutional state, which one must not think of as a dome under whose cupola, immediately under the roof of the constitution, the members of parliament and government sit, while down on the ground individual voters float around, allowed to express their political will at the polls every so many years. Rather, as with the market, the "room in between" is filled with a dense system of private "third-realm" organizations (Miller 1993), which are interlocked and whose existence is legally guaranteed (in the Federal Republic of Germany by Article 9 GG, which guarantees the freedom of association and of forming coalitions). Among these private organizations are unions, employer's associations, commercial organizations, the political lobby, and political parties. In Germany, though, political parties, with regard to their function, are constitutional organs (Art. 21 GG). Their specific function, protected by the constitution, consists in serving to develop the political objectives of the state. But this is also done in a sense by numerous other organizations, not least the various pressure groups (often with dubious results, as shown in Olson 1965). As in the case of the market, we may also speak here of a network of more or less relational contracts between individuals or organizations that allow inhabitants or citizens of the state, who have no official political mandate, to influence (sometimes considerably) political decision making at the top. Moreover, this influence can be exercised on a daily basis (not only on voting days) in an open constitutional state. This may be another reason why political competition for voting shares in an open democratic state is generally less efficient than is economic competition for (direct) material gains (North 1994, 361).[8]

Certainly, the system of the constitutional state organized as a representative democracy is not without problems, as is a private ownership economy. The famous dictum of Churchill before the House of Commons (November 11, 1947) on democracy fits quite well to the conditions of the private ownership economy:

> No one pretends that democracy is perfect or all wise. Indeed, it has been said that democracy is the worst form of government except all those other forms that have been tried from time to time.

## 9.4.  International Relations

In principle, political transactions are of the same character, whether they are between the forces of national politics, between national states, or on economic markets between firms or private individuals. They are generally targeted at a change in the institutional framework of a social relationship—be it a town, a nation-state, the world community, a market, a firm, or a marriage. They are characterized by partially conflicting objectives and by bounded rationality of the decision makers. Competition between states (generally decision units) plays a role and may or may not lead to Pareto improvements. Competitive interdependence produces competitive uncertainty between states (as between firms). The desire to co-opt one's competitors, and thus reduce competitive uncertainty, is an important motive for entering into strategic alliances between states, as it is between firms and other decision units (Burgers, Hill, and Kim 1993). As for peaceful political transactions, the situation is comparable to that of a barter market. The rules of peaceful exchange apply, and these are based on (or closely connected with) David Hume's three fundamental laws of nature. As the central elements of the private-ownership economy, they require "the stability of possession, of its transferance by consent, and of the performance of promises" (Hume [1739–40] 1969, 578). In the relationship between states, as between individuals, "it is on the strict observance of those three laws, that the peace and security of human society entirely depend; nor is there any possibility of establishing a good correspondence among men, where these are neglected" (578).

---

8. Work on these "third-realm," to a greater or lesser extent voluntary, associations is only beginning. The rent-seeking approach deals with this issue (Tollison 1982, 1988; Tullock 1989). For an analysis of the political lobby, see Miller 1989, 1993. Tollison (1988, 341–42) stresses that "economists have little idea of how successful cost-effective interest groups are formed."

The problem with the order of international relationships is that it is not guaranteed by a superior world authority.[9] It is anarchical and self-organizing. International law, whether codified or not, cannot be enforced as national law can. International jurisdiction is voluntary. The single states are sovereign states and must rely "on the means they can generate and the arrangements they can make for themselves" (Waltz 1979, quoted in Keohane 1984, 7). These means consist of the whole spectrum of diplomatic activities, including the application of physical power, of war as a "mere continuation of policy by other means" (Clausewitz [1832] 1963)—though the application of military force is now generally prohibited by the Charter of the United Nations (Art. 2, no. 3). Anyway, wars are expensive and hazardous undertakings. It can be hoped that states will resort increasingly to sanctions as the weapon of first resort.

International political transactions are concerned with the evolution, guarantee, and administration of constitutional and operational rules (see sec. 6.1.1) of the international community. In particular, what is at issue is the definition, guarantee, and transfer of political or economic property rights. Transactions lead to implicit agreements, explicit (formal) treaties, or anything in between. In other words, the agreements are similar to the constitutions governing economic markets, and they involve relational contracts, as described in section 4.4.3. The distributional problem is central: who gets what out of a relationship? Strategy comes into play. Because of bounded rationality and lack of knowledge of what the future will bring, it is impossible for the parties to agree ex ante on all future eventualities that may affect the relationship. Nor do they have the ability to verify all relevant variables to outsiders such as international courts and arbitrators. Transaction-specific investments are generally necessary, and thus ex post opportunism of the parties may be invited. Ex ante safeguards against ex post opportunism have to be arranged—in international relations more so than in private or public long-term relationships under the "shadow" of national law. Ex post dangers of contracting include expropriation, debt repudiation, confiscation, reneging, and other forms of opportunism. International contracts are involved not only between governments but also between firms or firms and governments across borders with respect to the public regulation of contracts.

As in economic markets, it may be possible to reduce competitive uncertainty by means of cartels or *alliances,* whether military, technical, or economic. Just as high-tech firms may gain by complex forms of cooperation on

9. Note, however, that the Security Council of the United Nations may act like a world authority (Arts. 41 and 42 in combination with Art. 39 of the UN Charter). The first police action of the United Nations against an aggressor was the Gulf War of 1991 against the Iraq, which had occupied Kuwait.

R&D among competing firms (Teece 1992), strategic alliances (on certain issues) may be profitable for competing states. This is demonstrated presently by the technical and organizational assistance of developed nations to former socialist states, underdeveloped countries, and states within the European Union. Strategic alliances of states are similar to and occasionally overlap strategic alliances of industries, for example, those of the global auto industry (Burgers, Hill, and Kim 1993), which have also protective and aggressive purposes. Thus, comparisons between the political and the economic "alliance game" may be of interest—an area so far neglected by institutional economists.

The problem of alliances is how to *safeguard* or *enforce* such bilateral or multilateral international agreements. The various ex ante safeguards include those listed by Kronman (1985) for legally nonenforceable agreements; the enforcement mechanisms include anything from breaking off the relationship to "total war."

### 9.4.1. Safeguarding International Agreements

Kronman (1985) distinguishes four different ex ante safeguarding techniques, which we described in chapter 4ff. They will be repeated here briefly as they apply to the international scene.

1. *Hostages:* The hostage can be anything (or anyone) of value to the hostage giver. The hostage taker threatens to destroy the hostage if the other party fails to perform. An example from the field of international relations is Schelling's (1960, 136ff.) interpretation of the antiballistic missile treaty of 1972 between the United States and the Soviet Union as a mutual exchange of hostages—"an exchange intended to enhance the confidence of each side that the other will keep its word and refrain from starting a nuclear war" (Schelling, quoted in Kronman 1985, 12).
2. *Collaterals:* While the characteristic of a hostage "is that it is valued by the hostage giver but not necessarily by the recipient or anyone else." (Kronman 1985, 12), collaterals are valued by the collateral taker as well. In international relationships, an example is the occupation by French and Belgian troops of the Ruhr area of the German Reich in 1922 as collateral for the fulfillment of German reparations obligations.
3. *Hands tying:* This makes particular sense if the promisor has a reputation for keeping his promises. Hands tying is, in a general sense, similar to hostage giving: "in each case the promisor does something at the outset that has the effect of making a subsequent breach on his part more costly" (Kronman 1985, 18). This is similar to the self-enforcing

agreements theory described in chapters 4 and 5. The value of reputation plays a central role. Examples in international relations are provided by the repeated public declarations of the members of the European Community, now the European Union, concerning political-economic issues—for example, in the case of the Maastricht Treaty of February 7, 1992.

4. *Union:* As a method to reduce the risk of opportunism, union is interpreted by Kronman as "any arrangement that seeks to reduce divergence by promoting a spirit of identification of fellow-feeling between the parties" (1985, 21). In the case of the unification of formerly sovereign states into a federal state, an authority is created, which is able to enforce legally the obligations of the member states. In addition, if the federal state is a democracy, voters can credibly threaten not to reelect the present rulers or their parties. The enforcement problem of international public law disappears for the unionized states. Examples are the German unification of 1871 and the reunification of 1990.

## 9.4.2.  Enforcements of International Agreements

Kronman's safeguarding techniques are of a peaceful character. In political (as in economic) competition, tougher means like a "divorce for life" or attacks and counterattacks play an important role. They characterize the mechanism of *reciprocity* of political—and economic—competition.

5. *Termination:* The (credible) threat to terminate the agreement forever, as applied in the theory of self-enforcing agreements described in sections 4.4.3 and 5.6. As one recalls, this is based on the hypothesis that someone keeps his word only if it pays more than to break it (Telser 1980, 29). It is the model world of reputation equilibria. The Klein and Leffler (1981, 617) idea may be applied to states interpreted as revenue maximizing firms. Cheating (of the gorvernment) may be prevented and the supply of high-quality products (i.e., living or working conditions) may be secured if the states (their voters) are earning a continual stream of rental income that will be lost if low-quality output (policy) is deceptively produced (Haucap, Wey, and Barmbold 1995).

6. *"Tit-for-tat":* As described in chapter 4, tit-for-tat represents a special retaliatory strategy given symmetric information. It consists of the policy of cooperating on the first move and then doing whatever the other party did on the previous move (Axelrod 1984, 13). Axelrod developed this concept in a series of computer tournaments to explain the emergence of international cooperation. States have to live together in the future as well as in the present. Hence, choices made

today determine not only "the outcome of this move, but can also influence the later choices of the players. The future can therefore cast a shadow back upon the present and thereby affect the current strategic situation" (12).

Examples in international relations are retaliations or reprisals (such as suspending a treaty or violating it). "In serious cases of treaty breach, a state may also suspend other treaties or confiscate goods of the other state which has violated the treaty. The Vienna Convention on the Law of Treaties has sought to solve the problem by introducing a special procedure (Art. 65) to revoke or suspend a treaty under which one party must notify its respective intentions to the other party(ies)" (Ress 1994, 283).

Examples from economic life are answering price cuts with price cuts, advertising campaigns with similar campaigns, and product innovation with similar moves (on competitive responses in economic markets, see, e.g., Chen, Smith, and Grimm 1992). In case of asymmetric information, if the attack is subtle, immediate retaliation can be avoided. The rival may then not be able to respond effectively. This is an old wisdom (Chen and Miller 1994) applied, among others, by the military and diplomats.

These are comparatively "soft" enforcement techniques. The classical "tough" enforcement is the threat or carrying out of military force. The termination of the relation consists in this case not in a "divorce" but in a "fight" between the parties, the threat to destroy the other side. Equilibria are imaginable and can actually be observed under such conditions. The classical example is the balance of power system.

7. *Balance-of-power systems:* Examples are alliances like the Entente Cordiale versus the "Central Powers" and the North Atlantic Treaty Organization (NATO) versus (originally) the Warsaw Pact states. According to the balance of power theory, cooperation among states necessarily consists of political-military alliances of states against adversaries. The balance of power system may be interpreted as an implicit relational contract between the adversaries regarding the basic rules of the game, namely, to respect, in spite of occasional wars, the existence of each member.[10] It is probably one of the oldest types of strategic alliances between states.

Considering military force or power, a typical figure is the *hegemon,* a military and economically leading state. A corresponding concept is that of "hegemonic stability."

---

10. See, for example, Bernholz (1985, 35), on the European balance of power system of the eighteenth and nineteenth centuries.

8. *Hegemonic stability:* This system is based on the hegemon, a powerful state that creates and guarantees an international order or international regime. A system of norms and rules is created, which operates to the hegemon's advantage. Examples are the Pax Romana and later the Pax Britannica and the Pax Americana (Gilpin 1981, quoted in Keohane 1984, 31). Pure hegemony, though, is not a very realistic concept. Hegemony requires at least some cooperation to make and enforce rules, and thus the international order must also offer some advantages to the inferior states. Hegemonic stability theory predicts that institutions (e.g., international regimes) are only stable and effective "as long as the distribution of power underlying their construction remains stable" (Alt and Martin 1994, 266).

International cooperation continues in general in spite of the erosion of American and Russian hegemony, though there are counterexamples like the breakdown of the international petroleum regime and the actual workings of the International Monetary Fund. Still, American leadership in international affairs is unquestionably present, as in cases like the Gulf War but also in less dramatic world-order problems such as the handling of the international monetary order after the breakdown of the Bretton Woods system. In more local matters, other states assume or try to assume a leading role—such as France in case of the European Community and Russia among the follower states of the Soviet Union. Certainly, as in national politics, policy without any political entrepreneur (leadership) is hardly conceivable, and power, even if it is "only" economic power, as in the case of postwar Germany, will continue to be important in this connection.

In general, cooperation matters under hegemony. It becomes increasingly important "after hegemony" in its classical form. Keohane (1984, 46) uses in this context the term *hegemonic cooperation,* which he and other political scientists analyze by using the instruments of the New Institutional Economics.

9. *Hegemonic cooperation:* The cooperation of sovereign states under the leadership of a powerful state, is, as was just mentioned, a weak form of hegemony. The foundation of *international regimes* like the United Nations, the European Economic Community, and the International Monetary Fund are typical results of this kind of asymmetric international cooperation. For historic reasons, a number of states find themselves locked into a coalition, like the Western Allies after World War II on the one side and the Warsaw Pact states on the other. In each coalition, one state has a leading position—in our examples, the United States and the Soviet Union. The situation is comparable with

Williamson's fundamental transformation. The hegemon will behave opportunistically, though, within certain limits. Examples include the Louvre Accord of 1987 between the Group of Seven major industrial countries (the G–7) under the leadership of the United States (see, e.g., Richter 1989b and the agreement of 1992 to establish a European Monetary Union under the leadership—or insistence—of France. But the hegemon will also help to establish and guarantee some order, that is, an international regime, consisting of "principles, norms, rules, and decisionmaking procedures" (Keohane 1984, 59).

In the general game-theoretic sense, regimes are interpreted by political scientists as cooperative solutions to repeated collective action games. As Alt, Calvert, and Humes (1988, 447) put it, "rational actors . . . under appropriate circumstances have sufficient incentives to cooperate with each other. Among such actors, structured, regimelike interactions would appear and persist. Whether cooperation ensues in such games depends on the structure of payoffs, the probability of repeated interaction, and the number of players" (see also Oye 1985). Contrary to Axelrod's explanation of the evolution of the international cooperation, the argument is that spontaneous cooperation "in these repeated games seldom occurs and that stable regimes depend instead upon the fostering actions of a dominant state. The hegemonic state provides an international order that furthers its own self-interest, although the resulting cooperation may work to the advantage of other states as well" (Snidal 1985, 587)" (quoted in Alt, Calvert, and Humes 1988, 447).

International regimes are, of course, special cases of relational contracts. They are legally unenforceable (because of the sovereignty of nations), but, like contracts, they help to organize relationships in mutually beneficial ways. "The rules are changed, bent or broken to meet their exigencies of the moment. . . . They are often matters of negotiation and renegotiation" (Keohane 1984, 89).[11] Because of the cost of creating international regimes, once they exist they will tend to be maintained and will continue to foster cooperation "even under conditions that would not be sufficiently benign to bring about their creation" (50).

In this sense, international regimes are institutions that help to stabilize international relationships. They are responses to problems of specific investments, uncertainty, and transaction costs. They reduce the range of expected behavior. Thus, as "uncertainty declines, and information becomes more

---

11. "Broader than formal agreements, regimes include principles (stating purposes), norms (general injuctions or definitions of legitimacy), rules (specific rights and obligations), and procedures (formal indications of means rather than substance)" (Alt, Calvert, and Humes 1988, 446).

widely available, the asymmetry of its distribution is likely to lessen." (Keohane 1984, 97). In short, international regimes enable states to make mutually beneficial agreements that would otherwise be difficult or impossible to obtain.

Keohane (1984) and Alt, Calvert, and Humes (1988) also consider the reputational effects of international regimes or institutions.

> By making past behavior common knowledge, and enhancing the future value of cooperation, institutions can lead states to put a higher value on having a reputation for living up to international agreements. (Alt and Martin 1994, 266)

> Garrett and Weingast (1993) and Calvert (1992) consider the impact of institutions in coordination situations. They see institutions as providing focal points or otherwise allowing states to settle on a particular outcome in multiple equilibria situations. (266)

> Models of international institutions that rely on considerations of information, reputation, credibility, and coordination all acknowledge the importance and draw on the insights of the NIE. (266)

Examples from the literature are provided in section 9.5.

### 9.5.  A Brief Guide to the Literature on the Economics of the State and International Relations

### 9.5.1.  The State

The literature on the theory of the state, even when limited to its economic variant, is far too extensive to be reported on here. Of interest from the viewpoint of the New Institutional Economics, or the New Economics of Organization, are the early arguments on the contract theory of the state by Locke ([1823] 1963, vol. 2, chap. 8), which go much further than the arguments by North (1981) that were presented. According to Locke, men agree freely with each other

> to join and unite into a community, for their comfortable, safe, peacable living one amongst another, in a secure enjoyment of their properties, and a greater security against any that are not of it. ([1823] 1963, 394)

Somewhat later, Locke says that men will do this only if "the power of society, or legislative constituted by them, can never be supposed to extend farther than the common good," which according to Locke is the preservation of man himself, his liberty and property (414).

The contract theory of the state can be interpreted as a convention between individuals in the sense of Hume ([1739–40] 1969, 40) and later Lewis (1969). Menger ([1883] 1963, bk. 3, chap. 2) also argues in this manner. He writes that states may have developed through the cooperation between heads of families without any agreement, determined only by their members' progressive realization of individual interests. The underlying problem is, in modern terms, that of the cooperative solution of a reiterative prisoner's dilemma game. As Axelrod (1984) showed, the tit-for-tat strategy may be successful. Schotter (1981, 45–51) has presented a model based on Nozick's (1975) work, according to which a state can emerge first by means of a social contract of a small group of people, and it can grow afterward, by adding more and more citizens, if the marginal costs of protection against violence, theft, and so on decrease as the number of people protected increases (Bernholz 1992). Binmore (1994) argues that game theory provides a systematic tool for investigating social cooperation and coordination and criticizes much of the present literature. Calvert (1995a, 224), a political scientist, argues along the same lines, explaining institutions as equilibria in an underlying game (see also Calvert 1995b). He addresses not only the *cooperation* but also the *coordination* problem and concludes that "any theory of institutions must offer a solid conceptual basis for explaining self-contained incentives for cooperation in an institution (1995a, 225). Greif (1994) interprets Genoa's political systems during the twelfth and thirteenth centuries as self-enforcing agreements. While previous studies emphasized the need to limit the ability of rulers to abuse rights, the history of Genoa seems to indicate "the importance of examining the institutional basis that determines the boundaries of political factions, the endogenous process through which the 'ruler' emerges, the ruler's incentives to advance growth, and the incentives to cooperate with the ruler" (285–86).

For an understanding of a modern open society, it is helpful to view the state as a voluntarily concluded contract in the sense of an implicit long-term contract between its constituents (the principals) and their agents (for a critical review of this approach, see March and Olsen, 1989). Specific investments of the constituents and informational asymmetries help to explain the rulers' opportunism. That is also true for the understanding of the dangers of totalitarianism of which Hayek warned in his book *The Road to Serfdom* (1944). In fact, the need to safeguard individual freedom is a central topic of the contract literature on the state at least since Locke. Hayek's *The Constitution of Liberty* (1960) is to be mentioned. The German theories of "economic order" (Böhm 1937; Eucken 1950) and American constitutional economics initiated by Buchanan (1987) have their roots in this theme. Buchanan's (1975) contractarian model of government was later extended by Holcombe (1994), who developed an exchange model of government.

The application of the instruments of the NIE to the theory of the state was initiated and furthered by North, who, as an economic historian, is particularly interested in the analysis of the causes of institutional change. His hypothesis is that institutional change occurs wherever it promises to be profitable. He develops and illustrates his hypothesis in a series of books (1971, 1973, 1981, the first two with Thomas) and summarizes the latest development of his theory in his book *Institutions, Institutional Change, and Economic Performance* (1990).[12] Levi (1988) extends North's hypothesis that rulers are predatory and illustrates this argument with case studies. Later authors drew attention to the parallels between the theories of the state and of the firm. They show, for example, that congressional institutions are designed to further the goals of legislators similar to those developed in the theory of the firm (see Shepsle and Weingast 1987; Weingast 1989, 1988; and Weingast and Marshall 1988). And they show that bureaucratic institutions parallel closely the issue of the delegation of decision rights by shareholders to managers (see Moe 1984, 1991; Weingast 1984; and McCubbins, Noll, and Weingast 1989). Not only the state but also the firm can be "accurately portrayed" as a political system (Eisenhardt and Zbaracki 1992, 35). Furthermore, constitutions may be interpreted as self-enforcing constraints of a polity, as North and Weingast (1989) assert. Constitutional economists like Gifford (1991) and Vanberg (1992) point out that not only the state but also the firm (or other organizations) can be understood as a constitutional system, that is, "a set of interdependent explicit or implicit contracts" (Gifford 1991, 104), which can be thought of as a constitution like that of a nation. Bureaucrats and their much criticized lack of productivity and accountability can be discussed, in an analogy to the separation of ownership and control problem of the firm, as a two-tier principal agent problem, with politicians and bureaucrats as agents (supervisors and workers) and constituents as principals. Yet, "unlike owners of firm, voters are unlikely to posses a distinct common objective, and this affects the ability of voters to organize effectively to monitor both politicians and bureaucrats" (Johnson and Libecap 1994a, 159). This, together with (in the United States) the competition between the president and Congress over the bureaucracy as an entrenched interest group—conclude Johnson and Libecap (159)—deserves more attention in the literature concerned with the reform of the civil service systems. A general argument in this literature is that institutions help to stabilize representative democracies (Moe 1990). As in case of the firm, the organizational culture matters—or, as Weingast (1994) puts it, "ideas matter" as a method to coordi-

---

12. Inefficiencies may, however, persist for quite some time "because rulers would not antagonize powerful constituents by enacting efficient rules that were opposed to their interests or because the costs of monitoring, metering, and collecting taxes might very well lead to a situation in which less efficient property rights yielded more tax revenue than efficient property rights" (North 1990, 52). The point is also stressed by Miller (1989).

nate hierachically activities under uncertainty. So does the "belief system" (North), that is, the institution of public and private education.

The *Journal of Law, Economics, and Organization* published conference issues on "The Organization of Political Institutions" (1990) and "The Economics and Politics of Administrative Law and Procedures" (1992), which survey lively developments in this field that are based on the application of NIE methods. The *Journal of Institutional and Theoretical Economics* (JITE) published a symposium issue on the application of NIE methods to the analysis of state and society (Furubotn and Richter 1994).

## 9.5.2. International Relations

First, there exists a wide literature on the economics of international relations, dealing largely with the organization and the consequences of international trade and finance. Marxist *imperialism theory* is an old and famous branch of this literature, surveyed, for example, by Amsden (1987). Neoclassical *international political economics* is another, newer branch, reviewed, for example, by Frey (1984a) and Frieden and Lake (1987).

Second, in addition to or overlapping with this literature, there exist studies that apply the economic style of reasoning to the analysis of the norms and institutional arrangements regulating not only trade but international relations in general. See, for example, contributions by Bernholz (1985, 1992), or the literature on arms races and deterrence by Rapoport (1960, 1967), Schelling (1960, 1966), Tullock (1974), and others. Most of this literature has a strong game-theoretic component.

The application of the methods of the NIE to the analysis of international relations, touched upon in this chapter, is the youngest branch of the economic analysis of international relations. It is applied to both the organization and consequences of international trade and finance as well as to the evolution and control of international political transactions in general. While the earlier approaches were introduced by economists, with political scientists standing skeptically aside, the NIE approach to international relations was introduced interestingly by political scientists themselves, like Keohane (1984), who discussed the concept of international regimes in the style of Williamson's transaction-cost approach. Alt, Calvert, and Humes (1988) added game-theoretic techniques and stressed the reputational effects of institutions, which was also mentioned by Keohane. Soon economists took up the issue. Thus, Richter (1989b) and Richter and Schmidt-Mohr (1992) analyzed the Louvre Accord of the Group of Seven major industrial countries by means of a combination of NIE concepts and the concept of hegemonic cooperation. Schmidtchen and Schmidt-Trenz (1990) and Schmidt-Trenz and Schmidtchen (1991) discuss the multinational firm using the NIE concept. Yarbrough and

Yarbrough (1992) developed, on the basis of the NIE concept, a "strategic organizational approach" to international relations. They use concepts drawn from Williamson, Keohane, and others to argue that organizational variety reflects alternate governance structures that are used to facilitate and enforce agreements, and they develop different hypotheses to explain various epochs of the organization of international trade since the nineteenth century. Political scientists continued in this vein. Martin (1993) argued that institutions allow states to make more credible threats and promises. Alt and Martin (1994) discussed the institutional approach to international contracting. Specialists in international law such as Ress (1994) became active and discussed international public law issues by considering ex ante safeguards against ex post opportunism.

### 9.6. Suggested Readings for Chapter 9

On the economic analysis of the institution of *the state,* begin by reading Locke's contract theory of the state ([1823] 1963, vol. 2, chap. 8). Continue with Buchanan's "The Limits of Liberty" (1975), a contractarian model of government. North's simple neoclassical theory of the state (1981, chap. 3) provides an instructive exercise in the economic analysis of a given ruler. Moe (1990) gives an excellent example of the application of NIE methodology to the analysis of public bureaucracy.

As an introduction to the public choice style of analysis of *international relations,* read Frey 1984a. For an early application of NIE techniques to an interesting and important topic, international regimes, read Keohane 1984. His concept of hegemonic cooperation helps to improve understanding of multi-lateral self-enforcing contracts. Keohane gives older examples for what he calls hegemonic cooperation. For a more recent example, analyzed with the use of NIE techniques plus the concept of hegemonic cooperation (the Louvre Accord of 1987), you might wish to read Richter 1989b.

CHAPTER 10

# Future Development of the New Institutional Economics

Looking back at the evolution of the field we now know as the New Institutional Economics, it seems clear that much has already been achieved by the scholarly work undertaken in the area. Certainly, we have improved understanding today of the role institutions play in economic life. From the outset, of course, a basic objective of neoinstitutionalist writing was to obtain greater insight into economic behavior by moving away from some of the more extreme simplifications and abstractions of orthodox neoclassical theory and focusing instead on a different, more empirically robust model. In any event, as the limitations of the received doctrine became increasingly evident during the postwar period, there occurred a major expansion of research interest in modern institutional economics. Not only did the volume of institutionally oriented research and publication grow over time, but in addition modern institutionalism began to secure recognition as a distinct and legitimate area of study. In short, there can be no doubt that the institutionalist enterprise is alive and under way; a more difficult issue, though, is to determine how the field will develop in the future.

Relative to this last matter, several things should be kept in mind. First, it is important to realize that neoinstitutionalist scholars do not speak with one voice and that the boundaries of the field have not been established with any great precision. This is so, in part, because the NIE was not developed in systematic fashion by individuals sharing a common vision or by those who saw themselves as engaging in a bold new movement designed to bring about revolutionary changes in economic theory. Rather, theoretical advance took place largely through innovative work undertaken in various subfields such as transaction-cost economics, property-rights analysis, law and economics, comparative systems, and constitutional economics. Indeed, during the formative years of modern institutionalism, the writings produced in the different specialized areas tended to be rather diverse in style and methodology as well as in content. Moreover, even today, there are major disagreements among scholars about how best to treat institutional and organizational questions in economics. It is true, of course, that shared intellectual ground does exist. The core element that binds the separate groups of neoinstitutionalist writers together is the conviction that orthodox neoclassical analysis rests on highly specialized assumptions and is incapable, *without some modification,* of dealing effectively with many problems of interest to theorists, empirical researchers, and policymakers.

At first glance, it might seem that exponents of the new institutionalism would show some interest in the work of the old institutionalists (of the German Historical School and the American institutionalist movement). After all, both groups are, to a greater or lesser degree, critical of neoclassical theory as expounded in the standard literature. Such concern with past work, however, is not found in the attitudes of neoinstitutionalists. While there may be some exceptions to the rule, most neoinstitutionalist scholars have been at pains to disassociate themselves from the central ideas put forward by the old institutionalists. What gave the original NIE advocates such confidence that they could disregard the older work on institutions was the belief that standard neoclassical analysis could be readily *generalized or "extended" to treat institutional problems.* The position taken reduced to this. Although neoinstitutionalists felt considerable dissatisfaction with what mainstream economists were doing, the dissatisfaction was not so much with the theory being used as with the manner in which it was used. Thus, it could be argued that:

> What distinguishes the modern institutional economists is not that they speak about institutions, the American institutionalists after all did this, nor that they have introduced a new economic theory, although they may have modified the existing theory in various ways, but that they use standard economic theory to analyze the working of these institutions and to discover the part they play in the operation of the economy. (Coase 1984, 230)

In this connection, it should be observed that if Coase was able to make this statement about the continued usefulness of basic neoclassical methodology other economists, such as those more committed to formal theory, were predisposed to be even more enthusiastic about the "generalization" approach to institutional analysis.

For most economists operating in the postwar period, there was something very satisfying about the notion that a straightforward transition could be made to a more flexible, institutionally oriented theory by simply changing certain neoclassical assumptions while holding others unchanged. The procedure seemed to promise the best of all outcomes. By following this approach, the NIE could presumably expand understanding of institutional questions while simultaneously preserving the rigor of the deductive neoclassical model. Moreover, extension of the neoclassical model permitted continued use of the standard technical tools that were part of the neoclassical legacy. Under these terms, research could be conducted more or less as usual. In particular, there was no need to engage in the kind of massive historical-descriptive studies that were associated with the old institutionalism. Rather, modern empirical and econometric work could be undertaken. What emerged, as a consequence, was a "renaissance of institutionalism" based on modern empirical and theoretical studies undertaken in a variety of specialized fields (Williamson 1975, 1). Despite certain methodological problems inherent in the early neoinstitutional writings, there can be no doubt that they served to clarify the role of institutional arrangements in an economy. At a minimum, the growing NIE literature made it clear that institutions count.

The systematic consideration of transaction costs and property-rights structures by neoinstitutionalist writers represented a crucial development in modern institutional thought because, once having moved in this direction, microeconomic theory could no longer return to a position that suggested institutional arrangements were *neutral* elements having no independent effect on economic behavior. Nevertheless, the approach initially taken by most NIE scholars, with its heavy reliance on neoclassical perspectives, had the effect of *oversimplifying* problems and often of moving discussion in less productive directions. Thus, while helpful in some respects, the NIE analysis could still mislead the unwary. The crux of the difficulty lay in the way in which the "extended neoclassical model" was specified. It was true, of course, that since positive transaction costs and bounded rationality were assumed to exist, there was recognition that the neoinstitutional approach had to be somewhat different from the approach used in the "frictionless" neoclassical model. As a result, constraints not found in the orthodox case were introduced and accepted as important in the new work (Eggertsson 1990, 6). However, what did not seem to be appreciated at first was the fact that the new assumptions employed by the NIE had very far-reaching consequences, and that the changed view of the world they represented implied results *different* from those established by the simple modeling of the early NIE contributors. In other words, as neoinstitutionalist thinking matured, some writers began to challenge NIE works whose methodology did not depart very far from neoclassical orthodoxy.

From one standpoint, the growing body of neoinstitutionalist writing can be seen as leading to greater "realism" in economic theory. Whether a movement in this direction represents a revolutionary development is open to question. But it is perhaps worth pointing out that many of the opinions expressed today concerning the limitations of neoclassicism are very similar to the criticisms made by Keynes when he introduced his famous General Theory:

I shall argue that the postulates of the classical theory are applicable to a special case only and not to the general case, the situation which it assumes being a limiting point of the possible positions of equilibrium. Moreover, the characteristics of the special case assumed by the classical theory happen not to be those of the economic society in which we actually live, with the result that its teaching is misleading and disastrous if we attempt to apply it to the facts of experience. (1936, 3)

These remarks could be applied to contemporary discussions of neoinstitutionalism with virtually no modification. We certainly know that the "frictionless," perfect-competition, perfect-market model of neoclassical tradition defines an abstract, hypothetical system that is only remotely related to real-world conditions. Given its emphasis on costless transactions and complete rationality, the model is indeed a special case. Thus, some form of change would seem necessary.

Insofar as the neoclassical model is recognized as a special case, relating to a special universe, speculation arises about whether this original model can be modified and extended to take account of the new theoretical themes being considered by neoinstitutionalist scholars or whether a shift must be made to a fundamentally different paradigm. Serious controversy still surrounds this issue, and the debate has by no means been settled. What is significant, however, is the fact that the term *revolution* is being used, in some quarters, to describe the situation that is unfolding as a result of the changed theoretical approach being promoted by the New Institutional Economics. The idea that major turning points exist in the development of economic theory is important in itself and has clear relevance for the way institutionalism is to be viewed.

The increasing interest in, or recognition of these processes of major change or revolution in the subject seems to have come about in three main phases. It probably originated mainly with the Keynesian phenomenon—which is still considered by some to be the only valid case of a "revolution." Further interest was then sharply stimulated in the 1960s by T. S. Kuhn's challenging book . . . *The Structure of Scientific Revolutions.* . . . Then, thirdly, in the early 1970s, interest in the concept of a revolution in economics was further reinforced by the actual emergence in those years of what was widely referred to, or claimed to be, some kind of fundamental "crisis," or "revolutionary situation," in the subject. Hence understanding the present state and prospects of the subject involved understanding the nature of "revolutions." (Hutchinson 1978, ix)

Obviously, if major changes in the economic paradigm are thought to be possible from time to time, it is of the greatest interest today to determine whether a shift to the methodological perspectives of the New Institutional Economics would represent such a critical transformation. Thus, in the final chapter of this book, it seems essential to broach this basic question and in particular to discuss at some length the feasibility of developing the New Institutional Economics through the extension of existing neoclassical theory.

## 10.1.   Institutionalism as Extended Neoclassical Theory

To gain some insight into the question of how the NIE may develop in the future, it is necessary to take a closer look at some of the basic ideas that animated the early writings on modern institutional economics. As suggested above, the intention of most contributors to the field during the 1960s and 1970s was not to reject marginalism but to extend its scope. There was confidence that the standard neoclassical techniques could be applied fruitfully to a wide array of new problems and new institutional settings.

Central to the changed approach that was being advocated was the understanding that, while the rationality assumption and mathematically based optimization procedures could be retained, other modifications had to be made in the neoclassical model. Thus, it was urged that:

1. Institutions are no longer to be regarded as neutral elements that exercise no significant effect on economic behavior.
2. More than one pattern of property rights can exist, and profit or wealth maximization is not assured.
3. The economic system is not a frictionless machine. Transaction costs arise in connection with the exchange process and their magnitudes affect the way in which economic activity is organized and carried out.
4. The analytical focus must be on the individual decision maker rather than on the organization or collectivity. Individuals have different goals, but each person can be conceived as maximizing his utility subject to the limits imposed by the existing institutional structure.

What was particularly stressed was that property-rights arrangements and transaction costs affected individual incentives and hence behavior. From this position, it followed that if the institutional environment in which economic activity occurred were specified with precision behavior could be predicted with some accuracy.

Not all scholars in the neoinstitutional camp were concerned with the way in which their work could be related to traditional theory, but for many there was acceptance of the view that a close linkage existed between the new thinking and the neoclassical model. It was even suggested in some circles that microeconomic theory, properly developed, was the property-rights/transaction-cost approach. Attitudes, however, have changed over time, and today there is less agreement on this basic issue. Nevertheless, it is certainly true the supporters of the "extended-model" concept still exist in large numbers. In this connection, it is interesting to note that current writers such as Richard Posner (1993a) argue that the New Institutional Economics has contributed more in the way of terminological changes than in significant theoretical advances and that there is in fact little to distinguish the New Institutional Economics from contemporary neoclassical economics. In this assessment, the NIE, and much of the work of Coase and Williamson, is best understood as an excursion into "case studies." If Posner's position is granted, the NIE can scarcely be seen as leading to any revolutionary change in the basic economic paradigm, as some neoinstitutionalists would like to believe. But the debate is still in progress. The vigorous response of Coase (1993) and Williamson (1993c) to Posner's criticisms (1993b), together with the increasingly sharp attacks on neoclassical theory from many sides, suggest that the question of how the NIE will evolve in the future is alive and important.

Given certain simplifying assumptions, neoclassical theory asserts that a competitive capitalist economy will reach an equilibrium that is also a first-best Pareto-optimal configuration of the economy. In this conception, markets are interpreted as the institutional means by which the marginal equivalencies for the general equilibrium of production and exchange are met. Although institutions play only a passive role in this pure neoclassical formulation, they are at least understood to exist. Thus, when it was recognized that differences in transaction costs and property-rights structures led to differences in economic behavior, it was an easy step to the representation of institutions as special constraints that had to be given serious consideration within the standard neoclassical framework.

> We may say that institutions consist of a set of constraints on behavior in the form of rules and regulations; a set of procedures to detect deviations from the rules and regulations; and finally, a set of moral, ethical behavioral norms which define the contours that constrain the way in which the rules and regulations are specified and enforcement is carried out. This framework rests on three fundamental assumptions which we must explore. First, an individualistic behavioral assumption; second, an assumption that specifying and enforcing the rules that underlie contracts is costly; and third, an assumption that ideology modifies maximizing behavior. (North 1984b, 8)

The ideas expressed in this passage are consonant with the view that the basic structure of neoclassical theory can be preserved when attention is turned to institutional questions. While it is suggested that individual maximizing behavior may be affected somewhat by ideological factors, rational choice is still seen as dominant. Rational choice will operate to shape economic behavior in a more complex system that now reflects positive transaction costs and various institutional constraints. Essentially the same interpretation had been offered in 1983 by DeAlessi, who argued that neoclassical theory could accommodate new elements through the simple expedient of introducing additional constraints into the orthodox model.

> Neoclassical theory . . . can be generalized to eliminate some of these limitations. A major step is to end the dichotomy between the theory of consumer choice and the theory of the firm by extending the utility-maximization hypothesis to all individual choices, including those made by business managers, and government employees. Another step is to broaden the concept of the limits on individual choices to include institutional constraints (the system of property rights) as well as more of the constraints (for example, including transaction and adjustment costs) imposed by nature and the state of the arts. (1983, 66)

This "generalization" of the neoclassical apparatus seemed to be an obvious way to proceed. No radical conceptual changes had to be made, and standard technical procedures could be put to work as usual. Certainly, in the case of the firm, the shift to utility as the maximand opened up new possibilities for studying business operations in various socioeconomic environments, and permitted the analysis of different patterns of managerial behavior. Moreover, the requirements of the new approach were straightforward. It was necessary to define the particular utility function that reflected the decision maker's preferences and then to determine the actual set of options open to the decision maker. Given these elements, the formal problem was one of maximizing the utility function subject to the constraint imposed by the opportunity set (Furubotn and Pejovich 1972a, 1138). But unfortunately, despite its apparent reasonableness, this theoretical treatment has some serious flaws.

## 10.2. The Initial Approach Reconsidered

It is argued by some economists (e.g., Stiglitz 1985; and Wiseman, 1991) that neoclassical theory tends to be viewed with some misgivings these days not primarily because neoinstitutionalists and others have put forward such convincing arguments against it but because the theory's own technological development has made possible a deeper appreciation of its limitations.

> The economists of the twentieth century, by pushing the neoclassical model to its logical conclusion, and thereby illuminating the absurdities of the world which they had created, have made an invaluable contribution

to the economics of the coming century: they have set the agenda, work on which has already begun. (Stiglitz 1991, 136)

While there is truth in this position, it is also clear that strong arguments can be advanced by neoinstitutionalists to question the legitimacy of the neoclassical model. Quite simply, it does not appear possible to relax certain of the highly specialized assumptions of neoclassical theory without changing the whole nature of the analysis. The problem is not just one of introducing complications from the real world and securing results that are "less than perfect" and only approximate those promised in pure theory. Rather, in models where transactions costs, incomplete information, and bounded rationality play key roles, the very process by which economic solutions are generated is quite different from the process envisioned in the neoclassical case. In what follows, then, an attempt will be made to justify these adverse judgments on neoclassicism and explain some of the major reasons why the orthodox model does not seem to provide a suitable basis for dealing with institutional problems.

## 10.2.1.  Contradictory Assumptions

The idea that neoclassical theory could be "generalized" by introducing additional constraints into the traditional model was appealing to the early neo-institutional writers, and many scholars still have faith in this approach. As noted, what seems to be promised is a straightforward way of studying economic behavior in a world of frictions. The practical effect of this line of research, however, was to produce what may be called "hybrid" models. That is, such models are composite in the sense that they are based on assumptions drawn from two disparate universes. Some traditional neoclassical assumptions are rejected, but others are retained. Thus, while useful new concepts are given attention (e.g., nonzero transaction costs), the resulting mix of the new and the old leads to structures that are *internally inconsistent.* In the so-called hybrid models that are found so widely in the literature, a consistent point of view is not maintained. Inter alia, decision makers are taken to have split economic personalities. They are perfectly informed about some matters yet completely ignorant about others.[1] Or, alternately, different economic actors in the same model show fundamentally different motivations and capabilities. For example, in the modern capitalist corporation, the hired manager is said to have some freedom to pursue his own independent interest at the expense of stockholders because of the high monitoring and enforcement costs that stockholders face. By contrast, it is assumed (at least implicitly) that the corporate manager in question is completely rational and knows precisely how to ad-

---

1. Such economic agents might be characterized as "partially omniscient."

vance his own welfare. Presumably, he knows everything about the technological alternatives confronting the firm, the internal organization of the firm, the behavior of the firm's board of directors, the willingness of the firm's employees and suppliers to honor their contracts, and so on. The manager can, in short, formulate both his utility function and the constraint set with accuracy and, thus, solve his constrained maximization problem optimally. An approach more in keeping with the perspectives of the New Institutional Economics would require quite different assumptions about the manager's information endowment. Once a realistic position is taken with respect to the existence of positive transaction costs in a system, it follows that all of the elements traditionally taken as data in neoclassical theory can no longer be accepted as objectively given to all decision makers. Thus, in the theory of the firm, the decision maker has to do more than find the profit-maximizing position or other desired point on the boundary of a clearly delineated production set. When operations are conducted in a world of frictions and uncertainty, the extent of the technological knowledge possessed by the manager of a productive organization is a variable to be determined as a part of a more general optimization process. Similarly, the levels of information about factor quality, employee effort, prices, and so on are also variables to be determined. Questions arise, therefore, about where, how far, and by whom the information search should be extended and about how specific institutional arrangements should be structured to generate appropriate productivity-enhancing incentives in a world of uncertainty.

The problem of inconsistent assumptions is not confined to simple deterministic models of the firm such as the one considered earlier, but rather it seems to be ubiquitous. For example, the large body of writings on formal principal-agent theory shows similar difficulty. There, different economic actors are assumed to possess quite different and specialized information structures. As was noted earlier, the basic situation envisioned is one in which the principal is "blind" as a direct monitor of his agent but otherwise has full knowledge of his agent's characteristics (i.e., the agent's preference function) as well as precise knowledge of the distribution function of the external disturbances in the system that affect economic performance. In short, the principal is assumed to have essentially unlimited information in some directions and none whatsoever in other directions—a situation that implies the coexistence of positive and zero transaction costs. Similarly, dubious assumptions are encountered in the literature on "mechanism design," an area that also maintains close connections with orthodox neoclassical theory. Thus, it is argued that even when positive transaction costs exist and individuals possess private information, cleverly conceived government intervention can bring about first-best efficiency solutions while private bargaining cannot (Farrell 1987, 118). What is not explained, though, is how the addition of binding constraints to a system in the form of transaction costs (and/or the recognition of bounded rationality) can be consistent with the first-best outcomes.

There is certainly a question, then, as to whether these analytic procedures are defensible. To ignore real and unavoidable restrictions on human activities, such as those associated with positive transaction costs, is to flirt with the nirvana fallacy. It is often legitimate to abstract from certain complications of the real world in order to permit a given problem to be solved under simpler conditions. Nevertheless, as Morgenstern has noted:

> One has to remain aware, of course, that whatever is said then is subject to grave limitations and that one has to state what they are. The abstraction made would be faulty if it bypasses a fundamental feature of economic reality and if the analysis of the radically simplified situation will never point towards its own modification in such a manner that eventually the true problem can be tackled. . . . Radical simplifications are allowable in science so long as they do not go against the essence of the given problem. (1964, 4)

Relative to this standard, it seems fair to say, at the very least, that the limitations of hybrid models are not emphasized sufficiently in the literature. The results they achieve depend critically on special assumptions; if these assumptions change, the results change. At the same time, the assumptions used in hybrid models define a type of universe that has little in common with the real world with which we are concerned. The situation here may be clarified with the use of an analogy. In Newtonian mechanics, it is possible to establish the equation for the trajectory of a projectile. The analysis can be accomplished by making various simplifying assumptions such as viewing the projectile as a mass point, disregarding the effect of the rotation of the earth, and neglecting the influence of the atmospheric temperature variations. Simplifications of the sort just mentioned do not affect the basic conclusions or predictions given by the trajectory equation. In other words, assuming that air temperature is inconsequential does not change the results in a fundamental way. The state of the air temperature is not a *crucial* assumption for the basic conclusions reached. By contrast, if the gravitational coefficient is assumed to be zero, the trajectory equation is changed profoundly, and the equation no longer provides any useful information about the behavior of the projectile in the physical world in which we are interested. Moreover, a trajectory equation based on the assumption of zero gravity would not seem to offer any foundation for learning more about the path of a projectile in the earthly world we know. The gravity assumption is a *crucial* assumption in this context. The point, then, for economics is straightforward. As long as we want to understand economic behavior as it occurs in an actual economic system, and as long as we believe that transaction costs and bounded rationality *affect real-life economic behavior significantly,* we cannot assume these "frictions" away and work with a model based in part on costless transactions and completely rational decision makers. Similarily, we cannot legitimately suggest that behavior occurs "as if" these special conditions hold and an individual can be simultaneously boundedly and unboundedly rational.

It is also true that transaction costs and bounded rationality play such central roles in actual economic life that the assumptions made about these phenomena are crucial not merely in one or two cases but in *all* economic contexts. Thus, if any real-world behavior is to be explored, it is inappropriate to abstract from transaction costs and bounded rationality. The credibility of hybrid models is undermined precisely because of this latter condition. It would be too extreme, of course, to say that hybrid models have nothing to offer and cannot contribute anything to our understanding of economic phenomena. Yet, it remains true that these models are vague about the fundamental significance of transaction costs and bounded rationality (Denzau and North 1994). All too frequently, the technical discussion moves back and forth haphazardly between different levels of abstraction. Economic activities that are supposedly carried out within one universe are judged relative to an efficiency standard or other considerations that have their origin and justification in a completely different universe. Ultimately, it would seem that analysis cannot be "half" neoclassical and "half" neoinstitutional.[2] All economic phenomena must be understood to be embedded in an environment in which costly transactions, incomplete information, and bounded rationality rule everywhere.

To simplify analysis, one might assert that all of the "frictions" in an economy are forms of transaction costs. Given this interpretation, it would seem to follow that the existence of nonzero transaction costs, as discussed previously, must produce an economic universe that is *strikingly different* from the one envisioned in neoclassical theory. This conclusion is inevitable unless it is believed that transaction costs can be introduced into the neoclassical model in a *selective* way. That is, the argument must be that transaction costs are (simultaneously) positive in some areas of the economy and zero in all others. By adopting this special convention, it might seem possible to say that decision makers are fully informed about all technological alternatives, or about existing commodities, but face nontrivial costs in using the price mechanism (Coase 1937, 390) and exchanging ownership titles (Demsetz 1968a, 35).

---

2. It has been noted in connection with the traditional neoclassical model that "we have learned that much of what we believed before is of limited validity; . . . the theory is not robust to slight alterations in the informational assumptions. It is but a special—and not very plausible— 'example' among the possible set of informational assumptions which can be employed to characterize an economy" (Stiglitz 1985, 21).

Reflection, however, suggests the inconsistency of this approach.[3] Why should the same general types of information gathering, communication, and enforcement operations be *costless* when the problem is, for example, one of individuals securing information on production technology or of establishing private ownership rights in resources and yet be *costly* when there is an attempt to use markets to acquire or sell products? In any event, some empirical justification for these assertions would have to be forthcoming. We would have to ask how large the costs are in each area and what specific factors account for the positive or zero costs stipulated. Such questions, though, have no easy answers. Indeed, the idea that zero transaction costs and positive transaction costs can hold simultaneously in an economic universe does not seem defensible conceptually. Actually, the case against the "dual-cost" universe is stronger than the discussion suggests so far. What must be recognized is that the movement to introduce positive transaction costs into the economic model is motivated, in part, by a desire to establish a different, more realistic conception of decision makers. To say that individuals have to use time and resources to secure information, and that they have limited ability to handle data and formulate plans, is merely to make reasonable assumptions concerning the character of the decision makers in the system. Indeed, there is general agreement that the "model of man" used in economic theory has to be made more flexible. But, insofar as individuals are conceived as possessing the particular characteristics just noted, it is clear that they must incur what we call "transaction costs" and that positive transaction costs will be encountered no matter what area of the economy the decision makers are conducting operations in or what type of activity they are performing. Transaction costs must appear *everywhere* in the system because of the nature of the individuals making decisions. Put differently, the point is that as long as individuals have to use scarce resources (human and nonhuman) in order to acquire and process information transaction costs must exist *wherever people make decisions*—that is, wherever economic activity takes place. Thus, once we reject the notion of the omniscient decision maker who is "completely rational," the economic model undergoes a basic transformation[4] and a change in paradigm appears to be unavoidable.

If the argument just advanced is correct, this position on transaction costs has some interesting implications for the interpretation of hybrid models. By definition, hybrid models are those that assume conditions in which some positive transaction costs coexist with zero transaction costs. Reflection suggests, however, that if such a mixed system is to be found, a necessary condi-

---

3. This tendency to employ what are effectively contradictory assumptions is widespread. For a recent example of the practice, see DeMeza and Gould 1992, 564.

4. According to one widely accepted definition: "A completely rational individual has the ability to foresee everything that might happen and to evaluate and optimally choose among available courses of action, all in the blink of an eye and at no cost (Kreps 1990b, 745).

tion for its existence is that *at least some individuals making decisions must be "completely rational."* If no decision maker can be described as completely rational, we have the outcome just discussed and there can be no zero transaction costs.[5] In short, all hybrid models require the retention of the extreme assumption concerning rational actors. Moreover another problem surfaces when it is assumed that even one "completely rational" decision maker is operating in an economy. That is, there seems to be a problem of internal logical consistency because it is difficult to see how boundedly rational individuals, characterized by significant cognitive limitations, can compete for long with hyperefficient and essentially omniscient decision makers. Presumably, the system would soon be run exclusively by the elite group. But models reflecting this kind of polarized structure pertain to a highly abstract and empirically uninteresting world.

While there may be substantial agreement on the general meaning of *bounded rationality,* the profession has found it difficult to come together on a precise definition of the term. *Bounded rationality* refers broadly to purposive behavior that is conditioned by the cognitive limits of decision makers. But, beyond the acceptance of this basic view, understandings of the concept differ. Thus, in commenting on the results of a recent conference concerning bounded rationality, Scott noted:

As I listened to the various presentations and discussions, it seemed to me that the concept of bounded rationality was being employed in at least three reasonably distinct ways. (1) Some authors were referring to the consequences of the fact that there can be significant cost to acquiring and processing information. (2) Some were referring to capacity constraints— to the limits of the present stock of scientific knowledge or of the unaided information storage and reasoning capacity of the human mind. (3) Some were referring to the asserted existence of systematic distortions in human perception or thinking. (1994, 315)

This summary of views is instructive because it underscores the conflicting positions that exist and suggests that problems may be encountered in relating ideas about bounded rationality to mainstream economic theory.

What must be emphasized here, however, is that, regardless of which of the three views of bounded rationality is held, no problem is created for the interpretation of transaction costs presented earlier. However one construes the particulars of cognitive limitations, it is clear that these limitations must lead to costs in decision making. And, since all economic activity involves human

---

5. It might be argued, if not very convincingly, that some decision makers may be only "partially omniscient" or "selectively omniscient." Then, in principle, zero transaction costs could exist in some sectors of the system.

decision making, positive transaction costs must be ubiquitous. See also the case made by Conlisk (1996) for incorporating bounded rationality into economic models.

At the very least, there would seem to be good reason to question the continued usefulness of the orthodox neoclassical assumptions concerning "perfect information" and "complete rationality." Discontent with these assumptions is significant, of course, because they relate to areas that are of prime interest to the NIE—transaction costs, asymmetrical information, and bounded rationality.[6] Nevertheless, while neoinstitutionalist writers may raise objections to the lack of realism in mainstream theory, and to the legitimacy of assuming strict maximizing behavior on the part of decision makers, such criticisms have not had the greatest impact on the profession. The reluctance to depart very far from neoclassical perspectives is based on a number of factors, but it is certainly understandable that economists are hesitant about moving to a fundamentally different form of analysis. We know that:

1. Neoclassical thinking exerts an enormous influence on mainstream economics and shapes attitudes toward current research (Frey 1993). Further, there is fear that abandonment of the neoclassical model would leave the profession without an analytical focus and open the door to a flood of dubious, nonrigorous theorizing.
2. The early development of transaction-cost/property-rights analysis was accomplished through the incorporation of new themes into the standard model, and this approach, which produced some useful results, has proved hard to desert.
3. Despite the contributions that have been made to economic understanding by Austrian economics, the NIE, and other nonstandard approaches, there is as yet no well-articulated and generally accepted alternative theory that appears to produce the same range and richness of results as neoclassical theory does.

Change, it appears, will not come about easily.

### 10.2.2. Predictive Accuracy

At a more fundamental level, attempts have been made to discredit criticisms of the neoclassical model by appealing to the requirements of scientific meth-

---

6. As Wiseman has observed: "The growing dissatisfaction with the dominant neoclassical orthodoxy manifests itself in several ways. The major one is the emergence of more-or-less-fundamentally competitive schools of thought. Notable examples are the Austrian School, the New Institutionalists . . . , evolutionary economics, public choice, constitutional economics, behavioral economics, and the radical subjectivists personified by Shackle" (1991, 150–51).

odology. Thus, it has been argued strongly by Friedman (1953, 30) and others that the predictive value of a theory, not the realism of its assumptions, is the prime consideration for evaluating the theory. Specific examples were used to bring home the correctness of this position. Hence, it was noted that, in a biological model, one could assume that each leaf of a plant deliberately seeks to maximize its exposure to the sun's rays. And then, even though the notion of such volitional action on the part of a leaf is *unrealistic,* good predictive results about plant behavior could still be obtained. The issue, though, does not end there. However persuasive the Friedman example may be (Mayer, 1993; Koopmans 1957, 137–40), there should be no confusion over the fact that an acceptable theory must be structured so that it contains no *contradictory* assumptions. For example, if, in addition to the "optimizing-leaf" assumption, the model also assumed that the physical characteristics of a leaf were such that it could not make any change in its orientation, the model would be fundamentally flawed. The two assumptions about leaf behavior are incompatible. But this condition of conflicting assumptions is precisely what is found in hybrid neoinstitutional models. Characteristically, these constructs presuppose the simultaneous existence of: (1) bounded rationality, (2) positive transaction costs, (3) complete knowledge of essential data, and (4) rational choice decision making. Models of this type have to be rejected because, under conditions in which all decisions are *costly* (as they must be when bounded rationality and positive transaction costs hold), decision makers simply cannot operate in the manner implied by the models. The solutions reached by hybrid models are defective because they are based on structures of inconsistent assumptions; in effect, solutions are derived from data that cannot be in the possession of the relevant actors and from decision methods that are too costly to be of practical use.

The difficulties just alluded to could be overcome if the neoinstitutional assumptions concerning bounded rationality and transaction costs were discarded. But then the models would obviously revert to the traditional neoclassical (frictionless) form, and there would be no neoinstitutional theory to discuss. From an analytical standpoint, the whole point of modern institutionalism is to take systematic account of certain constraints on economic activity that previously have been neglected. Insofar as we wish to understand economic behavior as it occurs in the real world, we cannot abstract from *fundamental features* of economic reality, and bounded rationality and transaction costs represent such fundamental features. We know from everyday experience that decision makers have only limited cognitive ability and limited time per period to devote to choice problems. Thus, economization is necessary. Similarly, we appreciate that the acquisition of information requires the use of scarce resources and that the initiation and completion of transactions involves a variety of contracting costs. Arguably, the special costs associated with bounded rationality can be conceived of as a particular class of transaction costs (or "frictions"). Whatever the classification system used, though, it is true that, together, bounded-rationality costs and the more conventional transaction costs exercise a profound effect on economic outcomes.

The analysis so far points to the fact that the hybrid models put forward in much of the neoinstitutional literature are based on inconsistent assumptions and are, by their inherent nature, incapable of yielding accurate predictions of events in the real world. Despite this criticism, however, it is often suggested by the defenders of hybrid models that, although these constructs embody certain "simplifications," they are still able to generate useful results and do indeed have empirical support for their predictions. The question arises, then, as to how such claims can be made. And, interestingly, one reason for the confusion would seem to be that the standards used to assess "predictive accuracy" are extremely loose. Traditional analysis, carried on in formal terms at high levels of abstraction, tends to produce solutions that, while plausible technically, carry very little real content. Thus, with respect to the standard neoclassical model of demand, Thaler has observed:

> Economists rarely draw the distinction between normative models of consumer choice and descriptive or positive models. Although the theory is normatively based (it describes what rational consumers *should* do), economists argue that it also serves well as a descriptive theory (it predicts what consumers in fact do). This paper argues that exclusive reliance on the normative theory leads economists to make systematic, predictable errors in describing or forecasting consumer choices.
>
> In some situations the normative and positive theories coincide. If a consumer must add two (small) numbers together as part of a decision process then one would hope that the normative answer would be a good predictor. So if a problem is sufficiently simple the normative theory will be acceptable. Furthermore, the sign of the substitution effect, the most important prediction in economics, has been shown to be negative even if consumers choose at random (Becker 1962). Recent research has demonstrated that even rats obey the law of demand (Kagel and Battalio 1975). (1994, 3–4)

If the existence of downward-sloping demand schedules in the economy can be taken as evidence of the predictive accuracy of a hybrid model of demand, it seems clear that the empirical testing process is not very rigorous. But such a relaxed approach is the norm. Various detailed questions about consumption are routinely ignored in purely formal analysis. For example, in an *n* commodity system, it would be interesting to know what the theory's predictions are with respect to such questions as: (1) how many distinct types of goods are consumed at equilibrium and (2) what is the consumption level of each type of good selected for consumption? We know the theory is flexible, but is it reasonable to believe that the consumer may specialize deliberately in the consumption of a single good, or that he may decide to consume simultaneously each type of consumer good produced in the system, or that he will show an infinite demand for any good that carries a zero price? Regardless of what even casual empiricism suggests, a hybrid model tied to orthodox utility analysis is consistent with the realization of any of the solutions just noted (Furubotn 1974b).

Actually, the problem with the hybrid models goes deeper, and there is no reason to believe that such constructs can ever make accurate predictions given their premises. Consider an example from the area of production economics. While the typical hybrid model may recognize that the firm's entrepreneur must incur costs in order to learn about input prices and input quality, the model assumes (implicitly) that the entrepreneur is able to use a *fully defined* production function in his optimizing adjustments. The latter information about technology, despite its extent and complexity, is assumed to be freely available. But this position is in conflict with other assumptions of the model that accept positive transaction costs and bounded rationality. Of course, if the fully defined production function is employed in the mathematical formulation of the problem, the solution is *inevitably biased.* This is so because the model makes it appear that search for the firm's ideal operating position can extend over a far greater range of technical alternatives than when the production alternatives have to be discovered by the entrepreneur through a costly discovery program. When discovery is necessary, the production function is attenuated and appears merely in *partial form.* Quite possibly, the partial (discontinuous) function, as established through the imperfect perception and limited cognitive capabilities of the human entrepreneur, can be so attenuated that what are, in theory, the most advantageous technical options available in society will not even be represented in the production set being reviewed by the entrepreneur. In short, the solution generated by the hybrid model of our discussion will not reflect real-world constraints and cannot be regarded as a suitable device for achieving accurate prediction of real-world behavior.

This pessimistic conclusion is reinforced when it is realized that hybrid models also presuppose that optimization involves the use of rational choice and maximization procedures based on the calculus. Such an approach implies costs that are not accounted for within the hybrid framework but have an important effect on what can actually be chosen by decision makers operating in a real-life system. The analysis of optimization costs will be the topic of the next section.

## 10.2.3.  Optimization Costs

As a practical matter, individuals incur costs in discovering options and choosing among them. Such "optimization costs" (or deliberation costs), as they may be called, are important because they exert a major influence on economic behavior. Unfortunately, however, such costs are either totally ignored in neoclassical theory or else given only partial treatment. For example, in the hybrid neoclassical models mentioned previously, some costs associated with the process of optimization may be considered while other significant forms of optimization costs are completely neglected. In any event, this general area deserves greater attention, and in what follows the objective is to explain more fully the nature of optimization costs and to demonstrate how they affect the ways in which decisions are reached in any economy characterized by "frictions." In order to simplify exposition, it will be convenient to conduct the discussion in terms of the elementary theory of the firm.

According to neoclassical doctrine, when decisions concerning the firm are made by "completely rational" individuals functioning within a world of costless transactions, the process of optimization is straightforward and takes place instantly (and costlessly). The institutional arrangements envisioned are rudimentary. The entrepreneur or owner-manager is assumed to possess unattenuated property rights in the "classical" firm and to make all decisions on enterprise policy (Alchain and Demsetz 1972). Then, in the special environment postulated, decisions are costless and each owner-manager can count on having comprehensive and accurate information about the firm's production function, prevailing market prices, factor qualities, and so on. Given this extensive information base, he is able to compare *all* of the "efficient" operating alternatives that are open and range in on the best, or profit-maximizing, option. However, things change radically when a shift is made to a world of frictions. When entrepreneurs have limited cognitive abilities and are forced to use time and other scarce resources to acquire and process information, the whole nature of the firm's optimization problem is altered. What occurs is not simply a transition to a moderately changed environment in which only a few variables have been affected. Rather, the new environment is one in which many crucial elements have changed simultaneously. The so-called hybrid models are unacceptable precisely because they take account of *only* some of the costs that have to be met in optimization (such as the cost of determining current input prices via search) while ignoring the costs of others (such as the cost of establishing the set of "efficient" production alternatives).

Given frictions, it is appropriate to assume that the entrepreneur controlling the firm has less than complete knowledge of the economic environment in which he is to function. This situation implies that when the structure of the firm is first established it will be based on the entrepreneur's imperfect initial knowledge endowment and influenced by his need to economize on the cost of decision making. Depending on how well the initially chosen structure is adapted to actually existing technological and market conditions, the firm's profits will be greater or lesser. Of course, in any time period (including the initial one) the entrepreneur is aware that his understanding of economic alternatives is restricted and that he may conceivably be able to increase his welfare level by *allocating greater resources to securing and processing information.* The urgency of the entrepreneur's desire for improved enterprise performance is likely to be related closely to the organization's level of profitability. Low profits imply modest rewards for the entrepreneur who is the residual claimant and may signal difficulties that can imperil the firm's survival. Obviously, factors other than profit can affect the decision in question. Individual owner-managers differ with respect to their willingness to assume risk, the aggressiveness with which they seek profits, and their capacity to make good decisions. But, regardless of the details here, the very nature of the real-world environment postulated ensures that firm adjustment will tend to take place over time.

We assume, then, that optimization is an ongoing process involving period by period adjustments as resources are made available at various dates for search and as learning by doing takes place. Insofar as the firm's activities lead to progressively greater knowledge of production options and improved economic arrangements, there will be successive reformulations of the firm's profit function, and a series of new operating solutions will be established over time. It is true, of course, that in any period (including the initial one), the cognitive and financial resources that can be devoted to maintaining or enhancing the firm's profit position are necessarily limited. Despite the constraints in existence, however, there should be continuing movement and structural adjustment as long as the entrepreneur believes that the prospective gains from corrective action are greater than the costs of such action.

This interpretation of enterprise behavior indicates that the optimization process (and the costs of such optimization) will tend to be spread out over time. There are still questions, of course, about precisely how the entrepreneur is likely to carry out the optimization process. What should be clear, too, is that optimization costs, which are not accounted for adequately in neoclassical analysis, have central importance for the neoinstitutional firm. That is, in order to realize a normal profit and remain in the industry in the long run, a firm must be careful about its outlays but take deliberate steps to maintain a reasonable level of efficiency over time. Given the fluid situation in existence, the firm must try to keep up with other firms in the industry, which are themselves continually seeking to improve their positions through the use of better decision procedures and the acquisition of new information. Only in this way can a firm ensure that its revenue from commodity sales each period will be sufficient to cover its per period outlays on the factors employed directly in commodity production, the array of routine transaction costs, and the various current costs attributable to the process of decision making and optimization. The general conclusion to be drawn, then, is that optimization activities, which generate both benefits and costs, are integral to a balanced theory of the firm (Pingle 1992, 5).

Taking a broad view of the optimization process, it is possible to distinguish three basic categories of optimization costs. These are (1) decision-method costs, (2) data costs, and (3) selection costs. In terms of our example concerning the theory of the firm, the following connections can be made. First, it is clear that since a fully defined production function is not known to the firm's decision maker automatically, the individual must make efforts to gather at least some information on technical production alternatives.[7] He must, therefore, select a particular *decision method,* from among the various possible decision methods extant, to guide his accumulation of data. In other words, the so-called rational choice approach is not the only decision method available. If an entrepreneur wishes to economize on decision time, he is able to use other methods, such as random choice or imitation, for the process of deciding which technical information to collect. But one must recognize that it is also costly, in terms of the entrepreneur's time and resources, to select a decision method.

The latter task is important, however, because the method chosen will determine (1) how intensively and in what manner the subsequent search for technical information will be conducted and (2) the costs that will be incurred in applying the decision method to the search process. Precisely how much in the way of resources the entrepreneur will be willing to commit at any time period to the process of selecting a decision method (or search plan) is a subjective matter. What has to be noted, though, is that the pool of relevant technical knowledge in the economy is very large relative to the capacity of any one (small) firm to discover and utilize new information. Thus, if the entrepreneur is to economize on the overall use of his valuable time (and other resources), he must give enough attention to the choice of a decision method to avoid the mistake of using a method (such as rational choice) that attempts systematic and close consideration of the system's *total* knowledge stock (Conlisk 1996, 675). It would seem that any search plan chosen and employed would have to be quite selective and would be designed to do no more than sample certain areas of technological information that the entrepreneur views as likely to be promising.

7. According to orthodox microeconomic theory, the production function supplies a decision maker with all of the information he needs to make an efficient choice of technical production arrangements for the firm. Arguably, however, if input prices vary systematically with the way in which the inputs are utilized in production, the whole production set will be needed to ensure an efficient (or profit-maximizing) choice (see Furubotn 1996).

Decision-method costs are the costs associated with the process of selecting a particular decision rule. Of course, whatever the decision rule or search plan chosen, additional costs will be incurred when the rule is *applied* to secure technological information. The costs in question may be termed *data costs*. The entrepreneur is free to determine how much total investment he is willing to make in each period in order to expand his perception of available production techniques. Nevertheless, he will not possess, either at the outset of operations or subsequently, anything like a comprehensive production function. In practice, information on technology is so extensive and complex that the total stock possessed by society will never be assembled by any single individual facing finite transaction costs.[8] The collection of data, like any other economic activity, is subject to the discipline imposed by cost-benefit calculus. Beyond some point, the cost of additional information will outweigh the perceived benefits of that information.

Depending on the judgment exercised by the entrepreneur, the firm will have established, in any period, a certain set of alternative production techniques. This highly attenuated "production function" will then represent a key datum facing the entrepreneur. It is from among the possibilities in this set of technological options that he must choose the particular production arrangement that he believes will result in the greatest net profit for the enterprise. But choice among options is not a costless process. Consequently, the entrepreneur must use some care in selecting another *decision method* (from among contending possibilities) that will be able to deal with the technological choice problem efficiently. It can be reemphasized here that, while the rational choice method (which underlies neoclassical optimization) will necessarily lead to the best solution theoretically attainable from the attenuated production set, the method will be costly in terms of decision time (and other resources) because it implies that *all* of the alternative options being surveyed will be considered and compared (Day and Pingle 1991; Gottinger 1982). In other words, the rational choice method is undeniably best in a zero-transaction-cost, unboundedly rational world where optimization costs are nil. In the real world, however, the situation is quite different. On balance, a decision method that is less systematic and exacting in pursuing the search for the "ideal" production arrangement (e.g., random choice) can be superior to the maximizing behavior of rational choice.

What we may call *selection costs* emerge at the final stage of the firm's optimization process in any period. These costs, which can be taken as essen-

---

8. The standard definition of the production function "presupposes technical efficiency and states the maximum output obtainable from *every possible input combination*" (Henderson and Quandt 1980, 66; italics added). It does not have to be emphasized that the consideration of every possible input combination represents a tall order. See also Nelson and Winter (1982, 59–65).

tially one-period flow costs, appear after the firm's set of technical production options is in place as a datum and when the entrepreneur must apply his chosen decision method to select what he believes to be the best solution from among the known options. The arrangement in question is the one that promises to yield the greatest net profit for the firm when followed, given the existence of the various costs of optimization, standard transaction costs, and the other significant limitations under which the entrepreneur must operate. Conceivably, quite significant outlays can be made by a firm in choosing decision methods, applying them to the problems of securing needed technological information, and deciding on which technical production alternative to use. It is obvious, of course, that the greater these optimization costs the greater must be the departure of the enterprise model from the orthodox neoclassical model, which assumes that optimization costs are zero.

### 10.2.4. Infinite Regress

Once the existence of optimization costs is recognized, it is no longer possible to defend the assumption that purposive individuals always reach their decisions on the basis of orthodox maximizing behavior. In short, the idea that rational choice is a universally used decision method has to be rejected. This is so because, when bounded rationality holds and all decisions made by human agents are costly, the concept of rational choice leads to a logical dilemma (Winter 1975; Gottinger 1982; Conlisk 1988).

> This difficulty with strict optimization theory has become known as the "circularity problem"—there does not exist an optimization problem which can be solved that fully incorporates the cost of decision making. (Pingle 1992, 10)

In the terminology introduced earlier, it is "decision-method costs" that reveal the workings of the circularity problem. We noted that the firm's decision maker had to incur cost (especially time cost) in deciding on the particular decision method (say A) to use in, for example, selecting the optimal production option for the firm from the known set of alternative technical options. What is apparent, however, is that no attention was given to the question of how the entrepreneur happened to choose the method (say B) that was used to choose among the array of possible decision methods (of which A was one element) or of the cost of selecting method B. A *higher order* problem was totally ignored. That is, some method (say C) must have been employed (at some cost) to choose B from among the different possible methods for selecting decision methods (of which B was one option). But then a further question emerges: how was C chosen? The general situation here indicates that the methodological problem of *infinite regress* obtains, and thus certain costs associated with rational-choice decision making cannot be taken into account. Indeed, we know that

> the decision-cost associated with solving the higher order problem is necessarily larger than that associated with the lower order problem. It follows that decision-costs act to limit the extent to which rationality can be displaced to higher levels. There must come a point where . . . the "rational thing to do is to be irrational" and simply choose a choice method without reason. Otherwise, all resources would be used in decision-making. (Pingle 1992, 11)

What is often overlooked in mainstream economic analysis is the fact that different modes of decision making behavior exist, and that no one method will always be utilized by decision makers. Indeed, given the high costs of the rational choice method in terms of decision time and other resources, it must be expected that, in practice, individuals will normally avoid rational choice procedures and economize by using alternative decision methods. Contrary to the neoclassical model and hybrid neoinstitutional models that are linked to rational choice, the general rule would seem to be that the entrepreneur, the consumer, and other decision makers will act according to rules of thumb or similar "short-cut" devices when seeking solutions that are, on balance, the best attainable (Conlisk 1996, 677).

It should also be understood that movement away from rational choice decision-making behavior forces a reconsideration of neoclassical concepts of efficient allocation. If there is a general tendency for decision makers to employ decision methods different from rational choice, it is clear that first-best Pareto efficiency will not be realized in the system. It is equally true, however, that second-best Pareto optimality, or constrained Pareto optimality, will not be realized either.[9] This point has some interest because the literature that sees modern institutionalism as extended neoclassical theory is based on the idea that adding constraints to the orthodox model can lead to outcomes that reflect "constrained efficiency" (Demsetz 1969, 11). From this perspective (of comparative institutional analysis), a correctly formulated equilibrium model must reach beyond the oversimplified neoclassical structure and include all of the real-life constraints that decision makers face when seeking to maximize profit or utility. But the approach has only superficial plausibility. In the context of a neoinstitutional environment in which transaction costs and bounded ratio-

---

9. See (Stiglitz, 1994, chaps. 3, 4), for a useful summary of the problems that arise in welfare economics when the orthodox assumptions about perfect information and complete markets are dropped.

nality exist, optimization costs also exist, and it is easy to show that second-best Pareto optimality is an illusion. Specifically, we know that if limited cognitive capacity is a universal condition of humankind individuals must find it costly to make decisions. Under such conditions, though, there will surely be attempts to reduce decision costs by adopting modes of decision-making behavior other than rational choice optimization. And, of course, when other decision methods are used, the characteristic, constrained-Pareto efficient solution cannot appear.

A consistent theme of section 10.2 has been the impossibilty of formulating an acceptable body of neoinstitutionalist theory through the simple strategy of changing a few neoclassical assumptions while leaving others unchanged. It is true, of course, that so-called hybrid models, reflecting this approach, appear prominently in the literature. Nevertheless, these models reveal serious logical difficulties and cannot be sustained. In summary, we can say that the case against hybrid models reduces ultimately to four basic considerations. (1) The models are unsatisfactory because they are constructed on the basis of contradictory assumptions. Specifically, the assumptions made about the information possessed by decision makers are inconsistent with the assumptions (made simultaneously) concerning bounded rationality and positive transaction costs, assumptions that are crucial to neoinstitutional analysis. (2) As a result of the information structure assumed in hybrid models, the characteristic decision problem for such models presupposes the availability of data (e.g., a comprehensively defined production function or utility function) that cannot be known to boundedly rational individuals operating in a neoinstitutional environment. (3) Only one mode of decision-making behavior is admitted (rational choice), even though other decision methods would likely bring about preferable solutions by reducing decision costs and even though rational choice leads to a logical dilemma (infinite regress) in a system in which all decisions are recognized as costly. (4) The solution reached by a hybrid model (which, by definition, involves both neoclassical and neoinstitutional elements) may appear plausible in purely formal terms, but it is fundamentally misleading because it is derived from data and decision procedures that are effectively beyond the power of real-life individuals to achieve.

## 10.2.5.  Economic Efficiency

Since the shift to a neoinstitutionalist universe has the effect of changing profoundly the nature of economic relationships and the kinds of solutions that are attainable, it is not surprising that the traditional neoclassical concept of economic efficiency must also undergo change. In the early period, however, writers of the NIE school were content merely to modify the neoclassical definition of efficiency. The revision contemplated was consistent with the position taken on the legitimacy of hybrid models. That is, these writers were critical of the orthodox approach because they did not believe that a definition based on the working of an idealized, frictionless system could serve as an adequate foundation for deciding allocation policy in the real world. Presumably, additional constraints had to be recognized since the orthodox general equilibrium model was seen as highly abstract and limited.

> It is a central characteristic of welfare economics that economic outcomes derived from the basic neoclassical model are used as a criterion of efficiency. Outcomes that deviate from outcomes in models based on fully defined exclusive rights [in property] and costless transaction are called "inefficient." (Eggertsson 1990, 21)

The basic conclusion, then, is that it is inappropriate to focus attention exclusively on hypothetical or "ideal" solutions. Indeed, it is obvious that once there is a shift from a "frictionless" universe scarce resources have to be used to effect transactions, protect property rights, and so on. This means, in turn, that the system's total resource endowment can no longer be devoted solely to the production of normal commodities (Dahlman 1979 150–56). The implication is, of course, that relative to the idealized neoclassical benchmark all real-world situations can be no more that second best.

The neoinstitutionalist argument was that, for the purposes of positive economics, the only outcomes that are meaningful are those that are potentially attainable in the real world.

> The view that now pervades much public policy economics implicitly presents the relevant choice as between an ideal norm and an existing "imperfect" institutional arrangement. This *nirvana* approach differs considerably from a *comparative institution* approach in which the relevant choice is between alternative real institutional arrangements. In practice, those who adopt the nirvana viewpoint seek to discover discrepancies between the ideal and the real and, if discrepancies are found, they deduce that the real is inefficient. Users of the comparative institution approach attempt to assess which alternative real institutional arrangement seems best able to cope with the economic problem. (Demsetz 1969, 1)

It follows from this interpretation of the problem that if each decision maker is rational and behaves consistently with the maximization postulate, the best *attainable* option will always be sought and reached. Thus, it can be argued that efficiency is being defined as constrained maximization. Efficiency conditions are seen as the properties of a determinate (equilibrium) solution implied by a given theoretical construct. On this view, a system's solutions are always efficient if they meet the constraints that characterize it. (DeAlessi 1983, 69)

There can be no doubt that this conception of efficiency concentrates attention on real choices and ends the dubious neoclassical practice of comparing observed outcomes to purely hypothetical and unrealizable solutions.[10] Nevertheless, the definition has unsettling aspects, and it can be asked whether the identification of efficiency with constrained maximization represents an acceptable way of proceeding.

As was suggested earlier, what the constrained maximization theory of efficiency does, in essence, is to accept the basic neoclassical definition and then extend it to cover situations in which additional constraints hold. The approach asserts that the *effective* opportunity set (which is established on the basis of actually existing constraints) always lies inside the hypothetical efficiency frontier of orthodox neoclassical theory. It follows from this position, of course, that the most a decision maker can do is to reach the boundary of the effective set. In the absence of saturation, an individual has motivation to exploit all of his options to the fullest extent so as to increase his welfare. Thus, if his perceived opportunity set is A, he will maximize and reach an equilibrium point on the frontier of this set. At the same time, any failure to reach the boundary of A can be interpreted to mean that the original opportunity set A was not specified properly. Presumably, some neglected constraint must exist, which, if accounted for, would help to generate a different opportunity set, B, and a different attainable optimum on the boundary of B. In short, any outcome can be rationalized as efficient. Using this logic, the exponents of "generalized" neoclassical theory attempt to defend the idea that behavior is always efficient and choice always optimal in properly specified models. On first view, the argument has a claim to reasonableness because it is difficult to assert that positive transaction costs and other real-world constraints that set limits on human action are the *causes* of inefficiency. Insofar as certain obstacles encountered in economic life are *unavoidable,* they must be represented as constraints in the maximization problem or the nirvana fallacy will obtain. The basic issue of efficiency, however, cannot be reduced to these simple terms and

---

10. Since no one other than an omniscient "observing economist" can have the information that would permit a system to reach full efficiency at the hypothetical, grand utility-possibility frontier, there is no chance for normal market participants to bring about the ideal results discussed in traditional welfare theory. See (Hayek, 1937, 1945, 1978).

then dismissed.[11] At the very least, the assumptions underlying this attempted "generalization" require fuller discussion.

Writers such as Leibenstein, whose views are somewhat more sympathetic to orthodox neoclassical theory, have been critical of the constrained maximization definition of efficiency on the grounds that it is tautological and contradicts common-sense interpretation. Leibenstein says:

> Any decision procedure that does not permit nonoptimal choices denies the essential meaning of the word optimization, that is, the necessarily comparative element involved. (1985, 11)

This point is well taken. Understanding is not advanced very far when any observed outcome can be rationalized as "efficient." But Leibenstein tends to play down the importance of unavoidable, real-world constraints. He argues that constraints merely explain why suboptimal decisions are made; they do not change the preference ordering of the options and do not alter the fact that suboptimal decisions have been made (Leibenstein 1985, 13, 15). Similarly, he rejects the argument that any apparent inefficient choice can be attributed to a misspecified objective or preference function. Thus, a quandary seems to exist. According to one school of thought, efficiency results when the conditions for constrained maximization are met and all relevant constraints are taken into account. But, on the other hand, efficiency is said to exist only when the idealized Pareto conditions for the optimum are met. Then an inefficient choice is defined as one that deviates from the frontier of the idealized opportunity set—a deviation that is inevitable in the real world. Depending on which explanation one accepts, *all solutions are efficient or all are inefficient.* Clearly, neither of the two approaches provides us with much comfort. And the fundamental difficulty is traceable to their close connection with the neoclassical model. Although the literature of the New Institutional Economics attempted a reformulation of the efficiency concept, it did not go far enough. It is not sufficient merely to add supplementary constraints to the optimization problem. What has to be recognized is that once positive transaction costs and bounded rationality are assumed the whole structure of the new world model becomes significantly different from that of the orthodox one. Inter alia, decision makers are placed in a different position with respect to the elements

---

11. There is no way of escaping the effects of those basic constraints that bind *every* decision maker. Problems appear, however, because constraints cannot always be separated neatly on a priori grounds into the avoidable and the unavoidable. Some constraints, especially those relating to personal qualities, tastes, and capabilities of individuals, do not lend themselves to straightforward classification. It follows that whether a particular constraint is or is not avoidable may depend on who the economic actor is. This situation, of course, creates difficulties for any definition of efficiency based on the concept of operative constraints.

traditionally taken as data, and the behavior of an economy cannot be interpreted as if it emerged from the solution to a set of straightforward maximization problems. Familiar efficiency benchmarks such as the welfare frontier disappear. Thus, nothing less than a radical transformation of conventional theory appears to be required. Precisely why all this is so, and the problems to be faced in the new theoretical environment, will be taken up in section 10.3.

## 10.2.4.  Coordination of Activity

It is well known that the basic neoclassical model is not particularly helpful in analyzing the problems of economic adjustment in a system characterized by positive transaction costs and imperfect information. Thus, relative to the issue of system stability, it had been pointed out that:

> Virtually all formal theory is concerned with equilibrium conditions. Very little formal theorizing has been concerned with the question of how a private enterprise system gets to equilibrium, or how it would stay there in the face of perturbations. Even in the context of partial equilibrium models of private enterprise, the question of dynamic response to a shift in a demand curve or factor supply conditions can involve some complications, particularly if responses are discrete—think of the corn-hog cobweb cycle. In a general equilibrium context, where changes in output response to changes in demand influence factor prices and personal incomes which in turn may feed back to further change demands, the question of stability is even more complicated. To someone who proposes that private enterprise responds accurately to changed market conditions, the failure of general equilibrium theorists to prove stability, save under very stringent conditions, should be a severe embarrassment. (Nelson 1981, 102–3)

Along similar lines, it has been noted that in the case of imperfect information *efficient* resource allocation cannot be achieved under decentralization of activity unless the government intervenes and introduces a whole set of subsidies and taxes. These critical comments suggest the difficulties that exist in this area of analysis once the simplifying assumptions of the neoclassical model are relaxed.

What is not so clear, however, is whether the operation of a decentralized system of the real world can be assessed with the aid of conventional measures of efficiency or whether the results of general equilibrium analysis, based on idealized assumptions, can be used to say much about stability. In circumstances in which positive transaction costs and bounded rationality play key roles, the very process by which economic solutions are reached is quite different from that contemplated by the neoclassical (perfect information) case. From the new perspective, data in the orthodox sense do not directly shape outcomes. In effect, economic reality is only subjectively, not objectively, knowable. And the consequence is that there is no clear-cut efficiency standard for a system comparable to either the Pareto optimum or the second-best optimum.

Serious problems of business planning arise inevitably in the kind of economy explored by the New Institutional Economics because transaction costs rule out anything like a complete set of forward (and risk) markets. Then, in considering potential investment projects, for example, decision makers have no straightforward way of securing accurate information on the intentions of other investors or of determining the likely consequences of their own investment plans. The loss of the ability to test intentions and the emergence of secondary or social uncertainty are important. Each decision maker has to adjust his behavior to what he *expects* others will know and do. But, given the different ways in which expectations can be formed and the inherent difficulty of using incomplete information to establish good projections, there can be no presumption that the decisions made will possess sharp optimality properties. Behavior in a world of frictions can be quite varied because individuals will see both the present and the future differently. It is also true that other mechanisms than the market may have to be used to permit responses to changed economic conditions to proceed in a more orderly and coordinated manner.

Stiglitz has remarked that the notion of decentralization associated with neoclassical theory seems to reflect a structure that is best adapted to the solution of a *once and for all* problem (1985, 35). What is needed to deal with a world of frictions and uncertainty, however, is something quite different. A model consistent with neoinstitutionalist perspectives should project an institutional structure that is able to adapt and respond to a series of new and changing problems. Thus, attention must be directed to the "architecture" of an economic system or the pattern of organization of individuals in the system.

Problems of information gathering, communication, and decision making are central to this view. Individuals have finite capacities to gather and process information, while communication of information between individuals is both costly and imperfect. Information gathering and decision making takes real time, and both because of positive discounting and because the environment is constantly changing (so that information quickly becomes obsolete) there is a return to making decisions quickly. The consequences of these simple observations is that how individuals are organized to gather information, how information is communicated, and how decisions are made is critical to the performance of the economic system. (Stiglitz 1985, 36)

The problems addressed by the New Institutional Economics go beyond those considered here, which are concerned especially with the informational aspects of organization. Nevertheless, it does seem obvious that any new construct promising greater insight into questions of interest to the New Institutional Economics must represent more than a simple extension of the neoclassical model (Nermuth 1982, 3–4).

If nothing else, developments within the New Institutional Economics have made it apparent that the profession must move away from narrow preoccupation with the neoclassical concept of "efficiency." Insofar as transaction costs and bounded rationality constitute fundamental features of an economic system, it is unrealistic to expect that decision makers can achieve either the conditions for Pareto optimality or those for *constrained* Pareto optimality. Moreover, the neoclassical approach is, by its nature, unable to deal easily with the problem of how institutions change and evolve over time. As DeAlessi has noted,

> current concepts of efficiency are firmly rooted in the mathematics of constrained optimization that characterize neoclassical economics and focus on the comparison of alternative equilibrium conditions. To compare institutions on the basis of equilibrium conditions that will never be attained in a world of change and uncertainty, however, ignores all information about the process of change itself. (1992, 340)

Presumably, neoclassicism must be replaced with a less mechanistic and rigid theory, but at best the outlines of a superior alternative can be seen only dimly today.

### 10.3.  The Basis of a New Paradigm

When a transition is made to a "neoinstitutional" environment, there is no denying the fact that the economic problem changes radically from the neoclassical conception. What happens is that decision makers find themselves in a quite different position with respect to the things traditionally assumed to be data. That is, individuals are not "fully informed," as in a neoclassical model of general equilibrium. Rather, each individual has only *partial* knowledge of the options known to society as a whole. In other words, it is no longer possible to assume that each decision maker has perfect information concerning all existing technological options, the true properties of every commodity, and so on. Moreover, at each cross section of time, each person's knowledge endowment or information structure tends to be somewhat different from those of others.[12]

---

12. It seems reasonable to say that once positive transaction costs are assumed and informa-

The *subjective* data, on the basis of which individual decision makers actually take action, are quite distinct from what might be called the *objective* data of the system. The latter, of course, are the data that are known in full only to the total collectivity of decision makers.

The reinterpretations just noted are essential, but a satisfactory neoinstitutional model must take account of other data. It is not appropriate to ignore institutional arrangements or to assume that institutions are merely neutral in their effects on economic behavior. We know that institutions exert powerful influence on activity by determining both the structure of incentives and, along with technology, the magnitudes of transaction costs. As North has said:

> Institutions are the humanly devised constraints that structure human interaction. They are made up of formal constraints (rules, laws, constitutions), informal constraints (norms of behavior, conventions, and self-imposed codes of conduct), and their enforcement characteristics. Together they define the incentive structure of societies and specifically economies. (1994, 4)

This passage suggests that if institutions are to be introduced into a model that broadly parallels the neoclassical construct, these new constraints must appear at two levels. First, there will be a set of institutions at the "constitutional" level. In North's terms, this is the "institutional environment" (North and Thomas 1971). These arrangements will have the function of setting limits to what new institutions or behavioral codes will be permitted in the society. Obviously, basic change in the system will be easier or harder depending on the ways in which these higher level economic, political, and social institutions are defined. Second, there will be, at any moment in time, a finite set of institutional possibilities and organizational forms (North calls these the "institutional arrangements" [6]) that is consistent with the constitutional constraints extant and known to the collectivity of decision makers in the community. But, just as in the case of technological alternatives, individual decision makers will have different understandings of the options available. Some individuals will have greater initial knowledge than others, and each may, if he thinks it useful, devote resources to the discovery of additional options from among those in the system's existing set, or to the discovery of entirely new options.

Under the conditions sketched, there is, as usual, diversity in the initial positions of the system's decision makers. What distinguishes this case from the neoclassical model of general equilibrium, however, is the inevitability of short-run data shifts. Even if what we have termed the objective data are held to

---

tion is imperfect it will be inevitable that different individuals will have different knowledge endowments. People cannot be assumed to be uniform in their access to or capacity to utilize the information channels of the system.

be fixed, there will still be continuing movement in the economic situation of individuals. How much change will occur in the so-called subjective data linked to individuals depends, in a complicated way, on the character of institutions, the attitudes of decision makers, the state of technology, and so on. For example, consider the question of individual ownership of the means of production. While the distribution of property rights in assets is taken as a datum in the neoclassical case, things are not so straightforward in a neoinstitutional model. Since in the type of system being studied transactions cannot be effected without the use of real resources and human intellectual effort, completely accurate monitoring and full enforcement of property rights are impossible. This is true if for no other reason than that such ideal results would be prohibitively expensive to achieve. Nevertheless, if ideal results cannot be achieved, there is still room for greater or lesser enforcement of private property rights. As was suggested earlier, how far an individual owner can go in protecting his position will vary with such factors as his own determination, the availability and cost of information, and the design of existing institutional and organization arrangements. Thus, in contrast to the neoclassical conception, the resource endowment possessed by an individual is not merely given[13] but can vary with his own efforts and events taking place within the system. Hence, his endowment may become effectively larger or smaller.

Even without further discussion of the complex neoinstitutionalist world, there can be no doubt that the theory pertaining to it must be significantly different from orthodox neoclassical theory. In the case of a general equilibrium model of the neoclassical type, the optimization problem stands out clearly, and it is possible to proceed smoothly from the precisely specified data and initial conditions of the system to the determination of the Pareto-optimal solution. In effect, everything necessary for the solution is known at the outset. But a comparable approach applied to the neoinstitutional problem does not seem feasible. One crucial difference is that, in this latter case, there are some basically *unknowable* elements that affect results. Wiseman has explained the situation lucidly as follows:

Human plans and decisions concern the future. In adapting to the future people have available to them incomplete information about the past and partial information about the continuous present (the moving points of actual decision). They can have no "information" about the future. Since it has yet to happen, there can be only opinion about it. In Shackle's graphic term, the future is characterized by "unknowledge." People will

13. Neoclassical theory recognizes, of course, that individual decision makers have control over the level of effort they wish to supply to the market. For a widely accepted summary of the neoclassical approach to welfare theory, see Bator (1957).

of course hold some opinions with more confidence than others. . . . [some] will be strong enough to render the difference between subjective and objective probability meaningless in respect to them. But in general the future is not of that kind: we expect it to contain events which we did not foresee. For it is of the essence of unknowledge that the future is unbounded. The problem is not simply that we do not know which of a possible set of futures will be the actual future; it is that we do not know the content of the possible set. In these circumstances, people will behave "probabilistically" only insofar as they conceive this to be an efficient way of coping with knowability, in which case a satisfactory explanation of their decision behavior must explain not only the attachment of probabilities to conceived outcomes, but also the selection process by which the unknowable future is reduced by decision-makers to those finite "relevant" outcomes. (1991, 151–52)

What has to be dealt with, then, is the dynamic nature of the neoinstitutional problem. While there may be some initially given conditions that influence the evolution of the system, new and unexpected forces are sure to be met over time. Thus, it is hard to believe that the dynamic system's time path can be predicted with great confidence.

Certainly a neoinstitutional economy's path is not "on rails" in the sense that the paths of some simpler dynamic models can be said to be. In principle, if precise information were available on the system's initial conditions and its structural characteristics, the system's evolution could possibly be "approximated." But the information necessary for even this type of solution is simply not obtainable. For one thing, in the circumstances described earlier, it is inherently difficult to decide which elements of the model are endogenous and which are exogenous. Indeed, since each individual is free to decide how far, and how frequently, to push the search for new or enhanced information, what we have termed the objective data of the system can only be known by some hypothetical, omniscient observer (Hayek 1945). No individual within the economy has full understanding of what all of the other decision makers in the system have accomplished because all operate more or less independently and secondary or social uncertainty abounds. At the same time, of course, the failure to possess a clear picture of the elements that are exogenous make theorizing about the system's development difficult.

## 10.3.1.  Diffusion of Information

In order to talk more easily about the peculiarities of the neoinstitutional economy, it will be convenient to assume initially that the so-called objective data of the system are fixed. Then the problems associated with the unknowable future are somewhat less sharp than was suggested earlier. Even under these simplified conditions, however, the neoclassical model can be shown to be ill adapted to the requirements of the New Institutional Economics. Difficulties arise because what begins as a static, neoclassical problem based on fixed data turns into a dynamic problem. At any moment, decision makers operating subject to positive transaction costs and bounded rationality can be assumed to have only partial and unequal knowledge of the system's fundamental data.[14] But some diffusion of information will inevitably be taking place over time. In one fashion or another—as a result of interaction among people, the free movement of workers, deliberate search programs, and so on—information transfers will be occurring. The very fact that monitoring and enforcement activities are costly means that individual knowledge stocks (even if they are recognized as private intellectual property) cannot be maintained completely inviolate. Thus, a progressively more equal distribution of knowledge will tend to evolve.

Ideally, a process of change and adjustment could go forward until all of the system's (fixed) knowledge stocks are utilized as fully as possible by decision makers and the limits to change imposed by the data are reached. At each step, changed information in the hands of the public will lead to corresponding change in production arrangements, organizational structures, preference ordering, and so on. Under these conditions, allocation will be altered appropriately from period to period, and system output will be progressively increased. In short, with this optimistic interpretation the model suggests that knowledge diffusion brings about economic changes similar to those found in a growing economy.

Such a view of the process, is too simplistic, however.[15] Indeed, unless the structure of the diffusion model is specified in much greater detail, it is difficult to say anything very definite about outcomes. Some improvement in output, at least in certain sectors, seems likely, but it is not clear how rapidly the knowledge dissemination activities will go forward or what channels will be used most. Firms will not, in general, be optimally adapted to existing economic conditions. Moreover, strong competition need not hold in all sectors since particular firms may achieve a degree of market power on the basis of differential knowledge. What has to be recognized, too, is the fact that at each step in

---

14. Precisely how great informational differences are in the initial period considered depends on how long the adjustment process has proceeded before analysis begins and the initial period is chosen.

15. Since, contrary to our simplifying assumption, the objective data of the system are also changing over time, there can be a more or less unending process of adjustment taking place in the economy, and it is far from clear that "long-run" equilibrium solutions will ever be attained. What is critical here is the speed of the diffusion process relative to the rate of change of the so-called objective data.

the dissemination process decision makers will be operating in a world in which some choices must be made subject to Knightian uncertainty. This situation does not prevent purposive behavior from taking place. But while, for example, information-search programs may be initiated in order to allow individuals or firms to make superior choices, there is no compelling reason to believe that such activities can assess the costs and benefits of search accurately. Some writers would argue that: "Information becomes a valued but expensive factor of production and decisions, to be used efficiently like any other" (Scott 1994, 316). From this standpoint, information fits into the general body of neoclassical analysis quite smoothly. The trouble is, however, that, unless some very extreme and dubious assumptions are made about the possibilities for predicting the net benefits from search as it is pushed, no great efficiency is achieved. There seems to be no way to avoid the uncertainty and fuzziness of results that are characteristic of the diffusion economy.

Any changes going forward in the evolving system must proceed under the influence of a particular institutional structure, and, of course, some of the changes that occur involve institutional and organizational restructuring. All of this means that political processes are also set in motion by the forces of information dissemination. But, again, uncertainty is generated because political markets are known to be even less efficient than economic markets are.

> Measuring and enforcing agreements in political markets is far more difficult. What is being exchanged (between constituents and legislators in a democracy) is promises for votes. The voter has little incentive to become informed because the likelihood that one's vote matters is infinitesimal; further, the complexity of the issues produces genuine uncertainty. Enforcement of political agreements is beset by difficulties. Competition is far less effective than in economic markets. For a variety of simple, easy-to-measure and important-to-constituent-well-being policies, constituents may be well informed, but beyond such straightforward policy issues ideological stereotyping takes over . . . (North 1994, 6)

In any event, if state sanction and support are needed for the practical implementation of a proposed property-rights or institutional change, a political process must be entered into by the parties interested in the change. Political bargaining occurs inevitably because modification of the institutional structure affects distribution as well as production and tends to bring about shifts in individual holdings of wealth and political power. Presumably, self-seeking behavior predominates in the system. Thus, the attitudes of decision makers toward a given reorganizational plan will be influenced strongly by the net gains they *expect* to receive from the restructuring. If significant parties cannot be compensated adequately through a gains-sharing solution reached by the political process, they are likely to withhold their support of reorganization and in this way possibly hinder the development of a more productive institutional environment. In short, it appears that distributional considerations influence the feasible set of institutional alternatives (Libecap 1989a; Johnson and Libecap 1994a).

Given the numerous complications that arise in the kind of universe presupposed by the information-diffusion model, we may wonder how people in such a system form their expectations or opinions about future developments. There is no question that expectations play a crucial role in shaping the path of an economy. However, in the case of an economy characterized by transaction costs, asymmetrical information, and bounded rationality it is not reasonable to assume that each decision maker follows the precepts of the "rational expectations" hypothesis. Rather, in light of the substantial differences among agents at any moment,[16] it seems likely that each individual makes his projections of future events using a different "model of economic reality." Precisely how people undertake purposive behavior in the face of an unknowable future is still an open question. It is interesting to note, however, that Keynes did not believe that outcomes were dominated by waves of irrational psychology.

> On the contrary, the state of long-term expectation is often steady, and even when it is not, the other factors exert their compensating effects. We are merely reminding ourselves that human decisions affecting the future, whether personal or political or economic, cannot depend on strict mathematical expectation, since the basis for making such calculations does not exist; and that it is our innate urge to activity which makes the wheels go round, our rational selves choosing between the alternatives as best we are able, calculating where we can, but often falling back to our motive on whim or sentiment or chance. (1936, 162)

Taking a broad view of the situation, it can simply be said that what actually emerges in the system is the result of all of the varied choices made by individuals. These decision makers can be conceived of as acting independently rather than in groups, but each person has to take some account of the anticipated behavior of others in the system. In contrast to the relatively straightforward, price-directed responses assumed in the neoclassical model, each consumer or producer in the neoinstitutional world faces more complex

---

16. The differences in knowledge endowments can be explained fundamentally by differences in personal qualities such as intelligence and energy and by the different opportunities people have for learning and development during the time interval before they enter the system as active decision makers.

choice problems. The neoinstitutionalist perspective, which emphasizes uncertainty, differential information endowments, optimization costs, and so on, also suggests why it is so difficult to establish a new formal model to deal with the phenomena of the New Institutional Economics. At the moment, there just seem to be too many alternative models that can be constructed—with each proceeding from different, but plausible, structural assumptions and initial conditions.

### 10.3.2. Shifting Preferences

In the economic system being considered, the consumer's preference map at any moment is determined by his reactions to the particular set of commodities of which he has current knowledge. Obviously, he cannot define preferences for commodities of whose existence he is ignorant and whose properties he does not know. At the same time, it is not realistic to assume that a decision maker is able to formulate a subjective probability distribution that will give him probabilistic information about when he will discover particular new goods in the future and about the specific properties these future goods will possess. It is true, of course, that since information concerning new options does not appear randomly but can be obtained through deliberate search, an individual may be able to reach at least some understanding of the likely direction of discovery. Nevertheless, it is difficult to believe that any significant or reliable knowledge can be had of the *properties* of the items to be discovered. There is no real basis for deciding in advance what the properties of yet to be discovered products will be, and decision makers must appreciate this fact. The consumer must move myopically from one period to the next; he cannot define preferences meaningfully in terms of anticipated future discoveries. There can be no reliable multiperiod utility functions in the system. This general situation means, however, that from an analytical standpoint problems arise when newly encountered goods require accommodation within the preference framework. Specifically, the original preference ordering must be discarded and replaced by a completely new ordering involving the new, enlarged set of goods. The newly discovered items cannot simply be added to an otherwise unchanged preference function; all information about preferences on the original set of goods becomes obsolete and valueless.

At this point, various objections might be raised against the explanation of events just presented. Thus, it has been argued that tastes and preferences can reasonably be regarded as *stable* over time and similar among people (Stigler and Becker 1977). This interesting conclusion is arrived at through the use of a reformulated theory of consumer choice that synthesizes production theory and consumption theory. Hicks (1956) made the suggestion that individual preferences are established in terms of certain ends or objectives that are not, in general, market goods. Rather, market goods are seen as the *means* to the attainment of objectives. This theme was developed by Morishima (1959) and Furubotn (1963) and in the well-known work of Becker (1965) and Michael and Becker (1973). As employed by Stigler and Becker (1977), the new consumer theory is drawn upon to show that unchanging preferences are consistent with the existence of such phenomena as addiction, advertising, and fads. However, from the standpoint of the New Institutional Economics, what is notable about this approach is that its results hold only if decision makers are "completely rational" and have the ability to foresee future events (Kreps 1990b, 745).

If one accepts the fact that the future is unknowable and information about the current situation is always incomplete, it is difficult to place much credence in any theory that assumes absolute permanence or changelessness of some underlying preference ordering—even an ordering pertaining to "basic needs." It would seem that an underlying preference ordering must have a limited perspective initially unless its originator can predict all future developments perfectly. In the Stigler-Becker model (1977), the utility function relating to the ultimate objects of choice is $U = U(Z_1, Z_2, \ldots, Z_m)$, and it is this function that reflects the individual's *preferences*. Then, in $U$, the relative importance of the different "objectives" $Z_1, Z_2, \ldots, Z_m$ must be given by means of some weighting system. Stability of tastes requires that these "weights" never vary over time, but this type of outcome holds only under very special conditions. Presumably, an individual might suffer a serious change in his health status and subsequently value "health services" more highly than some other objective. If the change in circumstances was foreseen accurately by the individual, a *multiperiod* utility function could be stable. Such a construct, however, would still imply preference change over time.

A more important problem here concerns the treatment of qualitative change in an individual's consumption options. Stigler and Becker assume that each $Z_i$ appearing in the basic preference function $U$ is produced with a single production function, $f_i$, involving market goods, a time input, human capital, and so on. Yet, if an object of choice, such as $Z_i$, is defined rather broadly, it seems clear that more than one production relation can be relevant. For example, "transportation services" can be provided by an oxcart or a Mercedes. And, in this case, selecting the oxcart because it offers the same, undifferentiated "transportation services" at lower cost than the automobile would likely be a mistake. On the other hand, higher quality choice objects can be interpreted as distinct outputs (elements of the set $Z_1, Z_2, \ldots, Z_m$) whose fabrication requires different productive techniques and different inputs (e.g., different market goods). In other words, relative to the preceding example, $Z_j$ can represent one type of transportation service and $Z_k$ can represent a similar service of different quality. This approach, though, solves one problem only at the cost of introducing another. If choice objects of different quality (based on inputs of different market goods) are all to be represented in the preference ordering $U = U(Z_1, Z_2, \ldots, Z_m)$, it is clear that all of the innovations that lead to quality changes in consumption options have to be anticipated when the ordering is first formulated.[17] Quite simply, if preferences are to be stable over time, despite the periodic appearance of new market goods, the decision makers in the system must be "completely rational."

Looking at the other side, and assuming that decision makers operate subject to bounded rationality, we find that a further difficulty besets the concept of stable preferences. The argument is straightforward. Theoretical models in the orthodox neoclassical tradition normally presuppose that an individual is able to establish a *comprehensive* map of his preferences, one that shows how he will react to all possible choices extant. What is required of the individual by the theory is, however, beyond his powers. Granting cognitive limitations, it is extremely unlikely that an imperfect choosing agent can order a very large number of options with complete consistency. Hence, at any moment, he will probably consider only a small subset of the *m* alternatives available. Indeed, recognizing that transaction costs are positive and that ordering alternatives is a time- and resource-using process, he has no compelling economic incentive to establish a fully comprehensive map. He will find it expedient to define only a few indifference curves or indifference manifolds, and he will specify only a limited segment of each curve drawn. Presumably, his choice of the zones to investigate and specify will be based on his current information about economic conditions (e.g., his income) and his expectations concerning future developments. But, if the boundedly rational individual proceeds in this fashion, there can be no confidence that his successive (partial) preference orderings will be mutually consistent or show stability over time. This whole discussion of preference stability illustrates, once again, how far we move from the simplifications of neoclassical theory when we introduce the assumptions of positive transaction costs and bounded rationality.

---

17. It has also been argued that if preferences are defined in terms of essential *characteristics* of goods rather that of the goods themselves (Lancaster 1966a, 1966b), preference orderings could be stable even though new goods were continually being discovered by consumers over time. Apart from everything else, for this argument to have real significance for the diffusion hypothesis and preference shifting, *all or most* of the new goods in question would have to be of special types. That is, the newly discovered goods at each round of adjustment would have to possess the same "characteristics" as those goods already known to consumers, but they must possess such characteristics in different proportions. The model that recognizes the role of information dispersion, though, asserts that it is not simply new forms of known types of commodities that consumers encounter during the ongoing discovery process but completely different types of goods not previously sampled. Thus, widening consumer experience (even in an environment in which the objective data are fixed) would seem to lead inevitably to changing preference orderings period by period.

The process of information diffusion, which is unavoidable in an economy of "frictions," carries major consequences for the concept of economic efficiency. Some of the problems have already been discussed. But a fundamental difficulty exists because individual tastes or preferences undergo change continually as people, who start with incomplete and unequal information endowments, broaden their knowledge of the system and discover "new" products. In effect, essentially *different individuals* are in existence at different points in time. Under these conditions, however, no consistent standards of reference are available with which to work, and there is no firm basis on which to make judgments about alternative economic plans. Preferences are simply not comparable from one period to the next. Note, however, that this view contrasts with the traditional interpretation. It was normally suggested in the mainstream literature that, while preferences might drift over time, the process of change was relatively slow. Thus, it was said that constructs like index numbers of real income change could be formulated provided the interval over which comparisons were to be made was short. What the transition to the neoinstitutionalist perspective does is bring this type of neoclassical analysis into serious question. It is not just long-run change in preferences that has to be accepted but also short-run change.

From a theoretical standpoint, it is also important to note that, even at any given moment of time, individual preference orderings will have one configuration or another depending on the particular structure of the economy at that time and the choices made by the people within it. In part, preferences are endogenous. It is not simply that one individual's preference function is affected by the consumption choices made by another, as in the standard theory of interdependence. In that case, it is assumed that all the relevant linkages between functions are known. Rather, the situation is one in which many different forces can influence what an individual knows about options and how he forms his preferences. But, since we do not as yet have a clear understanding of all the economic interconnections in a world of imperfect information and bounded rationality, preference functions are necessarily vague constructs. Hence, even comparative statical analysis is compromised; we cannot use preference functions to compare two hypothetical or conjectural situations at a given moment of time.

It follows from the argument presented that the Pareto criterion is not a device that can be employed meaningfully in assessing economic policy. And this is true whether or not there is agreement concerning the income (or welfare) distribution that is to be used as the basis for determining Pareto improvement. Indeed, if the problems exposed by the New Institutional Economics are as recondite as they now seem, nothing in the new, or the new new, welfare economics will be of much help to economists.

### 10.3.3. Efficiency Reconsidered

If the neoclassical efficiency standard is not used, a dilemma of sorts is created because it does not seem possible to find an alternative concept of efficiency that has the analytical rigor suggested by Pareto optimality or constrained Pareto optimality. One way of proceeding, of course, is to give up any attempt to measure efficiency with precision, or on a systemwide basis, and merely establish definitions ad hoc to meet the requirements of particular problems as they arise. For example, in considering the merits of different institutions, comparative institutional analysis might be employed. While a careful assessment of alternative institutional arrangements may have some usefulness, the insight provided is limited. Typically, only broad qualitative estimates are made of relevant characteristics (Demsetz 1969; Furubotn 1988). More important, however, is the fact that the number of alternatives that can be considered in any study is small. Therefore, although it may be true that, for example, option A is preferable to option B in the opinion of those who will be affected by the choice, this says little about ultimate efficiency. Moreover, in the literature of the New Institutional Economics, the criteria used to determine whether A is more efficient than B are normally static or one-period criteria, and such treatment seems ill adapted to the nature of the basic problem faced. After all, as Williamson has so often insisted, the choice of institutional forms takes place in the context of an ongoing, dynamic system. What has to be considered, to whatever extent possible in a world of pervasive uncertainty, is optimization over time, not one-period optimization. And the efficiency criteria used should be consistent with this requirement.

Another possible approach to the efficiency question is to define the criteria for efficiency in terms of the ability of a system to ensure the appearance of "reasonable" solutions for the economic problems of society. Then an economy would be regarded as efficient if it displayed tendencies to eliminate high-cost producers, force the movement of resources in directions desired by consumers, promote the innovation of new products and technologies, generate an acceptable distribution of income, maintain generally full employment, and so on. Consistency of the respective objectives might be a difficulty here, but if the requirements are not specified too rigidly there presumably will be some systems that can meet the standard (Buck 1982). Efficiency on this accounting is merely approximate; at best, there can be only a rough differentiation of the efficient from the inefficient. Moreover, since significant questions about the measurement of welfare are left unanswered, the approach is not particularly satisfying. All of this is unfortunate if not avoidable.

In his writings on institutional change, North has sketched an approach to efficiency that is perhaps best adapted to the type of economic environment contemplated by the New Institutional Economics. What is suggested, in effect, is that economic growth can be interpreted as a development that enhances social welfare and an "efficient" system is one that creates institutional and other conditions that serve to promote growth. From this standpoint, the traditional focus on allocative efficiency and the Pareto rule is not of prime interest. Rather, attention must be directed toward "adaptive efficiency," which is concerned with overall structure and the influence of structure on how the system can evolve over time. Thus, the assessment of efficiency involves consideration of such characteristics as "the willingness of a society to acquire knowledge and learning, to induce innovation, to undertake risk and creative activity of all sorts, as well as to resolve problems and bottlenecks of the society through time" (North 1990, 80).

North recognizes, of course, that the search for societal elements that make for adaptive efficiency is open ended. Understandably, however, he is convinced that institutional structure plays a key role.

> The incentives embedded in the institutional framework direct the process of learning by doing and the development of tacit knowledge that will lead individuals in decision making processes to evolve systems gradually that are different from the ones that they had to begin with. We need only to read, again, Armen Alchian (1950) to understand this. In a world of uncertainty, no one knows the correct answer to the problems we confront and no one therefore can, in effect, maximize profits. The society that permits the maximum generation of trials will be most likely to solve problems through time (a familiar argument of Hayek 1960). Adaptive efficiency, therefore, provides the incentives to encourage the development of decentralized decision making processes that will allow societies to maximize the efforts required to explore alternative ways of solving problems. We must also learn from failures, so that change will consist of the generation of organizational trials and the elimination of organizational errors. (1990, 81; see also Pejovich 1995, 159–67)

The general logic of North's position is clear, but, like other attempts of this type, the concept of adaptive efficiency scarcely lends itself to formalization. Further, once the matter of quantification is broached, it might be asked whether a society cannot invert too heavily in search (trials) at the cost of reasonable current consumption and intergenerational fairness. In any event, when loose definitions of efficiency are put forward, they may seem to compare unfavorably with the neoclassical efficiency standard. Superficially at least, the orthodox definition appears to provide more in the way of precise "scientific" information. This is perhaps one reason for its continued acceptance by much of the profession. Questionable though they may be, the nice regularities of the neoclassical model have appeal and are not easily discarded. Economists frequently speak of "efficiency," but one consequence of the movement into the territory of the New Institutional Economics is that we are left without a standard that can be described as comprehensive in its applicability and rigorous in its formulation.

## 10.4. Modern Institutionalism: The Opportunities for Progress

It is probably accurate to say that currently there are still many neoinstitutionalist writers who seek to deal with institutional questions through the use of extended neoclassical theory. In other words, despite their methodological problems, hybrid models of one sort or another remain in vogue. This tendency exists in part because neoclassical thinking continues to have a strong influence on economists and in part because it is impossible as yet to point to any well-articulated alternative theory that can replace existing neoclassical doctrine. To recognize that a new paradigm may be needed is one thing; to actually construct a comprehensive neoinstitutionalist model is another. If the objective is to create a "grand design" comparable in scope and detail with the general equilibrium models of neoclassical theory, a major task lies before us. For, as various writers have observed (e.g., Varian 1993, 1), the difficulties surrounding the construction of such a model are very great, indeed. It will be necessary to move into some relatively unexplored areas of study and set out the interconnections that exist among the economic, political, and social elements of the system. Since dynamic analysis will be involved, and since many of the things formerly relegated to the category of data will now be shifted to the status of active variables, complexity is unavoidable. Thus, the fully developed model we might like to have cannot reasonably be expected to appear in the near future, or perhaps ever.

To say that we cannot achieve our most ambitious objectives in a short span of time should not be too disheartening, however. It is not as though no progress has been made. As previous chapters of this book have indicated, a substantial foundation exists for future research, and certain topics in the areas of contract theory, transaction-cost economics, and the economics of the firm have shown substantial development. The literature concerned with the contracting process is particularly significant, of course, because it relates to a fundamental issue in economic theory—the explanation of how economic transactions between individuals can be coordinated through mutual agreement. In the neoclassical model, the characteristic transaction takes place instantaneously and the parties to it do not have any special interest in continued trade. Consequently, the understanding is that transactions are accomplished with the aid of the "complete" or "classical" contract. The latter, which

478    Institutions and Economic Theory

assumes perfect rationality on the part of decision makers, is quite specialized. It is comprehensive, its provisions are fixed ex ante for all eventualities and for the entire duration of the contract, the beginning and end of the contract can be determined unambiguously, and third-party adjudication can be relied upon for enforcement. In short, the clean and precisely specified "classical" contract mirrors the characteristics of the neoclassical world.

If transactions costs were zero and, for example, productive factors were costlessly mobile, classical contracts would be plausible. But, in fact, we know that there are significant costs to reallocation, that transactions take place repeatedly between the same parties over long periods of time, that markets are not impersonal, and that information is incomplete. Thus, the concept of the "relational" contract is used to explain the cooperation between individuals in a world with unforeseeable events. Relational contracting goes together with the assumption of bounded rationality and is fully consonant with neoinstitutionalist thought. Depending on circumstances, relational contracts are "administered," "organized," or "governed" by different "governance structures," "orders," or "constitutions" that are explicitly or implicitly developed through the efforts of cooperating individuals. The presumption is that contracting parties will formulate a constitution for their contractual association in such a way as to minimize the cost of adapting to the constantly changing conditions of the environment in which they are operating. This approach, which has already been given substantial development through work on incomplete contracts, self-enforcing agreements, and so on, forms an essential part of the New Institutional Economics. Lowering the cost of enforcing contracts and efficiently completing exchanges is an essential function for institutions and an indispensable element of the functioning of markets and economic "efficiency" (Wiggins 1991).

Earlier discussion has indicated that the general area of relational contracting is one from which an increasing flow of research contributions can be expected to emerge with time. Such research helps to underscore the limitations of the neoclassical model, and points the way to a deeper understanding of markets. It should be emphasized, however, that work in this area represents only one example of the writing that is enlarging institutional knowledge. A great deal of activity is taking place today in a variety of subfields connected with the New Institutional Economics. The theoretical and empirical studies being produced are not intended, of themselves, to create a comprehensive economic model that will supplant neoclassical theory, but the studies do introduce new ideas. And their findings must inevitably modify, or at least call into question, various aspects of neoclassical thought. It is true, of course, that insofar as progress in modern institutional economics takes the form of specialized studies in subareas we can anticipate that different lines of research, involving different approaches, will be pursued and the NIE will continue its development as a somewhat fragmented field.

An impression of the way in which the New Institutional Economics is now evolving can be gained by considering some of the themes being explored in the literature. Not surprisingly, transaction-cost economics continues to have its own adherents and remains a subject of major research interest. Application of the approach has yielded promising results in several areas. For example, when problems of industrial organization are viewed from the standpoint of transactions, important insights can be secured. As Masten has noted:

> Rather than stress strategic pricing and output decisions, these studies emphasize transactors' efforts to discover and adopt organizational arrangements that constrain strategic behavior and facilitate mutually beneficial transactions, efforts whose success depends in important ways on the content, operation, and limitations of the legal system. But the feature that most distinguishes this literature from the mainstream is its empirical content and, especially, the progress researchers have made identifying and collecting detailed transaction-level information on organizational practices and the nature and attributes of transactions. (Masten 1996, vii)

In a somewhat different direction, rent-seeking behavior represents another topic that has importance for current neoinstitutional research (Tullock 1975; Buchanan, 1980; Tollison 1982). Economic theory defines *rent* as a return to a resource owner in excess of the opportunity return the owner would otherwise receive. What is pointed out in this literature, of course, is that rents are frequently made possible by government action. Specifically, government can restrict entry into certain markets or grant special privileges through regulation and thus create artificial scarcity. Such scarcity permits profits to be made, and self-seeking individuals have an incentive to compete for the government dispensations that will allow them to capture the profits. The competition for government favors, however, involves a wastage of resources in (unproductive) lobbying activities, bribes, legal fees, and so on. In short, rent seeking often leads people to use scarce resources to try to capture transfers rather than create wealth. Various illustrations of the process can be found (e.g., Bates 1981), and the analysis of specific cases has interest because detailed discussion can reveal how various elements of the NIE (transaction costs, bounded rationality, secondary uncertainty, etc.) affect economic outcomes. An interesting issue here concerns the question of whether these are conditions under which rent seeking may be regarded as "efficient."

Since private parties are sometimes able to exercise monopoly power or undertake coercion, government is, of course, not the only agency that can lead to inefficient utilization of resources. Moreover, in a neoinstitutionalist environment in which information is costly to obtain and process, there would seem to be more scope for actions that limit competition and permit pressure groups to coerce others in the system. Transaction costs may indeed push an economy toward inefficient allocation, but it is also arguable that in a world of positive transaction costs it is harder to form stable coalitions that can carry out sustained exploitation of the public. As a counter to this latter argument, though, the NIE literature has indicated that various contractual devices, such as hostage giving, may be used to prevent defections from collusive agreement. What is apparent is that this general area opens up a host of difficult and far-reaching questions. Ultimately, it seems necessary to consider such things as the role of government, the relation between political and economic events, and the means for controlling force within a society. Finally, there is the matter of how efficiency is to be defined. Any theory that speaks of efficient allocation should define clearly the efficiency criterion it accepts. But, as we have seen, neoinstitutionalist writings have made this a murky proposition.

At another level, modern institutional research is beginning to consider some departures from principal-agent theory and the presumption that sharply defined optimization problems can be formulated. There is a growing belief in some quarters that theory should move away from models of a highly mechanistic type, which presuppose the possibility of precise optimizing solutions (engineered by rational actors). As was noted in chapter 8, it has been suggested that the problem of organizational control in a firm can be thought of in a new way (Miller 1992). One may say that the function of the manager in a hierarchial firm is not to shape the behavior of subordinates by designing an optimal system of incentives but rather to provide *leadership* so that individuals are induced to cooperate in achieving the firm's objectives. This conception of the problem is generally consistent with the idea that rational choice maximization becomes less and less appropriate for model building as information about economic variables becomes more and more uncertain and difficult to obtain and as human motivations are recognized as complex and beyond simple categorization.

In recent work, Arrow, too, has taken a more critical position with respect to orthodox doctrine. He argues that to understand economic events one must go beyond the set of individual decisions in the search for explanatory variables and consider the roles of social knowledge and societal learning.

> It is a touchstone of accepted economics that all explanations must run in terms of the actions and reactions of individuals. Our behavior in judging economic research in peer review of papers and research, and in promotions, includes the criterion that in principle the behavior we explain and the policies we propose are explicable in terms of individuals, not of other

social categories. I want to argue today that a close examination of even the most standard economic analysis shows that social categories are in fact used in economic analysis all the time and that they appear to be absolute necessities of the analysis, not just figures of speech that can be eliminated if need be. I further argue that the importance of technical information in the economy is an especially significant case of an irreducibly social category in the explanatory apparatus of economics. (1994, 1)

From the evidence of this and other writings in the neoinstitutionalist vein, it does seem to be true that there is a growing movement toward broader, empirically richer, economic models. More concern is being shown with the interrelations between economics and other phenomena. For example, North, as an economic historian interested in institutions, wishes to study the numerous factors that influence the performance of economies through time. Given this viewpoint, he sees serious deficiencies in the neoclassical approach.

A theory of economic dynamics is also crucial for the field of economic development. There is no mystery why the field of development has failed to develop during the five decades since the end of World War II. Neoclassical theory is simply an inappropriate tool to analyze and prescribe policies that will induce development. It is concerned with the operation of markets, not with how markets develop. How can one prescribe policies when one doesn't understand how economies develop? The very methods employed by neoclassical economists have dictated the subject matter and militated against such a development. That theory in the pristine form that gave it mathematical precision and elegance modeled a frictionless and static world. When applied to economic history and development it focused on technological development and more recently human-capital investment but ignored the incentive structure embodied in institutions that determined the extent of social investment in those factors. In the analysis of economic performance through time it contained two erroneous assumptions: (i) that institutions do not matter and (ii) that time does not matter. (1994, 359)

The belief in the nonseparability of economics from other phenomena is also forcing the NIE literature to pay more heed to the significance of such "esoteric" factors as the moral rules of behavior, fairness, trust, human learning, and legal evolution. In this limited sense, at least, the NIE can perhaps be said to be drawing closer to the old institutionalism.

While it seems quite clear that economic science is not about to make a shift to a comprehensive new paradigm in the immediate future, there is no denying the fact that discontent with orthodox theoretical formulations is increasing. Important new concepts have been introduced into economics by the NIE, and what appears to be needed now is action to assess the current theoretical scene and consolidate basic findings. The book has attempted to give a coherent account of how the literature of neoinstitutionalism has developed over time and how progress has been made in defining the key questions of the subject. It is not unreasonable to say that enough has been learned by the profession already to establish the agenda for future work. We know that some of the ideas about institutional analysis that were put forward in earlier years have limited validity and that numbers of significant questions have yet to be answered. Nevertheless, new insights have also been forthcoming, so there is real hope for theoretical advance. The next few decades could well see the creation of a more potent and focused body of neoinstitutionalist thought.

# Glossary

**Adverse Selection:** The problem of *adverse selection* is said to arise if the principal (e.g., a supplier) knows less about the agent (his customer) than the agent knows about himself. The existence of such asymmetrical information provides an opportunity for the agent to engage in ex ante opportunistic behavior. Example: A potential purchaser of life insurance, having private information about his health status, is in a better position to estimate his residual life expectancy than the seller of the life insurance, and the individual can conceivably gain advantage from this self-knowledge. (F&R, 150, 180)

**Attenuation of Property Rights:** Attenuation refers to the fact that property rights in an asset (whether held by a private party or the state) can be restricted through legal provisions or by other means. Example: An individual's property rights in an asset are attenuated when he cannot legally transfer ownership in the asset to another party for a price higher than the ceiling price stipulated by the government. (F&R, 88, 390–91)

**Bonding Expenditures:** The *bonding expenditures* or *bonding costs* of an agent serve as a guarantee "that he will not take certain actions which would harm the principal, or to ensure that the principal will be compensated if he does take such actions" (Jensen and Meckling 1976, 309). See also *Hostages*. (F&R, 344)

**Bounded Rationality:** It is argued that, in the real world, "bounded rationality" exists because "the capacity of the human mind for formulating and solving problems is very small compared with the size of the problems whose solution is required for objectively rational behavior in the real world—or even for a reasonable approximation to such objective reality" (Simon 1957, 198). The literature indicates that different interpretations of bounded rationality are accepted, but there is wide agreement that (1) significant costs attach to acquiring and processing information, (2) individuals have limited ability to store, retrieve, and utilize information, and (3) systematic distortions in human perceptions or thinking tend to exist. In practice, then, all decision makers (entrepreneurs, consumers, politicians, etc.) act subject to imperfect information and limited cognition. (F&R, 4, 164–66)

483

**Brand-Name Capital:** This term denotes the *specific investments* (expenditures) made by a firm in a "brand name." Example: Advertising campaigns may be undertaken to promote the firm's name. Similarly, representational expenses, in the form of outlays for the construction of a prestigious headquarters building, or for the design and use of a firm logo, may be approved in an effort to enhance the name and significance of the enterprise. Remark: The term *brand-name capital* is not to be confused with that of the goodwill of a firm. The latter denotes the firm's market value (i.e., a present value, not expenses). (F&R, 160, 306 ff.)

**Coase Theorem:** The Coase theorem (in its strong form) asserts that private bargaining can overcome the difficulties posed by an externality situation and lead to a first-best allocative solution. Hence, the initial assignment of property rights or legal entitlements is irrelevant to Pareto optimal resource allocation. For such efficiency to be achieved, however, it is recognized that a number of very special conditions have to be met in addition to the assumption of zero transaction costs. Example: In the case of a firm that has no property rights in a stream, allocative efficiency requires that pollution of the stream by the firm goes forward as long as the marginal benefit of pollution to the firm (and society) is greater than the marginal cost of pollution to the owner of the stream. The surplus that results from this arrangement can then be divided, via costless bargaining, between the firm and the stream owner. By assumption any agreement reached via private bargaining can also be monitored and enforced at zero cost. (F&R, 91 ff.)

**Commitment Problem:** The *commitment problem* deals with the credibility of a promise. It is particularly important for cases in which the legal enforcement of a promise is impossible or too expensive. A commitment is made credible by, among other things, pre-contractual specific investments (*bonding expenditures*) of the promisor which serve as *hostages* in the hands of the promisee. Example: Specific investments may range from symbolic small expenses for gifts to heavy investments in brand-name capital (in particular advertising expenditures). (F&R, 257)

**Common Pool Resources (CPRs):** *Common pool resources* may be either open for anybody or only to a limited number of individuals. In the first case one speaks of open-access CPRs, in the second of closed-access CPRs. Examples: Open-access CPRs include the open sea, the atmosphere, outer space; closed-access CPRs include the communally owned alpine meadows in the Swiss, Austrian, or Bavarian Alps. (F&R, 98)

**Contract Theory (Formal):** Formal (economic) *contract theory* seeks to explain the contractual arrangements that can arise in systems characterized by perfect individual rationality, asymmetric information and incomplete foresight, or the impossibility of verification to third parties. Examples: see

*Principal-Agent Theory (Formal)* and *Incomplete Contract Theory.* (F&R, 181 ff.)

**Convention:** *Convention* is reflected by regularity in behavior. Each individual, based on his experience, expects that everybody is going to follow the ruling convention. "Given this expectation, each person finds it in his interest to follow the convention . . . . In addition, anyone who is favored by the convention on at least some occasions is likely to regard any breach of the convention as an indirect threat to himself" (Sugden 1989, 95). Examples: The consensual character of rights as the evolution of right lane traffic (left lane traffic)—as a simple case—or of private ownership—as a more complex case (Lewis 1969). (F&R, 107 ff.)

**Corporate Culture:** See *Organizational Culture.*

**Ex Ante Opportunism:** *Ex ante opportunism* (or *precontractual opportunism*) arises because individuals, desirous of pursuing their own special interests, are not always wholly trustworthy and may take advantage of the existence of asymmetrical information when negotiating contracts. That is, the informed party has an incentive to give the uninformed party incomplete or distorted information about the quality of his promised performance. Examples: Job seekers misrepresent their abilities to an employer offering work; sellers of low quality used cars misrepresent the true quality of their *lemons* to potential buyers. Remark: Precontractual opportunism is modeled in *Principal Agent Theory* of the *Adverse Selection* type. (F&R, 130 ff.)

**Ex Post Opportunism:** *Ex post opportunism* or *postcontractual opportunism* occurs in cases in which transaction-specific investments play a role. Examples: The tenant, once moved in, does not pay the agreed upon rent on time; the worker, once employed, does not show up or shirks at work. (F&R, 131, 136, 138)

**Exclusion costs:** *Exclusion costs* are the costs of defining, monitoring, and enforcing private property rights. Examples: the costs of surveying land, keeping a real estate register, building a fence. (F&R, 98, 110)

**Focal Principle:** The term *focal principle* is used by Kreps (1990a) to describe a behavioral principle that may be followed, under normal circumstances, by the management of a firm. This usage follows from the concept of the "focal point" as expounded by Schelling (1960). According to Kreps, the focal principle "gives hierarchical inferiors an idea ex ante how the organization will react to circumstances as they arise" (1990a, 125). Example: The management may promise not to fire anyone as long as fluctuations and sales variations are the result of seasonal or routine business fluctuations. In the case of a major structural break, however, this principle would not apply. (F&R, 164, 174, 269)

**Fundamental Transformation:** Williamson (1985/61) speaks of a *fundamen-*

*tal transformation* in cases in which "what was a large-number bidding condition at the outset is effectively transformed into one of bilateral supply thereafter." Example: In the labor market a fundamental transformation occurs if an originally unskilled worker acquires firm-specific human capital during his employment with the firm. At that point, the firm becomes increasingly dependent on the worker's firm-specific abilities, and he represents a significant supplier of services to the firm who can bargain as an independent agent. (F&R, 159)

**Governance Structure:** A *governance structure* is understood as a system of norms inclusive of their enforcement instruments. Examples: Williamson distinguishes between the following governance structures: (a) market governance; (b) trilateral governance (the use of third-party assistance); (c) bilateral governance (the parties to the contract safeguard themselves against ex post opportunism through a mix of court ordering and private ordering); (d) unified governance (e.g., vertical integration). (F&R, 5, 167 ff.)

**Hegemonic Cooperation:** The term *hegemonic cooperation* is used by political scientists to describe the cooperation between sovereign states under the leadership of a powerful state: the hegemon. A system of norms and rules is created, which operates to the hegemon's advantage. Examples: The Pax Romana, the Pax Britannica and, after World War II until the sixties, the Pax Americana (Gilpin, 1981). Remark: The concept of hegemonic cooperation can also be applied in industrial organization, for example, to explain the role of the Big Three or Four in the U.S. automobile or tobacco industries. (F&R, 297, 428)

**Hold-Up:** When one party, say A, is locked into a contractual relationship with another party B because A has undertaken significant transaction-specific investment, A is vulnerable to exploitation. The term *hold-up* is used in the NIE literature for the postcontractual "robbery" by B of the appropriable quasi rent from the locked-in contractual partner A. Example: The steel mill that is built next to a power station in order to get electricity cheaply. "Once the steel mill incurs costs that become sunk, the power company would raise power prices," and so on (Alchian and Woodward 1988, 67). Remark: This is an example of *ex post opportunism*. (F&R, 131)

**Hostages:** *Hostages* in the sense of the NIE are specific investments undertaken by a promisor with the objective of making his promise credible. (See also *Commitment Problem*). Example: Advertising expenditures made by the supplier of experience goods. Such expenditures are, in effect, hostages in the hands of consumers who may "destroy" these hostages if the seller does not keep his word and supply acceptable commodities. The destruction of the hostages would be accomplished if consumers stopped buying the supplier's output. In the extreme case, the seller would be driven out of the market. Remark: A collateral has a direct use or exchange value to the person who takes it while a hostage is something of value to the hostage-giver, not necessarily to its recipient or anyone else. (F&R, 160, 425)

**Ideology:** North (1994, 363, n. 6) defines *ideologies* as "shared frameworks of mental models possessed by groups of individuals that provide both an interpretation of the environment and a prescription as to how that environment should be ordered." Remark: Ideologies can be understood as implicit agreements on informal rules for social action which help to reduce uncertainty. See also *Social Capital.* (F&R, 27 ff.)

**Implicit Contracts:** The term *implicit contracts* is used for, among other things, self-enforcing agreements (F&R, 156) but also for the so-called Azariadis-Bailey-Gordon (ABG) model of wage theory (F&R, 228 ff.). In the latter case, symmetric information of the parties (employers/employees) is assumed. Owners of firms are able to diversify their portfolios, while workers, who do not own much more than themselves, cannot do so. Workers tend to be risk averse, capital owners risk neutral. Under certain assumptions, both parties will prefer not to enter a "spot auction" market and instead agree on a fixed real wage. Then, the risk of the uncertain labor income stream is shifted to the risk-neutral capital owners. Example: Sticky wages and the resulting difference between workers' wages and the marginal (revenue) product of labor.

**Incentive Compatibility:** The term *incentive compatibility* is used in principal-agent theory. It describes an agency contract in which the principal maximizes his utility subject to the utility-maximizing behavior of his agent. Example: The principal, knowing his agent's response function, offers him a certain profit share as an incentive. (F&R, 188 ff., 193 ff.)

**Incentive Contracts:** We speak of an *incentive contract* if the contractual party, who is unable to observe the other party's quality or activity, offers the other side an economic incentive to tell the truth or behave well. Examples: In the *principal-agent* model with *moral hazard,* the incentives are embodied in the incentive schedule offered by the principal to the agent. In the *adverse selection* model, incentives are reflected by the self-selection constraints offered by the principal. (F&R, 247)

**Incomplete Contract Theory:** The *theory of incomplete contracts* explores the nature of contractual arrangements when certain specialized assumptions hold. The assumptions in question include: incomplete foresight by decision makers, symmetric information between the contractual parties, and the inability of an individual to verify a breach of contract to third parties (e.g., the courts). A characteristic problem considered is whether some specific investments, designed to increase the probability of a later improvement of the product, should be undertaken or not. A second-best optimum may be reached if the parties agree about some distribution of decision rights (i.e., property rights). Example: See F&R, 233.

**Institution:** An *institution* may be defined as a set of formal, or informal, rules, including their enforcement arrangements. These constraints are, in effect, the rules of the game whose purpose is to steer individual behavior in some particular direction. Examples: Ownership, marriage, guardianship, market system, monetary system, the state, the firm, etc. (F&R, 6)

**Institutional Arrangements:** Davis and North (1971, 6) use the term *institutional arrangements* for the agreed upon *governance structures* (Williamson 1993a, 53) of micro-level relationships between actors. Examples: The vertical integration between two firms, or a labor contract between a firm and its employee. Remark: Williamson's transaction cost economics deals exactly with this issue with the *institutional environment* assumed to be given. (F&R, 265 ff.)

**Institutional Economics, New:** See *New Institutional Economics.*

**Institutional Economics, Old:** See *Old Institutionalism.*

**Institutional Environment:** Davis and North (1971, 6) use the term *institutional environment* for macro-level relationships, viz., the general institutional framework (the constitution) that constrains the *contractual arrangements* of individuals. Example: The elementary constitutional rules of the classical liberal state. (F&R, 11, 267)

**International Regimes:** *International regimes* are a *terminus technicus* of the theory of international policy. They denote forms of bilateral or multilateral cooperation among states. Theoretically, they are understood as cooperative solutions of repeated collective action games (Alt, Calvert, and Humes 1988, 447). Examples: The United Nations, the European Union, the International Monetary Fund. Remark: International regimes are special cases of *relational contracts.* They are legally unenforceable (because of the sovereignty of nations). Like contracts, they help to organize relationships in mutually beneficial ways. (F&R, 429 ff., 271)

**Lemons Problem:** The *lemons problem* or *lemons principle* (introduced by Akerlof 1970) is a special case of *adverse selection* in which the bad products (lemons) tend to drive out the good ones. As a result, the market breaks down. Example: The market for used cars. Remark: Counteracting institutions can be introduced to offset the deleterious effects of the lemons problem. These include: guarantees, reputation, diplomas or licenses offered by a trustworthy source, etc. (F&R, 222 ff.)

**Lock-In Effect:** A contractual party can be effectively "locked in" if it has undertaken significant transaction-specific investments. The party with the greater specific investments may become the victim of a *hold-up* and some or all of its appropriable *quasi rent* may be secured by its contractual partner.

Example: The steel mill that is built next to a power station in the hope of getting electricity cheaply. In practice, however, the owner of the power company may take advantage of the mill's presence once it has actually been built. Specifically, he can raise power prices to the mill and capture the expected quasi rent of the mill owner. (F&R, 131)

**Market Screening:** The term *market screening* is used in the theory of *adverse selection* to describe the situation that exists when the party lacking information (e.g., a firm offering a job) proposes a menu of contracts to the informed party (e.g., the job seeker). By selecting one of the proffered contracts, the job seeker reveals his true quality, and the firm gains valuable information (Kreps 1990b, 651). (F&R, 222)

**Market Signaling:** In the theory of *adverse selection, market signaling* refers to the fact that an informed party is free to undertake activities that "signal" its quality. Example: A high level of educational attainment can be interpreted as a signal for high labor productivity because advanced education is more likely to be acquired by a more productive worker than by a less productive one. Remark: The term *signal* is used by Spence (1973, 357) for an observable but alterable attribute of an individual (or good, title, etc.). Thus, education is a signal, while age or sex are not. Spence calls the latter "indices." (F&R, 221 ff.)

**Moral Hazard:** The term *moral hazard* is used to identify situations in which, after the conclusion of a contract, the agent is either better informed than the principal (hidden information), or the agent's effort level is unobservable by the principal (hidden action). The agent is, in such cases, tempted to engage in *postcontractual opportunism.* Examples: (a) The hidden information case exists when the information known to a subordinate office or department is not available to a hierarchically superior office; (b) the hidden action case holds when the effort level of a manager (agent) is not observable by the firm's owners (the manager's principals). (F&R, 180)

**Network Externalities:** The utility of a commodity that is part of a network (e.g., a telephone network) depends on the number of potential connections (telephone connections) the commodity can achieve. *Network externalities* may be positive or negative. Examples: "Positive network externalities arise when a good is more valuable to a user the more users adopt the same good or compatible ones. The externality can be direct (a telephone user benefits from others being connected to the same network; computer software, if compatible, can be shared). It can also be indirect; because of increasing returns to scale in production, a greater number of complementary products can be supplied—and at a lower price—when the network grows" (Tirole 1988, 405). (F&R, 290)

**New Institutional Economics (NIE):** The term was introduced by Williamson (1975, 1). It is used in a narrower and in a wider sense. Positive *transaction* *costs,* methodological individualism and (bounded or perfect) rational choice are assumed in both. In its narrower sense, NIE deals with *institutional arrangements.* In its wider sense it deals with *institutional environments.* Examples: (a) transaction cost economics in the sense of Williamson (1985); (b) the new institutional approach to economic history in the sense of North (1981). (F&R, 29 ff.)

**Nirvana Fallacy:** Once positive transaction costs are recognized, it becomes obvious that an economy can never achieve the idealized Pareto optimal solution described in neoclassical theory. In the real world, all solutions are "inefficient" relative to the orthodox neoclassical criteria. It is argued, however, that unless an outcome found in the world can be improved upon in actual practice, there is no valid reason to say that it is inefficient. As Demsetz has noted, "The view that now pervades much public policy economics implicitly presents the relevant choice as between an ideal norm and an existing 'imperfect' institutional arrangement. This nirvana approach differs considerably from a comparative institution approach in which the relevant choice is between alternative real institutional arrangements" (1969, 1). Example: In the case of *principal-agent theory* with *moral hazard,* the principal suffers welfare loss relative to what his position would be in a "frictionless" system. (F&R, 8 ff., 199, 444, 460)

**Old Institutionalism (Old Institutional Economics, American institutionalists):** An analytic style, opposing neoclassical marginalism and methodological individualism, represented by American institutionalists like Thorstein Veblen, John R. Commons, Wesley Mitchell, and Clarence Ayres. Commons is the most important writer from the standpoint of the NIE. (F&R, 33 ff.)

**Opportunism:** Williamson (1985, 47) defines "opportunism" as "self-interest seeking with guile." In other words, individuals are likely to be less than completely trustworthy in the sense that they may disguise preferences, distort data, deliberately confuse issues, etc. in order to gain advantage. Remark: Asymmetric information provides a basis for opportunistic behavior as, for example, in the cases of *adverse selection* and *moral hazard.* The existence of transaction-specific investments provides another opportunity for such "dishonest" behavior. (F&R, 129 ff.)

**Order (Social Structure):** An *order* is defined as a system of rules and the enforcement arrangements for the rules. It constrains individual choice. Examples: The constitution of a state, civil law, criminal law, etc. Remark: The terms *order* and *institution* are, in essence, synonyms. (F&R, 5 ff., 265–69)

**Organization:** An *organization* is understood to be an institution together with the people taking advantage of it (North, 1990). An organization may be formal or informal or both. A formal organization (e.g., the military, a firm) is generally assumed to be hierarchically structured. Examples: The United States Army, the General Electric Corporation. Other possibilities, however, include the New York Stock Exchange and the DM currency 1948 to 1998. Remark: Market and organization are frequently described as opposites. See, for example, Albert (1967, 393) who defines an organization as a social construct, "for which a central authority exists" and a market "as a construct in which this is not the case." Analogously, Williamson (1975) distinguishes between market and hierarchy. Yet hierarchical structures may also be found in markets (e.g., for standardized products). (F&R, 7, 270 ff.)

**Organizational Culture:** The term *organizational culture* is used to suggest the mutually reinforcing behavioral expectations of the members of an organization. A special case is *corporate culture.* Kreps interprets it as a *focal principle* which "gives hierarchical inferiors an idea ex ante how the organization will react to circumstances as they arise" (Kreps 1990a, 125). (F&R, 163 ff.)

**Path Dependency:** When the historical development of a system has the effect of generating constraints that limit subsequent choice sets, *path dependency* is said to exist. "Path dependence means that history matters. We cannot understand today's choices . . . without tracing the incremental evolution of institutions" (North 1990, 100). (F&R, 28)

**Plasticity:** Alchian and Woodward (1987) use the term *plasticity* to describe the range of possible uses of a resource. Examples: Money has the highest degree of plasticity. In the case of a money loan, the debtor is de facto free to use the proceeds of the loan for any purpose he deems appropriate. Not quite as extensive, but still quite substantial, is the plasticity of the R&D department of a firm. At the lower end of the scale are specific assets like oil derricks. The greater the plasticity of a resource the greater its monitoring costs, for example. (F&R, 137 ff.)

**Principal-Agent Approach:** The *principal-agent approach* deals with cases of asymmetric information between contractual parties before or/and after the conclusion of a contract. The party offering a contract (the "principal") knows or observes less than the party accepting or rejecting the offer (the "agent"). As a result, the agent has an incentive to behave opportunistically. See also *Adverse Selection, Moral Hazard.* (F&R, 148 ff.)

**Principal-Agent Theory (Formal):**
**a) Moral hazard type:** This approach deals with the problem of post-contractual opportunism. Two subcases can be distinguished: (1) *hidden action:* The actions of the agent are unobservable by the principal; (2) *hidden information:* The agent has information which the principal has not. Example for (1): The shareholders are unable to observe the effort levels of their managers. Under certain assumptions, however, the shareholders (the principals) are able to offer incentive contracts to their managers (the agents)

that induce the managers to act so as to maximize the stockholders' utility together with their own utility. In the case of uncertain results only a second-best optimum obtains (*moral hazard* with *hidden action*). (F&R, 181 ff., 186 ff.)

**b) Adverse selection type:** This approach deals with the problem of pre-contractual opportunism. The principal cannot observe (fully) the qualities of the individual agents before the contract is concluded. As a result, the agent is tempted to misrepresent his qualifications. To avoid this, the principal proposes a suitable *incentive contract* that leads the individual agent to reveal his type (qualities) and, at the same time, promote the principal's welfare. Again, only a second-best optimum is obtained for the principal. (F&R, 182, 202 ff.)

**Private Ordering:** *Private ordering,* as opposed to court ordering, is a substitute for, or a supplement to, legal protection in non-legal relationships, or in legal relationships that would be difficult or impossible to verify before a court. Private ordering is not to be confused with self-help à la Wild West. It consists of the choice of a suitable *governance structure* to help resolve disputes. Examples: Enforcement by the explicit or implicit threat to terminate an agreement, tit-for-tat, the agreement to use private arbitrators to resolve disputes, the "union" of contractual parties as, for example, vertical integration. (F&R, 160 ff.)

**Property Rights:** *Property rights* in the sense of the *property-rights approach* are sanctioned ownership rights in material and immaterial things or claims from contractual or noncontractual obligations. The prevailing system of property rights in a society can be described as the set of economic and social relations defining the position of each individual with respect to the utilization of scarce resources. There exist (a) property rights in the legal sense, and (b) in the non-legal sense.

**a) Property rights in the legal sense:** In Anglo-American common law, property rights are related to both, tangibles (physical objects) and intangibles (patents, copyrights, contract rights, etc.). Examples: Private ownership of land, copyright, human rights, rights from either freely concluded contracts or legal claims from tortuous acts. (F&R, 76 ff.)

**b) Property rights in the non-legal sense:** Rights which are not sanctioned by law but by convention. Example: The customer relationship. (F&R, 83 ff.)

**Property-Rights Approach:** The *property-rights approach* assumes that the average individual behaves rationally and thus will try to get "the most" out of his property rights. One can, therefore, fairly well predict how (on the average) specific property rights will affect the allocation and use of economic resources. Example: Full ownership of land as opposed to usufruct rights. The holder of usufruct rights cannot sell or otherwise transfer the property to another party. Thus, as a rational utility maximizing individual, the usufruct holder might try to exploit the land ruthlessly (and avoid all maintenance activities) over the period of his contract. To prevent such an outcome, the owner of the land must require the usufruct holder to observe certain limits in the exercise of his usufruct rights. For example, the contract could demand that the usufruct holder maintain the economic integrity and character of the land. Enforcement of this provision would, of course, lead to special measurement, monitoring, and policing costs—costs that would not appear under full private ownership. (F&R, 71 ff., 79)

**Quasi Rent:** The returns to temporarily specialized productive services are called *quasi rents*. In the case of a firm operating in the short run, quasi rents are simply the excess of total receipts over total variable costs. Remark: "Marshall, who first formulated the theory of quasi-rents, defined them as total returns to temporarily specialized services *minus* costs of maintenance and replacement (1920, 426n). This definition . . . is not consistent with the general theory of rents in the sense of noncost outlays, nor can Marshall's quasi-rents easily be illustrated in the conventional cost diagrams of the firm" (Stigler, G.J. 1947. *The Theory of Price.* New York: Macmillan, 180). (F&R, 131, 136, 306 ff.)

**Quasi Rent (Appropriable):** The *appropriable* quasi rent (i.e., appropriable by a contractual partner) is that part of a quasi rent that exceeds its value to the second-best user (Klein, Crawford, Alchian 1978, 298). (F&R, 306 ff.)

**Relational Contract:** *Relational contracts* are long-term agreements between parties that take into account the fact of incomplete foresight, and establish contractual provisions so that future unforeseen contingencies can be accommodated. The contractual parties agree, either explicitly or implicitly, about the procedure (the constitution) that will be employed to deal with problems that may arise. In other words, legal enforcement is supplemented, or substituted for, by *private ordering.* Example: Something akin to relational contracts are employed to regulate relations between automobile assembly plants and their suppliers. Transactions are not coordinated by spot prices but by flexible long-term agreements about product deliveries, cost calculations, price fixing and profit sharing. (F&R, 143 ff., 158 ff.)

**Renegotiation-Proof Agreements:** An agreement is said to be *renegotiation proof* if the parties to a contract have no basis for improving their positions through renegotiation. Example: The Maastricht criteria for joining the European Monetary Union (EMU) were (implicitly) *not* renegotiation proof. Assume, first, that all of the members of the European Union were interested in becoming members of the EMU at the moment of its founding. Then, those states that did not fulfill the Maastricht criteria for membership had incentive to put the other states under pressure to either renegotiate the criteria or, at least, to interpret them broadly. This strategy had plausibility because the states that fulfilled the Maastricht criteria had a strong interest in the timely realization of the EMU. Thus, it was possible to reckon on their willingness to make concessions to the financially weaker states (as actually happened) (Richter 1994, 44). (F&R, 254)

**Rent Seeking:** In essence, *rent seeking* involves the expenditure of scarce resources to change existing legal and other constraints so that monopoly rents can be captured. Example: A taxi cab association makes expenditures on lobbying in order to secure legislation from a municipal government that will limit the number of cabs permitted in the city. (F&R, 104 ff.)

**Reputation:** The *reputation* of keeping one's word plays a significant role in the theory of credible commitments as, e.g., in the case of *self-enforcing agreements*. Example: The brand name of a product. (F&R, 240 ff.)

**Reputation Equilibrium:** A *reputation equilibrium,* in the sense of the theory of self-enforcing agreements, occurs when a steady state of individual expectations exists about the behavior of, for example, a firm. Example: A seller maintains the quality of his product over time and, as a result, the buyers' expectations are always fulfilled and the product price remains constant. Remark: Multiple equilibria may exist. For example, there may be both a high-quality equilibrium and a low-quality one. In this case, one would have an extreme *lemons situation.* (F&R, 241 ff.)

**Self-Enforcing Agreements:** The theory of *self-enforcing agreements* deals with the *private ordering* of legally nonbinding agreements (friendships, customer relations, etc.). The promised performance is "enforced" by the explicit or implicit threat to discontinue the agreement (Telser 1980, 27). Note: "A basic hypothesis of this approach is that someone is honest only if honesty, or appearance of honesty, pays more than dishonesty" (Telser 1980, 29). Example: The seller of a high-quality product continues to sell the high-quality as long as it is more profitable for him to do this instead of "milking his reputation" by suddenly lowering the quality of his product and making a short term higher profit. (F&R, 156 ff., 239 ff.)

**Set-Up Costs:** *Set-up costs* are the costs of establishing or restructuring an organization. Examples: The costs of establishing a state, the costs of the transformation of an economy from a centrally planned economy to a market economy, the costs of the establishment of a market for a new product. (F&R, 40)

**Shirking:** The term *shirking* is used in the NIE to describe *opportunistic behavior* in team production—as when an individual deliberately reduces his effort level so that he can enjoy more "leisure" or "utility" on the job. Attempts can be made to reduce the severity of this problem by metering, monitoring and disciplining jointly used inputs. Example: The joint lifting of a heavy burden by several persons. The issue concerns how much of the load is carried by each individual. (F&R, 65)

**Social Capital:** *Social capital* is represented by the level of trust within a society. It consists of a set of obligations, expectations, and mutually developed norms that have evolved from prior social interactions (Starr and MacMillan 1990, 80). Trust in an individual's word, cooperative behavior, the exchange of information, the offer of help without a direct quid pro quo, etc. all play parts here (Arrow 1974). Examples: Friendship, public spirit. Remark: It is important for the efficiency of an economic system that people follow the rules without being monitored. (F&R, 271 ff., 84, 27)

**Social Network:** A *social network* consists of actors, their attributes, and their bilateral relations. The latter are understood in a wide sense, not only as the transfer of material resources or information between actors. Examples: Relations between actors include such "non-economic" relationships as associations or affiliations among actors; their movements between places; physical connections (a road, a telephone line); legal relationships (the formal debtor/creditor relation); biological relationships (kinship, descent); mental relationships (common views, beliefs, convictions, culture, etc.). The market may be understood as a network of customer relationships between buyers and sellers, the firm as a network between management and employees. (F&R, 270 ff.)

**Solidarity (Weak):** Lindenberg (1988, 48) characterizes *weak solidarity* by the following four properties: (a) performance-oriented distribution within a group; (b) no open opportunistic behavior; (c) application of a clear sign that solidarity norms exist such as gift giving; (d) willingness to repair the relation if something goes wrong. Remark: Relational contracts reflect weak solidarity. "Peace is valued in its own right" (Macneil 1983, 362). (F&R, 160 ff.)

**Specific Investments (Asset Specificity):** *Specific investments* (or *specific assets*) are investments that generate higher returns in a particular employment (i.e., in a transaction-specific relation) than elsewhere. Examples: The purchase of tools that have highly specialized uses ("physical asset specificity"), the learning of skills that pertain only to a specialized job ("human capital specificity"). (F&R, 128 ff.)

**Sunk Cost:** *Sunk costs* denote expenditures that are not completely salvageable or not salvageable at all—in other words, investments that cannot be resold without loss (Klein and Leffler 1981, 619). Example: The search-, inspection-, and bargaining-costs of a sales contract that fails to be completed; the costs of introducing a new worker to his job when the worker leaves the job soon after his break-in period; the advertising expenditures made for a new product that turns out to be a flop. (F&R, 51, 139, 170, 175, 415)

**Tit-for-Tat Strategy:** The *tit-for-tat strategy* is one possible form of retaliatory behavior. Its first rule is that a decision maker should not initiate predatory behavior—in other words, "never be the first to defect" (Axelrod 1984, 27 ff.). If this rule is ignored by the other side, retaliation (or defection) is the appropriate move at the next round. Remark: This approach is discussed by Axelrod (1984) in relation to the prisoner's dilemma game. (F&R, 162)

**Transaction:** A *transaction* describes: (a) a technological procedure, as the transfer of a good across a technologically separable interface, or (b) the transfer of property rights. Examples: (a) The famous division of labor example by Adam Smith (1776/1976): a transaction takes place each time a pin changes hands within a factory; (b) The transfer of property rights from seller to buyer as during the execution of a sales contract. (F&R, 41 ff.)

**Transaction costs:** *Transaction costs* can be thought of in general terms as the costs of running an economic system or a social system. They consist of fixed transaction costs (e.g., the specific investments made in setting up institutional arrangements), and variable transaction costs (e.g., the outlays that depend on the number or volume of transactions). Examples of variable transaction costs include: search and information costs, bargaining and decision costs, supervisory and enforcement costs. (F&R, 43 ff.)

**Union:** A *union* in the sense of the NIE is "any arrangement that seeks to reduce divergence by promoting a spirit of identification or fellow-feeling between the parties" (Kronmann 1985, 21). Examples: Parent-child relationship, marriage, a firm, vertical integration. Williamson speaks of "unified governance" (Williamson 1985, 78). (F&R, 163, 168 ff.)

**Williamson Puzzle:** Williamson (1985, 131) asked: "Why can't a large firm do everything that a collection of small firms can do and more?" This became known in the literature as the *Williamson Puzzle* (Tirole 1988). Remark: The Williamson Puzzle deals with the problem of optimal firm size and with the role that property rights play in influencing incentives. (F&R, 336 ff.)

# References

Acheson, J. M. 1985. "The Maine Lobster Market: Between Market and Hierarchy," *Journal of Law, Economics, and Organization* 1:385–98.

Aghion, P., and P. Bolton. 1992. "An Incomplete Contracts Approach to Financial Contracting." *Review of Economic Studies* 59:473–94.

Aghion, P., M. Dewatripont, and P. Rey. 1990. "On Renegotiation Design." *European Economic Review* 34:322–29.

Aghion, P., M. Dewatripont, and P. Rey. 1991. "Renegotiation Design with Unverifiable Information." Mimeo.

Aivazian, V. A., J. L. Callen, and I. Lipnowski. 1987. "The Coase Theorem and Coalitional Stability." *Economica* 54:517–20.

Akerlof, G. A. 1970. "The Market for 'Lemons': Quality Uncertainty and the Market Mechanism." *Quarterly Journal of Economics* 84:488–500.

Akerlof, G. A. 1982. "Labor Contracts as Partial Gift Exchange." *Quarterly Journal of Economics* 97:543–69.

Akerlof, G. A. 1986. Reprint of Akerlof 1982. In Akerlof and Yellen 1986.

Akerlof, G. A., and H. Miyazaki. 1980. "The Implicit Contract Theory of Unemployment Meets the Wage Bill Argument." *Review of Economic Studies* 47:321–38.

Akerlof, G. A., and J. L. Yellen. 1986. "Introduction." In G. A. Akerlof, and J. L. Yellen, eds., *Efficiency Wage Models of the Labor Market,* 1–21. Cambridge: Cambridge University Press.

Albert H. 1967. *Marktsoziologie und Entscheidungslogik—Ökonomische Probleme in soziologischer Perspektive. Soziologische Texte,* Vol. 36. Neuwied und Berlin: Luchterhand.

Alchian, A. A. 1950. "Uncertainty, Evolution, and Economic Theory." *Journal of Political Economy* 58:211–21.

Alchian, A. A. 1958. "Private Property and the Relative Cost of Tenure." In P. D. Bradley, ed., *The Public Stake in Union Power.* Charlottesville: University of Virginia Press. Reprinted in Alchian 1977a.

Alchian, A. A. 1961. "Some Economics of Property." RAND D–2316. Santa Monica, Calif.: RAND Corporation.

Alchian, A. A. 1965a. "The Basis of Some Recent Advances in the Theory of Management of the Firm." *Journal of Industrial Economics* 14:30–41.

Alchian, A. A. 1965b. "Some Economics of Property Rights." *Il Politico* 30:816–29. Reprinted in Alchian 1977a.

Alchian, A. A. 1967. "Pricing and Society." Occasional Papers, no. 17. Westminster: Institute of Economic Affairs.

Alchian, A. A. 1969. "Information Costs, Pricing, and Resource Unemployment." *Western Economic Journal* 7:109–28.

Alchian, A. A. 1977a. *Economic Forces at Work.* Indianapolis: Liberty Press.

Alchian, A. A. 1977b. "Why Money?" *Journal of Money, Credit, and Banking* 9:133–40.

Alchian A. A. 1984. "Specificity, Specialization, and Coalitions," *Zeitschrift für die gesamte Staatswissenschaft* 140:34–49.

Alchian, A. A., and H. Demsetz. 1972. "Production, Information Costs, and Economic Organization." *American Economic Review* 72:777–95.

Alchian, A. A., and R. A. Kessel. 1962. "Competition, Monopoly, and the Pursuit of Pecuniary Gain." In National Bureau of Economic Research, *Aspects of Labor Economics,* 157–75. Princeton: Princeton University Press.

Alchian, A. A., and S. Woodward. 1987. "Reflections on the Theory of the Firm." *Journal of Institutional and Theoretical Economics* 143:110–37.

Alchian, A. A., and S. Woodward. 1988. "The Firm is Dead; Long Live the Firm: A Review of Oliver E. Williamson's *The Economic Institutions of Capitalism.*" *Journal of Economic Literature* 26:65–79.

Allen, F. 1985. "Repeated Principal-Agent Relationships with Lending and Borrowing." *Economics Letters* 17:27–31.

Alston, L. J., G. D. Libecap, and R. Schneider. 1996. "The Determinants and Impact of Property Rights: Land Titles on the Brazilian Frontier." *Journal of Law, Economics, and Organization* 12:25–61.

Alston, L. J., G. J. Libecap, and B. Mueller. 1997. "Violence and the Development of Property Rights to Land in the Brazilian Amazon." In J. N. Drobak and J. V. C. Nye, *The Frontiers of New Institutional Economics,* 145–63. San Diego: Academic Press.

Alt, J. R., R. Calvert, and B. Humes. 1988. "Reputation and Hegemonic Stability: A Game Theoretic Analysis." *American Political Science Review* 82:445–66.

Alt, J. R., and L. L. Martin. 1994. "Contracting and the Possibility of Multilateral Enforcement." *Journal of Institutional and Theoretical Economics* 150:265–71.

Amsden, A. H. 1987. "Imperialism." In J. Eatwell, M. Milgate, and P. Newman, eds., *The New Palgrave: A Dictionary of Economics,* 2:728–33. London: Macmillan.

Anderson, T. L., and P. J. Hill. 1975. "The Evolution of Property Rights: A Study of the American West." *Journal of Law and Economics* 18:163–79.

Anderson, T. L., and P. Hill. 1983. "Privatizing the Commons: An Improvement?" *Southern Economic Journal* 54:438–50.

Aoki, M. 1983. "Managerialism Revisited in the Light of Bargaining-Game Theory." *International Journal of Industrial Organization* 1:1–21.

Aoki, M. 1984. *The Co-operative Game Theory of the Firm.* London: Oxford University Press.

Archibald, G. C. 1987. "The Theory of the Firm." In J. Eatwell, M. Milgate, and P. Newman, eds., *The New Palgrave: A Dictionary of Economics,* 2:357–62. London: Macmillan.

Aristoteles. 1950. *The Politics of Aristotle,* with an introduction, two prefatory essays, and notes, critical and explanatory, by W. L. Newman. Reprint. Oxford: Clarendon.

Aron, R. 1967. *The Industrial Society.* London: Weidenfeld and Nicolson.

Arrow, K. J. 1962. "Economic Welfare and the Allocation of Resources for Invention." In National Bureau of Economic Research, *The Rate and Direction of Inventive Activity: Economic and Social Factors.* Princeton: Princeton University Press.

Arrow, K. J. 1969. "The Organization of Economic Activity: Issues Pertinent to the Choice of Market versus Non-Market Allocation." In *The Analysis and Evaluation of Public Expenditures: The PBB-System,* Joint Economic Committee, 91st Cong., 1st sess., vol. 1. Washington, D.C.: Government Printing Office.

Arrow, K. J. 1970. *Essays in the Theory of Risk-Bearing.* Amsterdam: North-Holland.

Arrow, K. J. 1974. *The Limits of Organization.* New York: W. W. Norton.

Arrow, K. J. 1979. "The Property Rights Doctrine and Demand Revelation under Incomplete Information." In M. J. Boskin, ed., *Economics and Human Welfare: Essays in Honor of Tibor Scitovsky,* 23–39. New York: Academic Press.

Arrow, K. J. 1985a. "Informational Structure of the Firm." *American Economic Review, Papers and Proceedings* 75:303–7.

Arrow, K. J. 1985b. "The Economics of Agency." In J. W. Pratt and R. J. Zeckhauser, eds., *Principals and Agents: The Structure of Business,* 37–51. Boston: Harvard Business School Press.

Arrow, K. J. 1994. "Methodological Individualism and Social Knowledge." *American Economic Review* 84:1–9.

Auerbach, N. Z. 1985. "A Transactional Approach to Lease Analysis." *Hofstra Law Review* 13:309–73.

Aumann, R. I., and S. Sorin. 1990. "Cooperation and Bounded Recall." *Games and Economic Behavior* 1:5–39.

Axelrod, R. 1984. *The Evolution of Cooperation.* New York: Basic Books.

Ayers, I., and R. Gertner. 1991. "Strategic Contractual Inefficiency and the Optimal Choice of Legal Rules." Working Papers, no. 83. Stanford: Stanford Law School.

Azariadis, C. 1975. "Implicit Contracts and Underemployment Equilibria." *Journal of Political Economy* 83:1183–1203.

Azariadis, C. 1983. "Employment with Asymmetric Information." *Quarterly Journal of Economics, Supplement* 98:157–72.

Azariadis, C. 1987. "Implicit Contracts." In J. Eatwell, M. Milgate, and P. Newman, eds., *The New Palgrave: A Dictionary of Economics,* 2:733–37. London: Macmillan.

Azariadis, C., and R. Cooper. 1985. "Nominal Wage-Price Rigidity as a Rational Expectation Equilibrium." *American Economic Review, Papers and Proceedings* 75:31–35.

Azariadis, C., and J. E. Stiglitz. 1983. "Implicit Contracts and Fixed Price Equilibria." *Quarterly Journal of Economics, Supplement* 98:1–22.

Backhaus, D. 1979. *Ökonomik der Partizipativen Unternehmung.* Tübingen: Y. C. B. Mohr (Paul Siebeck).

Bailey, M. J. 1974. "Wages and Employment under Uncertain Demand." *Review of Economic Studies* 41:37–50.

Bain, J. 1956. *Barriers to New Competition.* Cambridge: Harvard University Press.

Bain, J. 1987. "The Ratchet, Tautness, and Managerial Behavior in Soviet-Type Economies." *European Economic Review* 31:1173–1201.

Bajt, A. 1968. "Property in Capital and in the Means of Production in Socialist Economies." *Journal of Law and Economics* 11:1–4.

Baker, G. P., M. C. Jensen, and K. J. Murphy. 1988. "Compensation and Incentives: Practice vs. Theory." *Journal of Finance* 43:593–616.

Baldwin, R. 1985. *The Political Economy of U.S. Import Policy.* Cambridge: MIT Press.

Baltensperger, E. 1987. "Credit." In: J. Eatwell, M. Milgate, and P. Newman, eds., *The New Palgrave: A Dictionary of Economics,* 1:715–17. London: Macmillan.

Bamberg, G., and K. Spremann. 1981. "Implications of Constant Risk Aversion." *Zeitschrift für Operations Research* 25:205–24.

Banfield, E. C. 1958. *The Moral Basis of a Backward Society.* New York: Free Press.

Barnard, C. [1938] 1962. *The Functions of the Executive.* 15th ed. Cambridge: Harvard University Press.

Baron, D. P. 1989. "Design of Regulatory Mechanisms and Institutions." In R. Schmalensee, and R. D. Willig, eds., *Handbook of Industrial Organization,* 2:1347–1447. Amsterdam: North-Holland.

Baron, D. P., and D. Besanko. 1987. "Commitment and Fairness in a Dynamic Regulatory Relationship." *Review of Economic Studies* 54:413–36.

Barro, R. J. 1972. "A Theory of Monopolistic Price Adjustment." *Review of Economic Studies* 39:17–26.

Barro, R. J. 1977. "Long-Term Contracting, Sticky Prices, and Monetary Policy." *Journal of Monetary Economics* 3:305–16.

Barzel, Y. 1982. "Measurement Cost and the Organization of Markets." *Journal of Law and Economics* 25:27–48.

Barzel, Y. 1984. "The Entrepreneur's Reward for Self-Policing." *Economic Inquiry* 25:103–16.

Barzel, Y. 1985. "Transaction Costs: Are They Just Costs?" *Journal of Institutional and Theoretical Economics* 141:4–16.

Barzel, Y. 1989. *Economic Analysis of Property Rights.* Cambridge: Cambridge University Press.

Bates, R. H. 1981., *Markets and States in Tropical Africa.* Berkeley: University of California Press.

Bator, F. 1957. "The Simple Analytics of Welfare Maximization." *American Economic Review* 47:22–59.

Batstone, E., and P. Davies. 1976. *Industrial Democracy: European Experience.* London: Her Majesty's Stationery Office.

Baumol, W. J. 1952. "The Transaction Demand for Cash: An Inventory Theoretic Approach." *Quarterly Journal of Economics* 66:545–56.

Baumol, W. J. 1959. *Business Behavior, Value, and Growth.* London: Macmillan.

Baumol, W. J., and R. D. WILLIG. 1981. "Fixed Costs, Sunk Costs, Entry Barriers, and Sustainability of Monopoly." *Quarterly Journal of Economics* 96:405–31.

Becker, G. S. 1962. "Irrational Behavior and Economic Theory." *Journal of Political Economy* 70:1–13.

Becker, G. S. 1965. "A Theory of the Allocation of Time." *Economic Journal* 75:493–517.

Becker, G. S. 1975. *Human Capital.* 2nd ed. New York: Columbia University Press for the National Bureau of Research. First edition, 1964.

Becker, G. S., and G. J. Stigler. 1974. "Law Enforcement, Malfeasance, and Compensation of Enforcers." *Journal of Legal Studies* 3:1–18.

Beckmann, M. J. 1978. *Rank in Organizations: Lecture Notes in Economics and Mathematical Systems.* Berlin: Springer.

Beckmann, M. J. 1988. *Tinbergen Lectures on Organization Theory.* Berlin: Springer.

Benham, L., and P. Keefer. 1991. "Voting in Firms: The Role of Agenda Control, Size, and Voter Heterogeneity." *Economic Inquiry* 29:706–19.

Ben-Porath, Y. 1980. "The F-Connection: Families, Friends, and Firms and the Organization of Exchange." *Population and Development Review* 6:1–30.

Bentley, A. F. 1949. *The Process of Government.* Evanston, Ill.: Principia.

Berle, A., and G. Means. 1932. *The Modern Corporation and Private Property.* London: Macmillan.

Berliner, C., and J. A. Brimson. 1988. *Cost Management for Today's Advanced Manufacturing: The CAM-I Conceptual Design.* Boston: Harvard Business School Press.

Berliner, J. S. 1957. *Factory and Manager in the Soviet Union.* Cambridge: Harvard University Press.

Bernheim, D., and M. D. Whinston. 1985. "Common Marketing Agency as a Device for Facilitating Collusion." *Rand Journal of Economics* 16:269–81.

Bernholz, P. 1965. "Aufbewahrungs- und Transportkosten als Bestimmungsgründe der Geldnachfrage." *Schweizerische Zeitschrift für Volkswirtschaft und Statistik* 101:1–15.

Bernholz, P. 1967. "Erwerbskosten, Laufzeit, und Charakter zinstragender Forderungen als Bestimmungsgründe der Geldnachfrage der Haushalte." *Zeitschrift für die gesamte Staatswissenschaft* 123:9–24.

Bernholz, P. 1985. *The International Game of Power, Past, Present, and Future.* Berlin: Mouton Press.

Bernholz, P. 1992. "The Economic Approach to International Relations." In G. Radnitzky, ed., *Universal Economics: Assessing the Achievements of the Economic Approach.* New York: Paragon. 339–400.

Bernstein, L. 1992. "Opting Out of the Legal System: Extralegal Contractual Relations in the Diamond Industry." *Journal of Legal Studies* 21:115–57.

Besanko, D., and A. Thakor. 1987. "Collateral and Rationing: Sorting Equilibria in Monopolistic and Competitive Markets." *International Economic Review* 28:671–89.

Besen, S. M., and L. J. Raskind. 1991. "An Introduction to the Law and Economics of Intellectual Property." *Journal of Economic Perspectives* 5, no. 1:3–27.

Bils, M. 1989. "Pricing in a Customer Market." *Quarterly Journal of Economics* 104:699–717.

Bindseil, U. 1994. "Verfügungsrechte an organisierten Wertpapiermärkten. Untersucht auf der Grundlage der Theorie unvollständiger Verträge." Ph.D. diss., Universität des Saarlandes, Saarbrücken.

Binger, B. R., and E. Hoffmann. 1989. "Institutional Persistence and Change: The Question of Efficiency." *Journal of Institutional and Theoretical Economics* 145:67–84.

Binmore, K. 1987. "Modelling Rational Players I." *Economics and Philosophy* 3:179–214.

Binmore, K. 1988. "Modelling Rational Players II." *Economics and Philosophy* 4:9–55.

Binmore, K. 1992. *Fun and Games: A Text on Game Theory.* Lexington, Mass.: D. C. Heath.

Binmore, K. 1994. *Game Theory and the Social Contract I: Playing Fair.* Cambridge, Mass.: MIT Press.

Binmore, K., and L. Samuelson. 1992. "Evolutionary Stability in Repeated Games Played by Finite Automata." *Journal of Economic Theory* 57:278–305.

Black, D. 1958. *The Theory of Committees and Elections.* Cambridge: Cambridge University Press.

Black, H. C. 1990. *Black's Law Dictionary: Definitions of the Terms and Phrases of American and English Jurosprudence, Ancient and Modern,* by J. R. Nolan and J. M. Nolan-Haley. 6th ed. St. Paul, Minn.: West Co.

Blanchard, O. J., and S. Fischer. 1989. *Lectures on Macroeconomics.* Cambridge, Mass.: MIT Press.

Blau, P. 1964. *Exchange and Power in Social Life.* New York: John Wiley.

Blaug, M. 1958. "The Classical Economists and the Factory Acts: A Re-examination." *Quarterly Journal of Economics* 72:211–26.

Blaug, M. 1976. "The Empirical Status of Human Capital Theory: A Slightly Jaundiced Survey." *Journal of Economic Literature* 14:827–55.

Blaug, M. 1985. *Economic Theory in Retrospect.* 4th ed. Cambridge: Cambridge University Press.

Blinder, A. S. 1991. "Why Are Prices Sticky? Preliminary Results from an Interview Study." *American Economic Review, Papers and Proceedings* 81:89–96.

Böhm, F. 1937. *Die Ordnung der Wirtschaft als geschichtliche Aufgabe und rechtsschöpferische Leistung.* Stuttgart and Berlin: W. Kohlhammer.

Böhm, F., W. Eucken, and H. Grossmann-Doerth. 1936. "Vorwort der Herausgeber von F. Lutz, *Das Grundproblem der Geldverfassung.*" Heft 2 der Schriftenreihe Ordnung der Wirtschaft. Stuttgart and Berlin: W. Kohlhammer.

Böhm-Bawerk, E. 1881. *Rechte und Verhältnisse vom Standpunkte der Volkswirtschaftlichen Güterlehre.* Innsbruck: Verlag der Wagner'schen Universitäts-Buchhandlung.

Bonin, J. P. 1985. "Labor Management and Capital Maintenance: Investment Decisions in the Socialist Labor-Managed Firm." In D. C. Jones and J. Svejnar, eds., *Advances in the Economic Analysis of Participatory and Labor-Managed Firms,* 1:55–69. Greenwich, Conn.: JAI Press.

Bonus, H. 1991. "Umweltpolitik in der Sozialen Marktwirtschaft." Das Parlament, Aus Politik und Zeitgeschichte, no. B10/91, 1 (March), 37–46. Bonn: Bundeszentrale für Politische Bildung.

Bonus, H. 1992. "Preis- und Mengenlösungen in der Umweltpolitik." *Jahrbuch für Sozialwissenschaft* 41:343–58.

Bornstein M. 1979. *Comparative Economic Systems—Models and Cases.* Homewood, Ill.: Richard D. Irwin.

Bornstein, M., and D. Fusfeld. 1970. *The Soviet Economy: A Book of Readings.* Homewood, Ill.: Irwin.

Börsch-Supan, A. 1986. "On the West German Tenants' Protection Legislation." *Journal of Institutional and Theoretical Economics* 142:380–404.

Bössmann, E. 1978. "Information." In W. Albers et al., eds., *Handwörterbuch der Wirtschaftswissenschaft,* 4:184–200. Stuttgart: Gustav Fischer, J. C. B. Mohr (Paul Siebeck), and Vandenhoek and Ruprecht.

Bössmann, E. 1981. "Weshalb gibt es Unternehmungen? Der Erklärungsansatz von Ronald H. Coase." *Zeitschrift für die gesamte Staatswissenschaft/Journal of Institutional and Theoretical Economics* 137:667–74.

Bowles, S. 1985. "The Production Process in a Competitive Economy: Walrasian, Neo-Hobbesian, and Marxian Models." *American Economic Review* 75:16–36.

Bradley, M., and L. M. Wakeman. 1983. "The Wealth Effects of Targeted Share Repurchases." *Journal of Financial Economics* 11:310–28.

Brennan, G., and J. M. Buchanan. 1985. *The Reasons of Rules.* Cambridge: Cambridge University Press.

Brentano, L. 1878. "Die Arbeiter und die Produktionskrisen." *Jahrbuch für Gesetzgebung,Verwaltung, und Volkswirtschaft* 2:565–632.

Brunner, K., and W. H. Meckling. 1977. "The Perception of Man and the Conception of Government." *Journal of Money, Credit, and Banking* 3:70–85.

Buchanan, J. M. 1973. "The Coase Theorem and the Theory of the State." *Natural Resources Journal* 14:579–94.

Buchanan, J. M. 1975. *The Limits of Liberty: Between Anarchy and Leviathan.* Chicago: University of Chicago Press.

Buchanan, J. M. 1980a. "Reform in a Rent Seeking Society." In J. M. Buchanan, R. D. Tollison, and G. Tullock, eds., *Toward a Theory of a Rent-Seeking Society,* 359–67. College Station: Texas A&M University Press.

Buchanan, J. M. 1980b. "Rent Seeking and Profit Seeking." In J. M. Buchanan, R. D. Tollison, and G. Tullock, eds., *Toward a Theory of a Rent-Seeking Society,* 3–15. College Station: Texas A&M University Press.

Buchanan, J. M. 1987. "Constitutional Economics." In J. Eatwell, M. Milgate, and P. Newman, eds., *The New Palgrave: A Dictionary of Economics,* 1:585–88. London et al.: Macmillan.

Buchanan, J. M. 1990. "The Domain of Constitutional Economics." *Constitutional Political Economy* 1:1–18.

Buchanan, J. M., R. D. Tollison, and G. Tullock, eds. 1980. *Toward a Theory of a Rent-Seeking Society.* College Station: Texas A&M University Press.

Buchanan, J. M., and Tullok, G. 1962. *The Calculus of Consent.* Ann Arbor: University of Michigan Press.

Bücher, K. 1922. *Die Entstehung der Volkswirtschaft, Erste, und zweite Sammlung.* Tübingen: H. Laupp'schen Buchhandlung.

Buck, T. 1982. *Comparative Industrial Systems: Industry under Capitalism, Central Planning, and Self-Management.* London: Macmillan.

Bull, C. 1987. "The Existence of Self-Enforcing Implicit Contracts." *Quarterly Journal of Economics* 98:147–59.

Burgers, W. P., C. W. Hill, and W. G. Kim. 1993. "A Theory of Global Strategic Alliances: The Case of the Global Auto Industry." *Strategic Management Journal* 14:419–32.

Butters, G. 1977. "Equilibrium Distribution of Prices and Advertising." *Review of Economic Studies* 44:465–92.

Cable, J. 1985. "Capital Market Information and Industrial Performance: The Role of West German Banks." *Economic Journal* 95:118–32.

Calabresi, G. 1970. *The Costs of Accidents.* New Haven: Yale University Press.

Calamari, J. D., and J. M. Perillo. 1987. *Contracts.* 3d ed. St. Paul, Minn.: West.

Calvert, R. L. 1995a. "The Rational Choice Theory of Social Institutions: Cooperation, Coordination, and Communication." In J. S. Banks and E. A. Hanushek, eds., *Modern Political Economy: Old Topics, New Directions,* 216–69. Cambridge: Cambridge University Press.

Calvert, R. L. 1995b. "Rational Actors, Equilibrium, and Social Institutions." In J. Knight and I. Sened, eds., *Explaining Social Institutions,* 57–93. Ann Arbor: University of Michigan Press.

Calvo, G. A. 1978. "Optimal Seigniorage from Money Creation: An Analysis of the Optimal Balance of Payments Deficit Problem." *Journal of Monetary Economics* 4:503–17.

Calvo, G. A., and S. Wellisz. 1979. "Hierarchy, Ability, and Income Distribution." *Journal of Political Economy* 87:991–1010.

Carlton, D. W. 1983. "Equilibrium Fluctuations When Price and Delivery Lag Clear the Market." *Bell Journal of Economics* 14:562–72.

Carlton, D. W. 1986. "The Rigidity of Prices." *American Economic Review* 76:637–58.

Carlton, D. W. 1989. "The Theory and the Facts of How Markets Clear: Is Industrial Organization Valuable for Understanding Macroeconomics?" In R. Schmalensee and R. D. Willig, eds., *Handbook of Industrial Organization,* 1:909–46. Amsterdam: North-Holland.

Carmichael, H. L. 1989. "Self-Enforcing Contracts, Shirking, and Life Cycle Incentives." *Journal of Economic Perspectives* 3, no. 4:65–83.

Carr, J. L., and J. T. Landa. 1983. "The Economics of Symbols, Clan Names, and Religion." *Journal of Legal Studies* 12:135–56.

Carr, J. L., and F. Mathewson. 1990. "The Economics of Law Firms: A Study in the Legal Organization of the Firm." *Journal of Law and Economics* 233:307–30.

Chandler, A. D., Jr. 1977. *The Visible Hand: The Managerial Revolution in American Business.* Cambridge: Harvard University Press.

Chen, M.-J., and D. Miller. 1994. "Competitive Attack, Retaliation, and Performance: An Expectancy-Valence Framework." *Strategic Management Journal* 15:85–102.

Chen, M.-J., K. G. Smith, and C. M. Grimm. 1992. "Action Characteristics as Predictors of Competitive Responses." *Management Science* 38:439–55.

Cheung, S. N. S. 1969. "Transaction Costs, Risk Aversion, and the Choice of Contractual Arrangements." *Journal of Law and Economics* 12:23–45.

Cheung, S. N. S. 1970. "The Structure of a Contract and the Theory of a Non-exclusive Resource." *Journal of Law and Economics* 13:49–70.

Cheung, S. N. S. 1974. "A Theory of Price Control." *Journal of Law and Economics* 17:53–71.

Cheung, S. N. S. 1983. "The Contractual Nature of the Firm." *Journal of Law and Economics* 26:1–22.

Chung, T.-Y. 1991. "Incomplete Contracts, Specific Investments, and Risk Sharing." *Review of Economic Studies* 58:1031–42.

Ciriacy-Wantrup, S. V., and R. C. Bishop. 1975. "'Common Property' as a Concept in Natural Resource Policy." *Natural Resources Journal* 15:713–27.

Clark, C. W. 1977. "The Economics of Over-exploitation." In G. Hardin and J. Baden, eds., *Managing the Commons,* 82–95. San Francisco: Freeman.

Clarkson, K. W. 1977. *Intangible Capital and Rates of Return.* Washington D.C.: American Institute for Public Policy Research.

Clausewitz, C. Von. [1832] 1963. *Vom Kriege.* Reinbeck: Rowohlt.

Coase, R. H. 1937. "The Nature of the Firm." *Economica* 4:386–405.

Coase, R. H. 1959. "The Federal Communications Commission." *Journal of Law and Economics* 2:1–40.

Coase, R. H. 1960. "The Problem of Social Cost." *Journal of Law and Economics* 3:1–44.

Coase, R. H. 1972. "Industrial Organization: A Proposal for Research." In V. R. Fuchs, ed., *Policy Issues and Research Opportunities in Industrial Organization,* 59–73. New York: National Bureau of Economic Research.

Coase, R. H. 1984. "The New Institutional Economics." *Journal of Institutional and Theoretical Economics* 140:229–31.

Coase, R. H. 1988a. "R. H. Coase Lectures, 2: The Nature of the Firm—Meaning." *Journal of Law, Economics, and Organization* 4:19–32.

Coase, R. H. 1988b. *The Firm, the Market, and the Law.* Chicago and London: University of Chicago Press.

Coase, R. H. 1993. "Coase on Posner on Coase." *Journal of Institutional and Theoretical Economics* 149:96–98.

Coleman, J. S. 1988. "Social Capital in the Creation of Human Capital." *American Journal of Sociology, Supplement* 94:95–120.

Coleman, J. S. 1990. *Foundations of Social Theory.* Cambridge: Belknap Press of Harvard University Press.

Coleman, J. S. 1991. "Constructed Organization, First Principles." *Journal of Law, Economics, and Organization* 7:7–23.

Colson, E. 1974. *Tradition and Contract: The Problem of Order.* Chicago: Aldine.

Commons, J. R. 1934. *Institutional Economics.* Madison: University of Wisconsin Press.

Conlisk, J. 1988. "Optimization Cost." *Journal of Economic Behavior and Organization* 9:213–28.

Conlisk, J. 1996. "Why Bounded Rationality?" *Journal of Economic Literature* 34:669–700.

Cooper, R. 1988a. "The Rise of Activity-Based Costing, Part One: What Is an Activity-Based Cost System?" *Journal of Cost Management* 2 (Summer):45–54.

Cooper, R. 1988b. "The Rise of Activity-Based Costing, Part Two: When Do I Need an Activity-Based Cost System?" *Journal of Cost Management* 2 (Fall):41–48.

Cooter, R., and J. T. LANDA. 1984. "Personal versus Impersonal Trade: The Size of Trading Groups and Contract Law." *International Review of Law and Economics* 4:15–22.

Cooter, R., and T. Ulen. 1988. *Law and Economics.* Glenview, Ill.: Scott, Foresman.

Cournot, A. 1838. *Recherches sur les Principles Mathématiques de la Théorie des Richesses.* Paris: Riviere.

Crawford, V. P. 1988. "Long-Term Relationships Governed by Short-Term Contracts." *American Economic Review* 78:485–99.

Cremer, J. 1986. "Cooperation in Ongoing Organizations." *Quarterly Journal of Economics* 101:33–49.

Crocker, K. J., and S. E. Masten. 1991. "Pretia Ex Machina? Prices and Process in Long-Term Contracts." *Journal of Law and Economics* 34:69–99.

Cyert, R. M., and J. G. March. 1963. *A Behavioral Theory of the Firm.* Englewood Cliffs, N.J.: Prentice-Hall.

Dahlman, C. J. 1979. "The Problem of Externality." *Journal of Law and Economics* 22:141–62.

Dann, L. Y., and H. DeAngelo. 1983. "Standstill Agreements, Privately Negotiated Stock Repurchases, and the Market for Corporate Control." *Journal of Financial Economics* 11:275–300.

Dasgupta, P. 1988. "Trust as a Commodity." In D. Gambetta, ed., *Trust: Making and Breaking Cooperative Relations,* 49–72. Oxford: Basil Blackwell.

Dasgupta, P., and E. Maskin. 1986. "The Existence of Equilibrium in Discontinuous Economic Games I: Theory." *Review of Economic Studies* 53:1–26.

Day, R., and M. Pingle. 1991 "Economizing Economizing." *Handbook of Behavioral Economics* 2B:511–24.

DeAlessi, L. 1980. "The Economics of Property Rights: A Review of the Evidence." *Research in Law and Economics* 2:1–47.

DeAlessi, L. 1983. "Property Rights, Transaction Costs, and X-Efficiency: An Essay in Economic Theory." *American Economic Review* 73:64–81.

DeAlessi, L. 1987. "Property Rights and Privatization." In S. Hanke, ed., *Prospects for Privatization,* 24–35. New York: Academy of Political Science.

DeAlessi, L. 1989. "Subjective Value in Contract Law." *Journal of Institutional and Theoretical Economics* 145: 561–77.

DeAlessi, L. 1990. "Form, Substance, and Welfare Comparison in the Analysis of Institutions." *Journal of Institutional and Theoretical Economics* 146:5–23.

DeAlessi, L. 1992. "Efficiency Criteria for Optimal Laws: Objective Standards of Value Judgements?" *Constitutional Political Economy* 3:321–42.

Debreu, G. 1959. *Theory of Value: An Axiomatic Analysis of Economic Equilibrium.* New York and London: Wiley.

DeGeorge, R. T. 1900. *Business Ethics.* 3d ed. London: Macmillan.

De Jasay, A. 1989. *Social Contract, Free Ride: A Study of the Public Goods Problems.* Oxford: Clarendon.

De Meza, D., and J. P. Gould. 1992. "The Social Efficiency of Private Decisions to Enforce Property Rights." *Journal of Political Economy* 100:561–80.

Demsetz, H. 1964. "The Exchange and Enforcement of Property Rights." *Journal of Law and Economics* 7:11–26.

Demsetz, H. 1966. "Some Aspects of Property Rights." *Journal of Law and Economics* 9:61–70.

Demsetz, H. 1967. "Toward a Theory of Property Rights." *American Economic Review, Papers and Proceedings* 57:347–59.

Demsetz, H. 1968a. "The Cost of Transacting." *Quarterly Journal of Economics* 82:33–53.

Demsetz, H. 1968b. "Why Regulate Utilities?" *Journal of Law and Economics* 11:55–66.

Demsetz, H. 1969. "Information and Efficiency: Another Viewpoint." *Journal of Law and Economics* 12:1–22.

Demsetz, H. 1982. *Economic, Legal, and Political Dimensions of Competition.* Amsterdam: North-Holland.

Demski, J. S., and D. E. M. Sappington. 1984. "Optimal Incentive Contracts with Multiple Agents." *Journal of Economic Theory* 33:152–71.

Denzau, A. T., and D. C. North. 1994. "Shared Mental Models: Ideologies and Institutions." *Kyklos* 47:3–31.

De Vany, A. 1996. "Information, Chance, and Evolution: Alchian and the Economics of Self-Organization." *Economic Inquiry* 34:427–43.

Dewatripont, M. F. 1986. "On the Theory of Commitment with Applications to the Labor Market." Ph.D. diss. Harvard University, Department of Economics.

Diamond, D. 1984. "Financial Intermediation and Delegated Monitoring." *Review of Economic Studies* 51:393–414.

DiMaggio, P. J., and W. W. Powell. 1991. "Introduction." In W. W. Powell and P. J. DiMaggio, eds., *The New Institutionalism in Organizational Analysis,* 1–38. Chicago: University of Chicago Press.

Dnes, A. W. 1992a. *Franchising: A Case-Study Approach.* Avebury: Aldershot.

Dnes, A. W. 1992b. "'Unfair' Contractual Practices and Hostages in Franchise Contracts." *Journal of Institutional and Theoretical Economics* 148:484–504.

Dnes, A. W. 1996. "The Economic Analysis of Franchise Contracts." *Journal of Institutional and Theoretical Economics* 152:1–28.

Domar, E. D. 1966. "The Soviet Collective Farm as a Producer Cooperative." *American Economic Review* 56:734–57.

Dorfman, R., and P. O. Steiner. 1954. "Optimal Advertising and Optimal Quality." *American Economic Review* 44:826–45.

Downs, A. 1957. *An Economic Theory of Democracy.* New York: Harper and Row.

Dreier, R. 1986. "Der Begriff des Rechts." *Neue Juristische Wochenzeitschrift* 14:890–96.

Drèze, J. H. 1976. "Some Theories of Labor Management and Participation." *Econometrica* 44:1125–40.

Drobak, J. N., and J. V. C. Nye, eds. 1997. *The Frontiers of the New Institutional Economics.* San Diego: Academic Press.

Dürig, G. 1958. "Eigentum." In *Staatslexikon,* 6th ed. Freiburg:

Dwarkin, R. 1977. *Taking Rights Seriously.* London: Duckworth.

Dye, R. 1985. "Costly Contract Contingencies." *International Economic Review* 26:233–50.

Eaton, B., and D. Eaton. 1988. *Microeconomics.* New York: W. H. Freeman.

Eekhoff, J. 1981. "Zur Kontroverse um die ökonomischen Auswirkungen des Zweiten Wohnraumkündigungsschutzgesetzes." *Journal of Institutional and Theoretical Economics* 137:62–77.

Eggertsson, T. 1990. *Economic Behavior and Institutions.* Cambridge: Cambridge University Press.

EIRR 1990. "Employee Participation in Europe." *European Industrial Relations Review.* Reports no. 4. London: Eclipse.

Eisenhardt, K. M., and M. J. Zbaracki. 1992. "Strategic Decision Making." *Strategic Management Journal* 13:17–37.

Ellickson, R. C. 1987. "A Critique of Economic and Sociological Theories of Social Control." *Journal of Legal Studies* 16:67–100.

Elster, J. 1979. *Ulysses and the Sirens: Studies in Rationality and Irrationality.* New York: Cambridge University Press.

Elster, J. 1989. *The Cement of Society.* Cambridge: Cambridge University Press.

Eser, G. 1994. "Europarechtliche Aspekte der Arbeitermitbestimmung in Multinationalen Unternehmen." *Arbeit und Recht* Heft 3:91–100.

Etzioni, A. 1988. *The Moral Dimension.* New York: Free Press.

Eucken, W. 1940. "Wissenschaft im Stile Schmollers." *Weltwirtschaftliches Archiv* 52:468–506.

Eucken, W. 1947. *Die Grundlagen der Nationalökonomie.* 2d ed. Godesberg: Helmut Küpper, vormals Georg Bondi.

Eucken, W. 1950. *The Foundations of Economics.* Translated by T. W. Hutchison. Edinburgh: Hodge.

Eucken, W. 1951. *The Unsuccessful Age.* Edinburgh: Hodge.

Eucken, W. 1952. *Grundsätze der Wirtschaftspolitik.* Edited by E. Eucken and K. P. Hensel. Tübingen: J. C. B. Mohr (Paul Siebeck).

Fama, E. 1980. "Agency Problems and the Theory of the Firm." *Journal of Political Economy* 88:288–307.

Fama, E., and M. Jensen. 1983. "Separation of Ownership and Control." *Journal of Law and Economics* 26:301–25.

Farnsworth, E. A. 1990. *Contracts.* 2d ed. Boston and Toronto: Little, Brown.

Farrell, J. 1987. "Information and the Coase Theorem." *Journal of Economic Perspectives* 1, no. 2:113–29.

Farrell, J., and G. Saloner. 1985. "Standardization, Compatibility, and Innovation." *Rand Journal of Economics* 16:70–83.

Fellner, W. 1949. *Competition among the Few: Oligopoly and Similar Market Structures.* New York: Knopf.

Fischer, S. 1977. "Long-Term Contracts, Rational Expectations, and the Optimal Money Supply Rule." *Journal of Political Economy* 85:191–205.

Fisher, F. M., and J. J. McGowan. 1983. "On the Misuse of Accounting Rates of Return to Infer Monopoly Profits." *American Economic Review* 73:83–98.

Fisher, I. 1912. *The Nature of Capital and Income.* New York and London: Macmillan.

Flath, D. 1980. "The Economics of Short-Term Leasing." *Economic Inquiry.* 18:247–59.

Foley, D. K. 1970. "Economic Equilibrium with Costly Marketing." *Journal of Economic Theory* 2:276–91.

Frank, R. H. 1990. "A Theory of Moral Sentiments." In J. J. Mansbridge, ed., *Beyond Self-Interest,* 71–96. Chicago and London: University of Chicago Press.

Frank, R. H. 1992. "Melding Sociology and Economics: James Coleman's Foundations of Social Theory." *Journal of Economic Literature* 30:147–70.

Frase, R. 1966. "Comments on Hurt and Schuchman, The Economic Rationale of Copyright." *American Economic Review, Papers and Proceedings* 56:435–39.

Freixas, X., R. Guesnerie, and J. Tirole. 1985. "Planning under Incomplete Information and the Ratchet Effect." *Review of Economic Studies* 52:173–91.

Frey, B. S. 1984a. *International Political Economy.* Oxford: Basil Blackwell.

Frey, B. S. 1984b. "A New View of Economics: Comparative Analysis of Institutions." *Economia della Scelte Pubbliche* 1:3–16.

Frey, B. S. 1993. "An Economic Analysis of the New Institutional Economics." *Journal of Institutional and Theoretical Economics* 149:351–59.

Frey, B. S., and F. Schneider. 1981. "Central Bank Behavior: A Positive Empirical Analysis." *Journal of Monetary Economics* 7:291–315.

Fried, C. 1981. *Contract as a Promise: A Theory of Contractual Obligations.* Cambridge: Harvard University Press.

Frieden, J. A., and D. A. Lake. eds. 1987. *International Political Economy.* New York: St. Martin's.

Friedman, D. 1977. "A Theory of the Size and Shape of Nations." *Journal of Political Economy* 85–I:59–77.

Friedman, M. 1953. *Essays in Positive Economics.* Chicago: University of Chicago Press.

Fröhlich, W. 1940. "Das afrikanische Marktwesen." *Zeitschrift für Ethnologie* 72:234–328.

Fudenberg, D., B. R. Holmstrom, and P. Milgrom. 1990. "Short-Term Contracts and Long-Term Agency Relationships." *Journal of Economic Theory* 51:1–31.

Fudenberg, D., and J. Tirole. 1991. *Game Theory.* Cambridge: MIT Press.

Furubotn, E. G. 1963. "On Some Applications of the Utility Tree." *Southern Economic Journal* 30:128–43.

Furubotn, E. G. 1971a. "Economic Organization and Welfare Distribution." *Swedish Journal of Economics* 73:409–16.

Furubotn, E. G. 1971b. "Toward a Dynamic Model of the Yugoslav Firm." *Canadian Journal of Economics* 4:182–97.

Furubotn, E. G. 1974a. "Bank Credit and the Labor-Managed Firm: The Yugoslav Case." In E. G. Furubotn and S. Pejovich, eds., *The Economics of Property Rights,* 257–76. Cambridge: Ballinger.

Furubotn, E. G. 1974b. "The Quasi-Concave Utility Function and the Number of Distinct Commodities Chosen at Equilibrium." *Weltwirtschaftliches Archiv* 110:228–307.

Furubotn, E. G. 1976a. "The Long-Run Analysis of the Labor-Managed Firm: An Alternative Interpretation." *American Economic Review* 66:104–23.

Furubotn, E. G. 1976b. "Worker Alienation and the Structure of the Firm." In S. Pejovich, ed., *Government Controls and the Free Market,* 195–225. College Station: Texas A&M University Press.

Furubotn, E. G. 1978. "The Economic Consequences of Codetermination on the Rate and Sources of Private Investment." In S. Pejovich, ed., *The Codetermination Movement in the West: Labor Participation in the Management of Business Firms,* 131–67. Lexington, Mass.: D. C. Heath.

Furubotn, E. G. 1980. "The Socialist Labor-Managed Firm and Bank Financed Investment: Some Theoretical Issues." *Journal of Comparative Economics* 4:184–91.

Furubotn, E. G. 1985. "Codetermination Productivity Gains and the Economics of the Firm." *Oxford Economic Papers* 37:22–39.

Furubotn, E. G. 1986. "Efficiency and the Maximization Postulate: Another Interpretation," *Journal of Behavioral Economics* 15:41–48.

Furubotn, E. G. 1987. "Privatizing the Commons: Comment." *Southern Economic Journal* 54:219–24.

Furubotn, E. G. 1988. "Codetermination and the Modern Theory of the Firm: A Property-Rights Analysis." *Journal of Business* 61:165–81.

Furubotn, E. G. 1989a. "Distributional Issues in Contracting for Property Rights: Comment." *Journal of Institutional and Theoretical Economics* 145:25–31.

Furubotn, E. G. 1989b. "Organizational Economics and the Analysis of Codetermination." *Annals of Public and Cooperative Economics* 60:463–74.

Furubotn, E. G. 1990. "Different Approaches to the Economic Analysis of Institutions: Some Concluding Remarks." *Journal of Institutional and Theoretical Economics* 146:226–32.

Furubotn, E. G. 1991. "General Equilibrium Models, Transaction Costs, and the Concept of Efficient Allocation in a Capitalist Economy." *Journal of Institutional and Theoretical Economics* 147:662–86.

Furubotn, E. G. 1994. "Future Development of the New Institutional Economics: Extension of the Neoclassical Model or New Construct?" *Lectiones Jenenses* 1:3–42.

Furubotn, E. G. 1995. "Income Transfers, Entrepreneurial Effort, and the Coase Theorem: The Case for Efficiency Reconsidered." *European Journal of Law and Economics* 2:99–118.

Furubotn, E. G. 1996. "The Neoclassical Production Function: Useful Construct or Red Herring?" Unpublished manuscript. Center for the Study of the New Institutional Economics, Universität des Saarlandes, Saarbrüken, Germany.

Furubotn, E. G., and S. Pejovich. 1970a. "Tax Policy and Investment Decisions of the Yugoslav Firm." *National Tax Journal* 23:335–48.

Furubotn, E. G., and S. Pejovich. 1970b. "Property Rights and the Behavior of the Firm in a Socialist State: The Example of Yugoslavia." *Zeitschrift für Nationalökonomie* 30:431–54.

Furubotn, E. G., and S. Pejovich. 1972a. "Property Rights and Economic Theory: A Survey of Recent Literature." *Journal of Economic Literature* 10:1137–62.

Furubotn, E. G., and S. Pejovich. 1972b. "The Soviet Manager and Innovation: A Behavioral Model of the Soviet Firm." *Revue De L'Est* 3:29–45.

Furubotn, E. G., and S. Pejovich. eds. 1974. *The Economics of Property Rights.* Cambridge, Mass.: Balinger.

Furubotn, E. G., and S. Pejovich. 1991. "The Role of the Banking System in Yugoslav Economic Planning, 1946–1969." *Revue Internationale D'Historie De La Banque* 4:51–91.

Furubotn, E. G., and R. Richter. 1991. "The New Institutional Economics: An Assessment." In E. G. Furubotn and R. Richter, eds., *The New Institutional Economics,* 1–32. Tübingen: J. C. B. Mohr (Paul Siebeck).

Furubotn, E. G., and R. Richter. 1994. "The New Institutional Economics: Bounded

Rationality and the Analysis of State and Society." *Journal of Institutional and Theoretical Economics* 150:1–34.

Furubotn, E. G., and S. N. Wiggins. 1984. "Plant Closings, Worker Reallocation Costs, and Efficiency Gains to Labor Representation on Boards of Directors." *Journal of Institutional and Theoretical Economics* 140:176–92.

Galbraith, J. K. 1952. *American Capitalism: The Concept of Countervailing Power.* London: Hamish Hamilton.

Galbraith, J. K. 1967. *The New Industrial State.* Boston: Houghton Mifflin.

Garrett, G., and B. R. Weingast. 1993. "Ideas, Interests, and Institutions: Constructing the European Community's Internal Market." In J. Goldshein and R. Keohane, eds., *Ideas and Foreign Policy,* 173–206. Ithaca, N.Y.: Cornell University Press.

Garvy, G. 1944. "Rivals and Interlopers in the History of the New York Security Market." *Journal of Political Economy* 52:128–43.

Gibbons, R. 1992. *A Primer in Game Theory.* New York: Harvester.

Gifford, A., Jr. 1991. "A Constitutional Interpretation of the Firm." *Public Choice* 68:91–106.

Gilpin, R. 1981. *War and Change in World Politics.* Cambridge: Cambridge University Press.

Gilson, R. J., and R. H. Mnookin. 1989. "Coming of Age in a Corporate Law Firm: The Economics of Associate Career Patterns." *Stanford Law Review* 41:567–95.

Goetz, C. J., and R. E. Scott. 1981. "Principles of Relational Contracts." *Virginia Law Review* 67:1089–1150.

Goldberg, V. 1976. "Regulation and Administered Contracts." *Bell Journal of Economics* 7:426–52.

Goldberg, V. 1980. "Relational Exchange: Economic and Complex Contracts." *American Behavioral Scientist* 23:337–46.

Goldberg, V. 1990. "Aversion to Risk Aversion in the New Institutional Economics." *Journal of Institutional and Theoretical Economics* 146:216–22.

Gordon, D. F. 1974. "A Neoclassical Theory of Keynesian Unemployment." *Economic Inquiry* 12:431–49.

Gordon, H. S. 1954. "The Economic Theory of a Common Property Resource: The Fishery." *Journal of Political Economy* 62:124–42.

Gossen, J. H. [1854] 1889. *Entwicklung der Gesetze des menschlichen Verkehrs.* New ed. Berlin: Prager.

Gottinger, H. 1982. "Computational Costs and Bounded Rationality." In W. Stegmuller, W. Balzer, and W. Spohn, eds., *Studies in Contemporary Economics,* 223–38. Berlin: Springer.

Gould, J. P. 1968. "Adjustment Costs in the Theory of Investment of the Firm." *Review of Economic Studies* 35:47–55.

Gould, J. P. 1980. "The Economics of Markets: A Simple Model of the Market-Making Process." *Journal of Business* 53:167–87.

Grandmont, J. M. 1974. "On the Short Run Equilibrium in a Monetary Economy." In J. Drèze, ed., *Allocation under Uncertainty, Equilibrium, and Optimality,* 213–28. Proceedings of an International Economic Association Workshop in Economic Theory, Bergen, Norway. London: Macmillan.

Grandmont, J. M. 1977. "Temporary General Equilibrium Theory." *Econometrica* 45:535–72.

Grandmont, J. M., and Y. Younes. 1972. "On the Role of Money and the Existence of a Monetary Equilibrium." *Review of Economic Studies* 39:355–72.

Grandmont, J. M., and Y. Younes. 1973. "On the Efficiency of a Monetary Equilibrium." *Review of Economic Studies* 40:149–65.

Granovetter, M. 1985. "Economic Action and Social Structure: The Problem of Embeddedness." *American Journal of Sociology* 91:481–501.

Gravelle, H., and R. Rees. 1987. *Microeconomics.* London: Longman.

Green, J. R., and J. J. Laffont. 1979. *Incentives in Public Decision-Making.* Amsterdam: North-Holland.

Green, M., et al. 1979. "The Case for a Corporate Democracy Act of 1980." *Public Citizens' Congress Watch.* Washington, D.C., 1–127.

Greenwald, B. C. 1986. "Adverse Selection in the Labour Market." *Review of Economic Studies* 53:325–48.

Greif, A. 1989. "Reputation and Coalitions on Medieval Trade: Evidence on the Maghribi Traders." *Journal of Economic History* 49:857–82.

Greif, A. 1994. "On the Political Foundations of the Late Medieval Commercial Revolution: Genoa during the Twelfth and Thirteenth Centuries." *Journal of Economic History* 54:271–87.

Greif, A. 1997a. "Microtheory and Recent Developments in the Study of Economic Institutions Through Economic History." In D. M. Kreps and K. F. Wallis, eds., *Advances in Economics and Econometrics: Theory and Application.* Proceedings of the Seventh World Congress of the Econometrics Society, Vol. III, 79–113. Cambridge University Press.

Greif, A. 1997b. "On the Interrelations and Economic Implications of Economic, Social, Political, and Normative Factors: Reflections from Two Late Medieval Societies." In S. N. Drobak and J. V. C. Nye, eds., *The Frontiers of the New Institutional Economics,* 57–94. San Diego: Academic Press.

Greif, A., P. Milgrom, and B. R. Weingast. 1990. "The Merchant Gild as a Nexus of Contracts." Working Papers in Economics, no. E–90–23. Palo Alto: Hoover Institution, Stanford University.

Grossman, G., and C. Shapiro. 1984. "Informative Advertising with Differentiated Products." *Review of Economic Studies* 51:63–82.

Grossman, S. J. 1981. "The Role of Warranties and Private Disclosure about Product Quality." *Journal of Law and Economics* 24:461–83.

Grossman, S. J., and O. D. Hart. 1981. "Implicit Contracts, Moral Hazard, and Unemployment." *American Economic Review, Papers and Proceedings* 71:301–07.

Grossman, S. J., and O. D. Hart. 1982. "Corporate Financial Structure and Managerial Incentives." In J. J. McCall, ed., *The Economics of Information and Uncertainty,* 107–40. Chicago: University of Chicago Press.

Grossman, S. J., and O. D. Hart. 1983a. "An Analysis of the Principal Agent Problem." *Econometrica* 51:7–46.

Grossman, S. J., and O. D. Hart. 1983b. "Implicit Contracts under Asymmetric Information." *Quarterly Journal of Economics, Supplement* 98:123–56.

Grossman, S. J., and O. D. Hart. 1986. "The Costs and Benefits of Ownership: A Theory of Vertical and Lateral Integration." *Journal of Political Economy* 94:691–719.

Grossman, S. J., and O. D. Hart. 1987. "Vertical Integration and the Distribution of Property Rights." In A. Razin, eds., *Economic Policy and Practice*. London: Macmillan.

Grout, P. 1984. "Investment and Wages in the Absence of Binding Contracts: A Nash Bargaining Approach." *Econometrica* 52:449–60.

Gwartney, J., R. Lawson, and W. Block. 1995. *Economic Freedom of the World, 1975–1995*. Vancouver: Fraser Institute.

Haas, and Deseran 1981. "Trust and Symbolic Exchange." *Social Science Quarterly* 44:7–9.

Hadfield, G. K. 1990. "Problematic Relations: Franchising and the Law of Incomplete Contracts." *Stanford Law Review* 42:927–92.

Hahn, F. H. 1971. "Equilibrium with Transaction Costs." *Econometrica* 39:417–39.

Hahn, F. H. 1973. "On Transaction Costs, Inessential Sequence Economics, and Money." *Review of Economic Studies* 40:449–61.

Hall, R. E., and E. P. Lazear. 1984. "The Excess Sensitivity of Layoffs and Quits to Demand." *Journal of Labour Economics* 2:231–57.

Hamilton, G. G., and R. C. Feenstra. 1995. "Varieties of Hierarchies and Markets: An Introduction." *Industrial and Corporate Change* 4:51–92.

Hansmann, H. 1988. "Ownership of the Firm." *Journal of Law, Economics, and Organization* 4:267–304.

Hardin, G. 1968. "The Tragedy of the Commons." *Science* 162:1243–48.

Harsanyi, J. 1967. "Games with Incomplete Information Played by Bayesian Players I: The Basic Model." *Management Science* 14:159–82.

Hart, H. L. A. 1961. *The Concept of Law*. Oxford: Clarendon.

Hart, O. D. 1983a. "Optimal Labour Contracts under Asymmetric Information: An Introduction." *Review of Economic Studies* 50:3–35.

Hart, O. D. 1983b. "The Market Mechanism as an Incentive Scheme." *Bell Journal of Economics* 14:366–82.

Hart, O. D. 1987. "Incomplete Contracts." In J. Eatwell, M. Milgate, and P. Newman, eds., *The New Palgrave: A Dictionary of Economics*, 2:752–59. London: Macmillan.

Hart, O. D. 1989. "An Economist's Perspective on the Theory of the Firm." *Columbia Law Review* 89:1757–74.

Hart, O. D. 1990. "Is 'Bounded Rationality' an Important Element of a Theory of Institutions?" *Journal of Institutional and Theoretical Economics* 146:696–702.

Hart, O. D. 1995. *Firms, Contracts, and Financial Structure*. Oxford: Clarendon.

Hart, O. D., and B. R. Holmstrom. 1987. "The Theory of Contracts." In T. Bewley, ed., *Advances in Economic Theory*, 71–55. Cambridge: Cambridge University Press.

Hart, O. D., and J. Moore. 1988. "Incomplete Contracts and Renegotiation." *Econometrica* 56:755–85.

Hart, O. D., and J. Moore. 1989. "Default and Renegotiation: A Dynamic Model of Debt." Mimeo.

Hart, O. D., and J. Moore. 1990. "Property Rights and the Nature of the Firm." *Journal of Political Economy* 98:1119–58.

Haucap, J., C. Wey, and J. Barmbold. 1995. "Location Choice and Implicit Franchise Contracts." Discussion Papers, no. 9506. Department of Economics, University of Saarland.

Hausman, D. M. 1989. "Economic Methodology in a Nutshell." *Journal of Economic Perspectives* 3:115–27.

Hax, H. 1996. "Hare and Hedgehog Revisited: Comment." *Journal of Institutional and Theoretical Economics* 151:182–85.

Hayek, F. A., ed. 1935. *Collectivist Economic Planning.* London: Routledge and Kegan Paul.

Hayek, F. A. 1937. "Economics and Knowledge." *Economica* 4:35–54.

Hayek, F. A. 1944. *The Road to Serfdom.* London: Routledge and Kegan Paul.

Hayek, F. A. 1945. "The Use of Knowledge in Society." *American Economic Review* 35:519–30.

Hayek, F. A. 1960. *The Constitution of Liberty.* London: Routledge and Kegan Paul.

Hayek, F. A. 1973. *Law, Legislation, and Liberty.* Vol. 1. Chicago: University of Chicago Press.

Hayek, F. A. 1978. *New Studies in Philosophy, Politics, Economics, and the History of Economic Ideas.* London: Routledge and Kegan Paul.

Heller, W. P. 1972. "Transitions with Set-up Costs." *Journal of Economic Theory* 4:465–78.

Hellwig, M. 1987. "Some Recent Developments in the Theory of Competitive Markets with Adverse Selection." *European Economic Review* 31:319–25.

Hellwig, M. 1988a. "Kreditrationierung und Kreditsicherheiten bei asymmetrischer Information: Der Fall des Monopolmarkets." Discussion Papers, no. A–167, Universität Basel.

Hellwig, M. 1988b. "Equity, Opportunism, and the Design of Contractual Relations: Comment." *Journal of Institutional and Theoretical Economics* 144:200–207.

Hellwig, M. 1989. "Asymmetric Information, Financial Markets, and Financial Institutions." *European Economic Review* 33:277–85.

Hemmer, T. 1995. "On the Interrelation between Production Technology, Job Design, and Incentives." *Journal of Accounting & Economics* 19:209–45.

Henderson, J. M., and R. E. Quandt. 1958. *Microeconomic Theory: A Mathematical Approach.* New York, Toronto, and London: McGraw Hill.

Hennart, J.-F. 1988. "A Transaction Costs Theory of Equity Joint Ventures." *Strategic Management Journal* 9:361–74.

Hennart, J.-F. 1991. "The Transaction Costs Theory of Joint Ventures: An Empirical Study of Japanese Subsidiaries in the United States." *Management Science* 37:483–97.

Hermalin, B. E., and M. L. Katz. 1991. "Moral Hazard and Verifiability: The Effects of Renegotiation in Agency." *Econometrica* 59:1735–53.

Hess, J. D. 1983. *The Economics of Organization.* Amsterdam: North-Holland.

Hicks, J. R. 1932. *The Theory of Wages.* London: Macmillan.

Hicks, J. R. 1935. "A Suggestion for Simplifying the Theory of Money." *Economica* n.s., 2:1–19. Reprinted in F. A. Lutz, and L. W. Mints, eds., *Readings in Monetary Theory,* 13–32. New York, Philadelphia, and Toronto: Blakiston Company, 1951.

Hicks, J. R. 1946. *Value and Capital: An Inquiry into Some Fundamental Principles of Economic Theory.* 2d ed. Oxford: Clarendon.

Hicks, J. R. 1956. *A Revision of Demand Theory.* Oxford: Clarendon.

Hicks, J. R. 1967. "The Two Triads, Lecture I." In *Critical Essays in Monetary Theory,* 1–16. Oxford: Clarendon.

Hinds, M. 1990. *Issues in the Introduction of Market Forces in Eastern European Socialist Economies.* World Bank Reports, no. IDP–0057. Washington, D.C.: World Bank.

Hippel, E. von. 1963. *Die Kontrolle der Vertragsfreiheit nach anglo-amerikanischem Recht.* Frankfurt: Klostermann.

Hirschman, A. O. 1969. *Exit, Voice, and Loyalty: Responses to Decline in Firms, Organizations, and States.* Cambridge: Harvard University Press.

Hirshleifer, J. 1973. "Exchange Theory: The Missing Chapter." *Western Economic Journal* 11:129–46.

Hirshleifer, J., and J. G. Riley. 1979. "The Analytics of Uncertainty and Intermediation: An Expository Survey." *Journal of Economic Literature* 17:1375–1421.

Hodgson, G. 1982. "Theoretical and Policy Implications of Variable Productivity." *Cambridge Journal of Economics* 6:213–26.

Hoff, T. 1981. *Economic Calculation in the Socialist Society.* Indianapolis: Liberty.

Holcombe, R. G. 1994. *The Economic Foundations of Government.* London: Macmillan.

Holmstrom, B. R. 1979. "Moral Hazard and Observability." *Bell Journal of Economics* 10:74–91.

Holmstrom, B. R. 1982. "Moral Hazard in Teams." *Bell Journal of Economics* 13:324–40.

Holmstrom, B. R. 1983. "Equilibrium Long-Term Labor Contracts." *Quarterly Journal of Economics, Supplement* 98:23–54.

Holmstrom, B. R., and P. Milgrom. 1987. "Aggregation and Linearity in the Provision of Intertemporal Incentives." *Econometrica.* 55:303–28.

Holmstrom, B. R., and P. Milgrom. 1991. "Multitask Principal-Agent Analyses: Incentive Contracts, Asset Ownership, and Job Design." *Journal of Law, Economics, and Organization* 7:S24–52.

Holmstrom, B. R., and J. Ricart i Costa. 1986. "Managerial Incentives and Capital Management." *Quarterly Journal of Economics* 97:835–60.

Holmstrom, B. R., and J. Tirole. 1989. "The Theory of the Firm." In R. Schmalensee and R. D. Willig, eds., *Handbook of Industrial Organization,* 1:63–133. Amsterdam: North-Holland.

Holmstrom, B. R., and J. Tirole. 1991. "Transfer Pricing and Organizational Form." *Journal of Law, Economics, and Organization* 7:201–28.

Homann, K., and F. Blome-Drees. 1992. *Wirtschafts- und Unternehmensethik.* UTB für Wissenschaft. Göttingen: Vandenhoeck.

Homans, G. C. 1950. *The Human Group*. New York: Harcourt, Brace.

Homans, G. C. 1958. "Social Behaviour as Exchange." *American Journal of Sociology* 62:606–27.

Horn, N., H. Kötz, and H. G. Leser. 1982. *German Private and Commercial Law: An Introduction*. Oxford: Clarendon.

Horvat, B. 1971. "Yugoslav Economic Policy in the Post-War Period: Problems, Ideas, Institutional Developments." *American Economic Review, Supplement* 61:69–169.

Horvat, B., M. Markovic, and R. Supek, eds. 1975. *Self-Governing Socialism: A Reader.* White Plains, N.Y.: International Arts and Sciences Press.

Hughes, A. 1987. "Managerial Capitalism." In J. Eatwell, M. Milgate, and P. Newman, eds., *The New Palgrave: A Dictionary of Economics*, 3:293–96. London: Macmillan.

Hughes, J. 1988. "The Philosophy of Intellectual Property." *Georgetown Law Review* 77:287–366.

Humboldt, W. Von. [1792] 1967. *Ideen zu einem Versuch, die Grenzen der Wirksamkeit des Staates zu bestimmen*. Stuttgart: Philipp Reclam, Jr.

Hume, D. [1739–40] 1969. *A Treatise of Human Nature*. Edited by E. C. Mossner. London: Penguin.

Hurwicz, L. 1960. "Optimality and Informational Efficiency in Resource Allocation Mechanisms." In K. J. Arrow, S. Karlin, and P. Suppes, eds., *Mathematical Methods in the Social Sciences*, 27–46. Stanford: Stanford University Press.

Hurwicz, L. 1973. "The Design of Mechanisms for Resource Allocation." *American Economic Review, Papers and Proceedings* 63:1–30.

Hurwicz, L. 1986. "Incentive Aspects of Decentralization." In K. J. Arrow and M. Intriligator, eds., *Handbook of Mathematical Economics*, 3:1441–82. Amsterdam: North-Holland.

Hutchison, T. W. 1953. *A Review of Economic Doctrines*. Oxford: Clarendon.

Hutchison, T. W. 1978. *On Revolutions and Progress in Economic Knowledge*. Cambridge: Cambridge University Press.

Hutchison, T. W. 1979. "Notes on the Effects of Economic Ideas of the German Social Market Economy." *Zeitschrift für die gesamte Staatswissenschaft/Journal of Institutional and Theoretical Economics* 135:424–41.

Hutchison, T. W. 1984. "Institutionalist Old and New." *Journal of Institutional and Theoretical Economics* 140:20–29.

IDE [Industrial Democracy in Europe. International Research Group]. 1993. *Industrial Democracy in Europe Revisited*. Oxford: Oxford University Press.

Ireland, N., and P. Law. 1982. *The Economics of Labour-Managed Enterprises*. London: Croom Helm.

Isaac, M. R., and J. M. Walker. 1988. "Communication and Free Riding Behavior: The Voluntary Contribution Mechanism," *Economic Inquiry* 26:585–608.

Itoh, H. 1992. "Cooperation in Hierarchical Organizations: An Incentive Perspective." *Journal of Law, Economics and Organization* 8:321–45.

Jaffee, D. M., and T. Russell. 1976. "Imperfect Information, Uncertainty, and Credit Rationing." *Quarterly Journal of Economics* 90:651–66.

Jehle, E. 1982. "Gemeinkosten-Management." *Die Unternehmung* 36, no. 1:59–76.

Jensen, M. C. 1983. "Organization Theory and Methodology." *Accounting Review* 58:319–39.

Jensen, M. C. 1986. "Agency Costs of Free Cash Flow, Corporate Finance, and Takeovers." *American Economic Review, Papers and Proceedings* 76:323–29.

Jensen, M. C., and W. H. Meckling. 1976. "Theory of the Firm: Managerial Behavior, Agency Costs and Ownership Structure." *Journal of Financial Economics* 3:305–60. Reprinted in Putterman 1986a, 209–29.

Jensen, M. C., and W. H. Meckling. 1979. "Rights and Production Functions: An Application to Labor-Managed Firms and Codetermination." *Journal of Business* 52:469–506.

Jensen, M. C., and K. J. Murphy. 1990. "Performance Pay and Top-Management Incentives." *Journal of Political Economy* 98:225–64.

Johnson, R. N., and G. D. Libecap. 1994a. *The Federal Civil Service System and the Problem of Bureaucracy: The Economics and Politics of Institutional Change.* Chicago: University of Chicago Press.

Johnson, R. N., and G. D. Libecap. 1994b. "Patronage to Merit and Control of the Federal Government Labor Force," *Explorations in Economic History* 31:91–119.

Jones, D., and J. Svejnar, eds. 1989–92. *Advances in the Economic Analysis of Participatory and Labor-Managed Firms.* Vols. 1–4, Greenwich, Conn.: JAI.

Joskow, P. L. 1985a. "Vertical Integration and Long-Term Contracts: The Case of Coal-Burning Electric Generating Plants." *Journal of Law, Economics, and Organization* 1:33–80.

Joskow, P. L. 1985b. "Long Term Vertical Relationships and the Study of Industrial Organization and Government Regulation." *Journal of Institutional and Theoretical Economics* 141:586–93.

Joskow, P. L. 1988. "Asset Specificity and Structure of Vertical Relationship: Empirical Evidence." *Journal of Law, Economics, and Organization* 4:95–118.

Kagel, J., and R. Battalio. 1975. "Experimental Studies of Consumer Behavior Using Laboratory Animals." *Economic Inquiry* 13:22–38.

Kahneman, D. 1994. "New Challenges to the Rationality Assumption." *Journal of Institutional and Theoretical Economics* 150:18–36.

Kaldor, N. 1950. "The Economic Aspects of Advertising." *Review of Economic Studies* 18:1–27.

Kennan, J., and R. Wilson. 1993. "Bargaining with Private Information." *Journal of Economic Literature* 31:45–104.

Kenney, R. W., and B. Klein. 1983. "The Economics of Block Booking." *Journal of Law and Economics* 26:497–540.

Keohane, R. O. 1984. *After Hegemony: Cooperation and Discord in the World Political Economy.* Princeton: Princeton University Press.

Keynes, J. M. 1936. *The General Theory of Employment, Interest, and Money.* London: Macmillan.

Kirzner, I. M. 1973. *Competition and Entrepreneurship.* Chicago: University of Chicago Press.

Klein, B. 1980. "Transaction Cost Determinants of 'Unfair' Contractual Arrangements." *American Economic Review, Papers and Proceedings* 70:356–62.

Klein, B. 1985. "Self-Enforcing Contracts." *Journal of Institutional and Theoretical Economics* 141:594–600.

Klein, B., R. G. Crawford, and A. A. Alchian. 1978. "Vertical Integration, Appropriable Rents, and the Competitive Contracting Process." *Journal of Law and Economics* 28:297–326.

Klein, B., and K. B. Leffler. 1981. "The Role of Market Forces in Assuring Contractual Performance." *Journal of Political Economy* 89:615–41.

Knight, F. 1922. *Risk, Uncertainty, and Profit.* New York: Harper and Row.

Knight, J., and I. Sened, eds. 1995. *Explaining Social Institutions.* Ann Arbor: University of Michigan Press.

Koopmans, T. 1957. *Three Essays on The State of Economic Science.* New York: McGraw-Hill.

Krahnen, J. P. 1990. "Objektfinanzierung und Vertragsgestaltung. Eine theoretische Erklärung der Struktur langfristiger Leasingverträge." *Zeitschrift für Betriebswirtschaftslehre* 60:21–38.

Krahnen, J. P., and G. Meran. 1989. "Why Leasing? An Introduction to Comparative Contractual Analysis." In G. Bamberg and K. Spremann, eds., *Agency Theory, Information, and Incentives,* 255–80. Heidelberg: Springer.

Kranton, R. E. 1996. "The Formation of Cooperative Relationships." *Journal of Law, Economics, and Organization* 12:214–33.

Kreps, D. M. 1990a. "Corporate Culture and Economic Theory." In J. E. Alt and K. A. Shepsle, eds., *Perspectives on Positive Political Economy,* 90–143. Cambridge: Cambridge University Press.

Kreps, D. M. 1990b. *A Course in Microeconomic Theory.* New York: Harvester.

Kreps, D. M. 1990c. *Game Theory and Economic Modelling.* Oxford: Clarendon.

Kreps, D. M., P. Milgrom, J. Roberts, and R. Wilson. 1982. Rational Cooperation in the Finitely Repeated Prisoners Dilemma." *Journal of Economic Theory* 27:245–52.

Kreps, D. M., and R. Wilson. 1982. "Reputation and Imperfect Information." *Journal of Economic Theory* 27:253–79.

Kronman, A. T. 1985. "Contract Law and the State of Nature." *Journal of Law, Economics, and Organization* 1:5–32.

Kydland, F. E., and E. C. Prescott. 1977. "Rules Rather Than Discretion: The Inconsistency of Optimal Plans." *Journal of Political Economy* 85:473–91.

La Croix, S. J. 1989. "Homogeneous Middleman Groups: What Determines the Homogeneity?" *Journal of Law, Economics, and Organization* 5:211–22.

Laffont, J.-J. 1989. *The Economics of Uncertainty and Information.* Cambridge: MIT Press.

Laffont, J. J., and E. Maskin. 1982. "The Theory of Incentives: An Overview." In W. Hildenbrand, ed., *Advances in Economic Theory,* 31–94. Cambridge: Cambridge University Press.

Laffont, J. J., and J. Tirole. 1986. "Using Cost Observations to Regulate Firms." *Journal of Political Economy* 94:614–41.

Laffont, J. J., and J. Tirole. 1988. "The Dynamics of Incentive Contracts." *Econometrica* 56:1153–75.

Lambert, R. A. 1983. "Long-Term Contracts and Moral Hazard." *Bell Journal of Economics* 14:441–52.

Lancaster, K. 1966a. "Change and Innovation in the Technology of Consumption." *American Economic Review* 56:14–23.

Lancaster, K. 1966b. "A New Approach to Consumer Technology." *Journal of Political Economy* 74:132–57.

Lancaster, K. 1969. *Introduction to Modern Microeconomics.* Chicago: Rand McNally.

Landa, J. T. 1981. "A Theory of the Ethnically Homogeneous Middleman Group: An Institutional Alternative to Contract Law." *Journal of Legal Studies* 10:349–62.

Landes, W. M., and R. A. Posner. 1987. "Trademark Law: An Economic Perspective." *Journal of Law and Economics* 30:265–309.

Landes, W. M., and R. A. Posner. 1989. "An Economic Analysis of Copyright Law." *Journal of Legal Studies* 18:325–66.

Lange, O. 1938. "On the Economic Theory of Socialism." In O. Lange, F. M. Taylor, and B. E. Lippincott, eds., *On the Economic Theory of Socialism,* 57–143. Minneapolis: University of Minnesota Press.

Langlois, R. H. 1982. "Economics as a Process." New York University.

Langlois, R. H. 1986. "The New Institutional Economics: An Introductionary Essay." In R. H. Langlois, ed., *Economics as a Process: Essays in the New Institutional Economics,* 1–26. New York and Cambridge: Cambridge University Press.

Larenz, K. 1982. *Lehrbuch des Schuldrechts.* 1. Band: Allgemeiner Teil, 2. Band: Besonderer Teil. Munich: Beck.

Latham, E. 1952. *The Group Basis of Politics.* Ithaca, N.Y.: Cornell University Press.

Lawson, F. H., and B. Rudden. 1982. *The Law of Property.* Oxford: Clarendon.

Lazear, E. P. 1979. "Why Is There Mandatory Retirement?" *Journal of Political Economy* 87:1261–84.

Lazear, E. P. 1981. "Agency, Earnings Profiles, Productivity, and Hours Restrictions." *American Economic Review* 71:606–20.

Lazear, E. P. 1987. "Incentive Contracts." In J. Eatwell, M. Milgate, and P. Newman, eds., *The New Palgrave: A Dictionary of Economics,* 2:744–48. London: Macmillan.

Lazear, E. P. 1989. "Pay Equality and Industrial Politics." *Journal of Political Economy* 97:561–80.

Lazear, E. P. 1991. "Labor Economics and the Psychology of Organizations." *Journal of Economic Perspectives* 5, no. 2:89–110.

Lazear, E. P., and S. Rosen. 1981. "Rank-Order Tournaments as Optimum Labor Contracts." *Journal of Political Economy* 89:841–64.

Leibenstein, H. 1966. "Allocative Efficiency vs. 'X-Efficiency.'" *American Economic Review* 56:392–415.

Leibenstein, H. 1979. "A Branch of Economics Is Missing: Micro-Micro Theory." *Journal of Economic Literature* 17:477–502.

Leibenstein, H. 1985. "On Relaxing the Maximization Postulate." *Journal of Behavioral Economics* 14:5–19.

Leland, H. E., and D. H. Pyle. 1977. "Informational Asymmetries, Financial Structure, and Financial Intermediation." *Journal of Finance* 32:371–87.

Levi, M. 1988. *Of Rule and Revenue.* Berkeley: University of California Press.

Lewis, D. 1969. *Convention: A Philisophical Study.* Cambridge: Harvard University Press.

Libecap, G. D. 1989a. "Distributional Issues in Contracting for Property Rights." *Journal of Institutional and Theoretical Economics* 145:6–24.

Libecap, G. D. 1989b. *Contracting for Property Rights.* New York: Cambridge University Press.

Libecap, G. D., and S. N. Wiggins. 1985. "The Influence of Private Contractual Failure on Regulation: The Case of Oil Field Unitization." *Journal of Political Economy* 93:690–714.

Lindenberg, S. 1988. "Contractual Relations and Weak Solidarity: The Behavioral Basis of Restraints on Gain-Maximization." *Journal of Institutional and Theoretical Economics* 144:39–58.

Llewellyn, K. N. 1931–32. "What Price Contract? An Essay in Perspective." *Yale Law Journal* 40:704–51.

Locke, J. 1823 [1963]. "Two Treaties of Government: In the Former, the False Principles and Foundation of Sir Robert Rilmer, and His Followers, Are Detected and Overthrown; the Latter is an Essay Concerning the True Origin, Extent, and End of Civil Government." In *The Works of John Locke,* 5. London: J. M. Dent and Sons. Reprint, Aalen: Scientia Verlag.

Luhmann, N. 1984. *Soziale Systeme.* Frankfurt: Suhrkamp.

Ma, C.-T., J. Moore, and S. Turnbull. 1988. "Stopping Agents from 'Cheating,'" *Journal of Economic Theory* 46:355–72.

Macaulay, S. 1963. "Non-Contractual Relations in Business: A Preliminary Study." *American Sociological Review* 28:55–67.

Macey, J., and H. Kanda. 1990. "The Stock Exchange as a Firm: The Emergence of Close Substitutes for the New York Stock Exchange." *Cornell Law Review* 75:1007–52.

Macneil, I. R. 1974. "The Many Futures of Contracts." *Southern California Law Review* 47:691–816.

Macneil, I. R. 1978. "Contracts: Adjustment of Long-Term Economic Relations under Classical, Neoclassical, and Relational Contract Law." *Northwestern University Law Review* 72:854–905.

Macneil, I. R. 1980. *The New Social Contract: An Inquiry into Modern Contractual Relations.* New Haven and London: Yale University Press.

Macneil, I. R. 1983. "Values in Contract: Internal and External." *Northwestern University Law Review* 79:340–418.

Mailath, G. J., and A. Postlewaite. 1990. "Asymmetric Information: Bargaining Problems with Many Agents." *Review of Economic Studies* 57:351–67.

Malcomson, J. M., and F. Spinnewyn. 1988. "The Multiperiod Principal-Agent Problem." *Review of Economic Studies* 55:391–408.

Manne, H. G. 1965. "Mergers and the Market for Corporate Control." *Journal of Political Economy* 73:110–20.

Manne, H. G. 1967. "Our Two Corporate Systems: Law and Economics." *Virginia Law Review* 53:259–85.

March, J. G., and J. P. Olsen. 1989. *Rediscovering Institutions: The Organizational Basis of Politics.* New York: Free Press.

Marris, R. 1964. *The Economic Theory of "Managerial" Capitalism.* London: Macmillan.

Marris, R. 1974. *The Corporate Society.* London: Macmillan.

Marris, R. 1987. "Corporate Economy." In J. Eatwell, M. Milgate, and P. Newman, eds., *The New Palgrave: A Dictionary of Economics,* 1:671–75. London: Macmillan.

Marris, R., and D. C. Mueller. 1980. "The Corporation, Competition, and the Invisible Hand." *Journal of Economic Literature* 18:32–63.

Marris, R., and A. Wood, eds. 1971. *The Corporate Economy: Growth, Competition, and Innovation Potential.* Cambridge: Harvard University Press.

Marschak, J. 1971. "Economics of Information Systems." In M. D. Intriligator, ed., *Frontiers of Quantitative Economics,* 32–107. Amsterdam: North-Holland.

Marschak, J. 1979. "Efficient Organizational Design." In H. I. Greenfield, et al., eds., *Economic Theory for Economic Efficiency: Essays in Honor of A. P. Lerner,* 110–19. Cambridge: MIT Press.

Marschak, T. 1986. "Organization Design." In K. J. Arrow and M. D. Intriligator, eds., *Handbook of Mathematical Economics,* 3:1359–1440. Amsterdam: North-Holland.

Marschak, T., and R. Radner. 1971. *Economic Theory of Teams.* New Haven: Yale University Press.

Marshall, A. 1920. *Principles of Economics.* 8th ed. London: Macmillan.

Martin, D. L. 1972. "Job Property Rights and Job Defections." *Journal of Law and Economics* 15:385–410.

Martin, D. L. 1977. "The Economics of Employment Termination Rights." *Journal of Law and Economics* 20:187–204.

Martin, D. L. 1993. "Costs, Credibility, and Institutions: Cooperation on Economic Sanctions." *World Politics* 45:406–32.

Martinek, M. 1987. *Franchising—Grundlagen der zivil- und wettbewerbsrechtlichen Behandlung der vertikalen Gruppenkooperation bei Absatz von Waren und Dienstleistungen.* Heidelberg: V. Decker.

Martinek, M. 1991. *Moderne Vertragstypen. Band I: Leasing und Factoring.* Munich: C. H. Beck.

Martinek, M. 1992. *Moderne Vertragstypen. Band II: Franchising, Know-How-Verträge, Management- und Consultingverträge.* Munich: C. H. Beck.

Martinek, M. 1993. *Moderne Vertragstypen. Band III: Computerverträge, Kreditkartenverträge sowie sonstige moderne Vertragstypen.* Munich: C. H. Beck.

Marx, K., and F. Engels. 1848. *Kommunistisches Manifest.* London: N.p., printed in the office of "Bildungsanstalt für Arbeiter" of D. E. Burghard.

Mason D. 1992. "Attitudes towards the Market and the State in Post-Communist Europe." Paper presented at the annual meeting of the American Association for the Advancement of Slavic Studies, Phoenix, Arizona.

Masten, S., ed. 1996. *Case Studies in Contracting and Organization.* New York and Oxford: Oxford University Press.

Masulis, R. 1987. "Changes in Ownership Structure: Conversions of Mutual Savings and Loans to Stock Charter." *Journal of Financial Economics* 18:29–59.

Matthews, R. C. O. 1986. "The Economics of Institutions and the Sources of Growth." *Economic Journal* 96:903–18.

Mayer, T. 1993. "Friedman's Methodology of Positive Economics: A soft Reading." *Economic Inquiry* 31:213–23.

Mayers, D., and C. Smith. 1986. "Ownership Structure and Control: The Mutualization of Stock Life Insurance Companies." *Journal of Financial Economics* 16:73–98.

Maynes, E. S. 1976. *Decision-Making for Consumers: An Introduction to Consumer Economics.* London: Macmillan.

McCain, R. 1980. "A Theory of Codetermination." *Zeitschrift für Nationalökonomie* 40:65–90.

McCubbins, M. D., R. G. Noll, and B. R. Weingast. 1989. "Structure and Process, Politics and Policy: Administrative Arrangements and the Political Control of Agencies." Working Papers, no. P–89–4, Hoover Institution, Stanford University.

McGuire, M. C., and M. Olson, Jr. 1996. "The Economics of Autocracy and Majority Rule: The Invisible Hand and the Use of Force." *Journal of Economic Literature* 34:72–96.

McKean, 1941. *The Basic Works of Aristotle.* New York: Random House.

McManus, J. 1972. "An Economic Analysis of Indian Behavior in the North American Fur Trade." *Journal of Economic History* 32:36–53.

Meade, J. 1972. "The Theory of Labour-Managed Firms and of Profit Sharing." *Economic Journal, Supplement* 82:402–28.

Meade, J. 1986. *Alternative Systems of Business Organization and of Workers' Remuneration.* London: Allen and Unwin.

Medicus, D. 1985. *Schuldrecht II, Besonderer Teil.* 2d ed. Munich: Beck.

Medicus, D. 1992. *Schuldrecht I, Allgemeiner Teil,* 6th ed. Munich: Beck.

Mehren, A. T. von, and J. R. Gordley. 1977. *The Civil Law System.* 2d ed. Boston and Toronto: Little, Brown.

Melumad, N., D. Mookherjee, and S. Reichelstein. 1992. "A Theory of Responsibility Centers." *Journal of Accounting and Economics* 15:445–84.

Menell, P. S. 1991. "The Limitations of Legal Institutions for Addressing Environmental Risks." *Journal of Economic Perspectives* 5, no. 3:93–113.

Menger, C. [1883] 1963. *Problems of Economics and Sociology.* Translated by F. J. Nock from the German edition of 1883. Edited by L. Schneider. Urbana: University of Illinois Press.

Menger, C. 1884. *Die Irrtümer des Historismus.* Vienna: Hoelder.

Merryman, J. H. 1974. "Ownership and Estate (Variations on a Theme by Lawson)." *Tulane Law Review* 48:916–45.

Merryman, J. H. 1985. *The Civil Law Tradition: An Introduction to the Legal System of Western Europe and Latin America.* 2d ed. Stanford: Stanford University Press.

Merton, R. 1949. *Social Theory and Social Structure.* New York: Free Press.

Michael, R., and G. S. Becker. 1973. "On the New Theory of Consumer Behavior." *Swedish Journal of Economics* 75:378–96.

Milde, H., and J. G. Riley. 1988. "Signalling in Credit Markets." *Quarterly Journal of Economics* 102:101–29.

Milgrom, P. R., D. C. North, and B. R. Weingast. 1989. "The Role of Institutions in the Revival of Trade: The Law Merchant, Private Judges, and the Campagne Fairs." *Economics and Politics* 2:1–23.

Milgrom, P., and J. Roberts. 1982. "Predation, Reputation, and Entry Deterrence." *Journal of Economic Theory* 27:280–312.

Milgrom, P., and J. Roberts. 1986. "Price and Advertising Signals of Product Quality." *Journal of Political Economy* 94:796–821.

Milgrom, P., and J. Roberts. 1987. "Informational Asymmetries, Strategic Behavior, and Industrial Organization." *American Economic Review, Papers and Proceedings* 77:184–93.

Milgrom, P., and J. Roberts. 1988. "An Economic Approach to Influence Activities in Organizations." *American Journal of Sociology* 94:154–79.

Milgrom, P., and J. Roberts. 1990a. "Bargaining Costs, Influence Costs, and the Organization of Economic Activity." In J. Alt and K. Shepsle, eds., *Perspectives on Positive Political Economy*, 57–89. Cambridge: Cambridge University Press.

Milgrom, P., and J. Roberts. 1990b. "The Economics of Modern Manufacturing: Technology, Strategy, and Organization." *American Economic Review* 80:511–28.

Mill, J. S. [1848] 1902. *Principles of Political Economy.* London: Longmans, Green.

Mill, J. S. 1857. *Principles of Economics.* 4th ed. London: Parker.

Miller, G. J. 1992. *Managerial Dilemmas: The Political Economy of Hierarchy.* Cambridge: Cambridge University Press.

Miller, G. P. 1989. "Public Choice at the Dawn of the Special Interest State: The Story of Butter and Margarine." *California Law Review* 77:83–131.

Miller, G. P. 1993. "The Industrial Organization of Political Production: A Case Study." *Journal of Institutional and Theoretical Economics* 149:769–74.

Miller, J. G., and T. E. Vollmann. 1985. "The Hidden Factory." *Harvard Business Review* 55, no. 5:142–50.

Mills, F. C. 1927. *The Behavior of Prices.* New York: National Bureau of Economic Research.

Mincer, J. 1958. "Investment in Human Capital and Personal Income Distribution." *Journal of Political Economy* 66:281–302.

Minsky, M. 1967. *Computation: Finite and Infinite Machines.* Englewood Cliffs, N.J.: Prentice Hall.

Mirrlees, J. A. 1974. "Notes on Welfare Economics, Information, and Uncertainty." In M. S. Balch, D. L. McFadden, and S. Y. Wu, eds., *Essays on Economic Behavior under Uncertainty*, 243–58. Amsterdam: North-Holland.

Mirrlees, J. A. 1976. "The Optimal Structure of Incentives with Authority within an Organization." *Bell Journal of Economics* 7:105–31.

Mises, L. von. [1920] 1935. "Economic Calculation in a Socialist Commonwealth." In F. A. Hayek, ed., *Collectivist Economic Planning*, 87–130. London: Routledge and Kegan Paul.

Mises, L. von. [1932] 1981. *Socialism: An Economic and Sociological Analysis.* Indianapolis: Liberty Classics. Translation of L. Mises, *Die Gemeinwirtschaft*, 2d ed. Munich: Philosophia.

Mnookin, R. H., and L. Kornhauser. 1979. "Bargaining in the Shadow of the Law: The Case of Divorce." *Yale Law Journal* 88:950–97.

Modigliani, F., and M. Miller. 1958. "The Cost of Capital, Corporation Finance, and the Theory of Investment." *American Economic Review* 48:261–97.

Mody, A. 1993. "Learning through Alliances." *Journal of Economic Behavior and Organizations* 20:151–70.

Moe, T. M. 1984. "The New Economics of Organization." *American Journal of Political Science* 28:739–77.

Moe, T. M. 1990. "Political Institutions: The Neglected Side of the Story." *Journal of Law, Economics, and Organization, Special Issue* 6:213–53.

Moe, T. M. 1991. "Politics and the Theory of Organization." *Journal of Law, Economics, and Organization, Special Issue* 7:106–29.

Möller, H. 1940. "Wirtschaftsordnung, Wirtschaftssystem, und Wirtschaftsstil." *Schmollers Jahrbuch für Gesetzgebung und Verwaltung* 64:75–98.

Monteverde, K., and D. J. Teece. 1982. "Supplier Switching Costs and Vertical Integration in the Automobile Industry." *Bell Journal of Economics* 13:206–13.

Montinola, G., Y. Qian, and B. R. Weingast. 1995. "Federalism, Chinese Style: The Political Basis for Economic Success in China." *World Politics* 48:50–81.

Mookherjee, D. 1984. "Optimal Incentive Schemes with Many Agents." *Review of Economic Studies* 51:433–46.

Morgenstern, O. 1964. "Pareto Optimum and Economic Organization." Working paper, Econometric Research Program, Princeton University.

Morishima, M. 1959. "The Problem of Intrinsic Complementarity and Separability of Goods." *Metroeconomica* 11:188–202.

Morris, C. 1980. *The Cost of Good Intentions.* New York: Norton.

Motive 1888. *Motive zu dem Entwurfe eines Bürgerlichen Gesetzbuches für das Deutsche Reich,* Band III, *Sachenrecht.* Berlin and Leipzig: J. Guttentag.

Mulherin, J. H., J. M. Netter, and J. A. Overdahl. 1991. "Prices are Property: The Organization of Financial Exchanges from a Transaction Cost Perspective." *Journal of Law and Economics* 34:591–644.

Müller-Graff, P. C. 1988. "Franchising: A Case of Long-Term Contracts." *Journal of Institutional and Theoretical Economics* 144:122–44.

Müller-Hagedorn, L. 1995. "The Variety of Distribution Systems." *Journal of Institutional and Theoretical Economics* 151:186–211.

Mussa, M. 1981. "Sticky Prices and Disequilibrium Adjustment in a Rational Model of the Inflationary Process." *American Economic Review* 71:1020–27.

Myerson, R. 1991. *Game Theory: Analysis of Conflict.* Cambridge: Harvard University Press.

Nalebuff, B., and J. Stiglitz. 1983. "Information, Competition, and Markets." *American Economic Review, Papers and Proceedings* 73:278–83.

Nasse, E. 1879. "Über die Verhütung von Productionskrisen durch staatliche Fürsorge." *Jahrbuch für Gesetzgebung, Verwaltung und Volkswirtschaft im Deutschen Reich* 3:145–89.

Negishi, T. 1979. *Microeconomic Foundations of Keynesian Macroeconomics.* Amsterdam: North-Holland.

Nelson, P. 1970. "Information and Consumer Behavior." *Journal of Political Economy* 78:311–29.

Nelson, P. 1974. "Advertising as Information." *Journal of Political Economy* 82:729–54.

Nelson, R. 1981. "Assessing Private Enterprise: An Exegesis of Tangled Doctrine." *Bell Journal of Economics* 12:93–111.

Nelson, R., and S. G. Winter. 1982. *An Evolutionary Theory of Economic Change.* Cambridge: Belknap Press of Harvard University Press.

Nerlove, M., and K. J. Arrow. 1962. "Optimal Advertising Policy under Dynamic Conditions." *Economica* 29:129–42.

Nermuth, M. 1982. *Information Structures in Economics.* Heidelberg: Springer.

Netting, R. M. 1981. *Balancing on an Alp.* Cambridge: Cambridge University Press.

Nicholls, W. H. 1951. *Price Policy in the Cigarette Industry: A Study of "Concerted Action" and Its Social Control, 1911–50.* Nashville: Vanderbilt University Press.

Nichols, T. 1969. *Ownership, Control, and Ideology.* London: Allen and Unwin.

Niehans, J. 1969. "Money in a Static Theory of Optimal Payment Arrangements." *Journal of Money, Credit, and Banking* 1:706–26.

Niehans, J. 1971. "Money and Barter in General Equilibrium with Transaction Costs." *American Economic Review* 61:773–83.

Niehans, J. 1975. "Interest and Credit in General Equilibrium with Transaction Costs." *American Economic Review* 65:548–66.

Niehans, J. 1978. *The Theory of Money.* Baltimore and London: Johns Hopkins University Press.

Niskanen, W. 1968. "Nonmarket Decision Making: The Peculiar Economics of Bureaucracy." *American Economic Review, Papers and Proceedings* 58:293–305.

North, D. C. 1978. "Structure and Performance: The Task of Economic History." *Journal of Economic Literature* 16:963–78.

North, D. C. 1981. *Structure and Change in Economic History.* New York and London: Norton.

North, D. C. 1984a. "Government and the Cost of Exchange." *Journal of Economic History* 44:255–64.

North, D. C. 1984b. " Transaction Costs, Institutions, and Economic History." *Zeitschrift für die gesamte Staatswissenschaft* 140:7–17.

North, D. C. 1990. *Institutions, Institutional Change, and Economic Performance.* Cambridge: Cambridge University Press.

North, D. C. 1993. "Institutions and Credible Commitment." *Journal of Institutional and Theoretical Economics* 149:11–23.

North, D. C. 1994. "Economic Performance through Time." *American Economic Review* 84:359–68. Alfred Nobel Memorial Prize Lecture in Economic Science.

North, D. C. 1997. "Prologue." In J. N. Drobak and J. V. C. Nye, eds., *The Frontiers of the New Institutional Economics,* 3–12. San Diego: Academic Press.

North, D. C., and R. P. Thomas. 1971. "The Rise and Fall of the Manorial System: A Theoretical Model." *Journal of Economic History* 31:777–803.

North, D. C., and R. P. Thomas. 1973. *The Rise of the Western World: A New Economic History.* Cambridge: Cambridge University Press.

North, D. C., and R. P. Thomas. 1977. "The First Economic Revolution." *Economic History Review* 30:229–41.

North, D. C., and B. R. Weingast. 1989. "The Evolution of Institutions Governing Public Choice in 17th Century England." *Journal of Economic History* 49:803–32.

Noyes, C. R. 1936. *The Institution of Property: A Study of the Development, Substance, and Arrangement of the System of Property in Modern Anglo-American Law.* New York and Toronto: Longmans, Green.

Nozick, R. 1975. *Anarchy, State, and Utopia.* New York: Basic Books.

Nugent, J. B., and N. Sanchez. 1989. "The Efficiency of the Mesta: A Parable." *Explorations in Economic History* 20:261–84.

Nutter, G. W. 1968. "Markets without Property: A Grand Illusion." In N. A. Beadles and L. A. Dewry, Jr., eds., *Money, the Market, and the State,* 137–45. Athens: University of Georgia Press.

Obin, J. 1965. "Money and Economic Growth." *Econometrica* 33:671–84.

O'Guin, M. 1990. "Focus the Factory with Activity-Based Costing." *Management Accounting* 71, no. 2:36–41.

Oi, W. Y. 1990. "Productivity in the Distributive Trades: The Shopper and the Economies of Massed Reserves." Economic and Legal Organization Workshop, University of Rochester. Mimeo.

Okun, A. M. 1981. *Prices and Quantities: A Macroeconomic Analysis.* Oxford: Blackwell.

Olson, M. 1965. *The Logic of Collective Action: Public Goods and the Theory of Groups.* Cambridge: Harvard University Press.

Oppenheimer, F. 1922. *Grossgrundeigentum und soziale Frage: Versuch einer neuen Grundlegung der Gesellschaftswissenschaft.* 2d ed. Jena: Fischer.

Ordeshook, P. C. 1990. "The Emerging Discipline of Political Economy." In J. E. Alt and S. Shepsle, eds., *Perspectives on Positive Political Economy,* 9–30. Cambridge: Cambridge University Press.

Ostrom, E. 1990. *Governing the Commons: The Evolution of Institutions for Collective Action.* Cambridge: Cambridge University Press.

Ostroy, J. M., and R. M. Starr. 1990. "The Transaction Role of Money." In B. M. Friedman, ed., *Handbook of Monetary Economics,* 3–62. Amsterdam: North-Holland.

Oye, K. 1985. "Explaining Cooperation under Anarchy: Hypotheses and Strategies." *World Politics* 38:1–24.

Pease, J. G., and H. Chitty. 1958. *Pease and Chitty's Law of Markets and Fairs.* 2d ed. Edited by H. Parrish. London: C. Knight.

Pejovich, S. 1969. "Liberman's Reforms and Property Rights in the Soviet Union." *Journal of Law and Economics* 12:155–62.

Pejovich, S. 1972. "Economic Reforms in the Soviet Union: Their Causes and Purpose." *Modern Age* 16:68–76.

Pejovich, S. 1973. "The Banking System and the Investment Behavior of the Yugoslav Firm." In M. Bornstein, ed., *Plan and Market,* 294–301. New Haven: Yale University Press.

Pejovich, S. 1978. *The Codetermination Movement in the West.* Lexington, Mass.: Lexington Books.

Pejovich, S. 1990. *The Economics of Property Rights: Towards a Theory of Comparative Systems.* Dordrecht, Netherlands: Kluwer Academic.

Pejovich, S. 1995. *Economic Analysis of Institutions and Systems.* Boston: Kluwer Academic.

Persson, T. 1988. "Credibility of Macroeconomic Policy: An Introduction and a Broad Survey." *European Economic Review* 32:519–32.

Persson, T., and G. Tabellini. 1990. *Macroeconomic Policy, Credibility, and Politics.* Chur: Harwood Academic.

Phlips, L. 1988. *The Economics of Imperfect Information.* Cambridge: Cambridge University Press.

Pingle, M. 1992. "Costly Optimization: An Experiment." *Journal of Economic Behavior and Organization* 17:3–30.

Plant, A. 1934. "The Economic Aspects of Copyrights in Books." *Economica* 1:167–95.

Pommerehne, W. W., L. P. Feld, and A. Hart. 1994. "Voluntary Provision of a Public Good: Results from a Real World Experiment." *Kyklos* 47:505–18.

Popper, K. R. 1945. *The Open Society and Its Enemies.* Vol. 1: *The Spell of Plato.* London: Routledge and Kegan Paul.

Popper, K. R. 1957. *The Poverty of Historicism.* 2d ed. London: Routledge and Kegan Paul.

Porter, M. E. 1990. *The Competitive Advantage of Nations.* New York: Free Press.

Posner, R. A. 1972a. "The Appropriate Scope of Regulation in the Cable Television Industry." *Bell Journal of Economics and Management Science* 3:98–129.

Posner, R. A. 1972b. *The Economic Analysis of Law.* Boston and Toronto: Little, Brown.

Posner, R. A. 1980. "A Theory of Primitive Society with Special Reference to Primitive Law." *Journal of Law and Economics* 23:1–53.

Posner, R. A. 1993a. "The New Institutional Economics Meets Law and Economics." *Journal of Institutional and Theoretical Economics* 149:73–87.

Posner, R. A. 1993b. "Reply." *Journal of Institutional and Theoretical Economics* 149:119–21.

Powell, W. W. 1990. "Neither Market nor Hierarchy: Network Forms of Organization." *Research in Organizational Behavior* 12:295–336.

Powell, W. W., and P. J. DiMaggio, eds. 1991. *The New Institutionalism in Organizational Analysis.* Chicago: University of Chicago Press.

Prescott, E. C., and M. Visscher. 1980. "Organization Capital." *Journal of Political Economy* 88:446–61.

Prybyla, J. 1969. *Comparative Economic Systems.* New York: Appleton-Century-Crofts.

Putterman, L. 1984. "On Some Recent Explanations of Why Capital Hires Labor." *Economic Inquiry* 22:171–87.

Putterman, L., ed. 1986a. *The Economic Nature of the Firm: A Reader.* Cambridge: Cambridge University Press.

Putterman, L. 1986b. "Corporate Governance, Risk-Bearing, and Economic Power: A Comment on Recent Work by Oliver Williamson." *Journal of Institutional and Theoretical Economics* 143:422–34.

Radbruch, G. 1956. *Rechtsphilosophie.* 5th ed. Stuttgart: K. F. Koehler.

Radner, R. 1981. "Monitoring Cooperative Agreements in a Repeated Principal-Agent Relationship." *Econometrica* 49:1127–48.

Rapoport, A. 1960. *Fights, Games, and Debates.* Ann Arbor: University of Michigan Press.

Rapoport, A. 1967. *Games Which Simulate Deterrence and Disarmament.* Clarkston, Ont.: Canadian Peace Research Institute.

Rasmusen, E. 1989. *Games and Information: An Introduction to Game Theory.* Oxford: Basil Blackwell.

Rayner, B. 1987. "Accounting for Change in the Electronic Industry." *Electronic Business,* October 15, 118–23.

Reinganum, J., and L. Wilde. 1986. "Settlement, Litigation, and the Allocation of Litigation Costs." *Rand Journal of Economics* 17:557–66.

Reny, P. 1985. "Rationality, Common Knowledge, and the Theory of Games." Department of Economics, Princeton University. Mimeo.

Ress, G. 1994. "Ex Ante Safeguards against Ex Post Opportunism and International Treaties: The Boundary Question." *Journal of Institutional and Theoretical Economics* 150:279–303.

Rey, P., and B. Salanie. 1987. "Long-term, Short-term, and Renegotiation." Working Papers, no. 8715, Institut National de la Statistique et des Etudes Economiques, Paris.

Rey, P., and J. Tirole. 1986. "The Logic of Vertical Restraints." *American Economic Review* 76:921–39.

Rheinstein, M. 1935–36. "Some Fundamental Differences in Real Property Ideas of the 'Civil Law' and the 'Common Law Systems.'" *Chicago Law Review* 3:624–35.

Richter, R. 1979. "Currency and Economic Reform: West Germany after World War II, a Symposium, Editorial Preface." *Zeitschrift für die gesamte Staatswissenschaft/ Journal of Institutional and Theoretical Economics* 135:297–300.

Richter, R. 1989a. *Money: Lectures on the Basis of General Equilibrium Theory and the Economics of Institutions.* Heidelberg: Springer.

Richter, R. 1989b. "The Louvre Accord from the Viewpoint of the New Institutional Economics." *Journal of Institutional and Theoretical Economics.* 145:704–19.

Richter, R., ed. 1990. "Views and Comments on Bounded Rationality as Applied to Modern Institutional Economics." *Journal of Institutional and Theoretical Economics* 146:648–748.

Richter, R. 1992a. "A Socialist Market Economy: Can It Work?" *Kyklos* 45:185–207.

Richter, R. 1992b. "Über Papierstandards, Währungsunionen und das Ende der D-Mark. Wirtschaftstheoretische Kritikpunkte zum Thema Europäische Währungsunion." Discussion Paper, Universität des Saarlandes, Saarbrücken.

Richter, R. 1993. "'Stability Culture' as a Problem of Modern Institutional Economics." Translated from the German by M. Hudson. Working Paper, Center for the Study of the New Institutional Economics, Universität des Saarlandes, Saarbrücken.

Richter, R. 1994. "'Stabilitätskultur' als Problem der Institutionenökonomik." In H. Hesse and O. Issing, eds., Symposium *Geld und Moral,* 73–90. Munich: F. Vahlen.

Richter R. 1996a. "Bridging Old and New Institutional Economics: Gustav Schmoller, the Leader of the Younger German Historical School, Seen with Neoinstitutionalists' Eyes." *Journal of Institutional and Theoretical Economics* 152:568–92.

Richter, R. 1996b. "Die Neue Institutionenökonomik des Marktes." Lectiones Jenensis, Heft 5. Jena: Max-Planck-Institut zur Erforschung von Wirtschaftssystemen.

Richter, R., and E. G. Furubotn. 1996. *Neue Institutionenokonomik: Einfuhrung und Kritische Wurdigung.* Tubingen: J. C. B. Mohr (Paul Siebeck).

Richter, R., and U. Schmidt-Mohr. 1992. "An Institutional Analysis of the Louvre Accord." In H. Giersch, ed., *Money, Trade, and Competition: Essays in Honor of Egon Sohmen,* 59–86. Berlin: Springer.

Riker, W. H., and D. L. Weimer. 1995. "The Political Economy of Transformation: Liberalization and Property Rights." In J. S. Banks and E. A. Hanushek, eds., *Modern Political Economy: Old Topics, New Directions,* 80–107. Cambridge: Cambridge University Press.

Riley, J. G. 1975. "Competitive Signalling." *Journal of Economic Theory* 10:174–86.

Riley, J. G. 1979a. "Informational Equilibrium." *Econometrica* 47:331–59.

Riley, J. G. 1979b. "Noncooperative Equilibrium and Market Signalling." *American Economic Review, Papers and Proceedings* 69:303–07.

Riley, J. G. 1985. "Competition with Hidden Knowledge." *Journal of Political Economy* 93:958–76.

Rinkes, J. G., and G. H. Samuel. 1992. *Contractual and Non-contractual Obligations in English Law: Systematic Analysis of the English Law of Obligations in Comparative Context of the Netherlands Civil Code.* Nijmwegen: Ars Aequi Libri.

Rogerson, W. P. 1984. "Efficient Reliance and Damage Measures for Breach of Contract." *Rand Journal of Economics* 15:39–53.

Rogerson, W. P. 1985. "Repeated Moral Hazard." *Econometrica* 53:69–76.

Rogoff, K. 1985. "The Optimal Degree of Commitment to an Intermediate Monetary Target." *Quarterly Journal of Economics* 50:1169–89.

Rogoff, K. 1987. *Reputational Constraints on Monetary Policy,* 141–82. Carnegie-Rochester Conference Series on Public Policy, no. 26. Amsterdam: North-Holland.

Rosen, S. 1985. "Implicit Contracts: A Survey." *Journal of Economic Literature* 23:1144–75.

Rosen, S. 1987. "Human Capital." In J. Eatwell, M. Milgate, and P. Newman, eds., *The New Palgrave: A Dictionary of Economics,* 2:681–90. London: Macmillan.

Rosenthal, J. L. 1990. "The Development of Irrigation in Provence, 1700–1860: The French Revolution and Economic Growth." *Journal of Economic History* 50:615–38.

Ross, S. 1973. "The Economic Theory of Agency: The Principal's Problem." *American Economic Review, Papers and Proceedings* 63:134–39.

Roth, A. E. 1995. "Introduction to Experimental Economics." In J. H. Kagel and A. E. Roth, eds., *The Handbook of Experimental Economics,* 3–109. Princeton: Princeton University Press.

Rothschild, M., and J. Stiglitz. 1976. "Equilibrium in Competitive Insurance Markets: An Essay on the Economics of Imperfect Information." *Quarterly Journal of Economics* 80:629–49.

Rubin, P. 1978. "The Theory of the Firm and the Structure of the Franchise Contract." *Journal of Law and Economics* 21:223–33.

Rubinstein, A. 1986. "Finite Automata Play the Repeated Prisoner's Dilemma." *Journal of Economic Theory* 39:83–96.

Rubinstein, A. 1987. "A Sequential Strategic Theory of Bargaining." In T. Bewley, ed.,

*Advances in Economic Theory,* 197–224. Cambridge: Cambridge University Press.

Rubinstein, A., and M. E. Yaari. 1980. "Repeated Insurance Contracts and Moral Hazard." Hebrew University, Jerusalem. Mimeo.

Rumelt, R. P., D. Schendel, and D. J. Teece. 1991. "Strategic Management and Economics." *Strategic Management Journal* 12:5–29.

Sah, R. K. 1991. "Fallibility in Human Organizations and Political Systems." *Journal of Economic Perspectives* 5, no. 2:67–88.

Salop, J., and S. Salop. 1976. "Self-Selection and Turnover in the Labor Market." *Quarterly Journal of Economics* 90:619–27.

Samuelson, P. A. 1947. *Foundations of Economic Analysis.* Cambridge: Harvard University Press.

Samuelson, P. A. 1957. "Wage and Interest: A Modern Dissection of Marxian Economic Models." *American Economic Review* 47:884–912.

Samuelson, P. A. 1968. "What Classical and Neoclassical Monetary Theory Really Was." *Canadian Journal of Economics* 1:1–15.

Sappington, D. E. M. 1991. "Incentives in Principal-Agent Relationships." *Journal of Economic Perspectives* 5, no. 2:45–66.

Sauermann, H., and R. Selten. 1959. "Ein Oligopolexperiment," *Zeitschrift für die gesamte Staatswissenschaft/Journal of Institutional and Theoretical Economics* 115:427–71.

Sauermann, H., and R. Selten. 1962. "Anspruchsanpassungstheorie der Unternehmung." *Zeitschrift für die gesamte Staatswissenschaft/Journal of Institutional and Theoretical Economics* 118:577–97.

Schäffle, A. E. F. [1874] 1885. *Die Quintessenz des Sozialismus.* 8th ed. Gotha: Perthes.

Schanze, E. 1995. "Hare and Hedgehog Revisited: The Regulation of Markets That Have Escaped Regulated Markets." *Journal of Institutional and Theoretical Economics* 151:162–76.

Schein, E. H. 1986. *Organizational Culture and Leadership,* San Francisco: Jossey-Bass.

Schelling, T. C. 1960. *The Strategy of Conflict.* Cambridge: Harvard University Press.

Schelling, T. C. 1966. *Arms and Influence.* New Haven: Yale University Press.

Scherer, F. M. 1980. *Industrial Market Structure and Economic Performance.* 2d ed. Chicago: Rand McNally.

Scherer, F. M. 1987. "Selling Costs." In J. Eatwell, M. Milgate, and P. Newman, eds., *The New Palgrave: A Dictionary of Economics,* 4:300–301. London: Macmillan.

Schlicht, E. 1978. "Labor Turnover, Wage Structure, and Natural Unemployment." *Journal of Institutional and Theoretical Economics* 134:337–46.

Schlicht, E. 1983. "The Tenant's Decreasing Willingness to Pay and the Rent Abatement Phenomenon." *Journal of Institutional and Theoretical Economics* 139:155–59.

Schlicht, E. 1984. "Cognitive Dissonance in Economics." In H. Todt, ed., *Normengeleitetes Verhalten in den Sozialwissenschaften,* 61–82. Berlin: Duncker und Humblot.

Schlicht, E. 1997. *On Custom in the Economy.* Oxford: Clarendon Press.

Schmalensee, R. 1972. *The Economics of Advertising.* Amsterdam: North-Holland.

Schmalensee, R. 1986. "Inter-industry Studies of Structure and Performance." In R. Schmalensee and R. D. Willig, eds., *Handbook of Industrial Organization,* 2:951–1009. Amsterdam: North-Holland.

Schmalensee, R. 1987. "Industrial Organization." In J. Eatwell, M. Milgate, and P. Newman, eds., *The New Palgrave: A Dictionary of Economics,* 2:803–8. London: Macmillan.

Schmidt-Mohr, U. 1992. "Informationsökonomische Theorien der Bankunternehmung und des Bankverhaltens." Ph.D. diss., Universität des Saarlandes, Saarbrücken.

Schmidt-Trenz, H.-J., and D. Schmidtchen. 1991. "Private International Trade in the Shadow of the Territoriality of Law: Why Does It Work?" *Southern Economic Journal* 58:329–38.

Schmidtchen, D. 1984. "German 'Ordnungspolitik' as Institutional Choice." *Zeitschrift für die gesamte Staatswissenschaft/Journal of Institutional and Theoretical Economics* 140:54–70.

Schmidtchen, D., and H.-J. Schmidt-Trenz. 1990. "New Institutional Economics of International Transactions." In E. Boetcher et al., eds., *Jahrbuch für Neue Politische Ökonomie,* 3–34. Tübingen: J. C. B. Mohr (Paul Siebeck).

Schmoller, G. von. 1881. "Die Gerechtigkeit in der Volkswirtschaft." *Jahrbuch für Gesetzgebung, Verwaltung, und Volkswirtschaft im deutschen Reich* 5:19–54.

Schmoller, G. von. 1883. "Zur Methodologie der Staats- und Socialwissenschaften." *Jahrbuch für Gesetzgebung, Verwaltung und Volkswirtschaft im deutschen Reich* 7:965–94.

Schmoller, G. von. 1900. *Grundriss der Allgemeinen Volkswirtschaftslehre.* Munich and Leipzig: Duncker and Humblot.

Schotter, A. 1981. *The Economic Theory of Social Institutions.* Cambridge: Cambridge University Press.

Schultz, T. 1963. *The Economic Value of Education.* New York: Columbia University Press.

Schumpeter, J. A. [1918] 1954. "The Crisis of the Tax State." Translated by W. F. Stolper and A. Musgrave. In A. Peacock et al., eds., *International Economic Papers,* 4:5–38. London: Macmillan.

Schumpeter, J. A. 1926. "Gustav Schmoller und die Probleme von heute." *Schmollers Jahrbuch für Gesetzgebung und Verwaltung* 50:337–88.

Schumpeter, J. A. 1942. *Capitalism, Socialism, and Democracy.* New York: Harper.

Schumpeter, J. A. 1955. *History of Economic Analysis.* New York: Oxford University Press.

Schumpeter, J. A. 1970. *Das Wesen des Geldes.* Edited by F. K. Mann. Göttingen: Vandenhoeck and Ruprecht.

Schwartz, A. 1992. "Relational Contracts in the Courts: An Analysis of Incomplete Agreements and Judical Strategies." *Journal of Legal Studies* 21:271–318.

Schweizer, U. 1988. "Externalities and the Coase Theorem: Hypothesis or Result?" *Journal of Institutional and Theoretical Economics* 144:245–66.

Scott, K. 1994. "Bounded Rationality and Social Norms: Concluding Comment." *Journal of Institutional and Theoretical Economics* 150:315–19.

Scott, R. E. 1990. "A Relational Theory of Default Rules for Commercial Contracts." *Journal of Legal Studies* 29:597–616.

Selten, R. 1965. "Spieltheoretische Behandlung eines Oligopolmodells mit Nachfrageträgheit." *Zeitschrift für die gesamte Staatswissenschaft* 121:301–24.

Selten, R. 1967. "Die Strategiemethode zur Erforschung des eingeschränkt rationalen Verhaltens im Rahmen eines Oligopolexperiments." In H. Sauermann, ed., *Contributions to Experimental Economics,* 1:136–68. Tübingen: J. C. B. Mohr (Paul Siebeck).

Selten, R. 1970. "Ein Marktexperiment." In H. Sauermann, ed., *Contributions to Experimental Economics,* 2:33–98. Tübingen: J. C. B. Mohr (Paul Siebeck).

Selten, R. 1975. "Reexamination of the Perfectness Concept for Equilibrium Points in Extensive Games." *International Journal of Game Theory* 4:25–55.

Selten, R. 1990. "Bounded Rationality." *Journal of Institutional and Theoretical Economics* 146:649–58.

Sen, A. 1990. *On Ethics and Economics.* Oxford: Basic Blackwell.

Sertel, M. 1982. *Workers and Incentives.* Amsterdam: North-Holland.

Seyffert, R. 1966. *Wege und Kosten der Distribution der industriell gefertigten Konsumwaren.* Cologne and Opladen: Westdeutscher.

Shapiro, C. 1983. "Premiums for High Quality Products as Returns to Reputations." *Quarterly Journal of Economics* 97:659–79.

Shapiro, C., and J. E. Stiglitz. 1984. "Equilibrium Unemployment as a Worker Discipline Device." *American Economic Review* 74:433–44.

Shavell, S. 1979. "Risk Sharing and Incentives in the Principal Agent Relationship." *Bell Journal of Economics* 80:55–73.

Shavell, S. 1980. "Damage Measures for Breach of Contract." *Bell Journal of Economics* 11:466–90.

Shelanski, H. A., and P. G. Klein. 1995. "Empirical Research in Transaction Cost Economics: A Review and Assessment." *Journal of Law, Economics, and Organization* 11:335–61.

Shell, G. R. 1991. "Opportunism and Trust in the Negotiation of Commercial Contracts: Towards a New Cause of Action." *Vanderbilt Law Review* 44:221–82.

Shepsle, K. A. 1978. *The Grant Jigsaw Puzzle: Democratic Committee Assignments in the Modern House.* Chicago: University of Chicago Press.

Shepsle, K. A., and B. R. Weingast. 1987. "The Institutional Foundations of Committee Power." *American Political Science Review* 81:85–104.

Shleifer, A. 1985. "A Theory of Yardstick Competition." *Rand Journal of Economics* 16:319–27.

Siegel, S., and L. E. Fouraker. 1960 *Bargaining and Group Decision Making: Experiments in Bilateral Monopoly.* New York: McGraw-Hill.

Simmel, G. 1978. *The Philosophy of Money.* Translated by T. Bottomore and D. Frisby. London: Routledge and Kegan Paul.

Simon, H. A. 1951. "A Formal Theory of the Employment Relationship." *Econometrica* 19:293–305.

Simon, H. A. 1957. *Models of Man.* New York: Wiley.

Simon, H. A. 1987. "Bounded Rationality." In J. Eatwell, M. Milgate, and P. Newman, eds., *The New Palgrave: A Dictionary of Economics,* 1:266–68. London: Macmillan.

Simon, H. A. 1991. "Organizations and Markets." *Journal of Economic Perspectives* 5, no. 2:25–44.

Singer, A. E. 1994. "Strategy as Moral Philosophy." *Strategic Management Journal* 15:191–214.

Smith, A. [1776] 1976. *An Inquiry into the Nature and Causes of the Wealth of Nations.* General editors R. H. Campbell and A. S. Skinner, Textual editor W. B. Todd. Oxford: Clarendon Press.

Smith, A. [1790] 1975. *The Theory of Moral Sentiments.* Rev. ed. Oxford: Clarendon Press.

Smith, B. D. 1984. "Private Information, Deposit Interest Rates, and the 'Stability' of the Banking System." *Journal of Monetary Economics* 14:293–317.

Smith, C. 1982. "Pricing Mortgage Originations." *AREUEA Journal* 10 (Fall):313–30.

Smith, C., and L. Wakeman. 1985. "Determinants of Corporate Leasing Policy." *Journal of Finance* 40:895–908.

Smith, V. L. 1969. "On Models of Commercial Fishing." *Journal of Political Economy* 77:181–98.

Snidal, D. 1985. "The Limits of Hegemonic Stability Theory." *International Organization* 39:579–614.

Sohmen, E. 1976. *Allokationstheorie und Allokationspolitik.* Tübingen: J. C. B. Mohr (Paul Siebeck).

Solow, R. M. 1979. "Another Possible Source of Wage Stickiness." *Journal of Macroeconomics* 1:79–82.

Solow, R. M. 1985. "Economic History and Economics." *American Economic Review, Papers and Proceedings* 75:328–31.

Spence, A. M. 1973. "Job Market Signalling." *Quarterly Journal of Economics* 87:355–74.

Spence, A. M. 1974. *Market Signalling: Information Transfer in Hiring and Related Screening Processes.* Cambridge: Harvard University Press.

Spence, A. M. 1976. "Informational Aspects of Market Structure: An Introduction." *Quarterly Journal of Economics* 90:591–97.

Spence, A. M. 1977. "Consumer Misperceptions, Product Failure, and Producer Liability." *Review of Economic Studies* 44:561–72.

Spence, A. M., and R. Zeckhauser. 1971. "Insurance, Information, and Individual Action." *American Economic Review, Papers and Proceedings* 61:380–87.

Spremann, K. 1987. "Agency Theory and Risk Sharing." In G. Bamberg and K. Spremann, eds., *Agency Theory, Information, and Incentives,* 3–37. Heidelberg: Springer.

Starr, J. A., and I. C. MacMillan. 1990. "Resource Cooptation via Social Contracting: Resource Acquisition Strategies for New Ventures." *Strategic Management Journal* 11:79–92.

Starret, D. A. 1973. "Inefficiency and the Demand of 'Money' in a Sequence Economy." *Review of Economic Studies* 40:347–448.

Steinherr, A. 1977. "On the Efficiency of Profit Sharing and Labor Participation in Management." *Bell Journal of Economics* 8:545–55.

Stigler, G. J. 1961. "The Economics of Information." *Journal of Political Economy* 69:213–25.

Stigler, G. J. 1968. *The Organization of Industry.* Chicago: University of Chicago Press.

Stigler, G. J. 1972. "The Law and Economics of Public Policy: A Plea to Scholars." *Journal of Legal Studies* 1:1–12.

Stigler, G. J. 1974. "Free Riders and Collective Action: An Appendix to Theories of Economic Regulation." *The Bell Journal of Economics and Management Science* 5:359–65.

Stigler, G. J., and G. S. Becker. 1977. "De Gustibus Non Est Disputandum." *American Economic Review* 67:76–90.

Stiglitz, J. E. 1974. "Incentives and Risk Sharing in Sharecropping." *Review of Economic Studies* 41:219–55.

Stiglitz, J. E. 1975. "The Theory of 'Screening,' Education, and the Distribution of Income." *American Economic Review* 65:283–300.

Stiglitz, J. E. 1985. "Information and Economic Analysis: A Perspective." *Economic Journal, Supplement* 95:21–41.

Stiglitz, J. E. 1987. "The Causes and Consequences of the Dependence of Quality on Price." *Journal of Economic Literature* 25:1–48.

Stiglitz, J. E. 1991. "Another Century of Economic Science." *Economic Journal* 101:134–41.

Stiglitz, J. E. 1994. *Whither Socialism.* Cambridge: MIT Press.

Stiglitz, J. E., and A. Weiss. 1981. "Credit Rationing in Markets with Imperfect Information." *American Economic Review* 71:393–410.

Stole, L. A. 1991. "Mechanism Design under Common Agency." Working Paper, MIT, July.

Stützel, W. 1959. "Liquidität." In E. von Beckerath, ed., *Handwörterbuch der Sozialwissenschaften,* 6:622–29. Stuttgart: Gustav Fischer, J. C. B. Mohr (Paul Siebeck), and Vandenhoeck and Ruprecht.

Sugden R. 1986. *The Economics of Rights, Co-operation, and Welfare.* Oxford: Blackwell.

Sugden, R. 1989. "Spontaneous Order." *Journal of Economic Perspectives* 3, no. 4:85–97.

Sutton, J. 1986. "Non-cooperative Bargaining Theory: An Introduction." *Review of Economic Studies* 53:709–24.

Sutton, J. 1990. "Explaining Everything, Explaining Nothing? Game Theoretic Models in Industrial Economics." *European Economic Review* 34:505–12.

Sutton, J. 1992. *Sunk Costs and Market Structure.* Cambridge: MIT Press.

Swedberg, R. 1990. *Economics and Sociology, Redefining Their Boundaries: Conversations with Economists and Sociologists.* Princeton: Princeton University Press.

Taylor, P. 1987. "The Simple Analytics of Implicit Labour Contracts." In J. D. Hey and P. J. Lambert, eds., *Surveys in the Economics of Uncertainty,* 151–72. Oxford: Basil Blackwell.

Teece, D. J. 1977. "Technology Transfer by Multinational Firms: The Resource Cost of Transferring Technological Know-How." *Economic Journal* 87:242–61.

Teece, D. J. 1992a. "Competition, Cooperation, and Innovation." *Journal of Economic Behavior and Organization* 18:1–25.

Teece, D. J. 1992b. "Strategies for Capturing the Financial Benefits from Technological Innovation." In N. Rosenberg, R. Sandau, and D. C. Mowrey, eds., *Technology and the Wealth of Nations,* 174–205. Stanford: Stanford University Press.

Telser, L. G. 1980. "A Theory of Self-Enforcing Agreements." *Journal of Business* 53:27–44.

Telser, L. G. 1981. "Why There Are Organized Futures Markets." *Journal of Law and Economics* 24:1–22.

Thaler, R. H. 1994. *Quasi Rational Economics.* New York: Russell Sage Foundation.

Thomas, L. G. 1989. "Advertising in Consumer Goods Industries: Durability, Economics of Scale, and Heterogeneity." *Journal of Law and Economics* 32:163–93.

Tietz, R. 1990. "On Bounded Rationality: Experimental Work at the University of Frankfurt/Main." *Journal of Institutional and Theoretical Economics* 146:659–72.

Tirole, J. 1986. "Hierarchies and Bureaucracies: On the Role of Collusion in Organization." *Journal of Law, Economics and Organization* 2:182–214.

Tirole, J. 1988. *The Theory of Industrial Organization.* Cambridge: MIT Press.

Tirole, J. 1994. "Incomplete Contracts: Where Do We Stand?" Walras-Bowley lecture, delivered at the 1994 North American summer meetings of the Econometric Society, Quebec City.

Tobin, J. 1956. "The Interest-Elasticity of Transaction Demand for Cash." *Review of Economics and Statistics* 38:241–47.

Tollison, R. D. 1982. "Rent-Seeking: A Survey." *Kyklos* 35:575–602.

Tollison, R. D. 1988. "Public Choice and Legislation." *Virginia Law Review* 74:339–71.

Townsend, R. 1982. "Optimal Multiperiod Contracts and the Gain from Enduring Relationships under Private Information." *Journal of Political Economy* 90:1166–86.

Tullock, G. 1974. *The Economics of War and Revolution,* Blacksburg, Va.: Center for Study of Public Choice, Virginia Polytechnic Institute.

Tullock, G. 1975. The Transitional Gains Trap." *Bell Journal of Economics* 6:671–78.

Tullock, G. 1989. *The Economics of Special Privilege and Rent Seeking.* Dordrecht: Kluwer.

Ullmann-Margalit, E. 1978. *The Emergence of Norms.* Oxford: Oxford University Press.

Ulph, A. M., and D. T. Ulph. 1975. "Transaction Costs in General Equilibrium Theory: A Survey." *Economica* 42:355–72.

Vanberg, V. J. 1992. "Organizations as Constitutional Systems." *Constitutional Political Economy* 3:223–53.

Vanberg W. 1982. *Markt und Organisation: Individualistische Sozialtheorie und das Problem korperativen Handelns.* Tübingen: J. C. B. Mohr (Paul Siebeck).

Vanek, J. 1969. "Decentralization under Workers' Management: A Theoretical Appraisal." *American Economic Review* 59:1006–14.

Vanek, J. 1970. *The General Theory of Labor-Managed Market Economics.* Ithaca, N.Y.: Cornell University Press.

Vanek, J. 1977. *The Labor-Managed Economy.* Ithaca and New York: Cornell University Press.

Vanek, J. 1990. "On the Transition from Centrally Planned to Democratic Socialist Economies." *Economic and Industrial Democracy* 11:179–203.

Varian, H. R. 1987. *Intermediate Microeconomics: A Modern Approach.* New York and London: Norton.

Varian, H. R. 1992. *Microeconomic Analysis.* 3d ed. New York and London: Norton.

Varian, H. R. 1993. "What Use Is Economic Theory?" Working Paper, Department of Economics, University of Michigan.

Veljanovski, C. 1991. "Privatization in Transition Economics." Paper delivered to the Anglo-Soviet Symposium on Public International Law, London.

Wagner, A. 1894. *Grundlegung der Politischen Ökonomie. Zweiter Teil. Volkswirtschaft und Recht, besonders Vermögensrecht.* 3d ed. Leipzig: C. F. Winter'sche.

Wagner, A. 1907. *Theoretische Sozialökonomik oder Allgemeine und Theoretische Volkswirtschaftslehre: Grundriss tunlichst in prinzipieller Behandlungsweise.* Erste Abteilung. Leipzig: C. F. Winter'sche.

Wallis, J. J., and D. C. North. 1988. "Measuring the Transaction Sector in the American Economy, 1870–1970." In S. L. Engerman and R. E. Gallman, eds., *Long-Term Factors in American Economic Growth,* 95–161. Studies in Income and Wealth, no. 51. Chicago and London: University of Chicago Press.

Walras, L. 1954. *Elements of Pure Economics or the Theory of Social Wealth.* Translated by W. Jaffé. London: Allen and Unwin. (Translation of the edition définitive (1926) of *Eléments d'Economie Politique Pure.*

Waltz, K. 1979. *Theory of World Politics.* Reading, Mass.: Addison-Wesley.

Ward, B. 1958. "The Firm in Illyria: Market Syndicalism." *American Economic Review* 48:566–89.

Watts, R., and J. Zimmerman. 1986. *Positive Accounting Theory.* Englewood Cliffs, N.J.: Prentice-Hall.

Weber, M. 1905. "Die Protestantische Ethik und der 'Geist' des Kapitalismus." *Archiv für Sozialwissenschaft und Sozialpolitik, Neue Folge* 2:1–54.

Weber, M. 1930. *The Protestant Ethic and the Spirit of Capitalism.* London: Allen and Unwin. English translation of Weber 1905.

Weber, M. 1968. *Economy and Society: An Outline of Interpretative Sociology.* Edited by G. Roth and C. Wittich. Berkeley: University of California Press.

Weber, M. 1990. *Wirtschaft und Gesellschaft,* Edited by J. Winckelmann. Tübingen: J. C. B. Mohr (Paul Siebeck). Reprint of the 5th edition; first edition 1918.

Weingast, B. R. 1984. "Congressional-Bureaucratic System: A Principal Agent Perspective (with Applications to SEC)." *Public Choice* 44:147–91.

Weingast, B. R. 1988. "Political Institutions and Public Performance in Modern America: The Paradox of Public Policy Performance." Hoover Institution, Stanford University. Mimeo.

Weingast, B. R. 1989. "The Political Institutions of Representative Government." Working Papers, no. P–89–14. Hoover Institution, Stanford University.

Weingast, B. R. 1993. "Constitutions as Governance Structures: The Political Foundations of Secure Markets." *Journal of Institutional and Theoretical Economics* 149:286–311.

Weingast, B. R. 1994. "A Rational Choice Perspective on Shared Belief Systems: The Role of Sovereignity." Hoover Institution, Stanford University. Mimeo.

Weingast, B. R. 1995. "The Economic Role of Political Institutions: Market Preserving Federalism and Economic Development." *Journal of Law, Economics, and Organization* 11:1–31.

Weingast, B. R., and W. Marshall. 1988. "The Industrial Organization of Congress." *Journal of Political Economy* 96:132–63.

Weiss, A. 1991. *Efficiency Wages: Models of Unemployment, Layoffs, and Wage Dispersion.* Oxford: Clarendon.

Weiss, L. W., G. Pascoe, and S. Martin. 1983. "The Size of Selling Costs." *Review of Economics and Statistics* 65:668–72.

Weitzman, M. L. 1980. "The 'Ratchet Principle' and Performance Incentives." *Bell Journal of Economics* 11:302–08.

Weitzman, M. L. 1981. "Toward a Theory of Contract Types." MIT. Mimeo.

Weizsäcker, C. C. 1971. "Die zeitliche Struktur des Produktionsprozesses und das Problem der Einkommensverteilung zwischen Kapital und Arbeit." *Weltwirtschaftliches Archiv* 106:1–33.

Weizsäcker, C. C. von 1993. "Wirtschaftsordnung und Unternehmung." In W. Wittmann, et al., eds., *Handwörterbuch der Betriebswirtschaft,* Teilband 3:4721–33. 5th ed. Stuttgart: Schäfer-Poeschel.

Whitcomb, D. 1972. *Externalities and Welfare.* New York: Columbia University Press.

White, L. 1982. *The Regulation of Air Pollutant Emissions from Motor Vehicles.* Washingtion, D.C.: American Enterprise Institute for Public Policy Research.

Wiggins, S. N. 1991. "The Economics of the Firm and Contracts: A Selective Survey." *Journal of Institutional and Theoretical Economics* 147:603–61.

Williamson, O. E. 1963. "Managerial Discretion and Business Behavior." *American Economic Review* 53:1032–55.

Williamson, O. E. 1967. "Hierarchical Control and Optimum Firm Size." *Journal of Political Economy* 75:123–38.

Williamson, O. E. 1971. "The Vertical Integration of Production: Market Failure Considerations." *American Economic Review, Papers and Proceedings* 61:112–23.

Williamson, O. E. 1973. "Markets and Hierarchies: Some Elementary Considerations." *American Economic Review, Papers and Proceedings* 63:316–25.

Williamson, O. E. 1975. *Markets and Hierarchies: Analysis and Antitrust Implications.* New York: Free Press.

Williamson, O. E. 1976. "Franchise Bidding for Natural Monopolies—in General and with Respect to CATV." *Bell Journal of Economics* 7:73–104.

Williamson, O. E. 1979. "Transaction-Cost Economics: The Governance of Contractual Relations." *Journal of Law and Economics* 22:233–61.

Williamson, O. E. 1980. "The Organization of Work." *Journal of Economic Behavior and Organization* 1:5–38.

Williamson, O. E. 1981. "The Modern Corporation: Origin, Evolution, Attributes." *Journal of Economic Literature* 19:1537–68.

Williamson, O. E. 1983. "Credible Commitments: Using Hostages to Support Exchange." *American Economic Review* 73:519–40.

Williamson, O. E. 1984. "The Economics of Governance: Framework and Implications." *Journal of Institutional and Theoretical Economics* 140:195–223.

Williamson, O. E. 1985. *The Economic Institutions of Capitalism*. New York: Free Press.

Williamson, O. E. 1988. "Corporate Finance and Corporate Governance." *Journal of Finance* 43:567–91.

Williamson, O. E. 1991. "Economic Institutions: Spontaneous and Intentional Governance." *Journal of Law, Economics, and Organization* 7:159–87.

Williamson, O. E. 1993a. "The Evolving Science of Organization." *Journal of Institutional and Theoretical Economics* 149:36–63.

Williamson, O. E. 1993b. "Contested Exchange versus the Governance of Contractual Relations." *Journal of Economic Perspectives* 7, no. 1:103–8.

Williamson, O. E. 1993c. "Transaction Cost Economics Meets Posnerian Law and Economics." *Journal of Institutional and Theoretical Economics* 149:99–118.

Williamson, O. E. 1993d. "Transaction Cost Economics and the Evolving Science of Organization." May. Mimeo.

Williamson, O. E. 1993e. "Transaction Cost Economics and Organization Theory." *Industrial and Corporate Change* 2:107–56.

Williamson, O. E. 1994. "Concluding Comment." *Journal of Institutional and Theoretical Economics* 150:320–24.

Williamson, O. E. 1996. *The Mechanisms of Governance*. New York and Oxford: Oxford University Press.

Williamson, O. E., M. L. Wachter, and J. E. Harris. 1975. "Understanding the Employment Relation: The Analysis of Idiosyncratic Exchange." *Bell Journal of Economics* 6:250–80.

Williamson, S. D. 1986. "Costly Monitoring, Financial Intermediation, and Equilibrium Credit Rationing." *Journal of Monetary Economics* 18:159–79.

Williamson, S. D. 1987. "Costly Monitoring, Loan Contracts, and Equilibrium Credit Rationing." *Quarterly Journal of Economics* 102:135–79.

Wilson, C. 1977. "A Model of Insurance Markets with Incomplete Information." *Journal of Economic Theory* 16:167–207.

Winter, S. 1964. "Economic 'Natural Selection' and the Theory of the Firm." *Yale Economics Essays* 4:225–72.

Winter. S. 1975. "Optimization and Evolution in the Theory of the Firm." In R. Day and T. Graves, eds., *Adaptive Economic Models,* 73–118. New York: Academic.

Wiseman, J. 1991. "The Black Box." *Economic Journal* 101:149–55.

Worrall, T. 1989. "Labor Contract Theory." In F. Hahn, ed., *The Economics of Missing Markets, Information, and Games,* 336–48. Oxford: Clarendon.

Yarbrough, B. V., and R. M. Yarbrough. 1992. *Cooperation and Governance in International Trade*. Princeton: Princeton University Press.

Yellen, J. 1984. "Efficiency Wage Models of Unemployment." *American Economic Review* 74:200–208.

Zaleski, E. 1967. *Planning Reforms in the Soviet Union, 1962–1966*. Translated by M. C. MacAndrew and G. W. Nutter. Chapel Hill: University of North Carolina Press.

Zender, J. 1991. "Optimal Financial Instruments." *Journal of Finance* 46:1645–65.

# Author Index

Acheson, J. M., 319
Aghion, P., 260, 261
Akerlof, G. A., 33, 130, 136, 157, 158,
  222, 223, 225, 226, 254, 258, 263,
  316
Albert, H., 272
Alchian, A. A., 19, 29, 31, 32, 64, 65,
  72, 76, 87, 116, 117, 119, 131, 136,
  137, 154, 155, 173, 174, 176, 177,
  251, 263, 270, 289, 298, 299, 300,
  306, 307, 308, 317, 319, 328, 329,
  344, 345, 347, 351–52, 364, 366, 391,
  392, 406, 407, 409, 410, 411, 476
Alston, L. J., 113
Alt, J. R., 413, 428, 429, 430, 433, 434
Amsden, A. H., 433
Anderson, T. L., 89, 101, 102
Aoki, M., 347, 374
Archibald, G. C., 405
Aron, R., 250
Arrow, K. J., 1, 6, 7, 9, 10, 20, 22, 27,
  28, 37, 40, 42, 63, 64, 66, 70, 81, 84,
  92, 93, 95, 117, 119, 142, 145, 146,
  148, 149, 150, 177, 180, 198, 200,
  202, 226, 247, 249, 263, 275, 276,
  280, 281, 297, 315, 480, 481
Auerbach, N. Z., 133
Axelrod, R., 162, 248, 426, 427, 429,
  431
Azariadis, C., 228, 231, 232, 258, 259,
  263, 316

Backhaus, D., 390
Bailey, M. J., 228, 232, 258, 316
Bain, J., 283, 297, 411
Bajt, A., 411

Baker, G. P., 155, 173, 252
Baldwin, R., 319
Baltensperger, E., 138
Bamberg, G., 194
Banfield, E. C., 20
Barmbold, J., 426
Barnard, C., 18, 19, 24, 405, 410
Baron, D. P., 251, 256, 257
Barro, R. J., 259, 316
Barzel, Y., 31, 130, 280, 289, 293, 294,
  319, 329, 349, 351, 411
Bates, R. H., 479
Bator, F., 466
Batstone, E., 390
Battalio, R., 450
Baumol, W. J., 66, 250, 289, 405
Becker, G. S., 33, 82, 450, 471, 472
Beckmann, M. J., 280
Benham, L., 384
Bentley, A. F., 54
Berle, A., 149, 250
Berliner, C., 51
Berliner, J. S., 257
Bernheim, D., 253
Bernholz, P., 66, 427, 431, 433
Bernstein, L., 162, 310, 311, 319
Besanko, D., 256, 257
Besen, S. M., 80, 81, 119
Bils, M., 316
Bindseil, U., 301
Binger, B. R., 102
Binmore, K., 175, 267, 279, 281, 365,
  431
Bishop, R. C., 98
Black, D., 21
Black, H. C., 132, 135, 137

539

Blanchard, O. J., 231, 263
Blau, P., 271, 280, 315
Blaug, M., 82, 116, 172, 404
Blinder, A. S., 285, 319
Block, W., 54, 298, 313
Böhm, F., 116, 275, 279, 431
Bolton, P., 261
Bonus, H., 103
Bornstein, M., 374
Bössmann, E., 45, 328
Bowles, S., 409
Bradley, M., 343
Brennan, G., 315
Brentano, L., 115
Brimson, J. A., 51
Brunner, K., 4
Buchanan, J. M., 9, 21, 32, 36, 54, 105, 118, 119, 280, 315, 418, 431, 434, 479
Buck, T., 411, 475
Bull, C., 262
Burgers, W. P., 423, 425
Butters, G., 293

Calabresi, G., 83
Calamari, J. D., 127, 142, 176
Calvert, R. L., 158, 164, 173, 174, 429, 430, 433
Calvo, G. A., 253
Carlton, D. W., 285, 319
Carmichael, H. L., 174, 239, 262, 264
Carr, J. L., 311, 400
Chandler, A. D., Jr., 8, 288, 317, 405, 410
Chen, M.-J., 427
Cheung, S. N. S., 64, 111, 280, 366
Chitty, H., 319
Chung, T.-Y., 239, 260
Clark, C. W., 118
Clarkson, K. W., 51
Clausewitz, C. von, 424
Coase, R. H., 9, 29, 31, 34, 35, 39, 43, 63, 76, 78, 91, 93–97, 116, 117, 119, 176, 271, 283, 289, 291, 301, 314, 319, 327, 328, 332, 336, 340, 351, 352, 405, 410, 411, 436, 440, 445

Coleman, J. S., 5, 7, 27, 33, 84, 95, 96, 107, 156, 177, 271, 280, 281
Commons, J. R., 2, 34, 37, 41, 42, 48, 54, 67, 172, 174, 404
Conlisk, J., 165, 175, 176, 448, 456
Cooper, R., 46, 259
Cooter, R., 33, 83, 131, 132, 172, 311
Cournot, A., 283, 285
Crawford, R. G., 174, 176, 177, 263, 306–8, 317, 319, 406
Crawford, V. P., 259
Cremer, J., 334
Crocker, K. J., 411
Cyert, R. M., 175, 253, 405

Dahlman, C. J., 44, 61, 62, 66, 67, 459
Dann, L. Y., 343
Dasgupta, P., 26, 255
Davies, P., 390
Day, R., 455
DeAlessi, L., 31, 97, 116, 118, 119, 148, 460, 464
DeAngelo, H., 343
Debreu, G., 1, 66, 70, 142, 145, 146, 247, 404
DeGeorge, R. T., 268
Demsetz, H., 9, 31, 63, 65–67, 74, 76, 87, 90, 108, 109, 116, 117, 119, 154, 155, 173, 177, 251, 270, 309, 310, 318, 328, 329, 344, 345, 347, 351, 364, 366, 391, 406, 407, 409, 411, 420, 445, 452, 457, 459, 475
Denzau, A. T., 165, 269, 445
Deseran, 160
Dewatripont, M., 20, 260
Diamond, D., 137, 274, 310, 312
Dnes, A. W., 317
Domar, E. D., 377
Dorfman, R., 297
Downs, A., 21
Dwarkin, R., 17
Dye, R., 259

Eaton, B., 325, 354
Eaton, D., 325, 354
*Economist,* 290, 297, 341

Eggertsson, T., 32, 85, 98, 101, 102, 109, 110, 410, 411, 437, 459
Eisenhardt, K. M., 177, 413, 422, 432
Elster, J., 280
Engels, F., 85
Etzioni, A., 315
Eucken, W., 11, 12, 32, 36, 72, 75, 116, 123, 124, 275, 279, 281, 283, 431
Fama, E., 31, 151, 152, 153, 154, 173, 177, 345, 346, 347, 350, 406
Farnsworth, E. A., 126, 128, 176
Farrell, J., 93, 94, 290, 443
Feld, L. P., 96
Fellner, W., 290, 296, 297, 316
Fischer, S., 231, 259, 263
Fisher, F. M., 51
Fisher, I., 5, 84, 116, 119
Flath, D., 317
Foley, D. K., 55, 66, 67
Fouraker, L. E., 249
Frank, R. H., 26, 107, 156, 161, 177
Frase, R., 81
Freixas, X., 257
Frey, B. S., 30, 433, 434, 448
Fried, C., 141, 142
Frieden, J. A., 433
Friedman, M., 449
Fröhlich, W., 316, 319
Fudenberg, D., 254, 301
Furubotn, E. G., 11, 14, 31, 55, 62, 63, 72, 76, 95, 100–102, 105, 107, 116–19, 123, 135, 136, 148, 150, 167, 257, 324, 325, 329, 364, 366, 367, 375, 381, 383, 385, 387, 391, 398, 402, 409, 410–12, 433, 441, 451, 454, 472, 475

Galbraith, J. K., 54, 250
Garrett, G., 430
Garvy, G., 316, 319
Gibbons, R., 245, 264
Gifford, A., Jr., 432
Gilpin, R., 428
Gilson, R. J., 399
Goetz, C. J., 143
Goldberg, V., 32, 76, 131, 162, 163, 175,

176, 177, 271, 291, 310, 318, 411
Gordley, J. R., 126, 160
Gordon, D. F., 228, 258
Gordon, H. S., 101, 111
Gossen, J. H., 115
Gottinger, H., 455, 456
Gould, J. P., 66, 275, 317, 446
Grandmont, J. M., 66
Granovetter, M., 33
Gravelle, H., 262
Green, J. R., 96
Green, M., 390
Greenwald, B. C., 256
Greif, A., 302, 303
Grimm, C. M., 427
Grossman, G., 293
Grossman, S. J., 32, 232–34, 238, 250, 251, 256, 258, 259, 260, 261, 263, 331, 351, 407
Grout, P., 259
Guesnerie, R., 257
Gwartney, J., 54

Haas, 160
Hadfield, G. K., 159, 175, 317
Hahn, F. H., 66
Hall, R. E., 160, 259
Hamilton, G. G., 35, 273, 285, 314, 315
Hansmann, H., 342, 411
Hardin, G., 98, 100, 101, 118
Harris, J. E., 406
Harsanyi, J., 407
Hart, A., 96
Hart, H. L. A., 17
Hart, O. D., 18, 32, 202, 228, 232, 233, 234, 238, 240, 247, 250, 251, 258, 259, 260, 261, 263, 331, 350, 351, 407, 410, 411
Haucap, J., 426
Hax, H., 318, 416
Hayek, F. A., 6, 7, 24, 36, 74, 115, 275, 278, 279, 281, 288, 431, 460, 476
Heller, W. P., 61
Hellwig, M., 222, 255, 257
Hemmer, T., 253

Henderson, J.M., 283, 322, 455
Hennart, J. -F., 289, 317
Hess, J. D., 123
Hicks, J. R., 62, 129, 180, 471
Hill, C. W., 423, 425
Hill, P. J., 89, 101, 102
Hinds, M., 125, 138
Hippel, E. von, 12
Hirschman, A. O., 272
Hirshleifer, J., 44, 45, 119
Hodgson, G., 412
Hoff, T., 411
Hoffmann, E., 102
Holcombe, R. G., 431
Holmstrom, B. R., 30, 31, 136, 186,
  199, 202, 228, 232, 239, 247, 250,
  251, 252, 253, 254, 257, 261, 263,
  326, 334, 350, 408, 411
Homann, K., 268
Homans, G. C., 271, 315, 413
Horn, N., 120, 129, 141, 176, 421
Horvat, B., 385, 387, 411
Hughes, A., 263
Humboldt, W. Von, 11
Hume, D., 36, 37, 69, 70, 75, 76, 106,
  107, 115, 119, 122, 249, 271, 278,
  281, 423, 431
Humes, B., 429, 430, 433
Hurwicz, L., 280
Hutchison, T. W., 33, 36, 115, 119, 279

IDE, 390
Ireland, N., 409, 411
Isaac, M. R., 96
Itoh, H., 253

Jaffee, D. M., 256, 257
Jehle, E., 51
Jensen, M. C, 31, 48, 65, 76, 149–55,
  172, 173, 177, 200, 202, 252, 324,
  326, 343–47, 384, 389, 406, 409–12
Johnson, R. N., 432, 470
Jones, D., 409
Joskow, P. L., 128, 129, 176, 177, 300,
  319, 330, 407, 411

Kagel, J., 450
Kahneman, D., 176
Kaldor, N., 297
Keefer, P., 384
Kennan, J., 301
Kenney, R. W., 293, 295, 349
Keohane, R. O., 21, 32, 271, 424, 428,
  429, 430, 433, 434
Kessel, R. A., 116
Keynes, J. M., 276, 437, 438, 470
Kim, W. C., 423, 425
Kirzner, I. M., 33, 275
Klein, B., 20, 31, 32, 140, 156, 160,
  174, 176, 177, 226, 241, 244, 261,
  263, 264, 276, 281, 289, 292, 293,
  294, 295, 296, 297, 305, 306, 307,
  308, 317, 319, 347, 349, 406, 411,
  426
Knight, F., 17, 34, 404
Knight, J., 32
Kornhauser, L., 162
Krahnen, J. P., 317
Kranton, R. E., 169
Kreps, D. M., 3, 4, 23, 32, 45, 135, 163,
  164, 187, 221, 222, 245, 255, 262,
  263, 264, 269, 272, 281, 301, 315,
  332, 333, 334, 339, 351, 352, 407,
  419, 420, 446, 472
Kronman, A. T., 177, 425, 426
Kydland, F. E., 281

La Croix, S. J., 311
Laffont, J. J., 96, 188, 256, 257
Lake, D. A., 433
Lambert, R. A., 254
Lancaster, K., 1, 473
Landa, J. T., 311
Landes, W. M., 81
Lange, O., 9, 13, 115
Langlois, R. H., 33
Larenz, K., 124, 129
Law, P., 409, 411
Lawson, F. H., 76, 77, 78, 120, 132
Lawson, R., 54
Lazear, E. P., 174, 190, 247, 251, 252,
  259, 262

Leffler, K. B., 20, 32, 156, 160, 174, 176, 226, 241, 244, 261, 264, 276, 281, 292, 294, 295, 296, 297, 305, 306, 319, 347, 426
Leibenstein, H., 350, 461
Leland, H. E., 256
Leser, H. G, 120, 176
Levi, M., 21, 32, 47, 54, 432
Lewis, D., 107, 108, 142, 279, 288, 431
Libecap, G. D., 32, 104, 110, 111, 112, 113, 114, 411, 432, 470
Lindenberg, S., 33, 160, 161, 272, 420
Llewellyn, K. N., 141, 142, 172
Locke, J., 75, 81, 430, 431, 434

Macaulay, S., 144, 145, 168, 177
Macneil, I. R., 9, 18, 32, 142, 143, 158, 159, 160, 175, 177, 310
Manne, H. G., 9, 343, 345, 351
March, J. G., 175, 253, 405, 421
Markovic, M., 411
Marlin, A., 390
Marris, R., 250
Marschak, J., 280
Marschak, f., 280
Marshall, A., 1, 33, 283, 314
Marshall, W., 418, 432
Martin, D. L., 118, 434
Martin, L. L., 428, 430, 434
Martin, S., 50
Martinek, M., 317
Marx, K., 27, 34, 85
Maskin, E., 255
Mason, D., 89
Masten, S. E., 479
Mathewson, F., 400
Matthews, R. C. O., 37
Maynes, E. S., 49, 50
McCain, R., 412
McCubbins, M. D., 432
McGowan, J. J., 51
McKean, 115
McManus, J., 109
Meade, J., 389, 411
Means, G., 149, 250
Meckling, W. H., 4, 31, 48, 65, 76, 149,

151, 152, 172, 173, 177, 200, 324, 326, 343, 344, 345, 389, 406, 409, 410, 411, 412
Mehren, A. T. von, 126, 160
Melumad, N. D., 253
Menell, P. S., 104
Menger, C., 6, 36, 37, 278, 431
Meran, G., 317
Miller, D., 427
Miller, G. J., 155, 158, 173, 174, 177, 332, 334–36, 407, 408, 480
Miller, G. P., 422, 423
Miller, J., 411
Miller, J. G., 42, 46, 47, 67
Miller, M., 9, 344, 348
Mills, F. C., 285
Mincer, J., 82
Mirrlees, J. A., 250
Mises, L., 36, 115
Miyazaki, H., 258
Mnookin, R. H., 162, 399
Modigliani, F., 9, 344, 348
Mody, A., 298
Moe, T. M., 7, 32, 270, 280, 413, 417, 418, 419, 421, 432, 434
Möller, H., 279
Monteverde, K., 308, 309
Montinola, G., 419
Mookherjee, D., 251
Moore, J., 259, 260, 261
Morgenstern, O., 95, 193, 194, 229, 230, 444
Mueller, D. C., 250
Mulherin, J. H., 270, 291, 301, 316, 319
Murphy, K. J., 155, 173, 202, 252
Mussa, M., 316
Myerson, R., 249, 301

Nalebuff, B., 251, 252
Nasse, E., 115
Negishi, T., 316
Nelson, P., 292, 306, 315
Nelson, R., 33, 175, 374, 455, 462
Nerlove, M., 297
Netter, J. M., 301, 316

Netting, R. M., 103
Nicholls, W. H., 296
Nichols, T., 250
Niehans, J., 62, 66
Niskanen, W., 118
Noll, R. G., 432
North, D. C., 3, 6, 7, 15, 17, 21, 22, 27, 29, 32, 35, 37, 38, 49, 51–53, 65, 67, 88, 89, 100, 105, 106, 108–10, 165, 173, 265, 266, 268, 269, 280, 302, 303, 365, 413–20, 422, 423, 427, 430, 432–34, 440, 445, 465, 469, 475, 476, 481
Noyes, C. R., 82, 137
Nozick, R., 431
Nutter, G. W., 75, 366, 411

Oi, W. Y., 52, 58
Okun, A. M., 157, 232, 259, 316
Olsen, J. P., 421
Olson, M., 21, 32, 47, 48, 54, 65, 108, 273, 284, 314
Oppenheimer, F., 110
Ordeshook, P. C., 21
Ostrom, E., 6, 98, 101, 102, 103, 118, 119
Ostroy, J. M., 66
Overdahl, J. A., 301, 316, 319
Oye, K., 429

Pascoe, G., 50
Pease, J. G., 319
Pejovich, S., 31, 72, 76, 105, 116, 117, 119, 150, 257, 329, 364, 366, 367, 375, 381, 390, 409, 411, 441, 476
Perillo, J. M., 127, 142, 176
Persson, T., 20, 281, 419
Pingle, M., 454, 455, 456, 457
Plant, A., 81
Pommerehne, W. W., 96
Popper, K. R., 7, 24, 28, 38, 272
Porter, M. E., 298
Posner, R. A., 15, 33, 74, 81, 172, 176, 440
Prescott, E. C., 275, 281
Prybyla, J., 374

Putterman, L., 48, 408, 409, 410
Pyle, D. H., 256

Qian, Y., 419
Quandt, R. E., 283, 322, 455

Radbruch, G., 69
Radner, R., 254, 280
Rapoport, A., 433
Raskind, L. J., 80, 81, 119
Rasmusen, E., 180, 200, 203
Rayner, B., 51
Rees, R., 262
Reichelstein, S., 253
Reinganum, J., 256
Reny, P., 365
Ress, G., 427, 434
Rey, P., 252, 254, 260
Rheinstein, M., 79, 88
Ricart i Costa, J., 251
Richter, R., 14, 16, 35, 36, 66, 67, 115, 167, 177, 268, 269, 273, 279, 389, 411, 429, 433, 434
Riker, W. H., 22, 89, 419, 421
Riley, J. G., 44, 45, 119, 255, 257
Rinkes, J. G., 177
Roberts, J., 262, 271, 292, 301, 339, 340, 348, 349, 352, 401, 402, 403, 407
Rogerson, W. P., 259
Rogoff, K., 281
Rosen, S., 82, 232, 251, 258, 263
Rosenthal, J. L., 114
Ross, S., 65, 250
Roth, A. E., 249
Rothschild, M., 150, 220, 255, 256
Rubin, P., 317
Rubinstein, A., 175, 254, 301
Rudden, B., 76, 77, 78, 120, 132
Rumelt, R. P., 411

Salanie, B., 254
Saloner, G., 290
Samuel, G. H., 177
Samuelson, L., 175
Samuelson, P. A., 9, 70, 323

Sappington, D. E. M., 192, 193, 263
Sauermann, H., 175, 249
Schanze, E., 318, 418
Schein, E. H., 173
Schelling, T. C., 281, 333, 420, 425, 433
Schendel, D., 411
Scherer, F. M., 50, 343
Schlicht, E., 19, 27, 115, 134, 271, 316
Schmalensee, R., 283, 293, 297, 318, 319
Schmidtchen, D., 36, 123, 433
Schmoller, G. von, 2, 6, 7, 27, 34, 35, 36, 37, 116, 172, 174, 267, 272, 278, 279, 315, 420
Schneider, R., 113
Schotter, A., 24, 431
Schultz, T., 82
Schumpeter, J. A., 34, 35, 116, 172, 420
Schweizer, U., 117, 179
Scott, K., 69, 121, 447, 469
Scott, R. E., 143
Selten, R., 164, 165, 171, 175, 176, 249, 281, 407
Sen, A., 21
Sened, I., 32
Sertel, M., 412
Seyffert, R., 50
Shapiro, C., 174, 241, 243, 244, 261, 264, 293, 316
Shavell, S., 31, 198, 250, 259
Shelanski, H. A., 176
Shell, G. R., 131, 160, 162, 300
Shepsle, K. A., 21, 32, 418, 432
Shleifer, A., 252
Siegel, S., 249
Simmel, G., 25, 26
Simon, H. A., 4, 135, 161, 164, 175, 177, 272, 274, 275, 277, 287, 326, 332, 405
Singer, A. E., 171
Smith, A., 21, 33, 41, 47, 149, 172, 278
Smith, B. D., 256
Smith, K. G., 427
Smith, V. L., 118
Snidal, D., 297, 429
Sohmen, E., 95

Solow, R. M., 1, 316
Sorin, S., 175
Spence, A. M., 31, 45, 130, 135, 136, 150, 221, 222, 226, 250, 254, 255, 256, 263
Spremann, K., 263
Starr, J. A., 271, 272, 315, 413
Starr, R. M., 66
Starret, D. A., 66
Steiner, P. O., 297
Stigler, G. J., 10, 44, 65, 187, 292, 315, 318, 471, 472
Stiglitz, J. E., 30, 31, 61, 62, 150, 174, 187, 220, 222, 232, 250–52, 255–59, 262, 263, 315, 316, 323, 365, 374, 441, 442, 445, 457, 463
Stole, L. A., 253
Stützel, W., 125
Sugden, R., 249, 271, 278, 279
Supek, R., 411
Sutton, J., 256, 301, 318
Svejnar, J., 409
Swedberg, R., 33

Tabellini, G., 20, 419
Taylor, P., 228
Teece, D. J., 297, 308, 309, 411, 425
Telser, L. G., 32, 76, 156, 173, 174, 240, 261, 263, 281, 316, 426
Thakor, A., 257
Thaler, R. H., 450
Thomas, L. G., 296
Thomas, R. P., 32, 109, 110, 432
Tietz, R., 175, 249
Tirole, J., 136, 233, 235, 236, 237, 239, 241, 242, 244, 245, 252, 253, 256, 257, 261, 263, 264, 290, 293, 301, 318, 326, 334, 336, 350, 407, 408, 411
Tobin, J., 66
Tollison, R. D., 32, 105, 314, 423, 479
Townsend, R., 254
Tullock, G., 9, 21, 105, 118, 280, 418, 423, 433, 479

Ulph, A. M., 66
Ulph, D. T., 66

Vanberg, V. J., 270, 272, 432
Vanek, J., 9, 13, 14, 377, 387, 388, 389
Varian, H. R., 91, 93, 98, 187, 192, 205, 207, 220, 221, 226, 263, 477
Visscher, M., 275

Wachter, M. L., 406
Wagner, A., 2, 32, 116, 172
Wakeman, L. M., 343
Walker, J. M., 96
Wallis, J., 32, 49, 51, 52, 53, 67
Walras, L., 261, 289
Waltz, K., 424
Ward, B., 377, 379
Weber, M., 5, 7, 19, 25, 35, 42, 143, 172, 174, 269, 273, 279, 280, 314, 315, 319
Weimer, D. L., 22, 89, 419
Weingast, B. R., 21, 22, 32, 268, 302, 303, 413, 418, 419, 430, 432
Weiss, A., 256, 257
Weiss, L. W., 50
Weitzman, M. L., 257, 259
Wellisz, S., 253
Wey, C., 426
Whinston, M. D, 253
Whitcomb, D., 119
White, L., 33, 104
Wiggins, S. N., 20, 113, 128, 136, 330, 411, 478
Wilde, L., 256
Williamson, O. E., 4, 5, 7, 18, 19, 24, 29, 30–34, 37, 41, 42, 45, 46, 55, 64, 67, 76, 122, 123, 128, 129, 131, 134, 135, 148, 152, 159, 160, 162, 163, 165–77, 182–84, 201, 232, 249, 250, 263, 265, 266, 270, 273, 276, 280–82, 288, 289, 291, 292, 294, 296, 297, 299, 304, 308, 309, 310, 314, 318, 319, 329, 330, 336–41, 347, 348, 351, 352, 405, 406, 407, 409, 411, 412, 417, 418, 429, 433, 434, 437, 440, 475
Willig, R. D., 289
Wilson, C., 255
Wilson, R., 245, 262, 301, 407
Winter, S. G., 33, 175, 323, 455, 456
Wiseman, J., 365, 374, 441, 448, 466, 467
Wood, 250
Woodward, S., 19, 131, 136, 137, 176, 298, 299, 300, 319
Worrall, T., 136, 263

Yaari, M. E., 254
Yarbrough, B. V., 433, 434
Yarbrough, R. M., 433, 434
Yellen, J. L., 136, 263, 316
Younes, Y., 66

Zaleski, E., 374
Zbaracki, M. J., 177, 413, 422, 432
Zeckhauser, R., 250
Zender, J., 261

# Subject Index

Page numbers in italics signify on which pages the entry in question is dealt with in greater detail.

absolute property rights, 77, *80,* 82, 85, 169, 271

abusus (change of form of an asset, its substance and location), 16

activity based costing (*Prozeßkosten-rechnung*), 46

adaptive efficiency, 476

administered contracts, 310

adverse selection, 135, 138, *139,* 180–82, 202, 206, 219, 222, 247, 248, 254–56, 258

advertising, 50, 226, 292, 293, *296–98,* 306, 472

advocate of capital, 125

agency, *22, 23,* 31, 142, 146, 147, *148,* 151–54, 156, 253, 303, 317, 346, 347, 406, 408

agency costs, *48,* 65, 151, 152, 170, *200,* 201, *343–45*

agent, 22, 23, 26, 48, *148,* 149–53, 186–207, 227, 254, 415, 417–20, 443

air pollution, 103

allocative efficiency, 1, 13, 362, 476. *See also* efficiency

appropriability, 387

asset specificity, *128,* 270, 330, 406, 408

asymmetric information, 15, 130, 131, 135, 136, *179, 180,* 417, 427

auction markets, *288,* 316

Austrian School, 36, 448

authority relationship, *135,* 332, 351

bargaining costs, 8, 300, 349, *350*

barriers to entry, 275, *302,* 313

bilateral governance, 168

bilateral monopoly, 229, 247, 299, 304

bonding, 48, 87, 150, 151, 152, 160, 200, 344, 345

bonding costs, 48, 151, 345

bounded rationality, 4, 39, 164–66, 171, 175, 176, 405, 418, 424, 442, 445, *447–49,* 456, 462, 464, 468, 470, 473, 474, 478, 479

capital market discipline of management, *353*

capital structure, 9, 328, 344, 353, 408 optimal, *344*

cartel, 295

certainty equivalent, 194, 196, 230, 231

citizen, 84, *416,* 422

classical contract, 172, 175, 406, 478

classical firm, *154,* 328, 329, 353

classical liberal state, 14, 71

Coase theorem, *91, 93,* 95

codetermination, 353, *389–*91, 395–98, 410, 412
  legislation, 389
  voluntary, 391

Codetermination Law (Germany), *391,* 396

coercive force (of the state), 47, *106,* 280

collateral, 19, 138, 257, 425

collective action, *20,* 34, 98, 140, 265, 266, 275, 429

collectivism, 69
commitment problem, 26, 161, 175, *257*,
    317
common knowledge, 117, 245, 430
common property, 16, *100*, 109, 118,
    415
competition, 22, 45, 55, *75*, 107, 123,
    147, 252, 268, *287, 288*, 301, 350,
    420–23, 426
competition order, *75*, 123
complete contract, 4, 8, *142*, 146, 227,
    239, 246, 247
conclusion of contracts, 269, 302
conflict of interests, 34
consensus ideology, 28
constitution, *18*, 166, 270, 271, 407,
    422, *432*
constitutional economics, *32*, 280, 431,
    435
constitutional rules, 11, 32, *266–69*, 275
constrained Pareto optimality, 61, 457,
    464, 475
contract(s)
    administered, 310
    classical, 172, 175, 406, 478
    complete, 4, 8, *142*, 146, 227, 239,
        246, 247
    conclusion of, 269, 302
    costs of concluding, 44
    employment, *134–36*, 157, 328, 332,
        351, 391
    failure, 131
    implicit, *156, 157*, 170, 173, 174, 181,
        182, 227, 228, 231, 232, 239, 258,
        262, 339
    implicit employment *157*
    incentive, *247*, 250, 251, 253
    incomplete, 31, 32, 158, 159, *233*,
        *234, 259–63*, 407, 478
    international, 424
    joint venture, *260*
    lease, 129, *132, 133*, 307
    loan, *137–40*
    long-term, 143, 145, 175, 182, 228,
        233, 254, 272, 274, *300*, 302, 309,
        *310*, 398, 431

market, 229, 231
pooling, 220, 221
principle of freedom of, *11, 123, 124*,
    135, 267
relational, 32, 142, 143, 146, *158–60*,
    171, 172, 175, 176, 265, 266, 267,
    *277, 278*, 284, 300, 333, 478
right, 5, 30, 40, 76, 172, 414
sales, *129*, 172, 274
self-enforcing, (self-enforcing agree-
    ment), 32, 146, 147, *156*, 157, 160,
    162, 163, 170, 173, 174, 177, 180,
    181, 182, 239, 240, *244, 246, 247*,
    261, 305, 314, 351, 419, 426, 434,
    478
theory of incomplete, 4, 407
theory of the state, 430, 431, 434
third-party enforced, (third-party en-
    forcement), 162, 170, 171, 313
contractual obligations, *83, 121–23*,
    125–27, 267, 343
control rights (allocated to labor), *392*,
    *393*, 397, 400, 403, 410
convention, 36, 37, 76, *106–8*, 141, 142,
    431, 445
cooperation, 34, 108, 265, 273, 290,
    291, 325, 326, 407, 427, *428–31*,
    434
copyrights, 77, *80*, 81, 119
corporate culture, 147, *163, 164*, 262,
    334, 339, 407, 420
Corporate Democracy Act, 390
corporate finance, *348*
costs
    of acquisitions, *338*
    of concluding contracts, 44
    of monitoring and enforcing, *44*, 47,
        85
    of using the market, *43, 44*, 302
court ordering, 122, *131*, 162, 201, 277,
    284, 303
CPRs (Common Pool Resources), *98*,
    100, *101–3*, 114
credibility, *20*, 89, 157, 170, *281*, 417,
    430, 445
credible commitments, 29, 89, 183, 268,

*276, 277,* 281, 418, 419
credit rationing, 147, 256, 257
creditor, *137, 138*
customer markets, 288, *316*
custom, *19,* 37, 76, 202, 266, 278

damages, *78,* 83, 93, 162
De Beers Group, *295*
debtor, *137, 138*
decision costs, 31, *45,* 458
declaration of will, 126, *141*
democratic socialist state, *13*
department stores, 296
development economics, 22, 49
diffusion of information, 356, *467*
disciplining management, 343, *345*
discretion, *23,* 170, 250, 348, 368, 418
division of labor, *41,* 48, 49, 84, 199,
  280
division of powers, 277
domestication of coercive force, *47*

economic analysis of law, 33, 81, 131,
  *172,* 304
economic constitution, 275, *279*
economic efficiency, 14, 62, 78, *97, 98,*
  140, 152, *458,* 474
economic order, 279, 431
economics of socialist transition, 49
economies of scale, 169, 270, 414
education, 21, 40, 45, 49, 82, 136, *221,*
  *222,* 226, 255, 268, 269, 272
efficiency, 12–14, 61, 62, 85, *97,* 98,
  103, 104, 108, 109, 115–17, 123,
  316, 318, 350, 398, *457–64,* 474–
  78
  adaptive, 476
  allocative, 1, 13, 362, 476
  economic, 14, 62, 78, *97, 98,* 140,
    152, *458,* 474
  Pareto, 12, 389, 457
  political, 105, 422
elementary constitutional rules, 11, *267,*
  *268*
elementary operational rules, *268*
emergence of property rights, *105,* 110

employers' associations, 296
employment contract, *134–36,* 157, 328,
  332, 351, 391
enforcement, 6, 11, 19, 20, 28, 29, 45,
  86, 106–8, 170, 171, 278, *302–5,*
  329, 418, 422, 425, *426, 427,* 440,
  442, 446, 465, 466, 468, 478
  costs, 31, 45, 280, 442
  third party, 162, 170, 171, 313
entrepreneur, 60, *152,* 271, *275, 322,*
  327–29, *332,* 402, 428, *451–57*
environmental problems, 71
ethics, 21, 202, *268*
evolution of markets, *316, 317*
evolutionary approach to economics, 33
evolutionary rationalism, 6
ex ante opportunism, 160, 182
ex post opportunism, 160, 169, 181,
  280, 306–8, 318, 417, 424
exchange, 67, 269, 270, 274, 275, *289,*
  *301, 302,* 316, 319, 398, 406, 415,
  418, 421–23, 425, 439, 440
  political, 42, 418, 422
  simultaneous, 128, 304
  stock, 269, 270, 289, *301, 302,* 313
  voluntary 5, 11
exclusion costs, *85,* 98, 101, 110
exit, 303, 414
experience goods, 156, 288, *292*
"extended" neoclassical theory, 439,
  457, 477
external effects, 63, *89, 90,* 109, 290

fairs, 269, 296, 303, 319
feeling, *25–27,* 83, 161, 171
financial intermediaries, 55, *137,* 296
firm, 9, 10, *63–65, 155–57,* 265, 266,
  272, 315–18, *321–414,* 441–43,
  452, 453, 469
  classical, *154,* 328, 329, 353
  joint-investment, *394,* 395, 397–400
  labor-managed, 14, *73,* 327, 353,
    *375–411*
  labor-owned, 327, *399,* 400
  law, 164, 270, *399, 400*
  leasing, 296

managerial theory of the, *181, 182,*
184, 186, 250, 251, 405
property-rights theory of the, 329, *353*
right of the owner of the, *155*
separation of ownership and control in
the, 23, 147, *149,* 342
size, 163, 332, 338, 339, 340, 341
Soviet type, *148,* 327, 353, *366–428*
theory of the, 3, 175, 181, 182, 250,
251, *321, 323, 326, 329, 334, 336,*
*339, 344*
trading, 296, *317*
transaction, *57, 58*
fixed transaction costs, 46
focal point, 164, 174, *333,* 420, 430
focal principle, 164, 174, 269, 339. *See*
*also* focal point
formal organization, 7, 18, 19, 37
formal rules, 15, 106, *279*
franchising, 162, *306, 307,* 310, *317*
free market economy, 36, 123, *125,* 140,
279
free-rider problem, *96,* 154, 251
friction, *10, 62. See also* transaction
costs
fulfillment of contractual obligations,
44
fundamental laws of nature, 70, *122,*
279, 423
fundamental transformation, *159,* 168,
169, 304, 309, 318

game theory, 249, *281,* 318, 321, 333,
365, 408, 431
general equilibrium theory (general
equilibrium model), 11, 12, 14, 55,
61, 66, 70, 129, 179, 249, 298, 459,
466
general principles of private property,
*11,* 88, 267
gift, *157, 158, 160, 161,* 171
givebacks, *399*
governance
bilateral, 168
failure, *101*
structure, *5,* 55, 123, 165–71, 266,

270–73, 280, 312, 330, 347, *348,*
351, 392, 406, 478
trilateral, 168, 310
unified, 163, 330
greenmail, *343*
Gresham's law, 222, 223

hegemon, *271,* 275, 428, 429
hegemonial cooperation, *297*
hidden action, *148, 149,* 180, 183, 187,
200
hidden information, *148,* 180, 183, 200,
263
hierarchical transactions, *135,* 269, *272,*
274, 275, 287, 334, 419
hierarchy, 123, 147, 155, 164, *253,* 278,
347, 348
Historical School, 2, 34, *36, 37,* 110,
278, 279, 436
hold up, *131,* 139, 299, 306, *331,* 417
homo oeconomicus, 17, *35*
homo sociologicus, *35*
horizontal cooperation, *289–91,* 296,
305
hostages, 19, *160, 161,* 170, 226, *425*
human capital, *82,* 136, 159, 182, 228,
330, *342,* 353, 391, 392, 393, 394,
395, 397, 399, 407
hybrid models, *356,* 365, 441, 442, 444–
47, 449–52, 458, 459
hysteresis effect, *27*

ideology, 3, 21, *27,* 28, 420, 440
immaterial rights, *80*
implicit contract, *156, 157,* 170, 173,
174, 181, 182, 227, 228, 231, 232,
239, 258, 262, 339
implicit employment contract, *157*
incentive(s), 31, 71, 74, 80, 87, 115,
116, 146, 161, 173, 198, *227,* 247,
288, 289, 326, 328–30, *334–37,*
340, 374, 465, 476
compatibility, incentive compatible,
*206, 207,* 213, 215, 299
constraint (IC), *188,* 191, 196, 207,
215

contract, *247,* 250, 251, 253
neutrality, *340*
scheme, *188,* 202, 251, 359
structure, 6, 388, 391, 397, 465
incomplete contract, 31, 32, 158, 159,
   *233, 234, 259–63,* 407, 478
individual rationality, *3, 4,* 74, 174, 315
individualistic theory of ownership, 70
industrial democracy, 73, 375, 384, 389,
   390, 391, 396, 410
industrial organization, 256, 283, *318,*
   *319,* 407, 479
infinite regress, 323, 456–58
influence costs, *271,* 339, 352
informal organization, *7,* 19
informal rules, 6, 15, 18, 19, 21, *278,*
   *279,* 415
information, asymmetric, 15, 130, 131,
   135, 136, *179, 180,* 417, 427
   costs, 31, *44, 45,* 65, 170, 179, 201,
      221, 248
   diffusion of, 356, *467*
   economics, *187,* 263
   hidden, *148,* 180, 183, 200, 263
   perfect, *10,* 15, 63, 74, 179, 201, 374,
      448, 457, 463, 464
   suppression of, *298,* 313
   symmetric, 70, 145, 182, 194, 195,
      228, 426
inspection, 269, 273, 274, 284, 285,
   *290–94,* 351, 422
institution, *6, 7,* 8, 19, 34, 430
institutional
   arrangement, *265, 266,* 302, 312, 313,
      391, 465
   change, 24, 28, 29, *113, 114,* 469, 475
   environment, *21, 265, 266,* 273, 288,
      439, 465
   equilibrium, *24, 25*
   neutrality, 1, *10, 408*
   stability, *23, 24*
institutionalism (old), *33, 34,* 36, 437,
   481
integration, 64, *329–32,* 338, *352,* 406,
   408
intellectual property, *80, 81,* 119, 468

internal discipline, *352*
internalization of external effects, *90*
international contracts 424
international regime, *271,* 428, 429, 430,
   433, 434
international relations, 424, 425, 427,
   429, 433, 434
investment
   joint-investment firm, *394,* 395, 397–
      400
   specific, 43, *128, 129,* 136, 329, 330
   transaction-cost, 42, 128, 131
invisible hand, *16,* 18, 20, 21, 22, 25,
   28, 108, 274, 278

joint-investment firm, *394,* 395, 397–
   400
joint-venture contracts, *260*
joint ventures, 296, *317*

*Kleinblittersdorf,* 96
Knightian uncertainty, 140, 182, 469

labor
   division of, *41,* 48, 49, 84, 199, 280
   -managed economy, 9, 375–411
   -managed firm, 14, *73,* 327, 353,
      *375–411*
   market discipline, 350, *532*
   -owned firms, 327, *399,* 400
labor director (*Arbeitsdirektor*), *396*
laissez-faire, 13, 123, 279
lateral integration, 305, 307, 308
law firm, 164, 270, *399, 400*
lease (Pacht), 79, 132, 133, 273, 274,
   307, 393
lease contract, 129, *132, 133,* 307
leasing, 87, 132, 135, 147, 169, *317*
leasing firm, 296
legal obligations, *124*
legal principles, *17*
lemons problem, *222,* 254, 263, 277,
   315
liability, *11,* 83, 267
loan contract, *137–40*
lobbying expenditures, *105*

lock-in effect, *136*, 259, 274, 299
long-term business relationship, *156*, 158, 276, 299
long-term contract, 143, 145, 175, 182, 228, 233, 254, 272, 274, *300*, 302, 309, *310*, 398, 431
loyalty, 84, *161*, 272

maladaptation costs, *347, 348*
managerial capitalism, 263
managerial theory of the firm, *181, 182*, 184, 186, 250, 251, 405
managerial transaction costs, 43, *46, 47*, 50, 51, 352
marginal productivity of the transaction process, *56*
market(s), 72, *169, 170*, 265, 266, 268, 269, 270, 271, 272, *273–79, 284*, *285*, 311, 312, 313, 314, 315, 316, 478
  auction, *288*, 316
  contract, 229, 231
  for corporate control, 343, 345
  costs of using the, *43, 44*, 302
  customer, 288, *316*
  evolution of, *316, 317*
  failure, 60, *63, 64*, 101, 102, 131, 139, 254, 276, 309, *313, 315*
  open, 84, *289*, 309, 340. *See also* perfect
  organized, 274
  perfect, 123, 142, *289*, 291, 298, 302, 311–14. *See also* open
  political 22, *105*, 422, 469
  screening, 222
  socialism, 9, *12–14*
  transaction costs, *43*, 46, 50, 51
  uncertainty, 44
  value risk, 133
measurement costs, *293, 294*
mechanism design, 321, 443
merger, 337, 338, 340, *341*
methodological individualism, *2*, 374, 414
mineral rights, *110–12*
mobility, 391

modern institutional economics, *2, 7*, 31, 33, 34, 265, 332, 408, *477*
money, 16, *26*, 36, *62*, 137–39, 225, 268, 279
monitor, 86, 87, *154, 155*, 251, 406
monitoring, 44, 85–87, *150–52*, 251, 363, 397, 400, 406
monopoly power, 11, *233*, 301, 309
moral, *20*, 269, 315, 440, 481
moral hazard, 26, 34, 134, *138, 139*, 150, 180, *186, 187*, 248

Neo-Austrian economics, *33*
neoclassical theory, 1, *8*, 10, *325*, 365, 367, 375, 377, 401, 404, 405, 408–11, *439–45*, 477, 478
neoclassical theory of the State, 88, *414–17*, 434
neoinstitutionalism, 2, 318, 438, 482
network, 140, 253, *270, 272, 273*, 422
network externalities, 290
new economics of organization, 7, *32*, 270, 280, 405, 413, 419, 430
new institutional approach to economic history, 4, *32*
New Institutional Economics, 1, 2, 3, 29, 30, 39, 40, 409, 410, 411, *435*
new political economics, 24
New York Diamond Dealers Club (DDC), 274, *310, 312*
nirvana fallacy, 444, 460
non-labor income, 387, 388
non-normative principal-agent approach, 150
nonprofit organization, 361, 365

objective function, 7, 321, 408
obligations, 36, *82, 83, 121–27*, 140, 143, 146
once and for all solution, 463
open access, 78, 98
open market, 84, *289*, 309, 340. *See also* perfect market
opportunism, 48, 83, 84, *128–31*, 166, 168, 169, 170, 306, 307, 308, 408, 417

ex ante, 160, 182
ex post, 160, 169, 181, 280, 306–8, 318, 417, 424
postcontractual, 31, 129, 146
*See also* opportunistic behavior
opportunistic behavior (opportunism), 83, 84, *128*
optimal firm size, 341
optimization cost, 403, *451–58*
order, *5–8,* 11, 12, 47, 265, 266, 267, 268, 278, 279
  competition, *75,* 123
  economic, 279, 431
  spontaneous, 6, 106
  theory of economic, *279*
*Ordnungspolitik* (German), *36,* 60, 123, 279
organization, *7, 8,* 18, 34, 37, 40, 164, 270–75, *280–83,* 287–91
  formal, 7, 18, 19, 37
  informal, *7,* 19
  new economics of, 7, *32,* 270, 280, 405, 413, 419, 430
  nonprofit, 361, 365
  theory of, *280, 282,* 331
organizational capital, 27, 275
organizational culture, *163, 164,* 171, 269, 334, 339, 419, 420, 432
organized markets, 274
original majority, 385, 386
overhead costs, 41, *46,* 50, 51, 53, 67
oversearching, 295
overuse, 86, 98
owner manager, 179, 181
ownership of physical things, 42

Pareto efficiency, 12, 389, 457
  improvement, 5, 107, 423, 474
  optimality, 1, 61, 98, 336, 389, 457, 458, 464, 475
participation constraint (PC), *189,* 195, 196, 204, 230
patents, 76, 77, *80, 81,* 302
path dependent, 28
perfect foresight, *8,* 10, 15, 70, 201, 227
perfect information, *10,* 15, 63, 74, 179,

201, 374, 448, 457, 463, 464
perfect market, 123, 142, *289,* 291, 298, 302, 311–14. *See also* open market
physical asset specificity, *131,* 330, 348
physical things, 42
piecemeal social engineering, 28, 38
plasticity, *137, 138,* 267
political economics, 24, *32,* 433
political efficiency, 105, 422
political entrepreneur, 428
political exchange, 42, 418, 422
political institutions, 418
political market, 22, *105,* 422, 469
political parties, 2, 47, 276, *420, 422*
political property rights, 277, *421, 422*
political science, 24, 297, 335, 410
political transaction costs, 43, *47, 48,* 53, 82, 269
pollution certificates, 103
pooling contract, 220, 221
positive agency approach (theory) 150, 151, 170, 172, 173, 177
postcontractual opportunism, 31, 129, 146
posted prices, *299,* 319
preestablished harmony, 70
preference ordering, 91, 461, 468, 471, 472, 473, 474
preferences, 3, 4, 91, 383–85, 471–74
prerogative, 88, 105
pressure group, 11, 12, 47, 48, 54, 276, 285, 319, 329, 422, 480
price competition, 290, 302
  flexibility, 285
  leadership, 296–98, 300, 313
  rigidity, *285,* 299, 300, 302, 316
principal, 22, 23, 26, *148–51*
principal-agent theory, 23, 65, 134, 136, 151, *177,* 232, *250, 254,* 343
principle of freedom of contract, *11, 123, 124,* 135, 267
principle of private ownership, 71, 123
prisoner's dilemma, 106, 162
*Privatautonomie,* 12
private ordering, 122, *160, 162,* 170, 311

private property, 11, *85,* 107, 114, 115, 466
product guarantees, 130
product market discipline (of management), 353
production costs, 41, 43, 50, 60, 61, 184, 185, 238, 248
production set, 403, 443, 451, 455
profit maximization, 2, 168, 249, *324,* 375, 398
property, 14, 16, *85–89,* 106–21
property rights, 4, 5, 11, 69–72, *74–86,* 114–16, 271–73, 439, 441, 452, 459, 466
  absolute, 77, *80,* 82, 85, 169, 271
  analysis, 76, 77, 81
  approach, 117, 261, 413
  common, 16, *100,* 109, 118, 415
  emergence of, *105,* 110
  political, 277, *421, 422*
  relative, 77, *82, 83, 121,* 139, 169, 271
  theory (of the firm), 329, *353*
public goods, 47, 54, 64, 78, *96,* 270
public regulation, 252, 256, 257, 269, 305, *311*
public-choice theory, 3, 280, 416

qualitative competition, 290, 302
quality control, 45, 47, 175, 317
quantitative economic policy, 60
quasi agreement, 296, 300
quasi rent, 131, 136, 139, *306,* 308, 392, 410

rank-order tournaments, 251
ratchet principle (ratchet effect), *257,* 372
rational formation of expectations, *277*
reactive equilibrium, *255*
regimes, 271, *428–30,* 433, 434
regulation. *See* public regulation
relational contract, 32, 142, 143, 146, *158–60,* 171, 172, 175, 176, 265, 266, 267, *277, 278,* 284, 300, 333, 478

relationships, 25–27, 73, *83–85,* 142, 143, 158, 159, 161, 163, 458
relative property rights, 77, *82, 83, 121,* 139, 169, 271
REMM, 4
renegotiation, *254,* 260, 296, 300, 429
rent, 110, 177, 210–12, 243, 244, 479
rent seeking, *105,* 479
repeat purchases, *131,* 174, 245
reputation, 107, 168, 170, 226, *240,* 247, 261, 262, 352, 407, 426, 430
reputation capital, 170, 400
reputation equilibrium, *241,* 243, 245
research and development, 41, 338
reservation price, *191,* 192, 199
residual decision rights, *238,* 400, 407
residual loss, *48,* 151, 344
residual rights of control, 260, *331,* 332
right, *14*
  of the owner of the firm, *155*
  of ownership, *72,* 124, 382
  of self-determination, *81,* 85
rights to membership, 76
risk
  aversion, 131, 152, 193, 197, 199, 228, 229, 248, 294
  bearing, 150, *152–54,* 170, 345–47, 406
  neutral, 131, 193, 198, 207, 228, 260
  preference, 385
  premium, *194*
rules
  constitutional, 11, 32, *266–69,* 275
  vs. discretion, 23
  elementary constitutional, 11, *267, 268*
  elementary operational, *268*
  formal, 15, 106, *279*
  informal, 6, 15, 18, 19, 21, *278, 279,* 415
  specific operational, *269,* 284, 288
sales contract, *129,* 172, 274
sanctions, *6,* 160, 272, 276, 334, 424
scientific revolution, 438
screening, 215, *222,* 256
search, *44, 45,* 50, 269, 274, 291, 292

search costs, 50, 65, 298, 327
search goods, 288, 292
second best solution, *61*, 246, 459
selective intervention, *337*
self-enforcing contract (self-enforcing
    agreement), 32, 146, 147, *156*, 157,
    160, 162, 163, 170, 173, 174, 177,
    180, 181, 182, 239, 240, *244, 246,
    247*, 261, 305, 314, 351, 419, 426,
    434, 478
self-managed work teams, 407
self-selection constraint, *207*, 219, 247,
    248
selling costs, *50*
separation equilibrium, *219*
separation of ownership and control in
    the firm, 23, 147, *149*, 342
set-up costs, 8, 39, *40*, 49
shifting preferences, *471*
shirking, *65*, 154, 155, 344
signal, *130*, 222, *226, 254–56*
signaling-equilibria, 255
simultaneous exchange, 128, 304
single crossing property, *217*, 220
site specificity, *131*, 330
slack, 253, 350, 353
social actions, 6, *27*, 42
social capital, *27*, 40, 84, 171
social consensus, 26, 28
social costs, 95
social relationships, 25, 27, 42, *83–85*,
    143, 271, 413
social transactions, *42*, 271, 315
socialism, *13, 14, 73*, 89, 381
socialist market economy, *13*, 14, 245
soft budgeting, *125*
sorting costs, *130*
sovereignty, 417
Soviet manager, *367–72*
Soviet type firm, *148*, 327, 353, *366–
    428*
span, 164, *339*, 352, 477
specific investments, 43, *128, 129*, 136,
    329, 330
specific operational rules, *269*, 284, 288
specification costs, *89*

spontaneous order, 6, 106
stable preferences, 3, 473
standards *291, 307*
state, 3, 89, 105, 277, *413–17, 420,
    422–23, 426, 427–34*
stock exchange, 269, 270, 289, *301, 302,*
    313
strategic alliances, *296*, 423, 425, 427
strong solidarity, 160
structure-conduct performance hypoth-
    esis, *283*
sunk cost, *51*, 85, 133, 139, 170, 175,
    289, 415
supervisory board, 389, 390
suppression of information, *298*, 313
symmetric information, 70, 145, 182,
    194, 195, 228, 426
synallagmatique agreements, 127, 129

takeover threat (hostile takeover), 9, 353
target profit scheme, *192*
team production, 65, *154*, 328, 344, 357
theory of economic order, *279*
theory of incomplete contracts, 4, 407
theory of organization, *280, 282*, 331
theory of the firm, 3, 175, 181, 182, 250,
    251, *321, 323, 326, 329, 334, 336,
    339, 344*
third-party enforced contracts (third-
    party enforcement), 162, 170, 171,
    313
time-inconsistency problem, 281
tit-for-tat strategy, 19, *162*, 248, 296,
    426, 431
tort law, 83, 304
tortious act (tort), 11, *83*, 267, 304
trade secrets, 80, 119
trading firms, 296, *317*
transaction, 2, 4, 8, 10, 11, 12, 13, 14,
    33, 34, *40*, 41, 42, 43, 44, 46, 166–
    68, 170, 271, 272, 273, 274, 275
    activities, 49, 50, *269*, 292, *304*
    capital, *48, 49*
    curve, *56, 57*
    firm, *57, 58*
    function, 43, *56, 57*

transaction cost(s), *8,* 30, 31, *42–44,*
   *46–56,* 63–67, 146, 147, 323
   analysis, 4, 53
   economics, *31,* 64, *165,* 176, 406
   fixed, 46
   investments, 42, 128, 131, 146, 169,
      329, 424
   managerial, 43, *46, 47,* 50, 51, 352
   market, *43,* 46, 50, 51
   political, 43, *47, 48,* 53, 82, 269
   variable *46,* 122, 284
transfer, 5, *11,* 34, 40–42, 72, 86, 88,
   90, 124, 267
trilateral governance, 168, 310
trust, *20, 21,* 25, 26, 27, 49, 76, 84,
   141
truth-telling constraint, *207,* 227

uncertainty, 42, 44, 112, 113, 119, 162,
   166, 231, 232, 277, 307, 308, 310,
   463, 464, 467, 469, 475
unified governance, 163, 330
union, *163,* 313, 314, 426
unknowable elements, 466
usus, 14, *16,* 132
usus fructus, 14, 16, 132

variable transaction costs, *46,* 122, 284
vertical cooperation, *289,* 296, 304, 305
vertical integration, 64, 147, 163, 294,
   *305, 307,* 329, 330
voice, 414, 435
voluntary exchange, 5, 11
Von Neumann-Morgenstern utility, 193,
   194, 229, 230

wage fund, 368
wage maximization, 375, 377, 379, 380,
   382, 384
wage rigidity, 147, *259*
warranty, 128, *226*
weak solidarity, *161,* 171, 420
wealth maximization, *377,* 439
welfare economics, 1, 225, 297, 457,
   459
welfare loss, 136, 199, *200, 201,* 211,
   212, 219, 225, 227, 246, 248, 344
Williamson Puzzle, 336
workers' council, 375, *376,* 378, 380,
   382, 384

yardstick approach, *362*
yardstick competition, *252*